Women's Almanac

2000

Doris Weatherford

ORYX PRESS
2000

The rare Arabian Oryx is believed to have inspired the myth of the unicorn. This desert antelope became virtually extinct in the early 1960s. At that time several groups of international conservationists arranged to have 9 animals sent to the Phoenix Zoo to be the nucleus of a captive breeding herd. Today the Oryx population is over 1,000, and over 500 have been returned to the Middle East.

Published by The Oryx Press, Inc.
4041 North Central at Indian School Road; Phoenix, Arizona 85012-3397
www.oryxpress.com

© 2000 by The Moschovitis Group, Inc.
339 Fifth Avenue; New York, New York 10016
www.mosgroup.com

Produced by The Moschovitis Group, Inc.

Editor-in-Chief and Author:	Doris Weatherford
Executive Editor:	Valerie Tomaselli
Senior Editor:	Hilary W. Poole
Adjunct Writer:	Jo Lynn Southard
Researchers:	Aysan Celik, Brett Halsey, Stephanie Schreiber
Design and Layout:	Annemarie Redmond
Editorial Coordinator:	Stephanie Schreiber
Editorial Assistant:	Rachael Shook
Copyediting:	Andrea Balinson, Carole Campbell
Proofreading:	Joseph Reilly
Index:	AEIOU, Inc.

Published simultaneously in Canada
Printed and Bound in the United States of America

ISBN: 1-57356-341-2
ISSN: 1529-5311

♾ The paper used in this publication meets the minimum requirements of the American National Standard for Information Sciences—Permanence of Paper for Printed Library Materials, ANSI Z39.48-1984.

Table of Contents

About the Authors

Doris Weatherford is an acclaimed author in the field of women's history. Her book *A History of the American Suffragist Movement* was selected as a 1998 Honor Book by the Society of School Librarians International. Her other books include *Milestones: A Chronology of American Women's History*, *American Women's History: An A-Z of People, Organizations, Issues and Events*; *Foreign and Female: Immigrant Women in America, 1840-1920*; and *American Women in World War II*. Weatherford is an adjunct professor at the University of South Florida, is active in the political arena, and has been extensively recognized for her contributions to the field of women's studies. In 1995, she received one of five awards conferred by the Florida Commission on Human Relations at Florida's Annual Civil Rights Conference, and in 1994, she received the National Order of Women Legislators Hall of Fame Award.

Adjunct writer **Jo Lynn Southard** is associate editor of the *Maine Lawyers Review*. She is also a writer and was a contributing author to *Human Rights: The Essential Reference* (Oryx Press, 1999).

Introduction

At the turn of the first millennium, from 999 to 1000 C.E., the status of women was indisputably lower than when we moved from 1999 to 2000. Yet, as you can see in the timeline of Women in World History (Part Five), some women at the last turn-of-the-millennium were achievers in ways that most people today do not realize. The timeline entry for 1000 C.E., for instance, tells of Japanese literature in an era when women wrote literary masterpieces. This almanac is designed to introduce readers to many women and their achievements, as well as to women's problems and needs, both past and present. We have gathered much and varied information on women—current and topical as well as historical, international as well as national—to meet a wide variety of research needs and to offer readers a starting point for a vast range of questions on women, their history, and their current status and condition.

Of the thousands of years discussed here, no century comes close in importance to women as the one just ended. In 1900, for example, the only nation in the world that offered women full voting rights was the tiny outpost of New Zealand; at the end of the century, only a few nations still exclude women from the polls. The story of this vital expansion of basic civil rights is incredibly complex, involving partial rights in some places at some times for some women, with repeals and regression as well as forward progress. You will find details in several places: in the Women in World History and Women in U.S. History timelines (Part Five); in the News (Part One) on nations where women are just beginning to be considered as full citizens; and in the Profiles (Part Four) of some of the many women involved in the movement, and in the Women's History, State-by-State (Part Five).

These state histories, in fact, may be unique to this almanac. Although painfully aware that not all events could be covered and that almost any sentence in the work could be expanded into a book, we took up the challenge of presenting the story of American women by their locales—something that is rarely done. You will find, for instance, the fact that Florida women did not serve on juries until 1947, although Wyoming women had begun sitting on juries in 1870. As late as the 1960s, Alabama, Mississippi, and South Carolina still barred women from juries completely—but South Carolina was the second state to have two women in Congress simultaneously, and Alabama was the third state to elect a woman as governor. The story of the states, we believe, brings a fresh perspec-

tive to the study of American women: each history tells the story of that state's gains and losses for women in fields from politics to science, art, literature, and more.

Another useful section is the Calendar of Historical Anniversaries (Appendix One). Although shorter than most sections, it can provide the basis for countless speeches to organizations, articles for periodicals, and so forth. If, for instance, you are scheduled to speak in October to your local chapter of the National Organization for Women, you might begin by asking your audience to join you in celebrating the fact that NOW was founded in October 1966. Or you can talk about the World's Fair that began in October 1892 for the 400th anniversary of Christopher Columbus' first voyage—and how women used that opportunity for an international convocation that attracted 150,000 attendees. Or you could begin your speech with the October anniversary of the first national women's rights convention, held 1850—and celebrating its 150th anniversary in Worcester, Massachusetts, in October 2000.

A much longer section on Statistical Indicators (Part Three) also offers revealing information to thoughtful users. From Afghanistan to Zimbabwe, we include data on population, life expectancy, contraceptive use, literacy, education, maternity benefits, female legislators, and more. Often women are compared with men, so that the reader can readily see the relative status of women. We find, for example, that more than half of Algerian women are illiterate, while only a quarter of Algerian men are; on the other hand, women hold nearly 7 percent of the seats in Algeria's lower house, a rate not so different from the almost 12 percent that women have in the United States House of Representatives.

Sex ratios make for another interesting set of statistics: the ratio compares the number of men per 100 women in each nation. In Sweden and Switzerland, for example, where female health is a higher priority than in many other countries, we find a male-to-female ratio of 98:100—but in Bahrain, there are 133 males for every 100 females, suggesting that female nutrition and health is neglected. This one-line statistic thus becomes a worrisome bit of data meriting attention from the world community.

For Americans, one of the more important things that can be learned from perusing these statistics is how much better off women can be in other nations, especially in societal recognition of parental needs. In Austria, women get eight weeks of paid maternity leave before delivery and six weeks afterward; Bulgarian women get 120 days, which increases to 150 and 180 days for the second and third child; and even Qatar—where women voted for the first time in 1999—covers 100 percent of wages for 60 days (30 days for noncitizens).

The almanac also offers a section on Contemporary Issues (Part Two) that runs the alphabetical gamut from "abortion" to "working mothers." Many of these issues are further addressed in the News section (Part One), a lengthy analysis of the news as it relates to women—from the repression of women in Afghanistan to the progress in women's athletics.

Some of the most fascinating reading may be in the several hundred brief biographies of women in various places and times. We had to exclude many women who arguably merit inclusion, but we tried to systematize those included by profiling the women who have passed the milestones that mark society's recognition of women's achievements. We made a point of systematically including, for example, all women who have won Nobel Prizes and all women who have been elected as heads of state. In the United States timeline, for another example, we included all women who have received the unusual honor of being depicted on a stamp by the U.S. Post Office.

Reading about the last group offers still another approach to women's history, for the omissions can be as thought-provoking as the inclusions: the Post Office existed for more than a century before it created a stamp depicting a woman—and then the honor went to a non-American, Queen Isabella of Spain. A decade passed before the second was issued, but the 1902 honor went to Martha Washington, the wife of a famous man. Not until 1936 did the Post Office finally release a stamp that recognized an American woman of individual achievement, when Susan B. Anthony was honored on the thirtieth anniversary of her death. Still, women's history—whether in recognizing Washington's support of her husband or Anthony's impressive political achievements—develops when official venues such as the Post Office put a certified "stamp" on the historical record.

Another set of useful tools can be found in the Resources section at the back. It includes profiles of many women's organizations and agencies, lists of publications that provide further reading material, as well as web sites devoted to women's issues. Finally, we strongly encourage you to explore the cross-references and, especially, to use the index. If, for example, you read the entry on contraception in the Contemporary Issues section, you then could turn to the index and find many more entries on the subject: it will turn up in the Global and American timelines, in some state histories, in the biographies of women who worked on the issue, as well as in News (Part One).

Indeed, the subject of contraception is another one in which particularly revealing information can be mined from the data in the section on Statistical Indicators (Part Three). A thoughtful researcher will discover, for example, that despite the longtime ban of the Roman Catholic Church, women in nations that are largely Catholic practice birth control at nearly the same rate those as in non-Catholic societies: from Belgium and Brazil to Paraguay and Portugal, appreciably more than half of women in traditionally Catholic countries are actively controlling their reproductive lives. The lower rates of contraceptive practice instead are found in underdeveloped nations: Belgium's 79 percent rate, for instance, contrasts with 6 percent in Nigeria and 4 percent in Ethiopia.

Reference works are especially likely to encourage the one-thing-leads-to-another method of reading and thinking, and thinking about birth control leads naturally to thinking about those who took on tremendous societal disapproval to change attitudes on this subject. You will find biographies of Margaret Sanger, Marie Stopes, Mary Ware Dennett, and other women whose names have been appallingly absent in the end-of-the-millennium lists of those who mattered.

In addition to the 150th anniversary of the first national women's rights convention held in Worcester, Massachusetts, in October, the year 2000 will also feature one of the United Nations meetings devoted to women's issues held every five years. The others were convened elsewhere, but the 2000 meeting will be held in New York City from June 5-9. Among the items on the 2000 agenda are forced marriages, the sale of women as sexual slaves, and similar horrors that Susan B. Anthony, Elizabeth Cady Stanton, and others began addressing at the first international women's rights convention more than a century ago.

Indiana's May Wright Sewall chaired these conventions for many years—and yet most people today do not even know her name, let alone credit her and others who dedicated their lives and fortunes to champion women's rights around the world. We hope that this *Women's Almanac* will remind us all of the millions who have gone before us, and that, armed with the knowledge of where we have been and where we are now, women will find a straighter path to a more fulfilling future.

—*Doris Weatherford*

World News

A First for Women

A global precedent was set just weeks before the century's end, when New Zealand became the first nation in history to have a woman succeed a woman as an elected head of state.

In the general election held on Saturday, November 20, 1999, with almost 90 percent of New Zealanders voting, many conservatives were replaced with liberals. A solid majority for the Labor Party meant that party leader Helen Clark defeated incumbent Prime Minister JENNY SHIPLEY. Clark, age 49, pledged "a fair society, good education, good health system, and an absolute commitment to a growing economy which shares opportunity."

In no other nation has a woman succeeded a woman in the top office. This may not be surprising if historical context is considered: in 1893 New Zealand was the first nation in the world to fully enfranchise all of its women.

Panama's New President

Panama elected its first female president in May 1999, when Mireya Moscoso, 54, surprised pundits by upsetting the ruling party.

It was a sweet victory for Moscoso, whose husband, liberal Arnulfo Arias, was elected three times by the people of Panama and then toppled by conservative coups three times; during one of his administrations, Panamanian women got the vote. Moscoso went into exile with him when he fell for the final time in 1968. They lived in Miami for 20 years prior to his death in 1988.

Mireya Moscoso celebrates her inauguration as Panama's president. (AP/Wideworld Photos)

Subsequently Moscoso returned to Panama and took up the democratic cause. At a news conference upon her victory, she promised "a democratic country, with guaranteed freedoms, with judicial stability and social justice."

Political scientists called her election the most important since Panama's 1903 founding, particularly because—in accordance with the treaty signed during President Carter's administration—the United States ceded control of the Panama Canal Zone at the beginning of 2000. Although the outgoing president had cancelled its funding, Moscoso's September inauguration was free of violence and thousands cheered as she was sworn in at the National Stadium. She also included women in her inaugural speech, saying: "We begin to make real the hopes of thousands of Panamanian women over the centuries who . . . have nourished the hope that our society recognize their ability."

ELECTIONS

A Woman Wins, Yet Loses, In Indonesia

Although women have headed primarily Islamic countries for more than a decade, Indonesians spent much of 1999 arguing about whether or not the Koran permitted Megawati Sukarnoputri, the daughter of Indonesia's founding President Sukarno, to assume the presidency to which she was elected in June.

The June 1999 election was the most fairly conducted of any since Indonesia won its independence from the Netherlands in 1945. Although ballot counting in this nation of more than 200 million people on 13,000 islands took weeks, the final tally gave Megawati a clear lead, and five opposition parties (accounting for more than 90 percent of the votes) agreed that the results were accurate.

In the next months, however, East Timor voted to become independent of Indonesia, and the Indonesian military began committing gross violations of human rights against these civilians, including raping women. Although international headlines were full of news from Indonesia, virtually no media representatives asked the president-elect for her views—and when the parliament met to confirm the election in October, Megawati was pushed into second place.

She was forced to accept the vice presidency, while the top position was given to Abdurrahman Wahid, a popular but frail Islamic cleric whose party won just 12 percent of the vote in the June election. According to the Associated Press, his defeat of "the popular daughter of the country's founding father set off a wave of violent protests by her dis-

illusioned supporters." Megawati did not encourage the rioters and instead indicated her willingness to use the secondary position to its best advantage.

HONOR CODES

Developments in Egypt, India, and Bangladesh

Women's lives have historically been constricted by many moral codes that do not apply to men; in various societies at various times, families feel that they must avenge perceived wrongs to restore the family "honor." Egyptian President Hosni Mubarak recently decreed an end to a long legal tradition that "restored" family honor by allowing a rapist who married his victim to go free. Meanwhile, killings in India and Bangladesh drew worldwide attention to the issue of honor codes.

The Egyptian law, which dates to the days of British colonialism, was criticized by the government newspaper *Al-Ahram* because, by forcing the woman into marriage, it "encouraged the criminals...instead of deterring them" and allowed the rapist to escape prison. Debate in parliament over ratification of the decree was heated: some male legislators argued that family honor was at stake, while others averred that the law protected the raped women, who would be undesirable on the marriage market. The law was officially repealed in April 1999.

In India, a family in the town of Shimla (7,000 residents) in the northern Haryana province killed a young couple to enforce honor codes. In Haryana, all members of a village are considered to be kin: relationships between them are thought to be incestuous, and marriages are allowed only with members of another village. When Desh Raj, 23, and Nirmala, a 17-year-old with no surname, eloped in late March, they paid with their lives.

Nirmala's family killed Desh Raj, and then—apparently to avoid an appearance of unfairness—killed its own daughter. Hundreds watched as the couple were beaten and hacked to death with farm implements; their bodies were cremated on the village funeral pyre without ceremony. The groom's mother raged, "We blame the girl . . . It's always the girl who instigates these things." A police official found the thought of prosecution incomprehensible: "This couple was guilty of a social evil," he said. "But it is over now. The village has taken care of it."

In Bangladesh, civil authorities objected to the honor code that took the life of Bedi Begum, 18 years old, but did little to track down her killer when he fled. Although Bangladesh is primarily Islamic, it is not a theocracy, and

An Iranian woman surfs the Internet in Tehran's first cybercafe. (AFP/CORBIS)

religious authorities took the law into their own hands when they condemned her to death. An unidentified Islamic cleric and a council of male elders found her guilty of having premarital sex and of trying to induce an abortion with herbs that the 25-year-old father of her child gave her. Buried to the waist in the mud of her family's hut in the remote village of Batsail, she was flogged with a bamboo cane more than 100 times. The cleric prevented her family from going for medical help, and she died the next day.

HUMAN RIGHTS

Hope Springs Lightly in Iran

Although Iran is a theocracy that strictly governs women's lives—especially their appearance and sexual behavior—its mullahs are making concessions to a restive population, many of whom have lived in the West or have become familiar with western culture through the international media, especially the Internet.

Unlike in Afghanistan and Saudi Arabia, women are allowed to drive in Iran. Moreover, some important aspects of their status are measurably higher under the current theocracy than they were under the shah: According to Fen Montaigne of *National Geographic*, 74 percent of Iranian women are now literate, compared with 35 percent when the monarchy was overthrown in 1979; they have risen from one-third to one-half of university students. One in every three physicians is a woman—a higher rate

than most western nations. Because the government is worried about overpopulation, it offers free contraception, including free vasectomies. Birth control is strongly encouraged in compulsory and explicit premarital sex education classes—where, according to the Associated Press, men and women sit on opposite sides of the room.

New York Times correspondent Elaine Sciolino recently reported that Teheran movie audiences cheered at the end of Tamineh Milani's *Two Women* (1999), when the film's female protagonist frees herself of her heartless father and husband, and says: "I have to go to computer class. I have to learn how to drive." Montaigne also observed the difference between public and private behavior: although women do not dare to appear in public without Islamic clothing, behind the closed doors of a wedding reception in Teheran, women danced in tight, short dresses as though they were in the West. Change seems to come more slowly in rural areas and among the lower economic classes. In the desert oasis town of Khvor, for instance, boys often go on to school, but girls typically drop out at the fifth grade and begin weaving carpets to earn money for their dowries.

HUMAN RIGHTS

Women Protest in South Africa

Some 5,000 black South African women assembled in Kwathema in August 1999 and tried to reclaim their history. "You go to any library," said WINNIE MADIKIZELA-

MANDELA, "and the struggle of women has been ignored when the history of this country was written." The women not only dedicated a monument to civil rights leader Margaret Gazo, who died in 1974, but also took on current issues. Policewomen in uniform carried a banner reading, "Police Combat Violence Against Women." They pointed out that about 64,000 South African women are raped each year, a rate that is nearly three times greater than in the United States (which itself has a high rate). A disproportionate number of the South African victims are young girls: rapists target them because of a belief—also common in nineteenth-century Mediterranean cultures—that contact with a virgin cures venereal disease.

HUMAN RIGHTS
Student Speaks Out

When representatives of French-speaking nations met in Canada's New Brunswick province in late summer 1999, Anne-Marie Kabongo, a 25-year-old law student from the Democratic Republic of the Congo, addressed the assembly about the abuse of human rights that regularly occurs in her own and other member nations. According to the *Washington Post*, her voice trembled as she looked the 52 heads of state "straight in the eye" and told them that "their murderous military campaigns . . . had robbed their countries of hope." Although loudly applauded at the end of her speech, none of the leaders in the audience followed through in any meaningful way. Kabongo, who faced an uncertain future back in her dictatorial homeland, nonetheless vowed: "I don't care what they do to me. The truth had to be told."

MARRIAGE AND FAMILY
Brides for Sale in China

China's policy of one child per family is having unintended results for the current generation. Because boys have been favored over girls for thousands of years of Chinese history, when the communist government of the 1970s limited couples to just one child, many couples tried to make sure that their child was male—aborting or abandoning the girls—with the current result that, especially in rural areas, young men cannot find women to marry.

Although the communists had largely ended bride purchase, according to the All-China Women's Federation, this practice has begun again. Many of the young women sold as brides are actually kidnap victims, many from Vietnam. The International Organization for Migration estimates that 10,000 Vietnamese women recently have been sold into sexual slavery; women are also illegally brought in from Myanmar, North Korea, and even Russia. Most are lured to China by attractive job offers, and then find themselves physically forced into brothels or into marriages.

Women are both victims and exploiters, for the usual representative of a Chinese groom's family is his mother, who pays from $250 to $800 for a daughter-in-law. The fee is split between the initial kidnappers and traders who—exactly like the nineteenth-century slave trade—put prospective brides on the auction block for inspection. The further from the border a woman is taken, the higher the price traders demand for her—and the harder for her to escape.

The practice has increased especially on China's border with North Korea, as famine there has encouraged parents to sell daughters. Some see this as a favor to their daughters: A 24-year-old whose mother sold her for the equivalent of $47, for example, reported that her mother's last words were, "Don't worry about us any more and live a better life in China." The young woman summarized to Good Friends, Inc. of Seoul, "I understand her. She cried a lot."

MARRIAGE AND FAMILY
Polygamy in Africa and Russia

Although Kenya's Commission on the Status of Women hopes that polygamy is declining in the modern economy, the practice is still widespread across Africa; in Kenya, more than half of men have multiple wives. Ancentus Akuku Oguela, 81 and nicknamed "Danger," told the *Los Angeles Times* that he is separated from more than 80 wives, but currently has 37 in several homes in western Kenya. The youngest of his 172 children was just four months old when he was interviewed in March of 1999.

Far more typical are men with two or three wives, but health authorities nonetheless worry that such multiple partnerships are responsible for Africa's high rate of sexually transmitted disease, especially AIDS. The thinking of the ruling class is exemplified by a tribal spokesman in Nyanza province who argued that, to maintain their wealth, affluent men need multiple wives as a source of free labor: "Instead of employing somebody," said Alfred Odongo of South Kaganda, "you can have wives who . . . look after things on your behalf."

Akuku's youngest wife, age 20, is the mother of his newest baby. She says that she prefers her relationship with the octogenarian to that with her first husband, a much younger man who beat her when she did not become pregnant.

Automatically blaming women for infertility also continues in a large number of places throughout the world. Millions of women also are unfairly punished, especially in

Asia, for bearing a girl instead of a boy—even though Dr. NETTIE MARIA STEVENS discovered early in the twentieth century that the male chromosome determines the sex of a child. Although this ignorance brings huge pain to countless women, few scientific or feminist agencies make it a priority to educate the public on these biological facts.

The desire for more sons was a prime motivation for President Aushev of Ingushetia, a Russian republic in the Caucacus Mountains, when he signed an August decree that reinstated polygamy. It had been outlawed when the Soviet Union dominated the area, but Aushev, who took office in this primarily Islamic state in 1993, legalized it again.

Some area men already have multiple wives, and Aushev saw multiple marriages as particularly justified for a man whose first wife failed to bear sons, saying "The more boys there are in a family, the better." Aushev also noted that "If I did not have a son already, I am dead sure I would take advantage of the decree myself." Russia's Deputy Prime Minister Valentina Matviyenko was outraged: "This is amoral and offensive for women," she said.

POLITICS

The First Lady Tours Africa

In March of 1999, Hillary Rodham Clinton made a 12-day tour of northern Africa and met with the Moroccan king prior to his death, as well as with the president of Egypt and the prime minister of Tunisia. Clinton found that Tunisian women are making exceptionally good gains: she visited a family planning clinic there and met with the women who hold 7 percent of parliamentary seats.

In a speech on women's rights delivered in Tunisia's parliament building, Clinton decried the condition of women oppressed by religious fundamentalists from Algeria to Afghanistan. Girls' legs have been burned with acid, she said, because an ankle peeked from a skirt; teenagers are raped and forced into slavery; experienced professionals with skills to offer their nations are denied the right to work because they are female.

This tour was a milestone, marking visits by the American first lady to 75 nations. It was another of the spring break trips that she began taking with her daughter Chelsea in 1995: in the first, they drew particular attention to infanticide of girls in Southeast Asia, as well as the burning of brides in India when their families failed to pay dowries due to the grooms' families. This year, Uganda's ambassador, Edith Grace Sempala, summarized the feelings of many when she said, "In Mrs. Clinton, women all over the world have a friend."

POLITICS

"I Am the Boss": Women Take Charge in India

In 1993, India adopted a constitutional amendment that reserves one third of municipal governing seats for women—and within that, sets aside a percentage for low-caste women. The Center for Women's Development Studies in New Delhi announced in May that, as a result of the amendment, almost a million women have been elected to local governing councils and as mayors.

Rani, who has no surname, is an example: although illiterate and low-caste, she is intelligent and motivated. Elected mayor of the northern Indian village of Chijarasi, she rides a bus to government-sponsored training sessions and works to acquire electricity, latrines, and paved streets for her constituents.

"I am the boss," Rani says—something that enrages Brahman Alam Singh, who complained to *New York Times* reporter Celia W. Dugger: "We are the rulers, but now she is ruling." He and other men acknowledge that even if Rani does a good job, they will not vote for her in the next election—when her seat no longer will be reserved for a low-caste woman.

In more conservative areas, it is only the letter, not the spirit, of the law that is upheld. Munni Yadav is mayor of the village of Khoda, for instance, but her husband behaves as though he is—with his wife's approval. "Women," she said to the female reporter, "are not supposed to come out of the house and speak to strangers."

TALIBAN

Afghanistan's War on Women

The most striking story on the status of women in 1999 may be the crusade against female freedom that is being conducted by religious fundamentalists in Afghanistan and the international response—or lack thereof. The lesson of Afghanistan is that historical progress is not inevitable: women there had been as liberated as those in many nations, but their condition has reverted to the most oppressed state in the contemporary world.

Late in 1996, an extremely conservative Muslim group called the Taliban (which means "students") took over the government of Afghanistan, at the end of two decades of civil war and war with the former Soviet Union. Following a radical interpretation of Islam, they banished women and girls to the home. If a woman goes outside at all, she must be accompanied by a close male relative and

An Afghani woman wearing a burqa begs for help to feed her child. (AP/Wideworld Photos)

must wear a burqa that covers every inch of her body, including the eyes and nose; she sees the world from behind thick mesh. Women are not to speak—even the shoes they wear must be silent.

Schools, which were formerly coeducational, are now closed to girls and women, and women cannot hold any paying jobs. Many women with a lifetime of professional experience have been reduced to starvation or silent begging. Taliban theory is that every woman should be dependent on a man, but this ignores the fact that some 30,000 men died in the recent warfare, leaving thousands of widows with children to support.

Prior to the Taliban takeover, 40 percent of Afghanistan's doctors were women, but now female physicians are no longer allowed to practice and male physicians are forbidden to examine women. The health care system, dependent on female nurses who now are not allowed to work, has largely collapsed. Because 70 percent of teachers had been women, the same has happened in education. A woman who conducted a school in her home recently was shot in front of her students, and parents are forbidden to teach their daughters to read. Thousands of Afghanis watched in April 1999 when a 25-year-old woman was flogged with 100 lashes just days after giving birth to an out-

of-wedlock child; her mother, who helped hide the pregnancy from religious authorities, was beaten with 39 lashes.

Alarmed by the situation and concerned about a lack of international publicity, in October 1998 Mavis Leno and her husband, talk show host Jay Leno, kicked off an awareness campaign by donating $100,000 to the Feminist Majority Foundation's Campaign to Stop Gender Apartheid in Afghanistan. In March, Mavis Leno wrote a letter to "Dear Abby" that reached millions who had not heard about the Taliban. With Linda Bloodworth-Thompson, producer of *Designing Women* and other television shows, Leno organized a Hollywood fundraiser, which led to broadcasts on Radio Free Europe and Voice of America. Leno also asked people to call the campaign at 888-93WOMEN; by July, 45,000 readers had called to join.

In July, Mavis Leno said that "reporters told me the reason the Afghan situation had received so little coverage was that their editors thought Americans aren't interested in this kind of news." They were wrong, Leno concluded, adding that the State Department says the volume of mail on this issue is historic. She and her board have met with President Clinton and with United Nations officials, and they are hearing, according to Leno, that the Taliban is "allowing SOME home-schooling for girls and SOME segregated hospital wards for women."

VOTING RIGHTS

Democracy Comes to Parts of the Middle East

A century ago, women were just beginning global agitation for the vote: within the first few decades of the twentieth century, almost all women in Australia, Europe, and both Americas were fully enfranchised. As the century ends, the issue is not yet fully resolved worldwide.

In Qatar, a tiny emirate with no legislative body in the Persian Gulf, women voted for the first time in February of 1999. They cast their ballots for a municipal council that has advisory powers only. Six women were among the 248 candidates for 29 seats, but none won.

In Kuwait only a fraction of people are voters, and none are women. Of 2.3 million residents, fewer than 800,000 are citizens, and, of those, only 113,000 are registered voters. In May, Sheik Jaber al-Ahmed al-Sabah promised women the vote and the right to hold office in 2003—at the same time that he dissolved Kuwait's legislature, the only one in the Persian Gulf region.

While some Kuwaiti men argued that Islam has no religious prohibition against women's involvement in politics, others believe the opposite—and some attempt the same arguments against women's suffrage that were used in the West a century ago. An 18-year-old male university student, for example, told the Associated Press that women should not vote "because their minds are too small."

WARFARE

Kosovo: Will It Set Precedents on Rape?

When survivors of Serb attacks in Kosovo poured over the borders to safety in Albania and Macedonia, many told of women who were raped, often in front of their families, or were murdered after being gang raped. Officials of the U.S. Department of Defense said that as many as 20 women had been raped and killed at an army training camp in April, while United Nations war crimes prosecutor Patricia Sellers confirmed that rape was widespread and systematic, apparently a militarily sanctioned tool of war.

Although rape has gone hand-in-hand with warfare for millennia, only very recently have international peace keepers begun to see it as a crime worthy of prosecution. The outrages against Muslim women—whose culture makes virginity crucial—caused United Nations officials to issue the first indictments for rape as a war crime: in 1996, eight Serbian men were charged with rape and enslavement of Muslim women in Bosnia; among other specifics, U.N. casework accuses the men of selling a woman to other soldiers for German currency.

A year earlier, two Serbian military leaders were indicted for a series of crimes, including rape—but when the 1999 Kosovo war broke out, neither had been arrested. Many conclude that nothing has changed. In April 1999, Pentagon spokesman Kenneth Bacon informed the media that reports coming out of Kosovo indicated that Albanian women had been herded into camps, raped, and then killed. Said Bacon, "this is a very eerie and disturbing echo of documented instances of rape and killing of women in Bosnia during the Bosnian war, and its obviously outrageous that this is occurring."

WARFARE

Women in War: Contrasting African Models

At least 3,300 women have been kidnapped and held in sexual slavery during the last six years of political turmoil in northern Algeria. The estimate by Salima Tlemcani, a reporter for the newspaper *El Watan*, may well be low, due to the severe stigma against rape survivors.

Aicha Otemane, a 44-year-old mother of eight, is reported to be sorry that she told anyone about her nightmare experience. She was working as a shepherd when 11 men grabbed her; for the next three weeks, she was repeatedly raped at night; during the day, she was expected to cook and do laundry. When one of the men showed her clothing that belonged to her predecessor and said they had slit the woman's throat when they tired of her, Otemane determined to escape. Slipping out of the tent while the men slept, she returned to her village and reported the crime, which she now regrets.

New threats from the families of her captors forced her to flee to Algiers, where she and five of her children moved into a center operated by SOS—Women in Distress. The future is uncertain: Algerian society offers little solace to a raped woman, and her former friends resent that Otemane had the temerity to identify her rapists. Meanwhile, she aches for "my sheep, my goats, my little house."

A traveler going east from Algeria and crossing through Libya and Sudan (where slavery also exists) would arrive at Eritrea—and a very different scene of women and warfare. Eritrean women have served in the military for years: they can handle assault weapons as well as men, and rape by their compatriots is not an issue. Eritrea is again at war with Ethiopia, from which it won its independence in 1991—but female soldiers have the encouraging model of their mothers.

During its 30-year war for independence, women served in combat: one-third of the estimated 65,000 deaths were of female soldiers, who, like men, continue to perform a mandatory term of national service. Female veterans now serve at top levels of government, including the ministers of justice and labor, as well as the ambassador to the European Union. At the same time, Eritrean women acknowledge that cultural habits die hard: although genital mutilation is illegal, for example, some still practice it. On the whole, though, women's status is exceptionally high: as soldier Daniel Gitensae told the *New York Times*, "In the 30 years' struggle for freedom, there were ladies, so the ladies must now be with us."

WOMEN IN INTERNATIONAL GOVERNMENT

Promotions at the United Nations

When the United Nations indicted Yugoslavian President Slobodan Milosevic for war crimes in May, the chief prosecutor was Quebec's Louise Arbour. She soon resigned to accept the top position on Canada's Supreme Court, but the United Nations Security Council replaced her with another woman: in September, Switzerland's Carla del Ponte began focusing not only on crimes in the Balkans, but also in Rwanda. A former Swiss attorney general, del Ponte has headed international corruption investigations from Mexico to Russia; in 1988, she was the target of a bomb in Sicily, where she was investigating organized crime.

Arbour and del Ponte argued their cases before a 14-member panel of judges at the World Court in The Hague; the panel was also headed by a woman, Gabrielle Kirk McDonald. A Texan and a graduate of Howard University in Washington, D.C., McDonald was elected by her peers to a six-year term that ended in November 1999. Her replacement was also an American, 70-year-old Judge Patricia M. Wald of Washington.

Other women also have risen to the top at the United Nations in recent years: Its second-highest position, deputy secretary general, is held by Canadian Louise Frechette; in addition, women have been appointed to head six major agencies that deal with children, food, health, human rights, population, and refugees. Finland's Elisabeth Rehn controls the largest budget of any U.N. mission, supervising the representatives of 43 nations who police the Balkans. Nafis Sadik of Pakistan heads the population agency: she points out that U.N. surveys consistently show that women do not wish to have large numbers of children, but lack information on how to prevent pregnancy. In addition to family planning programs, Sakid also works to end genital mutilation; she reports that 15 of the 28 countries where the practice was common have now outlawed it.

World News Briefs

- By an 8 to 1 vote, Canada's Supreme Court ruled that an exclusively heterosexual definition of "spouse" is unconstitutional, thereby entitling same-sex partners to the legal advantages of common law marriages. The case was brought by an Ontario woman who sued her former partner for financial support.
- As the century ends, Luxembourg appointed its first female ambassador. Arlette Conzemius represents Luxembourg in the United States, while the U.S. sent its first openly gay ambassador, James Hormel, to Luxembourg.
- Debate in Thailand over a bill to allow women to retain their surnames after marriage was hung up by Interior Ministry bureaucrats, concerned that a commoner male might marry an aristocratic female, adopt her name, and pass himself off as a noble.
- Less than three years after Cristina Sanchez, 27, became Europe's first female professional matador, she held a Madrid news conference to announce her retirement. It was not the bulls in the ring that she found threatening, but instead her human counterparts. Describing her treatment by other matadors as "unfair" and "very difficult," Sanchez added, "I'm happy that there are other women bullfighters" who are following her lead.
- "We are making progress inch by inch," said Mo Mowlan, Britain's Secretary for Northern Ireland, after American First Lady Hillary Clinton visited Belfast in May to again urge peace there. The two women pointed to the vital work of women in ending violence—such as MAIRÉAD CORRIGAN-MAGUIRE and BETTY WILLIAMS, Irish recipients of the 1976 Nobel Peace Prize—and Clinton met with Northern Ireland's 14 female legislators. Further south, Galway granted her "the freedom of the city," the first woman so honored since the independent nation of Ireland began in 1922.
- Fed up with corrupt policemen who failed to enforce traffic laws, Mexico City's police chief created an all-female force in August, taking ticket-writing authority from some 900 men. Public Security spokesman Valentin Perez told the *Washington Post*, "Women, by nature, are more moral. They take the straighter road."
- Japan, which has long maintained its small families through a high abortion rate, authorized the sale of birth control pills—in the last year of the century and after 35 years of debate that centered on potential female promiscuity. Viagra went on the Japanese market just six months after its introduction in the West.
- The families of four American female missionaries who were raped and murdered in El Salvador in 1980 have filed a wrongful death suit against two former Salvadorian military officers now living in south Florida.
- In Chile, authorities were so quick to seize *The Black Book of Chilean Justice* upon its April release that author Alejandra Matus was unable to buy a copy for herself. She fled to Miami, while two editors in Santiago were arrested within hours of publication. Ironically, by August, the book was in its fourth printing in neighboring Argentina—a nation that itself has a history of censorship and other human rights abuse.
- In March, the Vatican confirmed its previous refusal to allow women to serve as deacons, a step below priests in the hierarchy of the Roman Catholic Church. Cardinal Dario Castrillon Hoyos explained that the church offers women "so many other opportunities."

U.S. News

Politics

CAMPAIGN 2000
Dole Drops Out

Elizabeth Dole became the first serious female presidential candidate in more than a quarter century when she ran for president in 1999. Her campaign, however, was short-lived. Dole reached her highest point in the polls immediately after announcing in the spring and went downhill from there. Although she placed second among more than a half-dozen male candidates at the beginning, she dropped out in October 1999, citing an inability to raise funds. "The bottom line," she said, "remains money." She could not compete with the $60 million amassed by George W. Bush or the deep pockets of billionaire Steve Forbes.

Dole's difficulties, however, were not simply a matter of money. The biggest problem may have been the fact that her resume in government consisted solely of appointed positions. She had never even run for local office, and that inexperience showed when she attempted to build a national network of supporters. What most distinguished her from other candidates, of course, was the fact that she was a woman—but although female, Dole has never identified herself with feminist goals. In the jargon of political scientists, the campaign lacked a message, and the subliminal one aimed at her gender was contradicted by the absence of a matching issue agenda.

Instead of indicating that voters will not support a woman for president, the campaign arguably demonstrated the opposite: Dole's credentials alone would not have gotten her far in a presidential race, and most voters who support her explicitly said they did so because they wanted to vote for a woman. Many who were initially supportive, however, were disappointed in this particular woman and ended up telling pollsters that they saw someone who appeared to be more style than substance.

Media coverage of the campaign displayed a continuing ignorance of women's history. They repeatedly referred to Dole as the first serious female contender for the presidency, although in fact both parties passed this milestone decades ago. Dole dropped out of the race three months prior to the first primary, whereas MARGARET CHASE SMITH ran in several Republican primaries in 1964, staying in long enough to amass 27 delegates for the convention. In 1972, SHIRLEY CHISHOLM competed in Democratic primaries and got 151 convention votes. Colorado's Patricia Schroeder, a veteran congresswoman, also ran a campaign more credible than Dole's in the 1988 presidential election.

CAMPAIGN 2000
Senator Clinton?

A precedent was set this year when First Lady Hillary Clinton began exploring a possible Senate run in New York: no other first lady has ever pursued an independ-

Hillary Rodham Clinton. (AP/Wideworld Photos)

ent political career. She was recruited by retiring Democratic Senator Daniel Patrick Moynihan, who hosted an introductory press conference for her. After spending the summer on a "listening tour" throughout the state, Clinton bought a house in New York in the fall of 1999—she announced that she had made a final decision in February 2000.

In most states, someone who is not a longtime resident would have little chance of winning, but Robert Kennedy showed decades ago that New Yorkers will elect a nationally known, non-local candidate. Like Kennedy, Clinton is an attorney with longtime family ties to the inner circles of government, and New Yorkers may show a similar willingness to vote for her.

Clinton has long identified herself with Eleanor Roosevelt, another controversial first lady. It would be historically appropriate if Roosevelt's home state chose to advance the progressive causes that she advocated a half-century ago by electing her ideological heir.

PROTEST

Dangerous Woman?

Kathleen Rumpf, a Catholic lay worker, was released from federal prison in Texas after friends in her hometown of Syracuse, New York, raised $2,000 to pay the fine that she received—along with a year in prison—for defacing a sign.

Rumpf had rewritten a sign at the School of the Americas at Fort Benning, Georgia, to read "School of Shame." The school trains Latin American military men in the techniques of brutal interrogation that have long violated human rights in most of Central and South America.

At 48, Rumpf has been arrested 80 times for her peace activism, but this arrest differed from earlier ones: under the provisions of an obscure statute, the warden refused to release her unless she promised to pay the $2,000 from her extremely limited income. The Syracuse *Herald-Tribune* summarized sarcastically, "Americans can feel safer in their beds at night with this dangerous [woman] behind bars."

PROTEST

Octogenarian Marches for Campaign Reform

On New Year's Day 1999, Doris Haddock headed east from Pasadena, California, intent on walking across the United States to draw attention to what she sees as the end of democracy because of the excessive influence of corporate money on politicians.

On January 24—her eighty-ninth birthday—she again donned the steel brace she wears to support her arthritic back and headed down the highway, undaunted even by four days of hospitalization because of dehydration caused by her walk across the Mojave Desert. Her emphysema improved after that, and by July, Haddock was in Texas—at the same time that George W. Bush announced he had amassed an unprecedented $36 million campaign chest in four months.

"It just infuriates me!" said Haddock, who spent her life in factory and office jobs. "I feel we are losing our democracy. The corporations are taking over and deciding

Doris Haddock, known as "Granny D," on her cross-country walk for campaign finance reform. (AP/Wideworld Photos)

who gets elected." She has some backing from Common Cause, but most of the trip's expenses are paid by supporters Haddock meets along the way. Her son and daughter-in-law also devoted 1999 to the cause, trailing along behind her in an old van with a bed in the back for the rests she takes as she hikes 10 miles a day.

Haddock asks supporters to contact their representatives in Congress for support of the McCain–Feingold Campaign Finance Reform Bill, sponsored by Democrat Russell Feingold of Wisconsin and Republican John McCain of Arizona. It would put teeth into campaign finance law by prohibiting large contributions to the national political parties from corporations, unions, and wealthy individuals—the loophole known as "soft money."

"Granny D," as Haddock calls herself, is nonpartisan and has not endorsed any of the presidential candidates. She stood in silent protest as Al Gore campaigned in Little Rock, Arkansas in August. And she had harsh words for Bush: "We don't know anything about his ideals or what he stands for. Apparently he stands for being able to raise a lot of money."

Haddock arrived in Washington, D.C., right on schedule, on February 29, 2000—about one month after her 90th birthday. More than 2,000 fellow protesters marched with her to the Capitol, where Haddock spoke on the east steps.

Granny D. continues to agitate for campaign finance reform, urging voters to reject anti-reform candidates in the upcoming November elections. "If we lose control of our government," she says, "then we lose our ability to dispense justice and human kindness." More details on her venture can be found at www.grannyd.com. Visitors to the site can sign an online petion, check the Activists' Calendar, discuss reform, and get the latest news on Granny's activities.

Science, Health, and Technology

ABORTION

Reproductive Rights Under Fire in Congress

In a June 1999 vote of 217-214, the House reinforced its edict of a year earlier, when it forbade the testing, development, or approval of any drug that acts as an abortifacient for women who suspect they are pregnant. Since the 1994 Republican takeover of the House, more than 100 pieces of anti-abortion legislation have been introduced; all but a handful have passed—and then met presidential veto. Both parties are following the mandates of their 1996 platforms; in particular, the Republican platform allowed no abortion whatsoever, not even in cases of rape or to protect the mother's life.

Controversy also continues over the small number of late-term, or "partial birth," abortions. A Virginia law banning them was struck down in July, when a federal judge ruled that the law "infringes upon the fundamental right to choose an abortion because it imposes an undue burden . . . and contains no health exception and an inadequate life exception."

In the same month, however, the House passed a new form of choice restriction by adopting legislation that would punish adults who assist a minor in obtaining an abortion without parental consent. The leadership refused to allow amendments that would have exempted counselors and medical providers from sentences of a year in prison and/or a $100,000 fine, which the bill imposes on anyone who crosses a state line to assist a minor in terminating a pregnancy.

Missouri joined the controversy in September, when legislators overrode Governor Mel Carnahan's May veto of what may be the harshest anti-abortion legislation ever passed. The law, which could force both physicians and their patients into life in prison, never uses the word "abortion" and instead substitutes "infanticide"—even though it could affect pregnancies as early as six weeks. The legislation contained no exception for a mother's health, an issue that Carnahan addressed in his veto message: "A dying woman could be arrested if she sought and obtained an abortion to save her life."

A spokesman for the Center for Reproductive Law and Policy termed the law "unprecedented in modern American jurisprudence." Federal courts had struck down comparable laws in 19 states, and the Supreme Court told Missouri in an earlier case that it could not put "unreasonable burdens" on women who seek to safely end a pregnancy.

Planned Parenthood quickly obtained an injunction against the legislation. And a week later, the eighth Circuit Court of Appeals struck down comparable legislation in Nebraska, Iowa, and Arkansas.

In late October, however, the seventh Circuit Court of Appeals upheld similar laws in Wisconsin and Illinois. With appellate courts ruling in direct opposition to each other, the issue heads to the U.S. Supreme Court. The situation illustrates the vital role that presidents have in appointing the federal judiciary.

Finally, in late October the Senate passed a ban on "partial birth" abortions—and in the course of the debate, also passed a historic confirmation of *Roe* v. *Wade*, the 1973 Supreme Court decision that legalized abortion. The ban passed 63-34 (two votes short of overriding President Clinton's expected veto), but several senators effectively voted both ways: By 51-47, the Senate also supported a resolution stating that the *Roe* decision established "an important constitutional right" and should not be overturned. The Senate had never before taken such a vote, and it was viewed as a surprising victory for its Democratic sponsor, Senator Tom Harkin of Iowa. All but two Democrats voted for it; 45 of the 54 Republicans were opposed.

BREAST CANCER
Recent Developments

Perhaps the most interesting contribution of space technology to women's health may be in breast cancer: a camera-like device developed for the Hubble Space Telescope is now being used to photograph suspicious breast tissue. The "camera" provides a much clearer image than previous technology, allowing a physician to go directly to a tiny area and extract a tissue sample with a needle instead of a knife. The new procedure cuts biopsy time in half, reduces costs 75 percent, causes no scars, and is far less painful than traditional surgery. NASA and the University of South Florida also are researching the Bioreactor, a tissue culture chamber that tests sensitivity to chemotherapy and hormonal therapy—something of great potential in the treatment of breast and ovarian cancer.

Breast cancer drew public attention in July, when Dr. Jerri Nielsen, the only physician at the South Pole, found a lump in her breast. Evacuation from Antarctica's 80-degree-below-zero winter was impossible, so the Air Force dropped equipment for Nielsen—who was anonymous in early reports—to treat herself. She performed her own biopsy during satellite communication with cancer specialists in the United States and, after confirming that the lump was cancerous, began chemotherapy on herself. When Antarctica's "spring" reached 58 degrees below zero in October, a replacement doctor quickly landed and Dr. Nielsen was returned to her native Ohio.

HEART DISEASE
Beyond Breast Cancer

Despite media attention to breast cancer, heart disease is the greatest killer of American women. Every year since 1984, heart attacks, strokes, and other cardiovascular diseases have killed more women than men, even though most of the public continues to believe the myth that men are most vulnerable to heart attacks. Instead, women are not only more likely than men to have heart disease, it kills more women than the next 16 causes of death combined.

According to the National Institutes of Health and other sources, more than half of all women alive today will die of cardiovascular disease. This compares with 12.5 percent who are diagnosed with—but do not necessarily die of—breast cancer. The most common form of cancer among women is skin cancer, which is largely preventable by reducing exposure to the Sun. Although both it and breast cancer occur more often than in the past, both also are becoming more treatable and less fatal. The most deadly form of cancer is lung cancer, which surpassed breast cancer as the leading cause of women's cancer deaths in 1987.

The public again seems unaware of this reality: while women are becoming more conscientious about doing monthly breast self-examinations and getting annual mammograms, young women are beginning to smoke at a higher rate than young men. More than 28 percent of women ages 25 to 34 are smokers; the American Lung Association predicts that women will reach equality in this unfortunate area in 2000.

REPRODUCTIVE TECHNOLOGY
Breakthrough

The year's most impressive scientific breakthrough may be that, for the first time in human history, we appear to be on the edge of extending female fertility past menopause. In a September 1999 report to the American Society of Reproductive Medicine in Toronto, Canada, physicians from the United States and England disclosed that they had removed parts of a woman's ovary, frozen them, and then reimplanted them when she was older; the ovary grew to normal size, and she began menstruating. The anonymous woman has not yet tried to become pregnant, but there appears to be no reason why she could not.

SPACE SCIENCE
Historic Launch

Air Force Colonel Eileen Collins became the first woman to command a spacecraft when she led a five-person team that flew the $2.7-billion Chandra X-ray Observatory into space in July 1999. During a five-day flight, Chandra was

In July 1999, Commander Eileen Collins makes a log entry aboard the space shuttle Columbia. *(AFP/CORBIS)*

released approximately 150 miles above the Earth, where rockets boosted it into an orbit that extends 87,000 miles—x-rays that it emits will travel far beyond that. Astronomers anticipate that these x-rays will offer a look at the very origins of the universe.

It was Collins's third trip into space, and the second for Lieutenant Colonel Cady Coleman, 38, a mission specialist with a doctorate in polymer science and engineering from the Massachusetts Institute of Technology. In 1990, Colonel Collins, 42, was the first female pilot chosen to be an astronaut by the National Aeronautics and Space Administration (NASA). NASA had a long history of hiring men whose expertise was as aviators. Women had performed as well as men in 1961 tests, but NASA excluded them from the space program.

Instead of aviators, NASA's female astronauts have been primarily scientists. Earlier female astronauts—SALLY RIDE, MAE JEMISON, Kathy Sullivan, Eileen Ochoa, and Shannon Lucid—all had doctorates. Conversely, the dozens of male astronauts hired often had relatively slim scientific credentials.

In honor of this ninety-fifth shuttle mission, the first commanded by a woman, NASA invited several dozen representatives of women's organizations and media to witness the historic launch of *Columbia* at Florida's Cape Canaveral. Health and Human Services Secretary Donna Shalala spoke of the scientific advances brought about by space exploration, while NASA's head, Dan Goldin, introduced women who now hold top jobs as engineers and other project heads, including chief scientist Kathie L. Olsen and Jennifer A. Harris, Mars 2001 operations system development manager.

However, the launch was cancelled when the system's computers shut it down just six seconds before liftoff because a faulty sensor falsely detected a hydrogen leak.

A second attempt the next night also was cancelled; the mission finally took off on July 23. Seconds later, an electrical short knocked out the computers controlling two of the three main engines, and Collins's spaceship was potentially in danger. She nonetheless accomplished the mission and, despite a second hydrogen problem, brought *Columbia* safely in on schedule at California's Edwards Air Force Base, where she accomplished another first by being the first woman to land a spacecraft.

The launch, which NASA termed "There's Space in My Life," was a family reunion of female astronauts, who reminisced on the past and offered updates on their current lives. The first in space, Sally Ride, left NASA in 1987 after her second flight and is currently a professor of physics at the University of California at San Diego.

The first woman to walk in space, Kathryn Sullivan, flew three missions between 1984 and 1992, and then returned to her first love, oceanography, and the U.S. Navy. She served in the Persian Gulf War and, in 1992, was named chief scientist at the National Oceanic and Atmospheric Administration. Dr. Sullivan now teaches at Ohio State and serves on numerous corporate and charitable boards, especially those related to girls and science.

Although less known to the public, Donna Shirley is one of NASA's most accomplished women. She recently retired after more than three decades as an engineer, including heading the team that built *Sojourner*—named in part for SOJOURNER TRUTH—which was delivered to Mars by the successful Pathfinder project in 1997. *Sojourner* explored the surface of Mars for nearly three months, which was more than 10 times its expected lifetime. Shirley, who is a mother and the author of *Managing Martians* (1998), returned to her native Oklahoma and is teaching at the University of Oklahoma.

A current project of NASA's Jet Propulsion Laboratory in Pasadena, California, concerns Mars and has women in all of its top jobs, a first in NASA's history. Project manager Sarah Gavit, chief scientist Suzanne Amrekar, and chief engineer Kari Lewis led a 55-member team that launched two probes in January. The women, who range in age from 25 to 37, designed instruments to slam into the red planet at speeds high enough to force them three feet into its surface—and strong enough to endure this crash landing and radio back information on their findings. That the team's leaders are all women was accidental, but their youth was a deliberate management choice: "They didn't want people with the old ways of thinking," Gavit said, "because they knew it was a really challenging mission."

TEENAGE PREGNANCY

Teen Moms on the Decline

Teenage pregnancy rates are falling dramatically, dropping 17 percent during the 1990s to the lowest level since 1973. "We have made real progress—and must do more—to encourage young people to delay parenthood," said Vice President Al Gore at a roundtable discussion with teenagers at the White House. Out-of-wedlock births are declining among both black and white women, and the Department of Health and Human Services (HHS) reports that the nation's overall birthrate is at an all-time low. Moreover, the babies that women do deliver are healthier: prenatal checkups are at a historic high, while maternal tobacco use is falling.

About one-third of pregnancies were terminated in 1997, the year of the HHS report, but the abortion rate is dropping as more women use more reliable contraception. Fear of AIDS also contributed to greater male use of condoms, with a resultant drop in pregnancies. The major responsibility for birth control continues to fall on women, and the Alan Guttmacher Institute—which has long promoted family planning—particularly pointed to young women's acceptance of new implants and injections such as Norplant and Depo-Provera, which provide long-term contraception without the need to remember a daily pill.

The institute also announced that the birth rate for unmarried black women is now at the lowest since it began keeping records in 1969. Yet even though teenage motherhood is declining everywhere, rates vary greatly by state: Vermont's 26.9 per 1,000 births is lowest, while Mississippi's is highest at 73.7. Some observers have explained the variances by suggesting that young women avoid pregnancy in direct correlation to cultural expectations and to their perception of realistic opportunity in areas other than early motherhood.

Science, Health, and Technology News in Brief

- Wal-Mart—the nation's largest retailer with 2,400 pharmacies in its stores—announced that it would not sell Preven, commonly known as the "morning after pill." If taken within 72 hours of unprotected sex, Preven prevents pregnancy. Wal-Mart alleged that it was not taking a moral stance, but instead feared the product would not sell well enough to justify stocking it.

- Sixty organizations representing women asked the Equal Employment Opportunity Commission in June to rule that employers must include contraception in insurance packages. Arguing that excluding this aspect of health coverage amounts to illegal sex discrimination, they pointed especially to the eagerness with which many insurance plans embraced the male impotence drug Viagra—something that is not nearly as essential to maintaining health.

- Greater numbers of women in top positions at NASA have led to direct research benefits for women, especially in health. When early studies showed gender differences in response to space radiation, for example, environmental scientists revised their recommendations on toxic tolerance levels. Studies on the effect of zero gravity on bone density are especially applicable to women—who lose bone mass at a significantly greater rate than men, causing many women to suffer debilitating osteoporosis.

- Without permission from governmental authorities, volunteer women are running human milk banks from coast to coast. New mothers with an excess of milk volunteer to supply the banks, which require a doctor's prescription for use. Families pay $2.50 an ounce to cover processing and delivery, and most milk goes to premature babies and those with allergies to other milks. The Human Milk Bank Association has adopted guidelines to ensure safety, but the Federal Food and Drug Administration does not yet fully support the effort.
- A study by Yale University's Dr. Sally Shaywitz showed increased activity in the brains of women who took estrogen, compared with brain scans of women who received a placebo instead of estrogen. Hoping that the hormone may help women avoid Alzheimer's and other diseases, Shaywitz's research team pointed out that, without estrogen supplements, the average woman spends at least half of her adult life with inadequate levels.

Business, Law, and the Workplace

MILITARY MILESTONES
Graduations and a Promotion

In the last year of the century, the first women graduated from the two military academies that were America's last to admit women. At Virginia Military Institute, which accepted women in 1997, transfer students Chinh-Yuan Ho and Melissa Kay Graham were the first female graduates in the school's 160-year history. Nancy Mace was the first to graduate from The Citadel, the Charleston, South Carolina, school that fought applicant Shannon Faulkner all the way to the U.S. Supreme Court in 1995.

Two decades earlier, pressure from feminists forced Congress to admit women to the national military academies, and this year, Mary Godfrey was the top graduate at the U.S. Naval Academy. Josephine Nguyen ranked second and—in an impressive display of merit—half of the top 10 of the graduating class at Annapolis were women, although women composed just 15 percent of the class. In 1995, Rebecca Marier graduated first in her class at the U.S. Army's West Point Military Academy.

Also, in 1999 Rear Admiral Evelyn Fields became the first woman and the first African-American to head the National Oceanic and Atmospheric Administration. She will command some 400 officers, all of whom are scientists or engineers.

PAY EQUITY
Women's Work and Worth

Equal Pay Day—when women's average wages caught up with those of men for the previous year—was April 8, 1999. In other words, on average a woman must work 16 months to earn what a man makes in 12. Women's wages have risen from 59 percent of the average male wage when feminists first began drawing attention to the issue in the 1970s, but the number seems stuck at about 74 percent. One trend has remained unchanged for the last three decades: black college–educated women still make less than white high school–educated men.

Equal Pay Day effectively draws attention to the issue, but a solution requires national effort. Because women are more likely than men to work at low-wage jobs, congressional approval of boosting the minimum wage to $6.15 an hour—as proposed by President Clinton and Labor Secretary Alexis Herman—could prove beneficial. Many business experts predicted disaster when this was done in 1996, but instead the economy flourished. Experience shows, too, that any raise in the minimum wage not only benefits those directly affected, but also makes it likely that pay levels slightly above the minimum also rise, thus benefiting the vast majority of women.

Income inequity also is being tackled with new enthusiasm by organized labor, which ran radio ads on the subject in 1999. Recently elected AFL-CIO president John Sweeney is more open to the postindustrial worker than were some of his predecessors—and that worker is often a woman. In what was called the biggest union victory since the United Auto Workers organized General Motors in 1937, more than 70,000 Los Angeles health care workers voted in February to join Service Employees International. Most of the new union members were black and Hispanic women, paid the entry-level minimum wage of $5.65 an hour—an annual income that averages less than $12,000.

SEXUAL HARASSMENT
Supreme Court Ruling

In a 5-4 ruling, the Supreme Court declared in May that school districts can be held liable if they knowingly allow students to engage in sexually harassing behavior. The suit was brought by Georgia parents whose third-grade daughter was repeatedly subjected to obscene gestures and sexual demands from a boy in her class; the parents sued after their complaints to school officials were ignored.

Four dissenting justices argued that a positive ruling would lead to frivolous lawsuits. Justice Sandra Day O'Connor made it clear in the opinion she wrote for the court's majority that they were not encouraging trivial cases or excessive federal control of schools, but instead dealing with a genuine problem that has been ignored. Acknowledging the power of the prevailing attitude that "boys will be boys," she set a high standard of proof for future cases: "Damages are not available for simple acts of teasing and name-calling," O'Connor wrote. School officials, however, should be held liable when they are indifferent to sexual harassment "so severe, pervasive, and objectively offensive that it can be said to deprive the victims of access to educational opportunities."

SEX DISCRIMINATION

Legal Victories

In a victory for equal access, the Air Force backed its women in July 1999, when First Lieutenant Ryan Berry refused to work with a woman on missile silo duty at Minot, North Dakota. Berry, a 26-year-old husband and father, feared the presence of a woman on the two-person, 24-hour underground assignment would be too sexually tempting. Instead of eliminating women from the duty as Berry desired, the Air Force decertified his missile status. Backed by Archbishop Edwin F. O'Brien, the Roman Catholic official assigned to the military, Berry is appealing the decision.

Also in 1999, a New York City court freed 29-year-old Adelaide Abankwah from the immigration detention center where she languished for more than two years. Abankwah fled her native Ghana because she was about to be subjected to genital mutilation. Because she used a false passport, she was immediately detained. Immigration authorities argued that her fears were not sufficient to entitle her to asylum in the United States, but after several denials and a great deal of celebrity support, the U.S. court of appeals issued a decision supporting Abankwah in July.

Business Briefs

- Mary Ellen Heyde headed some 200 engineers on Ford's 1999 Windstar minivan—and sales soared after an ad campaign that featured some of the 50 female engineers who worked on its design. Among their family-friendly innovations are space for diapers and overheard lights that, when a door opens, do not glare in a sleeping baby's

eyes. The success of the project, said an anonymous male executive, proved "we could put a woman in charge of a vehicle line and not go to hell in a handbasket."

- Carleton Fiorina, 44, was named CEO of Hewlett-Packard in July, at a time when stock analysts called the California computer company "conservative, old-fashioned, and slow." Formerly with Lucent Technologies and its parent company, AT&T, Fiorina graduated from Stanford University with a B.A. in medieval history and philosophy prior to earning an M.B.A. from the University of Maryland. Although only two other women lead Fortune 500 companies—which, with her appointment, gives women six-tenths of 1 percent of the nation's top business positions—Fiorina declared, "there really is not a glass ceiling anymore."

- President Clinton directed the Labor Department in June to draft rules that will allow states to spend unemployment compensation funds for parents who choose to use the 1993 Family Leave Act. Because unemployment is so low, many of these funds are running great surpluses; as many as six million parents of newborns or newly adopted children could be eligible for 12 weeks of paid leave annually.

- Martha Barnett, 52, is the second woman to lead the American Bar Association. A Floridian, she considers her most important case to have been winning compensation in 1994 for descendants of black survivors from the town of Rosewood, which was destroyed by white rioters in 1923.

Sports

BASKETBALL

The WNBA

Now in its third year, the Women's National Basketball Association (WNBA) had a sellout crowd for its first all-star game. Almost two million people cheered for the players at regular season games, with attendance averaging more than ten thousand fans per game.

The league's Western Division currently includes Houston, Los Angeles, Minnesota, Phoenix, Sacramento, and Utah; the Eastern has Charlotte, Cleveland, Detroit, New York, Orlando, and Washington. Four expansion teams are targeted for 2000: the first to reach the WNBA's minimum requirement for season ticket sales was Indiana. The women arranged for the last necessary ticket to be bought by Indiana's former U.S. Senator Birch Bayh—who, almost three decades ago, wrote the legislation that in 1972 became Title IX, which insists on equity between funding for girls and boys in public schools athletics.

SOCCER
United States Wins World Cup

More than ninety thousand fans packed California's Rose Bowl in July 1999, when the United States—not a nation known for soccer—beat China in what may have been the most intensely watched competition between women's athletic teams ever.

In a larger context, many conservative U.S. newspapers directly attributed the American victory to Title IX, legislation that they opposed at its passage. After Title IX of the 1972 Education Act required gender equity in funding for school athletics, soccer became the team sport that schools offered to girls in lieu of football. A quarter century later, it paid off.

Even preliminary competition against Germany drew precedent-setting crowds to New Jersey's Giants Stadium, and ESPN audiences were as large as those for baseball games. The final victory was a dramatic one, coming after 120 scoreless minutes. When Brandi Chastain kicked the winning goal in the tiebreaker shootout, she exuberantly pulled off her shirt and waved it, a common practice among men in soccer leagues. Viewers shared her excitement, and the immediate news coverage had nothing but praise for her and the team—but later stories focused negatively on Chastain's "exposure" of her sports bra, a dark, halter-like garment less revealing than the average swimsuit.

Most observers, however, praised the women for their teamwork, their lack of egotism, their appreciation of fans—and contrasted this with the salary demands and frequent bad behavior all too common among professional athletes.

TENNIS
Champion Retires

"I have nothing left to prove," Germany's Stephanie Graf said in an August 1999 news conference in Heidelberg when she announced her retirement from tennis. Graf has continued to prove herself since 1988, when she became the third woman to win all four annual Grand Slam tennis tournaments. The first two were American Maureen Connolly in 1953 and Australian MARGARET COURT in 1970.) As both tennis and women's athletics generally have greatly increased in popularity, Graf won much more money than earlier contenders, taking home more than $21 million in career prizes.

Brandi Chastain rejoices at her team's victory over China in the 1999 Women's World Cup. (AFP/CORBIS)

TENNIS
The Williams Sisters

Millions were riveted to their television screens during the 1999 tennis season, with this year's stars being African American sisters Venus and Serena Williams. Venus, 19, won England's summer Wimbledon, and, in September, Serena, 17, eliminated 127 other women to win the U.S. Open. The next day, the sisters returned to the same court to win their first U.S. Open doubles crown and their second Grand Slam title as a team. The sisters' victories are the first for black women in tennis since ALTHEA GIBSON won these coveted titles four decades ago.

TRACK AND FIELD
Jaeger Breaks Record

At age 56, American Kathy Jaeger performed all too well during the World Veteran Athletic Games in the United Kingdom in July 1999. She shattered records by completing the women's 100-meter dash in 13.5 seconds. The victory was marred when Jaeger was forced to submit to tests, including a physical examination, to prove that she was, indeed, a woman. The mother of two felt compelled to pose in a dress that, according to the *Manchester Guardian*, "emphasized her femininity."

Contemporary Issues

Abortion

Recognition of a woman's right of access to abortion is a major advance in human rights in recent years. However, one-quarter of the world's women have severely limited access to abortion or no access at all.

Abortion was not illegal until the nineteenth century and, indeed, was not considered a moral issue; in the late nineteenth and early twentieth century, laws against contraception were enforced far more strongly than those against abortion. As awareness of women's human rights has grown, so has the understanding that fertility presents unique health concerns for women and, as a result, of the need to protect women's right to control their reproductive health. After years of being outlawed, abortion has now been recognized as a human right—although many still disagree, feeling that the willful termination of a pregnancy is tantamount to murder. The issue is so controversial that the Program of Action of the International Conference on Population and Development, held in 1994, stopped short of calling for the legalization of abortion, urging governments instead to "to deal with the health impact of unsafe abortion as a major public health concern."

Having too many children, having them too close together, or having them too early or too late in life is detrimental to the health of both mothers and children. While the greater availability of contraception and the increased education of women and girls lower the incidence of abortion, the need for safe abortion will never disappear. In countries where abortion is illegal or highly restricted, women still manage to terminate their pregnancies; however, they cannot do it safely. Concern, therefore, is not just access to abortion, but to safe abortion. According to the World Health Organization, approximately 20 million illegal abortions occur every year. The United Nations Children's Fund estimates that 75,000 women die every year from unsafe abortions. The legal status of abortion appears to have little effect on its incidence—the rate is higher in some countries where it is illegal than in ones where it is legal.

Abortion decreases where women have access to education and contraception; making abortions difficult to obtain has a lesser effect in the number of abortions performed. In Tunisia, for example, where abortion is provided on request, abortions have been declining because of increased availability of contraception. Conversely, in Chile where abortion is illegal without exception, it is estimated that one abortion occurs for every two births, giving Chile one of the highest abortion rates in Latin America. In Nigeria, less than 10 percent of women of reproductive age use contraception and abortion is illegal except to save the life of the mother. Nevertheless, approximately 20,000 women die each year as a result of unsafe abortions.

A drug developed in 1982 by a French pharmaceutical company has the potential to generate enormous changes in the way abortions are performed. RU 486, also known as mifepristone, can be used to induce abortion at the earliest confirmation of conception, and it can be taken in the privacy of the home. Mifepristone can also function as emergency contraception; a recent World Health Organization study found RU 486 to be effective up to five days after unprotected sex.

An often overlooked aspect of abortion is the issue of coerced abortion; that is, women forced to have abortions they don't want. This occurs legally in countries where restrictive population control policies limit the number of children that women may have. It also happens in cultures where boys are more highly desired than girls—where a woman's value is based on bearing a son. Although this issue receives little publicity, outlawing coerced abortions is as important as legalizing safe ones.

Contraception and abortion are parts of the same issue. Because contraception is not completely effective and human beings are not completely reliable in using it correctly, unwanted pregnancies will continue, and thus the necessity for access to safe abortions.

For Further Reading

Costa, Marie. *Abortion: A Reference Handbook*. Denver, Co: ABC-CLIO, 1996.

Pojman, Louis P., and Francis Beckwith, eds. *The Abortion Controversy: 25 Years After Roe v. Wade*. Davis, California: Wadsworth Publishing Company, 1998.

—*Jo Lynn Southard*

AIDS

Nearly half of the adults living with HIV/AIDS today are women. Infection rates among women are growing faster than among any other group; over two million women were newly infected with AIDS in 1998. Since the beginning of the epidemic, 4.7 million women have died of AIDS.

Discrimination against women with AIDS can be difficult to measure. Reactions range from being shunned by one's neighbors to being beaten by one's partner. Even when a woman is infected by her husband, she risks being battered and turned out from her home. The stigma attached to HIV/AIDS has helped fuel its spread. Denial of infection results in a reluctance to change risky behavior—medical care is avoided and the infection continues to spread. In some of the hardest hit countries, the average life expectancy has dropped by almost 30 years.

Initially, HIV/AIDS appeared to be restricted to small groups of people who engaged in particular behaviors. However, in the two decades of the epidemic, AIDS has spread more quickly among women than among any other population. In many cultures the inequality of women contributes greatly to their increased risk of infection: if women have few rights within the family, and if their only risk behavior is having sex with their husbands, there is little women can do to protect themselves. In countries with large-scale sex industries, like Cambodia, where approximately 43 percent of brothel workers were HIV positive in 1998, HIV is spread from male clients to sex workers, to other male clients, to the regular partners of those clients.

HIV/AIDS has hit hardest among sub-Saharan African women. Nearly half of the new infections that occur every day occur in this part of the world; eight of 10 women who are already infected live in this area. At some clinics in southern Africa, 45 percent of women tested during pregnancy are HIV positive. In central and western Africa, the percentage is approximately four. But HIV/AIDS infections in women are growing in the rest of the world as well. In Haiti, tests of pregnant women revealed that more than 8% were infected. In Brazil, as AIDS spreads among women, the male to female ratio of infection has decreased; in the state of Sao Paulo, AIDS is the leading cause of death for women aged 20 to 34 and has been since 1992. In the United States, 16 percent of persons with AIDS are female, in Canada, almost 22 percent, and in Western Europe, 20 percent are women. Worldwide, 43 percent of HIV positive adults are women.

Awareness, prevention, and treatment of HIV/AIDS are relatively high in industrialized nations, where new cases continue to decrease. However, most people with AIDS live in the developing world, where even discussion of the disease is stigmatized. The devastation of AIDS is also more severe in these countries, where millions of women have died, leaving millions of orphaned children and surviving partners. For women, equality—in the family and in economic life—must be achieved in order to halt the spread of AIDS among females.

For Further Reading

Long, Lynellyn D., and E. Maxine Ankrah. *Women's Experiences with HIV/AIDS: An International Perspective.* New York: Columbia University Press, 1997.

Roth, Nancy, and Linda K. Fuller. *Women and AIDS: Negotiating Safer Practices, Care, and Representation.* Binghamton, NY: Haworth, 1998.

—*Jo Lynn Southard*

Kenyan women receive information about living with AIDS. (AFP/Corbis)

Anorexia and Bulimia

Anorexia nervosa is an ailment in which a person attempts to reach and maintain a below-normal body weight and is unusually afraid of gaining weight; bulimia nervosa is a condition in which a person has repeated episodes of binge eating, followed by purging, including induced vomiting, abusing laxatives, excessive fasting, or extreme exercising. Ninety percent of anorexics and bulimics are women. Many young women alternate between anorexia and bulimia.

Anorexia has been clinically recognized for more than 100 years; bulimia has been identified only since 1979. Nonetheless, bulimia is the most common eating disorder among young women. Anorexia and bulimia represent both a desire to be fashionably thin and a desire to take control of one's life and body. Theories about anorexia and bulimia postulate that it is a problem largely in Western cultures and that it is the result of unrealistic media images of women. But, in fact, anorexia has been around much longer than the current ultrathin media standard for women, and doctors are now finding occurrences of anorexia and bulimia in cultures all around the world.

Anorexia is most likely to appear in early adolescence, when teenage dieting becomes an obsession. Bulimia more often occurs later in adolescence and may be triggered by a life change—such as leaving home to go to college. In the United States, an estimated 20 percent of young women suffer from an eating disorder; in addition, at any given time, half of the teenage girls in the U.S. are on a diet, the most common predictor of an eating disorder. Recent studies in Australia found an estimated 68 percent of 15-year-old girls to be dieting. In Europe, an estimated six in 10,000 women suffer from anorexia and 8.5 in 10,000 from bulimia. One in 10 Argentinean women suffer from anorexia or bulimia.

In cultures that value plumpness as a sign of fertility or prosperity, eating disorders of any kind are rare. However, their incidence is growing even in these cultures. In some cases, this may be the result of the intrusion of Western cultural standards; in some, such as India and Hong Kong, anorexia has been associated with a desire to fast for religious reasons.

Approximately 20 percent of anorexics die from the disorder. Other complications of anorexia include slow heart rate, low blood pressure, and hormonal imbalance. If hospitalized, where they receive nutritional rehabilitation and counseling, half of anorexics make a full physical and psychological recovery. The medical complications of bulimia include: erosion of dental enamel, dehydration, and heart problems. As bulimia was only recently identified, long-term recovery rates are unknown, however, psychotherapy appears to provide improvement for most bulimics, with medication being not quite as effective.

It is not entirely clear what media images of women contribute to the rise of anorexia and bulimia. Nor is it completely clear what role women's rights play, although incidences of eating disorders appear to be higher in cultures where women have more freedom. What is clear is that anorexia and bulimia grow out of a young woman's distorted image of her body and the world around her.

For Further Reading

Buckroyd, Julia. *Anorexia and Bulimia: Your Questions Answered.* Rockport, Mass.: Elements, 1996.
Costin, Carolyn. *The Eating Disorder Sourcebook.* Los Angeles: Lowell House, 1999.

—*Jo Lynn Southard*

Breast Cancer

The International Agency for Research on Cancer reports that breast cancer is the most common non-skin cancer among women in industrialized countries and the second most common in developing countries. A woman who dies of breast cancer dies an average of 20 years sooner than would otherwise be expected. As a result, two million person-years are lost in the United States and Europe each year.

The incidence of breast cancer in industrialized nations began increasing about 1940. By the 1970s, one in 20 women in the United States was at risk of developing breast cancer; by the 1990s, the number was one in eight. Beginning in the 1980s, women's groups advocated for increases in money for research and treatment of breast cancer. One major outcome of that movement has been the increased use of mammography screening. As a result, breast cancers can be detected earlier and are more treatable. This, in turn, has led to higher survival rates in the last decade.

The first World Conference on Breast Cancer was held in Ontario, Canada, in 1997, sponsored by the Women's Environmental and Development Organization and other women's groups. The Global Plan of Action for the Eradication of Breast Cancer was drafted at that conference and presented to the second conference in 1999. It outlines recommendations for breast cancer research, prevention, and treatment, and notes that most governments do not have a clear policy on how to reduce breast cancer. The conferences have highlighted the worldwide nature of the disease. Although rates of breast cancer are higher in industrialized countries, they are growing in other parts of the world. For example, the World Health Organization estimates that breast cancer incidences will increase 40-50 percent in the next few years in Central America; the rates are also increasing in the Caribbean, South America, India, China, and South Asia.

Although the death rate from breast cancer in Africa is a relatively low 3 per 100,000 (compared to 20 per 100,000 in industrialized countries), many experts are concerned because most women in nonindustrialized countries have little access to information about detection, treatment, and prevention of breast cancer. Also, certain cultural beliefs lead women to ignore symptoms until treatment is more difficult. A woman from Egypt attending the first World Conference noted that breast cancer is stigmatized in her country; women are ashamed to tell their families, and, if they have surgery, they want immediate reconstruction so no one will know.

Decreasing mortality rates in the United States and Europe demonstrate that breast cancer can be eradicated. The mammogram, in particular, is a simple and cost-effective method of detection. The Global Plan of Action calls on governments to provide funding for research on the treatment and causes of breast cancer and on ways for emerging nations to industrialize without contributing to increased incidences in breast cancer.

For Further Reading

Potts, Laura K., ed. *Ideologies of Breast Cancer: Feminist Perspectives.* New York: St. Martin's Press, 1999.

Raz, Hilda, ed. *Living on the Margins: Women Writers on Breast Cancer.* New York: Persea Books, 1999.

—*Jo Lynn Southard*

Child Custody

In the United States, mothers have primary custody of children after a divorce nearly 70 percent of the time. Although more fathers are gaining custody of their children, it remains overwhelmingly mothers who are primary caretakers.

Beginning with Roman law, and carrying over to English and then U.S. common law, children were viewed as the property of their father. However, during the Industrial Revolution, men went out to work and women generally remained at home as primary caregivers. As a result, mothers came to be preferred in custody decisions, based on the "tender years" doctrine, which held that young children needed to be nurtured by their mothers. By the early twentieth century, maternal preference had become fixed in U.S. law. This presumption remained for many decades. Other legal systems that grew out of Roman law developed similarly; on the other hand, legal traditions based on Islam still favor the father in custody decisions.

In the late twentieth century, the presumption that the mother would be the best caregiver began to be seen as sexist. Men felt that they should be given an equal chance to gain custody of their children. In addition, some women would have preferred their former husbands to have custody, but feared the stigma attached to not wanting custody of their children. As a result, the "tender years" doctrine has been replaced by a "best interest of the child" standard and a presumption that joint custody of children is preferred.

In spite of these changes, 1997 U.S. Census figures indicate that only 9 percent of fathers have primary custody of their children and only 22 percent of divorced parents have joint custody. The Department of Health and Human Services (DHHS) estimates that one-third of U.S. children of divorce lose contact with their noncustodial parent within a few years. In addition to the damage this causes the child, studies by the DHHS have indicated that the best way to ensure that noncustodial parents continue to pay child support is to have them remain in contact with their children. Many states now include parenting programs in their child-support collection programs to help noncustodial parents remain in contact with their children.

Currently, another major child custody issue is the refusal to grant custody to a gay parent. Although the U.S. Supreme Court has ruled it is unconstitutional to base a custody decision on race, only five states mandate that a parent's sexual orientation not be used in determining custody. Courts tend to reflect community beliefs, and studies show that most U.S. citizens think that being raised by a gay parent is not in the best interest of the child. Other studies show, however, that being raised by a gay parent has no effect on a child's mental health or sexual orientation.

At present, it is unclear how child custody may change in the future, except that more fathers may take a more active role in their children's lives. In addition, what role the issue of sexual orientation will play in custody decisions is still unclear.

For Further Reading

Chesler, Phyllis. *Mothers on Trial: The Battle for Children and Custody.* San Diego: Harcourt Brace Jovanovich, 1991.

Mason, Mary Ann. *From Father's Property to Children's Rights: The History of Child Custody in the United States.* New York: Columbia University Press, 1994.

—*Jo Lynn Southard*

Clinical Trials

Clinical trials—large-scale medical testing of, for example, experimental procedures or new medicines—have historically been conducted almost exclusively on men. As a result, medical information about the impact of treatment on women and about women-specific diseases has been lacking. In the United States, the National Institutes of Health (NIH) now require gender equity as a part of medical research trials.

The reasons why women have traditionally been kept out of clinical trials are complex. The horrific experiments conducted by the Nazis on Jews in concentration camps during World War II caused international law to declare the right of research subjects to fundamental dignity. This ideal, although not always practiced, was endorsed universally. Generally, medical research has been viewed as not particularly beneficial to the subjects, and it was commonly accepted that women and minorities would be exploited if used in trials. Particularly women of childbearing age, it was felt, should be protected from being involved in medical research.

In the 1980s, the number of women in both Congress and in medical research increased dramatically, both of which helped women's concerns to be pushed to the forefront. Dr. Bernadine Healey was appointed director of the NIH; meanwhile, the Women's Congressional Caucus, led at that time by Representative Patricia Schroeder, demanded more attention to women's health issues. A U.S. Public Health task force, established in 1984, determined that excluding women from clinical trials had had a negative impact on women's health information and care. Two years later, the NIH mandated the inclusion of women in clinical trials. But a study requested by the Women's Congressional Caucus found in 1990 that women were still being excluded from research—for example, from the well-known study that taking an aspirin each day may prevent heart attack was conducted on men. The Food and Drug Administration is considering requiring the inclusion of women in clinical trials before approving new drugs.

In addition to a lack of understanding of how the results of clinical trials will affect women, the emphasis on using only men in clinical trials also resulted in a lack of research on medical conditions that largely or exclusively affect women. For example, although a few men develop breast cancer, it is overwhelmingly a woman's disease and has only gained prominence as a public health issue relatively recently, thanks to the advocacy of various women's groups. Osteoporosis is also the subject of recently increased research. Another example is AIDS, which often manifests differently in women than in men, yet, initially, the majority of information about AIDS was about its effect on men.

The inclusion of women in clinical trials—or, in some instances, revisiting earlier trials that had excluded women—has resulted in new information about common public health problems. For example, several recent studies reported in the *Journal of the National Cancer Institute* have determined that, given the same exposure to smoke, a woman is more likely to develop lung cancer than a man. Women have also been found to have greater difficulty quitting smoking than men. Such information will help doctors to tailor their advice and treatment to their patients. Another recent discovery is that, in the United States, heart disease is the number one killer of women. This discovery is of great importance, as heart disease has traditionally been seen as a "man's disease." New research will target prevention and treatment of heart disease in women.

For Further Reading

Mastoianni, Anna C., Ruth Faden, and Daniel Federman, eds. *Women and Health Research: Ethical and Legal Issues of Including Women in Clinical Studies.* Washington, D.C.: National Academy Press, 1994.

Sechzer, Jeri A., Anne Griffin, and Sheila M. Pfafflin. *Forging a Women's Health Research Agenda: Policy Issues for the 1990s.* New York: New York Academy of Sciences, 1994.

—*Jo Lynn Southard*

Contraception

The 1994 International Conference on Population and Development placed women's reproductive rights at the center of an international agreement on population for the first time. In 1995, at the United Nations Fourth World Conference on Women, the reproductive health and rights of women were recognized as imperative for women's empowerment. When women have too many children, too close together, or at too young or advanced an age, the health and well-being of both mothers and children are put at risk.

Women have always searched for ways to control when and how often they get pregnant; however, their cultures were not always supportive. The issue of contraception is wrapped up with cultural values about sexuality,

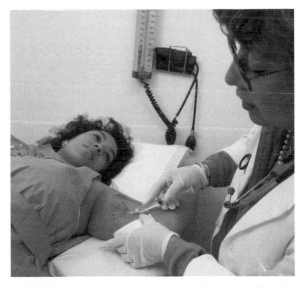

In New York, a nurse prepares to insert Norplant, an implanted birth control method. (Robert Maass/CORBIS)

marriage, and abortion. In addition, after wars or natural disasters decimated a population, it was often considered patriotic for women to give birth to many children in order to rebuild. Today, most countries recognize that family planning is necessary for healthy mothers and children. As a result, the rate of the global population increase has slowed in recent years.

Contraceptive use has increased greatly in the last generation. According to the United Nations Population Fund, thirty years ago less than 10 per cent of couples worldwide were using contraception; today, more than half are. As a result, the health of women and their children has improved. Usage varies greatly around the world, however. In countries such as Benin, Nigeria, Pakistan, Sudan, and Yemen, less than 10 percent of married women use modern methods of contraception; in Brazil, Indonesia, and Thailand, more than 50 percent do.

In addition to providing women with some control over their bodies, contraceptive use has other benefits. Women who plan their pregnancies are likely to know sooner that they are pregnant than women who do not; these women can seek out prenatal care sooner, improving their health and the health of their babies. In addition, children born more than two years apart have a greater chance of survival than those born at shorter intervals; as much as 20 percent of infant deaths could be prevented if births were spaced at least two years apart. The mother, who may not have regained her strength from the previous pregnancy, and the older child, who may be weaned too young, both suffer, as well as the new baby. Having mothers who are neither too young nor too old increases the chances of children surviving.

Although progress has been made in making contraceptives available to women, hundreds of millions of couples who desire family planning still have no access to programs. Some studies indicate that almost 40 percent of the 210 million pregnancies that occur each year are unplanned. Half a million women die each year as a result of pregnancy or childbirth; it is estimated that 100,000 of those women die from unsafe abortions. When contraception is not available, abortion may be a woman's only choice for family planning.

For a woman to control how many children she will have and when, she must have access to contraception for long periods of time. Many women will use contraceptives for 20 or even 30 years. In addition, both married and unmarried women need access to contraception and their male partners also need to be educated about their own birth control options. In 1990, there were one billion women of childbearing age throughout the world; by 2010, there will be half again as many. Although the availability of contraception has improved in recent years, it needs to be made available to many more women.

Further Reading

Department for Economic and Social Information and Policy Analysis, Population Division. *Reproductive Rights and Reproductive Health: A Concise Report.* New York: United Nations, 1996.

Wulf, Dierdre. *Hopes and Realities: Closing the Gap Between Women's Aspirations and Their Reproductive Experiences.* New York: The Alan Guttmacher Institute, 1995.

—*Jo Lynn Southard*

Depression

According to the World Health Organization, depression is currently the single most disabling disease among women. Studies show that in most cultures women suffer from depression twice as often as men. Yet, depression is still a misunderstood and underfunded disease.

Throughout much of history, depression was seen as a temporary mood condition rather than a disease. In the early twentieth century, depression was usually treated with Freudian psychoanalysis, although now many experts consider that treatment unproductive. Over time, the medical and psychological communities have learned that depression is a condition that requires active management. Currently, a combination of medication and therapy is the most common treatment for depression.

It is estimated by the World Health Organization that up to one quarter of women in developed nations will suffer from clinical depression at some point in their lives. Researchers do not know why so many more women than men suffer from depression. At one time, biology was the primary explanation for why women were more prone to depression; in the nineteenth century, hysterectomies were often performed to cure women of depression or, as it was then known, "hysteria." Some researchers still postulate that something in the biology of women makes them more susceptible to changes in the environment or that women's more variable levels of hormones explain the difference.

Proportionally more women than men seek treatment for depression; this difference was once explained as the result of women being more comfortable admitting a problem and seeking help. Most researchers now agree this explanation is too simple. Feminist researchers believe that the socialization of women is at least partly responsible for women's higher incidence of depression: girls and women are socialized to have low self-worth. In addition, far more women than men were sexually abused as children or adults and this abuse contributes to the onset of depression. Finally, women are more exposed to stresses that contribute to depression, such as poverty.

According to a Columbia University study, the incidence of depression has doubled in the last 50 years—and it continues to grow. With each succeeding generation born since 1915, depression has become more widespread. As with the actual causes of depression or theories of why women suffer more than men, the reasons for this increase are unclear; some of the causes cited include increased drug use, changes in traditional family and community structures, and environmental causes, such as pollution and overpopulation. It may also be that depression is more accurately diagnosed that it once was. Whatever the cause, the incidence of depression is increasing too fast to be explained entirely by genetics. In addition, some studies indicate that people of both genders are suffering from depression at younger ages and that episodes of depression are increasing in severity and frequency.

As women all over the world continue to have primary responsibility for child care, their impact on their children is of special concern. Studies have found that maternal depression has a negative influence on the social and psychological development of children. As the numbers of women suffering from depression continue to rise, so will the cost to society. Already, millions are spent in research and treatment as well as lost work. If current trends continue, the cost can only increase.

For Further Reading

Ferber, Jane S. *A Woman Doctor's Guide to Depression: Essential Facts and Up-To-The-Minute Information on Diagnosis, Treatment, and Recovery.* New York: Hyperion, 1997.

Raskin, Valerie Davis. *When Words Are Not Enough: The Women's Prescription for Depression and Anxiety.* New York: Broadway Books, 1997.

—Jo Lynn Southard

Divorce

By definition, the same number of women and men are involved in divorce at any given time; it would seem as though they would be affected in much the same way. However, women are significantly more disadvantaged by divorce than are men.

Like marriage, divorce has both civil and religious components. In most cases, government requirements must be met in order to obtain a divorce. For those who consider themselves members of a particular religious community, there are also religious strictures surrounding divorce. Societies vary greatly in the entanglement

between church and government. Sometimes the two are quite separate, as in the United States where the civil laws outline the procedures and requirements of divorce and religious concerns are left to the individuals. In other countries, where religious influence on government is particularly strong, civil divorce regulations reflect religious standards. For example, predominantly Roman Catholic countries such as Ireland, Brazil, and Spain only recently made divorce legal. Neither the Philippines nor Chile yet allow divorce, although annulment and legal separation are possible. On the whole, acceptance and legalization of divorce are increasing all over the world.

In some ways, divorce affects women and men in a similar fashion. Divorce appears to increase stress-related illnesses, physical and mental, for both men and women. However, women bear disproportionate economic burdens as the result of divorce. In the United States, studies indicate that women's post-divorce standard of living drops by 30 percent, while men's rises by 10 percent.

One recent change in U.S. divorce law is the advent of no-fault divorce. The goals of no-fault divorce are to make divorce less painful, expensive, and time consuming. As reliance on no-fault divorce has spread, other trends have emerged. For example, almost everywhere divorce rates have risen in the last several decades. Some people blame the availability of no-fault divorce for these rising rates. Another issue is how to adapt traditional questions of child custody, support, and alimony to no-fault divorce. In Japan, for example, 90 percent of divorces are mutually agreed upon no-fault divorces. In most of these cases, the parents usually agree to give the mother custody of the children, but fathers are not required to pay child support.

When government and religion are entangled, divorce laws can be confusing. In most South Asian and Middle Eastern countries, for example, family law is based on religion, so the laws that govern a couple's divorce depend on their religious affiliations. In many traditional religions, women and men are treated very differently. In some Islamic states, for example, husbands have the right to unilaterally divorce their wives, but wives do not have this option, nor do they have much right to share in the marital property after a divorce.

Generally, divorce laws are becoming more liberal around the world. However, conservative religious movements—in the United States and many other parts of the world—threaten to make divorces more difficult to obtain.

For Further Reading

DiFonzo, J. Herbie. *Beneath the Fault Line: The Popular and Legal Culture of Divorce in Twentieth-Century America.* Charlottesville: University Press of Virginia, 1997.

Everett, Craig A., ed. *The Consequences of Divorce: Economic and Custodial Impact on Children and Adults.* New York: Haworth, 1991.

—*Jo Lynn Southard*

Domestic Violence

Domestic violence is reported to be common everywhere in the world. According to *The State of Women in the World Atlas* by Joni Seager, it is the leading cause of injuries and death among women. Ninety-five percent of the victims of domestic violence are women. The economic costs of domestic violence equal those of cancer, heart disease, or AIDS, according to the World Bank.

Throughout history, men who abused their wives were viewed with tolerance, sympathy, and even humor. The phrase "rule of thumb" comes from English common law, in which a man could beat his wife with a stick or whip no bigger around than his thumb. In the United States, domestic violence was still a joke in the 1950s, when Jackie Gleason's TV persona threatened regularly to send his wife "Pow, straight to the Moon!" Only in the last generation has domestic violence been recognized as a social problem, and, indeed, the term itself is relatively new.

Surveys of women around the world conducted by the U.N. Commission on Human Rights reveal domestic violence rates of anywhere from 20 to 90 percent. In Pakistan, 80 percent of women report physical or emotional abuse. In Japan, New Guinea, Chili, Tanzania, and Sri Lanka, the percentage is 60 or more. In Barbados, Uganda, and Guatemala, nearly half the women report being victims of domestic violence. Canadian, Malaysian, and Zambian women report rates between 30 and 40 percent. In Norway and the United States, between 20 and 30 percent of women report being victims of domestic violence. In a single village in India, 82 of 109 wives—more than 89 percent—reported being beaten regularly. In 1997 UNICEF reported that between one quarter to one half of women around the world have been victims of domestic violence.

Each year, millions of women die at the hands of their husbands or boyfriends. One particularly virulent form of wife killing occurs in India. Known as "dowry death," it happens when a husband decides that his wife's dowry is not sufficient. She is killed to allow him to marry someone with a bigger dowry. Most often, these women are burned to death. In spite of new laws on the subject enacted by the Indian parliament, the number of dowry deaths continues to climb.

Daughters may be victims of domestic violence as well as wives and girlfriends. Severe overpopulation throughout the world—coupled with the fact that in nearly all cultures a majority of parents report a preference for sons—has led to female infanticide. For example, China has laws limiting married couples to one child. If that child is a girl, she may be killed so the couple can try again for a son. In other parts of the world, where girls' parents are expected to provide large dowries for their daughters to make good marriages, daughters may be killed for being too expensive. In many parts of the Middle East, a father, or other male relative, may kill his daughter if she disgraces him by marrying someone he does not approve of or losing her virginity before marriage.

For generations, governments turned a blind eye to domestic violence on the grounds that it was a private affair; this argument can still be heard occasionally. However, most countries now have laws making domestic violence illegal and are enforcing those laws, with greater and lesser degrees of success. Some international activists argue that domestic violence should be considered torture and prosecuted as an international human rights violation. In the United States, the issue is taken more seriously now than ever before; more shelters are available for women in crisis, and progress is being made toward educating both women and men about the problem.

For Further Reading

Berry, Dawn Bradley. *The Domestic Violence Sourcebook: Everything You Need to Know.* Los Angeles, Calif.: Lowell House, 1995.

Wallace, Harvey. *Family Violence: Legal, Medical, and Social Perspectives.* Needham Heights, Mass.: Allyn & Bacon, 1998.

—*Jo Lynn Southard*

Education

Two-thirds of the world's one billion illiterates are women. Currently, as many as 80 million young girls are denied access to a basic education; some have labeled it an apartheid of gender. Yet, education for women is the single most important tool for their advancement.

Virtually all the world's cultures have a tradition of preferring to educate boys. It was even argued that girls and women were incapable of learning and would be damaged by an attempt to teach them. Even as women received more education, the emphasis was on housekeeping over academics. In the nineteenth and even early-twentieth centuries in the United States and Europe, the feeling was that girls needed only a rudimentary education—arithmetic would not help a girl catch a husband and was therefore a waste of time. Women struggled to be accepted at each level—primary, secondary, and higher

In Dhaka, Bangladesh, a woman instructs a young girl. (Liba Taylor/Corbis)

education. In 1865 Vassar, the first women's college in the United States, was opened to great fanfare and a great many jokes about women wanting to be men.

In recent years North American, European, and Russian women have achieved literacy rates of more than 90 percent; indeed, slightly more men than women are illiterate in the United States. Most of the world, however, finds greater rates of illiteracy in women. In much of sub-Saharan Africa and the Indian subcontinent, more than 50 percent and as much as 75 percent of women are illiterate. In China, the Middle East, and much of South America, one-quarter to one-half of women are illiterate.

Over the last several decades, the United Nations and other organizations have targeted education for girls. As a result, the trend has been that more and more girls go to primary school every year. In many places, girls' enrollment rates have increased faster than those of boys—although the girls were quite far behind to begin with. In addition, more girls are staying in school longer than ever before. Unfortunately, in the last decade, this trend was reversed in many countries because of war and economic problems. As education for girls is a recent development, it may be among the first programs lost in times of crisis. In addition, education for girls and women may be among the first things to be discontinued when religious fundamentalists take over a government, e.g., the Taliban in Afghanistan.

Even the most basic rights and services are worthless to those who cannot read and understand them. Improved education of women has been shown to be the single most important factor in decreasing birthrates and increasing the standard of living of women all over the world. When girls are given a basic education, they grow up to have fewer and healthier children, who, in turn, receive better educations. Educated women are able to get better jobs, participate in their governments, and understand their basic human rights. Most important, education gives women the opportunity to reach their full potential, which is a benefit not only to them but to their community and her world. Depriving women of an education is one of the most effective ways to maintain them as second-class citizens.

For Further Reading

Heward, Christine, and Sheila Bunwaree, eds. *Gender, Education, And Development: Beyond Access to Empowerment.* New York: Zed Books, 1999.

Spring, Joel H. *Education and the Rise of the Global Economy.* Mahwah, N.J.: L. Erlbaum Associates, 1998.

—*Jo Lynn Southard*

Family Leave

In the United States, two-thirds of women with children work for pay; as medical advances enable people to live longer, many women may spend more years caring for elderly relatives than caring for their own children. Currently in the United States, over 22 million people, 72 percent of them women, are caring for an elderly relative at home. Family leave, the common name for an unpaid absence from work in order to attend to family illness or the birth or adoption of a child, is gaining increasing attention as workers—particularly female workers—struggle to balance job and family.

Since the Industrial Revolution, paid work has been designed with the idea that the average worker will be a man, usually with a wife at home. As millions of women joined the paid workforce, the "typical" worker began to change. Millions of workers now are also the primary caregivers for family members, usually children. Early in the twentieth century, some governments and companies began addressing the needs of some working women by providing maternity leave. This gave a woman a specific length of time to stay at home after the birth of her baby without losing her job. Although 120 countries provide for paid maternity leave, the United States does not; maternity leave in the United States is almost always unpaid.

In 1993, the United States expanded the concept of maternity leave with the Family Medical Leave Act (FMLA), which provides qualified workers with the right to take 12 weeks of unpaid leave a year to care for an ill family member or for maternity or adoption without risk of losing their jobs. This legislation is unique, in that it is gender neutral. Although in reality mothers more often take time off to care for family members, under the FMLA, fathers have the same rights. In fact, at least one U.S. court determined that it is illegal under the FMLA to offer a mother more leave for the birth of a child than a father. However, because the leave is unpaid, most workers who could qualify for leave indicate they do not apply for it because they cannot afford it.

An aging population means that workers have to be concerned not only about caring for their children but, often, about caring for elderly relatives as well. In 1997, one-quarter of U.S. households were providing care for an older relative, triple the number just 10 years earlier. The FMLA is groundbreaking in recognizing that workers may need leave from work to care for aging parents as well as children. The maternity leave that is common in the rest of the world does not address that issue. However, the FMLA only provides for unpaid leave; in November 1999, President Clinton proposed extending unemployment benefits to workers taking leave after the birth or adoption of a child. The proposal would allow states to redirect surplus unemployment funds to family leave.

When leave is provided only to women to care for children, only women's careers will be affected by the time they must take off from work. In addition, fathers suffer by not being given the option to help care for their children. However, as more women work outside the home, addressing the care of children with policies more extensive than maternity leave, is necessary. In addition, as the population ages, more elderly persons will be cared for in families' homes, necessitating more liberal family leave policies.

For Further Reading

Fried, Mindy. *Taking Time: Parental Leave Policy and Corporate Culture*. Philadelphia: Temple University Press, 1998.

Lewis, Suzan, and Jeremy Lewis, eds. *The Work-Family Challenge: Rethinking Employment*. Thousand Oaks, Calif.: Sage Publications, 1996.

—Jo Lynn Southard

Glass Ceiling

The phrase "glass ceiling" refers to artificial barriers that keep women from advancing their careers to the fullest extent. The expression was coined in a *Wall Street Journal* article in March 1986.

Traditionally, corporate culture was organized around the idea that men would work outside the home and women inside. Because working men had wives to care for home and family, corporations did not concern themselves with structuring jobs to allow time for family responsibilities. In the United States, passage of the Equal Pay Act of 1963 and the Civil Rights Act of 1964, coupled with the feminist movement of the 1970s, led to more women in traditionally male jobs. The difference was these women, by choice or necessity, did need to blend family and corporate concerns.

Although more and more women joined the workforce, corporate culture itself changed very little. As a result, women's job performances were based on the same standards that had been used for men—men who, largely, did not have the same family responsibilities as women. In many work settings, women were considered to be on the "mommy track"; that is, they would not be able to advance as far or as quickly as men in the corporation, because they would need time off from work to have and care for children.

Recent surveys indicate that women executives work an average of 56 hours a week—the same as male executives. When offered relocation in conjunction with a job, only 14 percent of women declined, as opposed to 20 percent of men. Nonetheless, stereotypes of women executives hold that they do not work long hours and cannot accept relocation because of family responsibilities. And while it is true that 82 percent of women who have taken a leave of absense from working have taken it for the birth of a child or other family reasons, only one-third of women executives took a leave of absence at all. Nonetheless, many women executives find themselves on the "mommy track," wherein their careers advance more slowly because of the assumption that they care (or will care) for their families at the expense of their careers.

A currently popular belief is that, if the glass ceiling did once exist, it no longer does. Surveys indicate this is also not true, either. A 1996 survey of the top companies in the United States by the Federal Glass Ceiling Commission shows that 95 percent of senior management positions are held by men and 97 percent of those men are white. Another survey, conducted by Financial Women International in 1990, found that 73 percent of male CEOs surveyed did not think there was a glass ceiling; 71 percent of female vice presidents did.

Military women also have begun to talk of a "brass ceiling" for mothers. Although women began to be promoted to top military ranks in 1970, thirty years later, no woman who is a mother has reached the level of general in the army or admiral in the navy. Colonel Lois Beard, mother of three and a veteran of the Persian Gulf War and the invasion of Panama, was seen as the most likely candidate for such appointment until late in 1999, when she opted to drop from the fast track to spend more time with her children. The Pentagon confirms that by far those most likely to be in top command positions are married men and unmarried women.

In recent years, cracks have begun to appear in the glass ceiling. The number of women holding high executive positions is increasing, although women are still a small percentage. In addition, of the executive positions held by women, 95 percent are held by white women; minority women are finding the glass ceiling even harder to crack. By 2005, an estimated 62 percent of the U.S. workforce will be made up of women and minorities. Sheer numbers may be the most important factor in shattering the glass ceiling.

For Further Reading

Albelda, Randy, and Chris Tilly. *Glass Ceilings and Bottomless Pits: Women's Work, Women's Poverty.* Boston, Mass.: South End Press, 1997.

Weiss, Ann. *The Glass Ceiling: A Look at Women in the Workforce.* Brookfield, Conn.: Twenty-First Century Books, 1999.

—*Jo Lynn Southard*

Human Rights

"Women's rights are human rights" has become a familiar phrase in the last few years. However, only recently have women's rights been granted human rights status.

Traditionally human rights have been most concerned with issues facing men for several reasons. One, the Universal Declaration of Human Rights established a hierarchy that gave prominence to civil and political rights—that is, rights that arise when a citizen interacts with his or her government. As women historically have spent more time in the private sphere than the public, these rights may be less meaningful for women. The foregrounding of political rights also established the idea that violations of human rights occur only when a government mistreats a citizen. Again, spending more of their time in the private realm, women are more likely to be mistreated by private actors. Finally, until only recently, men have been almost exclusively responsible for the definition and enforcement of human rights law; they understandably were concerned about the issues that were important to them.

Women's human rights are violated in a variety of ways. Very often, governments are directly involved, as when corrupt border guards facilitate traffic in women and girls. In some countries, laws directly discriminate against women, for example, when a woman's court testimony is given less weight than a man's or when a rape victim is prosecuted for adultery. Sometimes laws that seem to be gender neutral are applied in discriminatory ways—for example, when prostitutes are dealt with more harshly than their male customers or agents, or when men are excused for killing their adulterous wives.

The United Nations General Assembly adopted the Convention on the Elimination of All Forms of Discrimination Against Women (CEDAW) in 1979. The United States has not ratified the treaty. When countries sign on to treaties, they may enter reservations by which they exempt themselves from certain parts of the document. CEDAW has more reservations than any other human rights treaty.

Although the United Nations' recognition of the human rights of women was vitally important, violations of women's human rights still occur throughout the world. For example, early in 1999, the supreme court of Zimbabwe ruled that the nature of African society is such that women are not equal to men, particularly in their family relationships. Clearly, the ruling has profound implications for women's civil rights, and observers fear that the ruling will be used to "turn back the clock" on women's progress in Zimbabwe. Also in 1999, the Pakistani parliament declined to pass a resolution condemning the killing of women in the name of family honor, and the Iranian parliament passed a law making it illegal to discuss women's rights in the press. The most notorious example of human rights violations against women is the policies of the Taliban, who took over the government of Afghanistan in 1996. They have instituted a system of gender apartheid that denies women the right to have jobs, educate themselves, or even leave their homes without the accompaniment of a man.

Because women have been historically associated with home and family, women's human rights have often been considered a private matter, inappropriate for outside enforcement. For example, rape in wartime was seen as inevitable and essentially a private matter. Today, it is a recognized tactic of war, as evidenced in the former Yugoslavia. In addition, women have argued that, when governments turn a blind eye to domestic violence by refusing to enact laws or refusing to enforce the ones that exist, the government is sanctioning torture by a private actor. Until recently, discriminatory actions based on gender, such as veiling, restrictions on education, employment, and travel, and even female genital mutilation, were considered to be private cultural and religious matters, and were not accepted reasons for granting women asylum-seekers refugee status. Because of women's activism, more and more countries are recognizing gender discrimination as a basis for granting political asylum.

In the 1990s, several world conferences addressed the human rights of women, most notably the United Nations' Fourth World Conference on Women in Beijing, China, in 1995. In June 2000 the United Nations General Assembly will meet in New York City to assess how well the governments have done at living up to the commitments of the Beijing Conference.

For Further Reading

Lockwood, Carol Elizabeth, ed. *International Human Rights of Women: Instruments of Change.* Washington, D.C.: American Bar Association, 1998.

Neft, Naomi, and Ann D. Levine. *Where Women Stand: An International Report on the Status of Women in 140 Countries, 1997–1998.* New York: Random House, 1997.

—*Jo Lynn Southard*

Marriage

Statistically, most women and most men will spend most of their lives married. Marriage, however, can be a very different experience for women than for men.

Often—legally or traditionally—the husband is considered the head of the household. In some countries, women are the legal equivalent of minors, with their husbands completely controlling their lives; a wife cannot receive a passport or work outside the home without her husband's consent. In Ethiopia, wives by law owe their husbands obedience in all things; in Zaire, a wife may not open a bank account without her husband's assent; in Brazil, a husband may dispose of a couple's joint property without consulting his wife.

In several Caribbean countries, more than 20 percent of women over 45 have never married, but that is quite unusual. Marriage is considered in most cultures to be a normal state for women; unmarried women may be seen as unnatural. Even as more and more women around the world are becoming educated and having careers, marriage is often still considered to be a woman's primary purpose in life. Unmarried daughters are considered a burden on the family and divorced or separated women are often stigmatized.

Arranged marriages are common in many parts of the world. In India, an estimated 95 percent of marriages are arranged. This practice may seem to affect men and women equally; however, usually women's lives are more drastically changed by marriage than are men's because husbands often have control over wives. Forced marriage is often a response to poverty and a cultural preference for sons; fathers may simply sell their daughters. In other cases, criminal syndicates engage in large-scale kidnapping operations; women and girls are trafficked into prostitution or sold into marriage.

Although generally illegal, the marriage of children still occurs. For example, weddings between girls as young as six months and boys as young as nine years have been reported in India. In one state in India, 56 percent of women reported they were married before the age of 15; 14 percent before they were 10 and 3 percent before they were five.

In the United States, on the other hand, the most pressing marriage-related controversy is a very different one—whether or not same-sex couples should be permitted to marry. In recent years the concept of "domestic partnership" (which is available to both gay and straight couples) has been gaining gradual acceptance; increasing numbers of corporations, universities, and municipalities offer benefits to employees who register as domestic partners. A December 1999 ruling by the state supreme court in Vermont has opened up the possibility of same-sex unions being recognized at the state level, but it is still too soon to predict if other states will follow. Meanwhile, opponents of gay marriage have begun seeking legislation such as Proposition 22, recently passed in California, that limits the legal definition of marriage to opposite-sex couples only, even if the couple was married out of state.

For Further Reading

Minow, Martha, ed. *Family Matters: Readings on Family Lives and the Law.* New York: New Press, 1993.

Regan, Milton C. *Alone Together: Law and the Meanings of Marriage.* Oxford and New York: Oxford University Press, 1999.

—*Jo Lynn Southard*

Menopause

Menopause is the medical term for the end of a woman's menstrual periods. It occurs naturally when women are between the ages of 45 and 60, or anytime that the ovaries stop functioning or are surgically removed. When the ovaries cease functioning, a woman's body produces almost no estrogen.

In Western culture, menopause was traditionally viewed as something to be dreaded. One reason for the negative feelings about menopause is the youth-worshipping nature of the culture; menopause means a woman is getting old in a society that devalues age and leaving her fertile years behind in a society that, despite its progress, still values women for their ability to bear children. Furthermore, the medical profession viewed menopause as a disease. Even in 1999, the American Association of Clinical Endocrinologists called menopause "adult-onset ovarian failure" that should be managed and treated by a doctor.

The feminist movement, on the other hand, has been sending the message that menopause is a natural part of aging that should be celebrated, not feared. Because people are living longer, it is not unusual for a woman to live one-third or more of her life after menopause. Currently in the United States, about one-third of the female population has gone through menopause. Although about 75 percent of women report some annoying symptoms during menopause, for the most part these symptoms last only a short time.

Medical research has confirmed a link between decreased estrogen and an increased tendency to develop osteoporosis. Exercise and diet can help correct this problem; in addition, hormone replacement therapy (HRT) can be used to increase the level of estrogen. HRT can also be used to treat the short-term symptoms of menopause, such as hot flashes and sleep disturbance. In the past several years, HRT has become very popular in the United States and most women are at least offered the possibility of HRT by their doctors. Although HRT can ease menopause symptoms, little is known about possible side effects of the therapy. Research on HRT for menopausal women has been done on women who are experiencing problems with menopause. Millions of women experience few or no problems, but in many cases their doctors will prescribe HRT routinely.

To help address the deficiency in medical research surrounding HRT and menopause, in 1991, the National Institutes of Health established the Women's Health Initiative, the largest medical study of women's health ever. This 15-year study is concerned with the most common causes of death and disability among postmenopausal women and the effects of HRT.

At the same time that the medical community is beginning to pay more attention to women's health issues, women are beginning to re-define events such as menopause as natural changes that result from aging, as well as rites of passage. There is a movement among some women to celebrate menopause as a passage to the second part of adulthood. Some women even perform "crone ceremonies," which are recreations of ancient rites of passage that celebrate and honor older women.

Menopause has physical, emotional, and psychological aspects. A congruence of medical and feminist research into menopause will help demystify and ease the process. The Women's Health Initiative promises to contribute substantially to easing fears of menopause that many women have.

For Further Reading

Greer, Germaine. *The Change: Women, Aging, and the Menopause.* New York: Random House, 1992.

Love, Susan M. *Making Informed Choices About Menopause.* New York: Random House, 1997.

—*Jo Lynn Southard*

Midwifery

Midwives are health professionals—who may or may not also be nurses—who attend women through prenatal care, labor, and birth. Only about 7 percent of the babies born in the United States in 1997 were delivered by midwives. However, a majority of babies worldwide are born with midwives in attendance. It is believed that billions of health care dollars can be saved by utilizing midwives more effectively.

In spite of the old joke, midwifery is probably the world's oldest profession. Traditionally, women assisted one another during labor and birth and some women began practicing midwifery as a profession. Periodically throughout history, various organizations have attempted to eliminate midwifery as a profession. For example, midwives and other women healers were targeted during the European witch trials of the Middle Ages—although midwifery recovered and is flourishing in Europe today.

In the United States, native peoples have a long tradition of midwifery, as did European settlers; the first midwife in the United States was probably Tryntje Jones, who emigrated from the Netherlands around 1630. Midwives attended most births in the United States until the mid-

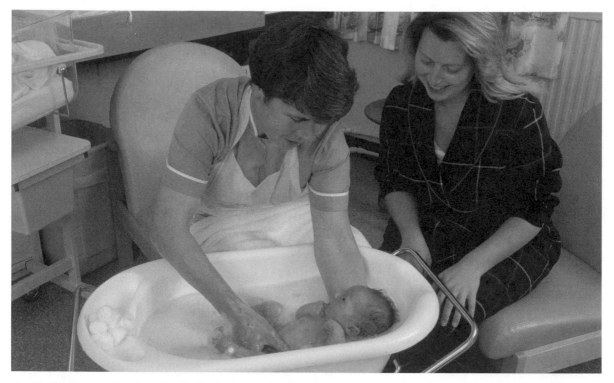

A midwife bathes a newborn baby. (Jennie Woodcock; Reflections Photolibrary/CORBIS)

nineteenth century. At that time, the American Medical Association and the American College of Gynecologists began a campaign to convince women that physicians were better able to attend births than midwives. They were so successful that the practice of midwifery was outlawed in many states. Midwifery began a resurgence in the 1920s in response to high rates of infant mortality in the United States. In the 1960s and 1970s, the women's movement encouraged the growth of the profession.

There are generally two kinds of midwives: midwives who work through a hospital or under the direction of a physician, and direct-entry midwives, who attend home or birthing-center births and do not work under the direction of a physician. Midwifery is now legal in all 50 states, although standards of certification or licensure vary. Also, some states do not allow direct-entry midwives to practice. Although only a small percentage of U.S. births are attended by a midwife, in other parts of the world a majority of babies are born with a midwife in attendance. The American Medical Association still maintains that physician-attended births are safer than midwife-attended ones. However, in Denmark, Sweden, Norway, and Finland, which have lower infant mortality rates than the United States or any other European country, over 70 percent of births are attended by midwives.

In many parts of the world, where medical professionals are scarce, a midwife may be the only medical professional that a woman sees routinely. The World Health Organization considers the promotion of midwifery to be vital to improving health care worldwide. Nurses and midwives are the most numerous health care providers in nearly every country in the world. However, they usually do not have the status or income of other medical professionals. The World Health Organization has been working to improve the training and working conditions of midwives around the world.

For Further Reading

Gaskin, Ina May. *Spiritual Midwifery.* 3rd ed. Summertown, Tenn.: Book Publishing Co., 1990.

Rooks, Judith Pence. *Midwifery and Childbirth in America.* Philadelphia, Penn.: Temple University Press, 1997.

—Jo Lynn Southard

Military, Women in

Although U.S. women have been denied the opportunity to serve in the military until recently, throughout history women have helped the military in times of war. Everyone is familiar with some famous women warriors, like JOAN OF ARC or MOLLY PITCHER, but most women in the military serve with much less fame.

In the United States, women were not allowed to become permanent members of the military until 1948. But since the Revolutionary War, women have served as nurses; women also on occasion entered the military disguised as men. It is impossible to know how many women did this, as most of them were found out only when they were wounded or killed. One woman who was discovered during the Mexican-American War had to appeal to the courts to receive her military pay.

Through the Spanish-American War, nurses who worked for the military were civilians who worked under contract, not members of military units. Contract nurses in that war served with such distinction that the result was the creation of the Army Nurse Corps in 1901 and the Navy Nurse Corps in 1908. This was the first time women became official members of the U.S. military. During the world wars, women served in a greater variety of military positions, but only on a temporary basis. In 1948, the Women's Armed Services Integration Act was signed into law, giving women permanent status in all branches of the U.S. military. However, the act restricted the number of women allowed to join the military and the number that could be promoted.

Women served in Korea and Vietnam and, by 1980, more than 170,000 women were on active duty. A greater number of jobs have become open to women in the military, although they still were not allowed to hold direct combat positions. The Persian Gulf war had 41,000 military women serving—making up 7 percent of the U.S. forces.

Integrating women into the military has not been without its problems. In 1991, 83 women, most of them naval officers, were sexually assaulted and harassed by fellow officers at the Tailhook convention. Over time, more charges of sexual assault and harassment in all branches of the military have occurred. In 1995, 55 percent of military women reported being victims of sexual harassment. During the 1990s, the Department of Defense has worked on implementing initiatives against sexual harassment.

A subset of the issue of women serving in the military is the question of whether women should be subject to the draft. One argument in favor of drafting women is that it would contribute to equalizing men and women in the military. However, the strong sentiment—both in the United States and elsewhere—against putting women in combat positions makes the draft for women highly unlikely. In Israel, women are subject to the draft—although they normally serve less time than men do and are, for the most part, restricted from combat jobs. The United States Congress debated the possibility of drafting

women for nursing corps duty during World War II, but the large number of volunteers made a draft unnecessary.

A more positive development on women in the military is reported by both the North Atlantic Treaty Organization and the United Nations, which have had great success with female members of peacekeeping forces and are considering increasing the proportion of women in these forces. Whether women are inherently better at peacekeeping than men or not, the collateral victims of war, like refugees, are more than two-thirds women and children, and some experts suggest that this fact alone requires that more women be involved in peacekeeping missions. In Bosnia, for example, women victims of the militarily sanctioned rape practiced in that war responded better to female peacekeepers than to male.

Currently, women make up about 14 percent of active duty military personnel in the United States. A few countries still entirely ban women from service, but many countries have an even larger proportion of women in the military.

For Further Reading

DePauw, Linda Grant. *Battle Cries and Lullabies: Women in War from Prehistory to the Present.* Norman: University of Oklahoma Press, 1998.

Holm, Jeanne M. *Women in the Military—An Unfinished Revolution.* Novato, Calif.: Presidio Press, 1992.

—*Jo Lynn Southard*

Pay Equity

Although women are working for pay in ever-increasing numbers all over the world, they continue to earn only 75 percent of men's salaries. In the United States, 99 percent of women will work for pay at some point in their lives. According to U.S. Census Bureau figures, those U.S. women will earn about 74 percent of what men earn, or $26 less for every $100 worth of work. According to calculations by the Institute for Women's Policy Research, that $26 dollar loss means that an average 25-year-old woman in the United States will lose $523,000 to unequal pay in the course of her lifetime.

In 1900, women constituted less than 18 percent of the paid workforce; by 1950 they were just under 30 percent, by 1997, just over 46 percent. By the year 2000, worldwide, as many women will be working for pay as men. Although women have always worked, they have not been—and are not—always paid for their work. Throughout history, "women's work" was to make life livable for their families. Even if, as in the case of farmers' wives, there was little difference in the actual work a husband and a wife did, her role was seen as supportive.

Even today, much of the work done by women is unpaid, including agricultural work and child care. By one estimate, women around the world are not paid for 66 percent of the work they do.

In 1963, the United States enacted equal pay laws. Some argue that current laws are not very effective. In 1960, working women in the United States earned 61 percent of what men earned. By 1990, this number had increased to 74 percent. Studies have shown that when the percentage of women rises in a particular occupation—when it starts to be seen as "women's work"— wages begin to fall. Jobs in which 70 percent or more of the workers are women usually pay less than jobs that are balanced or mostly male. Both the men and the women in those lower-paying jobs lose money.

Pay inequity is evident in all professions. Women lawyers and doctors in the United States earn hundreds of dollars less a week than males in those professions. Even in traditionally female dominated jobs, women do not receive equal pay. Although 95 percent of nurses are female, they earn $30 less a week than the 5 percent of male nurses. Waitresses' average weekly earnings are $50 less than that of waiters.

Salaries are not the only means of determining the pay equity of women compared to men. Increasingly, the benefits that come—or do not come—with employment are very important. For instance, in 1993 62 percent of male workers in the private sector received health insurance, while only 51 percent of women workers did. When it comes to pensions, 46 percent of male workers in the United States are covered under an employer's pension plan, but only 39 percent of women. Fourteen percent of working women have no sick leave and risk having their pay cut for missing even one day of work.

If single women earned as much as men in comparable jobs, their incomes would increase by more than 13 percent. If married women received pay equity with men, their families' incomes would increase by 6 percent. If single working mothers were paid equally with men, their families' incomes would rise 17 percent and their poverty rates would decrease by 50 percent. When women are paid equitably, and categories of jobs are no longer designated as women's jobs that receive lower pay, women, men, and children all benefit.

For Further Reading

Blau, Francine D., and Lawrence M. Kahn. *Wage Inequality: International Comparisons of Its Sources.* Washington, D.C.: AEI Press, 1996.

Gunderson, Morley. *Comparable Worth and Gender Discrimination: An International Perspective.* Geneva: International Labour Office, 1994.

—*Jo Lynn Southard*

Political Participation

The right to vote is the single most basic and important path to participation in any democratic system. When individuals or groups lack the ability to participate in the election of officials, they have little power to resist or change the government. However, it is also important that individuals have equal access to holding elected and appointed political offices. Therefore, women need not only the right to vote but the right to be elected.

With only one exception, women were not allowed to vote anywhere in the world until the twentieth century. New Zealand granted women the right in 1893; Australia was next in 1901. The majority of the world's women did not win the vote until the second half of the century; in the United States, the Nineteenth Amendment to the Constitution granted women full voting rights in 1920. Some parts Europe were faster to grant suffrage, while other parts of the world have been far slower. Women in Kuwait are still not allowed to vote, although that may finally be changing.

Political participation is about much more than voting. For women to be truly effective politically, they must hold offices in the government and in political parties. Yet, there are only 12 countries in the world where women make up more than one-quarter of the parliament. In 1999, of the 535 members of the U.S. Congress, 65 are women, or 12 percent. Twenty-two percent of state legislators throughout the United States are women.

Many industrialized countries—the United States, China, Japan, Germany, Australia, Russia and several others—have never elected a woman as head of state. Currently, 10 women worldwide hold such positions. Two of the most interesting of these women are SIRIMAVO BANDARANAIKE, prime minister of Sri Lanka, and her daughter, Chandrika Bandaranaike Kumaratunge, who is president; Sri Lanka is the first republic to have its top two offices held by democratically elected women. In addition, Sheikh Hasina Wajed is prime minister of Bangladesh, Mary McAleese is president of Ireland, Tarja Kaarina Halonen is president of Finland, Vaira Vike-Freiberga is president of Latvia, Helen Clark is prime minister of New Zealand, Domenica Michelotti is co-regent of San Marino, Mireya Elisa Moscoso is president of Panama, and Ruth Dreifuss is president of the Federal Council of Switzerland. There are also three women serving as royal heads of state: Queen Elizabeth of Great Britain, Margrethe II of Denmark, and Beatrix of the Netherlands.

In addition to having the right to vote and to be elected to office, women often need to be educated about their suffrage. Particularly in countries that have only recently granted the right to vote, women may be largely unaware of their rights and the mechanisms for exercising them. In many countries, a certain level of education is required in order for anyone to be qualified to vote. Where women routinely receive less education than men, fewer women will be able to meet this criterion and proportionally fewer women than men will be able to vote. The same is true of land ownership requirements or prerequisites that one had to have a voting ancestor. Obviously no restrictions or conditions on voting should apply to women that do not also apply to men.

As more and more governments are changing to various democratic approaches, the right to vote and be elected to office will be crucial. A brief look at history makes it all too clear what can happen to groups when they are not allowed a voice in their own governance.

For Further Reading

Christy, Carol A. *Sex Differences in Political Participation: Processes of Change in Fourteen Nations.* New York: Praeger, 1987.

Women in Parliaments, 1945-1995: A World Statistical Survey. Geneva: Inter-Parliamentary Union, 1995.

—*Jo Lynn Southard*

Poverty

One-half of the world's food is produced by women and two-thirds of all working hours are put in by women. Meanwhile, women own less than 1 percent of the world's property and earn only 10 percent of the world's income. Approximately one-quarter of the world's population lives in extreme poverty, subsisting on less than $1 per day. Seventy percent of these people—almost 900 million—are women.

According to the Census Bureau, 63 percent of adults living in poverty in the United States are women. In the 18-to 34 age group, twice as many women as men are poor; that gap decreases for people age 35 to 54, then rises: twice as many women over the age of 65 live in poverty than do men. Meanwhile, the "feminization" of poverty is evident all over the world. Over the last 20 years, the number of rural women living in poverty has doubled. In addition, the per capita income fell in at least 50 countries in the 1980s; since more women than men are poor, women are disproportionately represented.

Because the poor are overwhelmingly female, discrimination against people based on poverty affects women disproportionately. Poor people have greater difficulty receiving training for jobs or credit to start businesses. Poor women, therefore, are victims of a potent mix of sexism and classism. At least one study, by the Worldwatch

Institute, blames discrimination against women for the growing poverty numbers.

Many experts argue that the single most effective way to end poverty is to end discrimination against women. Women are subordinated by legal and traditional discrimination—such as restrictions on travel, education, and land ownership—in a number of countries. In addition, international aid most often targets men, even though women produce most of the world's food. For example, although women produce 80 percent of food in sub-Saharan Africa, 70 percent in India, and 50 percent in Latin America, in 1982 only 0.5 percent of the United Nations' aid programs for agriculture went to women's programs. This may happen because agencies granting aid assume that farm land is owned and worked by men, or because aid goes to the production of cash crops, which is the kind of farming men do while women tend to grow food for their families. Similarly, although women are usually responsible for obtaining water and fuel for their families, programs aimed at ending deforestation rarely even mention women.

Studies show that women not only work longer hours than men, but they use a larger proportion of the money they earn for their families. When women have their own income or control the household money, larger amounts are spent on food and children's education, helping to lift the family out of poverty. Men are more apt to earn a cash income than are women; however, when they do, they spend less of their income on the family—food, shelter, clothing, and health care. For example, in Mexico, research found that men spend 75 percent of their cash income on the family, while women spend 100 percent of theirs.

In many cultures it is assumed that a woman will be supported by a man—or, at least, that he will be the main wage earner in the family. Addressing these and other outmoded assumptions based on gender is a first step toward ending poverty.

For Further Reading

Alberti, Pilar, Marta Mercado, Jo Rowlands, et al. *Women and Power: Fighting Patriarchy and Poverty.* London: Zed Books, 2000.

Sidel, Ruth. *Keeping Women and Children Last: America's War on the Poor.* New York: Viking Penguin, 1996.

—*Jo Lynn Southard*

Prostitution

Estimating the number of women involved in prostitution is difficult. In the United States, the National Task Force on

Prostitution estimates that more than a million women have been involved at some time; the U.S. Department of Health and Human Services estimates that over 300,000 children currently work as prostitutes in the United States. In other countries, such as Thailand, entire economies are built on "sex tourism" and the prostitution of women and children.

An old cliché refers to prostitution as the world's oldest profession. For nearly as long, religious and governmental leaders have opposed it, while women have often resorted to it as one of the few ways they can earn a decent income (or any income). International laws prohibiting "trafficking" in women were created to end the practice of taking women across national boundaries and forcing them into a life of sexual slavery. Ironically, this issue was once called "white slavery," referring to European women being taken to Asia, Africa, and the Middle East. Today, most women come from poorer countries in Southern Africa, South America, and East Asia to Europe, North America, Japan, Australia, and the Middle East. By one estimate, over 30 million women have been "trafficked" since the 1970s. A new trend is the trafficking of impoverished Eastern European women to the West.

Another trend in recent years is the establishment of "sex tourism" as a major industry in several countries, especially in the impoverished countries of Southeast Asia. These countries, known for the availability of prostitutes, attract men from all over the world. Young women, desperate to make a decent living, often leave the rural areas for the "red-light" districts of major cities. Sometimes these women are kidnapped or even sold by their parents. Once they enter the life, they are forced to continue to work to pay ever-mounting debts they owe their employers. With growing awareness of AIDS, virgins are at a premium in the prostitution trade and younger and younger girls—and boys—are coerced into prostitution all the time. Some estimates indicate that Thailand has 800,000 child prostitutes, India 400,000, Brazil 250,000 and the Philippines 60,000. As long as foreign men are willing to pay for the services of prostitutes in these countries, the "industry" will continue.

In the industrialized world, prostitution is one of the most divisive issues in the women's movement. One school of thought favors decriminalizing prostitution totally, on the theory that the practice is inevitable and should therefore be regulated, as it is in the Netherlands. Some feminists argue that a woman's body is her own, and she should be free to do what she wants with it. Others want prostitution made illegal where it is currently legal and more strict enforcement of the current laws in order to save women from being coerced into prostitu-

A child prostitute in the mining town of Curionopolis, Brazil. (Stephanie Maze/Corbis)

tion. This group feels it is virtually impossible for women to freely choose prostitution in a sexist world. Both camps tend to agree that laws that target the prostitutes—rather than their customers or their agents—are misguided and that any legal effort against prostitution should concentrate on those who are coerced into the business and those who take advantage of them.

Prostitution will continue to be debated by women and the law enforcement community. Different cultures and countries will react in different ways, choosing paths of decriminalization, a shift in criminal emphasis, or zero tolerance for prostitution. However, most agree that the human rights of prostitutes should not be violated under any conditions.

For Further Reading

Jeffreys, Sheila. *The Idea of Prostitution*. North Melbourne, Australia: SpiniFex Press, 1998.

Kempadoo, Kamala, and Jo Doezema, eds. *Global Sex Workers: Rights, Resistance, and Redefinition*. New York: Routledge, 1998.

—*Jo Lynn Southard*

Rape

Rape is sexual intercourse achieved by the use of force or coercion and without the victim's consent. Its targets are overwhelmingly female. Rape, used as an instrument of terror and genocide in conflicts in Rwanda and the former Yugoslavia, has only recently come to be recognized as a human rights issue of international concern.

Rape is committed in times of peace and war, in private homes and in public institutions. Rape perpetrated in wartime has been a violation of international law since the earliest codification of the laws of warfare. However, like peacetime rape, it is an often overlooked crime. For example, the Charter of the International Military Tribunals at Nuremberg after World War II did not mention rape as a crime against humanity.

The recent conflict in the former Yugoslavia has spotlighted rape as a deliberate military tactic—an estimated 20,00 to 50,000 women were victims of systematic rape in that war. For the first time, the International Criminal Tribunals for Rwanda and the former Yugoslavia have said they will address rape as a human rights violation. Those conflicts were not particularly unique, however; in recent years mass rapes in military conflict have been reported in Afghanistan, Bangladesh, Burundi, Cambodia, Liberia, Peru, Rwanda, Somalia, and Uganda.

Judicial systems deal with rape in a variety of ways. Until recently in most countries, it was legally impossible for a husband to rape his wife. Now, the majority of countries technically outlaw marital rape; however, the laws are only enforced in a handful of states. In some countries, a woman who reports being raped can be jailed herself for committing adultery. In other situations, one or two eyewitnesses are required in order to prosecute a rapist. Under some legal systems, a rapist is only held responsible if the woman becomes pregnant; often, he may escape prosecution if he marries his victim. Women are also particularly vulnerable to rape when they are incarcerated—and the word of a convict is rarely believed over that of her jailer.

Rape is one of the world's most underreported crimes. It is estimated that in some parts of the world less than 5 percent of rapes are reported. It is also believed that, in a majority of cases, the rapist is known to the victim and that many of the victims of rape are children and adolescents. International enactments against rape have struggled to address the issue. Most mentions of rape in war categorize it as a crime against honor. Whose honor—the victim's, her family's, or her country's—is not clear. In virtually no setting is rape understood as a crime based on gender. Even the Convention on the Elimination of All Forms of Discrimination Against Women does not highlight rape as a gender-based hate crime. Recently, however, international law has begun to recognize rape as a crime committed because of the victim's gender. Currently, the United Nations is considering establishment of an International Criminal Court; this court may provide long-needed protection for victims of rape.

For Further Reading

Human Rights Watch. *The Human Rights Watch Global Report on Women's Human Rights.* New York: Human Rights Watch, 1995.

Miranda Davies, ed. *Women and Violence.* London: Zed Books, 1995.

—Jo Lynn Southard

Religion, Women and

Religion plays a central, defining role in the lives of many. For millions of women, however, the very religions in which they believe contribute to their oppression. However, many people believe that this domination of women is based more on cultural traditions than religious strictures.

The interaction of religious and cultural practices can be seen in the very different rituals of people who claim to practice the same religion. For example, many African Muslims and Christians practice female genital mutilation in the belief that it is a tenet of their religion; yet the custom has almost vanished in other parts of the world. Because cultures historically were dominated by men, religions came to be structured in the same way—but not necessarily for reasons of faith. The Buddha, for example, encouraged women to take an active role in religious life and permitted them to become nuns; over time, however, the ordination of women among Buddhists ceased in many areas. Similarly, Muhammad gave his word to all believers, men and women—yet in most parts of the Muslim world, women are legislated to second class citizenship in the name of religion.

Although some religious organizations still do not allow the ordination of women—for example, the Roman Catholic Church—others have ordained women for many years. The Society of Friends (Quakers) has ordained women since the 1800s. In the United States, the Presbyterian Church first ordained women in 1889, followed by most of the other Protestant denominations. In contrast to Orthodox Judaism, the Reform and Conservative branches have had female rabbis for many years. Native American traditions have always included both men and women healers, and in many pagan groups, priestesses have greater power than priests. Today, from 40 to 60 percent of students enrolled in seminaries are women. In the United States, as of 1996, one in eight clergypersons were women. However, women ministers generally earn less than men who hold similar positions, and are rarely senior pastors.

Today, in India, Israel, and most Middle Eastern countries, personal matters are governed by religious law. Therefore, for example, in Israel a Jewish woman cannot sue for divorce, but a Jewish man may. The current leadership of Afghanistan, called the Taliban, has legislated women out of public life entirely, citing a particularly repressive interpretation of Islam. In countries where government and religion are separate, civil law may provide a woman with the equality lacking in religious law. However, separation of church and state can also result in governments allowing religious organizations to engage in behavior that would be illegal in secular organizations. For example, in recent years there have been several lawsuits brought against Christian organizations in the United States for practicing sex discrimination in their employment practices; in most cases the employer's right to discriminate against women was upheld on religious grounds. Similarly, civil rights laws do not apply to the ordination of clergy.

Political issues of gender equality will continue to have an impact on religious organizations in the future. Many people are questioning at what point—if ever—it is appropriate for governments to intervene in religious practices or for religious practices to intervene in government.

For Further Reading

Chaves, Mark. *Ordaining Women: Culture and Conflict in Religious Organizations.* Cambridge, Mass.: Harvard University Press, 1999.

Zikmund, Barbara Brown, et al. *Clergy Women: An Uphill Calling.* Louisville, Ky.: Westminster John Knox Press, 1998.

—*Jo Lynn Southard*

Reproductive Technologies

In the last quarter of the twentieth century, advances in reproductive technology have changed childbearing immeasurably. In the United States an estimated more than six million couples have difficulty in conceiving a child. Assisted reproductive technologies provide an array of options for dealing with conception problems.

The oldest of the reproductive technologies are the test tube baby procedures—in vitro fertilization, sperm injection, and gamete intrafallopian transfer. The first test tube baby was born in 1978. Initially developed to assist women with blocked Fallopian tubes to become pregnant, these techniques are now used for other types of infertility as well.

Technology that allows for fertilization outside of the human body has led to the ability to freeze embryos for later implantation. Ethical problems may arise with this method, however. Once the embryos are frozen, they may become the subject of a custody battle for a divorcing couple. There may be legal questions about whether frozen embryos have inheritance rights, and there is also a question about what to do with abandoned frozen embryos. Advanced reproductive technology even allows postmenopausal women to bear children, leading to the possibility of children being born to deceased parents, if their eggs or sperm are available.

The use of donated eggs and sperm raises issues as well. Recently, a web page began offering the eggs of professional models for sale; many people feel this is a questionable practice. Legal problems can arise if an egg donor

Minister Kate Latimer is pictured at Yale University. (Shelley Gazin/Corbis)

later attempts to claim the child, or if the child wishes to seek out the donor. A recent case in California, in which a donor egg was fertilized with donor sperm and then implanted in a surrogate mother resulted in a child who—briefly—was legally found to have no parents. An appeals court later determined the couple who had arranged the procedures to be the child's parents.

Another procedure that involves a third party is surrogacy, in which a woman carries a child to term for someone else. The eggs may be provided by the surrogate or the mother; the sperm may be provided by the father or a donor. In one of the first legal cases involving surrogacy the woman who had contracted to carry "Baby M" to term for another couple had a change of heart and refused to relinquish the baby. Eventually, the court awarded custody to the biological father and gave the surrogate mother, who was in this case also the biological mother, visitation rights. The biological father's wife has no legal rights as the child's parent.

The use of reproductive technologies has also resulted in multiple births, most famously the McCaughey septuplets born in Iowa in 1997 and the Chukwu octuplets born in Texas in 1998. Although these births were hailed as medical miracles by some, other observers questioned the ethics of the parents and doctors involved in these multiple births, which strain the emotional, physical, and economic resources of the families and often leave several of the children in poor physical health.

According to the U.S. Centers for Disease Control, in 1995 nearly 60,000 reproductive procedures were performed in the United States, which resulted in over 11,000 deliveries. Currently more than 70,000 children in the United States have been born as the result of reproductive technology, a field that has only been in existence for two decades. Despite the thorny ethical issues involved, these numbers are likely to increase as reproductive technology improves.

For Further Reading

Franklin, Sarah. *Embodied Progress: A Cultural Account of Assisted Conception.* New York: Routledge, 1997.

Ginsburg, Faye D., and Rayna Rapp, eds. *Conceiving the New World Order: The Global Politics of Reproduction.* Berkeley: University of California Press, 1995.

—Jo Lynn Southard

Sexual Harassment

Sexual harassment is a form of sex discrimination involving unwanted sexual attention that humiliates or intimidates and is based on gender or sexual preference. Although both women and men may be victims, women are the overwhelming majority of targets. According to the National Organization for Women, studies suggest that most women will experience some form of sexual harassment at some point in their lives.

Sexual harassment as a concept did not exist until the 1970s. Prior to that time, what is now considered harassment was often just "normal" relations between the genders. The women's liberation movement identified and defined the existence of sexual harassment, and since then more women have become aware of their right to be free from harassment.

Sexual harassment in the United States is considered a violation of the victim's civil rights. Among the activities that may be held to be harassment are: suggestive comments about one's appearance; touching or other physical contact; sexual comments or jokes; exposure to sexually explicit material; and sexual advances. When women feel their jobs are in jeopardy unless they go along with the sexual behavior, they are victims of harassment. In addition, even if the harassment is not directed at a particular woman, it may create an environment that is hostile to her ability to function and is also considered harassment. Recent cases have applied sexual harassment laws to girls harassed in schools. Either men or women may be victims of harassment, although women most often are; either men or women may be perpetrators of harassment, although men most often are. A harasser's victim may be of the same gender or the opposite.

In many other countries, sexual harassment laws are nonexistent. Much as the United States was a generation ago, the concept of sexual harassment is a difficult one in many of these countries. Even when antiharassment laws are in place, they are often weak. Japanese companies, for example, are not prohibited from sex discrimination, just encouraged to "endeavor" to avoid it. Many times these laws only cover small numbers of workers by, for example, only covering government employees.

Many countries, such as members of the European Union, are in the process of drafting laws against sexual harassment. As with other laws that affect largely women, male-dominated legislatures often move slowly in enacting these laws.

For Further Reading

Bouchard, Elizabeth. *Everything You Need to Know About Sexual Harassment.* New York: Rosen Publishing Group, 1997.

Lemoncheck, Linda, and Mane Hajdin. *Sexual Harassment: A Debate.* Lanham, Maryland: Rowman & Littlefield, 1997.

—Jo Lynn Southard

Sexual Preference

Any time a woman is a member of another minority or oppressed group, she faces double oppression. Women who are lesbians and bisexuals are subject to persecution not only because they are women but also because of their sexual preference. Even in the few countries that have legislated against hate crimes, sexual orientation is often not included as a basis for action.

Historically, the fact that a woman is a lesbian or bisexual has been used to deny her various civil rights. For example, in all but a few U.S. states, an employee may be fired for her sexual orientation. Until only recently, lesbian and bisexual women were not allowed to adopt children. In many states, courts still use the fact of a woman's sexual orientation, by itself, as a reason to deny her custody of her children. In no state are lesbians and gay men allowed to marry a person of the same sex. Currently, sexual orientation is not included, for the most part, in sexual harassment or hate crimes laws.

In other countries, laws are often even more oppressive. In 1998, a Romanian lesbian was granted political asylum in the United States, because Romanian law makes "attempting to seduce another woman" a violation of criminal law. Another Romanian woman convicted under that law served three years in prison. In Zimbabwe, the government refused to allow a gay and lesbian rights exhibit at a book fair in 1995 and again in 1996; Zimbabwe's president noted that he did not believe homosexuals "have any rights at all." The culture of many Asian countries is not open to lesbians. At the Fourth United Nations World Conference on Human Rights, held in Vienna in 1993, the government of Singapore noted that it and "people in many other parts of the world" do not believe that homosexuality is an acceptable lifestyle. In many parts of Asia, disdain for lesbians results in lesbians themselves denying their own orientation. They may marry men and, although they continue to have relationships with women, deny that they are lesbians.

The United Nations has recently begun to address discrimination against lesbians and gay men. At the World Conference on Human Rights, three lesbian and gay organizations were accredited to the conference for the first time in U.N. history. In 1994, the Fourth World Conference on Women, held in Beijing, accredited 11 lesbian and gay organizations. Nonetheless, the final documents of both conferences avoided mentioning sexual orientation as an unacceptable form of discrimination, choosing instead to condemn discrimination in general.

Women's activists note that failure to defend the rights of lesbians is a failure to protect women's rights in general. All women should be allowed to determine their own sexuality and how to express it, where they want to work, whether or not to have children, and with whom they will live. Restricting the choices of lesbians in these areas affects all women.

For Further Reading

Levin, Michael, et al. *Sexual Preference and Human Rights.* Lanham, Maryland: Rowman & Littlefield, 1999.

Hendriks, Aart, et al. *The Third Pink Book: A Global View of Lesbian and Gay Liberation and Oppression.* Buffalo, N.Y.: Prometheus Books, 1993.

—*Jo Lynn Southard*

Sex Selection

Recent improvements in technology, coupled with a continuing preference for male children in many cultures, have resulted in the ratio of women to men decreasing in many countries. Under normal conditions, there will be 104 male babies born for every 100 females. Among some populations, the numbers are now from 118 to 159 males for every 100 females.

Historically, boy children have been preferred to girls in almost every culture. The preference for male children helped create large families: women with daughters continued having children until sufficient sons were born to assure at least one would live to adulthood. Today, the desire for sons still spurs increased fertility in many areas. It also means that daughters may receive less food, medical care, and education than sons. More daughters than sons die in childhood or grow up disadvantaged. In addition, where son preference is particularly strong and poverty is high, female infanticide has been and continues to be practiced. For example, in Pakistan, India, Bangladesh, and Egypt, female child mortality is almost two-thirds higher than male.

However, technology now allows son preference to be addressed before the child is born. In some cases, where technology such as amniocentesis is accessible, parents have an opportunity to abort unwanted female fetuses. In one clinic in India, of 8,000 abortions performed, 7,999 were performed on female fetuses. In China, what has come to be called "differential abortion" has resulted in the birth of 118 males for every 100 females. In some parts of the country the skew is even higher.

Other technologies are aimed at controlling the gender of a fetus at conception. Researchers have recently succeeded at helping couples choose the sex of their baby by "sperm sorting" and artificial insemination. Interestingly, the technique is most effective at ensuring the birth of a girl, rather than a boy. Those in favor of sex selection technology argue that families can use the techniques to balance their families and as a safeguard for couples at risk for sex-linked genetic diseases.

As technology improves and becomes cheaper and more accessible, it also becomes more difficult to regulate. As long as son preference remains strong, these technologies run the risk of skewing the ratio of the genders even further. In cultures with strong son preference, women could one day become scarce—a situation that has already arisen in parts of China, where young men are finding it difficult to find brides.

For Further Reading

Gosden, Roger. *Designing Babies: The Brave New World of Reproductive Technology.* New York: W. H. Freeman & Co., 1999.

Lublin, Nancy. *Pandora's Box: Feminism Confronts Reproductive Technology.* Lanham, Maryland: Rowman & Littlefield, 1998.

—*Jo Lynn Southard*

Single Mothers

Eighteen percent of all families in the United States are headed by a woman without a husband, according to the U.S. Census Bureau. Sixty-one percent of children will live in a single parent household—most likely with their mother—at some point in their lives.

Although some people question its basis in reality, for many years, the picture of the traditional family in the United States was that of two parents and children. However, the number of single parent families has been growing. In 1950, only 9 percent of U.S. households contained only one parent; now it is just under 20 percent. More than 80 percent of single parent households are headed by women.

Although the overall birth rate is falling in the United States, more than half of first births in 1998 were to single women; one-quarter of births overall are to single women.

Almost two-thirds of single parent households are created by divorce or marital separation. Never-married women head up just over one-quarter of the single parent families. The remainder of these families are created by the death of a spouse. Whether divorced, separated, or never married, less than 60 percent of single mothers are awarded child support. Of those due child support, about half receive no money or only partial payments. The National Center for Policy Analysis estimates that 30 million children who are due support are not receiving it. Although recent efforts have resulted in more money being collected, the percentage of child support awards being paid has remained about the same for several years.

Whether single mothers receive child support or not, female-headed single parent families have the highest poverty rate—46 percent—of any group in the United States. This group also contains the largest percentage of those receiving public assistance of some sort.

One of the biggest problems that single mothers face is the availability of affordable child care. Women who make cash payments for child care pay about 7 percent of their monthly income. However, poor women pay much more—more than a quarter of their income. Although some government subsidies are available to help low-income families pay for child care, they are currently only reaching one in 10 eligible children. The Children's Defense Fund estimates that nearly five million children are home alone after school, with no after school program available. With a low unemployment rate, more and more mothers will have the opportunity to work outside the home—but only if child care is available and affordable.

For Further Reading

Engber, Andrea, and Leah Klungness. *The Complete Single Mother: Reassuring Answers to Your Most Challenging Concerns.* Holbrook, Mass: Adams Media Corp., 1995.

Ludtke, Melissa. *On Our Own: Unmarried Motherhood in America.* New York: Random House, 1997.

—*Jo Lynn Southard*

Sports, Women in

Lack of opportunity for women in sports was addressed in the United States by Title IX, passed in 1972, which mandated equality of resources allocated to women's and men's athletics in schools, and the Amateur Sports Act, passed in 1978, which requires the U.S. Olympic Committee to operate in a nondiscriminatory fashion. Nonetheless, today only about one-third of amateur athletes in schools or the Olympics are women.

Since the passage of Title IX, women's participation in sports has increased. In 1972, less than 16 percent of college athletes and 7 percent of high school athletes were female. Thirty years later, almost 35 percent of college and 37 percent of high school athletes were women. There was a big jump in the number of women participating right after passage of Title IX, but in recent years the numbers have only grown about 5 percent.

In 1992, 37 percent of U.S. Olympic athletes were female; in the summer games that year, there were 159 events for men and 86 for women. In the winter games in 1994, the men participated in 34 events and the women 25. Internationally, the Olympics are faced with the reality that women from religiously fundamentalist countries may not be allowed to participate at all.

In addition to participation, funding for women's programs has not reached parity with that for men's. In colleges, the median expenditure on women's sports is less than one quarter that spent on men's. Universities often argue that men's athletics bring in more revenues than women's do. However, the majority of football and basketball programs actually lose money. Also, women's coaches are paid less than men's—for example, a head basketball coach for a men's team in 1995 earned an average of $71,511; for a women's team, $39,177. Even though a wide disparity remains, the salaries of women's coaches have gradually increased since the passage of Title IX. This has ironically resulted in more men being hired as coaches of women's teams. In 1972, 90 percent of women's teams were coached by women, now, half of the coaches are men. At the high school level, two-third of all coaches are men. Meanwhile, only 2 percent of men's teams are coached by women.

Amateur sports participation remains divided very much along traditional gender lines. For example, 86 percent of the participants in aerobic exercise are female; 81 percent of the participants in baseball are male. Although some sports are close to parity—volleyball, for example, is 48 percent male and 52 percent female—only bowling is truly equal, at 50-50.

If women's participation in sports continues to grow at the slow pace of the last several years, it will take about 40 years to achieve equality on the high school athletics level. After years of increases, however small, a study by the U.S. Department of Education found that the participation of high school sophomore girls in sports actually declined from 1980 to 1990. The growth of women's sports participation on the college level is hampered by the expenditures of college athletic departments. Only 24 percent of operating budgets and 18 percent of recruiting budgets are for women's athletics.

Women's participation in professional sports is growing, although slowly. After several failed attempts, the Women's National Basketball Association was launched in 1996 and is slowly but surely gaining fans and media attention. The most recent attempt at women's professional football debuted in 1999 with the creation of the Women's Professional Football League. Women's pro sports in general was given a major boost with the dramatic victory of the U.S. Women's Soccer Team during the 1999 World Cup. The successes of these women are expected to contribute greatly to increased participation by girls and women in amateur sports.

For Further Reading

Birrell, Susan, and Cheryl Cole, eds. *Women, Sport and Culture.* Champaign, Ill.: Human Kinetics, 1994.

Cahn, Susan. *Coming on Strong.* New York: Free Press, 1994.

—*Jo Lynn Southard*

Welfare

A majority of the people living in poverty worldwide are women and children. As a result, government assistance or welfare plays a role in the lives of many women at some point. Public debate on welfare usually centers on the adult receiving it; however, the most common recipient of welfare today is not an adult, but a child.

Modern-day welfare programs began in the United States during the Great Depression in the 1930s. Prior to that, religious and charitable organizations were charged with taking care of the disadvantaged. As the welfare system evolved, women—who were and are more likely to be poor, less educated, and paid lower wages than men—were also more likely to depend on welfare at some time in their lives.

Although the women who are or have been on welfare receive the payments for a variety of reasons, one factor underlies women's use of welfare more than any other: women are poorer than men. Women receive lower salaries and less education than men. (See entries in this section on PAY EQUITY and EDUCATION.) In addition, many women receive welfare in order to leave an abusive relationship. According to the Institute for Women's Policy Research, various surveys indicate that as many as 80 percent of women on welfare survived domestic violence or are in the process of escaping it. As long as domestic violence remains an issue in society, welfare will probably remain a necessity.

The Institute for Women's Policy Research also found that 25 percent of welfare recipients are caring for a chronically ill child. In many cases, these women have children with particular medical conditions that are costly—such as asthma, diabetes, and learning disabilities—but not serious enough to qualify the child for disability insurance. Without welfare, many women simply could not afford to obtain treatment for their children.

Welfare reform has been on the political agenda in the United States for some time. In 1996 President Bill Clinton signed the sweeping Welfare Reform Bill, which limited the amount of time people are allowed to be on welfare and substantially reduced the federal role in the welfare system, allowing many policies to be set by the states. In many states, recent changes have indeed resulted in shrinking welfare rolls, as more and more mothers receive an education and help finding a job, as well as subsidized day care and health insurance.

However, in 1999 the Children's Defense Fund reported that during the first year of widespread welfare reform, there was a 27 percent increase in the number of children in single-mother families living in "extreme poverty"—that is, with incomes that are less than half of the federally defined poverty line. Statistics like this lead some observers to question whether welfare reform is helping or hurting women and, most pressingly, their children. Some experts contend that in the long run, welfare reform programs will only succeed when they are aimed at the social ills that create the need for welfare—poverty, gender inequality, domestic violence, and lack of affordable child and health care.

For Further Reading

Seccombe, Karen. *So You Think I Drive a Cadillac: Welfare Recipients' Perspectives on the System and Its Reform*. Needham Heights, Mass.: Allyn & Bacon, 1998.

Zucchino, David. *Myth of the Welfare Queen: A Pulitzer Prize-Winning Journalist's Portrait of Women on the Line*. New York: Touchstone Books, 1999.

—*Jo Lynn Southard*

Working Mothers

Over one third of the paid workforce worldwide is made up of women. In the United States, almost two-thirds of women with children work. While men are praised for their ability to earn a good living, mothers are often made to feel guilty about working.

It would be disingenuous to imply that there was ever a time when mothers did not work. Raising children and caring for a home are certainly work. But, until the last half century, women in the United States who worked outside the home were relatively rare. The women's movement and changing economic realities have led to a huge increase in the number of mothers who work outside the

For mothers getting off welfare, affordable child care can be a major issue; at the Millhill Family Center in Trenton, N.J., a mother stops in to play with her daughter. (AP Photo/Daniel Hulshizer)

home. Even as these numbers have grown, studies show that mothers, even in two parent families, do most of the housework and child rearing.

Women continue to earn less than men. In addition, women tend to be clustered in jobs that are defined as "women's work" and are paid at lower rates than men in comparable jobs. Worldwide, these women's jobs include child care work, nursing, and elementary school teaching. In the United States, bank teller is a woman's job; in Austria, chimney sweeps tend to be women; in India, road builders; and in Russia, doctors. These are all lower-paying jobs in these societies. Around the world, women are responsible for growing the food and gathering the water for their families, yet these activities are often not considered "work," because women are not paid for doing them.

Women are the main providers in 23 percent of families in the United States. Nearly one-third of those families are living below the poverty level, because women's wages are lower. Many other families have come to depend on having two incomes, the mother's and the father's, in order to maintain their lifestyle. Other mothers work because they choose to, because they enjoy the work. Although the stereotype is that working mothers are bad for children, a recent study by the National Institute of Child Health and Human Development indicates that a child may actually benefit from having a working mother.

One of the major issues facing working mothers is the availability and affordability of child care. Most companies in the United States do not provide day care for their workers, nor does the federal government. Day care is hugely expensive, as much as two or three hundred dollars a week depending on the number of children. In addition, studies show that when children are sick, or there are school conferences to attend, mothers are more likely than fathers to take time off from work, often using vacation time or their own sick leave to do so.

Because working mothers, whether single or married, tend to have their workdays interrupted more by their children than do working fathers, employers may be reluctant to hire women with children. As opposed to the idea of a "fast track" at work—where an employee receives regular promotions and raises as he rises through the ranks—some women now consider themselves on the "mommy track." On the mommy track, it will take longer to receive promotions, good assignments, and raises, because being a mommy interferes with a woman's career.

In most parts of the world, work outside the home was designed for men—men who have wives at home taking care of their needs and taking care of their children. As more and more women join the workforce, it is becoming obvious that this model may not be appropriate for working mothers.

For Further Reading

Chira, Susan. *A Mother's Place: Taking the Debate About Working Mothers Beyond Guilt and Blame.* New York: Harper Collins, 1998.

Holcomb, Betty. *Not Guilty!: The Good News About Working Mothers.* New York: Scribners, 1998.

—*Jo Lynn Southard*

Country-by-Country Survey

The charts below present a broad-based global snapshot of some key indicators concerning the condition of women. Political entities considered to be independent and sovereign are included in the tables, even if little data are available for them; these countries have been included so that the reader will know that an error of omission has not occurred.

Data are presented from the following sources: the *CIA World Factbook*; the Population and Statistics Divisions of the United Nations Secretariat; United Nations Educational, Scientific, and Cultural Organization; the World Bank; and the World Health Organization.

Data are from 1997, the most recent year for which information has been collected, unless otherwise indicated. Contraceptive usage surveys were conducted of married women ages 15 to 49, unless otherwise noted. The symbol "n.a." represents data not available.

AFGHANISTAN

Estimated 1999 population, in thousands, total: 21,923
Estimated 1999 population, in thousands, female: 10,672
Sex ratio 1999 (males per 100 females): 105

Birth rate, crude (per 1,000 people): 51.5
Fertility rate, total (births per woman): 6.9
Life expectancy at birth, female (years): 46.0
Life expectancy at birth, male (years): 45.0

Mortality rate, adult, female (per 1,000 female adults): 410.0
Mortality rate, adult, male (per 1,000 male adults): 413.0
Mortality rate, infant (per 1,000 live births): 151.0

Illiteracy rate, adult female (percent of females aged 15+): 82.1
Illiteracy rate, adult male (percent of males aged 15+): 51.9
School life expectancy, 1995, female: n.a.
School life expectancy, 1995, male: n.a.

Contraceptive prevalence, percent
  Year: n.a.
  Any method: n.a.
  Modern method: n.a.

Maternity leave benefits, as of early 1990s
  Maternity leave: 90 days
  Percentage of wages covered: 100
  Provider of coverage: employer

Labor force, total: 10,485,292
Labor force, female (percent of total): 35.1

Women in parliament as of January 1997
  Single or lower house, percent of seats occupied by women: n.a.
  Upper house, percent of seats occupied by women: n.a.

ALBANIA

Estimated 1999 population, in thousands, total: 3,113
Estimated 1999 population, in thousands, female: 1,521
Sex ratio 1999 (males per 100 females): 105

Birth rate, crude (per 1,000 people): 19.3
Fertility rate, total (births per woman): 2.5
Life expectancy at birth, female (years): 74.7
Life expectancy at birth, male (years): 68.8

Mortality rate, adult, female (per 1,000 female adults): 65.0
Mortality rate, adult, male (per 1,000 male adults): 122.0
Mortality rate, infant (per 1,000 live births): 25.8

Illiteracy rate, adult female (percent of females aged 15+): n.a.
Illiteracy rate, adult male (percent of males aged 15+): n.a.
School life expectancy, 1995, female: n.a.
School life expectancy, 1995, male: n.a.

Contraceptive prevalence, percent
  Year: n.a.
  Any method: n.a.
  Modern method: n.a.

Maternity leave benefits, as of early 1990s
  Maternity leave: n.a.
  Percentage of wages covered: n.a.
  Provider of coverage: n.a.

Labor force, total: 1,628,907
Labor force, female (percent of total): 41.0

Women in parliament as of January 1997
  Single or lower house, percent of seats occupied by women: 12.1
  Upper house, percent of seats occupied by women: n.a.

ALGERIA

Estimated 1999 population, in thousands, total: 30,774
Estimated 1999 population, in thousands, female: 15,199
Sex ratio 1999 (males per 100 females): 102

Birth rate, crude (per 1,000 people): 27.1
Fertility rate, total (births per woman): 3.6
Life expectancy at birth, female (years): 72.0
Life expectancy at birth, male (years): 68.8

Mortality rate, adult, female (per 1,000 female adults): 125.0
Mortality rate, adult, male (per 1,000 male adults): 160.0
Mortality rate, infant (per 1,000 live births): 32.0

Illiteracy rate, adult female (percent of females aged 15+): 52.3
Illiteracy rate, adult male (percent of males aged 15+): 27.3
School life expectancy, 1995, female: 9.9
School life expectancy, 1995, male: 11.1

Contraceptive prevalence, percent*
  Year: 1995
  Any method: 52†
  Modern method: 49
  * Includes ever-married women.
  † Adjusted from source to exclude breastfeeding.

Maternity leave benefits, as of early 1990s
  Maternity leave: 14 weeks
  Percentage of wages covered: 100
  Provider of coverage: social security

Labor force, total: 9,381,680
Labor force, female (percent of total): 25.7

Women in parliament as of January 1997
  Single or lower house, percent of seats occupied by women: 6.6
  Upper house, percent of seats occupied by women: n.a.

ANDORRA

Estimated 1994 population, in thousands, total: 64
Estimated 1994 population, in thousands, female: 30
Sex ratio 1994 (males per 100 females): 113

Birth rate, crude (per 1,000 people): 10.7
Fertility rate, total (births per woman): 1.2
Life expectancy at birth, female (years): n.a.
Life expectancy at birth, male (years): n.a.

Mortality rate, adult, female (per 1,000 female adults): n.a.
Mortality rate, adult, male (per 1,000 male adults): n.a.
Mortality rate, infant (per 1,000 live births): 4.1

Illiteracy rate, adult female (percent of females aged 15+): n.a.
Illiteracy rate, adult male (percent of males aged 15+): n.a.
School life expectancy, 1995, female: n.a.
School life expectancy, 1995, male: n.a.

Contraceptive prevalence, percent
  Year: n.a.
  Any method: n.a.
  Modern method: n.a.

Maternity leave benefits, as of early 1990s
  Maternity leave: n.a.
  Percentage of wages covered: n.a.
  Provider of coverage: n.a.

Labor force, total: n.a.
Labor force, female (percent of total): n.a.

Women in parliament as of January 1997
  Single or lower house, percent of seats occupied by women: n.a.
  Upper house, percent of seats occupied by women: n.a.

ANGOLA

Estimated 1999 population, in thousands, total: 12,478
Estimated 1999 population, in thousands, female: 6,310
Sex ratio 1999 (males per 100 females): 98

Birth rate, crude (per 1,000 people): 48.4
Fertility rate, total (births per woman): 6.8
Life expectancy at birth, female (years): 48.1
Life expectancy at birth, male (years): 44.9

Mortality rate, adult, female (per 1,000 female adults): 355.0
Mortality rate, adult, male (per 1,000 male adults): 412.0
Mortality rate, infant (per 1,000 live births): 125.0

Illiteracy rate, adult female (percent of females aged 15+): n.a.
Illiteracy rate, adult male (percent of males aged 15+): n.a.
School life expectancy, 1995, female: n.a.
School life expectancy, 1995, male: n.a.

Contraceptive prevalence, percent
  Year: n.a.
  Any method: n.a.
  Modern method: n.a.

Maternity leave benefits, as of early 1990s
  Maternity leave: 90 days
  Percentage of wages covered: 100
  Provider of coverage: employer

Labor force, total: 5,363,090
Labor force, female (percent of total): 46.4

Women in parliament as of January 1997
  Single or lower house, percent of seats occupied by women: 9.5
  Upper house, percent of seats occupied by women: n.a.

ANTIGUA AND BARBUDA

Estimated 1996 population, in thousands, total: 69
Estimated 1996 population, in thousands, female: 36
Sex ratio 1996 (males per 100 females): 92

Birth rate, crude (per 1,000 people): 17.5
Fertility rate, total (births per woman): 1.7
Life expectancy at birth, female (years): 78.9
Life expectancy at birth, male (years): 72.2

Mortality rate, adult, female (per 1,000 female adults): 67.0
Mortality rate, adult, male (per 1,000 male adults): 135.0
Mortality rate, infant (per 1,000 live births): 17.3

Illiteracy rate, adult female (percent of females aged 15+): n.a.
Illiteracy rate, adult male (percent of males aged 15+): n.a.
School life expectancy, 1995, female: n.a.
School life expectancy, 1995, male: n.a.

Contraceptive prevalence, percent*
    Year: 1998
    Any method: 53
    Modern method: 51
    * All women aged 15-44 years.

Maternity leave benefits, as of early 1990s
    Maternity leave: n.a.
    Percentage of wages covered: n.a.
    Provider of coverage: n.a.

Labor force, total: n.a.
Labor force, female (percent of total): n.a.

Women in parliament as of January 1997
    Single or lower house, percent of seats occupied by women: 5.3
    Upper house, percent of seats occupied by women: 17.6

ARGENTINA

Estimated 1999 population, in thousands, total: 36,577
Estimated 1999 population, in thousands, female: 18,637
Sex ratio 1999 (males per 100 females): 96

Birth rate, crude (per 1,000 people): 19.9
Fertility rate, total (births per woman): 2.6
Life expectancy at birth, female (years): 76.8
Life expectancy at birth, male (years): 69.6

Mortality rate, adult, female (per 1,000 female adults): 80.0
Mortality rate, adult, male (per 1,000 male adults): 165.0
Mortality rate, infant (per 1,000 live births): 22.0

Illiteracy rate, adult female (percent of females aged 15+): 3.5
Illiteracy rate, adult male (percent of males aged 15+): 3.4
School life expectancy, 1995, female: n.a.
School life expectancy, 1995, male: n.a.

Contraceptive prevalence, percent
    Year: n.a.
    Any method: n.a.
    Modern method: n.a.

Maternity leave benefits, as of early 1990s
    Maternity leave: 13 weeks
    Percentage of wages covered: 60
    Provider of coverage: social security

Labor force, total: 14,270,728
Labor force, female (percent of total): 31.8

Women in parliament as of January 1997
    Single or lower house, percent of seats occupied by women: 25.3
    Upper house, percent of seats occupied by women: 2.8

ARMENIA

Estimated 1999 population, in thousands, total: 3,525
Estimated 1999 population, in thousands, female: 1,811
Sex ratio 1999 (males per 100 females): 95

Birth rate, crude (per 1,000 people): 11.7
Fertility rate, total (births per woman): 1.5
Life expectancy at birth, female (years): 77.3
Life expectancy at birth, male (years): 70.3

Mortality rate, adult, female (per 1,000 female adults): 81.0
Mortality rate, adult, male (per 1,000 male adults): 164.0
Mortality rate, infant (per 1,000 live births): 15.4

Illiteracy rate, adult female (percent of females aged 15+): n.a.
Illiteracy rate, adult male (percent of males aged 15+): n.a.
School life expectancy, 1995, female: n.a.
School life expectancy, 1995, male: n.a.

Contraceptive prevalence, percent
    Year: 1990
    Any method: 22
    Modern method: n.a.

Maternity leave benefits, as of early 1990s
    Maternity leave: n.a.
    Percentage of wages covered: n.a.
    Provider of coverage: n.a.

Labor force, total: 1,855,802
Labor force, female (percent of total): 48.2

Women in parliament as of January 1997
    Single or lower house, percent of seats occupied by women: 6.3
    Upper house, percent of seats occupied by women: n.a.

AUSTRALIA

Estimated 1999 population, in thousands, total: 18,705
Estimated 1999 population, in thousands, female: 9,415
Sex ratio 1999 (males per 100 females): 99

Birth rate, crude (per 1,000 people): 13.7
Fertility rate, total (births per woman): 1.8
Life expectancy at birth, female (years): 81.2
Life expectancy at birth, male (years): 75.5

Mortality rate, adult, female (per 1,000 female adults): 57.0
Mortality rate, adult, male (per 1,000 male adults): 110.0
Mortality rate, infant (per 1,000 live births): 5.3

Illiteracy rate, adult female (percent of females aged 15+): n.a.
Illiteracy rate, adult male (percent of males aged 15+): n.a.
School life expectancy, 1995, female: 16.1
School life expectancy, 1995, male: 16.3

Contraceptive prevalence, percent*
Year: 1986
Any method: 76
Modern method: 72
* Married women aged 20-49 years.

Maternity leave benefits, as of early 1990s
Maternity leave: 6 weeks before delivery and 6 weeks after
Percentage of wages covered: 100 (Only public servants at the federal level and in some states are entitled to paid maternity leave.)
Provider of coverage: n.a.

Labor force, total: 9,451,422
Labor force, female (percent of total): 43.0

Women in parliament as of January 1997
Single or lower house, percent of seats occupied by women: 15.5
Upper house, percent of seats occupied by women: 30.3

AUSTRIA

Estimated 1999 population, in thousands, total: 8,177
Estimated 1999 population, in thousands, female: 4,148
Sex ratio 1999 (males per 100 females): 97

Birth rate, crude (per 1,000 people): 10.1
Fertility rate, total (births per woman): 1.4
Life expectancy at birth, female (years): 80.6
Life expectancy at birth, male (years): 74.2

Mortality rate, adult, female (per 1,000 female adults): 61.0
Mortality rate, adult, male (per 1,000 male adults): 123.0
Mortality rate, infant (per 1,000 live births): 4.7

Illiteracy rate, adult female (percent of females aged 15+): n.a.
Illiteracy rate, adult male (percent of males aged 15+): n.a.
School life expectancy, 1995, female: 14.2
School life expectancy, 1995, male: 14.4

Contraceptive prevalence, percent
Year: 1981/82
Any method: 71
Modern method: 56

Maternity leave benefits, as of early 1990s
Maternity leave: 8 weeks before delivery and 6 weeks after
Percentage of wages covered: ave. earnings
Provider of coverage: health insurance

Labor force, total: 3,793,925
Labor force, female (percent of total): 40.3

Women in parliament as of January 1997
Single or lower house, percent of seats occupied by women: 26.8
Upper house, percent of seats occupied by women: 20.3

AZERBAIJAN

Estimated 1999 population, in thousands, total: 7,697
Estimated 1999 population, in thousands, female: 3,927
Sex ratio 1999 (males per 100 females): 96

Birth rate, crude (per 1,000 people): 17.5
Fertility rate, total (births per woman): 2.1
Life expectancy at birth, female (years): 74.6
Life expectancy at birth, male (years): 67.4

Mortality rate, adult, female (per 1,000 female adults): 101.0
Mortality rate, adult, male (per 1,000 male adults): 213.0
Mortality rate, infant (per 1,000 live births): 19.6

Illiteracy rate, adult female (percent of females aged 15+): n.a.
Illiteracy rate, adult male (percent of males aged 15+): n.a.
School life expectancy, 1995, female: n.a.
School life expectancy, 1995, male: n.a.

Contraceptive prevalence, percent
Year: 1990
Any method: 17
Modern method: n.a.

Maternity leave benefits, as of early 1990s
Maternity leave: n.a.
Percentage of wages covered: n.a.
Provider of coverage: n.a.

Labor force, total: 3,344,000
Labor force, female (percent of total): 44.1

Women in parliament as of January 1997
Single or lower house, percent of seats occupied by women: 12
Upper house, percent of seats occupied by women: n.a.

BAHAMAS

Estimated 1999 population, in thousands, total: 301
Estimated 1999 population, in thousands, female: 153
Sex ratio 1999 (males per 100 females): 97

Birth rate, crude (per 1,000 people): 20.2
Fertility rate, total (births per woman): 2.3
Life expectancy at birth, female (years): 77.1
Life expectancy at birth, male (years): 70.5

Mortality rate, adult, female (per 1,000 female adults): 78.0
Mortality rate, adult, male (per 1,000 male adults): 159.0
Mortality rate, infant (per 1,000 live births): 17.0

Illiteracy rate, adult female (percent of females aged 15+): 3.6
Illiteracy rate, adult male (percent of males aged 15+): 4.9
School life expectancy, 1995, female: 13.2
School life expectancy, 1995, male: 12.1

Contraceptive prevalence, percent*
 Year: 1988
 Any method: 62
 Modern method: 60
 * All women aged 15-44 years.

Maternity leave benefits, as of early 1990s
 Maternity leave: 8 weeks
 Percentage of wages covered: 100
 Provider of coverage: national insurance / employer

Labor force, total: 153,170
Labor force, female (percent of total): 46.9

Women in parliament as of January 1997
 Single or lower house, percent of seats occupied by women: 8.2
 Upper house, percent of seats occupied by women: 18.8

BAHRAIN

Estimated 1999 population, in thousands, total: 607
Estimated 1999 population, in thousands, female: 261
Sex ratio 1999 (males per 100 females): 133

Birth rate, crude (per 1,000 people): 23.9
Fertility rate, total (births per woman): 3.3
Life expectancy at birth, female (years): 75.3
Life expectancy at birth, male (years): 70.4

Mortality rate, adult, female (per 1,000 female adults): 105.0
Mortality rate, adult, male (per 1,000 male adults): 175.0
Mortality rate, infant (per 1,000 live births): 9.0

Illiteracy rate, adult female (percent of females aged 15+): 19.3
Illiteracy rate, adult male (percent of males aged 15+): 10.1
School life expectancy, 1995, female: 13.3
School life expectancy, 1995, male: 12.6

Contraceptive prevalence, percent*
 Year: 1995
 Any method: 61†
 Modern method: 30
 * Married women under 50 years.
 † Adjusted from source to exclude breastfeeding.

Maternity leave benefits, as of early 1990s
 Maternity leave: 45 days
 Percentage of wages covered: 100
 Provider of coverage: employer

Labor force, total: 279,000
Labor force, female (percent of total): 19.7

Women in parliament as of January 1997
 Single or lower house, percent of seats occupied by women: n.a.
 Upper house, percent of seats occupied by women: n.a.

BANGLADESH

Estimated 1999 population, in thousands, total: 126,948
Estimated 1999 population, in thousands, female: 61,947
Sex ratio 1999 (males per 100 females): 105

Birth rate, crude (per 1,000 people): 28.1
Fertility rate, total (births per woman): 3.2
Life expectancy at birth, female (years): 58.2
Life expectancy at birth, male (years): 58.1

Mortality rate, adult, female (per 1,000 female adults): 309.0
Mortality rate, adult, male (per 1,000 male adults): 285.0
Mortality rate, infant (per 1,000 live births): 75.0

Illiteracy rate, adult female (percent of females aged 15+): 72.6
Illiteracy rate, adult male (percent of males aged 15+): 50.1
School life expectancy, 1995, female: n.a.
School life expectancy, 1995, male: n.a.

Contraceptive prevalence, percent*
 Year: 1996/97
 Any method: 49
 Modern method: 42
 * Married women aged 10-49 years.

Maternity leave benefits, as of early 1990s
 Maternity leave: 6 weeks before delivery and 6 weeks after
 Percentage of wages covered: 100
 Provider of coverage: employer

Labor force, total: 63,052,604
Labor force, female (percent of total): 42.2

Women in parliament as of January 1997
 Single or lower house, percent of seats occupied by women: 9.1
 Upper house, percent of seats occupied by women: n.a.

BARBADOS

Estimated 1999 population, in thousands, total: 269
Estimated 1999 population, in thousands, female: 139
Sex ratio 1999 (males per 100 females): 94

Birth rate, crude (per 1,000 people): 13.5
Fertility rate, total (births per woman): 1.6
Life expectancy at birth, female (years): 78.7
Life expectancy at birth, male (years): 73.7

Mortality rate, adult, female (per 1,000 female adults): 69.0
Mortality rate, adult, male (per 1,000 male adults): 123.0
Mortality rate, infant (per 1,000 live births): 14.0

Illiteracy rate, adult female (percent of females aged 15+): n.a.
Illiteracy rate, adult male (percent of males aged 15+): n.a.
School life expectancy, 1995, female: n.a.
School life expectancy, 1995, male: n.a.

Contraceptive prevalence, percent*
   Year: 1988
   Any method: 55
   Modern method: 53
   * All women aged 15-44 years.

Maternity leave benefits, as of early 1990s
   Maternity leave: 12 weeks
   Percentage of wages covered: 100
   Provider of coverage: national insurance

Labor force, total: 137,732
Labor force, female (percent of total): 46.5

Women in parliament as of January 1997
   Single or lower house, percent of seats occupied by women: 10.7
   Upper house, percent of seats occupied by women: 28.6

BELARUS

Estimated 1999 population, in thousands, total: 10,275
Estimated 1999 population, in thousands, female: 5,449
Sex ratio 1999 (males per 100 females): 89

Birth rate, crude (per 1,000 people): 8.8
Fertility rate, total (births per woman): 1.2
Life expectancy at birth, female (years): 74.3
Life expectancy at birth, male (years): 62.9

Mortality rate, adult, female (per 1,000 female adults): 115.0
Mortality rate, adult, male (per 1,000 male adults): 333.0
Mortality rate, infant (per 1,000 live births): 12.4

Illiteracy rate, adult female (percent of females aged 15+): 1.5
Illiteracy rate, adult male (percent of males aged 15+): 0.4
School life expectancy, 1995, female: n.a.
School life expectancy, 1995, male: n.a.

Contraceptive prevalence, percent*
   Year: 1995
   Any method: 50
   Modern method: 42
   * Married women aged 18-34 years.

Maternity leave benefits, as of early 1990s
   Maternity leave: n.a.
   Percentage of wages covered: n.a.
   Provider of coverage: n.a.

Labor force, total: 5,338,840
Labor force, female (percent of total): 48.8

Women in parliament as of January 1997
   Single or lower house, percent of seats occupied by women: n.a.
   Upper house, percent of seats occupied by women: n.a.

BELGIUM

Estimated 1999 population, in thousands, total: 10,152
Estimated 1999 population, in thousands, female: 5,180
Sex ratio 1999 (males per 100 females): 96

Birth rate, crude (per 1,000 people): 11.0
Fertility rate, total (births per woman): 1.6
Life expectancy at birth, female (years): 80.4
Life expectancy at birth, male (years): 73.5

Mortality rate, adult, female (per 1,000 female adults): 62.0
Mortality rate, adult, male (per 1,000 male adults): 134.0
Mortality rate, infant (per 1,000 live births): 6.4

Illiteracy rate, adult female (percent of females aged 15+): n.a.
Illiteracy rate, adult male (percent of males aged 15+): n.a.
School life expectancy, 1995, female: 15.4
School life expectancy, 1995, male: 15.6

Contraceptive prevalence, percent*
   Year: 1991
   Any method: 79
   Modern method: 75
   * Married women aged 20-40 years.

Maternity leave benefits, as of early 1990s
   Maternity leave: 7 weeks before delivery and 8 weeks after
   Percentage of wages covered: 82
   Provider of coverage: social security

Labor force, total: 4,177,900
Labor force, female (percent of total): 40.5

Women in parliament as of January 1997
   Single or lower house, percent of seats occupied by women: 12
   Upper house, percent of seats occupied by women: 22.5

BELIZE

Estimated 1999 population, in thousands, total: 235
Estimated 1999 population, in thousands, female: 116
Sex ratio 1999 (males per 100 females): 103

Birth rate, crude (per 1,000 people): 31.5
Fertility rate, total (births per woman): 3.7
Life expectancy at birth, female (years): 76.1
Life expectancy at birth, male (years): 73.4

Mortality rate, adult, female (per 1,000 female adults): 90.0
Mortality rate, adult, male (per 1,000 male adults): 170.0
Mortality rate, infant (per 1,000 live births): 32.0

Illiteracy rate, adult female (percent of females aged 15+): n.a.
Illiteracy rate, adult male (percent of males aged 15+): n.a.
School life expectancy, 1995, female: 10.4
School life expectancy, 1995, male: 10.6

Contraceptive prevalence, percent*
Year: 1991
Any method: 47
Modern method: 42
* All women aged 15-44 years.

Maternity leave benefits, as of early 1990s
Maternity leave: 6 weeks before delivery and 6 weeks after
Percentage of wages covered: 80
Provider of coverage: social security

Labor force, total: 75,735
Labor force, female (percent of total): 23.4

Women in parliament as of January 1997
Single or lower house, percent of seats occupied by women: 3.4
Upper house, percent of seats occupied by women: 37.5

BENIN

Estimated 1999 population, in thousands, total: 5,937
Estimated 1999 population, in thousands, female: 3,011
Sex ratio 1999 (males per 100 females): 97

Birth rate, crude (per 1,000 people): 42.8
Fertility rate, total (births per woman): 5.8
Life expectancy at birth, female (years): 55.2
Life expectancy at birth, male (years): 51.7

Mortality rate, adult, female (per 1,000 female adults): 304.0
Mortality rate, adult, male (per 1,000 male adults): 362.0
Mortality rate, infant (per 1,000 live births): 88.0

Illiteracy rate, adult female (percent of females aged 15+): 79.1
Illiteracy rate, adult male (percent of males aged 15+): 52.3
School life expectancy, 1995, female: n.a.
School life expectancy, 1995, male: n.a.

Contraceptive prevalence, percent
Year: 1996
Any method: 16
Modern method: 3

Maternity leave benefits, as of early 1990s
Maternity leave: 14 weeks
Percentage of wages covered: 100
Provider of coverage: social security

Labor force, total: 2,608,241
Labor force, female (percent of total): 48.3

Women in parliament as of January 1997
Single or lower house, percent of seats occupied by women: 7.2
Upper house, percent of seats occupied by women: n.a.

BHUTAN

Estimated 1999 population, in thousands, total: 2,064
Estimated 1999 population, in thousands, female: 1,022
Sex ratio 1999 (males per 100 females): 102

Birth rate, crude (per 1,000 people): 39.2
Fertility rate, total (births per woman): 5.8
Life expectancy at birth, female (years): 62.0
Life expectancy at birth, male (years): 59.5

Mortality rate, adult, female (per 1,000 female adults): n.a.
Mortality rate, adult, male (per 1,000 male adults): n.a.
Mortality rate, infant (per 1,000 live births): 63.0

Illiteracy rate, adult female (percent of females aged 15+): n.a.
Illiteracy rate, adult male (percent of males aged 15+): n.a.
School life expectancy, 1995, female: n.a.
School life expectancy, 1995, male: n.a.

Contraceptive prevalence, percent
Year: 1994
Any method: 19
Modern method: 19

Maternity leave benefits, as of early 1990s
Maternity leave: n.a.
Percentage of wages covered: n.a.
Provider of coverage: n.a.

Labor force, total: 361,228
Labor force, female (percent of total): 39.7

Women in parliament as of January 1997
Single or lower house, percent of seats occupied by women: 2
Upper house, percent of seats occupied by women: n.a.

BOLIVIA

Estimated 1999 population, in thousands, total: 8,142
Estimated 1999 population, in thousands, female: 4,093
Sex ratio 1999 (males per 100 females): 99

Birth rate, crude (per 1,000 people): 33.2
Fertility rate, total (births per woman): 4.4
Life expectancy at birth, female (years): 63.2
Life expectancy at birth, male (years): 59.8

Mortality rate, adult, female (per 1,000 female adults): 220.0
Mortality rate, adult, male (per 1,000 male adults): 269.0
Mortality rate, infant (per 1,000 live births): 66.0

Illiteracy rate, adult female (percent of females aged 15+): 23.2
Illiteracy rate, adult male (percent of males aged 15+): 9.3
School life expectancy, 1995, female: n.a.
School life expectancy, 1995, male: n.a.

Contraceptive prevalence, percent
Year: 1994
Any method: 45
Modern method: 18

Maternity leave benefits, as of early 1990s
Maternity leave: 60 days
Percentage of wages covered: minimum wage + 80 percent of regular wage
Provider of coverage: national insurance

Labor force, total: 3,106,800
Labor force, female (percent of total): 37.5

Women in parliament as of January 1997
Single or lower house, percent of seats occupied by women: 6.9
Upper house, percent of seats occupied by women: 3.7

BOSNIA AND HERZEGOVINA

Estimated 1999 population, in thousands, total: 3,838
Estimated 1999 population, in thousands, female: 1,939
Sex ratio 1999 (males per 100 females): 98

Birth rate, crude (per 1,000 people): 13.3
Fertility rate, total (births per woman): n.a.
Life expectancy at birth, female (years): n.a.
Life expectancy at birth, male (years): n.a.

Mortality rate, adult, female (per 1,000 female adults): 93.0
Mortality rate, adult, male (per 1,000 male adults): 170.0
Mortality rate, infant (per 1,000 live births): 12.7

Illiteracy rate, adult female (percent of females aged 15+): n.a.
Illiteracy rate, adult male (percent of males aged 15+): n.a.
School life expectancy, 1995, female: n.a.
School life expectancy, 1995, male: n.a.

Contraceptive prevalence, percent
Year: n.a.
Any method: n.a.
Modern method: n.a.

Maternity leave benefits, as of early 1990s
Maternity leave: n.a.
Percentage of wages covered: n.a.
Provider of coverage: n.a.

Labor force, total: 1,079,362
Labor force, female (percent of total): 38.0

Women in parliament as of January 1997
Single or lower house, percent of seats occupied by women: n.a.
Upper house, percent of seats occupied by women: n.a.

BOTSWANA

Estimated 1999 population, in thousands, total: 1,597
Estimated 1999 population, in thousands, female: 813
Sex ratio 1999 (males per 100 females): 96

Birth rate, crude (per 1,000 people): 33.9
Fertility rate, total (births per woman): 4.4
Life expectancy at birth, female (years): 48.4
Life expectancy at birth, male (years): 46.2

Mortality rate, adult, female (per 1,000 female adults): 552.0
Mortality rate, adult, male (per 1,000 male adults): 600.0
Mortality rate, infant (per 1,000 live births): 58.0

Illiteracy rate, adult female (percent of females aged 15+): 23.1
Illiteracy rate, adult male (percent of males aged 15+): 28.2
School life expectancy, 1995, female: 10.7
School life expectancy, 1995, male: 10.5

Contraceptive prevalence, percent
Year: 1988
Any method: 33
Modern method: 32

Maternity leave benefits, as of early 1990s
Maternity leave: 12 weeks
Percentage of wages covered: 25
Provider of coverage: employer

Labor force, total: 674,520
Labor force, female (percent of total): 45.7

Women in parliament as of January 1997
Single or lower house, percent of seats occupied by women: 8.5
Upper house, percent of seats occupied by women: n.a.

BRAZIL

Estimated 1999 population, in thousands, total: 167,988
Estimated 1999 population, in thousands, female: 84,991
Sex ratio 1999 (males per 100 females): 98

Birth rate, crude (per 1,000 people): 20.6
Fertility rate, total (births per woman): 2.3
Life expectancy at birth, female (years): 71.0
Life expectancy at birth, male (years): 63.1

Mortality rate, adult, female (per 1,000 female adults): 139.0
Mortality rate, adult, male (per 1,000 male adults): 202.0
Mortality rate, infant (per 1,000 live births): 34.0

Illiteracy rate, adult female (percent of females aged 15+): 16.1
Illiteracy rate, adult male (percent of males aged 15+): 15.9
School life expectancy, 1995, female: n.a.
School life expectancy, 1995, male: n.a.

Contraceptive prevalence, percent
Year: 1996
Any method: 77
Modern method: 70

Maternity leave benefits, as of early 1990s
Maternity leave: 120 days
Percentage of wages covered: 100
Provider of coverage: social insurance

Labor force, total: 75,297,024
Labor force, female (percent of total): 35.3

Women in parliament as of January 1997
Single or lower house, percent of seats occupied by women: 6.6
Upper house, percent of seats occupied by women: 7.4

BRUNEI

Estimated 1999 population, in thousands, total: 321
Estimated 1999 population, in thousands, female: 153
Sex ratio 1999 (males per 100 females): 110

Birth rate, crude (per 1,000 people): 22.3
Fertility rate, total (births per woman): 2.8
Life expectancy at birth, female (years): 78.1
Life expectancy at birth, male (years): 73.4

Mortality rate, adult, female (per 1,000 female adults): 78.0
Mortality rate, adult, male (per 1,000 male adults): 132.0
Mortality rate, infant (per 1,000 live births): 9.0

Illiteracy rate, adult female (percent of females aged 15+): 14.0
Illiteracy rate, adult male (percent of males aged 15+): 6.3
School life expectancy, 1995, female: 12.1
School life expectancy, 1995, male: 11.8

Contraceptive prevalence, percent
Year: n.a.
Any method: n.a.
Modern method: n.a.

Maternity leave benefits, as of early 1990s
Maternity leave: n.a.
Percentage of wages covered: n.a.
Provider of coverage: n.a.

Labor force, total: 135,458
Labor force, female (percent of total): 34.6

Women in parliament as of January 1997
Single or lower house, percent of seats occupied by women: n.a.
Upper house, percent of seats occupied by women: n.a.

BULGARIA

Estimated 1999 population, in thousands, total: 8,280
Estimated 1999 population, in thousands, female: 4,249
Sex ratio 1999 (males per 100 females): 95

Birth rate, crude (per 1,000 people): 8.7
Fertility rate, total (births per woman): 1.1
Life expectancy at birth, female (years): 74.4
Life expectancy at birth, male (years): 67.2

Mortality rate, adult, female (per 1,000 female adults): 106.0
Mortality rate, adult, male (per 1,000 male adults): 213.0
Mortality rate, infant (per 1,000 live births): 17.5

Illiteracy rate, adult female (percent of females aged 15+): 2.4
Illiteracy rate, adult male (percent of males aged 15+): 1.2
School life expectancy, 1995, female: 12.5
School life expectancy, 1995, male: 11.8

Contraceptive prevalence, percent
Year: n.a.
Any method: n.a.
Modern method: n.a.

Maternity leave benefits, as of early 1990s
Maternity leave: 120 days (150 days for the second child, 180 days
for the third and 120 days for the fourth and subsequent children.)
Percentage of wages covered: 100
Provider of coverage: social insurance

Labor force, total: 4,239,156
Labor force, female (percent of total): 48.2

Women in parliament as of January 1997
Single or lower house, percent of seats occupied by women: 13.3
Upper house, percent of seats occupied by women: n.a.

BURKINA FASO

Estimated 1999 population, in thousands, total: 11,616
Estimated 1999 population, in thousands, female: 5,819
Sex ratio 1999 (males per 100 females): 100

Birth rate, crude (per 1,000 people): 44.8
Fertility rate, total (births per woman): 6.6
Life expectancy at birth, female (years): 45.2
Life expectancy at birth, male (years): 43.6

Mortality rate, adult, female (per 1,000 female adults): 520.0
Mortality rate, adult, male (per 1,000 male adults): 540.0
Mortality rate, infant (per 1,000 live births): 99.0

Illiteracy rate, adult female (percent of females aged 15+): 88.9
Illiteracy rate, adult male (percent of males aged 15+): 69.5
School life expectancy, 1995, female: 2.0
School life expectancy, 1995, male: 3.3

Contraceptive prevalence, percent
Year: 1993
Any method: 8†
Modern method: 4
† Excludes "prolonged abstinence," reported as the current method by 17 percent.

Maternity leave benefits, as of early 1990s
Maternity leave: 14 weeks
Percentage of wages covered: 100
Provider of coverage: soc. sec./employer

Labor force, total: 5,236,765
Labor force, female (percent of total): 46.6

Women in parliament as of January 1997
Single or lower house, percent of seats occupied by women: 3.7
Upper house, percent of seats occupied by women: 11.9

BURMA (MYANMAR)

Estimated 1999 population, in thousands, total: 45,059
Estimated 1999 population, in thousands, female: 22,633
Sex ratio 1999 (males per 100 females): 99

Birth rate, crude (per 1,000 people): 27.0
Fertility rate, total (births per woman): 2.4
Life expectancy at birth, female (years): 61.8
Life expectancy at birth, male (years): 58.5

Mortality rate, adult, female (per 1,000 female adults): 217.0
Mortality rate, adult, male (per 1,000 male adults): 263.0
Mortality rate, infant (per 1,000 live births): 79.0

Illiteracy rate, adult female (percent of females aged 15+): 21.2
Illiteracy rate, adult male (percent of males aged 15+): 11.5
School life expectancy, 1995, female: n.a.
School life expectancy, 1995, male: n.a.

Contraceptive prevalence, percent
Year: 1992
Any method: 17
Modern method: 14

Maternity leave benefits, as of early 1990s
Maternity leave: n.a.
Percentage of wages covered: n.a.
Provider of coverage: n.a.

Labor force, total: 23,263,210
Labor force, female (percent of total): 43.5

Women in parliament as of January 1997
Single or lower house, percent of seats occupied by women: n.a.
Upper house, percent of seats occupied by women: n.a.

BURUNDI

Estimated 1999 population, in thousands, total: 6,565
Estimated 1999 population, in thousands, female: 3,353
Sex ratio 1999 (males per 100 females): 96

Birth rate, crude (per 1,000 people): 42.8
Fertility rate, total (births per woman): 6.3
Life expectancy at birth, female (years): 43.8
Life expectancy at birth, male (years): 41.0

Mortality rate, adult, female (per 1,000 female adults): 491.0
Mortality rate, adult, male (per 1,000 male adults): 550.0
Mortality rate, infant (per 1,000 live births): 119.0

Illiteracy rate, adult female (percent of females aged 15+): 63.9
Illiteracy rate, adult male (percent of males aged 15+): 46.2
School life expectancy, 1995, female: 4.0
School life expectancy, 1995, male: 5.1

Contraceptive prevalence, percent
Year: 1987
Any method: 9
Modern method: 1

Maternity leave benefits, as of early 1990s
Maternity leave: 12 weeks
Percentage of wages covered: 90
Provider of coverage: employer

Labor force, total: 3,474,754
Labor force, female (percent of total): 48.9

Women in parliament as of January 1997
Single or lower house, percent of seats occupied by women: n.a.
Upper house, percent of seats occupied by women: n.a.

CAMBODIA

Estimated 1999 population, in thousands, total: 10,946
Estimated 1999 population, in thousands, female: 5,641
Sex ratio 1999 (males per 100 females): 94

Birth rate, crude (per 1,000 people): 34.3
Fertility rate, total (births per woman): 4.6
Life expectancy at birth, female (years): 55.4
Life expectancy at birth, male (years): 52.6

Mortality rate, adult, female (per 1,000 female adults): 303.0
Mortality rate, adult, male (per 1,000 male adults): 349.0
Mortality rate, infant (per 1,000 live births): 103.0

Illiteracy rate, adult female (percent of females aged 15+): n.a.
Illiteracy rate, adult male (percent of males aged 15+): n.a.
School life expectancy, 1995, female: n.a.
School life expectancy, 1995, male: n.a.

Contraceptive prevalence, percent
  Year: n.a.
  Any method: n.a.
  Modern method: n.a.

Maternity leave benefits, as of early 1990s
  Maternity leave: 90 days
  Percentage of wages covered: 100
  Provider of coverage: employer

Labor force, total: 5,449,470
Labor force, female (percent of total): 52.0

Women in parliament as of January 1997
  Single or lower house, percent of seats occupied by women: 5.8
  Upper house, percent of seats occupied by women: n.a.

CAMEROON

Estimated 1999 population, in thousands, total: 14,710
Estimated 1999 population, in thousands, female: 7,390
Sex ratio 1999 (males per 100 females): 99

Birth rate, crude (per 1,000 people): 39.2
Fertility rate, total (births per woman): 5.3
Life expectancy at birth, female (years): 57.7
Life expectancy at birth, male (years): 55.4

Mortality rate, adult, female (per 1,000 female adults): 352.0
Mortality rate, adult, male (per 1,000 male adults): 390.0
Mortality rate, infant (per 1,000 live births): 52.2

Illiteracy rate, adult female (percent of females aged 15+): 35.4
Illiteracy rate, adult male (percent of males aged 15+): 21.0
School life expectancy, 1995, female: n.a.
School life expectancy, 1995, male: n.a.

Contraceptive prevalence, percent
  Year: 1998
  Any method: 19
  Modern method: 7

Maternity leave benefits, as of early 1990s
  Maternity leave: 14 weeks
  Percentage of wages covered: 100
  Provider of coverage: social security

Labor force, total: 5,713,781
Labor force, female (percent of total): 37.7

Women in parliament as of January 1997
  Single or lower house, percent of seats occupied by women: 12.2
  Upper house, percent of seats occupied by women: n.a.

CANADA

Estimated 1999 population, in thousands, total: 30,857
Estimated 1999 population, in thousands, female: 15,583
Sex ratio 1999 (males per 100 females): 98

Birth rate, crude (per 1,000 people): 11.9
Fertility rate, total (births per woman): 1.6
Life expectancy at birth, female (years): 82.0
Life expectancy at birth, male (years): 76.0

Mortality rate, adult, female (per 1,000 female adults): 52.0
Mortality rate, adult, male (per 1,000 male adults): 106.0
Mortality rate, infant (per 1,000 live births): 6.1

Illiteracy rate, adult female (percent of females aged 15+): n.a.
Illiteracy rate, adult male (percent of males aged 15+): n.a.
School life expectancy, 1995, female: 17.8
School life expectancy, 1995, male: 17.2

Contraceptive prevalence, percent
  Year: 1995
  Any method: 75
  Modern method: 75

Maternity leave benefits, as of early 1990s
  Maternity leave: 17 weeks
  Percentage of wages covered: 57 for 15 weeks
  Provider of coverage: unemployment ins.

Labor force, total: 16,051,898
Labor force, female (percent of total): 45.3

Women in parliament as of January 1997
  Single or lower house, percent of seats occupied by women: 18
  Upper house, percent of seats occupied by women: 23.1

CAPE VERDE

Estimated 1999 population, in thousands, total: 418
Estimated 1999 population, in thousands, female: 223
Sex ratio 1999 (males per 100 females): 87

Birth rate, crude (per 1,000 people): 32.4
Fertility rate, total (births per woman): 3.6
Life expectancy at birth, female (years): 71.3
Life expectancy at birth, male (years): 65.5

Mortality rate, adult, female (per 1,000 female adults): 168.0
Mortality rate, adult, male (per 1,000 male adults): 190.0
Mortality rate, infant (per 1,000 live births): 56.0

Illiteracy rate, adult female (percent of females aged 15+): 37.6
Illiteracy rate, adult male (percent of males aged 15+): 17.9
School life expectancy, 1995, female: 8.6
School life expectancy, 1995, male: 9

Contraceptive prevalence, percent
Year: n.a.
Any method: n.a.
Modern method: n.a.

Maternity leave benefits, as of early 1990s
Maternity leave: n.a.
Percentage of wages covered: n.a.
Provider of coverage: n.a.

Labor force, total: 160,476
Labor force, female (percent of total): 39.0

Women in parliament as of January 1997
Single or lower house, percent of seats occupied by women: 11.1
Upper house, percent of seats occupied by women: n.a.

CENTRAL AFRICAN REPUBLIC

Estimated 1999 population, in thousands, total: 3,549
Estimated 1999 population, in thousands, female: 1,824
Sex ratio 1999 (males per 100 females): 95

Birth rate, crude (per 1,000 people): 36.9
Fertility rate, total (births per woman): 4.9
Life expectancy at birth, female (years): 46.9
Life expectancy at birth, male (years): 42.9

Mortality rate, adult, female (per 1,000 female adults): 476.0
Mortality rate, adult, male (per 1,000 male adults): 567.0
Mortality rate, infant (per 1,000 live births): 98.0

Illiteracy rate, adult female (percent of females aged 15+): 69.9
Illiteracy rate, adult male (percent of males aged 15+): 44.0
School life expectancy, 1995, female: n.a.
School life expectancy, 1995, male: n.a.

Contraceptive prevalence, percent
Year: 1994/95
Any method: 15
Modern method: 3

Maternity leave benefits, as of early 1990s
Maternity leave: 14 weeks
Percentage of wages covered: 50
Provider of coverage: social security

Labor force, total: n.a.
Labor force, female (percent of total): n.a.

Women in parliament as of January 1997
Single or lower house, percent of seats occupied by women: 3.5
Upper house, percent of seats occupied by women: n.a.

CHAD

Estimated 1999 population, in thousands, total: 7,458
Estimated 1999 population, in thousands, female: 3,771
Sex ratio 1999 (males per 100 females): 98

Birth rate, crude (per 1,000 people): 45.1
Fertility rate, total (births per woman): 6.5
Life expectancy at birth, female (years): 50.3
Life expectancy at birth, male (years): 46.9

Mortality rate, adult, female (per 1,000 female adults): 383.0
Mortality rate, adult, male (per 1,000 male adults): 448.0
Mortality rate, infant (per 1,000 live births): 100.0

Illiteracy rate, adult female (percent of females aged 15+): n.a.
Illiteracy rate, adult male (percent of males aged 15+): n.a.
School life expectancy, 1995, female: n.a.
School life expectancy, 1995, male: n.a.

Contraceptive prevalence, percent
Year: 1996/97
Any method: 4
Modern method: 1

Maternity leave benefits, as of early 1990s
Maternity leave: 14 weeks
Percentage of wages covered: 50
Provider of coverage: social security

Labor force, total: 3,433,445
Labor force, female (percent of total): 44.5

Women in parliament as of January 1997
Single or lower house, percent of seats occupied by women: 17.3
Upper house, percent of seats occupied by women: n.a.

CHILE

Estimated 1999 population, in thousands, total: 15,019
Estimated 1999 population, in thousands, female: 7,584
Sex ratio 1999 (males per 100 females): 98

Birth rate, crude (per 1,000 people): 19.6
Fertility rate, total (births per woman): 2.4
Life expectancy at birth, female (years): 78.3
Life expectancy at birth, male (years): 72.3

Mortality rate, adult, female (per 1,000 female adults): 73.0
Mortality rate, adult, male (per 1,000 male adults): 143.0
Mortality rate, infant (per 1,000 live births): 11.0

Illiteracy rate, adult female (percent of females aged 15+): 5.0
Illiteracy rate, adult male (percent of males aged 15+): 4.6
School life expectancy, 1995, female: 11.7
School life expectancy, 1995, male: 11.8

Contraceptive prevalence, percent
  Year: 1990
  Any method: 30
  Modern method: n.a.

Maternity leave benefits, as of early 1990s
  Maternity leave: 6 weeks before delivery and 12 weeks after
  Percentage of wages covered: 100
  Provider of coverage: social insurance

Labor force, total: 5,848,800
Labor force, female (percent of total): 32.5

Women in parliament as of January 1997
  Single or lower house, percent of seats occupied by women: 7.5
  Upper house, percent of seats occupied by women: 6.5

CHINA

Estimated 1999 population, in thousands, total: 1,266,838
Estimated 1999 population, in thousands, female: 615,024
Sex ratio 1999 (males per 100 females): 106

Birth rate, crude (per 1,000 people): 16.8
Fertility rate, total (births per woman): 1.9
Life expectancy at birth, female (years): 71.3
Life expectancy at birth, male (years): 68.1

Mortality rate, adult, female (per 1,000 female adults): 137.0
Mortality rate, adult, male (per 1,000 male adults): 165.0
Mortality rate, infant (per 1,000 live births): 32.0

Illiteracy rate, adult female (percent of females aged 15+): 25.5
Illiteracy rate, adult male (percent of males aged 15+): 9.1
School life expectancy, 1995, female: n.a.
School life expectancy, 1995, male: n.a.

Contraceptive prevalence, percent
  Year: 1992
  Any method: 83
  Modern method: 83

Maternity leave benefits, as of early 1990s
  Maternity leave: 56 days
  Percentage of wages covered: 100
  Provider of coverage: n.a.

Labor force, total: 736,305,984
Labor force, female (percent of total): 45.1

Women in parliament as of January 1997
  Single or lower house, percent of seats occupied by women: 21
  Upper house, percent of seats occupied by women: n.a.

Note: For statistical purposes, data do not include Hong Kong or Taiwan.

COLOMBIA

Estimated 1999 population, in thousands, total: 41,564
Estimated 1999 population, in thousands, female: 21,026
Sex ratio 1999 (males per 100 females): 98

Birth rate, crude (per 1,000 people): 24.5
Fertility rate, total (births per woman): 2.8
Life expectancy at birth, female (years): 73.4
Life expectancy at birth, male (years): 67.2

Mortality rate, adult, female (per 1,000 female adults): 115.0
Mortality rate, adult, male (per 1,000 male adults): 210.0
Mortality rate, infant (per 1,000 live births): 24.0

Illiteracy rate, adult female (percent of females aged 15+): 9.2
Illiteracy rate, adult male (percent of males aged 15+): 9.0
School life expectancy, 1995, female: n.a.
School life expectancy, 1995, male: n.a.

Contraceptive prevalence, percent
  Year: 1995
  Any method: 72
  Modern method: 59

Maternity leave benefits, as of early 1990s
  Maternity leave: 12 weeks
  Percentage of wages covered: 100
  Provider of coverage: social security

Labor force, total: 17,218,060
Labor force, female (percent of total): 37.9

Women in parliament as of January 1997
  Single or lower house, percent of seats occupied by women: 11.7
  Upper house, percent of seats occupied by women: 6.9

COMOROS

Estimated 1999 population, in thousands, total: 676
Estimated 1999 population, in thousands, female: 338
Sex ratio 1999 (males per 100 females): 100

Birth rate, crude (per 1,000 people): 34.9
Fertility rate, total (births per woman): 4.6
Life expectancy at birth, female (years): 60.8
Life expectancy at birth, male (years): 58.8

Mortality rate, adult, female (per 1,000 female adults): 250.0
Mortality rate, adult, male (per 1,000 male adults): 270.0
Mortality rate, infant (per 1,000 live births): 65.0

Illiteracy rate, adult female (percent of females aged 15+): 51.8
Illiteracy rate, adult male (percent of males aged 15+): 37.1
School life expectancy, 1995, female: n.a.
School life expectancy, 1995, male: n.a.

Contraceptive prevalence, percent
  Year: 1996
  Any method: 21
  Modern method: 11

Maternity leave benefits, as of early 1990s
  Maternity leave: 14 weeks
  Percentage of wages covered: 100
  Provider of coverage: employer

Labor force, total: 232,929
Labor force, female (percent of total): 42.4

Women in parliament as of January 1997
  Single or lower house, percent of seats occupied by women: 0
  Upper house, percent of seats occupied by women: n.a.

CONGO, DEM. REP. (ZAIRE)

Estimated 1999 population, in thousands, total: 50,336
Estimated 1999 population, in thousands, female: 25,432
Sex ratio 1999 (males per 100 females): 98

Birth rate, crude (per 1,000 people): 46.6
Fertility rate, total (births per woman): 6.4
Life expectancy at birth, female (years): 52.3
Life expectancy at birth, male (years): 49.2

Mortality rate, adult, female (per 1,000 female adults): n.a.
Mortality rate, adult, male (per 1,000 male adults): n.a.
Mortality rate, infant (per 1,000 live births): 92.0

Illiteracy rate, adult female (percent of females aged 15+): n.a.
Illiteracy rate, adult male (percent of males aged 15+): n.a.
School life expectancy, 1995, female: 4.4
School life expectancy, 1995, male: 6.8

Contraceptive prevalence, percent*
  Year: 1991
  Any method: 8
  Modern method: 2
  * Married women aged 12-49 years.

Maternity leave benefits, as of early 1990s
  Maternity leave: 14 weeks
  Percentage of wages covered: two thirds of remuneration
  Provider of coverage: employer

Labor force, total: 19,617,856
Labor force, female (percent of total): 43.5

Women in parliament as of January 1997
  Single or lower house, percent of seats occupied by women: 5
  Upper house, percent of seats occupied by women: n.a.

CONGO, REP.

Estimated 1999 population, in thousands, total: 2,864
Estimated 1999 population, in thousands, female: 1,464
Sex ratio 1999 (males per 100 females): 96

Birth rate, crude (per 1,000 people): 43.7
Fertility rate, total (births per woman): 6.1
Life expectancy at birth, female (years): 50.8
Life expectancy at birth, male (years): 46.3

Mortality rate, adult, female (per 1,000 female adults): 402.0
Mortality rate, adult, male (per 1,000 male adults): 464.0
Mortality rate, infant (per 1,000 live births): 90.0

Illiteracy rate, adult female (percent of females aged 15+): 30.3
Illiteracy rate, adult male (percent of males aged 15+): 15.4
School life expectancy, 1995, female: n.a.
School life expectancy, 1995, male: n.a.

Contraceptive prevalence, percent
  Year: n.a.
  Any method: n.a.
  Modern method: n.a.

Maternity leave benefits, as of early 1990s
  Maternity leave: 15 weeks
  Percentage of wages covered: 100
  Provider of coverage: employer/soc. sec.

Labor force, total: 1,110,116
Labor force, female (percent of total): 43.4

Women in parliament as of January 1997
  Single or lower house, percent of seats occupied by women: 1.6
  Upper house, percent of seats occupied by women: 3.3

COSTA RICA

Estimated 1999 population, in thousands, total: 3,873
Estimated 1999 population, in thousands, female: 1,939
Sex ratio 1999 (males per 100 females): 103

Birth rate, crude (per 1,000 people): 23.2
Fertility rate, total (births per woman): 2.8
Life expectancy at birth, female (years): 78.9
Life expectancy at birth, male (years): 74.3

Mortality rate, adult, female (per 1,000 female adults): 70.0
Mortality rate, adult, male (per 1,000 male adults): 117.0
Mortality rate, infant (per 1,000 live births): 12.0

Illiteracy rate, adult female (percent of females aged 15+): 4.9
Illiteracy rate, adult male (percent of males aged 15+): 5.0
School life expectancy, 1995, female: n.a.
School life expectancy, 1995, male: n.a.

Contraceptive prevalence, percent
  Year: 1992/93
  Any method: 75
  Modern method: 65

Maternity leave benefits, as of early 1990s
  Maternity leave: 1 month before delivery + 3 months after
  Percentage of wages covered: 100
  Provider of coverage: soc. sec./employer

Labor force, total: 1,350,960
Labor force, female (percent of total): 30.2

Women in parliament as of January 1997
  Single or lower house, percent of seats occupied by women: 15.8
  Upper house, percent of seats occupied by women: n.a.

CÔTE D'IVOIRE

Estimated 1999 population, in thousands, total: 14,527
Estimated 1999 population, in thousands, female: 7,133
Sex ratio 1999 (males per 100 females): 104

Birth rate, crude (per 1,000 people): 37.4
Fertility rate, total (births per woman): 5.1
Life expectancy at birth, female (years): 47.3
Life expectancy at birth, male (years): 46.1

Mortality rate, adult, female (per 1,000 female adults): 490.0
Mortality rate, adult, male (per 1,000 male adults): 510.0
Mortality rate, infant (per 1,000 live births): 87.0

Illiteracy rate, adult female (percent of females aged 15+): 66.3
Illiteracy rate, adult male (percent of males aged 15+): 48.9
School life expectancy, 1995, female: n.a.
School life expectancy, 1995, male: n.a.

Contraceptive prevalence, percent
  Year: 1994
  Any method: 11
  Modern method: 4

Maternity leave benefits, as of early 1990s
  Maternity leave: 14
  Percentage of wages covered: 100
  Provider of coverage: employer/soc. sec.

Labor force, total: 5,684,464
Labor force, female (percent of total): 33.0

Women in parliament as of January 1997
  Single or lower house, percent of seats occupied by women: 8.3
  Upper house, percent of seats occupied by women: n.a.

CROATIA

Estimated 1999 population, in thousands, total: 4,477
Estimated 1999 population, in thousands, female: 2,313
Sex ratio 1999 (males per 100 females): 94

Birth rate, crude (per 1,000 people): 10.0
Fertility rate, total (births per woman): 1.6
Life expectancy at birth, female (years): 76.9
Life expectancy at birth, male (years): 68.3

Mortality rate, adult, female (per 1,000 female adults): 78.0
Mortality rate, adult, male (per 1,000 male adults): 176.0
Mortality rate, infant (per 1,000 live births): 8.5

Illiteracy rate, adult female (percent of females aged 15+): 3.6
Illiteracy rate, adult male (percent of males aged 15+): 0.9
School life expectancy, 1995, female: 11.7
School life expectancy, 1995, male: 11.5

Contraceptive prevalence, percent
  Year: n.a.
  Any method: n.a.
  Modern method: n.a.

Maternity leave benefits, as of early 1990s
  Maternity leave: n.a.
  Percentage of wages covered: n.a.
  Provider of coverage: n.a.

Labor force, total: 2,240,786
Labor force, female (percent of total): 43.8

Women in parliament as of January 1997
  Single or lower house, percent of seats occupied by women: 7.9
  Upper house, percent of seats occupied by women: 4.4

CUBA

Estimated 1999 population, in thousands, total: 11,160
Estimated 1999 population, in thousands, female: 5,567
Sex ratio 1999 (males per 100 females): 100

Birth rate, crude (per 1,000 people): 13.7
Fertility rate, total (births per woman): 1.6
Life expectancy at birth, female (years): 78.0
Life expectancy at birth, male (years): 74.2

Mortality rate, adult, female (per 1,000 female adults): 80.0
Mortality rate, adult, male (per 1,000 male adults): 125.0
Mortality rate, infant (per 1,000 live births): 7.2

Illiteracy rate, adult female (percent of females aged 15+): 4.1
Illiteracy rate, adult male (percent of males aged 15+): 4.1
School life expectancy, 1995, female: 11.7
School life expectancy, 1995, male: 10.9

Contraceptive prevalence, percent
Year: 1987
Any method: 70
Modern method: 67

Maternity leave benefits, as of early 1990s
Maternity leave: 6 weeks before delivery + 12 weeks after
Percentage of wages covered: 100
Provider of coverage: social security

Labor force, total: 5,418,910
Labor force, female (percent of total): 38.6

Women in parliament as of January 1997
Single or lower house, percent of seats occupied by women: 22.8
Upper house, percent of seats occupied by women: n.a.

CYPRUS

Estimated 1999 population, in thousands, total: 779
Estimated 1999 population, in thousands, female: 390
Sex ratio 1999 (males per 100 females): 100

Birth rate, crude (per 1,000 people): 14.7
Fertility rate, total (births per woman): 2.0
Life expectancy at birth, female (years): 80.0
Life expectancy at birth, male (years): 75.5

Mortality rate, adult, female (per 1,000 female adults): 64.0
Mortality rate, adult, male (per 1,000 male adults): 109.0
Mortality rate, infant (per 1,000 live births): 8.1

Illiteracy rate, adult female (percent of females aged 15+): 6.5
Illiteracy rate, adult male (percent of males aged 15+): 1.6
School life expectancy, 1995, female: n.a.
School life expectancy, 1995, male: n.a.

Contraceptive prevalence, percent
Year: n.a.
Any method: n.a.
Modern method: n.a.

Maternity leave benefits, as of early 1990s
Maternity leave: n.a.
Percentage of wages covered: n.a.
Provider of coverage: n.a.

Labor force, total: 358,435
Labor force, female (percent of total): 38.5

Women in parliament as of January 1997
Single or lower house, percent of seats occupied by women: 5.4
Upper house, percent of seats occupied by women: n.a.

CZECH REPUBLIC

Estimated 1999 population, in thousands, total: 10,263
Estimated 1999 population, in thousands, female: 5,266
Sex ratio 1999 (males per 100 females): 95

Birth rate, crude (per 1,000 people): 9.2
Fertility rate, total (births per woman): 1.2
Life expectancy at birth, female (years): 77.5
Life expectancy at birth, male (years): 70.5

Mortality rate, adult, female (per 1,000 female adults): 82.0
Mortality rate, adult, male (per 1,000 male adults): 181.0
Mortality rate, infant (per 1,000 live births): 5.9

Illiteracy rate, adult female (percent of females aged 15+): n.a.
Illiteracy rate, adult male (percent of males aged 15+): n.a.
School life expectancy, 1995, female: 13.1
School life expectancy, 1995, male: 13.1

Contraceptive prevalence, percent*
Year: 1993
Any method: 69
Modern method: 45
* All women aged 15-44 years.

Maternity leave benefits, as of early 1990s
Maternity leave: n.a.
Percentage of wages covered: n.a.
Provider of coverage: n.a.

Labor force, total: 5,667,255
Labor force, female (percent of total): 47.4

Women in parliament as of January 1997
Single or lower house, percent of seats occupied by women: 15
Upper house, percent of seats occupied by women: n.a.

DENMARK

Estimated 1999 population, in thousands, total: 5,283
Estimated 1999 population, in thousands, female: 2,671
Sex ratio 1999 (males per 100 females): 98

Birth rate, crude (per 1,000 people): 12.8
Fertility rate, total (births per woman): 1.75
Life expectancy at birth, female (years): 78.0
Life expectancy at birth, male (years): 72.8

Mortality rate, adult, female (per 1,000 female adults): 81.0
Mortality rate, adult, male (per 1,000 male adults): 144.0
Mortality rate, infant (per 1,000 live births): 5.5

Illiteracy rate, adult female (percent of females aged 15+): n.a.
Illiteracy rate, adult male (percent of males aged 15+): n.a.
School life expectancy, 1995, female: 14.8
School life expectancy, 1995, male: 14.5

Contraceptive prevalence, percent*
  Year: 1988
  Any method: 78
  Modern method: 72
  * All sexually active women aged 15-44 years.

Maternity leave benefits, as of early 1990s
  Maternity leave: 4 weeks before delivery and 14 weeks after
  Percentage of wages covered: Daily cash benefits equivalent to the hourly wage or average earnings, up to a ceiling (2,556 Danish kroner) payable for 28 weeks.
  Provider of coverage: n.a.

Labor force, total: 2,959,163
Labor force, female (percent of total): 46.3

Women in parliament as of January 1997
  Single or lower house, percent of seats occupied by women: 33
  Upper house, percent of seats occupied by women: n.a.

DJIBOUTI

Estimated 1999 population, in thousands, total: 629
Estimated 1999 population, in thousands, female: 321
Sex ratio 1999 (males per 100 females): 96

Birth rate, crude (per 1,000 people): 37.9
Fertility rate, total (births per woman): 5.30
Life expectancy at birth, female (years): 52.0
Life expectancy at birth, male (years): 48.7

Mortality rate, adult, female (per 1,000 female adults): 321.0
Mortality rate, adult, male (per 1,000 male adults): 377.0
Mortality rate, infant (per 1,000 live births): 106.0

Illiteracy rate, adult female (percent of females aged 15+): n.a.
Illiteracy rate, adult male (percent of males aged 15+): n.a.
School life expectancy, 1995, female: n.a.
School life expectancy, 1995, male: n.a.

Contraceptive prevalence, percent
  Year: n.a.
  Any method: n.a.
  Modern method: n.a.

Maternity leave benefits, as of early 1990s
  Maternity leave: 14 weeks
  Percentage of wages covered: 50
  Provider of coverage: employer

Labor force, total: n.a.
Labor force, female (percent of total): n.a.

Women in parliament as of January 1997
  Single or lower house, percent of seats occupied by women: 0
  Upper house, percent of seats occupied by women: n.a.

DOMINICA

Estimated 1994 population, in thousands, total: 75
Estimated 1994 population, in thousands, female: 36
Sex ratio 1994 (males per 100 females): 108

Birth rate, crude (per 1,000 people): 21.5
Fertility rate, total (births per woman): 1.90
Life expectancy at birth, female (years): 78.0
Life expectancy at birth, male (years): 74.0

Mortality rate, adult, female (per 1,000 female adults): 77.0
Mortality rate, adult, male (per 1,000 male adults): 120.0
Mortality rate, infant (per 1,000 live births): 15.8

Illiteracy rate, adult female (percent of females aged 15+): n.a.
Illiteracy rate, adult male (percent of males aged 15+): n.a.
School life expectancy, 1995, female: n.a.
School life expectancy, 1995, male: n.a.

Contraceptive prevalence, percent*
  Year: 1987
  Any method: 50
  Modern method: 48
  * All women aged 15-44 years.

Maternity leave benefits, as of early 1990s
  Maternity leave: 9 weeks
  Percentage of wages covered: 60 percent ave. week + 50 percent of regular wage
  Provider of coverage: soc. sec./employer

Labor force, total: n.a.
Labor force, female (percent of total): n.a.

Women in parliament as of January 1997
  Single or lower house, percent of seats occupied by women: 9.4
  Upper house, percent of seats occupied by women: n.a.

DOMINICAN REPUBLIC

Estimated 1999 population, in thousands, total: 8,665
Estimated 1999 population, in thousands, female: 4,112
Sex ratio 1999 (males per 100 females): 103

Birth rate, crude (per 1,000 people): 25.6
Fertility rate, total (births per woman): 3.00
Life expectancy at birth, female (years): 73.1
Life expectancy at birth, male (years): 68.9

Mortality rate, adult, female (per 1,000 female adults): 94.0
Mortality rate, adult, male (per 1,000 male adults): 150.0
Mortality rate, infant (per 1,000 live births): 40.0

Illiteracy rate, adult female (percent of females aged 15+): 17.7
Illiteracy rate, adult male (percent of males aged 15+): 17.1
School life expectancy, 1995, female: 11.3
School life expectancy, 1995, male: 11.1

Contraceptive prevalence, percent
 Year: 1996
 Any method: 64
 Modern method: 59

Maternity leave benefits, as of early 1990s
 Maternity leave: 12 weeks
 Percentage of wages covered: 100
 Provider of coverage: soc. sec./employer

Labor force, total: 3,486,135
Labor force, female (percent of total): 29.7

Women in parliament as of January 1997
 Single or lower house, percent of seats occupied by women: 11.7
 Upper house, percent of seats occupied by women: 3.3

ECUADOR

Estimated 1999 population, in thousands, total: 12,411
Estimated 1999 population, in thousands, female: 6,178
Sex ratio 1999 (males per 100 females):

Birth rate, crude (per 1,000 people): 24.9
Fertility rate, total (births per woman): 3.02
Life expectancy at birth, female (years): 72.9
Life expectancy at birth, male (years): 67.7

Mortality rate, adult, female (per 1,000 female adults): 104.0
Mortality rate, adult, male (per 1,000 male adults): 180.0
Mortality rate, infant (per 1,000 live births): 33.1

Illiteracy rate, adult female (percent of females aged 15+): 11.2
Illiteracy rate, adult male (percent of males aged 15+): 7.3
School life expectancy, 1995, female: n.a.
School life expectancy, 1995, male: n.a.

Contraceptive prevalence, percent
 Year: 1994
 Any method: 57
 Modern method: 46

Maternity leave benefits, as of early 1990s
 Maternity leave: 2 weeks before delivery and 10 weeks after
 Percentage of wages covered: 100
 Provider of coverage: soc. sec./employer

Labor force, total: 4,536,060
Labor force, female (percent of total): 27.0

Women in parliament as of January 1997
 Single or lower house, percent of seats occupied by women: n.a.
 Upper house, percent of seats occupied by women: n.a.

EGYPT

Estimated 1999 population, in thousands, total: 67,226
Estimated 1999 population, in thousands, female: 38,130
Sex ratio 1999 (males per 100 females): 101

Birth rate, crude (per 1,000 people): 24.5
Fertility rate, total (births per woman): 3.22
Life expectancy at birth, female (years): 67.9
Life expectancy at birth, male (years): 64.7

Mortality rate, adult, female (per 1,000 female adults): 174.0
Mortality rate, adult, male (per 1,000 male adults): 198.0
Mortality rate, infant (per 1,000 live births): 51.0

Illiteracy rate, adult female (percent of females aged 15+): 59.5
Illiteracy rate, adult male (percent of males aged 15+): 35.3
School life expectancy, 1995, female: 8.8
School life expectancy, 1995, male: 10.8

Contraceptive prevalence, percent
 Year: 1995
 Any method: 47†
 Modern method: 46
 † Adjusted from source to exclude breastfeeding

Maternity leave benefits, as of early 1990s
 Maternity leave: 50 days
 Percentage of wages covered: 100
 Provider of coverage: soc. sec./employer

Labor force, total: 22,328,808
Labor force, female (percent of total): 29.4

Women in parliament as of January 1997
 Single or lower house, percent of seats occupied by women: 2
 Upper house, percent of seats occupied by women: n.a.

EL SALVADOR

Estimated 1999 population, in thousands, total: 6,154
Estimated 1999 population, in thousands, female: 3,135
Sex ratio 1999 (males per 100 females): 103

Birth rate, crude (per 1,000 people): 27.8
Fertility rate, total (births per woman): 3.17
Life expectancy at birth, female (years): 72.5
Life expectancy at birth, male (years): 66.5

Mortality rate, adult, female (per 1,000 female adults): 117.0
Mortality rate, adult, male (per 1,000 male adults): 207.0
Mortality rate, infant (per 1,000 live births): 32.0

Illiteracy rate, adult female (percent of females aged 15+): 25.8
Illiteracy rate, adult male (percent of males aged 15+): 19.8
School life expectancy, 1995, female: 9.9
School life expectancy, 1995, male: 9.6

Contraceptive prevalence, percent*
  Year: 1993
  Any method: 53
  Modern method: 48
  * All women aged 15-44 years.

Maternity leave benefits, as of early 1990s
  Maternity leave: 12 weeks
  Percentage of wages covered: 75
  Provider of coverage: social security

Labor force, total: 2,489,668
Labor force, female (percent of total): 35.1

Women in parliament as of January 1997
  Single or lower house, percent of seats occupied by women: 10.7
  Upper house, percent of seats occupied by women: n.a.

EQUATORIAL GUINEA

Estimated 1999 population, in thousands, total: 442
Estimated 1999 population, in thousands, female: 224
Sex ratio 1999 (males per 100 females): 96

Birth rate, crude (per 1,000 people): 41.0
Fertility rate, total (births per woman): 5.51
Life expectancy at birth, female (years): 51.6
Life expectancy at birth, male (years): 48.4

Mortality rate, adult, female (per 1,000 female adults): 324.0
Mortality rate, adult, male (per 1,000 male adults): 378.0
Mortality rate, infant (per 1,000 live births): 108.0

Illiteracy rate, adult female (percent of females aged 15+): 29.9
Illiteracy rate, adult male (percent of males aged 15+): 9.5
School life expectancy, 1995, female: n.a.
School life expectancy, 1995, male: n.a.

Contraceptive prevalence, percent
  Year: n.a.
  Any method: n.a.
  Modern method: n.a.

Maternity leave benefits, as of early 1990s
  Maternity leave: 6 weeks before delivery and 6 weeks after
  Percentage of wages covered: 75
  Provider of coverage: social security

Labor force, total: 176,560
Labor force, female (percent of total): 35.4

Women in parliament as of January 1997
  Single or lower house, percent of seats occupied by women: 8.8
  Upper house, percent of seats occupied by women: n.a.

ERITREA

Estimated 1999 population, in thousands, total: 3,720
Estimated 1999 population, in thousands, female: 1,874
Sex ratio 1999 (males per 100 females): 97

Birth rate, crude (per 1,000 people): 40.5
Fertility rate, total (births per woman): 5.80
Life expectancy at birth, female (years): 52.4
Life expectancy at birth, male (years): 49.3

Mortality rate, adult, female (per 1,000 female adults): 403.0
Mortality rate, adult, male (per 1,000 male adults): 450.0
Mortality rate, infant (per 1,000 live births): 62.0

Illiteracy rate, adult female (percent of females aged 15+): n.a.
Illiteracy rate, adult male (percent of males aged 15+): n.a.
School life expectancy, 1995, female: 3.5
School life expectancy, 1995, male: 4.6

Contraceptive prevalence, percent
  Year: 1995
  Any method: 5†
  Modern method: 4
  † Adjusted from source to exclude breastfeeding.

Maternity leave benefits, as of early 1990s
  Maternity leave: n.a.
  Percentage of wages covered: n.a.
  Provider of coverage: n.a.

Labor force, total: 1,886,500
Labor force, female (percent of total): 47.4

Women in parliament as of January 1997
  Single or lower house, percent of seats occupied by women: 21
  Upper house, percent of seats occupied by women: n.a.

ESTONIA

Estimated 1999 population, in thousands, total: 1,412
Estimated 1999 population, in thousands, female: 748
Sex ratio 1999 (males per 100 females): 99

Birth rate, crude (per 1,000 people): 9.1
Fertility rate, total (births per woman): 1.24
Life expectancy at birth, female (years): 76.0
Life expectancy at birth, male (years): 64.5

Mortality rate, adult, female (per 1,000 female adults): 95.0
Mortality rate, adult, male (per 1,000 male adults): 284.0
Mortality rate, infant (per 1,000 live births): 10.1

Illiteracy rate, adult female (percent of females aged 15+): n.a.
Illiteracy rate, adult male (percent of males aged 15+): n.a.
School life expectancy, 1995, female: 12.9
School life expectancy, 1995, male: 12.2

Contraceptive prevalence, percent*
Year: 1994
Any method: 70
Modern method: 56
* Married women aged 20-49 years.

Maternity leave benefits, as of early 1990s
Maternity leave:
Percentage of wages covered:
Provider of coverage:

Labor force, total: 801,895
Labor force, female (percent of total): 49.0

Women in parliament as of January 1997
Single or lower house, percent of seats occupied by women: 12.9
Upper house, percent of seats occupied by women: n.a.

ETHIOPIA

Estimated 1999 population, in thousands, total: 61,095
Estimated 1999 population, in thousands, female: 30,436
Sex ratio 1999 (males per 100 females): 89

Birth rate, crude (per 1,000 people): 45.8
Fertility rate, total (births per woman): 6.50
Life expectancy at birth, female (years): 44.3
Life expectancy at birth, male (years): 42.4

Mortality rate, adult, female (per 1,000 female adults): 510.0
Mortality rate, adult, male (per 1,000 male adults): 550.0
Mortality rate, infant (per 1,000 live births): 107.0

Illiteracy rate, adult female (percent of females aged 15+): 70.8
Illiteracy rate, adult male (percent of males aged 15+): 58.5
School life expectancy, 1995, female: n.a.
School life expectancy, 1995, male: n.a.

Contraceptive prevalence, percent*
Year: 1990
Any method: 4
Modern method: 3
* Excludes parts of Tigrai, Asseb, Ogaden, parts of Gondar and Wello, and nomadic populations; includes ever-married women.

Maternity leave benefits, as of early 1990s
Maternity leave: 90 days
Percentage of wages covered: 100
Provider of coverage: employer

Labor force, total: 25,692,500
Labor force, female (percent of total): 40.8

Women in parliament as of January 1997
Single or lower house, percent of seats occupied by women: 2
Upper house, percent of seats occupied by women: n.a.

FIJI

Estimated 1999 population, in thousands, total: 806
Estimated 1999 population, in thousands, female: 396
Sex ratio 1999 (males per 100 females): 104

Birth rate, crude (per 1,000 people): 22.4
Fertility rate, total (births per woman): 2.73
Life expectancy at birth, female (years): 74.8
Life expectancy at birth, male (years): 70.5

Mortality rate, adult, female (per 1,000 female adults): 103.0
Mortality rate, adult, male (per 1,000 male adults): 157.0
Mortality rate, infant (per 1,000 live births): 18.0

Illiteracy rate, adult female (percent of females aged 15+): 10.6
Illiteracy rate, adult male (percent of males aged 15+): 5.9
School life expectancy, 1995, female: n.a.
School life expectancy, 1995, male: n.a.

Contraceptive prevalence, percent
Year: 1986
Any method: 40
Modern method: 40

Maternity leave benefits, as of early 1990s
Maternity leave: 42 days before delivery + 42 days after
Percentage of wages covered: fixed daily amount
Provider of coverage: employer

Labor force, total: 317,714
Labor force, female (percent of total): 28.6

Women in parliament as of January 1997
Single or lower house, percent of seats occupied by women: 4.3
Upper house, percent of seats occupied by women: 8.8

FINLAND

Estimated 1999 population, in thousands, total: 5,165
Estimated 1999 population, in thousands, female: 2,647
Sex ratio 1999 (males per 100 females): 95

Birth rate, crude (per 1,000 people): 11.5
Fertility rate, total (births per woman): 1.85
Life expectancy at birth, female (years): 80.5
Life expectancy at birth, male (years): 73.4

Mortality rate, adult, female (per 1,000 female adults): 61.0
Mortality rate, adult, male (per 1,000 male adults): 141.0
Mortality rate, infant (per 1,000 live births): 4.0

Illiteracy rate, adult female (percent of females aged 15+): n.a.
Illiteracy rate, adult male (percent of males aged 15+): n.a.
School life expectancy, 1995, female: 16
School life expectancy, 1995, male: 15

Contraceptive prevalence, percent
  Year: n.a.
  Any method: n.a.
  Modern method: n.a.

Maternity leave benefits, as of early 1990s
  Maternity leave: 105 days
  Percentage of wages covered: 80 (Payable for a total of 275 working days.)
  Provider of coverage: social insurance

Labor force, total: 2,621,319
Labor force, female (percent of total): 47.9

Women in parliament as of January 1997
  Single or lower house, percent of seats occupied by women: 33.5
  Upper house, percent of seats occupied by women: n.a.

FRANCE

Estimated 1999 population, in thousands, total: 58,886
Estimated 1999 population, in thousands, female: 30,181
Sex ratio 1999 (males per 100 females): 95

Birth rate, crude (per 1,000 people): 12.4
Fertility rate, total (births per woman): 1.71
Life expectancy at birth, female (years): 82.1
Life expectancy at birth, male (years): 74.2

Mortality rate, adult, female (per 1,000 female adults): 51.0
Mortality rate, adult, male (per 1,000 male adults): 130.0
Mortality rate, infant (per 1,000 live births): 5.1

Illitcracy rate, adult female (percent of females aged 15+): n.a.
Illiteracy rate, adult male (percent of males aged 15+): n.a.
School life expectancy, 1995, female: 15.6
School life expectancy, 1995, male: 15.2

Contraceptive prevalence, percent*
  Year: 1994
  Any method: 75
  Modern method: 69
  * Married women aged 20-44 years.

Maternity leave benefits, as of early 1990s
  Maternity leave: 6 weeks before delivery and 10 weeks after (for the third and subsequent children, 8 weeks before delivery and 18 weeks after).
  Percentage of wages covered: 84
  Provider of coverage: social security

Labor force, total: 26,373,182
Labor force, female (percent of total): 44.6

Women in parliament as of January 1997
  Single or lower house, percent of seats occupied by women: 6.4
  Upper house, percent of seats occupied by women: 5.6

GABON

Estimated 1999 population, in thousands, total: 1,197
Estimated 1999 population, in thousands, female: 605
Sex ratio 1999 (males per 100 females): 98

Birth rate, crude (per 1,000 people): 36.5
Fertility rate, total (births per woman): 5.20
Life expectancy at birth, female (years): 53.8
Life expectancy at birth, male (years): 51.1

Mortality rate, adult, female (per 1,000 female adults): 340.0
Mortality rate, adult, male (per 1,000 male adults): 380.0
Mortality rate, infant (per 1,000 live births): 87.0

Illiteracy rate, adult female (percent of females aged 15+): n.a.
Illiteracy rate, adult male (percent of males aged 15+): n.a.
School life expectancy, 1995, female: n.a.
School life expectancy, 1995, male: n.a.

Contraceptive prevalence, percent
  Year: n.a.
  Any method: n.a.
  Modern method: n.a.

Maternity leave benefits, as of early 1990s
  Maternity leave: n.a.
  Percentage of wages covered: n.a.
  Provider of coverage: n.a.

Labor force, total: 541,755
Labor force, female (percent of total): 44.5

Women in parliament as of January 1997
  Single or lower house, percent of seats occupied by women: n.a.
  Upper house, percent of seats occupied by women: n.a.

GAMBIA

Estimated 1999 population, in thousands, total: 1,268
Estimated 1999 population, in thousands, female: 641
Sex ratio 1999 (males per 100 females): 98

Birth rate, crude (per 1,000 people): 43.0
Fertility rate, total (births per woman): 5.70
Life expectancy at birth, female (years): 55.0
Life expectancy at birth, male (years): 51.4

Mortality rate, adult, female (per 1,000 female adults): 339.0
Mortality rate, adult, male (per 1,000 male adults): 404.0
Mortality rate, infant (per 1,000 live births): 78.0

Illiteracy rate, adult female (percent of females aged 15+): 73.6
Illiteracy rate, adult male (percent of males aged 15+): 59.9
School life expectancy, 1995, female: 4.0
School life expectancy, 1995, male: 6.1

Contraceptive prevalence, percent
Year: 1990
Any method: 12
Modern method: 7

Maternity leave benefits, as of early 1990s
Maternity leave: n.a.
Percentage of wages covered: n.a.
Provider of coverage: n.a.

Labor force, total: 602,249
Labor force, female (percent of total): 44.9

Women in parliament as of January 1997
Single or lower house, percent of seats occupied by women: n.a.
Upper house, percent of seats occupied by women: n.a.

GEORGIA

Estimated 1999 population, in thousands, total: 5,005
Estimated 1999 population, in thousands, female: 2,613
Sex ratio 1999 (males per 100 females): 102

Birth rate, crude (per 1,000 people): 9.8
Fertility rate, total (births per woman): 1.50
Life expectancy at birth, female (years): 76.8
Life expectancy at birth, male (years): 68.5

Mortality rate, adult, female (per 1,000 female adults): 83.0
Mortality rate, adult, male (per 1,000 male adults): 197.0
Mortality rate, infant (per 1,000 live births): 17.3

Illiteracy rate, adult female (percent of females aged 15+): n.a.
Illiteracy rate, adult male (percent of males aged 15+): n.a.
School life expectancy, 1995, female: 10.4
School life expectancy, 1995, male: 10.1

Contraceptive prevalence, percent
Year: 1990
Any method: 17
Modern method: n.a.

Maternity leave benefits, as of early 1990s
Maternity leave: n.a.
Percentage of wages covered: n.a.
Provider of coverage: n.a.

Labor force, total: 2,659,377
Labor force, female (percent of total): 46.5

Women in parliament as of January 1997
Single or lower house, percent of seats occupied by women: 6.8
Upper house, percent of seats occupied by women: n.a.

GERMANY

Estimated 1999 population, in thousands, total: 82,177
Estimated 1999 population, in thousands, female: 41,980
Sex ratio 1999 (males per 100 females): 92

Birth rate, crude (per 1,000 people): 9.6
Fertility rate, total (births per woman): 1.35
Life expectancy at birth, female (years): 80.0
Life expectancy at birth, male (years): 73.5

Mortality rate, adult, female (per 1,000 female adults): 66.0
Mortality rate, adult, male (per 1,000 male adults): 133.0
Mortality rate, infant (per 1,000 live births): 4.9

Illiteracy rate, adult female (percent of females aged 15+): n.a.
Illiteracy rate, adult male (percent of males aged 15+): n.a.
School life expectancy, 1995, female: 14.8
School life expectancy, 1995, male: 15.4

Contraceptive prevalence, percent*
Year: 1992
Any method: 75
Modern method: 72
* Married women aged 20-39 years.

Maternity leave benefits, as of early 1990s
Maternity leave: 6 weeks before delivery and 8 weeks after
Percentage of wages covered: 100
Provider of coverage: soc. sec./employer

Labor force, total: 41,035,500
Labor force, female (percent of total): 42.1

Women in parliament as of January 1997
Single or lower house, percent of seats occupied by women: 26.2
Upper house, percent of seats occupied by women: 19.1

GHANA

Estimated 1999 population, in thousands, total: 19,678
Estimated 1999 population, in thousands, female: 9,885
Sex ratio 1999 (males per 100 females): 96

Birth rate, crude (per 1,000 people): 35.5
Fertility rate, total (births per woman): 4.90
Life expectancy at birth, female (years): 61.8
Life expectancy at birth, male (years): 58.3

Mortality rate, adult, female (per 1,000 female adults): 226.0
Mortality rate, adult, male (per 1,000 male adults): 278.0
Mortality rate, infant (per 1,000 live births): 66.0

Illiteracy rate, adult female (percent of females aged 15+): 43.5
Illiteracy rate, adult male (percent of males aged 15+): 23.5
School life expectancy, 1995, female: n.a.
School life expectancy, 1995, male: n.a.

Contraceptive prevalence, percent
  Year: 1993
  Any method: 20
  Modern method: 10

Maternity leave benefits, as of early 1990s
  Maternity leave: 6 weeks before delivery and 6 weeks after
  Percentage of wages covered: 50
  Provider of coverage: employer

Labor force, total: 8,452,757
Labor force, female (percent of total): 50.6

Women in parliament as of January 1997
  Single or lower house, percent of seats occupied by women: n.a.
  Upper house, percent of seats occupied by women: n.a.

GREECE

Estimated 1999 population, in thousands, total: 10,626
Estimated 1999 population, in thousands, female: 5,396
Sex ratio 1999 (males per 100 females): 99

Birth rate, crude (per 1,000 people): 9.8
Fertility rate, total (births per woman): 1.30
Life expectancy at birth, female (years): 80.5
Life expectancy at birth, male (years): 75.1

Mortality rate, adult, female (per 1,000 female adults): 61.0
Mortality rate, adult, male (per 1,000 male adults): 114.0
Mortality rate, infant (per 1,000 live births): 7.2

Illiteracy rate, adult female (percent of females aged 15+): 5.1
Illiteracy rate, adult male (percent of males aged 15+): 1.7
School life expectancy, 1995, female: 13.6
School life expectancy, 1995, male: 13.9

Contraceptive prevalence, percent
  Year: n.a.
  Any method: n.a.
  Modern method: n.a.

Maternity leave benefits, as of early 1990s
  Maternity leave: 15 weeks
  Percentage of wages covered: 100
  Provider of coverage: social insurance

Labor force, total: 4,524,460
Labor force, female (percent of total): 37.1

Women in parliament as of January 1997
  Single or lower house, percent of seats occupied by women: 6.3
  Upper house, percent of seats occupied by women: n.a.

GRENADA

Estimated 1991 population, in thousands, total: 85
Estimated 1991 population, in thousands, female: 43
Sex ratio 1991 (males per 100 females): 97

Birth rate, crude (per 1,000 people): 25.7
Fertility rate, total (births per woman): 3.60
Life expectancy at birth, female (years): 75.1
Life expectancy at birth, male (years): 68.6

Mortality rate, adult, female (per 1,000 female adults): 95.0
Mortality rate, adult, male (per 1,000 male adults): 180.0
Mortality rate, infant (per 1,000 live births): 24.0

Illiteracy rate, adult female (percent of females aged 15+): n.a.
Illiteracy rate, adult male (percent of males aged 15+): n.a.
School life expectancy, 1995, female: n.a.
School life expectancy, 1995, male: n.a.

Contraceptive prevalence, percent*
  Year: 1990
  Any method: 54
  Modern method: n.a.
  * All women aged 15-44 years.

Maternity leave benefits, as of early 1990s
  Maternity leave: 3 months
  Percentage of wages covered: 60
  Provider of coverage: national insurance

Labor force, total: n.a.
Labor force, female (percent of total): n.a.

Women in parliament as of January 1997
  Single or lower house, percent of seats occupied by women: 20
  Upper house, percent of seats occupied by women: n.a.

GUADELOUPE

Estimated 1999 population, in thousands, total: 450
Estimated 1999 population, in thousands, female: 230
Sex ratio 1999 (males per 100 females): 96

Birth rate, crude (per 1,000 people): 16.6
Fertility rate, total (births per woman): 1.90
Life expectancy at birth, female (years): 80.9
Life expectancy at birth, male (years): 73.6

Mortality rate, adult, female (per 1,000 female adults): 57.0
Mortality rate, adult, male (per 1,000 male adults): 129.0
Mortality rate, infant (per 1,000 live births): 9.0

Illiteracy rate, adult female (percent of females aged 15+): n.a.
Illiteracy rate, adult male (percent of males aged 15+): n.a.
School life expectancy, 1995, female: n.a.
School life expectancy, 1995, male: n.a.

Contraceptive prevalence, percent
  Year: n.a.
  Any method: n.a.
  Modern method: n.a.

Maternity leave benefits, as of early 1990s
  Maternity leave: n.a.
  Percentage of wages covered: n.a.
  Provider of coverage: n.a.

Labor force, total: 204,960
Labor force, female (percent of total): 45.1

Women in parliament as of January 1997
  Single or lower house, percent of seats occupied by women: n.a.
  Upper house, percent of seats occupied by women: n.a.

GUATEMALA

Estimated 1999 population, in thousands, total: 11,090
Estimated 1999 population, in thousands, female: 5,497
Sex ratio 1999 (males per 100 females): 102

Birth rate, crude (per 1,000 people): 33.7
Fertility rate, total (births per woman): 4.50
Life expectancy at birth, female (years): 67.2
Life expectancy at birth, male (years): 61.4

Mortality rate, adult, female (per 1,000 female adults): 193.0
Mortality rate, adult, male (per 1,000 male adults): 296.0
Mortality rate, infant (per 1,000 live births): 43.0

Illiteracy rate, adult female (percent of females aged 15+): 41.1
Illiteracy rate, adult male (percent of males aged 15+): 25.8
School life expectancy, 1995, female: n.a.
School life expectancy, 1995, male: n.a.

Contraceptive prevalence, percent*
  Year: 1995
  Any method: 31
  Modern method: 27
  * All women aged 15-44 years.

Maternity leave benefits, as of early 1990s
  Maternity leave: 30 days before delivery and 50 days after
  Percentage of wages covered: 100
  Provider of coverage: soc. sec./employer

Labor force, total: 3,786,747
Labor force, female (percent of total): 27.3

Women in parliament as of January 1997
  Single or lower house, percent of seats occupied by women: 12.5
  Upper house, percent of seats occupied by women: n.a.

GUINEA

Estimated 1999 population, in thousands, total: 7,359
Estimated 1999 population, in thousands, female: 3,658
Sex ratio 1999 (males per 100 females): 101

Birth rate, crude (per 1,000 people): 40.9
Fertility rate, total (births per woman): 5.51
Life expectancy at birth, female (years): 47.0
Life expectancy at birth, male (years): 46.0

Mortality rate, adult, female (per 1,000 female adults): 400.0
Mortality rate, adult, male (per 1,000 male adults): 399.0
Mortality rate, infant (per 1,000 live births): 120.0

Illiteracy rate, adult female (percent of females aged 15+): n.a.
Illiteracy rate, adult male (percent of males aged 15+): n.a.
School life expectancy, 1995, female: n.a.
School life expectancy, 1995, male: n.a.

Contraceptive prevalence, percent
  Year: 1992/93
  Any method: 2
  Modern method: 1

Maternity leave benefits, as of early 1990s
  Maternity leave: 14 weeks
  Percentage of wages covered: 100
  Provider of coverage: employer/soc. sec.

Labor force, total: 3,321,403
Labor force, female (percent of total): 47.3

Women in parliament as of January 1997
  Single or lower house, percent of seats occupied by women: 7
  Upper house, percent of seats occupied by women: n.a.

GUINEA-BISSAU

Estimated 1999 population, in thousands, total: 1,187
Estimated 1999 population, in thousands, female: 603
Sex ratio 1999 (males per 100 females): 97

Birth rate, crude (per 1,000 people): 42.0
Fertility rate, total (births per woman): 5.75
Life expectancy at birth, female (years): 45.2
Life expectancy at birth, male (years): 42.4

Mortality rate, adult, female (per 1,000 female adults): 416.0
Mortality rate, adult, male (per 1,000 male adults): 469.0
Mortality rate, infant (per 1,000 live births): 130.0

Illiteracy rate, adult female (percent of females aged 15+): 81.8
Illiteracy rate, adult male (percent of males aged 15+): 50.3
School life expectancy, 1995, female: n.a.
School life expectancy, 1995, male: n.a.

Contraceptive prevalence, percent
    Year: n.a.
    Any method: n.a.
    Modern method: n.a.

Maternity leave benefits, as of early 1990s
    Maternity leave: 60 days
    Percentage of wages covered: 100
    Provider of coverage: employer

Labor force, total: 534,418
Labor force, female (percent of total): 40.4

Women in parliament as of January 1997
    Single or lower house, percent of seats occupied by women: 10
    Upper house, percent of seats occupied by women: n.a.

GUYANA

Estimated 1999 population, in thousands, total: 855
Estimated 1999 population, in thousands, female: 433
Sex ratio 1999 (males per 100 females): 97

Birth rate, crude (per 1,000 people): 21.9
Fertility rate, total (births per woman): 2.32
Life expectancy at birth, female (years): 67.9
Life expectancy at birth, male (years): 61.1

Mortality rate, adult, female (per 1,000 female adults): 144.0
Mortality rate, adult, male (per 1,000 male adults): 260.0
Mortality rate, infant (per 1,000 live births): 58.0

Illiteracy rate, adult female (percent of females aged 15+): 2.5
Illiteracy rate, adult male (percent of males aged 15+): 1.3
School life expectancy, 1995, female: 9.7
School life expectancy, 1995, male: 9.4

Contraceptive prevalence, percent
    Year: n.a.
    Any method: n.a.
    Modern method: n.a.

Maternity leave benefits, as of early 1990s
    Maternity leave: 13 weeks
    Percentage of wages covered: n.a.
    Provider of coverage: social security

Labor force, total: 364,511
Labor force, female (percent of total): 33.3

Women in parliament as of January 1997
    Single or lower house, percent of seats occupied by women: 20
    Upper house, percent of seats occupied by women: n.a.

HAITI

Estimated 1999 population, in thousands, total: 8,087
Estimated 1999 population, in thousands, female: 4,114
Sex ratio 1999 (males per 100 females): 97

Birth rate, crude (per 1,000 people): 31.9
Fertility rate, total (births per woman): 4.38
Life expectancy at birth, female (years): 56.2
Life expectancy at birth, male (years): 51.4

Mortality rate, adult, female (per 1,000 female adults): 332.0
Mortality rate, adult, male (per 1,000 male adults): 427.0
Mortality rate, infant (per 1,000 live births): 71.1

Illiteracy rate, adult female (percent of females aged 15+): 56.6
Illiteracy rate, adult male (percent of males aged 15+): 51.7
School life expectancy, 1995, female: n.a.
School life expectancy, 1995, male: n.a.

Contraceptive prevalence, percent
    Year: 1994/95
    Any method: 18
    Modern method: 13

Maternity leave benefits, as of early 1990s
    Maternity leave: 12 weeks
    Percentage of wages covered: 100
    Provider of coverage: employer

Labor force, total: 3,296,480
Labor force, female (percent of total): 43.0

Women in parliament as of January 1997
    Single or lower house, percent of seats occupied by women: 3.6
    Upper house, percent of seats occupied by women: 0

HONDURAS

Estimated 1999 population, in thousands, total: 6,315
Estimated 1999 population, in thousands, female: 3,132
Sex ratio 1999 (males per 100 females): 102

Birth rate, crude (per 1,000 people): 33.5
Fertility rate, total (births per woman): 4.30
Life expectancy at birth, female (years): 72.0
Life expectancy at birth, male (years): 67.0

Mortality rate, adult, female (per 1,000 female adults): 115.0
Mortality rate, adult, male (per 1,000 male adults): 193.0
Mortality rate, infant (per 1,000 live births): 36.0

Illiteracy rate, adult female (percent of females aged 15+): 29.8
Illiteracy rate, adult male (percent of males aged 15+): 28.9
School life expectancy, 1995, female: n.a.
School life expectancy, 1995, male: n.a.

Contraceptive prevalence, percent*
　Year: 1996
　Any method: 50
　Modern method: 41
　* All women aged 15-44 years.

Maternity leave benefits, as of early 1990s
　Maternity leave: 4 weeks before delivery and 6 weeks after
　Percentage of wages covered: 100
　Provider of coverage: soc. sec./employer

Labor force, total: 2,154,841
Labor force, female (percent of total): 30.6

Women in parliament as of January 1997
　Single or lower house, percent of seats occupied by women: 7.8
　Upper house, percent of seats occupied by women: n.a.

HONG KONG, CHINA

Estimated 1999 population, in thousands, total: 6,801
Estimated 1999 population, in thousands, female: 3,212
Sex ratio 1999 (males per 100 females): 112

Birth rate, crude (per 1,000 people): 10.1
Fertility rate, total (births per woman): 1.25
Life expectancy at birth, female (years): 81.6
Life expectancy at birth, male (years): 75.9

Mortality rate, adult, female (per 1,000 female adults): 56.0
Mortality rate, adult, male (per 1,000 male adults): 108.8
Mortality rate, infant (per 1,000 live births): 4.5

Illiteracy rate, adult female (percent of females aged 15+): 11.7
Illiteracy rate, adult male (percent of males aged 15+): 3.9
School life expectancy, 1995, female: 12.7
School life expectancy, 1995, male: 12.6

Contraceptive prevalence, percent
　Year: 1992
　Any method: 86
　Modern method: 80

Maternity leave benefits, as of early 1990s
　Maternity leave: 4 weeks before delivery and 6 weeks after
　Percentage of wages covered: two thirds
　Provider of coverage: employer

Labor force, total: 3,381,040
Labor force, female (percent of total): 36.8

Women in parliament as of January 1997
　Single or lower house, percent of seats occupied by women: n.a.
　Upper house, percent of seats occupied by women: n.a.

HUNGARY

Estimated 1999 population, in thousands, total: 10,075
Estimated 1999 population, in thousands, female: 5,259
Sex ratio 1999 (males per 100 females): 92

Birth rate, crude (per 1,000 people): 10.0
Fertility rate, total (births per woman): 1.38
Life expectancy at birth, female (years): 75.1
Life expectancy at birth, male (years): 66.4

Mortality rate, adult, female (per 1,000 female adults): 138.0
Mortality rate, adult, male (per 1,000 male adults): 330.0
Mortality rate, infant (per 1,000 live births): 9.9

Illiteracy rate, adult female (percent of females aged 15+): 0.9
Illiteracy rate, adult male (percent of males aged 15+): 0.6
School life expectancy, 1995, female: 12.6
School life expectancy, 1995, male: 12.3

Contraceptive prevalence, percent*
　Year: 1992/93
　Any method: 73
　Modern method: 60
　* Married women aged 18-41 years.

Maternity leave benefits, as of early 1990s
　Maternity leave: 24 weeks
　Percentage of wages covered: 100
　Provider of coverage: social insurance

Labor force, total: 4,772,803
Labor force, female (percent of total): 44.6

Women in parliament as of January 1997
　Single or lower house, percent of seats occupied by women: 11.4
　Upper house, percent of seats occupied by women: n.a.

ICELAND

Estimated 1999 population, in thousands, total: 279
Estimated 1999 population, in thousands, female: 139
Sex ratio 1999 (males per 100 females): 101

Birth rate, crude (per 1,000 people): 15.3
Fertility rate, total (births per woman): 2.00
Life expectancy at birth, female (years): 80.8
Life expectancy at birth, male (years): 76.6

Mortality rate, adult, female (per 1,000 female adults): 60.0
Mortality rate, adult, male (per 1,000 male adults): 102.0
Mortality rate, infant (per 1,000 live births): 5.5

Illiteracy rate, adult female (percent of females aged 15+): n.a.
Illiteracy rate, adult male (percent of males aged 15+): n.a.
School life expectancy, 1995, female: n.a.
School life expectancy, 1995, male: n.a.

Contraceptive prevalence, percent
  Year: n.a.
  Any method: n.a.
  Modern method: n.a.

Maternity leave benefits, as of early 1990s
  Maternity leave: 1 month before delivery + 1 month after
  Percentage of wages covered: (variable) Daily cash benefits
  equivalent to the hourly wage or average earnings, up to a ceil-
  ing (2,556 Danish kroner) payable for 28 weeks.
  Provider of coverage: social security

Labor force, total: 151,984
Labor force, female (percent of total): 45.3

Women in parliament as of January 1997
  Single or lower house, percent of seats occupied by women: 25.4
  Upper house, percent of seats occupied by women: n.a.

INDIA

Estimated 1999 population, in thousands, total: 998,056
Estimated 1999 population, in thousands, female: 482,801
Sex ratio 1999 (males per 100 females): 107

Birth rate, crude (per 1,000 people): 27.2
Fertility rate, total (births per woman): 3.30
Life expectancy at birth, female (years): 63.9
Life expectancy at birth, male (years): 62.4

Mortality rate, adult, female (per 1,000 female adults): 202.0
Mortality rate, adult, male (per 1,000 male adults): 212.0
Mortality rate, infant (per 1,000 live births): 71.0

Illiteracy rate, adult female (percent of females aged 15+): 60.6
Illiteracy rate, adult male (percent of males aged 15+): 33.3
School life expectancy, 1995, female: n.a.
School life expectancy, 1995, male: n.a.

Contraceptive prevalence, percent*
  Year: 1992/93
  Any method: 41
  Modern method: 37
  * Married women aged 13-49 years.

Maternity leave benefits, as of early 1990s
  Maternity leave: 12 weeks
  Percentage of wages covered: ave. daily wage
  Provider of coverage: soc. sec./employer

Labor force, total: 423,446,176
Labor force, female (percent of total): 31.9

Women in parliament as of January 1997
  Single or lower house, percent of seats occupied by women: 7.2
  Upper house, percent of seats occupied by women: 7.8

INDONESIA

Estimated 1999 population, in thousands, total: 209,255
Estimated 1999 population, in thousands, female: 104,852
Sex ratio 1999 (males per 100 females): 100

Birth rate, crude (per 1,000 people): 23.9
Fertility rate, total (births per woman): 2.75
Life expectancy at birth, female (years): 67.0
Life expectancy at birth, male (years): 63.3

Mortality rate, adult, female (per 1,000 female adults): 188.0
Mortality rate, adult, male (per 1,000 male adults): 240.0
Mortality rate, infant (per 1,000 live births): 47.0

Illiteracy rate, adult female (percent of females aged 15+): 20.5
Illiteracy rate, adult male (percent of males aged 15+): 9.4
School life expectancy, 1995, female: 9.5
School life expectancy, 1995, male: 10.4

Contraceptive prevalence, percent
  Year: 1994
  Any method: 55
  Modern method: 52

Maternity leave benefits, as of early 1990s
  Maternity leave: 3 months
  Percentage of wages covered: 100
  Provider of coverage: employer

Labor force, total: 94,183,440
Labor force, female (percent of total): 40.1

Women in parliament as of January 1997
  Single or lower house, percent of seats occupied by women: 12.6
  Upper house, percent of seats occupied by women: n.a.

IRAN

Estimated 1999 population, in thousands, total: 66,796
Estimated 1999 population, in thousands, female: 32,910
Sex ratio 1999 (males per 100 females): 103

Birth rate, crude (per 1,000 people): 22.1
Fertility rate, total (births per woman): 2.80
Life expectancy at birth, female (years): 70.0
Life expectancy at birth, male (years): 68.5

Mortality rate, adult, female (per 1,000 female adults): 162.0
Mortality rate, adult, male (per 1,000 male adults): 165.0
Mortality rate, infant (per 1,000 live births): 32.0

Illiteracy rate, adult female (percent of females aged 15+): 34.2
Illiteracy rate, adult male (percent of males aged 15+): 19.3
School life expectancy, 1995, female: n.a.
School life expectancy, 1995, male: n.a.

Contraceptive prevalence, percent*
  Year: 1992
  Any method: 65
  Modern method: 45
  * All women aged 15-44 years.

Maternity leave benefits, as of early 1990s
  Maternity leave: 90 days
  Percentage of wages covered: two-thirds of earnings
  Provider of coverage: social security

Labor force, total: 18,278,622
Labor force, female (percent of total): 25.4

Women in parliament as of January 1997
  Single or lower house, percent of seats occupied by women: 4
  Upper house, percent of seats occupied by women: n.a.

IRAQ

Estimated 1999 population, in thousands, total: 22,450
Estimated 1999 population, in thousands, female: 11,031
Sex ratio 1999 (males per 100 females): 104

Birth rate, crude (per 1,000 people): 33.1
Fertility rate, total (births per woman): 4.70
Life expectancy at birth, female (years): 59.0
Life expectancy at birth, male (years): 57.0

Mortality rate, adult, female (per 1,000 female adults): 174.0
Mortality rate, adult, male (per 1,000 male adults): 198.0
Mortality rate, infant (per 1,000 live births): 112.0

Illiteracy rate, adult female (percent of females aged 15+): n.a.
Illiteracy rate, adult male (percent of males aged 15+): n.a.
School life expectancy, 1995, female: 7.1
School life expectancy, 1995, male: 9.4

Contraceptive prevalence, percent
  Year: 1989
  Any method: 14†
  Modern method: 10
  † Adjusted from source to exclude breastfeeding.

Maternity leave benefits, as of early 1990s
  Maternity leave: 62 days
  Percentage of wages covered: 100
  Provider of coverage: social security

Labor force, total: 5,898,690
Labor force, female (percent of total): 18.7

Women in parliament as of January 1997
  Single or lower house, percent of seats occupied by women: n.a.
  Upper house, percent of seats occupied by women: n.a.

IRELAND

Estimated 1999 population, in thousands, total: 3,705
Estimated 1999 population, in thousands, female: 1,866
Sex ratio 1999 (males per 100 females): 99

Birth rate, crude (per 1,000 people): 14.3
Fertility rate, total (births per woman): 1.91
Life expectancy at birth, female (years): 78.6
Life expectancy at birth, male (years): 73.4

Mortality rate, adult, female (per 1,000 female adults): 73.0
Mortality rate, adult, male (per 1,000 male adults): 135.0
Mortality rate, infant (per 1,000 live births): 5.1

Illiteracy rate, adult female (percent of females aged 15+): n.a.
Illiteracy rate, adult male (percent of males aged 15+): n.a.
School life expectancy, 1995, female: 13.8
School life expectancy, 1995, male: 13.5

Contraceptive prevalence, percent
  Year: n.a.
  Any method: n.a.
  Modern method: n.a.

Maternity leave benefits, as of early 1990s
  Maternity leave: 14 weeks
  Percentage of wages covered: 70
  Provider of coverage: social security

Labor force, total: 1,501,010
Labor force, female (percent of total): 33.7

Women in parliament as of January 1997
  Single or lower house, percent of seats occupied by women: 13.9
  Upper house, percent of seats occupied by women: 13.3

ISRAEL

Estimated 1999 population, in thousands, total: 6,101
Estimated 1999 population, in thousands, female: 3,075
Sex ratio 1999 (males per 100 females): 98

Birth rate, crude (per 1,000 people): 20.5
Fertility rate, total (births per woman): 2.70
Life expectancy at birth, female (years): 79.4
Life expectancy at birth, male (years): 75.5

Mortality rate, adult, female (per 1,000 female adults): 69.0
Mortality rate, adult, male (per 1,000 male adults): 111.0
Mortality rate, infant (per 1,000 live births): 6.5

Illiteracy rate, adult female (percent of females aged 15+): 6.6
Illiteracy rate, adult male (percent of males aged 15+): 2.5
School life expectancy, 1995, female: n.a.
School life expectancy, 1995, male: n.a.

Contraceptive prevalence, percent
  Year: n.a.
  Any method: n.a.
  Modern method: n.a.

Maternity leave benefits, as of early 1990s
  Maternity leave: 12 weeks
  Percentage of wages covered: 75
  Provider of coverage: sickness insurance

Labor force, total: 2,451,120
Labor force, female (percent of total): 40.3

Women in parliament as of January 1997
  Single or lower house, percent of seats occupied by women: 7.5
  Upper house, percent of seats occupied by women: n.a.

ITALY

Estimated 1999 population, in thousands, total: 57,343
Estimated 1999 population, in thousands, female: 29,513
Sex ratio 1999 (males per 100 females): 94

Birth rate, crude (per 1,000 people): 9.4
Fertility rate, total (births per woman): 1.20
Life expectancy at birth, female (years): 81.7
Life expectancy at birth, male (years): 74.9

Mortality rate, adult, female (per 1,000 female adults): 54.0
Mortality rate, adult, male (per 1,000 male adults): 117.0
Mortality rate, infant (per 1,000 live births): 5.4

Illiteracy rate, adult female (percent of females aged 15+): 2.2
Illiteracy rate, adult male (percent of males aged 15+): 1.2
School life expectancy, 1995, female: n.a.
School life expectancy, 1995, male: n.a.

Contraceptive prevalence, percent
  Year: n.a.
  Any method: n.a.
  Modern method: n.a.

Maternity leave benefits, as of early 1990s
  Maternity leave: 2 months before delivery + 3 months after
  Percentage of wages covered: 80
  Provider of coverage: social security

Labor force, total: 25,310,120
Labor force, female (percent of total): 38.0

Women in parliament as of January 1997
  Single or lower house, percent of seats occupied by women: 11.1
  Upper house, percent of seats occupied by women: 8

JAMAICA

Estimated 1999 population, in thousands, total: 2,561
Estimated 1999 population, in thousands, female: 1,291
Sex ratio 1999 (males per 100 females): 98

Birth rate, crude (per 1,000 people): 23.8
Fertility rate, total (births per woman): 2.70
Life expectancy at birth, female (years): 76.9
Life expectancy at birth, male (years): 72.3

Mortality rate, adult, female (per 1,000 female adults): 86.0
Mortality rate, adult, male (per 1,000 male adults): 141.0
Mortality rate, infant (per 1,000 live births): 11.6

Illiteracy rate, adult female (percent of females aged 15+): 10.4
Illiteracy rate, adult male (percent of males aged 15+): 18.8
School life expectancy, 1995, female: 11.1
School life expectancy, 1995, male: 10.8

Contraceptive prevalence, percent*
  Year: 1993
  Any method: 62
  Modern method: 58
  * All women aged 15-44 years.

Maternity leave benefits, as of early 1990s
  Maternity leave: 12 weeks
  Percentage of wages covered: 100
  Provider of coverage: employer

Labor force, total: 1,328,080
Labor force, female (percent of total): 46.2

Women in parliament as of January 1997
  Single or lower house, percent of seats occupied by women: 11.7
  Upper house, percent of seats occupied by women: 14.3

JAPAN

Estimated 1999 population, in thousands, total: 126,505
Estimated 1999 population, in thousands, female: 64,508
Sex ratio 1999 (males per 100 females): 96

Birth rate, crude (per 1,000 people): 9.5
Fertility rate, total (births per woman): 1.39
Life expectancy at birth, female (years): 83.2
Life expectancy at birth, male (years): 76.9

Mortality rate, adult, female (per 1,000 female adults): 46.0
Mortality rate, adult, male (per 1,000 male adults): 100.0
Mortality rate, infant (per 1,000 live births): 3.7

Illiteracy rate, adult female (percent of females aged 15+): n.a.
Illiteracy rate, adult male (percent of males aged 15+): n.a.
School life expectancy, 1995, female: 13.8
School life expectancy, 1995, male: 14.2

Contraceptive prevalence, percent
Year: 1994
Any method: 59
Modern method: 53

Maternity leave benefits, as of early 1990s
Maternity leave: 14 weeks
Percentage of wages covered: 60
Provider of coverage: health ins./soc. sec.

Labor force, total: 68,089,136
Labor force, female (percent of total): 41.0

Women in parliament as of January 1997
Single or lower house, percent of seats occupied by women: 4.6
Upper house, percent of seats occupied by women: 13.9

JORDAN

Estimated 1999 population, in thousands, total: 6,483
Estimated 1999 population, in thousands, female: 3,133
Sex ratio 1999 (males per 100 females): 107

Birth rate, crude (per 1,000 people): 31.3
Fertility rate, total (births per woman): 4.20
Life expectancy at birth, female (years): 72.6
Life expectancy at birth, male (years): 69.2

Mortality rate, adult, female (per 1,000 female adults): 121.0
Mortality rate, adult, male (per 1,000 male adults): 160.0
Mortality rate, infant (per 1,000 live births): 28.7

Illiteracy rate, adult female (percent of females aged 15+): 18.2
Illiteracy rate, adult male (percent of males aged 15+): 7.8
School life expectancy, 1995, female: n.a.
School life expectancy, 1995, male: n.a.

Contraceptive prevalence, percent*
Year: 1997
Any method: 50†
Modern method: 38
* Excluding the West Bank.
† Adjusted from source to exclude breastfeeding.

Maternity leave benefits, as of early 1990s
Maternity leave: 3 weeks before delivery and 3 weeks after
Percentage of wages covered: 50
Provider of coverage: employer

Labor force, total: 1,286,684
Labor force, female (percent of total): 22.6

Women in parliament as of January 1997
Single or lower house, percent of seats occupied by women: 1.3
Upper house, percent of seats occupied by women: 5

KAZAKHSTAN

Estimated 1999 population, in thousands, total: 16,269
Estimated 1999 population, in thousands, female: 8,352
Sex ratio 1999 (males per 100 females): 95

Birth rate, crude (per 1,000 people): 14.2
Fertility rate, total (births per woman): 2.00
Life expectancy at birth, female (years): 70.4
Life expectancy at birth, male (years): 59.7

Mortality rate, adult, female (per 1,000 female adults): 168.0
Mortality rate, adult, male (per 1,000 male adults): 383.0
Mortality rate, infant (per 1,000 live births): 24.0

Illiteracy rate, adult female (percent of females aged 15+): n.a.
Illiteracy rate, adult male (percent of males aged 15+): n.a.
School life expectancy, 1995, female: n.a.
School life expectancy, 1995, male: n.a.

Contraceptive prevalence, percent
Year: 1995
Any method: 59
Modern method: 46

Maternity leave benefits, as of early 1990s
Maternity leave: n.a.
Percentage of wages covered: n.a.
Provider of coverage: n.a.

Labor force, total: 7,584,480
Labor force, female (percent of total): 46.6

Women in parliament as of January 1997
Single or lower house, percent of seats occupied by women: 13.4
Upper house, percent of seats occupied by women: 8.5

KENYA

Estimated 1999 population, in thousands, total: 29,549
Estimated 1999 population, in thousands, female: 14,744
Sex ratio 1999 (males per 100 females): 100

Birth rate, crude (per 1,000 people): 36.5
Fertility rate, total (births per woman): 4.70
Life expectancy at birth, female (years): 53.0
Life expectancy at birth, male (years): 51.1

Mortality rate, adult, female (per 1,000 female adults): 397.0
Mortality rate, adult, male (per 1,000 male adults): 425.0
Mortality rate, infant (per 1,000 live births): 74.0

Illiteracy rate, adult female (percent of females aged 15+): 28.1
Illiteracy rate, adult male (percent of males aged 15+): 13.1
School life expectancy, 1995, female: n.a.
School life expectancy, 1995, male: n.a.

Contraceptive prevalence, percent
  Year: 1993
  Any method: 33
  Modern method: 27

Maternity leave benefits, as of early 1990s
  Maternity leave: 2 months
  Percentage of wages covered: annual leave forteited
  Provider of coverage: employer

Labor force, total: 14,591,906
Labor force, female (percent of total): 46.1

Women in parliament as of January 1997
  Single or lower house, percent of seats occupied by women: 3
  Upper house, percent of seats occupied by women: n.a.

KIRIBATI

Estimated 1995 population, in thousands, total: 77
Estimated 1995 population, in thousands, female: 39
Sex ratio 1995 (males per 100 females): 98

Birth rate, crude (per 1,000 people): 32.0
Fertility rate, total (births per woman): 4.20
Life expectancy at birth, female (years): 63.0
Life expectancy at birth, male (years): 58.0

Mortality rate, adult, female (per 1,000 female adults): 240.0
Mortality rate, adult, male (per 1,000 male adults): 330.0
Mortality rate, infant (per 1,000 live births): 60.0

Illiteracy rate, adult female (percent of females aged 15+): n.a.
Illiteracy rate, adult male (percent of males aged 15+): n.a.
School life expectancy, 1995, female: n.a.
School life expectancy, 1995, male: n.a.

Contraceptive prevalence, percent
  Year: 1988
  Any method: 37
  Modern method: 27

Maternity leave benefits, as of early 1990s
  Maternity leave: n.a.
  Percentage of wages covered: n.a.
  Provider of coverage: n.a.

Labor force, total: n.a.
Labor force, female (percent of total): n.a.

Women in parliament as of January 1997
  Single or lower house, percent of seats occupied by women: 0
  Upper house, percent of seats occupied by women: n.a.

KOREA, DEM. REP. (NORTH)

Estimated 1999 population, in thousands, total: 23,702
Estimated 1999 population, in thousands, female: 11,820
Sex ratio 1999 (males per 100 females): 101

Birth rate, crude (per 1,000 people): 20.9
Fertility rate, total (births per woman): 2.05
Life expectancy at birth, female (years): 65.0
Life expectancy at birth, male (years): 61.0

Mortality rate, adult, female (per 1,000 female adults): 207.0
Mortality rate, adult, male (per 1,000 male adults): 268.0
Mortality rate, infant (per 1,000 live births): 56.0

Illiteracy rate, adult female (percent of females aged 15+): n.a.
Illiteracy rate, adult male (percent of males aged 15+): n.a.
School life expectancy, 1995, female: n.a.
School life expectancy, 1995, male: n.a.

Contraceptive prevalence, percent
  Year: 1990/92
  Any method: 62
  Modern method: 53

Maternity leave benefits, as of early 1990s
  Maternity leave: n.a.
  Percentage of wages covered: n.a.
  Provider of coverage: n.a.

Labor force, total: 12,133,497
Labor force, female (percent of total): 43.4

Women in parliament as of January 1997
  Single or lower house, percent of seats occupied by women: 20.1
  Upper house, percent of seats occupied by women: n.a.

KOREA, REP. (SOUTH)

Estimated 1999 population, in thousands, total: 46,479
Estimated 1999 population, in thousands, female: 23,042
Sex ratio 1999 (males per 100 females): 102

Birth rate, crude (per 1,000 people): 15.3
Fertility rate, total (births per woman): 1.70
Life expectancy at birth, female (years): 76.0
Life expectancy at birth, male (years): 68.8

Mortality rate, adult, female (per 1,000 female adults): 97.0
Mortality rate, adult, male (per 1,000 male adults): 209.0
Mortality rate, infant (per 1,000 live births): 9.0

Illiteracy rate, adult female (percent of females aged 15+): 4.5
Illiteracy rate, adult male (percent of males aged 15+): 1.1
School life expectancy, 1995, female: 13.9
School life expectancy, 1995, male: 15.1

Contraceptive prevalence, percent*
 Year: 1991
 Any method: 79
 Modern method: 70
 * All women aged 15-44 years.

Maternity leave benefits, as of early 1990s
 Maternity leave: n.a.
 Percentage of wages covered: n.a.
 Provider of coverage: n.a.

Labor force, total: 22,995,500
Labor force, female (percent of total): 40.8

Women in parliament as of January 1997
 Single or lower house, percent of seats occupied by women: 3
 Upper house, percent of seats occupied by women: n.a.

KUWAIT

Estimated 1999 population, in thousands, total: 1,897
Estimated 1999 population, in thousands, female: 906
Sex ratio 1999 (males per 100 females): 109

Birth rate, crude (per 1,000 people): 22.4
Fertility rate, total (births per woman): 2.90
Life expectancy at birth, female (years): 79.5
Life expectancy at birth, male (years): 73.6

Mortality rate, adult, female (per 1,000 female adults): 65.0
Mortality rate, adult, male (per 1,000 male adults): 124.0
Mortality rate, infant (per 1,000 live births): 12.0

Illiteracy rate, adult female (percent of females aged 15+): 22.5
Illiteracy rate, adult male (percent of males aged 15+): 16.9
School life expectancy, 1995, female: 9.1
School life expectancy, 1995, male: 8.9

Contraceptive prevalence, percent*
 Year: 1987
 Any method: 35
 Modern method: 32
 * Married women under 50 years.

Maternity leave benefits, as of early 1990s
 Maternity leave: 3 weeks before delivery and 40 days after;
 mother must forfeit annual leave.
 Percentage of wages covered: 100
 Provider of coverage: employer

Labor force, total: 687,420
Labor force, female (percent of total): 31.2

Women in parliament as of January 1997
 Single or lower house, percent of seats occupied by women: 0
 Upper house, percent of seats occupied by women: n.a.

KYRGYZ REPUBLIC

Estimated 1999 population, in thousands, total: 4,669
Estimated 1999 population, in thousands, female: 2,380
Sex ratio 1999 (males per 100 females): 96

Birth rate, crude (per 1,000 people): 22.0
Fertility rate, total (births per woman): 2.79
Life expectancy at birth, female (years): 71.4
Life expectancy at birth, male (years): 62.6

Mortality rate, adult, female (per 1,000 female adults): 143.0
Mortality rate, adult, male (per 1,000 male adults): 305.0
Mortality rate, infant (per 1,000 live births): 28.2

Illiteracy rate, adult female (percent of females aged 15+): n.a.
Illiteracy rate, adult male (percent of males aged 15+): n.a.
School life expectancy, 1995, female: n.a.
School life expectancy, 1995, male: n.a.

Contraceptive prevalence, percent
 Year: 1997
 Any method: 60
 Modern method: 49

Maternity leave benefits, as of early 1990s
 Maternity leave: n.a.
 Percentage of wages covered: n.a.
 Provider of coverage: n.a.

Labor force, total: 1,946,700
Labor force, female (percent of total): 46.9

Women in parliament as of January 1997
 Single or lower house, percent of seats occupied by women: 1.4
 Upper house, percent of seats occupied by women: 11.4

LAO PDR

Estimated 1999 population, in thousands, total: 5,297
Estimated 1999 population, in thousands, female: 2,629
Sex ratio 1999 (males per 100 females): 101

Birth rate, crude (per 1,000 people): 38.4
Fertility rate, total (births per woman): 5.60
Life expectancy at birth, female (years): 55.0
Life expectancy at birth, male (years): 52.0

Mortality rate, adult, female (per 1,000 female adults): 323.0
Mortality rate, adult, male (per 1,000 male adults): 378.0
Mortality rate, infant (per 1,000 live births): 98.0

Illiteracy rate, adult female (percent of females aged 15+): n.a.
Illiteracy rate, adult male (percent of males aged 15+): n.a.
School life expectancy, 1995, female: 5.7
School life expectancy, 1995, male: 8.2

Contraceptive prevalence, percent*
  Year: 1993
  Any method: 19
  Modern method: 15
  * Not a nationally representative sample—national prevalence is probably lower than indicated.

Maternity leave benefits, as of early 1990s
  Maternity leave: 90 days
  Percentage of wages covered: 100
  Provider of coverage: soc. sec./employer

Labor force, total: n.a.
Labor force, female (percent of total): n.a.

Women in parliament as of January 1997
  Single or lower house, percent of seats occupied by women: 9.4
  Upper house, percent of seats occupied by women: n.a.

LATVIA

Estimated 1999 population, in thousands, total: 2,389
Estimated 1999 population, in thousands, female: 1,303
Sex ratio 1999 (males per 100 females): 83

Birth rate, crude (per 1,000 people): 8.0
Fertility rate, total (births per woman): 1.11
Life expectancy at birth, female (years): 74.9
Life expectancy at birth, male (years): 63.8

Mortality rate, adult, female (per 1,000 female adults): 100.0
Mortality rate, adult, male (per 1,000 male adults): 306.0
Mortality rate, infant (per 1,000 live births): 15.3

Illiteracy rate, adult female (percent of females aged 15+): 0.6
Illiteracy rate, adult male (percent of males aged 15+): 0.3
School life expectancy, 1995, female: 11.7
School life expectancy, 1995, male: 11.1

Contraceptive prevalence, percent*
  Year: 1995
  Any method: 48
  Modern method: 39
  * Married women aged 18-49 years.

Maternity leave benefits, as of early 1990s
  Maternity leave: n.a.
  Percentage of wages covered: n.a.
  Provider of coverage: n.a.

Labor force, total: 1,331,100
Labor force, female (percent of total): 50.2

Women in parliament as of January 1997
  Single or lower house, percent of seats occupied by women: 9
  Upper house, percent of seats occupied by women: n.a.

LEBANON

Estimated 1999 population, in thousands, total: 3,236
Estimated 1999 population, in thousands, female: 1,654
Sex ratio 1999 (males per 100 females): 96

Birth rate, crude (per 1,000 people): 21.8
Fertility rate, total (births per woman): 2.50
Life expectancy at birth, female (years): 71.7
Life expectancy at birth, male (years): 68.1

Mortality rate, adult, female (per 1,000 female adults): 134.0
Mortality rate, adult, male (per 1,000 male adults): 177.0
Mortality rate, infant (per 1,000 live births): 28.0

Illiteracy rate, adult female (percent of females aged 15+): 21.7
Illiteracy rate, adult male (percent of males aged 15+): 8.8
School life expectancy, 1995, female:
School life expectancy, 1995, male:

Contraceptive prevalence, percent
  Year: 1995
  Any method: 59†
  Modern method: 37
  † Adjusted from source to exclude breastfeeding.

Maternity leave benefits, as of early 1990s
  Maternity leave: 40 days
  Percentage of wages covered: 100
  Provider of coverage: social security

Labor force, total: 1,409,480
Labor force, female (percent of total): 28.8

Women in parliament as of January 1997
  Single or lower house, percent of seats occupied by women: 2.3
  Upper house, percent of seats occupied by women: n.a.

LESOTHO

Estimated 1999 population, in thousands, total: 2,108
Estimated 1999 population, in thousands, female: 1,070
Sex ratio 1999 (males per 100 females): 97

Birth rate, crude (per 1,000 people): 35.3
Fertility rate, total (births per woman): 4.75
Life expectancy at birth, female (years): 57.3
Life expectancy at birth, male (years): 54.7

Mortality rate, adult, female (per 1,000 female adults): 282.0
Mortality rate, adult, male (per 1,000 male adults): 320.0
Mortality rate, infant (per 1,000 live births): 93.0

Illiteracy rate, adult female (percent of females aged 15+): 7.5
Illiteracy rate, adult male (percent of males aged 15+): 28.6
School life expectancy, 1995, female: 9.0
School life expectancy, 1995, male: 7.6

Contraceptive prevalence, percent
Year: 1991/92
Any method: 23
Modern method: 19

Maternity leave benefits, as of early 1990s
Maternity leave: n.a.
Percentage of wages covered: n.a.
Provider of coverage: n.a.

Labor force, total: 825,703
Labor force, female (percent of total): 36.8

Women in parliament as of January 1997
Single or lower house, percent of seats occupied by women: 4.6
Upper house, percent of seats occupied by women: 24.2

LIBERIA

Estimated 1999 population, in thousands, total: 2,930
Estimated 1999 population, in thousands, female: 1,459
Sex ratio 1999 (males per 100 females): 101

Birth rate, crude (per 1,000 people): 45.7
Fertility rate, total (births per woman): 6.30
Life expectancy at birth, female (years): 48.5
Life expectancy at birth, male (years): 46.1

Mortality rate, adult, female (per 1,000 female adults): 374.0
Mortality rate, adult, male (per 1,000 male adults): 411.0
Mortality rate, infant (per 1,000 live births): 116.0

Illiteracy rate, adult female (percent of females aged 15+): 68.3
Illiteracy rate, adult male (percent of males aged 15+): 35.1
School life expectancy, 1995, female: n.a.
School life expectancy, 1995, male: n.a.

Contraceptive prevalence, percent
Year: 1986
Any method: 6
Modern method: 5

Maternity leave benefits, as of early 1990s
Maternity leave: n.a.
Percentage of wages covered: n.a.
Provider of coverage: n.a.

Labor force, total: 1,183,309
Labor force, female (percent of total): 39.5

Women in parliament as of January 1997
Single or lower house, percent of seats occupied by women: 5.7
Upper house, percent of seats occupied by women: n.a.

LIBYA

Estimated 1999 population, in thousands, total: 5,470
Estimated 1999 population, in thousands, female: 2,635
Sex ratio 1999 (males per 100 females): 108

Birth rate, crude (per 1,000 people): 29.1
Fertility rate, total (births per woman): 3.80
Life expectancy at birth, female (years): 72.2
Life expectancy at birth, male (years): 68.3

Mortality rate, adult, female (per 1,000 female adults): 135.0
Mortality rate, adult, male (per 1,000 male adults): 187.0
Mortality rate, infant (per 1,000 live births): 24.0

Illiteracy rate, adult female (percent of females aged 15+): 37.1
Illiteracy rate, adult male (percent of males aged 15+): 11.3
School life expectancy, 1995, female: n.a.
School life expectancy, 1995, male: n.a.

Contraceptive prevalence, percent
Year: 1995
Any method: 40†
Modern method: 26
† Adjusted from source to exclude breastfeeding.

Maternity leave benefits, as of early 1990s
Maternity leave: 50 days
Percentage of wages covered: 50
Provider of coverage: employer

Labor force, total: 1,508,293
Labor force, female (percent of total): 21.7

Women in parliament as of January 1997
Single or lower house, percent of seats occupied by women: n.a.
Upper house, percent of seats occupied by women: n.a.

LIECHTENSTEIN

Estimated 1987 population, in thousands, total: 28
Estimated 1987 population, in thousands, female: 14
Sex ratio 1987 (males per 100 females): 14

Birth rate, crude (per 1,000 people): n.a.
Fertility rate, total (births per woman): n.a.
Life expectancy at birth, female (years): n.a.
Life expectancy at birth, male (years): n.a.

Mortality rate, adult, female (per 1,000 female adults): n.a.
Mortality rate, adult, male (per 1,000 male adults): n.a.
Mortality rate, infant (per 1,000 live births): n.a.

Illiteracy rate, adult female (percent of females aged 15+): n.a.
Illiteracy rate, adult male (percent of males aged 15+): n.a.
School life expectancy, 1995, female: n.a.
School life expectancy, 1995, male: n.a.

Contraceptive prevalence, percent
  Year: n.a.
  Any method: n.a.
  Modern method: n.a.

Maternity leave benefits, as of early 1990s
  Maternity leave: 8 weeks after delivery
  Percentage of wages covered: 80
  Provider of coverage: sickness insurance

Labor force, total: n.a.
Labor force, female (percent of total): n.a.

Women in parliament as of January 1997
  Single or lower house, percent of seats occupied by women: 8
  Upper house, percent of seats occupied by women: n.a.

LITHUANIA

Estimated 1999 population, in thousands, total: 3,682
Estimated 1999 population, in thousands, female: 1,944
Sex ratio 1999 (males per 100 females): 89

Birth rate, crude (per 1,000 people): 10.3
Fertility rate, total (births per woman): 1.39
Life expectancy at birth, female (years): 76.8
Life expectancy at birth, male (years): 65.9

Mortality rate, adult, female (per 1,000 female adults): 88.0
Mortality rate, adult, male (per 1,000 male adults): 269.0
Mortality rate, infant (per 1,000 live births): 10.3

Illiteracy rate, adult female (percent of females aged 15+): 0.9
Illiteracy rate, adult male (percent of males aged 15+): 0.5
School life expectancy, 1995, female: n.a.
School life expectancy, 1995, male: n.a.

Contraceptive prevalence, percent*
  Year: 1994/95
  Any method: 59
  Modern method: 40
  * Married women aged 18-49 years.

Maternity leave benefits, as of early 1990s
  Maternity leave: n.a.
  Percentage of wages covered: n.a.
  Provider of coverage: n.a.

Labor force, total: 1,926,907
Labor force, female (percent of total): 47.9

Women in parliament as of January 1997
  Single or lower house, percent of seats occupied by women: 17.5
  Upper house, percent of seats occupied by women: n.a.

LUXEMBOURG

Estimated 1999 population, in thousands, total: 426
Estimated 1999 population, in thousands, female: 217
Sex ratio 1999 (males per 100 females): 96

Birth rate, crude (per 1,000 people): 12.6
Fertility rate, total (births per woman): 1.71
Life expectancy at birth, female (years): 79.6
Life expectancy at birth, male (years): 73.5

Mortality rate, adult, female (per 1,000 female adults): 63.0
Mortality rate, adult, male (per 1,000 male adults): 138.0
Mortality rate, infant (per 1,000 live births): 5.0

Illiteracy rate, adult female (percent of females aged 15+): n.a.
Illiteracy rate, adult male (percent of males aged 15+): n.a.
School life expectancy, 1995, female: n.a.
School life expectancy, 1995, male: n.a.

Contraceptive prevalence, percent
  Year: n.a.
  Any method: n.a.
  Modern method: n.a.

Maternity leave benefits, as of early 1990s
  Maternity leave: 6 weeks before delivery and 8 weeks after
  Percentage of wages covered: 100
  Provider of coverage: n.a.

Labor force, total: 181,245
Labor force, female (percent of total): 36.6

Women in parliament as of January 1997
  Single or lower house, percent of seats occupied by women: 20
  Upper house, percent of seats occupied by women: n.a.

MACEDONIA, FYR

Estimated 1999 population, in thousands, total: 2,011
Estimated 1999 population, in thousands, female: 1,006
Sex ratio 1999 (males per 100 females): 100

Birth rate, crude (per 1,000 people): 15.9
Fertility rate, total (births per woman): 1.90
Life expectancy at birth, female (years): 74.7
Life expectancy at birth, male (years): 70.3

Mortality rate, adult, female (per 1,000 female adults): 107.0
Mortality rate, adult, male (per 1,000 male adults): 164.0
Mortality rate, infant (per 1,000 live births): 15.7

Illiteracy rate, adult female (percent of females aged 15+): n.a.
Illiteracy rate, adult male (percent of males aged 15+): n.a.
School life expectancy, 1995, female: 10.3
School life expectancy, 1995, male: 10.3

Contraceptive prevalence, percent
　Year: n.a.
　Any method: n.a.
　Modern method: n.a.

Maternity leave benefits, as of early 1990s
　Maternity leave: n.a.
　Percentage of wages covered: n.a.
　Provider of coverage: n.a.

Labor force, total: 918,560
Labor force, female (percent of total): 41.1

Women in parliament as of January 1997
　Single or lower house, percent of seats occupied by women: 3.3
　Upper house, percent of seats occupied by women: n.a.

MADAGASCAR

Estimated 1999 population, in thousands, total: 15,496
Estimated 1999 population, in thousands, female: 7,804
Sex ratio 1999 (males per 100 females): 99

Birth rate, crude (per 1,000 people): 42.1
Fertility rate, total (births per woman): 5.80
Life expectancy at birth, female (years): 59.0
Life expectancy at birth, male (years): 56.0

Mortality rate, adult, female (per 1,000 female adults): 295.0
Mortality rate, adult, male (per 1,000 male adults): 332.0
Mortality rate, infant (per 1,000 live births): 94.0

Illiteracy rate, adult female (percent of females aged 15+): n.a.
Illiteracy rate, adult male (percent of males aged 15+): n.a.
School life expectancy, 1995, female: n.a.
School life expectancy, 1995, male: n.a.

Contraceptive prevalence, percent
　Year: 1997
　Any method: 19
　Modern method: 10

Maternity leave benefits, as of early 1990s
　Maternity leave: 14 weeks
　Percentage of wages covered: 50
　Provider of coverage: social security

Labor force, total: 6,649,654
Labor force, female (percent of total): 44.8

Women in parliament as of January 1997
　Single or lower house, percent of seats occupied by women: 3.7
　Upper house, percent of seats occupied by women: n.a.

MALAWI

Estimated 1999 population, in thousands, total: 10,640
Estimated 1999 population, in thousands, female: 5,366
Sex ratio 1999 (males per 100 females): 98

Birth rate, crude (per 1,000 people): 47.6
Fertility rate, total (births per woman): 6.43
Life expectancy at birth, female (years): 43.0
Life expectancy at birth, male (years): 42.6

Mortality rate, adult, female (per 1,000 female adults): 471.0
Mortality rate, adult, male (per 1,000 male adults): 454.0
Mortality rate, infant (per 1,000 live births): 132.5

Illiteracy rate, adult female (percent of females aged 15+): 56.6
Illiteracy rate, adult male (percent of males aged 15+): 27.2
School life expectancy, 1995, female: 9.9
School life expectancy, 1995, male: 11.0

Contraceptive prevalence, percent
　Year: 1996
　Any method: 22
　Modern method: 14

Maternity leave benefits, as of early 1990s
　Maternity leave: n.a.
　Percentage of wages covered: n.a.
　Provider of coverage: n.a.

Labor force, total: 4,932,523
Labor force, female (percent of total): 48.9

Women in parliament as of January 1997
　Single or lower house, percent of seats occupied by women: 5.6
　Upper house, percent of seats occupied by women: n.a.

MALAYSIA

Estimated 1999 population, in thousands, total: 21,830
Estimated 1999 population, in thousands, female: 10,765
Sex ratio 1999 (males per 100 females): 103

Birth rate, crude (per 1,000 people): 25.8
Fertility rate, total (births per woman): 3.18
Life expectancy at birth, female (years): 74.5
Life expectancy at birth, male (years): 69.6

Mortality rate, adult, female (per 1,000 female adults): 114.0
Mortality rate, adult, male (per 1,000 male adults): 187.0
Mortality rate, infant (per 1,000 live births): 11.0

Illiteracy rate, adult female (percent of females aged 15+): 19.0
Illiteracy rate, adult male (percent of males aged 15+): 9.8
School life expectancy, 1995, female: n.a.
School life expectancy, 1995, male: n.a.

Contraceptive prevalence, percent*
  Year: 1988
  Any method: 48
  Modern method: 31
  * Includes peninsular Malaysia only.

Maternity leave benefits, as of early 1990s
  Maternity leave: 60 days
  Percentage of wages covered: 100
  Provider of coverage: employer

Labor force, total: 8,666,800
Labor force, female (percent of total): 37.2

Women in parliament as of January 1997
  Single or lower house, percent of seats occupied by women: 7.8
  Upper house, percent of seats occupied by women: 17.4

MALDIVES

Estimated 1999 population, in thousands, total: 278
Estimated 1999 population, in thousands, female: 135
Sex ratio 1999 (males per 100 females): 106

Birth rate, crude (per 1,000 people): 31.5
Fertility rate, total (births per woman): 4.70
Life expectancy at birth, female (years): 68.0
Life expectancy at birth, male (years): 66.0

Mortality rate, adult, female (per 1,000 female adults): 198.0
Mortality rate, adult, male (per 1,000 male adults): 195.0
Mortality rate, infant (per 1,000 live births): 32.0

Illiteracy rate, adult female (percent of females aged 15+): 4.4
Illiteracy rate, adult male (percent of males aged 15+): 4.3
School life expectancy, 1995, female: n.a.
School life expectancy, 1995, male: n.a.

Contraceptive prevalence, percent
  Year: n.a.
  Any method: n.a.
  Modern method: n.a.

Maternity leave benefits, as of early 1990s
  Maternity leave: n.a.
  Percentage of wages covered: n.a.
  Provider of coverage: n.a.

Labor force, total: 104,853
Labor force, female (percent of total): 43.0

Women in parliament as of January 1997
  Single or lower house, percent of seats occupied by women: 6.3
  Upper house, percent of seats occupied by women: n.a.

MALI

Estimated 1999 population, in thousands, total: 10,960
Estimated 1999 population, in thousands, female: 5,551
Sex ratio 1999 (males per 100 females): 97

Birth rate, crude (per 1,000 people): 47.2
Fertility rate, total (births per woman): 6.60
Life expectancy at birth, female (years): 52.3
Life expectancy at birth, male (years): 48.5

Mortality rate, adult, female (per 1,000 female adults): 334.0
Mortality rate, adult, male (per 1,000 male adults): 416.0
Mortality rate, infant (per 1,000 live births): 118.0

Illiteracy rate, adult female (percent of females aged 15+): 71.8
Illiteracy rate, adult male (percent of males aged 15+): 56.9
School life expectancy, 1995, female: n.a.
School life expectancy, 1995, male: n.a.

Contraceptive prevalence, percent
  Year: 1995/96
  Any method: 7
  Modern method: 5

Maternity leave benefits, as of early 1990s
  Maternity leave: 14 weeks
  Percentage of wages covered: 100
  Provider of coverage: social security

Labor force, total: 5,042,228
Labor force, female (percent of total): 46.3

Women in parliament as of January 1997
  Single or lower house, percent of seats occupied by women: 2.3
  Upper house, percent of seats occupied by women: n.a.

MALTA

Estimated 1999 population, in thousands, total: 386
Estimated 1999 population, in thousands, female: 195
Sex ratio 1999 (males per 100 females): 98

Birth rate, crude (per 1,000 people): 12.4
Fertility rate, total (births per woman): 1.83
Life expectancy at birth, female (years): 79.2
Life expectancy at birth, male (years): 75.0

Mortality rate, adult, female (per 1,000 female adults): 70.0
Mortality rate, adult, male (per 1,000 male adults): 114.0
Mortality rate, infant (per 1,000 live births): 6.7

Illiteracy rate, adult female (percent of females aged 15+): 8.2
Illiteracy rate, adult male (percent of males aged 15+): 9.5
School life expectancy, 1995, female: 13.1
School life expectancy, 1995, male: 13.7

Contraceptive prevalence, percent
  Year: n.a.
  Any method: n.a.
  Modern method: n.a.

Maternity leave benefits, as of early 1990s
  Maternity leave: 13 weeks
  Percentage of wages covered: 100
  Provider of coverage: employer

Labor force, total: 142,500
Labor force, female (percent of total): 27.0

Women in parliament as of January 1997
  Single or lower house, percent of seats occupied by women: 5.8
  Upper house, percent of seats occupied by women: n.a.

MARSHALL ISLANDS

Estimated 1998 population, in thousands, total: 63
Estimated 1998 population, in thousands, female: 31
Sex ratio 1998 (males per 100 females): 104

Birth rate, crude (per 1,000 people): n.a.
Fertility rate, total (births per woman): n.a.
Life expectancy at birth, female (years): n.a.
Life expectancy at birth, male (years): n.a.
Mortality rate, adult, female (per 1,000 female adults): n.a.
Mortality rate, adult, male (per 1,000 male adults): n.a.
Mortality rate, infant (per 1,000 live births): n.a.

Illiteracy rate, adult female (percent of females aged 15+): n.a.
Illiteracy rate, adult male (percent of males aged 15+): n.a.
School life expectancy, 1995, female: n.a.
School life expectancy, 1995, male: n.a.

Contraceptive prevalence, percent
  Year: 1985
  Any method: 27
  Modern method: 18

Maternity leave benefits, as of early 1990s
  Maternity leave: n.a.
  Percentage of wages covered: n.a.
  Provider of coverage: n.a.

Labor force, total: n.a.
Labor force, female (percent of total): n.a.

Women in parliament as of January 1997
  Single or lower house, percent of seats occupied by women: n.a.
  Upper house, percent of seats occupied by women: n.a.

MAURITANIA

Estimated 1999 population, in thousands, total: 2,598
Estimated 1999 population, in thousands, female: 1,310
Sex ratio 1999 (males per 100 females): 98

Birth rate, crude (per 1,000 people): 40.6
Fertility rate, total (births per woman): 5.50
Life expectancy at birth, female (years): 55.1
Life expectancy at birth, male (years): 51.9

Mortality rate, adult, female (per 1,000 female adults): 294.0
Mortality rate, adult, male (per 1,000 male adults): 344.0
Mortality rate, infant (per 1,000 live births): 92.0

Illiteracy rate, adult female (percent of females aged 15+): 72.2
Illiteracy rate, adult male (percent of males aged 15+): 50.6
School life expectancy, 1995, female: n.a.
School life expectancy, 1995, male: n.a.

Contraceptive prevalence, percent
  Year: 1990
  Any method: 3†
  Modern method: 1
  † Adjusted from source to exclude breastfeeding.

Maternity leave benefits, as of early 1990s
  Maternity leave: 14 weeks
  Percentage of wages covered: ave. daily earnings
  Provider of coverage: social security

Labor force, total: 1,132,065
Labor force, female (percent of total): 43.8

Women in parliament as of January 1997
  Single or lower house, percent of seats occupied by women: 1.3
  Upper house, percent of seats occupied by women: 0

MAURITIUS

Estimated 1999 population, in thousands, total: 1,149
Estimated 1999 population, in thousands, female: 576
Sex ratio 1999 (males per 100 females): 99

Birth rate, crude (per 1,000 people): 17.4
Fertility rate, total (births per woman): 1.91
Life expectancy at birth, female (years): 75.1
Life expectancy at birth, male (years): 67.9

Mortality rate, adult, female (per 1,000 female adults): 97.0
Mortality rate, adult, male (per 1,000 male adults): 205.0
Mortality rate, infant (per 1,000 live births): 19.8

Illiteracy rate, adult female (percent of females aged 15+): 20.8
Illiteracy rate, adult male (percent of males aged 15+): 13.1
School life expectancy, 1995, female: n.a.
School life expectancy, 1995, male: n.a.

Contraceptive prevalence, percent
  Year: 1991
  Any method: 75
  Modern method: 49

Maternity leave benefits, as of early 1990s
  Maternity leave: n.a.
  Percentage of wages covered: n.a.
  Provider of coverage: n.a.

Labor force, total: 493,640
Labor force, female (percent of total): 31.9

Women in parliament as of January 1997
  Single or lower house, percent of seats occupied by women: 7.6
  Upper house, percent of seats occupied by women: n.a.

MEXICO

Estimated 1999 population, in thousands, total: 97,366
Estimated 1999 population, in thousands, female: 49,168
Sex ratio 1999 (males per 100 females): 98

Birth rate, crude (per 1,000 people): 24.6
Fertility rate, total (births per woman): 2.75
Life expectancy at birth, female (years): 75.1
Life expectancy at birth, male (years): 69.0

Mortality rate, adult, female (per 1,000 female adults): 83.0
Mortality rate, adult, male (per 1,000 male adults): 166.0
Mortality rate, infant (per 1,000 live births): 31.0

Illiteracy rate, adult female (percent of females aged 15+): 12.1
Illiteracy rate, adult male (percent of males aged 15+): 7.7
School life expectancy, 1995, female: n.a.
School life expectancy, 1995, male: n.a.

Contraceptive prevalence, percent
  Year: 1995
  Any method: 67
  Modern method: 58

Maternity leave benefits, as of early 1990s
  Maternity leave: 6 weeks before delivery and 6 weeks after
  Percentage of wages covered: 100
  Provider of coverage: social insurance

Labor force, total: 37,739,544
Labor force, female (percent of total): 32.3

Women in parliament as of January 1997
  Single or lower house, percent of seats occupied by women: 14.2
  Upper house, percent of seats occupied by women: 12.5

MICRONESIA

Estimated 1994 population, in thousands, total: 106
Estimated 1994 population, in thousands, female: 52
Sex ratio 1994 (males per 100 females): 105

Birth rate, crude (per 1,000 people): 27.9
Fertility rate, total (births per woman): 4.00
Life expectancy at birth, female (years): 69.0
Life expectancy at birth, male (years): 65.0

Mortality rate, adult, female (per 1,000 female adults): 185.0
Mortality rate, adult, male (per 1,000 male adults): 246.0
Mortality rate, infant (per 1,000 live births): 29.6

Illiteracy rate, adult female (percent of females aged 15+): n.a.
Illiteracy rate, adult male (percent of males aged 15+): n.a.
School life expectancy, 1995, female: n.a.
School life expectancy, 1995, male: n.a.

Contraceptive prevalence, percent
  Year: n.a.
  Any method: n.a.
  Modern method: n.a.

Maternity leave benefits, as of early 1990s
  Maternity leave: n.a.
  Percentage of wages covered: n.a.
  Provider of coverage: n.a.

Labor force, total: n.a.
Labor force, female (percent of total): n.a.

Women in parliament as of January 1997
  Single or lower house, percent of seats occupied by women: 0
  Upper house, percent of seats occupied by women: n.a.

MOLDOVA

Estimated 1999 population, in thousands, total: 4,379
Estimated 1999 population, in thousands, female: 2,283
Sex ratio 1999 (males per 100 females): 92

Birth rate, crude (per 1,000 people): 10.6
Fertility rate, total (births per woman): 1.60
Life expectancy at birth, female (years): 70.3
Life expectancy at birth, male (years): 62.9

Mortality rate, adult, female (per 1,000 female adults): 177.0
Mortality rate, adult, male (per 1,000 male adults): 316.0
Mortality rate, infant (per 1,000 live births): 20.0

Illiteracy rate, adult female (percent of females aged 15+): 2.6
Illiteracy rate, adult male (percent of males aged 15+): 0.7
School life expectancy, 1995, female: n.a.
School life expectancy, 1995, male: n.a.

Contraceptive prevalence, percent*
    Year: 1997
    Any method: 74
    Modern method: 50
    * All women aged 15-44 years.

Maternity leave benefits, as of early 1990s
    Maternity leave: n.a.
    Percentage of wages covered: n.a.
    Provider of coverage: n.a.

Labor force, total: 2,112,880
Labor force, female (percent of total): 48.5

Women in parliament as of January 1997
    Single or lower house, percent of seats occupied by women: 4.8
    Upper house, percent of seats occupied by women: n.a.

MONACO

Estimated 1990 population, in thousands, total: 30
Estimated 1990 population, in thousands, female: 16
Sex ratio 1990 (males per 100 females): 90

Birth rate, crude (per 1,000 people): n.a.
Fertility rate, total (births per woman): n.a.
Life expectancy at birth, female (years): n.a.
Life expectancy at birth, male (years): n.a.

Mortality rate, adult, female (per 1,000 female adults): n.a.
Mortality rate, adult, male (per 1,000 male adults): n.a.
Mortality rate, infant (per 1,000 live births): n.a.

Illiteracy rate, adult female (percent of females aged 15+): n.a.
Illiteracy rate, adult male (percent of males aged 15+): n.a.
School life expectancy, 1995, female: n.a.
School life expectancy, 1995, male: n.a.

Contraceptive prevalence, percent
    Year: n.a.
    Any method: n.a.
    Modern method: n.a.

Maternity leave benefits, as of early 1990s
    Maternity leave: n.a.
    Percentage of wages covered: n.a.
    Provider of coverage: n.a.

Labor force, total: n.a.
Labor force, female (percent of total): n.a.

Women in parliament as of January 1997
    Single or lower house, percent of seats occupied by women: 5.6
    Upper house, percent of seats occupied by women: n.a.

MONGOLIA

Estimated 1999 population, in thousands, total: 2,621
Estimated 1999 population, in thousands, female: 1,307
Sex ratio 1999 (males per 100 females): 101

Birth rate, crude (per 1,000 people): 22.9
Fertility rate, total (births per woman): 2.60
Life expectancy at birth, female (years): 67.3
Life expectancy at birth, male (years): 64.3

Mortality rate, adult, female (per 1,000 female adults): 170.0
Mortality rate, adult, male (per 1,000 male adults): 203.0
Mortality rate, infant (per 1,000 live births): 52.0

Illiteracy rate, adult female (percent of females aged 15+): n.a.
Illiteracy rate, adult male (percent of males aged 15+): n.a.
School life expectancy, 1995, female: 8.1
School life expectancy, 1995, male: 6.0

Contraceptive prevalence, percent
    Year: 1994
    Any method: 61
    Modern method: 25

Maternity leave benefits, as of early 1990s
    Maternity leave: 45 days before delivery and 56 days after
    Percentage of wages covered: n.a.
    Provider of coverage: n.a.

Labor force, total: 1,245,668
Labor force, female (percent of total): 46.8

Women in parliament as of January 1997
    Single or lower house, percent of seats occupied by women: 7.9
    Upper house, percent of seats occupied by women: n.a.

MOROCCO

Estimated 1999 population, in thousands, total: 27,866
Estimated 1999 population, in thousands, female: 13,920
Sex ratio 1999 (males per 100 females): 100

Birth rate, crude (per 1,000 people): 25.7
Fertility rate, total (births per woman): 3.10
Life expectancy at birth, female (years): 68.5
Life expectancy at birth, male (years): 64.8

Mortality rate, adult, female (per 1,000 female adults): 150.0
Mortality rate, adult, male (per 1,000 male adults): 207.0
Mortality rate, infant (per 1,000 live births): 51.0

Illiteracy rate, adult female (percent of females aged 15+): 67.3
Illiteracy rate, adult male (percent of males aged 15+): 40.7
School life expectancy, 1995, female: n.a.
School life expectancy, 1995, male: n.a.

Contraceptive prevalence, percent
  Year: 1995
  Any method: 50
  Modern method: 42

Maternity leave benefits, as of early 1990s
  Maternity leave: 12 weeks
  Percentage of wages covered: 100
  Provider of coverage: social security

Labor force, total: 10,650,900
Labor force, female (percent of total): 34.6

Women in parliament as of January 1997
  Single or lower house, percent of seats occupied by women: 0.6
  Upper house, percent of seats occupied by women: n.a.

MOZAMBIQUE

Estimated 1999 population, in thousands, total: 19,286
Estimated 1999 population, in thousands, female: 9,761
Sex ratio 1999 (males per 100 females): 98

Birth rate, crude (per 1,000 people): 40.6
Fertility rate, total (births per woman): 5.30
Life expectancy at birth, female (years): 46.9
Life expectancy at birth, male (years): 44.1

Mortality rate, adult, female (per 1,000 female adults): 354.0
Mortality rate, adult, male (per 1,000 male adults): 400.0
Mortality rate, infant (per 1,000 live births): 135.0

Illiteracy rate, adult female (percent of females aged 15+): 75.0
Illiteracy rate, adult male (percent of males aged 15+): 43.3
School life expectancy, 1995, female: 2.8
School life expectancy, 1995, male: 4.0

Contraceptive prevalence, percent
  Year: 1997
  Any method: 6
  Modern method: 5

Maternity leave benefits, as of early 1990s
  Maternity leave: 60 days
  Percentage of wages covered: 100
  Provider of coverage: employer

Labor force, total: 8,647,600
Labor force, female (percent of total): 48.4

Women in parliament as of January 1997
  Single or lower house, percent of seats occupied by women: 25.2
  Upper house, percent of seats occupied by women: n.a.

NAMIBIA

Estimated 1999 population, in thousands, total: 1,695
Estimated 1999 population, in thousands, female: 850
Sex ratio 1999 (males per 100 females): 99

Birth rate, crude (per 1,000 people): 35.8
Fertility rate, total (births per woman): 4.90
Life expectancy at birth, female (years): 56.6
Life expectancy at birth, male (years): 54.7

Mortality rate, adult, female (per 1,000 female adults): 341.0
Mortality rate, adult, male (per 1,000 male adults): 366.0
Mortality rate, infant (per 1,000 live births): 65.0

Illiteracy rate, adult female (percent of females aged 15+): 21.5
Illiteracy rate, adult male (percent of males aged 15+): 18.8
School life expectancy, 1995, female: n.a.
School life expectancy, 1995, male: n.a.

Contraceptive prevalence, percent
  Year: 1992
  Any method: 29
  Modern method: 26

Maternity leave benefits, as of early 1990s
  Maternity leave: 4 weeks before delivery and 8 weeks after
  Percentage of wages covered: n.a.
  Provider of coverage: n.a.

Labor force, total: 665,254
Labor force, female (percent of total): 40.8

Women in parliament as of January 1997
  Single or lower house, percent of seats occupied by women: 18.1
  Upper house, percent of seats occupied by women: n.a.

NAURU

Estimated 1995 population, in thousands, total: 10
Estimated 1995 population, in thousands, female: n.a.
Sex ratio 1995 (males per 100 females): n.a.

Birth rate, crude (per 1,000 people): 18.0 (1995 est.)
Fertility rate, total (births per woman): 2.0 (1995 est.)
Life expectancy at birth, female (years): 69.2 (1995 est.)
Life expectancy at birth, male (years): 64.3 (1995 est.)

Mortality rate, adult, female (per 1,000 female adults): n.a.
Mortality rate, adult, male (per 1,000 male adults): n.a.
Mortality rate, infant (per 1,000 live births): 40.6 (1995 est.)

Illiteracy rate, adult female (percent of females aged 15+): n.a.
Illiteracy rate, adult male (percent of males aged 15+): n.a.
School life expectancy, 1995, female: n.a.
School life expectancy, 1995, male: n.a.

Contraceptive prevalence, percent
Year: n.a.
Any method: n.a.
Modern method: n.a.

Maternity leave benefits, as of early 1990s
Maternity leave: n.a.
Percentage of wages covered: n.a.
Provider of coverage: n.a.

Labor force, total: n.a.
Labor force, female (percent of total): n.a.

Women in parliament as of January 1997
Single or lower house, percent of seats occupied by women: n.a.
Upper house, percent of seats occupied by women: n.a.

NEPAL

Estimated 1999 population, in thousands, total: 23,386
Estimated 1999 population, in thousands, female: 11,538
Sex ratio 1999 (males per 100 females): 103

Birth rate, crude (per 1,000 people): 34.4
Fertility rate, total (births per woman): 4.45
Life expectancy at birth, female (years): 57.1
Life expectancy at birth, male (years): 57.6

Mortality rate, adult, female (per 1,000 female adults): 314.0
Mortality rate, adult, male (per 1,000 male adults): 274.0
Mortality rate, infant (per 1,000 live births): 83.0

Illiteracy rate, adult female (percent of females aged 15+): 79.3
Illiteracy rate, adult male (percent of males aged 15+): 44.3
School life expectancy, 1995, female: n.a.
School life expectancy, 1995, male: n.a.

Contraceptive prevalence, percent
Year: 1996
Any method: 29
Modern method: 26

Maternity leave benefits, as of early 1990s
Maternity leave: 52 days (For a maximum of two children.)
Percentage of wages covered: 100
Provider of coverage: employer

Labor force, total: 10,267,734
Labor force, female (percent of total): 40.4

Women in parliament as of January 1997
Single or lower house, percent of seats occupied by women: 3.4
Upper house, percent of seats occupied by women: 8.3

NETHERLANDS

Estimated 1999 population, in thousands, total: 15,735
Estimated 1999 population, in thousands, female: 7,945
Sex ratio 1999 (males per 100 females): 98

Birth rate, crude (per 1,000 people): 11.9
Fertility rate, total (births per woman): 1.53
Life expectancy at birth, female (years): 80.5
Life expectancy at birth, male (years): 74.7

Mortality rate, adult, female (per 1,000 female adults): 62.0
Mortality rate, adult, male (per 1,000 male adults): 121.0
Mortality rate, infant (per 1,000 live births): 5.1

Illiteracy rate, adult female (percent of females aged 15+): n.a.
Illiteracy rate, adult male (percent of males aged 15+): n.a.
School life expectancy, 1995, female: 15.2
School life expectancy, 1995, male: 15.7

Contraceptive prevalence, percent*
Year: 1993
Any method: 79
Modern method: 76
* Married women aged 18-42 years.

Maternity leave benefits, as of early 1990s
Maternity leave: 16 weeks
Percentage of wages covered: 100
Provider of coverage: sickness insurance

Labor force, total: 7,335,290
Labor force, female (percent of total): 40.1

Women in parliament as of January 1997
Single or lower house, percent of seats occupied by women: 31.3
Upper house, percent of seats occupied by women: 22.7

NEW ZEALAND

Estimated 1999 population, in thousands, total: 3,828
Estimated 1999 population, in thousands, female: 1,942
Sex ratio 1999 (males per 100 females): 97

Birth rate, crude (per 1,000 people): 15.4
Fertility rate, total (births per woman): 1.94
Life expectancy at birth, female (years): 79.9
Life expectancy at birth, male (years): 74.5

Mortality rate, adult, female (per 1,000 female adults): 68.0
Mortality rate, adult, male (per 1,000 male adults): 132.0
Mortality rate, infant (per 1,000 live births): 6.6

Illiteracy rate, adult female (percent of females aged 15+): n.a.
Illiteracy rate, adult male (percent of males aged 15+): n.a.
School life expectancy, 1995, female: 16.7
School life expectancy, 1995, male: 16.0

Contraceptive prevalence, percent
  Year: 1995
  Any method: 75
  Modern method: 72

Maternity leave benefits, as of early 1990s
  Maternity leave: 14 weeks
  Percentage of wages covered: unpaid
  Provider of coverage: n.a.

Labor force, total: 1,880,500
Labor force, female (percent of total): 44.4

Women in parliament as of January 1997
  Single or lower house, percent of seats occupied by women: 29.2
  Upper house, percent of seats occupied by women: n.a.

NICARAGUA

Estimated 1999 population, in thousands, total: 4,938
Estimated 1999 population, in thousands, female: 2,483
Sex ratio 1999 (males per 100 females): 99

Birth rate, crude (per 1,000 people): 32.2
Fertility rate, total (births per woman): 3.90
Life expectancy at birth, female (years): 70.6
Life expectancy at birth, male (years): 65.8

Mortality rate, adult, female (per 1,000 female adults): 126.0
Mortality rate, adult, male (per 1,000 male adults): 202.0
Mortality rate, infant (per 1,000 live births): 43.0

Illiteracy rate, adult female (percent of females aged 15+): 36.7
Illiteracy rate, adult male (percent of males aged 15+): 36.6
School life expectancy, 1995, female: 9.4
School life expectancy, 1995, male: 8.9

Contraceptive prevalence, percent
  Year: 1992
  Any method: 49
  Modern method: 45

Maternity leave benefits, as of early 1990s
  Maternity leave: 4 weeks before delivery and 8 weeks after
  Percentage of wages covered: 60
  Provider of coverage: social security

Labor force, total: 1,823,913
Labor force, female (percent of total): 34.6

Women in parliament as of January 1997
  Single or lower house, percent of seats occupied by women: 10.8
  Upper house, percent of seats occupied by women: n.a.

NIGER

Estimated 1999 population, in thousands, total: 10,401
Estimated 1999 population, in thousands, female: 5,256
Sex ratio 1999 (males per 100 females): 98

Birth rate, crude (per 1,000 people): 52.4
Fertility rate, total (births per woman): 7.40
Life expectancy at birth, female (years): 49.5
Life expectancy at birth, male (years): 44.5

Mortality rate, adult, female (per 1,000 female adults): 342.0
Mortality rate, adult, male (per 1,000 male adults): 450.0
Mortality rate, infant (per 1,000 live births): 118.0

Illiteracy rate, adult female (percent of females aged 15+): 92.7
Illiteracy rate, adult male (percent of males aged 15+): 78.3
School life expectancy, 1995, female: n.a.
School life expectancy, 1995, male: n.a.

Contraceptive prevalence, percent
  Year: 1998
  Any method: 8
  Modern method: 5

Maternity leave benefits, as of early 1990s
  Maternity leave: 14 weeks
  Percentage of wages covered: 50
  Provider of coverage: social security

Labor force, total: 4,605,432
Labor force, female (percent of total): 44.2

Women in parliament as of January 1997
  Single or lower house, percent of seats occupied by women: n.a.
  Upper house, percent of seats occupied by women: n.a.

NIGERIA

Estimated 1999 population, in thousands, total: 108,945
Estimated 1999 population, in thousands, female: 54,912
Sex ratio 1999 (males per 100 females): 98

Birth rate, crude (per 1,000 people): 40.4
Fertility rate, total (births per woman): 5.31
Life expectancy at birth, female (years): 55.3
Life expectancy at birth, male (years): 51.8

Mortality rate, adult, female (per 1,000 female adults): 335.0
Mortality rate, adult, male (per 1,000 male adults): 398.0
Mortality rate, infant (per 1,000 live births): 77.0

Illiteracy rate, adult female (percent of females aged 15+): 49.1
Illiteracy rate, adult male (percent of males aged 15+): 31.4
School life expectancy, 1995, female: n.a.
School life expectancy, 1995, male: n.a.

Contraceptive prevalence, percent
  Year: 1990
  Any method: 6
  Modern method: 4

Maternity leave benefits, as of early 1990s
  Maternity leave: 12 weeks
  Percentage of wages covered: 50
  Provider of coverage: employer

Labor force, total: 47,158,828
Labor force, female (percent of total): 36.1

Women in parliament as of January 1997
  Single or lower house, percent of seats occupied by women: n.a.
  Upper house, percent of seats occupied by women: n.a.

NORWAY

Estimated 1999 population, in thousands, total: 4,442
Estimated 1999 population, in thousands, female: 2,241
Sex ratio 1999 (males per 100 females): 98

Birth rate, crude (per 1,000 people): 13.5
Fertility rate, total (births per woman): 1.86
Life expectancy at birth, female (years): 81.0
Life expectancy at birth, male (years): 75.5

Mortality rate, adult, female (per 1,000 female adults): 59.0
Mortality rate, adult, male (per 1,000 male adults): 114.0
Mortality rate, infant (per 1,000 live births): 4.1

Illiteracy rate, adult female (percent of females aged 15+): n.a.
Illiteracy rate, adult male (percent of males aged 15+): n.a.
School life expectancy, 1995, female: 15.2
School life expectancy, 1995, male: 14.7

Contraceptive prevalence, percent
  Year: 1988/89
  Any method: 74
  Modern method: 69

Maternity leave benefits, as of early 1990s
  Maternity leave: 12 weeks before delivery and 6 weeks after
  Percentage of wages covered: 100 (Full wages are paid for 42 weeks or 80 percent for 52 weeks.)
  Provider of coverage: employer/soc. ins.

Labor force, total: 2,290,132
Labor force, female (percent of total): 46.0

Women in parliament as of January 1997
  Single or lower house, percent of seats occupied by women: 39.4
  Upper house, percent of seats occupied by women: n.a.

OMAN

Estimated 1999 population, in thousands, total: 2,460
Estimated 1999 population, in thousands, female: 1,155
Sex ratio 1999 (males per 100 females): 113

Birth rate, crude (per 1,000 people): 29.5
Fertility rate, total (births per woman): 4.80
Life expectancy at birth, female (years): 74.4
Life expectancy at birth, male (years): 71.4

Mortality rate, adult, female (per 1,000 female adults): 108.0
Mortality rate, adult, male (per 1,000 male adults): 143.0
Mortality rate, infant (per 1,000 live births): 18.0

Illiteracy rate, adult female (percent of females aged 15+): 45.0
Illiteracy rate, adult male (percent of males aged 15+): 23.1
School life expectancy, 1995, female: 8.1
School life expectancy, 1995, male: 8.8

Contraceptive prevalence, percent*
  Year: 1995
  Any method: 22†
  Modern method: 18
  * Married women under 50 years.
  † Adjusted from source to exclude breastfeeding.

Maternity leave benefits, as of early 1990s
  Maternity leave: n.a.
  Percentage of wages covered: n.a.
  Provider of coverage: n.a.

Labor force, total: 609,120
Labor force, female (percent of total): 15.1

Women in parliament as of January 1997
  Single or lower house, percent of seats occupied by women: n.a.
  Upper house, percent of seats occupied by women: n.a.

PAKISTAN

Estimated 1999 population, in thousands, total: 152,330
Estimated 1999 population, in thousands, female: 73,698
Sex ratio 1999 (males per 100 females): 107

Birth rate, crude (per 1,000 people): 35.8
Fertility rate, total (births per woman): 5.00
Life expectancy at birth, female (years): 62.6
Life expectancy at birth, male (years): 60.8

Mortality rate, adult, female (per 1,000 female adults): 158.0
Mortality rate, adult, male (per 1,000 male adults): 175.0
Mortality rate, infant (per 1,000 live births): 95.0

Illiteracy rate, adult female (percent of females aged 15+): 74.7
Illiteracy rate, adult male (percent of males aged 15+): 44.8
School life expectancy, 1995, female: n.a.
School life expectancy, 1995, male: n.a.

Contraceptive prevalence, percent
Year: 1994/95
Any method: 18
Modern method: 13

Maternity leave benefits, as of early 1990s
Maternity leave: 6 weeks before delivery and 6 weeks after
Percentage of wages covered: ave. daily earnings
Provider of coverage: social security

Labor force, total: 47,529,204
Labor force, female (percent of total): 27.2

Women in parliament as of January 1997
Single or lower house, percent of seats occupied by women: n.a.
Upper house, percent of seats occupied by women: 3.4

PALAU

Estimated 1987 population, in thousands, total: 17
Estimated 1987 population, in thousands, female: 8
Sex ratio 1987 (males per 100 females): 115

Birth rate, crude (per 1,000 people): n.a.
Fertility rate, total (births per woman): n.a.
Life expectancy at birth, female (years): n.a.
Life expectancy at birth, male (years): n.a.

Mortality rate, adult, female (per 1,000 female adults): n.a.
Mortality rate, adult, male (per 1,000 male adults): n.a.
Mortality rate, infant (per 1,000 live births): n.a.

Illiteracy rate, adult female (percent of females aged 15+): n.a.
Illiteracy rate, adult male (percent of males aged 15+): n.a.
School life expectancy, 1995, female: n.a.
School life expectancy, 1995, male: n.a.

Contraceptive prevalence, percent
Year: n.a.
Any method: n.a.
Modern method: n.a.

Maternity leave benefits, as of early 1990s
Maternity leave: n.a.
Percentage of wages covered: n.a.
Provider of coverage: n.a.

Labor force, total: n.a.
Labor force, female (percent of total): n.a.

Women in parliament as of January 1997
Single or lower house, percent of seats occupied by women: 0
Upper house, percent of seats occupied by women: 7.1

PANAMA

Estimated 1999 population, in thousands, total: 2,812
Estimated 1999 population, in thousands, female: 1,393
Sex ratio 1999 (males per 100 females): 102

Birth rate, crude (per 1,000 people): 22.5
Fertility rate, total (births per woman): 2.63
Life expectancy at birth, female (years): 76.4
Life expectancy at birth, male (years): 71.8

Mortality rate, adult, female (per 1,000 female adults): 81.0
Mortality rate, adult, male (per 1,000 male adults): 137.0
Mortality rate, infant (per 1,000 live births): 21.0

Illiteracy rate, adult female (percent of females aged 15+): 9.6
Illiteracy rate, adult male (percent of males aged 15+): 8.3
School life expectancy, 1995, female: n.a.
School life expectancy, 1995, male: n.a.

Contraceptive prevalence, percent*
Year: 1984
Any method: 64
Modern method: 58
* All women aged 15-44 years.

Maternity leave benefits, as of early 1990s
Maternity leave: 6 weeks before delivery and 8 weeks after
Percentage of wages covered: 100 percent of average weekly wage, plus the difference with actual salary.
Provider of coverage: soc. sec./employer

Labor force, total: 1,114,790
Labor force, female (percent of total): 34.5

Women in parliament as of January 1997
Single or lower house, percent of seats occupied by women: 9.7
Upper house, percent of seats occupied by women: n.a.

PAPUA NEW GUINEA

Estimated 1999 population, in thousands, total: 4,702
Estimated 1999 population, in thousands, female: 2,279
Sex ratio 1999 (males per 100 females): 106

Birth rate, crude (per 1,000 people): 31.9
Fertility rate, total (births per woman): 4.30
Life expectancy at birth, female (years): 58.7
Life expectancy at birth, male (years): 57.2

Mortality rate, adult, female (per 1,000 female adults): 333.0
Mortality rate, adult, male (per 1,000 male adults): 348.0
Mortality rate, infant (per 1,000 live births): 61.0

Illiteracy rate, adult female (percent of females aged 15+): n.a.
Illiteracy rate, adult male (percent of males aged 15+): n.a.
School life expectancy, 1995, female: n.a.
School life expectancy, 1995, male: n.a.

Contraceptive prevalence, percent
Year: 1996
Any method: 26
Modern method: 20

Maternity leave benefits, as of early 1990s
Maternity leave: 6 weeks after (Period necessary for hospitalization before confinement.)
Percentage of wages covered: unpaid, unless annual leave or sick leave credits are converted into paid maternity leave by employer.
Provider of coverage: n.a.

Labor force, total: 2,205,461
Labor force, female (percent of total): 41.9

Women in parliament as of January 1997
Single or lower house, percent of seats occupied by women: 0
Upper house, percent of seats occupied by women: n.a.

PARAGUAY

Estimated 1999 population, in thousands, total: 5,359
Estimated 1999 population, in thousands, female: 2,657
Sex ratio 1999 (males per 100 females): 102

Birth rate, crude (per 1,000 people): 31.3
Fertility rate, total (births per woman): 3.80
Life expectancy at birth, female (years): 72.0
Life expectancy at birth, male (years): 67.5

Mortality rate, adult, female (per 1,000 female adults): 124.0
Mortality rate, adult, male (per 1,000 male adults): 185.0
Mortality rate, infant (per 1,000 live births): 23.0

Illiteracy rate, adult female (percent of females aged 15+): 8.9
Illiteracy rate, adult male (percent of males aged 15+): 6.2
School life expectancy, 1995, female: 9.1
School life expectancy, 1995, male: 9.2

Contraceptive prevalence, percent
Year: 1995/96
Any method: 56
Modern method: 41

Maternity leave benefits, as of early 1990s
Maternity leave: 6 weeks before delivery and 6 weeks after
Percentage of wages covered: 50
Provider of coverage: social security

Labor force, total: 1,881,450
Labor force, female (percent of total): 29.4

Women in parliament as of January 1997
Single or lower house, percent of seats occupied by women: 2.5
Upper house, percent of seats occupied by women: 11.1

PERU

Estimated 1999 population, in thousands, total: 25,230
Estimated 1999 population, in thousands, female: 12,716
Sex ratio 1999 (males per 100 females): 98

Birth rate, crude (per 1,000 people): 26.6
Fertility rate, total (births per woman): 3.20
Life expectancy at birth, female (years): 71.0
Life expectancy at birth, male (years): 66.2

Mortality rate, adult, female (per 1,000 female adults): 124.0
Mortality rate, adult, male (per 1,000 male adults): 200.0
Mortality rate, infant (per 1,000 live births): 40.0

Illiteracy rate, adult female (percent of females aged 15+): 16.3
Illiteracy rate, adult male (percent of males aged 15+): 6.1
School life expectancy, 1995, female: 11.8
School life expectancy, 1995, male: 12.9

Contraceptive prevalence, percent
Year: 1996
Any method: 64
Modern method: 41

Maternity leave benefits, as of early 1990s
Maternity leave: 45 days before delivery + 45 days after
Percentage of wages covered: 100
Provider of coverage: social security

Labor force, total: 9,017,270
Labor force, female (percent of total): 30.3

Women in parliament as of January 1997
Single or lower house, percent of seats occupied by women: 10.8
Upper house, percent of seats occupied by women: n.a.

PHILIPPINES

Estimated 1999 population, in thousands, total: 74,454
Estimated 1999 population, in thousands, female: 36,896
Sex ratio 1999 (males per 100 females): 102

Birth rate, crude (per 1,000 people): 28.6
Fertility rate, total (births per woman): 3.62
Life expectancy at birth, female (years): 70.2
Life expectancy at birth, male (years): 66.5

Mortality rate, adult, female (per 1,000 female adults): 153.0
Mortality rate, adult, male (per 1,000 male adults): 200.0
Mortality rate, infant (per 1,000 live births): 35.0

Illiteracy rate, adult female (percent of females aged 15+): 5.7
Illiteracy rate, adult male (percent of males aged 15+): 5.2
School life expectancy, 1995, female: 11.0
School life expectancy, 1995, male: 11.0

Contraceptive prevalence, percent
Year: 1998
Any method: 47
Modern method: 28

Maternity leave benefits, as of early 1990s
Maternity leave: 10 weeks before delivery and 4 weeks after
Percentage of wages covered: 100 for 60 days
Provider of coverage: employer

Labor force, total: 30,881,340
Labor force, female (percent of total): 37.4

Women in parliament as of January 1997
Single or lower house, percent of seats occupied by women: 10.8
Upper house, percent of seats occupied by women: 16.7

POLAND

Estimated 1999 population, in thousands, total: 38,741
Estimated 1999 population, in thousands, female: 19,909
Sex ratio 1999 (males per 100 females): 95

Birth rate, crude (per 1,000 people): 10.7
Fertility rate, total (births per woman): 1.50
Life expectancy at birth, female (years): 77.0
Life expectancy at birth, male (years): 68.5

Mortality rate, adult, female (per 1,000 female adults): 91.0
Mortality rate, adult, male (per 1,000 male adults): 238.0
Mortality rate, infant (per 1,000 live births): 10.2

Illiteracy rate, adult female (percent of females aged 15+): 0.4
Illiteracy rate, adult male (percent of males aged 15+): 0.3
School life expectancy, 1995, female: 13.3
School life expectancy, 1995, male: 13.0

Contraceptive prevalence, percent
Year: n.a.
Any method: n.a.
Modern method: n.a.

Maternity leave benefits, as of early 1990s
Maternity leave: 16 (18 weeks for the second and subsequent children.)
Percentage of wages covered: 100
Provider of coverage: social security

Labor force, total: 19,711,500
Labor force, female (percent of total): 46.2

Women in parliament as of January 1997
Single or lower house, percent of seats occupied by women: 13
Upper house, percent of seats occupied by women: 13

PORTUGAL

Estimated 1999 population, in thousands, total: 9,873
Estimated 1999 population, in thousands, female: 5,120
Sex ratio 1999 (males per 100 females): 93

Birth rate, crude (per 1,000 people): 11.4
Fertility rate, total (births per woman): 1.44
Life expectancy at birth, female (years): 78.7
Life expectancy at birth, male (years): 71.4

Mortality rate, adult, female (per 1,000 female adults): 72.0
Mortality rate, adult, male (per 1,000 male adults): 154.0
Mortality rate, infant (per 1,000 live births): 6.4

Illiteracy rate, adult female (percent of females aged 15+): 11.7
Illiteracy rate, adult male (percent of males aged 15+): 6.3
School life expectancy, 1995, female: 14.7
School life expectancy, 1995, male: 13.9

Contraceptive prevalence, percent
Year: 1979/80
Any method: 66
Modern method: 33

Maternity leave benefits, as of early 1990s
Maternity leave: 90 days
Percentage of wages covered: 100
Provider of coverage: social security

Labor force, total: 4,972,500
Labor force, female (percent of total): 43.6

Women in parliament as of January 1997
Single or lower house, percent of seats occupied by women: 13
Upper house, percent of seats occupied by women: n.a.

QATAR

Estimated 1999 population, in thousands, total: 589
Estimated 1999 population, in thousands, female: 204
Sex ratio 1999 (males per 100 females): 189

Birth rate, crude (per 1,000 people): 14.2
Fertility rate, total (births per woman): 2.80
Life expectancy at birth, female (years): 74.5
Life expectancy at birth, male (years): 74.2

Mortality rate, adult, female (per 1,000 female adults): 113.0
Mortality rate, adult, male (per 1,000 male adults): 118.0
Mortality rate, infant (per 1,000 live births): 12.0

Illiteracy rate, adult female (percent of females aged 15+): 18.8
Illiteracy rate, adult male (percent of males aged 15+): 20.4
School life expectancy, 1995, female: 11.6
School life expectancy, 1995, male: 10.6

Contraceptive prevalence, percent*
    Year: 1987
    Any method: 32
    Modern method: 29
    * Married women under 50 years.

Maternity leave benefits, as of early 1990s
    Maternity leave: 60 days (30 days for non-nationals.)
    Percentage of wages covered: 100
    Provider of coverage: employer

Labor force, total: 396,396
Labor force, female (percent of total): 13.7

Women in parliament as of January 1997
    Single or lower house, percent of seats occupied by women: n.a.
    Upper house, percent of seats occupied by women: n.a.

ROMANIA

Estimated 1999 population, in thousands, total: 22,402
Estimated 1999 population, in thousands, female: 11,400
Sex ratio 1999 (males per 100 females): 97

Birth rate, crude (per 1,000 people): 10.2
Fertility rate, total (births per woman): 1.32
Life expectancy at birth, female (years): 73.0
Life expectancy at birth, male (years): 65.2

Mortality rate, adult, female (per 1,000 female adults): 119.0
Mortality rate, adult, male (per 1,000 male adults): 270.0
Mortality rate, infant (per 1,000 live births): 22.0

Illiteracy rate, adult female (percent of females aged 15+): 3.3
Illiteracy rate, adult male (percent of males aged 15+): 1.1
School life expectancy, 1995, female: 11.4
School life expectancy, 1995, male: 11.5

Contraceptive prevalence, percent*
    Year: 1993
    Any method: 57
    Modern method: 15
    * All women aged 15-44 years.

Maternity leave benefits, as of early 1990s
    Maternity leave: 112 days
    Percentage of wages covered: 50 to 94, depending on length of service and number of children.
    Provider of coverage: n.a.

Labor force, total: 10,600,380
Labor force, female (percent of total): 44.4

Women in parliament as of January 1997
    Single or lower house, percent of seats occupied by women: 7
    Upper house, percent of seats occupied by women: 2.1

RUSSIAN FEDERATION

Estimated 1999 population, in thousands, total: 147,195
Estimated 1999 population, in thousands, female: 78,368
Sex ratio 1999 (males per 100 females): 88

Birth rate, crude (per 1,000 people): 8.6
Fertility rate, total (births per woman): 1.28
Life expectancy at birth, female (years): 73.1
Life expectancy at birth, male (years): 61.0

Mortality rate, adult, female (per 1,000 female adults): 130.0
Mortality rate, adult, male (per 1,000 male adults): 370.0
Mortality rate, infant (per 1,000 live births): 17.0

Illiteracy rate, adult female (percent of females aged 15+): 1.3
Illiteracy rate, adult male (percent of males aged 15+): 0.4
School life expectancy, 1995, female: n.a.
School life expectancy, 1995, male: n.a.

Contraceptive prevalence, percent
    Year: 1990
    Any method: 32
    Modern method: n.a.

Maternity leave benefits, as of early 1990s
    Maternity leave: 140 days
    Percentage of wages covered: 100
    Provider of coverage: social security

Labor force, total: 78,072,712
Labor force, female (percent of total): 48.7

Women in parliament as of January 1997
    Single or lower house, percent of seats occupied by women: 10.2
    Upper house, percent of seats occupied by women: 0.6

RWANDA

Estimated 1999 population, in thousands, total: 7,235
Estimated 1999 population, in thousands, female: 3,663
Sex ratio 1999 (males per 100 females): 98

Birth rate, crude (per 1,000 people): 45.9
Fertility rate, total (births per woman): 6.20
Life expectancy at birth, female (years): 41.7
Life expectancy at birth, male (years): 39.3

Mortality rate, adult, female (per 1,000 female adults): 534.0
Mortality rate, adult, male (per 1,000 male adults): 585.0
Mortality rate, infant (per 1,000 live births): 124.0

Illiteracy rate, adult female (percent of females aged 15+): 44.4
Illiteracy rate, adult male (percent of males aged 15+): 29.3
School life expectancy, 1995, female: n.a.
School life expectancy, 1995, male: n.a.

Contraceptive prevalence, percent
  Year: 1992
  Any method: 21
  Modern method: 13

Maternity leave benefits, as of early 1990s
  Maternity leave: 12 weeks
  Percentage of wages covered: one third
  Provider of coverage: employer

Labor force, total: 4,184,446
Labor force, female (percent of total): 48.9

Women in parliament as of January 1997
  Single or lower house, percent of seats occupied by women: 17.1
  Upper house, percent of seats occupied by women: n.a.

ST. KITTS AND NEVIS

Estimated 1996 population, in thousands, total: 42
Estimated 1996 population, in thousands, female: 21
Sex ratio 1996 (males per 100 females): 101

Birth rate, crude (per 1,000 people): 20.5
Fertility rate, total (births per woman): 2.40
Life expectancy at birth, female (years): 72.7
Life expectancy at birth, male (years): 67.5

Mortality rate, adult, female (per 1,000 female adults): 129.0
Mortality rate, adult, male (per 1,000 male adults): 209.0
Mortality rate, infant (per 1,000 live births): 22.0

Illiteracy rate, adult female (percent of females aged 15+): n.a.
Illiteracy rate, adult male (percent of males aged 15+): n.a.
School life expectancy, 1995, female: n.a.
School life expectancy, 1995, male: n.a.

Contraceptive prevalence, percent*
  Year: 1984
  Any method: 41
  Modern method: 37
  * All sexually active women aged 15-44 years.

Maternity leave benefits, as of early 1990s
  Maternity leave: n.a.
  Percentage of wages covered: n.a.
  Provider of coverage: n.a.

Labor force, total: n.a.
Labor force, female (percent of total): n.a.

Women in parliament as of January 1997
  Single or lower house, percent of seats occupied by women: 13.3
  Upper house, percent of seats occupied by women: n.a.

ST. LUCIA

Estimated 1991 population, in thousands, total: 136
Estimated 1991 population, in thousands, female: 70
Sex ratio 1991 (males per 100 females): 95

Birth rate, crude (per 1,000 people): 20.7
Fertility rate, total (births per woman): 2.40
Life expectancy at birth, female (years): 74.0
Life expectancy at birth, male (years): 67.0

Mortality rate, adult, female (per 1,000 female adults): 116.0
Mortality rate, adult, male (per 1,000 male adults): 232.0
Mortality rate, infant (per 1,000 live births): 16.0

Illiteracy rate, adult female (percent of females aged 15+): n.a.
Illiteracy rate, adult male (percent of males aged 15+): n.a.
School life expectancy, 1995, female: n.a.
School life expectancy, 1995, male: n.a.

Contraceptive prevalence, percent*
  Year: 1988
  Any method: 47
  Modern method: 46
  * All women aged 15-44 years.

Maternity leave benefits, as of early 1990s
  Maternity leave: 6 weeks before delivery and 1 week of
  confinement + 6 weeks after
  Percentage of wages covered: 60
  Provider of coverage: national insurance

Labor force, total: n.a.
Labor force, female (percent of total): n.a.

Women in parliament as of January 1997
  Single or lower house, percent of seats occupied by women: 0
  Upper house, percent of seats occupied by women: 36.4

ST. VINCENT AND THE GRENADINES

Estimated 1996 population, in thousands, total: 112
Estimated 1996 population, in thousands, female: 56
Sex ratio 1996 (males per 100 females): 100

Birth rate, crude (per 1,000 people): 20.7
Fertility rate, total (births per woman): 2.19
Life expectancy at birth, female (years): 76.7
Life expectancy at birth, male (years): 69.3

Mortality rate, adult, female (per 1,000 female adults): 85.0
Mortality rate, adult, male (per 1,000 male adults): 181.0
Mortality rate, infant (per 1,000 live births): 17.7

Illiteracy rate, adult female (percent of females aged 15+): n.a.
Illiteracy rate, adult male (percent of males aged 15+): n.a.
School life expectancy, 1995, female: n.a.
School life expectancy, 1995, male: n.a.

Contraceptive prevalence, percent*
  Year: 1988
  Any method: 58
  Modern method: 55
  * All women aged 15-44 years.

Maternity leave benefits, as of early 1990s
  Maternity leave: n.a.
  Percentage of wages covered: n.a.
  Provider of coverage: n.a.

Labor force, total: n.a.
Labor force, female (percent of total): n.a.

Women in parliament as of January 1997
  Single or lower house, percent of seats occupied by women: 9.5
  Upper house, percent of seats occupied by women: n.a.

SAMOA

Estimated 1999 population, in thousands, total: 177
Estimated 1999 population, in thousands, female: 85
Sex ratio 1999 (males per 100 females): 108

Birth rate, crude (per 1,000 people): 28.2
Fertility rate, total (births per woman): 4.15
Life expectancy at birth, female (years): 71.1
Life expectancy at birth, male (years): 67.5

Mortality rate, adult, female (per 1,000 female adults): 159.0
Mortality rate, adult, male (per 1,000 male adults): 209.0
Mortality rate, infant (per 1,000 live births): 22.0

Illiteracy rate, adult female (percent of females aged 15+): n.a.
Illiteracy rate, adult male (percent of males aged 15+): n.a.
School life expectancy, 1995, female: 11.7
School life expectancy, 1995, male: 11.4

Contraceptive prevalence, percent
  Year: 1990
  Any method: 34
  Modern method: 34

Maternity leave benefits, as of early 1990s
  Maternity leave: n.a.
  Percentage of wages covered: n.a.
  Provider of coverage: n.a.

Labor force, total: n.a.
Labor force, female (percent of total): n.a.

Women in parliament as of January 1997
  Single or lower house, percent of seats occupied by women: 4.1
  Upper house, percent of seats occupied by women: n.a.

SAN MARINO

Estimated 1995 population, in thousands, total: 24
Estimated 1995 population, in thousands, female: 13
Sex ratio 1995 (males per 100 females): n.a.

Birth rate, crude (per 1,000 people): 10.9 (1995 est.)
Fertility rate, total (births per woman): 1.5 (1995 est.)
Life expectancy at birth, female (years): 85.3 (1995 est.)
Life expectancy at birth, male (years): 77.3 (1995 est.)

Mortality rate, adult, female (per 1,000 female adults): n.a.
Mortality rate, adult, male (per 1,000 male adults): n.a.
Mortality rate, infant (per 1,000 live births): 5.6

Illiteracy rate, adult female (percent of females aged 15+): n.a.
Illiteracy rate, adult male (percent of males aged 15+): n.a.
School life expectancy, 1995, female: n.a.
School life expectancy, 1995, male: n.a.

Contraceptive prevalence, percent
  Year: n.a.
  Any method: n.a.
  Modern method: n.a.

Maternity leave benefits, as of early 1990s
  Maternity leave: n.a.
  Percentage of wages covered: n.a.
  Provider of coverage: n.a.

Labor force, total: n.a.
Labor force, female (percent of total): n.a.

Women in parliament as of January 1997
  Single or lower house, percent of seats occupied by women: n.a.
  Upper house, percent of seats occupied by women: n.a.

SAO TOME AND PRINCIPE

Estimated 1995 population, in thousands, total: 127
Estimated 1995 population, in thousands, female: 65
Sex ratio 1995 (males per 100 females): 96

Birth rate, crude (per 1,000 people): 32.5
Fertility rate, total (births per woman): 4.65
Life expectancy at birth, female (years): 66.0
Life expectancy at birth, male (years): 62.0

Mortality rate, adult, female (per 1,000 female adults): 188.0
Mortality rate, adult, male (per 1,000 male adults): 248.0
Mortality rate, infant (per 1,000 live births): 50.0

Illiteracy rate, adult female (percent of females aged 15+): n.a.
Illiteracy rate, adult male (percent of males aged 15+): n.a.
School life expectancy, 1995, female: n.a.
School life expectancy, 1995, male: n.a.

Contraceptive prevalence, percent
  Year: n.a.
  Any method: n.a.
  Modern method: n.a.

Maternity leave benefits, as of early 1990s
  Maternity leave: 70 days
  Percentage of wages covered: ave. daily wages
  Provider of coverage: soc. sec./employer

Labor force, total: n.a.
Labor force, female (percent of total): n.a.

Women in parliament as of January 1997
  Single or lower house, percent of seats occupied by women: 7.3
  Upper house, percent of seats occupied by women: n.a.

SAUDI ARABIA

Estimated 1999 population, in thousands, total: 20,899
Estimated 1999 population, in thousands, female: 9,333
Sex ratio 1999 (males per 100 females): 124

Birth rate, crude (per 1,000 people): 34.5
Fertility rate, total (births per woman): 5.90
Life expectancy at birth, female (years): 71.8
Life expectancy at birth, male (years): 69.4

Mortality rate, adult, female (per 1,000 female adults): 147.0
Mortality rate, adult, male (per 1,000 male adults): 171.0
Mortality rate, infant (per 1,000 live births): 21.0

Illiteracy rate, adult female (percent of females aged 15+): 37.6
Illiteracy rate, adult male (percent of males aged 15+): 19.0
School life expectancy, 1995, female: 8.4
School life expectancy, 1995, male: 9.0

Contraceptive prevalence, percent
  Year: n.a.
  Any method: n.a.
  Modern method: n.a.

Maternity leave benefits, as of early 1990s
  Maternity leave: 4 weeks before delivery and 6 weeks after
  Percentage of wages covered: 50 (Half pay for women who have worked one year or more with the same employer or full pay for women who have worked more than three years with the same employer.)
  Provider of coverage: employer

Labor force, total: 6,621,665
Labor force, female (percent of total): 14.2

Women in parliament as of January 1997
  Single or lower house, percent of seats occupied by women: n.a.
  Upper house, percent of seats occupied by women: n.a.

SENEGAL

Estimated 1999 population, in thousands, total: 9,240
Estimated 1999 population, in thousands, female: 4,632
Sex ratio 1999 (males per 100 females): 99

Birth rate, crude (per 1,000 people): 39.7
Fertility rate, total (births per woman): 5.55
Life expectancy at birth, female (years): 54.2
Life expectancy at birth, male (years): 50.5

Mortality rate, adult, female (per 1,000 female adults): 381.0
Mortality rate, adult, male (per 1,000 male adults): 453.0
Mortality rate, infant (per 1,000 live births): 70.0

Illiteracy rate, adult female (percent of females aged 15+): 75.2
Illiteracy rate, adult male (percent of males aged 15+): 55.5
School life expectancy, 1995, female: n.a.
School life expectancy, 1995, male: n.a.

Contraceptive prevalence, percent
  Year: 1997
  Any method: 13
  Modern method: 8

Maternity leave benefits, as of early 1990s
  Maternity leave: 14 weeks
  Percentage of wages covered: 100
  Provider of coverage: social security

Labor force, total: 3,955,671
Labor force, female (percent of total): 42.5

Women in parliament as of January 1997
  Single or lower house, percent of seats occupied by women: 11.7
  Upper house, percent of seats occupied by women: n.a.

SEYCHELLES

Estimated 1996 population, in thousands, total: 76
Estimated 1996 population, in thousands, female: 38
Sex ratio 1996 (males per 100 females): 100

Birth rate, crude (per 1,000 people): 20.8
Fertility rate, total (births per woman): 2.10
Life expectancy at birth, female (years): 75.0
Life expectancy at birth, male (years): 68.0

Mortality rate, adult, female (per 1,000 female adults): 103.0
Mortality rate, adult, male (per 1,000 male adults): 213.0
Mortality rate, infant (per 1,000 live births): 15.0

Illiteracy rate, adult female (percent of females aged 15+): n.a.
Illiteracy rate, adult male (percent of males aged 15+): n.a.
School life expectancy, 1995, female: n.a.
School life expectancy, 1995, male: n.a.

Contraceptive prevalence, percent
  Year: n.a.
  Any method: n.a.
  Modern method: n.a.

Maternity leave benefits, as of early 1990s
  Maternity leave: 14 weeks
  Percentage of wages covered: flat monthly rate for 10 weeks
  Provider of coverage: social security

Labor force, total: n.a.
Labor force, female (percent of total): n.a.

Women in parliament as of January 1997
  Single or lower house, percent of seats occupied by women: 27.3
  Upper house, percent of seats occupied by women: n.a.

SIERRA LEONE

Estimated 1999 population, in thousands, total: 4,717
Estimated 1999 population, in thousands, female: 2,402
Sex ratio 1999 (males per 100 females): 96

Birth rate, crude (per 1,000 people): 45.7
Fertility rate, total (births per woman): 6.06
Life expectancy at birth, female (years): 38.7
Life expectancy at birth, male (years): 35.8

Mortality rate, adult, female (per 1,000 female adults): 483.0
Mortality rate, adult, male (per 1,000 male adults): 544.0
Mortality rate, infant (per 1,000 live births): 170.0

Illiteracy rate, adult female (percent of females aged 15+): n.a.
Illiteracy rate, adult male (percent of males aged 15+): n.a.
School life expectancy, 1995, female: n.a.
School life expectancy, 1995, male: n.a.

Contraceptive prevalence, percent
  Year: n.a.
  Any method: n.a.
  Modern method: n.a.

Maternity leave benefits, as of early 1990s
  Maternity leave: n.a.
  Percentage of wages covered: n.a.
  Provider of coverage: n.a.

Labor force, total: 1,756,760
Labor force, female (percent of total): 36.4

Women in parliament as of January 1997
  Single or lower house, percent of seats occupied by women: 6.3
  Upper house, percent of seats occupied by women: n.a.

SINGAPORE

Estimated 1999 population, in thousands, total: 3,522
Estimated 1999 population, in thousands, female: 1,748
Sex ratio 1999 (males per 100 females): 101

Birth rate, crude (per 1,000 people): 12.7
Fertility rate, total (births per woman): 1.71
Life expectancy at birth, female (years): 78.5
Life expectancy at birth, male (years): 73.5

Mortality rate, adult, female (per 1,000 female adults): 77.0
Mortality rate, adult, male (per 1,000 male adults): 136.0
Mortality rate, infant (per 1,000 live births): 3.8

Illiteracy rate, adult female (percent of females aged 15+): 13.0
Illiteracy rate, adult male (percent of males aged 15+): 4.2
School life expectancy, 1995, female: n.a.
School life expectancy, 1995, male: n.a.

Contraceptive prevalence, percent*
  Year: 1982
  Any method: 74
  Modern method: 73
  * All women aged 15-44 years.

Maternity leave benefits, as of early 1990s
  Maternity leave: 4 weeks before delivery and 4 weeks after
  Percentage of wages covered: 100
  Provider of coverage: employer

Labor force, total: 1,551,750
Labor force, female (percent of total): 39.0

Women in parliament as of January 1997
  Single or lower house, percent of seats occupied by women: 2.5
  Upper house, percent of seats occupied by women: n.a.

SLOVAK REPUBLIC

Estimated 1999 population, in thousands, total: 5,381
Estimated 1999 population, in thousands, female: 2,759
Sex ratio 1999 (males per 100 females): 95

Birth rate, crude (per 1,000 people): 11.0
Fertility rate, total (births per woman): 1.43
Life expectancy at birth, female (years): 76.7
Life expectancy at birth, male (years): 68.9

Mortality rate, adult, female (per 1,000 female adults): 90.0
Mortality rate, adult, male (per 1,000 male adults): 208.0
Mortality rate, infant (per 1,000 live births): 8.7

Illiteracy rate, adult female (percent of females aged 15+): n.a.
Illiteracy rate, adult male (percent of males aged 15+): n.a.
School life expectancy, 1995, female: n.a.
School life expectancy, 1995, male: n.a.

Contraceptive prevalence, percent*
  Year: 1991
  Any method: 74
  Modern method: 41
  * All sexually active women aged 15-44 years.

Maternity leave benefits, as of early 1990s
  Maternity leave: n.a.
  Percentage of wages covered: n.a.
  Provider of coverage: n.a.

Labor force, total: 2,906,982
Labor force, female (percent of total): 47.8

Women in parliament as of January 1997
  Single or lower house, percent of seats occupied by women: 14.7
  Upper house, percent of seats occupied by women: n.a.

SLOVENIA

Estimated 1999 population, in thousands, total: 1,989
Estimated 1999 population, in thousands, female: 1,023
Sex ratio 1999 (males per 100 females): 94

Birth rate, crude (per 1,000 people): 9.4
Fertility rate, total (births per woman): 1.25
Life expectancy at birth, female (years): 78.6
Life expectancy at birth, male (years): 71.0

Mortality rate, adult, female (per 1,000 female adults): 76.0
Mortality rate, adult, male (per 1,000 male adults): 173.0
Mortality rate, infant (per 1,000 live births): 5.2

Illiteracy rate, adult female (percent of females aged 15+): 0.5
Illiteracy rate, adult male (percent of males aged 15+): 0.4
School life expectancy, 1995, female: n.a.
School life expectancy, 1995, male: n.a.

Contraceptive prevalence, percent
  Year: n.a.
  Any method: n.a.
  Modern method: n.a.

Maternity leave benefits, as of early 1990s
  Maternity leave: n.a.
  Percentage of wages covered: n.a.
  Provider of coverage: n.a.

Labor force, total: 992,980
Labor force, female (percent of total): 46.4

Women in parliament as of January 1997
  Single or lower house, percent of seats occupied by women: 7.8
  Upper house, percent of seats occupied by women: n.a.

SOLOMON ISLANDS

Estimated 1999 population, in thousands, total: 430
Estimated 1999 population, in thousands, female: 209
Sex ratio 1999 (males per 100 females): 106

Birth rate, crude (per 1,000 people): 35.3
Fertility rate, total (births per woman): 4.85
Life expectancy at birth, female (years): 72.7
Life expectancy at birth, male (years): 68.4

Mortality rate, adult, female (per 1,000 female adults): 127.0
Mortality rate, adult, male (per 1,000 male adults): 187.0
Mortality rate, infant (per 1,000 live births): 23.0

Illiteracy rate, adult female (percent of females aged 15+): n.a.
Illiteracy rate, adult male (percent of males aged 15+): n.a.
School life expectancy, 1995, female: n.a.
School life expectancy, 1995, male: n.a.

Contraceptive prevalence, percent
  Year: n.a.
  Any method: n.a.
  Modern method: n.a.

Maternity leave benefits, as of early 1990s
  Maternity leave: 12 weeks
  Percentage of wages covered: 25
  Provider of coverage: employer

Labor force, total: 205,530
Labor force, female (percent of total): 46.6

Women in parliament as of January 1997
  Single or lower house, percent of seats occupied by women: 2.1
  Upper house, percent of seats occupied by women: n.a.

SOMALIA

Estimated 1999 population, in thousands, total: 9,672
Estimated 1999 population, in thousands, female: 4,871
Sex ratio 1999 (males per 100 females): 99

Birth rate, crude (per 1,000 people): 52.3
Fertility rate, total (births per woman): 7.25
Life expectancy at birth, female (years): 48.6
Life expectancy at birth, male (years): 45.4

Mortality rate, adult, female (per 1,000 female adults): 352.0
Mortality rate, adult, male (per 1,000 male adults): 409.0
Mortality rate, infant (per 1,000 live births): 122.0

Illiteracy rate, adult female (percent of females aged 15+): n.a.
Illiteracy rate, adult male (percent of males aged 15+): n.a.
School life expectancy, 1995, female: n.a.
School life expectancy, 1995, male: n.a.

Contraceptive prevalence, percent
  Year: n.a.
  Any method: n.a.
  Modern method: n.a.

Maternity leave benefits, as of early 1990s
  Maternity leave: 14 weeks
  Percentage of wages covered: 50
  Provider of coverage: employer

Labor force, total: 3,773,065
Labor force, female (percent of total): 43.4

Women in parliament as of January 1997
  Single or lower house, percent of seats occupied by women: n.a.
  Upper house, percent of seats occupied by women: n.a.

SOUTH AFRICA

Estimated 1999 population, in thousands, total: 39,900
Estimated 1999 population, in thousands, female: 20,303
Sex ratio 1999 (males per 100 females): 97

Birth rate, crude (per 1,000 people): 25.0
Fertility rate, total (births per woman): 2.80
Life expectancy at birth, female (years): 68.3
Life expectancy at birth, male (years): 62.3

Mortality rate, adult, female (per 1,000 female adults): 160.0
Mortality rate, adult, male (per 1,000 male adults): 261.0
Mortality rate, infant (per 1,000 live births): 48.0

Illiteracy rate, adult female (percent of females aged 15+): 16.8
Illiteracy rate, adult male (percent of males aged 15+): 15.2
School life expectancy, 1995, female: 13.2
School life expectancy, 1995, male: 13.0

Contraceptive prevalence, percent*
  Year: 1988
  Any method: 50
  Modern method: 48
  * Married women under 50 years.

Maternity leave benefits, as of early 1990s
  Maternity leave: n.a.
  Percentage of wages covered: n.a.
  Provider of coverage: n.a.

Labor force, total: 15,835,420
Labor force, female (percent of total): 37.6

Women in parliament as of January 1997
  Single or lower house, percent of seats occupied by women: 25
  Upper house, percent of seats occupied by women: 17.8

SPAIN

Estimated 1999 population, in thousands, total: 39,633
Estimated 1999 population, in thousands, female: 20,250
Sex ratio 1999 (males per 100 females): 96

Birth rate, crude (per 1,000 people): 9.2
Fertility rate, total (births per woman): 1.15
Life expectancy at birth, female (years): 81.5
Life expectancy at birth, male (years): 74.5

Mortality rate, adult, female (per 1,000 female adults): 56.0
Mortality rate, adult, male (per 1,000 male adults): 124.0
Mortality rate, infant (per 1,000 live births): 5.0

Illiteracy rate, adult female (percent of females aged 15+): 3.8
Illiteracy rate, adult male (percent of males aged 15+): 1.6
School life expectancy, 1995, female: 15.9
School life expectancy, 1995, male: 15.1

Contraceptive prevalence, percent*
  Year: 1985
  Any method: 59
  Modern method: 38
  * Married women aged 18-49 years.

Maternity leave benefits, as of early 1990s
  Maternity leave: 16 weeks
  Percentage of wages covered: 75
  Provider of coverage: n.a.

Labor force, total: 16,908,890
Labor force, female (percent of total): 36.5

Women in parliament as of January 1997
  Single or lower house, percent of seats occupied by women: 24.6
  Upper house, percent of seats occupied by women: 13.3

SRI LANKA

Estimated 1999 population, in thousands, total: 18,639
Estimated 1999 population, in thousands, female: 9,412
Sex ratio 1999 (males per 100 females): 98

Birth rate, crude (per 1,000 people): 18.6
Fertility rate, total (births per woman): 2.20
Life expectancy at birth, female (years): 75.4
Life expectancy at birth, male (years): 70.9

Mortality rate, adult, female (per 1,000 female adults): 99.0
Mortality rate, adult, male (per 1,000 male adults): 156.0
Mortality rate, infant (per 1,000 live births): 14.2

Illiteracy rate, adult female (percent of females aged 15+): 12.4
Illiteracy rate, adult male (percent of males aged 15+): 6.0
School life expectancy, 1995, female: n.a.
School life expectancy, 1995, male: n.a.

Contraceptive prevalence, percent*
Year: 1993
Any method: 66
Modern method: 44
* Excluding areas containing roughly 15 percent of the population.

Maternity leave benefits, as of early 1990s
Maternity leave: 12 weeks for the first and second surviving child, 6 weeks for the third and subsequent surviving children.
Percentage of wages covered: 100
Provider of coverage: employer

Labor force, total: 7,977,360
Labor force, female (percent of total): 36.0

Women in parliament as of January 1997
Single or lower house, percent of seats occupied by women: 5.3
Upper house, percent of seats occupied by women: n.a.

SUDAN

Estimated 1999 population, in thousands, total: 28,882
Estimated 1999 population, in thousands, female: 14,402
Sex ratio 1999 (males per 100 females): 101

Birth rate, crude (per 1,000 people): 33.3
Fertility rate, total (births per woman): 4.61
Life expectancy at birth, female (years): 56.4
Life expectancy at birth, male (years): 53.6

Mortality rate, adult, female (per 1,000 female adults): 328.0
Mortality rate, adult, male (per 1,000 male adults): 373.0
Mortality rate, infant (per 1,000 live births): 71.0

Illiteracy rate, adult female (percent of females aged 15+): 58.7
Illiteracy rate, adult male (percent of males aged 15+): 34.6
School life expectancy, 1995, female: n.a.
School life expectancy, 1995, male: n.a.

Contraceptive prevalence, percent*
Year: 1992/93
Any method: 8†
Modern method: 7
* Includes North Sudan only.
† Adjusted from source to exclude breastfeeding.

Maternity leave benefits, as of early 1990s
Maternity leave: n.a.
Percentage of wages covered: n.a.
Provider of coverage: n.a.

Labor force, total: 10,817,379
Labor force, female (percent of total): 28.8

Women in parliament as of January 1997
Single or lower house, percent of seats occupied by women: 5.3
Upper house, percent of seats occupied by women: n.a.

SURINAME

Estimated 1999 population, in thousands, total: 416
Estimated 1999 population, in thousands, female: 210
Sex ratio 1999 (males per 100 females): 98

Birth rate, crude (per 1,000 people): 20.2
Fertility rate, total (births per woman): 2.21
Life expectancy at birth, female (years): 72.7
Life expectancy at birth, male (years): 67.5

Mortality rate, adult, female (per 1,000 female adults): 119.0
Mortality rate, adult, male (per 1,000 male adults): 193.0
Mortality rate, infant (per 1,000 live births): 29.0

Illiteracy rate, adult female (percent of females aged 15+): n.a.
Illiteracy rate, adult male (percent of males aged 15+): n.a.
School life expectancy, 1995, female: n.a.
School life expectancy, 1995, male: n.a.

Contraceptive prevalence, percent
Year: n.a.
Any method: n.a.
Modern method: n.a.

Maternity leave benefits, as of early 1990s
Maternity leave: n.a.
Percentage of wages covered: n.a.
Provider of coverage: n.a.

Labor force, total: 152,274
Labor force, female (percent of total): 32.7

Women in parliament as of January 1997
Single or lower house, percent of seats occupied by women: 15.7
Upper house, percent of seats occupied by women: n.a.

SWAZILAND

Estimated 1999 population, in thousands, total: 980
Estimated 1999 population, in thousands, female: 508
Sex ratio 1999 (males per 100 females): 93

Birth rate, crude (per 1,000 people): 37.3
Fertility rate, total (births per woman): 4.70
Life expectancy at birth, female (years): 62.5
Life expectancy at birth, male (years): 57.9

Mortality rate, adult, female (per 1,000 female adults): 215.0
Mortality rate, adult, male (per 1,000 male adults): 290.0
Mortality rate, infant (per 1,000 live births): 65.0

Illiteracy rate, adult female (percent of females aged 15+): 23.7
Illiteracy rate, adult male (percent of males aged 15+): 21.1
School life expectancy, 1995, female: 10.8
School life expectancy, 1995, male: 11.5

Contraceptive prevalence, percent
Year: 1988
Any method: 20
Modern method: 17

Maternity leave benefits, as of early 1990s
Maternity leave: 12 weeks
Percentage of wages covered: none
Provider of coverage: n.a.

Labor force, total: 344,992
Labor force, female (percent of total): 37.6

Women in parliament as of January 1997
Single or lower house, percent of seats occupied by women: 3.1
Upper house, percent of seats occupied by women: 20

SWEDEN

Estimated 1999 population, in thousands, total: 8,892
Estimated 1999 population, in thousands, female: 4,484
Sex ratio 1999 (males per 100 females): 98

Birth rate, crude (per 1,000 people): 10.1
Fertility rate, total (births per woman): 1.74
Life expectancy at birth, female (years): 81.8
Life expectancy at birth, male (years): 76.5

Mortality rate, adult, female (per 1,000 female adults): 54.0
Mortality rate, adult, male (per 1,000 male adults): 105.0
Mortality rate, infant (per 1,000 live births): 4.0

Illiteracy rate, adult female (percent of females aged 15+): n.a.
Illiteracy rate, adult male (percent of males aged 15+): n.a.
School life expectancy, 1995, female: 14.5
School life expectancy, 1995, male: 13.9

Contraceptive prevalence, percent*
Year: 1981
Any method: 78
Modern method: 71
* Married women aged 20-44.

Maternity leave benefits, as of early 1990s
Maternity leave: 6 weeks before delivery and 6 weeks after
Percentage of wages covered: 90 (Depending on the period of insurance.)
Provider of coverage: social security

Labor force, total: 4,778,698
Labor force, female (percent of total): 47.9

Women in parliament as of January 1997
Single or lower house, percent of seats occupied by women: 40.4
Upper house, percent of seats occupied by women: n.a.

SWITZERLAND

Estimated 1999 population, in thousands, total: 7,345
Estimated 1999 population, in thousands, female: 3,714
Sex ratio 1999 (males per 100 females): 98

Birth rate, crude (per 1,000 people): 11.2
Fertility rate, total (births per woman): 1.50
Life expectancy at birth, female (years): 82.2
Life expectancy at birth, male (years): 76.1

Mortality rate, adult, female (per 1,000 female adults): 50.0
Mortality rate, adult, male (per 1,000 male adults): 106.0
Mortality rate, infant (per 1,000 live births): 4.5

Illiteracy rate, adult female (percent of females aged 15+): n.a.
Illiteracy rate, adult male (percent of males aged 15+): n.a.
School life expectancy, 1995, female: 13.5
School life expectancy, 1995, male: 14.5

Contraceptive prevalence, percent
Year: 1980
Any method: 71
Modern method: 65

Maternity leave benefits, as of early 1990s
Maternity leave: 8 weeks
Percentage of wages covered: 100 (Depending on the period of service.)
Provider of coverage: employer

Labor force, total: 3,827,520
Labor force, female (percent of total): 40.0

Women in parliament as of January 1997
Single or lower house, percent of seats occupied by women: 21
Upper house, percent of seats occupied by women: 17.4

SYRIAN ARAB REPUBLIC

Estimated 1999 population, in thousands, total: 15,725
Estimated 1999 population, in thousands, female: 7,782
Sex ratio 1999 (males per 100 females): 102

Birth rate, crude (per 1,000 people): 29.4
Fertility rate, total (births per woman): 4.00
Life expectancy at birth, female (years): 71.2
Life expectancy at birth, male (years): 66.7

Mortality rate, adult, female (per 1,000 female adults): 141.0
Mortality rate, adult, male (per 1,000 male adults): 206.0
Mortality rate, infant (per 1,000 live births): 31.0

Illiteracy rate, adult female (percent of females aged 15+): 43.5
Illiteracy rate, adult male (percent of males aged 15+): 13.5
School life expectancy, 1995, female: 8.5
School life expectancy, 1995, male: 9.8

Contraceptive prevalence, percent
  Year: 1995
  Any method: 40
  Modern method: 28
Maternity leave benefits, as of early 1990s
  Maternity leave: 50 days
  Percentage of wages covered: 70
  Provider of coverage: employer
Labor force, total: 4,617,382
Labor force, female (percent of total): 26.2

Women in parliament as of January 1997
  Single or lower house, percent of seats occupied by women: 9.6
  Upper house, percent of seats occupied by women: n.a.

TAIWAN

Estimated 1995 population, in thousands, total: 21,500 (
Estimated 1995 population, in thousands, female: n.a.
Sex ratio 1995 (males per 100 females): n.a.

Birth rate, crude (per 1,000 people): 15.33 (1995 est.)
Fertility rate, total (births per woman): 1.8 (1995 est.)
Life expectancy at birth, female (years): 78.9 (1995 est.)
Life expectancy at birth, male (years): 72.7 (1995 est.)

Mortality rate, adult, female (per 1,000 female adults): n.a.
Mortality rate, adult, male (per 1,000 male adults): n.a.
Mortality rate, infant (per 1,000 live births): 5.6 (1995 est.)

Illiteracy rate, adult female (percent of females aged 15+): n.a.
Illiteracy rate, adult male (percent of males aged 15+): n.a.
School life expectancy, 1995, female: n.a.
School life expectancy, 1995, male: n.a.

Contraceptive prevalence, percent
  Year: n.a.
  Any method: n.a.
  Modern method: n.a.
Maternity leave benefits, as of early 1990s
  Maternity leave: n.a.
  Percentage of wages covered: n.a.
  Provider of coverage: n.a.
Labor force, total: n.a.
Labor force, female (percent of total): n.a.

Women in parliament as of January 1997
  Single or lower house, percent of seats occupied by women: n.a.
  Upper house, percent of seats occupied by women: n.a.

TAJIKISTAN

Estimated 1999 population, in thousands, total: 6,104
Estimated 1999 population, in thousands, female: 3,064
Sex ratio 1999 (males per 100 females): 99

Birth rate, crude (per 1,000 people): 23.2
Fertility rate, total (births per woman): 3.50
Life expectancy at birth, female (years): 71.2
Life expectancy at birth, male (years): 65.5

Mortality rate, adult, female (per 1,000 female adults): 143.0
Mortality rate, adult, male (per 1,000 male adults): 234.0
Mortality rate, infant (per 1,000 live births): 30.0

Illiteracy rate, adult female (percent of females aged 15+): 1.7
Illiteracy rate, adult male (percent of males aged 15+): 0.6
School life expectancy, 1995, female: n.a.
School life expectancy, 1995, male: n.a.

Contraceptive prevalence, percent
  Year: 1990
  Any method: 21
  Modern method: n.a.
Maternity leave benefits, as of early 1990s
  Maternity leave: n.a.
  Percentage of wages covered: n.a.
  Provider of coverage: n.a.
Labor force, total: 2,286,460
Labor force, female (percent of total): 44.1

Women in parliament as of January 1997
  Single or lower house, percent of seats occupied by women: 2.8
  Upper house, percent of seats occupied by women: n.a.

TANZANIA

Estimated 1999 population, in thousands, total: 32,792
Estimated 1999 population, in thousands, female: 16,541
Sex ratio 1999 (males per 100 females): 98

Birth rate, crude (per 1,000 people): 41.2
Fertility rate, total (births per woman): 5.50
Life expectancy at birth, female (years): 49.1
Life expectancy at birth, male (years): 46.8

Mortality rate, adult, female (per 1,000 female adults): 460.0
Mortality rate, adult, male (per 1,000 male adults): 502.0
Mortality rate, infant (per 1,000 live births): 85.0

Illiteracy rate, adult female (percent of females aged 15+): 38.1
Illiteracy rate, adult male (percent of males aged 15+): 18.3
School life expectancy, 1995, female: n.a.
School life expectancy, 1995, male: n.a.

Contraceptive prevalence, percent
  Year: 1996
  Any method: 18
  Modern method: 13

Maternity leave benefits, as of early 1990s
  Maternity leave: n.a.
  Percentage of wages covered: n.a.
  Provider of coverage: n.a.

Labor force, total: 15,971,211
Labor force, female (percent of total): 49.3

Women in parliament as of January 1997
  Single or lower house, percent of seats occupied by women: 17.5
  Upper house, percent of seats occupied by women: n.a.

THAILAND

Estimated 1999 population, in thousands, total: 60,856
Estimated 1999 population, in thousands, female: 30,482
Sex ratio 1999 (males per 100 females): 100

Birth rate, crude (per 1,000 people): 16.7
Fertility rate, total (births per woman): 1.74
Life expectancy at birth, female (years): 72.0
Life expectancy at birth, male (years): 65.8

Mortality rate, adult, female (per 1,000 female adults): 122.0
Mortality rate, adult, male (per 1,000 male adults): 219.0
Mortality rate, infant (per 1,000 live births): 33.4

Illiteracy rate, adult female (percent of females aged 15+): 7.2
Illiteracy rate, adult male (percent of males aged 15+): 3.3
School life expectancy, 1995, female: n.a.
School life expectancy, 1995, male: n.a.

Contraceptive prevalence, percent*
  Year: 1993
  Any method: 74
  Modern method: 72
  * All women aged 15-44 years.

Maternity leave benefits, as of early 1990s
  Maternity leave: 90 days
  Percentage of wages covered: 100 for 45 days
  Provider of coverage: employer

Labor force, total: 36,361,200
Labor force, female (percent of total): 46.4

Women in parliament as of January 1997
  Single or lower house, percent of seats occupied by women: 5.6
  Upper house, percent of seats occupied by women: 8.1

TOGO

Estimated 1999 population, in thousands, total: 4,512
Estimated 1999 population, in thousands, female: 2,275
Sex ratio 1999 (males per 100 females): 98

Birth rate, crude (per 1,000 people): 41.0
Fertility rate, total (births per woman): 6.05
Life expectancy at birth, female (years): 50.1
Life expectancy at birth, male (years): 47.6

Mortality rate, adult, female (per 1,000 female adults): 432.0
Mortality rate, adult, male (per 1,000 male adults): 477.0
Mortality rate, infant (per 1,000 live births): 86.0

Illiteracy rate, adult female (percent of females aged 15+): 61.7
Illiteracy rate, adult male (percent of males aged 15+): 31.3
School life expectancy, 1995, female: n.a.
School life expectancy, 1995, male: n.a.

Contraceptive prevalence, percent
  Year: 1998
  Any method: 14†
  Modern method: 7
  † Excludes "prolonged abstinence," reported as the current method by 10 percent.

Maternity leave benefits, as of early 1990s
  Maternity leave: n.a.
  Percentage of wages covered: n.a.
  Provider of coverage: n.a.

Labor force, total: 1,781,348
Labor force, female (percent of total): 39.9

Women in parliament as of January 1997
  Single or lower house, percent of seats occupied by women: 1.2
  Upper house, percent of seats occupied by women: n.a.

TONGA

Estimated 1994 population, in thousands, total: 97
Estimated 1994 population, in thousands, female: 48
Sex ratio 1994 (males per 100 females): 103

Birth rate, crude (per 1,000 people): 28.0
Fertility rate, total (births per woman): 3.60
Life expectancy at birth, female (years): 72.5
Life expectancy at birth, male (years): 68.5

Mortality rate, adult, female (per 1,000 female adults): 132.0
Mortality rate, adult, male (per 1,000 male adults): 187.0
Mortality rate, infant (per 1,000 live births): 22.0

Illiteracy rate, adult female (percent of females aged 15+): n.a.
Illiteracy rate, adult male (percent of males aged 15+): n.a.
School life expectancy, 1995, female: n.a.
School life expectancy, 1995, male: n.a.

Contraceptive prevalence, percent
  Year: 1998
  Any method: 74
  Modern method: 56

Maternity leave benefits, as of early 1990s
  Maternity leave: n.a.
  Percentage of wages covered: n.a.
  Provider of coverage: n.a.

Labor force, total: n.a.
Labor force, female (percent of total): n.a.

Women in parliament as of January 1997
  Single or lower house, percent of seats occupied by women: 0
  Upper house, percent of seats occupied by women: n.a.

TRINIDAD AND TOBAGO

Estimated 1999 population, in thousands, total: 1,288
Estimated 1999 population, in thousands, female: 647
Sex ratio 1999 (males per 100 females): 99

Birth rate, crude (per 1,000 people): 16.2
Fertility rate, total (births per woman): 1.90
Life expectancy at birth, female (years): 75.2
Life expectancy at birth, male (years): 70.5

Mortality rate, adult, female (per 1,000 female adults): 103.0
Mortality rate, adult, male (per 1,000 male adults): 168.0
Mortality rate, infant (per 1,000 live births): 12.0

Illiteracy rate, adult female (percent of females aged 15+): 3.0
Illiteracy rate, adult male (percent of males aged 15+): 1.3
School life expectancy, 1995, female: 11.3
School life expectancy, 1995, male: 10.1

Contraceptive prevalence, percent
  Year: 1987
  Any method: 53
  Modern method: 44

Maternity leave benefits, as of early 1990s
  Maternity leave: 6 weeks before delivery, 1 week of confinement and 6 weeks after
  Percentage of wages covered: 60
  Provider of coverage: national insurance

Labor force, total: 562,139
Labor force, female (percent of total): 33.4

Women in parliament as of January 1997
  Single or lower house, percent of seats occupied by women: 11.1
  Upper house, percent of seats occupied by women: 29

TUNISIA

Estimated 1999 population, in thousands, total: 9,460
Estimated 1999 population, in thousands, female: 4,682
Sex ratio 1999 (males per 100 females): 102

Birth rate, crude (per 1,000 people): 22.5
Fertility rate, total (births per woman): 2.80
Life expectancy at birth, female (years): 70.7
Life expectancy at birth, male (years): 68.4

Mortality rate, adult, female (per 1,000 female adults): 153.0
Mortality rate, adult, male (per 1,000 male adults): 171.0
Mortality rate, infant (per 1,000 live births): 30.0

Illiteracy rate, adult female (percent of females aged 15+): 44.2
Illiteracy rate, adult male (percent of males aged 15+): 21.9
School life expectancy, 1995, female: n.a.
School life expectancy, 1995, male: n.a.

Contraceptive prevalence, percent
  Year: 1994
  Any method: 60
  Modern method: 51

Maternity leave benefits, as of early 1990s
  Maternity leave: 30 days
  Percentage of wages covered: two-thirds of daily wage
  Provider of coverage: social security

Labor force, total: 3,501,700
Labor force, female (percent of total): 30.9

Women in parliament as of January 1997
  Single or lower house, percent of seats occupied by women: 6.7
  Upper house, percent of seats occupied by women: n.a.

TURKEY

Estimated 1999 population, in thousands, total: 65,546
Estimated 1999 population, in thousands, female: 32,436
Sex ratio 1999 (males per 100 females): 102

Birth rate, crude (per 1,000 people): 22.2
Fertility rate, total (births per woman): 2.50
Life expectancy at birth, female (years): 71.7
Life expectancy at birth, male (years): 66.5

Mortality rate, adult, female (per 1,000 female adults): 120.0
Mortality rate, adult, male (per 1,000 male adults): 165.0
Mortality rate, infant (per 1,000 live births): 39.9

Illiteracy rate, adult female (percent of females aged 15+): 26.1
Illiteracy rate, adult male (percent of males aged 15+): 7.6
School life expectancy, 1995, female: 8.7
School life expectancy, 1995, male: 10.6

Contraceptive prevalence, percent
  Year: 1993
  Any method: 63
  Modern method: 35

Maternity leave benefits, as of early 1990s
  Maternity leave: 6 weeks before delivery and 6 weeks after
  Percentage of wages covered: two-thirds
  Provider of coverage: social insurance

Labor force, total: 29,960,150
Labor force, female (percent of total): 36.7

Women in parliament as of January 1997
  Single or lower house, percent of seats occupied by women: 2.4
  Upper house, percent of seats occupied by women: n.a.

TURKMENISTAN

Estimated 1999 population, in thousands, total: 4,384
Estimated 1999 population, in thousands, female: 2,215
Sex ratio 1999 (males per 100 females): 98

Birth rate, crude (per 1,000 people): 24.2
Fertility rate, total (births per woman): 3.00
Life expectancy at birth, female (years): 69.3
Life expectancy at birth, male (years): 62.3

Mortality rate, adult, female (per 1,000 female adults): 159.0
Mortality rate, adult, male (per 1,000 male adults): 282.0
Mortality rate, infant (per 1,000 live births): 40.0

Illiteracy rate, adult female (percent of females aged 15+): n.a.
Illiteracy rate, adult male (percent of males aged 15+): n.a.
School life expectancy, 1995, female: n.a.
School life expectancy, 1995, male: n.a.

Contraceptive prevalence, percent
  Year: 1990
  Any method: 20
  Modern method: n.a.

Maternity leave benefits, as of early 1990s
  Maternity leave: n.a.
  Percentage of wages covered: n.a.
  Provider of coverage: n.a.

Labor force, total: 1,956,360
Labor force, female (percent of total): 45.5

Women in parliament as of January 1997
  Single or lower house, percent of seats occupied by women: 18
  Upper house, percent of seats occupied by women: n.a.

TUVALU

Estimated 1995 population, in thousands, total: 10
Estimated 1995 population, in thousands, female: n.a.
Sex ratio 1995 (males per 100 females): n.a.

Birth rate, crude (per 1,000 people): 24.8 (1995 est.)
Fertility rate, total (births per woman): 3.1 (1995 est.)
Life expectancy at birth, female (years): 64.3 (1995 est.)
Life expectancy at birth, male (years): 61.9 (1995 est.)

Mortality rate, adult, female (per 1,000 female adults): n.a.
Mortality rate, adult, male (per 1,000 male adults): n.a.
Mortality rate, infant (per 1,000 live births): 27.9 (1995 est.)

Illiteracy rate, adult female (percent of females aged 15+): n.a.
Illiteracy rate, adult male (percent of males aged 15+): n.a.
School life expectancy, 1995, female: n.a.
School life expectancy, 1995, male: n.a.

Contraceptive prevalence, percent
  Year: n.a.
  Any method: n.a.
  Modern method: n.a.

Maternity leave benefits, as of early 1990s
  Maternity leave: n.a.
  Percentage of wages covered: n.a.
  Provider of coverage: n.a.

Labor force, total: n.a.
Labor force, female (percent of total): n.a.

Women in parliament as of January 1997
  Single or lower house, percent of seats occupied by women: n.a.
  Upper house, percent of seats occupied by women: n.a.

UGANDA

Estimated 1999 population, in thousands, total: 21,143
Estimated 1999 population, in thousands, female: 10,620
Sex ratio 1999 (males per 100 females): 99

Birth rate, crude (per 1,000 people): 47.9
Fertility rate, total (births per woman): 6.60
Life expectancy at birth, female (years): 42.1
Life expectancy at birth, male (years): 42.8

Mortality rate, adult, female (per 1,000 female adults): 590.0
Mortality rate, adult, male (per 1,000 male adults): 580.0
Mortality rate, infant (per 1,000 live births): 99.0

Illiteracy rate, adult female (percent of females aged 15+): 46.9
Illiteracy rate, adult male (percent of males aged 15+): 24.7
School life expectancy, 1995, female: n.a.
School life expectancy, 1995, male: n.a.

Contraceptive prevalence, percent
  Year: 1995
  Any method: 15
  Modern method: 8

Maternity leave benefits, as of early 1990s
  Maternity leave: 8 weeks
  Percentage of wages covered: n.a.
  Provider of coverage: n.a.

Labor force, total: 10,158,620
Labor force, female (percent of total): 47.7

Women in parliament as of January 1997
  Single or lower house, percent of seats occupied by women: 18.1
  Upper house, percent of seats occupied by women: n.a.

UKRAINE

Estimated 1999 population, in thousands, total: 50,658
Estimated 1999 population, in thousands, female: 27,075
Sex ratio 1999 (males per 100 females): 87

Birth rate, crude (per 1,000 people): 8.7
Fertility rate, total (births per woman): 1.30
Life expectancy at birth, female (years): 73.0
Life expectancy at birth, male (years): 62.0

Mortality rate, adult, female (per 1,000 female adults): 135.0
Mortality rate, adult, male (per 1,000 male adults): 350.0
Mortality rate, infant (per 1,000 live births): 14.0

Illiteracy rate, adult female (percent of females aged 15+): n.a.
Illiteracy rate, adult male (percent of males aged 15+): n.a.
School life expectancy, 1995, female: n.a.
School life expectancy, 1995, male: n.a.

Contraceptive prevalence, percent
  Year: 1990
  Any method: 23
  Modern method: n.a.

Maternity leave benefits, as of early 1990s
  Maternity leave: n.a.
  Percentage of wages covered: n.a.
  Provider of coverage: n.a.

Labor force, total: 25,349,000
Labor force, female (percent of total): 48.6

Women in parliament as of January 1997
  Single or lower house, percent of seats occupied by women: 3.8
  Upper house, percent of seats occupied by women: n.a.

UNITED ARAB EMIRATES

Estimated 1999 population, in thousands, total: 2,397
Estimated 1999 population, in thousands, female: 876
Sex ratio 1999 (males per 100 females): 174

Birth rate, crude (per 1,000 people): 17.7
Fertility rate, total (births per woman): 3.50
Life expectancy at birth, female (years): 76.5
Life expectancy at birth, male (years): 73.9

Mortality rate, adult, female (per 1,000 female adults): 93.0
Mortality rate, adult, male (per 1,000 male adults): 127.0
Mortality rate, infant (per 1,000 live births): 8.0

Illiteracy rate, adult female (percent of females aged 15+): 23.2
Illiteracy rate, adult male (percent of males aged 15+): 26.0
School life expectancy, 1995, female: 10.3
School life expectancy, 1995, male: 9.8

Contraceptive prevalence, percent*
  Year: 1995
  Any method: 27†
  Modern method: 44
  * Married women under 50 years.
  † Adjusted from source to exclude breastfeeding.

Maternity leave benefits, as of early 1990s
  Maternity leave: 45 days
  Percentage of wages covered: 100
  Provider of coverage: employer

Labor force, total: 1,290,000
Labor force, female (percent of total): 13.8

Women in parliament as of January 1997
  Single or lower house, percent of seats occupied by women: 0
  Upper house, percent of seats occupied by women: n.a.

UNITED KINGDOM

Estimated 1999 population, in thousands, total: 58,744
Estimated 1999 population, in thousands, female: 29,910
Sex ratio 1999 (males per 100 females): 96

Birth rate, crude (per 1,000 people): 11.9
Fertility rate, total (births per woman): 1.70
Life expectancy at birth, female (years): 79.8
Life expectancy at birth, male (years): 74.5

Mortality rate, adult, female (per 1,000 female adults): 67.0
Mortality rate, adult, male (per 1,000 male adults): 123.0
Mortality rate, infant (per 1,000 live births): 5.9

Illiteracy rate, adult female (percent of females aged 15+): n.a.
Illiteracy rate, adult male (percent of males aged 15+): n.a.
School life expectancy, 1995, female: 16.6
School life expectancy, 1995, male: 16.1

Contraceptive prevalence, percent*
  Year: 1993
  Any method: 82
  Modern method: 82
  * Married women aged 16-41 years; excludes Northern Ireland.

Maternity leave benefits, as of early 1990s
  Maternity leave: 14 weeks
  Percentage of wages covered: 90
  Provider of coverage: national insurance

Labor force, total: 29,504,500
Labor force, female (percent of total): 43.6

Women in parliament as of January 1997
  Single or lower house, percent of seats occupied by women: 9.5
  Upper house, percent of seats occupied by women: 6.9

UNITED STATES

Estimated 1999 population, in thousands, total: 276,219
Estimated 1999 population, in thousands, female: 140,091
Sex ratio 1999 (males per 100 females): 97

Birth rate, crude (per 1,000 people): 14.6
Fertility rate, total (births per woman): 1.99
Life expectancy at birth, female (years): 79.2
Life expectancy at birth, male (years): 73.2

Mortality rate, adult, female (per 1,000 female adults): 80.0
Mortality rate, adult, male (per 1,000 male adults): 150.0
Mortality rate, infant (per 1,000 live births): 7.1

Illiteracy rate, adult female (percent of females aged 15+): n.a.
Illiteracy rate, adult male (percent of males aged 15+): n.a.
School life expectancy, 1995, female: 16.2
School life expectancy, 1995, male: 15.4

Contraceptive prevalence, percent*
  Year: 1990
  Any method: 71
  Modern method: 67
  * All women aged 15-44 years

Maternity leave benefits, as of early 1990s
  Maternity leave: 12 weeks
  Percentage of wages covered: unpaid
  Provider of coverage: n.a.

Labor force, total: 136,494,368
Labor force, female (percent of total): 45.5

Women in parliament as of January 1997
  Single or lower house, percent of seats occupied by women: 11.7
  Upper house, percent of seats occupied by women: 9

For an expanded statistical profile for the United States, please refer to Part Three: Spotlight on the United States.

URUGUAY

Estimated 1999 population, in thousands, total: 3,313
Estimated 1999 population, in thousands, female: 1,706
Sex ratio 1999 (males per 100 females): 94

Birth rate, crude (per 1,000 people): 17.7
Fertility rate, total (births per woman): 2.40
Life expectancy at birth, female (years): 77.7
Life expectancy at birth, male (years): 69.8

Mortality rate, adult, female (per 1,000 female adults): 76.0
Mortality rate, adult, male (per 1,000 male adults): 171.0
Mortality rate, infant (per 1,000 live births): 16.4

Illiteracy rate, adult female (percent of females aged 15+): 2.2
Illiteracy rate, adult male (percent of males aged 15+): 3.0
School life expectancy, 1995, female: n.a.
School life expectancy, 1995, male: n.a.

Contraceptive prevalence, percent
  Year: n.a.
  Any method: n.a.
  Modern method: n.a.

Maternity leave benefits, as of early 1990s
  Maternity leave: 6 weeks before delivery and 6 weeks after
  Percentage of wages covered: 100
  Provider of coverage: social security

Labor force, total: 1,469,727
Labor force, female (percent of total): 41.0

Women in parliament as of January 1997
  Single or lower house, percent of seats occupied by women: 7.1
  Upper house, percent of seats occupied by women: 6.5

UZBEKISTAN

Estimated 1999 population, in thousands, total: 23,941
Estimated 1999 population, in thousands, female: 12,054
Sex ratio 1999 (males per 100 females): 99

Birth rate, crude (per 1,000 people): 26.8
Fertility rate, total (births per woman): 3.30
Life expectancy at birth, female (years): 72.4
Life expectancy at birth, male (years): 66.1

Mortality rate, adult, female (per 1,000 female adults): 128.0
Mortality rate, adult, male (per 1,000 male adults): 230.0
Mortality rate, infant (per 1,000 live births): n.a.

Illiteracy rate, adult female (percent of females aged 15+): n.a.
Illiteracy rate, adult male (percent of males aged 15+): n.a.
School life expectancy, 1995, female: n.a.
School life expectancy, 1995, male: n.a.

Contraceptive prevalence, percent
  Year: 1996
  Any method: 56
  Modern method: 51

Maternity leave benefits, as of early 1990s
  Maternity leave: n.a.
  Percentage of wages covered: n.a.
  Provider of coverage: n.a.

Labor force, total: 9,703,470
Labor force, female (percent of total): 46.5

Women in parliament as of January 1997
  Single or lower house, percent of seats occupied by women: 6
  Upper house, percent of seats occupied by women: not applicable

VANUATU

Estimated 1999 population, in thousands, total: 186
Estimated 1999 population, in thousands, female: 93
Sex ratio 1999 (males per 100 females): 100

Birth rate, crude (per 1,000 people): 31.6
Fertility rate, total (births per woman): 4.70
Life expectancy at birth, female (years): 66.0
Life expectancy at birth, male (years): 63.3

Mortality rate, adult, female (per 1,000 female adults): 232.0
Mortality rate, adult, male (per 1,000 male adults): 267.0
Mortality rate, infant (per 1,000 live births): 37.0

Illiteracy rate, adult female (percent of females aged 15+): n.a.
Illiteracy rate, adult male (percent of males aged 15+): n.a.
School life expectancy, 1995, female: n.a.
School life expectancy, 1995, male: n.a.

Contraceptive prevalence, percent
  Year: 1991
  Any method: 15
  Modern method: 15

Maternity leave benefits, as of early 1990s
  Maternity leave: n.a.
  Percentage of wages covered: n.a.
  Provider of coverage: n.a.

Labor force, total: n.a.
Labor force, female (percent of total): n.a.

Women in parliament as of January 1997
  Single or lower house, percent of seats occupied by women: n.a.
  Upper house, percent of seats occupied by women: not applicable

VENEZUELA

Estimated 1999 population, in thousands, total: 23,706
Estimated 1999 population, in thousands, female: 11,776
Sex ratio 1999 (males per 100 females): 101

Birth rate, crude (per 1,000 people): 24.8
Fertility rate, total (births per woman): 2.98
Life expectancy at birth, female (years): 75.7
Life expectancy at birth, male (years): 70.0

Mortality rate, adult, female (per 1,000 female adults): 91.0
Mortality rate, adult, male (per 1,000 male adults): 160.0
Mortality rate, infant (per 1,000 live births): 21.0

Illiteracy rate, adult female (percent of females aged 15+): 8.5
Illiteracy rate, adult male (percent of males aged 15+): 7.5
School life expectancy, 1995, female: 10.7
School life expectancy, 1995, male: 10.2

Contraceptive prevalence, percent*
  Year: 1982
  Any method: 52
  Modern method: 40
  * All women aged 15-44 years.

Maternity leave benefits, as of early 1990s
  Maternity leave: 6 weeks before delivery and 12 weeks after
  Percentage of wages covered: 100
  Provider of coverage: social security

Labor force, total: 9,110,800
Labor force, female (percent of total): 33.8

Women in parliament as of January 1997
  Single or lower house, percent of seats occupied by women: 5.9
  Upper house, percent of seats occupied by women: 8

VIETNAM

Estimated 1999 population, in thousands, total: 78,705
Estimated 1999 population, in thousands, female: 39,858
Sex ratio 1999 (males per 100 females): 97

Birth rate, crude (per 1,000 people): 20.8
Fertility rate, total (births per woman): 2.40
Life expectancy at birth, female (years): 70.6
Life expectancy at birth, male (years): 65.8

Mortality rate, adult, female (per 1,000 female adults): 150.0
Mortality rate, adult, male (per 1,000 male adults): 205.0
Mortality rate, infant (per 1,000 live births): 29.0

Illiteracy rate, adult female (percent of females aged 15+): 11.0
Illiteracy rate, adult male (percent of males aged 15+): 4.9
School life expectancy, 1995, female: n.a.
School life expectancy, 1995, male: n.a.

Contraceptive prevalence, percent
Year: 1994
Any method: 65
Modern method: 44

Maternity leave benefits, as of early 1990s
Maternity leave: 4-6 months
Percentage of wages covered: 100 (An additional allowance equal to one month's salary for the first two children.)
Provider of coverage: social insurance

Labor force, total: 39,122,608
Labor force, female (percent of total): 49.1

Women in parliament as of January 1997
Single or lower house, percent of seats occupied by women: 18.5
Upper house, percent of seats occupied by women: not applicable

YEMEN, REP.

Estimated 1999 population, in thousands, total: 17,488
Estimated 1999 population, in thousands, female: 8,679
Sex ratio 1999 (males per 100 females): 101

Birth rate, crude (per 1,000 people): 40.0
Fertility rate, total (births per woman): 6.40
Life expectancy at birth, female (years): 54.8
Life expectancy at birth, male (years): 53.8

Mortality rate, adult, female (per 1,000 female adults): 330.0
Mortality rate, adult, male (per 1,000 male adults): 340.0
Mortality rate, infant (per 1,000 live births): 95.7

Illiteracy rate, adult female (percent of females aged 15+): 79.1
Illiteracy rate, adult male (percent of males aged 15+): 35.8
School life expectancy, 1995, female: n.a.
School life expectancy, 1995, male: n.a.

Contraceptive prevalence, percent
Year: 1997
Any method: 13†
Modern method: 10
† Adjusted from source to exclude breastfeeding.

Maternity leave benefits, as of early 1990s
Maternity leave: 70 days
Percentage of wages covered: 70
Provider of coverage: employer

Labor force, total: 5,143,008
Labor force, female (percent of total): 27.9

Women in parliament as of January 1997
Single or lower house, percent of seats occupied by women: 0.7
Upper house, percent of seats occupied by women: not applicable

YUGOSLAVIA, FR (SERBIA/MONTENEGRO)

Estimated 1999 population, in thousands, total: 10,637
Estimated 1999 population, in thousands, female: 5,351
Sex ratio 1999 (males per 100 females): 99

Birth rate, crude (per 1,000 people): 13.2
Fertility rate, total (births per woman): 1.88
Life expectancy at birth, female (years): 74.7
Life expectancy at birth, male (years): 69.6

Mortality rate, adult, female (per 1,000 female adults): 108.0
Mortality rate, adult, male (per 1,000 male adults): 180.0
Mortality rate, infant (per 1,000 live births): 14.0

Illiteracy rate, adult female (percent of females aged 15+): n.a.
Illiteracy rate, adult male (percent of males aged 15+): n.a.
School life expectancy, 1995, female: n.a.
School life expectancy, 1995, male: n.a.

Contraceptive prevalence, percent
Year: n.a.
Any method: n.a.
Modern method: n.a.

Maternity leave benefits, as of early 1990s
Maternity leave: n.a.
Percentage of wages covered: n.a.
Provider of coverage: n.a.

Labor force, total: 4,988,580
Labor force, female (percent of total): 42.5

Women in parliament as of January 1997
Single or lower house, percent of seats occupied by women: n.a.
Upper house, percent of seats occupied by women: 2.5

ZAMBIA

Estimated 1999 population, in thousands, total: 8,976
Estimated 1999 population, in thousands, female: 4,537
Sex ratio 1999 (males per 100 females): 98

Birth rate, crude (per 1,000 people): 42.3
Fertility rate, total (births per woman): 5.60
Life expectancy at birth, female (years): 43.3
Life expectancy at birth, male (years): 43.0

Mortality rate, adult, female (per 1,000 female adults): 524.0
Mortality rate, adult, male (per 1,000 male adults): 512.0
Mortality rate, infant (per 1,000 live births): 113.0

Illiteracy rate, adult female (percent of females aged 15+): 32.5
Illiteracy rate, adult male (percent of males aged 15+): 16.7
School life expectancy, 1995, female: 6.8
School life expectancy, 1995, male: 7.9

Contraceptive prevalence, percent
  Year: 1996
  Any method: 25†
  Modern method: 14
  † Adjusted from source to exclude breastfeeding.

Maternity leave benefits, as of early 1990s
  Maternity leave: 12 weeks
  Percentage of wages covered: 100
  Provider of coverage: employer

Labor force, total: 3,966,148
Labor force, female (percent of total): 45.2

Women in parliament as of January 1997
  Single or lower house, percent of seats occupied by women: 9.7
  Upper house, percent of seats occupied by women: not applicable

ZIMBABWE

Estimated 1999 population, in thousands, total: 11,529
Estimated 1999 population, in thousands, female: 5,806
Sex ratio 1999 (males per 100 females): 99

Birth rate, crude (per 1,000 people): 31.4
Fertility rate, total (births per woman): 3.80
Life expectancy at birth, female (years): 54.0
Life expectancy at birth, male (years): 50.8

Mortality rate, adult, female (per 1,000 female adults): 388.0
Mortality rate, adult, male (per 1,000 male adults): 449.0
Mortality rate, infant (per 1,000 live births): 69.0

Illiteracy rate, adult female (percent of females aged 15+): 12.4
Illiteracy rate, adult male (percent of males aged 15+): 5.7
School life expectancy, 1995, female: n.a.
School life expectancy, 1995, male: n.a.

Contraceptive prevalence, percent
  Year: 1994
  Any method: 48
  Modern method: 42

Maternity leave benefits, as of early 1990s
  Maternity leave: 90 days
  Percentage of wages covered: 60 (75 percent if annual
  leave is forfeitted)
  Provider of coverage: employer

Labor force, total: 5,275,326
Labor force, female (percent of total): 44.4

Women in parliament as of January 1997
  Single or lower house, percent of seats occupied by women: 14.7
  Upper house, percent of seats occupied by women: not applicable

Spotlight on the United States

Population

Resident Population, by Age and Sex: 1997

In thousands. Excludes Armed Forces overseas.

Year and Sex	Total, all years	Under 5 years	5–9 years	10–14 years	15–19 years	20–24 years	25–29 years	30–34 years	35–39 years
1997 total	267,636	19,150	19,738	19,040	19,068	17,512	18,869	20,741	22,625
1997 female	136,618	9,349	9,634	9,283	9,241	8,532	9,399	10,401	11,338

Year and sex	40–44 years	45–49 years	50–54 years	55–59 years	60–64 years	65–74 years	75–84 years	85 years and over
1997 total	21,373	18,470	15,163	11,757	10,056	18,499	11,706	3,871
1997 female	10,777	9,396	7,780	6,111	5,311	10,230	7,077	2,759

Source: U.S. Bureau of the Census, *Current Population Reports*, P25-1095; and Population Paper Listings 91.

Resident Population Projections, by Age and Sex: 1998 to 2050

In thousands.

Year and Sex	Total	Under 5 years	5–13 years	14–17 years	18–24 years	25–34 years	35–44 years	45–54 years	55–64 years	65–74 years	75–84 years	85 years and over
2000 Total (projection)	274,634	18,987	36,043	15,752	26,258	37,233	44,659	37,030	23,962	18,136	12,315	4,259
2000 Female (projection)	140,453	9,274	17,589	7,662	12,920	18,699	22,478	18,938	12,529	9,956	7,377	3,031

Source: U.S. Bureau of the Census, *Current Population Reports*, P25-1130.

Ratio of Males to Females, by Age Group: 1997 and Projected 2000

Number of males per 100 females. Total resident population.

Age	1997 (July 1)	2000 (July 1)	Age	1997 (July 1)	2000 (July 1)
All ages	95.9	95.5	25 to 44 years	99.5	98.9
Under 14 Years	104.9	104.8	45 to 64 years	93.9	93.8
14 to 24 years	105.8	104.1	65 years and over	69.8	70.4

Source: U.S. Bureau of the Census, *Current Population Reports*, P25-1095 and P25-1130; and Population Paper Listings PPL-91.

Live Births, Birth Rates, and Fertility Rates, by State and Race: 1995

Number of births, except rate. Registered births. Excludes births to nonresidents of the United States. By race of mother.

State	All races[1]	White		Black		Hispanic[2]	Birth Rate[3]	Fertility Rate[4]
		Total	Non-Hispanic	Total	Non-Hispanic			
United States	3,899,589	3,098,885	2,382,638	603,139	587,781	679,768	14.8	65.6
Alabama	60,329	39,759	39,073	19,868	19,830	758	14.2	61.9
Alaska	10,244	7,014	6,581	445	421	574	17.0	73.2
Arizona	72,463	63,777	38,474	2,238	2,166	25,504	17.2	79.5
Arkansas	35,175	26,984	25,962	7,676	7,648	1,004	14.2	65.0
California	552,045	449,889	196,695	40,260	39,284	254,001	17.5	76.6
Colorado	54,332	49,634	38,142	2,619	2,518	11,523	14.5	62.5
Connecticut	44,334	37,643	30,867	5,396	4,974	5,505	13.5	61.0
Delaware	10,266	7,689	7,134	2,362	2,326	585	14.3	61.2
Dist. of Columbia	9,014	2,023	1,354	6,780	6,736	685	16.3	65.3
Florida	188,723	142,326	108,831	42,142	41,191	34,509	13.3	64.9
Georgia	112,282	71,811	66,497	38,462	38,217	5,067	15.6	64.5
Hawaii	18,595	4,968	4,311	564	540	2,029	15.7	72.2
Idaho	18,035	17,477	15,375	74	71	2,040	15.5	70.5
Illinois	185,812	142,225	110,180	37,507	37,308	32,166	15.7	69.3
Indiana	82,835	73,145	70,525	8,737	8,674	2,546	14.3	62.2
Iowa	36,810	34,931	33,463	992	963	1,279	13.0	59.9
Kansas	37,201	33,125	30,010	2,890	2,857	2,828	14.5	66.1
Kentucky	52,377	47,127	46,634	4,784	4,759	493	13.6	59.0
Louisiana	65,641	37,519	36,448	26,844	26,784	1,158	15.1	65.2
Maine	13,896	13,554	13,248	79	66	112	11.2	49.7
Maryland	72,396	46,970	43,477	22,674	22,348	3,155	14.4	60.6
Massachusetts	81,648	70,242	63,067	7,778	6,272	8,109	13.4	57.9
Michigan	134,642	106,509	95,715	25,015	24,679	4,781	14.1	61.3
Minnesota	63,263	56,702	49,834	2,905	2,705	1,915	13.7	60.5
Mississippi	41,344	21,578	21,321	19,244	19,241	220	15.3	66.5
Missouri	73,028	60,720	59,423	11,017	10,990	1,288	13.7	61.5
Montana	11,142	9,858	9,226	40	33	282	12.8	60.2
Nebraska	23,243	21,294	19,289	1,220	1,209	1,615	14.2	64.5
Nevada	25,056	21,567	15,459	1,895	1,863	6,124	16.4	75.2
New Hampshire	14,665	14,386	13,659	89	75	214	12.8	54.2
New Jersey	114,828	87,435	69,375	20,973	19,518	18,835	14.5	64.8
New Mexico	26,920	22,694	9,914	508	473	12,900	16.0	71.6
New York	271,369	199,079	121,349	56,213	49,730	54,193	15.0	66.1
North Carolina	101,592	71,413	67,262	26,909	26,833	4,244	14.1	61.7
North Dakota	8,476	7,634	7,375	70	68	147	13.2	61.3
Ohio	154,064	129,185	126,215	22,802	22,702	2,801	13.8	61.0
Oklahoma	45,672	36,038	33,727	4,497	4,469	2,356	13.9	64.3
Oregon	42,811	39,736	34,781	873	860	5,002	13.6	62.2

Live Births, Birth Rates, and Fertility Rates, by State and Race: 1995 (*cont.*)

State	All races[1]	White Total	White Non-Hispanic	Black Total	Black Non-Hispanic	Hispanic[2]	Birth Rate[3]	Fertility Rate[4]
Pennsylvania	151,850	126,987	120,544	21,445	21,062	6,572	12.6	57.8
Rhode Island	12,776	11,289	8,256	915	683	1,554	12.9	57.3
South Carolina	50,926	31,875	31,127	18,410	18,393	763	13.9	59.3
South Dakota	10,475	8,693	8,590	100	97	116	14.4	66.9
Tennessee	73,173	55,964	54,875	16,156	16,130	1,111	13.9	60.6
Texas	322,753	275,090	137,816	38,727	38,434	137,131	17.2	74.5
Utah	39,577	37,610	34,496	243	231	3,110	20.3	86.2
Vermont	6,783	6,659	6,268	39	33	27	11.6	50.2
Virginia	92,578	67,450	62,660	21,307	21,209	4,841	14.0	58.6
Washington	77,228	67,306	56,839	2,962	2,757	8,502	14.2	62.1
West Virginia	21,162	20,237	20,162	807	806	90	11.6	52.7
Wisconsin	67,479	58,155	55,365	6,518	6,476	2,856	13.2	58.8
Wyoming	6,261	5,910	5,368	69	69	548	13.0	59.3

[1]Includes other races not shown separately. [2]Persons of Hispanic origin may be of any race. Births by Hispanic origin of mother. [3]Per 1,000 estimated population.
[4]Per 1,000 women aged 15-44 years estimated.
Source: U.S. National Center for Health Statistics, *Vital Statistics of the United States*, annual, and *Monthly Vital Statistics Report*.

Infant, Maternal, and Neonatal Mortality Rates and Fetal Mortality Ratios, by Race: 1995 and 1996

Deaths per 1,000 live births, except as noted. Excludes deaths of nonresidents of U.S. Race for live births tabulated according to race of mother, for infant and neonatal mortality rates. Race for live births tabulated according to race of mother, for maternal mortality rates and mortality rates.

Item	1995	1996
Infant Deaths[1]	7.6	7.2
White	6.3	6.0
Black and other	(NA)	(NA)
Black	15.1	14.2
Maternal Deaths[2]	7.1	(NA)
White	4.2	(NA)
Black and other	18.5	(NA)
Black	22.1	(NA)

Item	1995	1996
Neonatal Deaths[3]	4.9	4.7
White	4.1	3.9
Black and other	(NA)	(NA)
Black	9.8	9.2

NA Not available. [1]Represents deaths of infants under 1 year old, exclusive of fetal deaths. [2]Per 100,000 live births from deliveries and complications of pregnancy, childbirth, and the puerperium. [3]Represents deaths of infants under 28 days old, exclusive of fetal deaths.

Marriage and Pregnancy

Marriages and Divorces: 1996

Year	Marriages Number (1000)	Marriages Rate Per 1,000 population Total	Marriages Rate Per 1,000 population Unmarried women 15 yrs. old and over	Marriages Rate Per 1,000 population Unmarried women 15 to 44 yrs. old	Divorces and Annulments Number (1000)	Divorces and Annulments Rate per 1,000 population Total[1]	Divorces and Annulments Rate per 1,000 population Married women 15 yrs. old and over
1996 Provisional[1]	2,344	8.8	49.7	81.5	1,150	4.3	19.5

[1]Includes nonlicensed marriages registered in California.

Married-Couple Families—Number, by Work Experience of Husbands and Wives and Presence of Children: 1996

As of March 1997, Based on Current Population Survey. In thousands.

Work Experience of Husband or Wife	All married couple families	No related children	One or more related children under 18 years old		
			Total	One child	Two children or more
All married-couple families	53,604	27,420	26,184	10,011	16,173
Husband worked	42,953	18,138	24,815	9,343	15,472
Wife worked	32,453	13,848	18,605	7,477	11,128

Source: U.S. Bureau of the Census, *Current Population Reports*, P60-197; and Internet site, http://www.census.gov/hhes/income/histinc/index.html (accessed 25 March 1998).

Characteristics of Women Age 15 to 44 Who Have Had a Child in the Last Year: 1995

As of June. Covers civilian noninstitutional population. Since the number of women who had a birth during the 12-month period was tabulated and not the actual numbers of births, some small underestimation of fertility for this period may exist. Based on Current Population Survey (CPS).

Characteristic	Number of women (1,000)	Women who have had a child in the last year	
		Total births per 1,000 women	First births per 1,000 women
Total[1]	60,225	61.4	23.2
White	48,603	59.2	22.6
Black	8,617	70.6	26.4
Hispanic[2]	6,632	79.6	25.0
Currently married	31,616	85.5	30.3
Married, spouse present	29,202	87.2	31.4
Married, spouse absent[3]	2,414	64.5	17.4
Widowed or divorced	5,762	28.4	4.1
Never married	22,846	36.3	18.0
Educational attainment:			
Less than high school	12,629	57.3	19.6
High school, 4 years	18,404	67.4	25.5
College:			
Associate degree	4,663	56.9	19.2
Bachelor's degree	8,884	65.3	27.0
Grad. Or prof. Degree	2,921	59.2	26.8
Labor force status:			
Employed	39,989	46.5	20.9
Unemployed	3,287	53.5	22.8
Not in labor force	16,949	98.1	28.5

[1]Includes women of other races, not shown separately. [2]Persons of Hispanic origin may be of any race. [3]Includes separated women.

Source: U.S. Bureau of the Census, *Current Population Reports*, P20-375, P20-454, and P20-482.

Contraceptive Use by Women, 15 to 44 Years of Age: 1995

Based on samples of the female population of the United States; see source for details.

Contraceptive Status and Method	All Women	Age			Race		Hispanic
		15-24 years	25-34 years	35-44 years	Non-Hispanic White	Black	
All women (1,000)	60,201	18,002	20,758	21,440	42,522	8,210	6,702
Sterile[2]	29.7	2.6	25.0	57.0	30.2	31.5	28.4
Surgically sterile	27.9	1.8	23.6	54.0	28.5	29.7	26.3
Noncontraceptively sterile[3]	3.1	0.1	1.2	7.4	3.2	3.7	2.3
Contraceptively sterile[4]	24.8	1.7	22.4	46.6	25.3	26.0	24.0
Nonsurgically sterile[5]	1.7	0.7	1.3	2.8	1.6	1.8	2.0
Pregnant, postpartum	4.6	5.9	6.9	1.3	4.3	4.5	6.3
Seeking pregnancy	4.0	2.1	6.2	3.5	3.7	4.6	4.0
Other nonusers	22.3	44.4	13.3	12.6	21.1	23.1	26.3
Never had intercourse	10.9	30.8	3.4	1.4	10.4	8.9	12.1
No intercourse in last month[6]	6.2	7.0	5.3	6.5	5.7	7.2	8.6
Had intercourse in last month[6]	5.2	6.6	4.6	4.7	5.0	7.0	5.6
Nonsurgical contraceptors	39.7	45.0	49.1	26.1	41.2	36.1	35.1
Pill	17.3	23.1	23.7	6.3	18.8	14.8	13.6
IUD	0.5	0.1	0.6	0.8	0.5	0.5	0.9
Diaphragm	1.2	0.2	1.2	2.0	1.5	0.5	0.4
Condom	13.1	13.9	15.0	10.7	13.0	12.5	12.1
Periodic abstinence	1.5	0.5	1.8	2.0	1.6	0.7	1.3
Natural family planning	0.2	0	0.3	0.3	0.3	0	0.1
Withdrawal	2.0	1.6	2.3	1.9	2.1	0.9	2.0
Other methods[7]	3.9	5.6	4.2	2.1	3.4	6.2	4.7

[1]Includes other races, not shown separately. [2]Total sterile includes male sterile for unknown reasons. [3]Persons who had sterilizing operation and who gave as one reason that they had medical problems with their female organs. [4]Includes all other sterilization operations, and sterilization of the husband or current partner. [5]Persons sterile from illness, accident, or congenital conditions. [6]Prior to interview. [7]Includes implants, injectables, morning-after-pill, suppository, Today™ sponge, and less frequently used methods.

Source: U.S. National Center for Health Statistics, *Advance Data from Vital and Health Statistics*, No. 182

Education

School Enrollment, by Sex and Level: 1996

In millions. As of Oct. For the civilian noninstitutional population. Elementary includes kindergarten and grades 1-8; high school, grades 9-12; and college, 2-year and 4-year colleges, universities, and graduate and professional schools. Data for college represent degree-credit enrollment.

Year	All Levels[1]		Elementary		High School		College	
	Total	Female	Total	Female	Total	Female	Total	Female
1996	70.3	35.2	35.5	17.3	15.3	7.4	15.2	8.4

[1]Includes nursery schools, not shown separately.
Data beginnning 1986, based on a revised edit and tabulation package.
Source: U.S. Bureau of the Census, *Current Population Reports*, P20-500; and earlier reports.

Educational Attainment, by Race, Hispanic Origin, and Sex: 1960 to 1997

	All Races[1]		White		Black		Hispanic[2]	
	Male	Female	Male	Female	Male	Female	Male	Female
Completed 4 years of high school or more 1997	82.0	82.2	82.9	83.2	73.5	76.0	54.9	54.6
Completed 4 years of college or more 1997	26.2	21.7	27.0	22.3	12.5	13.9	10.6	10.1

NA Not available. [1]Includes other races, not shown separately. [2]Persons of Hispanic origin may be of any race.
Source: U.S. Bureau of the Census, *U.S. Census of Population, 1960, 1970, and 1980, Vol 1*; and *Current Population Reports*, P20-459, P20-493, P20-505; and unpublished data.

College Enrollment, by State: 1996

Opening fall enrollment of resident and extension students attending full time or part time. Excludes students taking courses for credit by mail, radio, or TV, and students in branches of U.S. institutions operated in foreign countries. In thousands.

State	1996 Enrollment, prel. Total	Female	State	1996 Enrollment, prel. Total	Female	State	1996 Enrollment, prel. Total	Female
United States	14,300	7,956	Louisiana	204	118	Oregon	165	89
Alabama	219	124	Maine	56	33	Pennsylvania	622	329
Alaska	29	17	Maryland	261	152	Rhode Island	72	40
Arizona	277	152	Massachusetts	410	231	South Carolina	174	102
Arkansas	101	58	Michigan	547	308	South Dakota	35	20
California	1,883	1,041	Minnesota	275	154	Tennessee	247	139
Colorado	243	132	Mississippi	126	72	Texas	955	519
Connecticut	155	88	Missouri	291	164	Utah	152	76
Delaware	45	26	Montana	43	23	Vermont	35	20
District of Columbia	74	41	Nebraska	119	66	Virginia	354	200
Florida	641	364	Nevada	73	41	Washington	292	164
Georgia	318	183	New Hampshire	64	37	West Virginia	86	48
Hawaii	61	34	New Jersey	328	186	Wisconsin	299	167
Idaho	60	33	New Mexico	104	60	Wyoming	31	18
Illinois	721	405	New York	1,028	591	U.S. military[1]	82	13
Indiana	286	155	North Carolina	373	213			
Iowa	177	96	North Dakota	41	20			
Kansas	172	95	Ohio	538	297			
Kentucky	178	104	Oklahoma	177	96			

[1]Service schools.
Source: U.S. National Center for Education Statistics, *Digest of Education Statistics*, annual.

Earned Degrees Conferred, by Level and Sex: 1995

In thousands except percent. Includes Alaska and Hawaii.

Year Ending	All Degrees		Associate's		Bachelor's		Master's		First Professional		Doctor's	
	Male	Female	Male	Female	Male	Female	Male	Female	Male	Female	Male	Female
1995	2,218	44.9	218	321	526	634	179	219	45	31	27	18

Source: U.S. National Center for Education Statistics, *Digest of Education Statistics*, annual.

Labor and Income

Civilian Labor Force and Participation Rates, With Projections: 1997 and 2006

For civilian noninstitutinal population 16 years old and over. Annual averages of monthly figures.
Rates are based on annual average noncivilian noninstitutional population of each specified group and represent proportion
of each specified group in the civilian labor force. Based on Current Population Survey.

Race, Sex, and Age	Civilian Labor Force (millions)		Participation Rate (percent)	
	1997[1]	2006, proj.	1997[1]	2006, proj.
Total[2]	136.3	148.8	67.1	67.6
White	114.7	123.6	67.5	68.1
Male	62.6	66.0	75.9	74.3
Female	52.1	57.6	59.5	62.0
Black	15.5	17.2	64.7	64.9
Male	7.4	8.0	68.3	69.6
Female	8.2	9.2	61.7	61.3
Hispanic[3]	13.8	17.4	67.9	67.4
Male	8.3	10.2	80.1	77.1
Female	5.5	7.2	55.1	57.2
Total Female	**63.0**	**70.6**	**59.8**	**61.4**

[1] Data not strictly comparable with data for earlier years. [2] Includes other races, not shown separately. [3] Persons of Hispanic origin may be of any race.

Source: U.S. Bureau of Labor Statistics, *Employment and Earnings*, monthly, January issues; *Monthly Labor Review*, November 1997; and unpublished data.

Employment Status of Women, by Marital Status and Presence and Age of Children: 1997

Based on Current Population Survey.

Item	Total			With Any Children								
				Total			Children 6 to 17 only			Children under 6		
	Single	Married[1]	Other[2]	Single	Married[1]	Other[2]	Single	Married[1]	Other[2]	Single	Married[1]	Other[2]
In Labor Force (mil.) 1997[3]	16.2	33.9	12.8	2.8	18.2	4.7	1.0	10.6	3.4	1.8	7.6	1.3
Participation Rate[4] 1997[3]	66.8	62.1	48.7	68.1	71.1	79.1	74.0	77.6	81.1	65.1	63.6	74.2
Employment (mil.) 1997[3]	14.7	32.8	12.1	2.3	17.5	4.3	0.9	10.3	3.1	1.4	7.3	1.1
Unemployment Rate[5] 1997[3]	8.8	3.2	5.8	16.9	3.5	9.0	13.5	2.9	7.9	18.8	4.4	11.7

[1] Husband present. [2] Widowed, divorced or separated. [3] Data not strictly comparable with data for earlier years. See February 1994, March 1996, and February 1997 issues of *Employment and Earnings*. [4] Percent of women in each specific category in the labor force. [5] Unemployed as a percent of civilian labor force in specified group.

Source: U.S. Bureau of Labor Statistics, *Bulletin 2307*; and unpublished data.

Employed Civilians, by Selected Occupation and Sex: 1997

For civilian noninstitutional population 16 years old and over. Annual average of monthly figures. Based on Current Population Survey.

Occupation	Total employed (1,000)	Female (percent of total)
TOTAL	129,558	46.2
Managerial and professional specialty	37,686	48.9
Executive, administrative, and managerial	18,440	44.3
Accountants and auditors	1,625	56.6
Architects	169	17.9
Engineers	2,036	9.6
Mathematical and computer scientists	1,494	30.4
Natural scientists	529	31.0
Physicians	724	26.2
Dentists	138	17.3
Registered nurses	2,065	93.5
Pharmacists	200	45.9
Dietitians	101	88.7
Therapists	455	75.4
Teachers, college and university	869	42.7
Teachers, except college and university	4,798	75.7
Librarians, archivists, and curators	217	77.1
Economists	135	52.2
Psychologists	256	59.3
Social workers	781	69.3
Clergy	350	13.6
Lawyers and judges	925	26.7
Authors	137	53.6
Designers	658	58.5
Musicians and composers	155	36.6
Actors and directors	136	38.2
Painters, sculptors, craft-artists, and artist printmakers	251	45.8
Photographers	132	29.2
Editors and reporters	257	51.2
Public relations specialists	148	65.7
Announcers	61	14.2
Athletes	92	27.0
Technical, sales, and administrative support	38,309	64.1
Clinical laboratory technologists and technicians	388	75.9
Dental hygienists	107	98.2
Licensed practical nurses	408	94.1

Occupation	Total employed (1,000)	Female (percent of total)
Electrical and electronic technicians	391	14.2
Drafting occupations	222	16.7
Surveying and mapping technicians	76	10.2
Biological technicians	106	57.2
Chemical technicians	85	22.8
Airplane pilots and navigators	120	1.2
Computer programmers	626	30.0
Legal assistants	346	83.9
Sales occupations	15,734	50.2
Insurance sales	594	42.8
Real estate sales	781	50.0
Securities and financial services sales	429	31.2
Advertising and related sales	173	56.6
Cashiers	3,007	78.4
Computer equipment operators	392	58.5
Secretaries, stenographers, and typists	3,692	97.9
File clerks	295	84.7
Bookkeepers, accounting, and auditing clerks	1,735	92.3
Telephone operators	173	83.5
Mail carrier, postal service	314	30.7
Stock and inventory clerks	454	41.1
Insurance adjusters, examiners, and investigators	434	72.5
General office clerks	818	80.6
Bank tellers	446	90.1
Service occupations	17,537	59.4
Child care workers	260	96.8
Cleaners and servants	512	94.9
Supervisors, police and detectives	108	17.4
Police and detectives	1,005	16.4
Firefighting and fire prevention	233	3.4
Sheriffs, bailiffs, and other law enforcement officers	142	22.2
Correctional institution officers	284	22.9
Guards	881	24.4
Bartenders	310	57.2
Waiters and waitresses	1,375	77.8
Cooks	2,126	41.8

Employed Civilians, by Selected Occupation and Sex: 1997 (cont.)

Occupation	Total employed (1,000)	Female (percent of total)	Occupation	Total employed (1,000)	Female (percent of total)
Kitchen workers, food preparation	278	72.6	Data processing equipment repairers	190	13.3
Maids and housemen	643	80.1	Construction trades	5,378	2.4
Janitors and cleaners	2,226	34.0	Carpenters	1,335	1.6
Barbers	79	22.8	**Operators, fabricators, and laborers**	18,399	24.7
Hairdressers and cosmetologists	748	90.3	Machine operators, assemblers, and inspectors	7,962	37.7
Attendants, amusement and recreation facilities	206	34.8	Textile, apparel, and furnishings machine operators	1,083	72.1
Precision production, craft, and repair	14,124	8.9	Motor vehicle operators	4,089	11.3
Mechanics and repairers	4,675	3.9	Laborers, except construction	1,323	21.3
Automobile mechanics	905	1.5	Farm workers	796	19.0
Aircraft engine mechanics	135	2.9	Forestry and logging occupations	108	5.1

Source: U.S. Bureau of Labor Statistics, *Employment and Earnings*, monthly, January issues; and unpublished data.

Money Income of Persons-Selected Characteristics, by Income Level: 1995

Constant dollars based on CPI-UX1 deflator. As of March of following year. Covers persons 15 years old and over. In thousands.

Item	Total	Under $5,000[1]	$5,000 to $9,999	$10,000 to $14,999	$15,000 to $24,999	$25,000 to $34,999	$35,000 to $49,999	$50,000 to $74,999	$75,000 and over	Median Income (dollars)
Male total	93,439	9,014	10,402	10,931	18,145	14,516	13,996	9,912	6,253	23,834
Female total	96,558	19,495	19,854	13,970	19,237	11,278	7,505	3,659	1,560	12,815
Females by characteristic:										
15 to 24 years old	13,502	6,064	3,168	1,913	1,666	495	137	40	18	5,881
25 to 34 years old	18,481	3,290	2,763	2,532	4,519	3,105	1,475	602	196	16,384
35 to 44 years old	20,637	3,336	2,789	2,485	4,554	3,309	2,459	1,140	565	18,447
45 to 54 years old	15,693	2,370	2,048	1,883	3,487	2,338	2,054	1,110	403	19,046
55 to 64 years old	10,220	2,057	1,982	1,468	2,077	1,099	833	506	197	13,316
65yr. old and over	18,026	2,377	7,103	3,690	2,933	933	547	262	180	9,626
Northeast	19,400	3,803	3,927	2,675	3,728	2,339	1,692	834	403	13,451
Midwest	23,219	4,597	4,679	3,414	4,876	2,783	1,726	825	320	13,051
South	37,954	6,916	7,224	4,979	6,805	3,921	2,393	1,094	440	12,357
West	22,807	4,179	4,024	2,902	3,828	2,235	1,695	906	397	12,831
White	88,756	16,252	16,242	11,867	15,970	9,481	6,365	3,175	1,389	12,961
Black	13,514	2,347	2,906	1,585	2,504	1,329	774	297	75	11,772
Hispanic[2]	7,744	2,036	2,003	1,242	1,366	602	309	148	39	9,484

[1]Includes persons with income deficit. [2]Persons of Hispanic origin may be of any race.
Source: U.S. Bureau of the Census, *Current Population Reports*, P60-197.

Median Income of Families, by Type of Family in Current (1996) Dollars: 1996.

Year		Current Dollars				
	Total	Married-couple families			Male householder, no wife present	Female householder, no husband present
		Total	Wife in paid labor force	Wife not in paid labor force		
1996	42,300	49,707	58,381	33,748	31,600	19,911

Source: U.S. Bureau of the Census, *Current Population Reports*, P60-197; and Internet site, http://www.census.gov/hhes/income/histinc/index.html (accessed 25 March 1998).

Health

Expectation of Life at Birth: 1996
In years. Excludes deaths of nonresidents of the United States.

Year	Total		White		Black	
	Male	Female	Male	Female	Male	Female
1996	73.0	79.0	73.8	79.6	66.1	74.2

Source: U.S. National Center for Health Statistics, *Vital Statistics of the United States*, annual, and *Monthly Vital Statistics Reports*.

Percent of Women, 15 to 44 Years Old, Who Received Selected Medical Services from a Medical Care Provider: 1995
In percent, except as indicated.

Characteristic	Number (1,000)	Pregnancy Test	Pap smear	Pelvic Exam	HIV test[1]	Other STD[2] test or treatment	Test or treatment for infection[3]
Total	60,201	16.0	61.9	61.3	17.3	7.6	21.0
Age at interview:							
15-19 years old	8,961	16.1	33.5	32.4	14.6	9.4	16.9
15-17 years old	5,452	11.4	23.0	23.4	12.1	7.1	12.2
18-19 years old	3,508	23.3	49.9	46.4	18.5	13.0	24.2
20-24 years old	9,041	27.4	68.7	66.5	23.7	14.0	28.1
25-29 years old	9,693	25.3	70.9	69.3	23.6	10.3	25.7
30-34 years old	11,065	17.4	69.5	70.3	18.5	6.5	21.8
35-39 years old	11,211	8.1	62.9	62.6	14.2	4.7	19.2
40-44 years old	10,230	4.3	62.7	63.2	10.0	2.2	15.1
Race and hispanic origin:							
Hispanic	6,702	19.8	52.2	52.6	21.9	7.2	20.4
Non-Hispanic White	42,522	14.8	63.2	63.2	14.5	7.1	20.9
Non-Hispanic Black	8,210	19.8	67.6	63.0	28.7	11.4	24.8
Non-Hispanic other	2,767	14.3	47.7	47.7	14.7	(B)	13.6
Marital status:							
Never married	22,679	15.5	52.1	49.8	18.9	10.7	20.1
Currently married	29,673	17.3	68.5	69.0	14.5	4.7	20.9
Formerly married	7,849	12.4	64.8	65.3	23.1	9.7	24.2

(B) Figure does not meet standard of reliability. [1]Excludes HIV (human immunodeficiency virus) tests done as part of blood donation. [2]STD is sexually transmitted disease. [3]Refers to vaginal, urinary tract, and pelvic infections.

Source: U.S. National Center for Health Statistics, *Fertility, Family Planning, and Women's Health: New data from the 1995 National Survey of Family Growth, Vital and Health Statistics*, Series 23, No. 19, 1997.

Hospital Utilization Rates: 1980 to 1996

Represents estimates of inpatients discharged from noninstitutional, short-stay hospitals, exclusive of federal hospitals. Excludes newborn infants.

Selected Characteristic	Days of Care per 1,000 Persons		Average Stay (days)	
	Total	Female	Total	Female
1996 total	606	665	5.2	4.9
Age:				
Under 1 year old	1,154	1,009	5.9	5.8
1 to 4 years old	140	128	3.3	3.5
5 to14 years old	92	81	4.3	4.1
15 to 24 years old	258	356	3.2	2.8
25 to 34 years old	360	477	3.5	3.0
35 to 44 years old	373	377	4.7	4.1
45 to 64 years old	624	592	5.3	5.2
65 to 74 years old	1,604	1,546	6.2	6.3
75 years old and over	3,075	3,025	6.8	6.8
Region:				
Northeast	803	855	6.2	5.9
Midwest	574	626	5.0	4.7
South	621	684	5.2	4.8
West	440	502	4.5	4.1

Source: U.S. National Center for Health Statistics, *Vital and Health Statistics*, series 13; and unpublished data.

Current Cigarette Smoking: 1995

In percent. Definition includes persons who smoke only "some days." Excludes unknown smoking status.

Sex, Age, and Race	1995
Male, total	27.0
18 to 24 years	27.8
25 to 34 years	(NA)
35 to 44 years	(NA)
45 to 64 years	27.1
65 years and over	14.3
Female, total	22.6
18 to 24 years	21.8
25 to 34 years	(NA)
35 to 44 years	(NA)
45 to 64 years	24.0
65 years and over	11.5

NA Not available.

Source: U.S. National Center for Health Statistics, *Health United States, 1996-97 and Injury Chartbook*, 1997, and U.S. Centers for Disease Control and Prevention, *Morbidity and Mortality Weekly Report*, Vol. 46, No. 51, December 26, 1997.

Use of Mammography for Women 40 Years Old and Over by Patient Characteristics: 1994

Percent of women having a mammogram within the past 2 years. Covers civilian noninstitutional population.

Characteristic	1994
Total[1]	60.9
40 to 49 years old	61.3
50 years old and over	60.6
50 to 64 years old	66.5
65 years old and over	55.0
White, non-Hispanic	61.3
Black, non-Hispanic	64.4
Hispanic origin[2]	51.9
Years of School Completed:	
Less than 12 years	48.2
12 years	61.0
13 years or more	69.7

[1]Includes all other races not shown separately and unknown education level and poverty status. [2]Persons of Hispanic origin may be of any race.

Source: U.S. National Center for Health Statistics, *Health United States, 1996-1997 and Injury Chartbook*, 1997.

Politics

Local Elected Officials, by Sex and Type of Government: 1992

Sex	Total	General Purpose			Special Purpose	
		County	Municipal	Township	School district	Special district
Total	493,830	58,818	135,531	126,958	88,434	84,089
Male	324,255	43,563	94,808	76,213	54,443	55,228
Female	100,531	12,525	26,825	27,702	24,730	8,749
Sex not reported	69,044	2,730	13,898	23,043	9,261	20,112

Source: U.S. Bureau of the Census, 1992 Census of Governments, Popularly Elected Officials (GC92(1)-2).

Members of 104th Congress

Representatives, Male: 388, Female: 47. Senators, Male: 92, Female: 8.

Women Holding State Public Offices, by Office and State: 1997

As of January.

State	Statewide elective executive office[1]	State legislature	State	Statewide elective executive office[1]	State legislature	State	Statewide elective executive office[1]	State legislature
United States	82	1,605	Kentucky	0	13	North Dakota	4	24
Alabama	3	6	Louisiana	1	17	Ohio	2	29
Alaska	1	8	Maine	0	48	Oklahoma	4	15
Arizona	4	34	Maryland	1	56	Oregon	1	23
Arkansas	2	23	Massachusetts	0	46	Pennsylvania	1	31
California	2	27	Michigan	2	34	Rhode Island	1	39
Colorado	3	35	Minnesota	3	62	South Carolina	1	22
Connecticut	2	54	Mississippi	0	22	South Dakota	4	18
Delaware	4	16	Missouri	2[2]	42	Tennessee	1	18
Florida	1	38	Montana	2	35	Texas	1	33
Georgia	1	39	Nebraska	2	13	Utah	2	17
Hawaii	1	13	Nevada	1	21	Vermont	0	60
Idaho	2	25	New Hampshire	1	130	Virginia	0	21
Illinois	2	46	New Jersey	1	20	Washington	4	58
Indiana	3	28	New Mexico	1	30	WestVirginia	0	20
Iowa	1	32	New York	1	39	Wisconsin	0	31
Kansas	3	49	North Carolina	1	29	Wyoming	2	16

[1]Excludes women elected to the judiciary, women appointed to state cabinet-level positions, women elected to executive posts by the legislature, and elected members of university Board of Trustees or board of education. [2]Includes one official who was appointed to an elective position.

Source: Center for the American Woman and Politics, Eagleton Institute of Politics, Rutgers University, New Brunswick, NJ, information releases (copyright).

Notable Women of U.S. History

ABBOTT, EDITH (1876–1957) The founding dean of the University of Chicago's School of Social Service Administration in 1924, Abbott earned a doctorate in economics in 1905 and wrote several innovative books about women and economics. Many of her students went on to implement Social Security and other New Deal programs that fundamentally changed American life.

ABBOTT, GRACE (1878–1939) Like her sister, EDITH ABBOTT, Grace Abbott was affiliated with JANE ADDAMS's Hull House. The longtime head of the Chicago Immigrant Protective League, she testified before Congress on immigration law in 1912 and wrote several books on the subject. In the 1920s, she headed the federal Children's Bureau, where she established free clinics for pregnant women.

ABZUG, BELLA (1920–1998) Elected to Congress from New York in 1970, Abzug was one of the most publicized women of the revitalized feminist movement in the 1970s. Her credentials were stronger than many realized: she had graduated from prestigious Hunter College in 1942 and from Columbia University Law School in 1945. Despite her long marriage to a supportive man, Abzug was often negatively portrayed in the media. She left the House of Representatives in 1976 to run for the Senate and subsequently lost several elections.

ADAMS, ABIGAIL SMITH (1744–1818) The second first lady, Adams maintained a voluminous correspondence with her husband, President John Adams, and others of the nation's founders. She was a strong supporter of the American Revolution, and her independent spirit was especially revealed in her request that the Continental Congress "remember the ladies" in drafting the Constitution. She was also the mother of President John Quincy Adams. The White House was completed while she was first lady, and she hung laundry in the unfinished East Room.

ADDAMS, JANE (1860–1935) The first American woman to win the Nobel Peace Prize (in 1931), Addams's political activism has been overshadowed by her founding of Chicago's Hull House, the best known of the "settlement houses" for immigrants, in 1899. Her efforts to help the poor pioneered modern social work and led Addams into activism in favor of women's suffrage, economic reform, civil liberties, and pacifism. The controversy over her opposition to World War I was forgotten by the time she died, when thousands of people paid their last respects. Much honored, Addams was depicted on a postage stamp in 1940.

ALBRIGHT, MADELEINE KORBEL (1937–) The highest-ranking member of the cabinet, Albright is the daughter of a Czech diplomat; her family immigrated to the United States in 1948. After marriage and divorce, she earned a Ph.D. from Georgetown University and began serving in a series of political and diplomatic positions. President Bill Clinton appointed her ambassador to the United Nations when he took office in 1993 and made her the nation's first female secretary of state in 1997. The news media then revealed that, unbeknownst to Albright, her family had been Jewish before converting to Christianity to escape the Holocaust.

ALLEN, FLORENCE ELLINWOOD (1884–1966) Elected to the Ohio Supreme Court in 1922, Allen was the first woman in the world to sit on a court of last resort. A 1904 graduate of Case Western Reserve University's College for Women, she earned her law degree at New York University. She and her mother were active in the Ohio suffrage movement, and after women were granted the right to vote, suffragists organized to elect her to the state supreme court at the next election. President Franklin Roosevelt appointed Allen to sit on the United States Court of Appeals in 1934—the first woman ever.

ANDERSON, MARIAN (1902–1993) Like other African Americans, Philadelphia singer Marian Anderson was acclaimed in Europe before she was in her homeland; she sang before royalty and was praised by music critics from Italy to Russia in the early 1930s. When she returned to the United States, however, the Daughters of the American Revolution canceled her rental of their hall for a concert when they realized that the audience would be integrated. With support from ELEANOR ROOSEVELT and others, the 1939 concert was famously relocated to the Lincoln Memorial. The first black to sing with the Metropolitan Opera, she had her debut there in 1955. Anderson was much honored in the next decades, and she received a Congressional Gold Medal in 1978.

ANDERSON, MARY (1872–1964) As head of the Women's Bureau of the Department of Labor for the first quarter century of its existence, Anderson made great strides for working women. A Swedish immigrant, she had supported herself from the time she was seventeen; she was thirty-nine when a 1910 strike in the Chicago garment industry brought her to full-time labor-union work. President Franklin Roosevelt admired Anderson so much that, over the objections of labor leaders, he appointed her to head the U.S. delegation to the International Labor Organization.

ANGELOU, MAYA (1928–) A contemporary African American poet and writer, Angelou has written several volumes of autobiography, including the best-selling *I Know Why the Caged Bird Sings* (1970), as well as poetry and plays. An Arkansan like President Bill Clinton, she wrote "On the Pulse of the Morning" for his 1993 inauguration.

ANTHONY, SUSAN BROWNELL (1820–1906) Known as the leader of the women's suffrage movement, Anthony spent her life speaking and writing in support of women's rights, but she was first active as an abolitionist and temperance advocate. A Quaker teacher, she attended her first women's rights convention in 1852, four years after ELIZABETH CADY STANTON and LUCRETIA MOTT organized the original one. She consciously stayed single, and while Stanton specialized in writing and in policy development for the movement, Anthony became the on-the-road organizer.

During the Civil War, Anthony and Stanton founded the Loyal League, and they followed that up by founding the National Woman Suffrage Association in 1869. Anthony was the primary fund-raiser for the association and its short-lived newspaper, the *Revolution*. When the Fifteenth Amendment used gender-neutral language to extend suffrage to non-whites, Anthony tried to vote in Rochester, New York, in

1872; she was arrested and fined. After the two rival suffrage associations merged in 1890, she served as president of the National American Woman Suffrage Association from 1892 to 1900, when she retired at age eighty.

Anthony outlived Stanton and other pioneers, but she died fourteen years before the Nineteenth Amendment granted all American women the vote. She is the only American woman depicted on a coin: the Susan B. Anthony dollar, which was first minted in 1978.

APGAR, VIRGINIA (1909–1974) Apgar, who is depicted on a 1995 postage stamp, created the standard test for assessing the health of newborns. Long associated with the March of Dimes and its campaign against birth defects, Apgar was the first woman at Columbia University's medical school to be granted a full professorship.

BAGLEY, SARAH (1806–?) Long before women were supposed to engage in political activity, Bagley led a group of women to testify before a committee of the Massachusetts legislature in 1845. They presented a petition with more than 2,000 signatures from women who objected to the long days and low wages of textile factories. When their Lowell legislator failed to support them, Bagley helped organize a campaign that defeated him. Blacklisted from local factories, she set another precedent by becoming the nation's first female telegraph operator.

BAKER, JOSEPHINE (1906–1975) The personification of the Jazz Age in Paris, Josephine Baker, an African American who was born in Saint Louis, created a sensation with her imaginative, seminude dances. She lived in France for most of her life and received the coveted Croix de Guerre for her espionage on behalf of the French during the German occupation. GRACE KELLY, princess of Monaco, gave her a home in Monaco in the late 1960s, where Baker struggled to support a "rainbow tribe" of ethnically diverse children she adopted.

BALCH, EMILY GREENE (1867–1961) Winner of the 1946 Nobel Peace Prize, Balch was the second American woman so honored (her friend JANE ADDAMS was the first, in 1931). An economist with international credentials, she was fired from Wellesley College for her opposition to World War I—losing her pension at age fifty-two. Under the aegis of the Women's International League for Peace and Freedom, she worked in Geneva through the 1920s and 1930s; despite being in her seventies during World War II, she intervened for Jewish refugees and for Japanese Americans imprisoned in their own country. The author of several books, Balch died where she was born, in Cambridge, Massachusetts.

BARTON, CLARA (1821–1912) Founder of the American Red Cross, Barton was a teacher in New Jersey until she went to Washington, D.C., in 1854, where she may have been the first female federal employee to work in a Washington office. When the Civil War began, she organized the donation and distribution of supplies to the troops; only briefly a nurse, her true genius was in supply procurement and distribution. At the end of the war, she set up the nation's first agency to find missing soldiers, personally going to the notorious prison-of-war camp in Andersonville, Georgia, and marking thousands of graves. In 1869, Barton went to Switzerland and became active with the International Red Cross, then returned to lobby the Senate to ratify the International Red Cross treaty. After the treaty's ratification in 1882, Barton was president of the American Red Cross until 1904.

BATES, DAISY GASTON (1922–1999) As head of the Arkansas branch of the National Association for the Advancement of Colored People (NAACP), Bates led the Little Rock school integration that rocked the nation in 1957, risking her life and bankrupting her business. The story is told in her book, *The Long Shadow of Little Rock* (1962).

BATES, KATHERINE LEE (1859–1929) Author of "America the Beautiful," Massachusetts English professor Bates wrote this poem after climbing Colorado's Pikes Peak in 1893. It was set to music and published in 1911.

BEARD, MARY RITTER (1876–1958) Increasingly recognized as the important historian she was, Beard struggled for recognition of women's history in her lifetime. Among her many books is the seminal *Woman as a Force in History* (1945). In addition to writing history, she lived it as a New York City leader in the suffrage movement.

BELMONT, ALVA ERSKINE SMITH VANDERBILT (1853–1933) Fantastically wealthy and generous, Belmont supported her feminist goals with time as well as money: she personally bailed out jailed women during the great 1909 New York City garment-industry strike, and as an officer of the national suffrage association, she paid the rent on its large Fifth Avenue office. Her summer home in Newport, Rhode Island, was the headquarters of the National Woman's Party. When she became the party's president in 1921, she bought the historic Capitol Hill house that still serves women in Washington. In an entire-

ly different side of her complex life, she built Vanderbilt mansions in the 1880s, restored a fifteenth-century European castle, and was one of the first women elected to the American Institute of Architects.

BENEDICT, RUTH FULTON (1887–1948) Ruth Benedict coined the word *racism* in her groundbreaking *Race: Science and Politics* (1939). Although she did not finish her Columbia University anthropology doctorate until she was thirty-seven, Benedict went on to profoundly influence American thought. *Her Patterns of Culture* (1934) introduced the concept of cultural relativism to the general public, and her work on Japanese society, *The Chrysanthemum and the Sword* (1946), was a best-seller that affected America's treatment of its former enemy. MARGARET MEAD studied under Benedict.

BETHUNE, MARY McLEOD (1875–1955) The founder of Bethune-Cookman College in Daytona Beach, Florida, Bethune was an outstanding leader of black women from the 1920s through the 1940s. Born in South Carolina, she was educated in Chicago and returned south to teach. She began her girls' school in 1904 and by 1929 had developed it into a coeducational college. President Franklin Roosevelt brought her into his administration in 1935, and President Harry Truman appointed her to the founding conference of the United Nations in 1945, where she was the only woman of color with official status. Bethune wrote regularly for black newspapers, was a founder of a life insurance company, and served on the advisory committee that developed the Women's Army Corps. An officer in many organizations, including Planned Parenthood, she was president of the National Association of Colored Women and the founding president of the National Council of Negro Women.

BICKERDYKE, MARY ANN BALL (1817–1901) The only woman whom General William Tecumseh Sherman allowed in his camps, Bickerdyke, who came from Illinois, saw far more Civil War combat than most soldiers did. Before joining Sherman, she worked as a nurse on hospital ships that traveled the Mississippi River and then worked through the terrible battles in Tennessee, including at Lookout Mountain, where "Mother Bickerdyke" was the only nurse for 2,000 wounded men. She was at the Battle of Atlanta and helped liberate starving men from the appalling prisoner-of-war camp at Andersonville, Georgia. She stayed with Sherman's armies until their final victory march in Washington and then retired to Kansas, where she finally was granted a pension two decades later.

BLACKWELL, ANTOINETTE BROWN (1825–1921) The first American woman ordained by a congregation of a mainstream church (in 1853 in Wayne County, New York), Antoinette Brown married Samuel Charles Blackwell, brother of ELIZABETH BLACKWELL, and also was the sister-in-law of LUCY STONE. Deeply involved in the women's rights movement, she preached and even ordained two female Congregationalist preachers. She was one of the few pioneer feminists still alive to vote in 1920.

BLACKWELL, ELIZABETH (1821–1910) The first credentialed female physician in the world, Blackwell immigrated to the United States from England with her family in 1832. She overcame poverty and hostility from her classmates to graduate at the head of her medical school class in Geneva, New York, in 1849. In 1857, she and her sister Emily, also a doctor, founded the New York Infirmary for Women and Children, which was staffed entirely by women. They also founded a women's medical college in 1868. Blackwell moved to London in 1869, where she practiced medicine and taught at the new London School of Medicine for Women. Her autobiography is *Pioneer Work in Opening the Medical Profession to Women* (1895).

BLAIR, BONNIE (1964–) Speed skater Bonnie Blair holds more Olympic gold medals than any other American woman, having won five in the Olympic Winter Games between 1988 and 1994. She retired to Florida in 1995.

BOURKE-WHITE, MARGARET (1906–1971) Most Americans regularly saw Bourke-White's photographs during her three decades with *Life* magazine. She is most famous for depicting the poor of the Great Depression and the horrors of World War II. The only foreign photographer in the Soviet Union when the Germans attacked, she also took the first photographs of Hitler's death camps. The author of several photo books, her autobiography is *Portrait of Myself* (1963).

BLOOMER, AMELIA JENKS (1818–1894) Bloomer edited a temperance-movement newspaper called the *Lily* in Seneca Falls, New York; after she wrote an 1849 article advocating that women wear loose-fitting long trousers under a knee-length skirt, people began calling the garments "bloomers" after her. She stopped wearing them within a few years, feeling that the outfit distracted attention from more important reforms, but continued to be an active suffragist after moving to Iowa.

BOW, CLARA (1905–1965) The silent movie star known as the "It girl," Bow embodied the emancipated flapper in the 1927 film *It*. Her trend-setting short hair was a large part of liberating fashions in the Roaring Twenties, when women shortened their dresses and stopped wearing rigid corsets and other confining clothing that had been standard for centuries.

BRADSTREET, ANNE DUDLEY (1612–1672) Born in England, Bradstreet immigrated to Massachusetts in 1630; while rearing eight children and twice serving as first lady of the new Puritan colony, she wrote poetry throughout her life. Her best-known poem is "To My Dear and Loving Husband," a surprisingly unpuritanical work. She became America's first published poet when, without her knowledge, her brother-in-law took her poems to London, where they were published as *The Tenth Muse Lately Sprung Up in America* (1650).

BRADWELL, MYRA COLBY (1831–1894) Bradwell passed the Illinois bar examination in 1869, but the Illinois Supreme Court refused to admit a woman to the state bar association. In *Bradwell v. Illinois* (1873), the United States Supreme Court refused to overturn that verdict, rejecting Bradwell's argument that it was a violation of the Fourteenth Amendment's equal-protection clause. The court not only ruled that states could exclude women from the practice of law—it also cited "the law of the Creator" as justification. Bradwell continued to edit the *Chicago Legal News*, and Illinois finally offered to admit her to the bar in 1890. In 1892, two years before her death, she was admitted to practice before the Supreme Court.

BRENT, MARGARET (1600?–1671?) In effect the governor of colonial Maryland, Margaret Brent was a descendant of English royalty. Lord Baltimore granted her a huge amount of land as an inducement to move to newly founded Catholic Maryland in 1638, where his brother, Leonard Calvert, was governor. When Calvert died in 1647, he named Brent executor of his will, and she therefore headed the propriety colony. Her handling of a rebellion by unpaid soldiers was so skilled that Maryland's legislators sent Lord Baltimore a resolution saying that without her, "all would have gone to ruin." Brent nonetheless left Maryland for Virginia in 1651, where she and her sister lived prosperously until her death sometime prior to 1671.

Modern feminists occasionally cite Brent as an early lawyer because she exercised the power of attorney; this activity was not as a lawyer for hire, but was instead in her role as a powerful political and business woman.

BROOKS, GWENDOLYN (1917–) A prolific poet and author, Brooks has published a dozen books of poetry as well as children's literature, a novel, and an autobiography. Her poetry was among the first to incorporate black patterns of speech. Among many other honors, Brooks won the Pulitzer Prize in poetry in 1950, the first black woman to do so.

BUCK, PEARL SYDENSTRICKER (1892–1973) Buck spent her childhood in China with her missionary parents and returned there after college, teaching at Chinese universities. Her second novel about China, *The Good Earth* (1931), won the Pulitzer Prize. After the political situation forced her to leave China in 1934, she continued to produce fiction and nonfiction about Asia at a furious rate for the rest of her life. She won the Nobel Prize in literature in 1938 and was the only American woman to do so until TONI MORRISON in 1993.

CABRINI, FRANCES XAVIER (1850–1917) The first American citizen to be canonized as a saint by the Roman Catholic Church, Mother Cabrini founded the international order of the Missionary Sisters of the Sacred Heart of Jesus while still in her native Italy. With six other sisters, she arrived in the United States in 1889 and began building schools, hospitals, and orphanages from New York to Los Angeles. She became an American citizen in 1909, and when she died at age sixty-seven, she left more than 1,500 "daughters" in sixty-seven convents throughout the world.

CALDWELL, SARAH (1924–) The first woman to conduct the New York Philharmonic and the Metropolitan Opera (in 1975), Caldwell's undergraduate musical education was at the University of Arkansas. After graduating from the New England Conservatory of Music, she staged her first opera in 1946, when she was just twenty-two.

CANNON, ANNIE JUMP (1863–1941) An astronomer at the Harvard Observatory, Cannon cataloged almost 400,000 celestial bodies. Although Harvard did not give her professorial rank until she had worked for almost a half century, she was well known in her lifetime and highly supportive of women in science. Oxford University granted Cannon the first honorary doctorate ever awarded to a woman.

CARAWAY, HATTIE WYATT (1878–1950) The first woman elected to the Senate, Caraway initially was appointed to her husband's Senate seat after his death in November 1931. Surprising the experts, Arkansas voters elected her in 1932 and 1938, before she lost to a liberal university president in 1944. A Democrat, Caraway was the first woman to preside over the Senate, to chair a Senate committee, and to be chosen as president pro tempore of the Senate.

CARSON, RACHEL (1907–1964) Carson's book *Silent Spring* (1962) alerted Americans to the environmental damage done by the pesticide DDT, inspiring the environmental movement. It won the National Book Award and became a long-term best-seller, but Carson was harshly attacked by the chemical and agricultural industries. By the time it was clear that her book would be the foundation of a major movement, Carson was dying of cancer.

CASSATT, MARY (1844–1926) Perhaps America's most famous female artist, Cassatt lived mostly in France, including through World War I. After studying at the Pennsylvania Academy of Fine Arts, in 1866 she persuaded her wealthy family to send her to Paris, where she remained for the rest of her life. The early impressionistic work of Edgar Degas greatly influenced Cassatt, who participated in the pioneering exhibits of the impressionists in the 1870s and 1880s. Her paintings had a feminine perspective, often depicting mothers and children. In 1967, a Cassatt painting became the first by a female artist to appear on an American postage stamp.

CATHER, WILLA (1873–1947) Novelist Willa Cather is best known for *O Pioneers* (1913) and *My Antonia* (1918), but she won the 1922 Pulitzer Prize for *One of Ours*, a novel about World War I. Although she is closely associated with her native Nebraska, which was the setting for much of her work, Cather actually lived in New York City most of her life. She was the managing editor of *McClure's*, one of the era's most popular magazines.

CATT, CARRIE LANE CHAPMAN (1859–1947) More politically astute than most of her colleagues in the suffrage movement, Catt provided the leadership that finally enfranchised all American women. An Iowa native, she was widowed young; when she remarried in 1890, her husband signed a notarized prenuptial agreement promising that she could travel for the suffrage movement four months of the year. She won campaigns in Colorado in 1893 and in Idaho in 1896, and when SUSAN B. ANTHONY retired from presidency of the National Woman Suffrage Association in 1900, she chose Catt as her successor. Unfortunately, Catt had to resign in 1904 because of her husband's illness.

After her husband died, Catt concentrated on the International Suffrage Association, presiding over its biannual meetings in Europe until World War I ended them.

She conducted a global tour between 1911 and 1913, speaking to women from Persia to China; it was the first time that many in these societies had ever heard of women's rights. By 1915, however, the national suffrage association was in such internal disarray that Catt was drafted to return to the presidency—and five years later, American women had the vote.

Catt not only handled the difficult process of obtaining a positive vote from two-thirds of both houses of Congress but also won ratification from the necessary three-quarters of state legislatures. She published a book about the campaign called *Woman Suffrage and Politics* (1923) and was the honorary president of the League of Women Voters for the rest of her life.

CHESNUT, MARY BOYKIN MILLER (1823–1886) The daughter of a senator from South Carolina, Chesnut spent most of her adult life on her husband's isolated plantations. She kept a detailed diary during the Civil War that is invaluable to historians, in part because her position as the wife of a Confederate cabinet member gave her access to important information.

CHILD, JULIA McWILLIAMS (1912–) A graduate of Le Cordon Bleu, Child introduced Americans to the possibility of making French cuisine at home through her coauthorship of *Mastering the Art of French Cooking* (1961) and her show on public television, "The French Chef." A Bostonian, she has written numerous other cookbooks.

CHILD, LYDIA MARIA FRANCIS (1802–1880) Child wrote more than two dozen books and countless pieces for periodicals to supplement her husband's limited income. Her books included a very popular book of domestic advice, *The Frugal Housewife* (1829), and an early antislavery book, *An Appeal in Favor of That Class of Americans Called Africans* (1833). This abolitionist work caused such controversy that canceled subscriptions bankrupted the juvenile magazine she edited, which was America's first. Child's works also include books sympathetic to Native Americans and an early feminist work, *The History of the Condition of Women* (1835). A brilliant thinker, she is perhaps best known for her 1844 Thanksgiving poem, "Over the River and Through the Woods."

CHISHOLM, SHIRLEY (1924–) The first black congresswoman, Chisholm was elected from the impoverished Bedford-Stuyvesant district of New York in 1968. She became a leader for women and minorities during the activist years of the 1960s and 1970s. As a candidate for president in 1972, she received the votes of 151 delegates at the Democratic National Convention. She remained active after her 1982 retirement from Congress, and in 1993, President Bill Clinton appointed her ambassador to Jamaica.

COCHRAN, JACQUELINE (1910?–1980) Cochran founded a cosmetics company that funded her real interest: flying. She beat a field of men to win a major race in 1938 and held seventeen speed records by 1940. In 1942, she organized the Women's Airforces Service Pilots, who performed military functions but were officially civilians and received no benefits. Cochran continued to fly after the war and in 1953 became the first woman to break the sound barrier.

COLEMAN, BESSIE (1893–1926) African American aviator Bessie Coleman, who is depicted on a 1995 postage stamp, went to France to learn to fly in 1921 because no American aviation school would accept her. She became the world's first black woman licensed to fly. Called "Queen Bess," she attracted large audiences—which she insisted be integrated—to daredevil shows all over the South, but she died just five years after being licensed. She was killed in Florida when she fell from the open cockpit of her plane—a death remarkably similar to that of HARRIET QUIMBY.

COLLINS, MARTHA LAYNE (1936–) Governor of Kentucky from 1983 to 1987, Martha Layne Collins was the nation's sixth female governor. A graduate of the University of Kentucky, she was a wife, mother, and teacher; she became active in Democratic politics, and in 1978, was elected lieutenant governor. Collins chaired the national association of lieutenant governors in 1982, and late that year, won Kentucky's gubernatorial election. Education and the environment were her top priorities; she raised academic standards and reduced strip mining—but the state had a one-term limit at the time, and she could not run for reelection.

COOPER, ANNA JULIA (1861–1965) Born in slavery, Cooper may have been the best-educated black woman in the world when she earned a 1925 doctorate at the Sorbonne. A Washington, D.C., educator for most of her life, she went to Paris after retiring, researched Haiti, and published two books in French. Earlier, she had published the autobiographical book *A Voice from the South* (1892). Cooper returned to Washington and lived to participate in the modern civil rights movement, dying at age 104.

CORBIN, MARGARET (1751–c. 1800) Like many Revolutionary War wives, Corbin was present on the battlefield at Manhattan's Fort Washington on November 16, 1776, when her husband was killed. Taking up his position as an artillery gunner, she continued firing until the end of the battle despite being wounded. The Continental Congress awarded her the first disabled soldier's pension granted to an American woman, and there is a monument at West Point that honors her.

CORI, GERTY RADNITZ (1896–1957) The first American woman to win the Nobel Prize in physiology or medicine, biochemist Cori won in 1947 for research on glucose enzymes and glycogen metabolism, which grew out of her work on malignant tumors. She shared the prize with her husband, Carl Cori; both earned their medical degrees in their native Prague and emigrated in 1922. They spent most of their working lives at Washington University in Saint Louis, but it was only after the Nobel honor that the university offered her a fully paid position. Sadly, it came just a decade prior to her death at age fifty-nine.

CROLY, JANE CUNNINGHAM (1829–1901) One of the best-known women of the Victorian era, Croly continued to work for New York newspapers as a journalist after her 1856 marriage and even after bearing five children. When she was excluded from an 1868 New York Press Club function for Charles Dickens, she founded Sorosis, perhaps the first professional women's association in the world. In 1890, she extended this principle nationally with the General Federation of Women's Clubs. Croly also wrote several books, most of which addressed women's issues.

DARE, VIRGINIA (1587–?) Virginia Dare was the first known child born to English parents in the Western Hemisphere. She disappeared along with her parents and the other members of the "Lost Colony" on North Carolina's Roanoke Island.

DENNETT, MARY COFFIN WARE (1872–1947) Although much less famous than MARGARET SANGER, Dennett's life closely paralleled Sanger's. Dennett took over the National Birth Control League in 1915 when Sanger fled to Europe; a decade later, she resigned in protest against what she saw as Sanger's acquiescence to physicians over women and free speech. *The Sex Side of Life*, a pamphlet she wrote for her sons in 1918, was widely distributed—even by the Young Men's Christian Association—until postal authorities deemed it obscene and began a decade of legal difficulties for Dennett. She nonetheless continued to write and speak for birth control, and when she finally won her court case in 1930, she celebrated with a book called *Who's Obscene?*

DICKINSON, EMILY (1830–1886) Dickinson lived a secluded life in her parents' home in Amherst, Massachusetts, while writing almost 1,800 poems. She did not seek publication during her lifetime, and when she died, literary critic Thomas Wentworth Higginson advised her family against publication, saying her work was "too crude." Dickinson, however, clearly intended her poems for posterity, and today she is considered one of the greatest American poets.

DIX, DOROTHEA (1802–1887) After a career as a teacher and author, Dix encountered the terrible conditions suffered by the mentally ill in jails and institutions. She toured Massachusetts and offered the legislature a report that motivated it to establish new mental hospitals. Dix then repeated the process in other states and Canada, providing the impetus for thirty-two new institutions. She was appointed superintendent of the United States Army Nurses during the Civil War, but when she became increasingly imperious, the War Department limited her authority in 1863.

DOUGLAS, MARJORY STONEMAN (1890–1998) Douglas wrote a great deal of fiction and nonfiction during her long life, but her best-known work was *The Everglades: River of Grass* (1947), which described the damage done to the unique Florida Everglades ecosystem by land developers and the Army Corps of Engineers. Her book eventually inspired action to protect the Everglades. A Massachusetts native, she remained mentally sharp until her death in Miami at age 107. President Bill Clinton awarded Douglas the Medal of Freedom in 1993.

DOVE, RITA (1952–) The youngest poet laureate of the United States, Dove served two terms as poet laureate in 1993-1995. Her latest book of poetry is *On the Bus With Rosa Parks* (1999). Among her many honors is a Pulitzer Prize for *Thomas and Beulah* (1986). She is the Commonwealth Professor of English at the University of Virginia.

DYER, MARY BARRETT (?–1660) A Quaker in the Puritan theocracy of the Massachusetts Bay Colony, Dyer was banished twice and threatened with execution, but she insisted on returning to preach in Boston, ignoring the pleas of her husband and five adult sons. She made a speech in favor of religious freedom before she was hanged for heresy. Her death was an important factor in lessening the power of the church in New England.

EARHART, AMELIA (1897–1937) Earhart was teaching English to immigrants in Boston in 1928 when the Putnam publishing firm conducted a search for a female pilot they could promote. Earhart, who was personable and attractive, was selected, and she flew across the Atlantic as a standby pilot. She became a national phenomenon and began to concentrate on earning her reputation. She set several records for speed and distance and was the first woman to fly solo across the Atlantic Ocean. Earhart set out on a round-the-world trip in June 1937; radio contact with her ceased on July 2 over the Pacific Ocean. Neither she nor her plane was ever found.

EDDY, MARY BAKER GLOVER PATTERSON (1821–1910) When she became physically ill after the death of her first husband in 1844, Eddy was treated with morphine, and she spent almost twenty years as a drugged invalid. After mesmerist Phineas Quimby convinced her that sickness was based on "false belief," she stopped taking medication and recovered her health. She began writing and teaching about her belief that prayer was superior to medication, attracting many followers as well as critics. In 1879 she formally founded the First Church of Christ, Scientist, and in 1908 she founded the *Christian Science Monitor*. When she died in Boston at age eighty-nine, Eddy left a well-established church and a $2 million estate.

EDERLE, GERTRUDE CAROLINE (1906–) The first woman to swim the English Channel, in 1926, Ederle did so almost two hours faster than any man had done. The achievement made her a huge celebrity in the Roaring Twenties, and New Yorkers organized a parade down Fifth Avenue in her honor.

ELION, GERTRUDE BELLE (1918–1999) One of the winners of the 1988 Nobel Prize in physiology or medicine, Elion worked to develop synthetic DNA, which can disrupt the reproductive cycles of viruses and bacteria. Her research made possible drugs that are used in treating leukemia, malaria, and other diseases; it also played a crucial role in overcoming tissue rejection in organ transplants. Elion, who lived in North Carolina after 1970, was a New Yorker. She earned a chemistry degree from Hunter College in 1937 but had to enroll in secretarial school to get her first job. She spent her career with the pharmaceutical firm of Burroughs Wellcome and held more than a dozen honorary doctorates.

EVERT, CHRIS (1954–) Born in Florida, Evert astonished the sports world by beating such tennis icons as MARGARET COURT and BILLIE JEAN KING while still a teenage amateur. She turned professional in 1972 and swept the international tournaments, winning the ladies' singles championship at Wimbledon at age nineteen. Holding at least seventeen major championships, she retired in 1989. Evert now does television appearances and runs a charitable foundation in Florida.

FAUSET, CRYSTAL BIRD (1893–1965) The first black woman in a state legislature, Faucet was elected to the Pennsylvania House of Representatives in 1938. The Democratic women who supported her—mostly whites—used the new method of a telephone campaign. Faucet inexplicably resigned from the legislature after only a year and returned to the Works Progress Administration. After she supported Republican Thomas Dewey against President Franklin Roosevelt in 1944, she no longer had a future in the Democratic Party, and the Republicans did not welcome her.

FELTON, REBECCA ANN LATIMER (1835–1930) The first woman sworn in as a member of the Senate, Felton had been politically active in her home state of Georgia since the 1870s, first with the Democratic Party and then with the Progressive Party. When a U.S. senator she had supported died in office, the governor appointed her to replace him. Congress had already adjourned, but at the beginning of the following term, the newly elected senator agreed to allow her to serve for one day. At age eighty-seven, Felton went to Washington and was sworn in November 21, 1922; she made a speech before resigning.

FERBER, EDNA (1885–1968) Best-selling novelist Ferber won the 1924 Pulitzer Prize for *So Big* and two years later had her biggest hit as a playwright with *Show Boat*. Most of her novels explored American historical settings; *Giant*, a sweeping Texas saga, became a hit movie for Elizabeth Taylor. Very popular with the public, she was perhaps the wealthiest author of her era.

FERRARO, GERALDINE (1935–) The first woman to be nominated for vice president of the United States by a major party, Ferraro was Walter Mondale's running mate in the 1984 election. A New Yorker, she is the daughter of an Italian immigrant. She earned a 1960 law degree from Fordham University and worked as a prosecutor while raising three children. She ran for Congress in 1978 and won a sound victory, replacing a thirty-year incumbent. A major women's advocate both in and out of office, Ferraro's autobiography is *My Story* (1985).

FINNEY, JOAN McINROY (1925-) Governor of Kansas between 1991 and 1995, Finney was the nation's tenth female governor. Her 1990 election was remarkable on several counts: Not only did she surprise pundits by upsetting the incumbent, she also won as a Democrat in a traditionally Republican state—and her victory made Kansas the first state to have women in both the U.S. Senate and the governor's mansion. Finney, who switched parties in 1974 after Republican leaders asked her to step aside for a man, became mayor of Topeka in 1973 and state treasurer the next year, a post she held until becoming governor.

FITZGERALD, ELLA (1918–1996) A leading jazz singer from 1938 on, Fitzgerald won countless awards. Her ability to improvise was especially valued by jazz aficionados, and despite the racial segregation that still existed for much of her career, she was greatly admired by both blacks and whites. The youngest person ever admitted to the American Society of Composers, Authors, and Publishers, she was honored at the White House in 1987 with the National Medal of the Arts.

FLEMING, WILLIAMINA STEVENS (1857–1911) Although she had worked as a teacher in her native Scotland, Fleming was forced to become a maid after her husband deserted her in Boston. Luckily her employer, the director of the Harvard Observatory, became so angry at his employees that he declared that his maid could do a better job, and he hired Fleming to do mathematical calculations in 1881. She eventually supervised dozens of female "computers" while also conducting independent scientific research—including the discovery of 222 variable stars. Her appointment as curator of astronomical photographs in 1898 was Harvard's first of a woman. She received honors in France and Mexico and was the first American woman elected to Britain's Royal Astronomical Society.

FLYNN, ELIZABETH GURLEY (1890–1964) When she was elected national chair of the Communist Party in 1961, Flynn had already spent her sixty-sixth birthday in federal prison. She spent a lifetime in leftist causes, beginning with speeches to miners for the Industrial Workers of the World in 1907. Her fiery red hair added to her attraction as a gifted orator, but Flynn was arrested several times in violation of her constitutional right to free speech. She supported World War II, but the repressive environment of the 1950s and the execution of ETHEL ROSENBERG further radicalized Flynn. She died in Moscow and had a state funeral in Red Square.

FOSTER, ABBY KELLY (1810–1887) A pioneer for abolitionism and women's rights, Foster spoke against slavery in the 1830s, when that was still a very risky position to take. Yet when William Lloyd Garrison rewarded her with an appointment to the business committee of the American Anti-Slavery Society in 1840, about half the male membership objected so strongly to the presence of a woman that they resigned. Her 1845 marriage to Stephen Symonds Foster was a very modern one: he tended their child while she continued her lecture tours. Progressives all their lives, the Fosters allowed their Massachusetts farm to be auctioned for taxes three times in the 1870s; friends bought the farm and returned it to them, but it made her point of no taxation without representation.

FOSTER, HANNAH WEBSTER (1758–1840) The anonymous author of one of America's first novels, Foster published *The Coquette* in 1797. The title page said it was by "A Lady of Massachusetts"; Foster's name did not appear on it until 1866, when she had been dead for more than a quarter century. Along with the work of SUSANNA ROWSON HASWELL, Foster's novel set precedents long before those of more famous male authors. *The Coquette*, which features a woman who rejects conventional standards, has been continually reprinted for two centuries.

FRIEDAN, BETTY NAOMI GOLDSTEIN (1921–) In 1963, Friedan's book *The Feminine Mystique* documented the dissatisfaction American women felt with their lives at midcentury. A best-seller, it led her to found the National Organization for Women (NOW) in 1966, with the goal of securing real equality for women. She stepped down from the presidency of NOW in 1970 and has continued to write about women's issues.

FULLER, MARGARET (1810–1850) A founder of the transcendentalist philosophical movement in the 1840s, Fuller edited its journal, the *Dial*. Horace Greeley, editor of the *New York Tribune*, noticed her writing and invited her to join his staff, making her the first professional book reviewer in the United States. Fuller also published *Woman in the Nineteenth Century* (1845), the leading book on American feminist thought for decades. In 1846 Greeley appointed her foreign correspondent; she went to Europe, married an Italian count, and participated in Italy's 1848 revolution. She and her husband, along with their baby—born before their marriage—drowned in a shipwreck returning to the United States.

GAGE, MATILDA JOSLYN (1826–1898) Although not nearly as well known as SUSAN B. ANTHONY and ELIZABETH CADY STANTON, Gage was a coequal author with them of the first three volumes of *The History of Woman Suffrage*. She met Anthony in 1854 when she paid Anthony's bills after her purse was stolen. Known for her stylish dress and happy marriage, Gage was in fact a deeper thinker than most other suffragists, who did not keep pace with her rise in consciousness. After the 1893 publication of her radical *Woman, Church and State*, Gage was almost entirely dropped by the suffragist leadership, but her books, including *Woman as Inventor* (1870) and *Woman's Rights Catechism* (1871), have remained fresh. She lived most of her life in Fayetteville, New York, but died in Chicago while visiting her daughter and her son-in-law L. Frank Baum, author of the *Wizard of Oz*.

GIBSON, ALTHEA (1927–) The first black American to play in the Wimbledon tennis tournament (in 1951), Gibson won the tournament in 1957 and was named Woman Athlete of the Year by the Associated Press. In 1960 she won the World Professional Tennis Championship. One of relatively few women in the Black Sports Hall of Fame, Gibson wrote *I Always Wanted to Be Somebody* (1958).

GINSBERG, RUTH BADER (1933–) Ginsberg graduated from Harvard Law School in 1959, when there were only nine women in the class. After several years as a law professor, she was appointed to the United States Court of Appeals for the District of Columbia in 1980. In 1993, President Bill Clinton appointed her to the United States Supreme Court, making Ginsberg the second woman to serve on the nation's highest court.

GLASGOW, ELLEN ANDERSON GHOULSON (1873–1945) Born in Virginia, Glasgow published the first of her critically acclaimed novels in 1902. Unlike almost any other major author, she also led her state's efforts for the vote for women. Her career climaxed with her election to the American Academy of Arts and Letters in 1940, and she won a Pulitzer Prize the following year. Glasgow's last novel appeared in 1966—more than two decades after her death.

GOLDMAN, EMMA (1869–1940) "Red Emma" was the best-known leftist woman of her time. From the 1890s through her deportation in 1918, she spoke and wrote against war and repressive capitalism and for free speech and free love. Repeatedly arrested, she published *Mother Earth*, a radical monthly, as well as several books, including the intellectual *Social Significance of Modern Drama* (1914). Deported after making antiwar speeches, Goldman was allowed to visit the United States again in 1934, after publication of *My Disillusionment in Russia* (1923). She lived in Canada while raising funds for Scandinavians and others who were resisting the Nazis.

GRAHAM, KATHARINE MEYER (1917–) Katharine Meyer's father owned the *Washington Post*, and her husband, Phil Graham, gradually took over the business from him. When Phil Graham committed suicide in 1963, Katharine Graham became president of the Washington Post Company. Her leadership of the paper, particularly the *Post*'s exposure of the Watergate scandal, has been widely admired, as was her 1998 autobiography, *Personal History*.

GRAHAM, MARTHA (1894?–1991) During a dance career that spanned the half century between 1920 and 1970, Graham became the nation's leading choreographer and the driving force behind modern dance. After retiring from the stage, she was director of the Martha Graham Center of Contemporary Dance.

GRASSO, ELLA TAMBUSSI (1919–1981) The first female governor whose career was independent of any male relative, Ella Grasso won the Connecticut governorship in 1974. A Democrat, she was the daughter of Italian immigrants, a 1952 Mount Holyoke graduate, and a congresswoman since 1970. She defeated a Republican congressman for the governorship and was reelected in a landslide in 1978; her colleagues demonstrated their esteem for her by choosing Grasso to chair the Democratic Governors Conference in 1979. She was being discussed as a possible presidential contender when cancer struck. She resigned in December 1980 and died a few weeks later. Thomas Grasso, her husband since 1942, survived her; he had kept such a low profile that when he died in 1999, many learned of his existence for the first time.

GRIMKÉ, SARAH (1792–1873) and ANGELINA (later WELD) (1805–1879) The Grimké sisters were born to a wealthy family in Charleston, South Carolina, where they saw the horror of slavery firsthand. They moved to Philadelphia, and in 1829 Angelina wrote a letter to William Lloyd Garrison's antislavery newspaper testifying to slavery's cruelty. Abolitionists welcomed this personal experience, and the Grimkés wrote and spoke against slavery as no other southerners would, attracting huge crowds throughout New England. The presence of black guests at Angelina's 1838 wedding to abolitionist Theodore Weld provoked a riot in Philadelphia.

Sarah Grimké lived with the Welds and edited *American Slavery as It Is: Testimony of a Thousand Voices* (1839) with Theodore Weld. They moved to Boston in 1863, and, after the Civil War ended, the sisters adopted their two biracial nephews. Sarah Grimké had added feminism to her abolitionism back in 1838, when she published *Letters on the Equality of the Sexes*, and in 1870 the Grimkés were among the Boston women who tested the gender-neutral language of the Fifteenth Amendment by attempting to vote. The ballots of these true American heroes were rejected because they were women. Both sisters died in Boston a few years later.

HAMER, FANNIE LOU TOWNSEND (1917–1977)

Hamer, a sharecropper, threw the 1964 Democratic National Convention into chaos when her "Mississippi Freedom" delegation of blacks challenged the credentials of the state's all-white representation. Earlier, she had endured jailings and beatings for civil rights actions in Mississippi and South Carolina. Her moving speech at the convention made national television, and she followed up with a trip to Africa. Hamer received several honorary degrees from black colleges before her death at age 59; although she died of cancer, she never completely recovered from kidney damage inflicted when she was beaten in a South Carolina jail.

HAMILTON, ALICE (1869–1970)

Hamilton, who is depicted on a 55-cent postage stamp, became a professor at the Woman's Medical School of Northwestern University in Chicago in 1897. She chose to live at Hull House, JANE ADDAMS's charitable center, where she became interested in the health problems caused by toxic industrial working conditions. Hamilton pioneered the study of toxicology and in 1919 became the first woman on the staff of Harvard Medical School. She published several classic works and remained active in progressive politics throughout her long life.

HANSBERRY, LORRAINE VIVIAN (1930–1965)

The first black female playwright to be produced on Broadway, Hansberry's big success came just six years before her premature death. Her play *A Raisin in the Sun* (1959) was highly autobiographical, reflecting the life of Hansberry's Chicago family. It won the New York Drama Critics Circle Award and continues to be frequently produced.

HARPER, FRANCES ELLEN WATKINS (1825–1911)

The most celebrated black poet of the nineteenth century was born free in Baltimore but moved north after the 1850 Fugitive Slave Act increased harassment of free blacks. She published *Poems on Miscellaneous Subjects* in 1854 but supported herself by lecturing against slavery throughout the Northeast. After the Civil War, Harper lectured in the South on the educational needs of freed slaves. An 1859 short story, "The Two Offers," was possibly the first published by a black woman. She is also known for an 1892 novel, *Iola Leroy*, or *Shadows Uplifted*.

HARRIS, PATRICIA ROBERTS (1924–1985)

The first black female ambassador, attorney Harris was appointed to Luxembourg in 1965 by President Lyndon Johnson. She also served in two cabinet positions for President Jimmy Carter: after heading the Department of Housing and Urban Development, she took over the Department of Health, Education, and Welfare in 1979. A graduate of Howard University and George Washington University Law School, Harris lost a 1982 race for mayor of Washington, D.C., to Marion Barry—shortly before he was convicted of drug felonies.

HEPBURN, KATHARINE (1909–)

Hepburn won four Academy Awards over the course of her fifty-year acting career. Most of her roles featured Hepburn as a smart, independent woman; many were played with her longtime lover, Spencer Tracy. Her films include *The Philadelphia Story* (1940), *The African Queen* (1952), *Guess Who's Coming to Dinner* (1967), *The Lion in Winter* (1968), and *On Golden Pond* (1981). She published her autobiography, *Me*, in 1981.

HOBBY, OVETA CULP (1905–1995)

Hobby was a lawyer and a newspaper executive before heading the Women's Army Corps from its 1942 creation at the beginning of World War II. She spent three years recruiting, training, and supervising almost 100,000 women stationed all over the globe, while dealing with the sexism of the military. After the war, Hobby returned to her native Texas, where she expanded her late husband's publishing business into a television network. President Dwight Eisenhower selected her to create a second federal agency in 1952, when she headed the new Department of Health, Education, and Welfare. She dealt with many difficult issues in this complex and massive department, especially controversy over distribution of the new polio vaccine. Hobby resigned in 1955 and returned to her very successful Houston businesses.

HOLIDAY, BILLIE (1915?–1959) Possibly the most important female jazz artist of all time, Holiday began singing in Harlem nightclubs as a teenager. She made her first record in 1936 and toured with Count Basie's and Artie Shaw's bands in 1937 and 1938. Throughout the 1940s and 1950s, she performed and recorded in both Europe and the United States, but she also struggled with an unhappy personal life, racial discrimination, and the drug addiction that killed her in 1959.

HOPPER, GRACE (1907–1992) Known with good reason as "Amazing Grace," Hopper programmed the nation's first large-scale digital computer to calculate targets for the D-day invasion of Europe while working as a mathematician for the United States Navy's female auxiliary, the WAVES (Women Accepted for Volunteer Emergency Service). She remained with the navy after the war and wrote many computer programs. The Data Processing Management Association named her Man of the Year in 1969. When she retired in 1986, at age seventy-nine, she was the nation's oldest military officer on active duty.

HORNEY, KAREN DANIELSON (1885–1952) The first psychologist to challenge Freudian assumptions about women, Horney published *New Ways in Psychoanalysis* in 1939. She earned her medical degree at the University of Berlin in 1911, immigrated to the United States in 1932, and developed a successful New York practice. When her ideas were rejected by many men in the profession because she questioned Freudian orthodoxy, she and her supporters founded the Association for the Advancement of Psychoanalysis in 1941.

HOWE, JULIA WARD (1819–1910) Howe achieved celebrity with the publication of her poem "The Battle Hymn of the Republic," which became the Union anthem of the Civil War. After the war, women's rights leaders capitalized on her popularity by making her the first president of the American Women Suffrage Association in 1869. She also lectured and wrote books and articles. In 1871 she became the founding president of the feminist group, New England Woman's Club. Although her marriage to Samuel Gridley Howe—an educator of the blind who was famous in his own right—was difficult, the public was unaware of it and regarded her as an affluent, intellectual Boston celebrity. She was much honored, and her likeness appeared on a 1988 postage stamp.

HUERTA, DOLORES (1930–) A founder of the United Farm Workers union in 1962, Huerta has given a lifetime to Chicana causes and especially those of migrant workers. A longtime Washington lobbyist, she also has led boycotts on grapes and other agricultural products to obtain minimum-wage contracts for those who harvest America's food.

HURSTON, ZORA NEALE (1901?–1960) Hurston was part of the vibrant 1930s literary scene called the Harlem Renaissance. She collaborated with poet Langston Hughes on a 1931 play and then published six books dealing with African American life. *Their Eyes Were Watching God* (1937) is her best-known work. In 1948 Hurston was falsely accused of sexual abuse, which ruined her career; she returned to her native Florida and lived in poverty. Since Robert Hemenway published a popular biography of her in 1977, much of Hurston's writing has been reissued.

HUTCHINSON, ANNE MARBURY (1591–1643) Hutchinson was the mother of nine when she immigrated to Boston from England in 1634. She developed beliefs that were less harsh than Puritan theology, and her charisma and leadership attracted followers, including many men, making her a threat to the leaders of the Massachusetts Bay Colony—where church and state were synonymous. Hutchinson was pregnant and almost forty-seven when she was tried for heresy and banished in 1638. Her family moved to the two-year-old colony of Rhode Island, and after her husband's death in 1642, she moved to New York, where Algonquians killed her and five of her children.

JACOBI, MARY PUTNAM (1842–1906) The first woman admitted to Paris's Ecole de Medecine, Mary Putnam had already earned an 1863 degree from Woman's Medical College of Pennsylvania. Her postgraduate work in France earned high honors, and when she returned to her prominent publishing family in New York in 1871, she established a strong practice. She continued to work after marriage and motherhood, supported suffrage, and, with the publication of over 100 scientific papers, was considered the preeminent female physician of the nineteenth century.

JEMISON, MAE (1956–) The first black female astronaut, Jemison earned a 1977 degree in chemical engineering at Stanford University and graduated from the Cornell University medical school in 1981. She joined the National Aeronautics and Space Administration (NASA) in 1987 and flew in space in 1992, experimenting with the physiological effects of zero gravity. Jemison resigned from NASA in 1993 to form her own research and development company.

JORDAN, BARBARA (1936–1996) When Jordan was elected to the Texas state senate as a young lawyer in 1966, she was the only woman and the only black person. She designed a Houston congressional district for herself in the reapportionment of 1972 and became the first black woman elected to Congress from the Deep South. During the 1974 Nixon impeachment proceedings, Jordan captured national attention with her oratorical skill and was invited to give the keynote speech at the 1976 Democratic National Convention, the first black and the first woman to do so. In 1978, she left the Senate to teach at the University of Texas and write her autobiography.

JOYNER-KERSEE, JACKIE (1962–) Joyner-Kersee was considered the world's best all-around female athlete in the late 1980s and early 1990s, as well as the greatest heptathlete ever. At the 1988 Olympic Summer Games, she set world and Olympic records in the heptathlon—which comprises seven different track and field events—as well as the Olympic record in the long jump. At the 1992 Olympic Summer Games, she again won the gold medal in the heptathlon.

JUDSON, (NANCY) ANN HASSELTINE (1789–1826) With HARRIET NEWELL, Judson was America's first overseas female missionary. She died in Burma, largely as a result of famine. During the fourteen years her after arrival in 1812, she bore and lost two children and saw her husband imprisoned, but she also translated English into Burmese and taught classes for native women.

KAEL, PAULINE (1919–) The *New York Times* film critic for many years, Kael has greatly influenced American life through her writing about film. She helped to define it as an art form, adding a new dimension to twentieth-century culture.

KELLER, HELEN (1880–1968) Blind and deaf since infancy, Keller would have passed her life in isolation but for the intervention of teacher Anne Sullivan, who remained with Keller for the rest of her life. After attending the Perkins School for the Blind and receiving some other schooling, Keller entered Radcliffe College and graduated cum laude in 1904. She then embarked on a career of writing, lecturing, and political activism for liberal causes. She raised $2 million for the American Foundation for the Blind and was especially effective in urging treatment for newborns to prevent blindness—an area that was controversial because infantile blindness was often caused by parental venereal disease.

KEMBLE, FANNY (1809–1893) Kemble began acting in her father's London theater in 1829 and toured the United States from 1832 to 1834, when she married a Georgia man. She left her husband in 1846, partly because of her opposition to slavery, and—in an era when men automatically got child custody—was reunited with her children only after their father died in 1867. Kemble supported herself in London and Massachusetts by giving readings of Shakespeare and by writing poems, essays, and plays. Her books included *Journal of a Residence on a Georgian Plantation* (1863) and a three-volume autobiography. She also introduced the garment that was later named for AMELIA BLOOMER.

KING, BILLIE JEAN MOFFITT (1943–) A tennis star since 1962, when she defeated MARGARET COURT at age eighteen, King held a record twenty Wimbledon championships by 1980. Feminists throughout the world were glued to their televisions in 1973, when King and Bobby Riggs played a match in Houston; he and most sports experts had denigrated her ability, and he had bragged that a woman could not beat a man, but she soundly trounced him. A founder of the Women's Sports Foundation, King probably has done more than anyone else to encourage girls in athletics.

KUNIN, MADELEINE MAY (1933–) Vermont's governor between 1985 and 1991, Kunin was born Jewish in Switzerland; her widowed mother brought her to the United States only months before the beginning of World War II. She worked her way through the University of Massachusetts and earned a master's degree from Columbia University in 1957. After she married and had children, Kunin volunteered with the League of Women Voters and was elected to the Vermont legislature in 1972. A Democrat in a traditionally Republican state, she won a close race for lieutenant governor in 1978, lost a 1982 gubernatorial attempt, and then won in 1984—defeating the incumbent Republican by a mere sixty votes. In her first two-year term, she managed to erase a $35 million debt and raise the education budget by 25%. She was reelected several times, and in 1990 she announced that she would not seek a fourth term.

KUSHNER, ROSE (1930–1990) A psychologist and medical writer, Kushner changed standard medical practice with her 1975 book, *What Every Woman Should Know About Breast Cancer to Save Her Life*. Although physicians initially scorned her, Kushner played a major role in reducing the number of radical mastectomies and in empowering women to use self-examination techniques that are now universally recommended by physicians.

LA FLESCHE, SUSAN (later PICOTTE) (1865–1915) The first female Native American physician, La Flesche was the youngest child of the chief of the Omaha tribe. She graduated at the top of her class from Woman's Medical College of Pennsylvania in 1889 and returned to Nebraska, where she continued to practice after her 1894 marriage and motherhood. She led a delegation of Omaha to Washington in 1906 and functioned as chief after her father's death.

LA FLESCHE, SUSETTE (later TIBBLES) (1854–1903) Using her native name "Bright Eyes" and wearing native dress, La Flesche created a sensation in eastern cities of the Victorian age. The oldest child of the chief of the Omaha tribe, she and her sisters were schooled in New Jersey and at Virginia's Hampton Institute, which was highly uncommon for American Indian girls at the time. La Flesche then taught on the Nebraska reservation until 1879, when she interpreted for Chief Standing Bear as he went on a national tour to publicize the deaths of a third of his tribe, the Ponca. It was the first time that many easterners heard anything from a Native American point of view, and she was invited to speak in Boston's historic Faneuil Hall. She married a white man in 1881 and, with his support, went on to testify before Congress at least twice. She lectured in England in 1886, lived briefly in Washington, D.C., and died back in Nebraska.

LATHROP, JULIA CLIFFORD (1858–1932) The first woman to head a federal bureau in Washington, Lathrop received this honor in 1912—before most women could vote. An 1880 graduate of Vassar College, she was a pioneer of social work and had lived two decades at JANE ADDAMS's Hull House in Chicago when Republican President William Howard Taft appointed her to head the new federal Children's Bureau. Democratic President Woodrow Wilson reappointed her when Taft was defeated a few months later. Lathrop led a crusade against child labor and for programs that benefited women as well as children, including mothers' pensions and maternal death prevention. She retired in 1921 but continued to serve on international committees, and she was honored by the governments of Poland and Czechoslovakia for her work in resettling World War I orphans.

LAZARUS, EMMA (1849–1887) Although they might not know Lazarus's name, almost every American knows her words: "Give me your tired, your poor, your huddled masses yearning to breathe free. . . ." Written to raise funds for the Statue of Liberty, her poem became so popular that it was inscribed at the statue's base. Lazarus's family had lived in America since the 1600s, but as a Sephardic Jew, she was a minority within a minority. She lived her entire life in New York City, where she wrote prose, a play, and books of poetry and died at age thirty-eight.

LEAVITT, HENRIETTA SWAN (1886–1921) Although less honored an astronomer than her contemporaries, ANNIE JUMP CANNON and WILLIAMINA FLEMING, Leavitt discovered some 2,400 variable stars—about half of those known in her time. Many male astronomers were delighted to have found one star, and Leavitt should have been far more recognized than she was. She began her work as a volunteer at the Harvard Observatory in 1895, was hired in 1902, and spent the rest of her life studying the heavens.

LEE, "MOTHER" ANN (1736–1784) Founder of the American religious community known as Shakers, Lee's influence long outlasted the decade that she lived in the United States. She spent most of her life in lower-class Manchester, England, where she was exposed to the Society of Friends (Quakers) and a subgroup called Shakers. Unhappily married, she continued to be known by her maiden name, and she bore four children, all of whom died. After mystical experiences around 1770, several friends began to see her as a prophet and saint; most were men, which was especially surprising given that the chief tenet of her new faith was celibacy. Twice jailed for dissident preaching, she and eight disciples immigrated to the Albany, New York, area in 1774. When the American Revolution broke out soon after, Lee was jailed again by Americans who suspected her of being a British agent, but part of her creed was pacifism. She conducted a successful tour of New England in 1781–1783, converting entire congregations, and when she died at age forty-eight, several thousand Americans had adopted her beliefs. Shakers went on to develop eighteen utopian colonies, where men and women lived without sexual relations, in eight states. They supported themselves by making quality furniture, brooms, and other crafts; several of their colonies are now museums.

LESLIE, MIRIAM FLORENCE FOLLINE (1836–1914) Divorced three times in an era when that was almost beyond comprehension, Leslie legally changed her name to that of her third husband, Frank Leslie, when he died in 1880. She inherited the empire of newspapers and magazines that he had named for himself and demonstrated great business acumen in paying his debts and streamlining operations. Termed "the empress of journalism," she wrote several books, but she is especially known for her suffrage work; she left nearly $2 million to CARRIE CHAPMAN CATT to be spent for that cause. Although probate reduced the amount, her support was so substantial that it may have been the single greatest factor contributing to women's enfranchisement just six years after her death.

LEVI-MONTALCINI, RITA (1901–) The winner of the 1986 Nobel Prize in physiology or medicine, neurologist Levi-Montalcini was born in Turin, Italy, to a father named Levi and a mother named Montalcini. She graduated from medical school summa cum laude in 1936, but her internship in neurology and psychiatry was soon interrupted by fascism and World War II. Levi-Montalcini worked as a physician for refugees and immigrated to the United States in 1947, becoming a citizen in 1956. A pioneer in neuroembryology, she also established a research unit in Rome in 1962; the next year, she was honored by the United Cerebral Palsy Association for developing techniques to selectively grow parts of the nervous system. She was affiliated with Washington University in Saint Louis for her entire American career. She retired in 1977 and published an autobiography, *In Praise of Imperfection*, in 1988.

LIN, MAYA (1959–) When the winner of an anonymous competition to select an architect for Washington's Vietnam Memorial was announced in 1980, the eight male judges were shocked to discover that from 1,421 entries, they had chosen a design by a twenty-one-year-old female Chinese American student. Lin's proposal—a long black granite wall chronologically listing each American who died in the war—became the target of bitter criticism, and some funders, including Texas billionaire Ross Perot, refused to sponsor it. Lin's design worked out beautifully, however, and millions of visitors testify to its great evocative power. Born in Ohio to parents who emigrated from China in the 1940s, Lin graduated from Yale University in 1981 and earned a master's degree there in 1986. Working out of New York, she has designed other significant works, including the Civil Rights Memorial in Montgomery, Alabama, and the Women's Table at Yale University.

LIVERMORE, MARY ASHTON RICE (1820–1905) Immensely popular in her time, Livermore served a role in the Civil War equivalent to that of CLARA BARTON. She headed the United States Sanitary Commission in the Midwest, developing 3,000 local units that provided soldiers with essential supplies. Happily married to a Unitarian minister, she founded the Illinois Suffrage Association in 1868, and she edited the *Woman's Journal* after moving to Boston. Her lecture tours were profitable for two decades. In 1873, she became the first president of the Association for the Advancement of Women, and she headed the American Woman Suffrage Association during the difficult times when its former president, the Reverend Henry Ward Beecher, was tried for adultery. With FRANCES WILLARD, she edited *A Woman of the Century* (1893), a biographical reference book that functioned much like *Who's Who*. Among several other books, Livermore had a best-seller with *My Story of the War* (1887).

LOCKWOOD, BELVA BENNETT McNALL (1830–1917) The first female attorney to practice before the United States Supreme Court, Lockwood did not come by her achievement easily. A widowed teacher, she was elected school superintendent in Lockport, New York, in 1857. At the end of the Civil War, she moved with her child to Washington, D.C., where she began a coeducational school. After remarrying, Lockwood began her quest to become a lawyer, but no local law school was willing to admit a woman until a new institution, National University Law School (now George Washington University), accepted her. She finished her course work in 1873, but school officials refused to grant her degree until President Ulysses S. Grant intervened on Lockwood's behalf. Then the federal courts refused to admit her (essential to practice in the District of Columbia, which lacks a state government). When she lost her appeal to the Supreme Court, Lockwood lobbied friends in Congress for enabling legislation, and finally—a decade after beginning law school—she was authorized to practice in 1879.

Meanwhile, Lockwood lectured nationally for suffrage. With support from women on the West Coast, she formed the National Equal Rights Party, and in 1884, the party emulated VICTORIA WOODHULL's 1872 campaign and audaciously nominated Lockwood for president. She won some 4,000 votes in six states among ten million cast, but the exercise nonetheless raised public awareness of women's issues and also provided Lockwood's law practice with excellent name recognition. Indeed, her most successful case came very late in life: she won $5 million for eastern Cherokees in 1906, arguing before the Supreme Court when she was seventy-six.

LONGWORTH, ALICE LEE ROOSEVELT (1884–1980) President Theodore Roosevelt once said of his teenage daughter Alice that he could either govern the country or govern Alice, but he couldn't do both. Two decades before the Roaring Twenties, she delighted in scandalizing the public by smoking, gambling, and otherwise defying Victorian norms. Her 1906 marriage to future Speaker of the House Nicholas Longworth—a Republican like her father—did not diminish her independence, and when she bore her only child at age forty-one, Washington was full of gossip that the fifty-six-year-old congressman was not the father. Although her social mores might be termed liberal, her politics were conservative, and when her first cousin ELEANOR ROOSEVELT entered the White House, newspapers soon learned that Longworth was available for colorful anti-Democratic comments. For decades, she was an often-quoted insider source.

LOW, JULIETTE MAGILL KINZIE GORDON (1860–1927)

Founder of the Girl Scouts, Low's personal life did not match the image most would assume. Her 1886 marriage was so unhappy that her husband sought to divorce her, but he could not under Georgia law. When he died after eighteen years of wedlock, he left most of his estate to his mistress, and Low had long legal battles for financial security.

Born in Savannah, Georgia, Low lived in Europe much of her life, and it was in Britain that she became aware of Boy Scouts and Girl Guides. After leading a troop in Scotland, she introduced the idea in Savannah in 1912; a troop in Tampa, Florida, organized by her friend Jessamine Flowers Link, soon followed. Low spent the remainder of her life building the Girl Scouts. She established a Washington headquarters in 1913, formalized the name in 1915, and began the famous cookie sales in the early 1920s, shortly before her death. With remarkable organizational ability, she had established a troop in every state in the nation within fifteen years.

LUCE, CLARE BOOTH (1903–1987)

One of the nation's best-known women at midcentury, she edited such sophisticated magazines as *Vogue* and *Vanity Fair* prior to her 1935 marriage to publishing tycoon Henry Luce. The next year, she published her second play, *The Women*, which was so presciently feminist that it was more popular at the end of the century than it was in the 1930s. Luce was elected to Congress from an affluent Connecticut district in 1942; quickly promoted, she gave the keynote address at the Republican National Convention in 1944, but she declined to run in the next election, primarily because of the death of her daughter.

When Republicans returned to the White House in 1952, President Dwight Eisenhower appointed Luce ambassador to Italy, the highest such appointment at that time; she left the post in 1956. Eisenhower named her as ambassador to Brazil in 1959, but Luce resigned only a

month after winning a bitter Senate confirmation fight. She had grown increasingly conservative, and as her earlier feminism was replaced with right-wing views, women no longer supported her. Luce retired to Hawaii until the 1980 election of Ronald Reagan, when she returned to Washington. President Reagan awarded her the Medal of Freedom in 1983, and she died in Washington at age eighty-four.

LUCY, AUTHERINE JUANITA (1930–)

Too often overlooked in the history of the modern civil rights movement, Lucy was the first black person to attempt to integrate the University of Alabama—in February 1956, less than two years after the Supreme Court's desegregation ruling. White students rioted when she enrolled, and three days later, the administration suspended her. Despite threats to her life, she returned to court and affirmed her right to enroll, but in March the administration expelled her. No civil rights officials pursued this obvious miscarriage of justice, and Lucy's courageous effort to integrate a Deep South institution is seldom noted.

LUDINGTON, SYBIL (later OGDEN) (1761–1838)

On the night of April 26, 1777, sixteen-year-old Ludington rode through Putnam County, New York, alerting sleeping soldiers to the burning of Danbury, Connecticut. Her forty-mile ride was much longer and more dangerous than that of famed Paul Revere, and both George Washington and Comte de Rochambeau of France came to thank her after the battle. The oldest of twelve children, she married a lawyer in 1784 and had six children. Bethel, Connecticut, honored Ludington with a large statue (sculpted by Anna Hyatt Huntington) in 1961, and when the nation celebrated its bicentennial in 1976, a postage stamp was issued in her honor.

LYON, MARY MASON (1791–1849)

A pioneer educator, Mary Lyon founded what was in fact the first college for women, although she did not risk public disfavor by calling it that. All higher education was closed to women at the time, but she eagerly studied on her own and started teaching at age seventeen. She visited EMMA WILLARD's girls' school in 1833 and went as far as Michigan observing the educational environment for women. Returning to Massachusetts, she literally went door to door seeking money, and within two years she raised some $15,000. With support from the town of South Hadley, she opened Mount Holyoke Female Seminary in 1837. The curriculum met the standards of modern colleges, and she established a work-study plan to make tuition affordable. The school's quick success demonstrated the desire of women to learn. Lyon is buried on the grounds of what is now Mount Holyoke College.

MAASS, CLARA (1876–1901) A 1976 postage stamp commemorates Maass, who gave her life in experiments to determine the cause of yellow fever. The daughter of German immigrants, she graduated from a Newark nursing school in 1895 and worked in the Spanish-American War, in which far more deaths resulted from yellow fever than from combat. The only woman in the postwar experiments, she earned $100 by allowing herself to be bitten by the mosquito suspected of carrying the disease. She died in Havana, Cuba, at age 25.

MADISON, DOLLEY PAYNE TODD (1768–1849) As first lady, Madison was the first to create a persona for herself and for the White House, and she set social standards that continued far into the future. Although her husband was the nation's fourth president, in many ways she was the first first lady; the White House did not exist during Washington's administration and was still under construction at the end of Adams's term, and Jefferson, the third president, was a widower. Immensely popular, she helped America's image with older nations, even though she smoked a pipe and played cards. She is particularly remembered for saving valuable papers and art when the British set the presidential home on fire during the War of 1812—while James Madison joined the retreating army.

MAHONEY, MARY ELIZABETH (1845–1926) Known as the first black professional nurse, Mahoney graduated from MARIE ZAKRZEWSKA's school of nursing in 1879. She had been born free in Boston but worked in menial jobs until entering nursing school at age thirty-three. Mahoney worked as a private nurse throughout the Northeast and ended her career running an orphanage on Long Island, New York. She joined white women in the American Nurses Association, but Mahoney also was a founder of the National Association of Colored Graduate Nurses in 1908.

MANKILLER, WILMA (1945–) Chief of the Cherokee Nation from 1985 to 1995, Mankiller was born in Oklahoma but grew up in San Francisco. She participated in a 1969 American Indian occupation of Alcatraz Island and then was unhappily married to a wealthy Ecuadoran before returning to Oklahoma in 1977. She had studied at two California colleges and graduated from Oklahoma's Flaming Rainbow College in 1977. Her work in economic development for the tribe was so successful that, less than a decade later, the nation's second-largest tribe chose her as its

first female chief. Governing from Tahlequah, Oklahoma, she tripled tribal membership and became an internationally known advocate for Indian rights. Mankiller—whose name dates back to an eighteenth-century ancestor—has since coedited a book with GLORIA STEINEM.

MAYER, MARIA GOEPPERT (1906–1972) In 1963, Mayer became the first American woman to win the Nobel Prize in physics, after a lifetime of largely unpaid jobs. Born in Germany, she entered the University of Göttingen in 1924, where she studied with pioneers in quantum mechanics. She married an American physicist and came to the United States in 1930. Mayer wrote an outstanding doctoral dissertation that same year and, while raising two children in the next decade, continued her research on nuclear structure, published monographs, and coauthored a widely used textbook. Like BARBARA McCLINTOCK and other female scientists, Mayer found opportunity with World War II, joining her friend Enrico Fermi on the Manhattan Project to build the atomic bomb. After the war, the University of Chicago gave her the rank of full professor—but without a salary. Her first genuine academic job came almost three decades after her Ph.D., when the University of California hired both her and her husband in 1959. Just five years later, she was awarded the Nobel Prize for her work in the 1940s, which demonstrated that atomic nuclei contain successive shells.

McAFEE, MILDRED (later HORTON) (1906–) As head of the United States Navy's female auxiliary, the WAVES (Women Accepted for Volunteer Emergency Service), during World War II, McAfee commanded some 100,000 women around the world. She created this naval unit with only the slightly older Women's Army Corps as a model. Called "Miss Mac" during most of her naval career, she never rose above captain, a rank given to men who command as few as 500. McAfee came to this position at age thirty-six, from the presidency of Wellesley College, and returned to academia at the war's end. She married during the war and conventionally took her husband's name, but that received almost no media attention; indeed, McAfee's remarkable ability to handle publicity was key to the smooth launch of naval women.

McCLINTOCK, BARBARA (1902–1992) Winner of the 1983 Nobel Prize in physiology or medicine, McClintock was only the third woman to win a Nobel in science that was not shared with other recipients. A pioneer geneticist, she won for her discovery of "jumping genes"—the idea that genes are capable of moving within a chromosome. Cells in corn plants were her primary research tool, and her theory was greeted with scorn when she first presented it. For most of her life, McClintock struggled as a woman in science. Despite a 1927 doctorate from Cornell University, she lived on money earned from part-time jobs until 1936, when she finally was offered an assistant professorship in Missouri. World War II opened opportunities for women, and McClintock moved to the Cold Spring Harbor Laboratory on Long Island, New York. She was elected president of the Genetics Society of America in 1944, but full recognition eluded her until she was in her seventies.

McCORMICK, ANNE ELIZABETH O'HARE (1880–1954)
The first female newspaper correspondent to win the Pulitzer Prize (1937), McCormick also was the first woman on the *New York Times* editorial board (1936). She did not grow up privileged; indeed, her deserted mother was so poor that young Anne peddled her poetry door to door. Marriage at age thirty gave her an opportunity to travel with her husband, and she made the most of it. In an era when most women were limited to the "women's pages" of newspapers, the *Times* gave her a permanent column in 1925, and she conducted interviews with Adolf Hitler, Joseph Stalin, Winston Churchill, and other giants of the era. Two collections of McCormick's columns were published after her death.

McCORMICK, RUTH HANNA (1880–1944)
Daughter of Republican kingmaker Mark Hanna, McCormick's early life closely paralleled that of RUTH BRYAN OWEN: both women won congressional elections in 1928, despite being widows with young children. An officer in the National American Woman Suffrage Association in the decade before women won the vote, McCormick grew more conservative during the 1920s, disavowing her former feminist associations when she ran for Congress. Illinois voters elected her, but she immediately began concentrating on the next race, filing for the Senate just two months after joining the House. Although Republicans nominated her, she resoundingly lost the 1930 general election.

McCULLERS, (LULU) CARSON SMITH (1917–1967)
Novelist McCullers lived in New York and Paris, but her hometown of Columbus, Georgia, provided the background for much of her fiction. *The Heart Is a Lonely Hunter* (1940) brought her almost instant fame at age twenty-three. She followed it up in 1941 with *Reflections in a Golden Eye* and won the O. Henry short story prize in 1942. She adapted her 1946 novel, *The Member of the Wedding*, for the stage; the play won the 1950 Drama Critics Award. Her personal life, however, was not happy:

confined to a wheelchair much of the time because of the effects of rheumatic fever, Carson McCullers had a tumultuous marriage, divorce, and remarriage prior to her husband's 1953 suicide. She attempted suicide in 1948 but lived to be elected to the National Institute of Arts and Letters in 1952. Her always fragile health gave out at age fifty.

McGEE, ANITA NEWCOMB (1864–1940)
Founder of the Army Nurse Corps, McGee was born in Washington, D.C., and earned her medical degree from Columbian (later George Washington) University as a young married woman in 1892. When the army began hiring nurses for the Spanish-American War in 1898, McGee was appointed acting assistant surgeon general to create the new corps. She drafted legislation that made the nurse corps permanent in 1901, chose her successor, and retired. She was commissioned as an army officer again in 1904 when, during the Russo-Japanese War, she inspected hospitals in Japan, Korea, and Manchuria. She was buried in Arlington National Cemetery with full military honors.

McPHERSON, AIMEE ELIZABETH KENNEDY SEMPLE (1890–1944)
The most celebrated female evangelist of the twentieth century, McPherson went to China as a missionary with her husband. He died there, leaving her a pregnant widow at age twenty. She remarried and had another child but soon left her family behind to conduct her first revival in 1915, when she was twenty-five. She preached from Maine to Florida in the next years, and a 1921 divorce did not lessen her popularity. With her mother as her agent, McPherson toured Australia in 1922 and, within six years of beginning her career, drew soldout audiences in the largest available buildings even in such cosmopolitan cities as San Francisco.

Settling in Los Angeles, she introduced radio evangelism and set up innovative telephone counseling; the 5,000 seats of her extravagant Angelus Temple filled almost every night and three times on Sundays, while thousands of students enrolled at her Bible College. A 1926 disappearance, in which she claimed to have been kidnapped, drew national headlines. A nervous breakdown took its toll in 1930, and another marriage and divorce, as well as lawsuits from former associates, damaged her credibility. She lost more of her audience when she grew politically conservative—at the same that her blue-collar believers were liberalizing with New Deal ideas. McPherson died of an overdose of sleeping pills just short of her fifty-fourth birthday. Her autobiography, *The Story of My Life*, was published posthumously in 1951.

MEAD, MARGARET (1901–1978) More famous than almost any other social scientist, Margaret Mead captured public imagination with her first book, *Coming of Age in Samoa* (1928). She made her first trip to the South Pacific in 1925 and earned her doctorate from Columbia University in 1929. She held a terminal degree from the most prestigious university in her field and had published to wide acclaim, but unfortunately, the Great Depression also began that year, and Mead never received the employment status she merited. Although the American Museum of Natural History hired her in 1926, she did not receive full curator status until 1964, when she was old enough to retire. The public loved Mead, however, and avidly read her books on alternative cultures. She lectured widely, spoke on radio and television, and popularized many new concepts in social science, especially in child rearing and gender roles. After a lifetime of original contributions to American thought, Fordham University invited Mead to chair its social science department in 1968, and she was elected to the National Academy of Sciences in 1973. Her autobiography is *Blackberry Winter* (1972); her daughter, linguist and anthropologist Mary Catherine Bateson, published *Through a Daughter's Eye* in 1984.

MILLS, SUSAN LINCOLN TOLMAN (1825–1912) Mills and her husband, Cyrus Mills, cofounded California's historic Mills College. The couple left Massachusetts in 1848 and went to Ceylon (modern Sri Lanka) as missionaries. They began a school in Hawaii in 1860, and in 1864 they settled in California, where they developed the school that became Mills College. He died in 1884, and after trustees gave up on another male president, they elected Susan Mills president in 1890. She successfully made the transition to college status, retiring in 1909 at eighty-four. The Oakland campus remains the oldest women's college on the West Coast.

MINOR, VIRGINIA LOUISA (1824–1894) Minor's 1874 Supreme Court case, *Minor v. Happersett*, was a huge loss for women, making it clear that the gender-neutral language of the recently adopted Fifteenth Amendment did not include them. President of the Missouri suffrage association, Minor (who had that name before and after her marriage to a cousin) sued a Saint Louis official named Happersett when he refused to register her to vote. With her attorney husband, she argued that the amendment's language—"the right of citizens of the United States to vote shall not be denied or abridged by the United States or by any State on account of race, color, or previous condition of servitude"—enfranchised women as well as black

men. The court unanimously ruled that the words did not mean what they said and that states could continue to deny the vote to women. The Minors, who had ardently supported the Union in the Civil War, continued to be active for women's rights the rest of their lives; in 1879, Minor refused to pay taxes because she could not vote.

MITCHELL, MARGARET (1900–1949) The phenomenally successful author of *Gone With the Wind* (1936), Mitchell never published another book. She lived in Atlanta all her life, except for a year spent at Smith College, and worked for the *Atlanta Journal*. She kept her maiden name when she married in 1925 and worked for a decade on her Civil War novel, which included much family lore. *Gone With the Wind* set a number of records, including the most copies (50,000) sold in a single day. It won the 1938 Pulitzer Prize and had sold eight million copies by the time she died. The movie, which won ten Academy Awards, became Hollywood's all-time most valuable property. The Nazis banned the book in Germany, presumably because of its independent women and clever blacks. Mitchell died at age forty-eight after being hit by a car.

MITCHELL, MARIA (1818–1889) Probably the nineteenth century's most famous female scientist, Mitchell discovered a comet in 1847, when she was just twenty-nine. She lived on Nantucket Island and, like other girls of her era, had little educational opportunity. She learned by reading during two decades as a librarian and spent evenings on the roof of a local bank, where she studied the stars. The United States Coastal Survey hired her at an annual salary of $300 to work on celestial-navigation problems; although she did not go to an office, she may have been the first female federal employee in a nonmenial job. Mitchell also was the first woman elected to the American Academy of Arts and Sciences, and almost a century would pass before another woman was so honored. Mitchell was highly supportive of other women and, among other offices, served as president of the 1876 Women's Congress, which was held in conjunction with the U.S. centennial. The comet she discovered is named for her, and she received many other honors as well.

MOON, LOTTIE DIGGES (1840–1912) If Baptists had saints, Moon would probably be one. Christmas offerings in her name still commemorate her 1911 death from starvation while working as a missionary in China. Born in Virginia, in 1861 she was probably the first southern woman to earn a master's degree, from Charlottesville's Albemarle Institute; her older sister, Orianna Moon

Andrews, was the first credentialed female physician in the South. She went to Asia in 1872, when Southern Baptists finally sponsored unmarried women as missionaries, and, except for serving in Japan during China's Boxer Rebellion, worked the rest of her life in the province of Shandong. When, in 1885, the Foreign Mission Board denied women the right to vote in meetings, Moon resigned in protest—and the board immediately reversed itself. She gave food to others during the 1911 famine and, after her condition was discovered, died on a ship headed home.

MORGAN, JULIA (1872–1957) Morgan designed many buildings, especially in California; the most prominent was Hearst Castle, the estate built at San Simeon for publishing magnate William Randolph Hearst. An 1894 graduate of the University of California in Berkeley, in 1902 Morgan became the first woman to graduate from Paris's Ecole des Beaux-Arts. Also California's first licensed female architect, she designed buildings for the University of California and for the Young Women's Christian Association, including in Hawaii. She rebuilt famous San Francisco structures after the 1906 earthquake and in 1929 designed the Berkeley City Club, a residence hotel for women. She continued her practice through the Great Depression and World War II, supervising construction as far east as Illinois. Although extremely successful, Morgan was shy and avoided publicity.

MORRISON, TONI (CHLOE ANTHONY) WOFFORD (1931–) The first black woman to win the Nobel Prize in literature, Morrison's 1993 award was just the second given to an American woman (the first having gone to PEARL BUCK in 1938). Born in Ohio, she graduated from Howard University in 1953 and earned a 1955 master's degree from Cornell University. When she married in 1958, she changed her name to Morrison; she had adopted "Toni" as her first name earlier. After her divorce, with two sons, Morrison worked as an editor at Random House and published her first book in 1970. *Song of Solomon* (1977) won the National Book Critics Circle Award, and *Beloved* won the 1988 Pulitzer Prize—after black authors signed a nationally publicized letter when it failed to win the National Book Award. Morrison teaches at Princeton University, and she was the first black woman to hold an endowed chair at an Ivy League school.

MOSELEY-BRAUN, CAROL (1947–) The first black woman in the Senate, Moseley-Braun was elected as a Democrat from Illinois in 1992. A Chicago native, she was elected to the state senate in 1978 and then held office in Cook County. She received support from women nationally and won the Senate race with fifty-three percent of the vote. She disappointed feminists, however, by giving up a seat on the Senate Judiciary Committee—where women's input was badly needed—to serve on the Finance Committee. Further criticized for her personal financial affairs, she lost a reelection bid in 1998; in 1999, she became ambassador to New Zealand.

MOSES, GRANDMA (ANNA MARY ROBERTSON MOSES) (1860–1961) Perhaps the most popular primitive artist of all time, Grandma Moses did not begin to paint until she was in her seventies, when arthritis made needlework too difficult. With lifelong frugality, she painted old boards white to use as her canvas, and rural scenes on a white background became her signature style. An art collector saw her work at a 1938 Woman's Exchange in her hometown of Hoosick Falls, New York; the next year, her work was exhibited at the Museum of Modern Art in New York. Success followed at a phenomenal rate, and during the two decades that remained of her exceptionally long life, she painted as many as 1,500 works.

MOTLEY, CONSTANCE BAKER (1921–) The first black woman on the federal judiciary, Motley was appointed to the district court of Manhattan by President Lyndon Johnson in 1966. A graduate of New York University and Columbia University Law School, she practiced with future Supreme Court justice Thurgood Marshall. Motley set another precedent in 1964, when she became the first black woman elected to the New York state senate.

MOTT, LUCRETIA COFFIN (1793–1880) Mott was one of the two organizers of the women's rights movement, and she may be said to have been the original one; although ELIZABETH CADY STANTON is better known, Mott was her inspiration. Born on Nantucket, she married James Mott, a liberal Quaker like herself, in 1811. They lived in Philadelphia, and, with six children, Mott became an official minister in 1821. She preached in black churches as early as 1829. A founder of the American Anti-Slavery Society in 1833, she also took a personal vow never to use anything made with slave labor—which meant finding substitutes for cotton, sugar, coffee, and other staples.

It was Mott's attendance at the 1840 World's Anti-Slavery Convention that made women's rights a second priority for her; although she and other women were elected as delegates from their societies, men in London refused to seat them. She and Stanton, who also was banned, planned then to hold a women's rights convention when they returned home. Eight years went by before that happened, but in 1848, hundreds of people attended the first, held in Seneca Falls, New York. In addition to these causes, in the post–Civil War era, Mott was a founder of Swarthmore College and the founding president of the American Equal Rights Association.

MURRAY, JUDITH SARGENT STEVENS (1751–1820) The highly original feminist philosophy of Judith Sargent Murray predates that of women who are much better known. As Judith Sargent Stevens, she wrote "Essay on the Equality of the Sexes" in 1779—years before English MARY WOLLSTONECRAFT published her famous 1792 work. Stevens's husband, a sea captain, died in the West Indies in 1786; she married again and bore her first children in her forties. Needing income in the 1790s, she began to write for money, including a 1793 play that may have been the first produced in the United States. In 1798, she published three volumes of the essays she had written as a lonely seaman's wife; an endorsement by George Washington boosted their sales, and some contemporaries ranked Murray alongside Noah Webster as an American literary pioneer. After living her entire life in the cultural center of Boston, as a widow Murray went to live with a married daughter. She moved to the wilderness of Mississippi in 1816 and died in Natchez.

NATION, CARRY MOORE GLOYD (1846–1911) One of the most lampooned American women, Nation merits more serious attention in the context of an era when women had few legal or economic resources. The Kansas resident joined the Women's Christian Temperance Union (WCTU) in 1890 and agitated in the conventional way for another decade. In May 1900, however, while men stared agape, the six-foot-tall Nation attacked saloons in Kiowa, Kansas, breaking liquor bottles and smashing furniture with the hatchet that became her trademark. For a year, she wrecked small-town "joints" almost at will, doubtless encouraged by the fact that she had some justification under Kansas law, which ostensibly prohibited their operation. But when she did thousands of dollars worth of damage at a Wichita hotel favored by elite men, she finally was arrested. Women gathered outside her jail to sing and pray, and they honored her at a temperance convention upon her release, drawing national attention.

Nation toured the country for the next decade, but the crowds she attracted were often less than respectful of her mission, and the WCTU increasingly distanced itself from her radical tactics. She sold hatchets and her autobiography, *The Use and Need of Carry Nation* (1904), to support herself and fight off legal battles; she even founded and attempted to fund a Kansas City shelter for families of alcoholics. Ironically, it was another woman who ended her career: when Nation attacked a Montana saloon in 1910, its female owner beat the sixty-four-year-old so badly that she never fully recovered. She collapsed at a 1911 Arkansas appearance and died in Kansas.

NESTOR, AGNES (1880–1940) The longtime leader of working women in Chicago, Nestor was a founder of the International Glove Workers Union in 1902. President Woodrow Wilson appointed her to several positions, and when the federal eight-hour-day law finally passed in 1937, her leadership was widely credited.

NEWELL, HARRIET ATWOOD (1793–1812) The first American missionary to die in foreign service, Newell sailed from Massachusetts just ten days after her wedding in February 1812. Both she and ANN HASSELTINE JUDSON married recent seminary graduates and set out for India with them. Meanwhile, the War of 1812 began, and they soon were expelled from this British colony. The Newells went to the island of Mauritius, where Harriet delivered a premature child and died in October, just weeks after her nineteenth birthday.

NICHOLS, CLARINA HOWARD CARPENTER (1810–1885) A pioneer feminist, Nichols persuaded the Vermont legislature to reform property law for married women in 1847—a year prior to the first women's rights convention. She also had managed to get a divorce in 1843, an unusual legal feat at the time. As editor of a Brattleboro newspaper, she raised public awareness of women's legal disabilities, and in 1852, the Vermont legislature invited her to speak. She and Lydia Folger Fowler, America's second woman to graduate from an established medical school, lectured in frontier Wisconsin in 1853. Nichols and her family then moved permanently to Kansas, where she founded that state's suffrage society, and she continued to write after an 1871 move to California. She died there, having spread the women's rights gospel from coast to coast.

NICHOLS, MARY SERGEANT GOVE (1810–1884) Probably the first American woman to advocate sex education and a more healthy lifestyle for women, Mary Gove began her career in the same Massachusetts town of Lynn that later produced MARY BAKER EDDY and LYDIA PINKHAM. She lectured in Boston on the verboten subject of female anatomy as early as 1838 and published *Lectures to Ladies on Anatomy and Physiology* in 1842. Her husband, Hiram Gove, took advantage of his legal right to seize both her earnings and their daughter, and because women could not sue for divorce, she had to wait until he chose to end the marriage. Thomas Nichols, whom she married in 1848, shared her interests; among their joint projects was *Marriage* (1854).

NORTON, MARY TERESA HOPKINS (1875–1951)
Elected to Congress from New Jersey in 1924, Norton set a number of precedents. She chaired the House Labor Committee from 1937 until her retirement in 1950. During the early portion of her tenure, she led passage of the Social Security Act and other legislation that ameliorated the effects of the Great Depression; during World War II, she dealt with a labor shortage so severe that legislation to draft women for industrial jobs was seriously considered. Although the equal pay law and child care programs that she championed were not adopted in her lifetime, Norton merits much more recognition from modern women than she has received.

NOVELLO, ANTONIA (1944–)
The first female surgeon general of the United States, Novello was born in Puerto Rico. She earned degrees at the University of Michigan and Johns Hopkins University and was with the National Institutes of Health when President George Bush appointed her in 1990. Novello drew particular attention for her innovative argument that violence was a national public health epidemic.

OAKLEY, ANNIE (1860–1926)
A very popular attraction at Wild West shows, Annie Oakley was amazingly skilled with a gun. Born Phoebe Ann Oakley Moses (or Mozee) in Ohio, she took "Annie Oakley" as her name and joined Buffalo Bill's traveling expo in 1885; her husband, Bill Butler, gave up his western showman career to manage hers. Among Oakley's feats were hitting a moving target while standing on a galloping horse, shooting dimes tossed in the air, and hitting a cigarette held in her husband's lips. Her career ended abruptly in 1901, at age forty-one, when she was injured in a train wreck.

O'CONNOR, SANDRA DAY (1930–)
The first woman appointed to the United States Supreme Court, O'Connor got her undergraduate degree at Stanford University and graduated from Stanford Law School in 1951; she married the next year, bore three children, and became active in Arizona Republican politics, which led to a state senate appointment in 1969. Reelected in 1970 and 1972, she rose to majority leader in just five years,

becoming the first female senate majority leader in the nation. O'Connor left the legislature for the judiciary in 1974. After five years as an elected judge, she was appointed to the state court of appeals in 1979, and a mere two years later she was named to the highest court in the land. Although there were women with stronger credentials, her moderate record and Republican affiliation made her acceptable to both ends of the political spectrum; hers was the last noncontroversial Supreme Court nomination of the Reagan administration. She acknowledged the barriers that women have had to overcome by recalling that she—like many qualified female attorneys in the 1950s—had been expected to work instead as a legal secretary.

O'KEEFFE, GEORGIA TOTTO (1887–1986)
Probably America's most famous female painter, Georgia O'Keeffe was born in Wisconsin. Her unusual middle name came from a Hungarian grandfather. She studied in Chicago and New York, where her work was first exhibited in 1916. She shared an open marriage with photographer Alfred Stieglitz after 1924, began visiting the Southwest in 1929, and moved permanently in 1946 to northern New Mexico. Her work often reflected this locale, especially her signature bleached-white animal bones contrasting against brilliantly colored desert rocks. Her uniquely American scenes and highly creative style won many honors, including election to the American Academy of Arts and Letters in 1969. President Jimmy Carter presented her with the Medal of Freedom in 1977, but she was increasingly reclusive; when too many visitors came to her tiny town of Abiquiu, O'Keeffe hid herself in a second home still farther back in the mountains. She painted past her ninetieth year.

ONASSIS, JACQUELINE LEE BOUVIER KENNEDY (1929–1994)
Perhaps the century's most captivating first lady, Jackie Kennedy was especially applauded for the dignified manner in which she handled her husband's assassination, which left her a widow at age thirty-three. Born on Long Island, New York, she attended Vassar College and the Sorbonne before graduating from George Washington University in 1951. She worked as a photojournalist for the *Washington Times-Herald* and married Senator John Kennedy in 1953; he was assassinated soon after their tenth anniversary, leaving her with two young children. Her 1968 marriage to Greek shipping magnate Aristotle Onassis ended with his death in 1975. For the rest of her life, Jackie Onassis earned the respect of many by working as an editor at Doubleday. She is buried in Arlington National Cemetery.

ORR, KAY (1939–) Governor of Nebraska from 1987 to 1991, Orr was the first female Republican governor in the nation; although seven women preceded her as governor, the first in 1924, they were all Democrats. The race that she won set another precedent: the first between two women for a governorship, with Orr defeating the former mayor of Lincoln, Helen Boosalis. Orr served just one term before losing to a businessman who accused her of raising taxes and supporting a nuclear waste dump.

O'SULLIVAN, MARY KENNY (1864–1943) The first female organizer for the American Federation of Labor (AFL), O'Sullivan worked from age twelve on. She organized her Chicago coworkers into Woman's Bookbinding Union #1, and the newly formed AFL hired her in 1891. Also a founder of the Women's Trade Union League and active in feminist causes, O'Sullivan spent more than a half century working for working women.

OWEN, RUTH BRYAN (later ROHDE) (1885–1954) The first American woman to hold a major diplomatic position, Owen was also the first congresswoman from the South and a pioneer with the United Nations. She was the daughter of Democratic presidential nominee William Jennings Bryan, and from an early age she had worked in his campaigns and with her mother in the suffrage movement. Eloping at age eighteen, she soon divorced and then married an Englishman named Owen. They lived in several countries, and she worked as a nurse in Egypt during World War I. She returned to the United States after the war and, with a disabled husband and four children, moved in with her retired parents in Miami. Just six years after Florida women got the vote, she ran for Congress in 1926, attracting attention by driving a car through a district that ran from Georgia to Key West. She lost, but only by 800 votes, and she won in 1928. Owen served until 1933, sponsoring legislation to preserve the Everglades and, less successfully, to create a cabinet-level Department of Home and Child. President Franklin Roosevelt appointed Owen minister to Denmark in 1933, the first such appointment given a woman. After leaving that post, Owen lectured and wrote, ultimately becoming the author of five books, mostly on world affairs. This specialty led Presidents Roosevelt and Truman to appoint her to positions with the new United Nations. She died in Copenhagen, where she had gone to accept a belated honor.

PALMER, ALICE FREEMAN (1855–1902) Much more famous in her time than she is now, Palmer was such an academic superstar that she became president of Wellesley College at age twenty-seven. She is primarily known for her affiliation with the University of Chicago; she was the first dean of women at that new institution in 1891, when she conducted a commuter marriage with her husband in Boston. A founder of the organization that became the American Association of University Women, Palmer was the seventh woman elected to the Hall of Fame of Great Americans.

PALMER, BERTHA HONORÉ (1849–1918) As head of an enormous women's exhibition at the World's Columbian Exposition in Chicago that commemorated the 400th anniversary of Christopher Columbus's voyage to America, Palmer demonstrated her tremendous executive ability. President William McKinley appointed Palmer to head women's participation at the exposition, and she recruited exhibits from forty-seven nations that showed the diversity of women's lives. Her work was so superlative that President McKinley made her the only female commissioner representing the nation at the Paris exposition in 1900. A real estate developer, among the many Chicago properties she owned was the famous Palmer House hotel. She also supported the Women's Trade Union League and other progressive causes. Palmer invested in Florida land and personally conducted cattle-breeding experiments. She died near Sarasota.

PARK, MAUDE WOOD (1875–1955) The first president of the League of Women Voters (1919–1924), Park founded the college-based Equal Suffrage League, which was formalized in 1908. A Bostonian and an 1898 graduate of Radcliffe College, her 1908 marriage was an extremely modern one: she neither took her husband's name nor lived with him. Instead, she spent most of the next decade traveling in college circles and recruiting younger women to the aging suffrage movement. Park published work on women's history during the 1930s and 1940s; her story of the vote, *Front Door Lobbying* (1960), was issued after her death.

PARKS, ROSA McCAULEY (1913–) The mother of the civil rights movement, Parks earned her place in history on December 1, 1955, when she refused to give her bus seat to a white man, as Alabama blacks were supposed to do. Her arrest led to the first massive resistance to segregation: a boycott of Montgomery buses that lasted more than a year, seriously disrupting an economy dependent on black workers paid so poorly that few owned cars.

Born in Tuskegee, Parks was working as a seamstress when she took this unplanned action; although she had courageously attempted to vote in 1945 and attended a civil rights school earlier in 1955, she had not intended to set off the chain of events that followed. Instead, she said, she was simply tired after a long work week; she wanted to sit and "be treated like a human being." The protest drew threats to her life, and after the 1963 Birmingham bombing that killed four girls, Parks and her husband moved to Detroit, where she continued to work for civil rights. She has been much honored in recent years; President Bill Clinton awarded her the Congressional Gold Medal in 1999, and every member of Michigan's congressional delegation attended the White House ceremony.

PATTERSON, ALICIA (1906–1963) The founder of *Newsday*, Patterson broke established business rules when she began this differently formatted newspaper in the seemingly unlikely location of Long Island, New York. In an era when papers were going bankrupt because of competition from television, she made *Newsday* a success. Unlike her male competitors, she understood that suburban housewives were untapped readers—not to mention buyers for advertisers' products. Emulating her aunt, CISSY PATTERSON, she bought a defunct paper in 1940 and quickly made it profitable and reputable. It won its first Pulitzer Prize in 1954. Her success flew in the face of contradictory advice from the Patterson men, who published conservative papers in Chicago and New York, but neither journalists nor women offered her the recognition she merited.

PATTERSON, CISSY (ELEANOR) (1881–1948) Publisher of the *Washington Herald*, Patterson's influence in the capital city during the Great Depression and World War II was comparable to that of KATHARINE GRAHAM at the modern *Washington Post*. She bought the paper in 1930, when it was nearly bankrupt, and with a liberal editorial policy—unlike the anti-Roosevelt men in her publishing family—had Washington's largest audience a decade later. She increased her personal wealth from $1 million to $16 million and, though twice married, left her estate to her employees.

PATTERSON, MARY JANE (1840–1894) America's first black female college graduate, Patterson graduated from Oberlin College in 1862. Born in North Carolina slavery, her father escaped and then brought his family to Ohio; they settled in Oberlin in about 1854. With her sisters, Patterson spent a lifetime working in education; for many years, she was the principal of the only black high school in Washington, D.C., which educated many of the nation's African American leaders.

PAUL, ALICE (1885–1977) The leader of the radical wing of the twentieth-century suffrage movement, Paul's participation was relatively brief but was the catalyst that revitalized the effort for the vote. She also was the primary author of the Equal Rights Amendment.

A 1905 graduate of Swarthmore College, Paul earned a Ph.D. from the University of Pennsylvania in 1912 as well as, later, three law degrees. She was introduced to the militant style of British suffragists while a graduate student in England and, after returning to the United States in 1910, organized the Congressional Union under the aegis of the mainstream National American Woman Suffrage Association. In 1916, her faction split off and formed the National Woman's Party. The group relentlessly picketed the White House, sought arrest, and went on hunger strikes in prison. These methods were, of course, very controversial—but they also commanded attention and ultimately may have been necessary to advance the long-stalled issue.

Paul never came close to similar success in the fifty-seven years of her life after the vote. She proposed the Equal Rights Amendment in 1923, but most progressive women opposed it because it would have nullified hard-won labor laws and other protections for women. From a Capitol Hill headquarters, she led the National Woman's Party for decades and worked for inclusion of women in the new United Nations. Paul lived to see the Equal Rights Amendment pass passed by Congress in 1972 but died as states were rejecting it.

PEABODY, ELIZABETH PALMER (1804–1894) One of the nineteenth century's most important educational innovators, Peabody also ran a publishing house in conjunction with her Boston bookstore. She published early works by men who became the nation's most famous writers, including her brother-in-law Nathaniel Hawthorne. In 1827, when female public speakers were still taboo, Peabody successfully charged fees for history lectures she delivered in homes. She and MARGARET FULLER were the only female charter members of the Transcendental Club, which evolved into America's first unique contribution to philosophy, and she published Henry David Thoreau's seminal essay "Civil Disobedience." The author of ten books, Peabody emphasized educational reform and introduced the German idea of kindergartens to the United States. Independently of another famous brother-in-law, Horace Mann, she set up schools and lectured across the nation.

PECK, ANNIE SMITH (1850–1935) Famous for planting a "Votes for Women" sign at the summit of Mt. Coropuna in the Andes at age sixty-one, Peck first drew worldwide attention with her 1885 ascent of the Matterhorn. She climbed higher than any man or woman in the Western Hemisphere, exploring unknown areas in Argentina, Bolivia, and other countries. Honored with a gold medal from Peru, she was elected a fellow of England's Royal Geographical Society in 1917. Peck, who was born and died in Rhode Island, climbed her last mountain at age eighty-two.

PEMBER, PHOEBE YATES LEVY (1823–1913) As the administrator of the world's largest military hospital up to that time, Pember ran Chimborazo Hospital in Richmond, Virginia, during the Civil War. A young Georgia widow, she supervised the care of more than 15,000 men by the war's end, sometimes carrying a gun to deal with physicians and others who resented her control over the hospital's precious supply of drugs and alcohol. Her sister, Eugenia Levy Phillips—whose husband had been an Alabama congressman at secession—was arrested in both Washington and Louisiana for treasonous activity against the Union, but Pember nonetheless went north after the war, dying in Pittsburgh. Her autobiography is *A Southern Woman's Story* (1879), and she was included in a 1995 Civil War stamp series.

PERKINS, FRANCES (1880–1965) The first woman cabinet member, Perkins also deserves immense credit for establishing fundamentals of the modern economy: Social Security, unemployment insurance, minimum wages, maximum hours, and other federal protection of workers that began during her tenure as secretary of labor.

Perkins graduated from Mount Holyoke College and Columbia University and worked in the settlement house and suffragist movements. In 1918, she became the highest-paid woman in New York government when she was appointed to its State Industrial Commission, where she implemented safety inspections and negotiated strikes. She rose to its chairmanship, and when Governor Franklin Roosevelt became president of the United States, he took her to Washington. Together they implemented a safety net for those most vulnerable to economic downturns. She dealt with a different set of labor problems during World War II and was one of just two cabinet members to stay with the Roosevelt administration until its end.

Perkins, who retained her maiden name when she married in 1913, also compassionately dealt with a husband who spent much of his time in mental sanatoriums—a fact that few knew. Many conservative commentators vilified her for the progressive changes she made, while male labor leaders also questioned her right to her position.

Excessively modest, Perkins did not receive the honors she merited in her lifetime, but in 1980 a postage stamp was issued in her memory.

PERRY, ANTOINETTE (1888?–1947) The namesake of theater's Tony Awards, Antoinette Perry Frueauff was called Tony Perry. An actor and producer, she directed her first major play at age twenty-eight. Among her most successful Broadway productions was *Harvey*, which won the 1945 Pulitzer Prize for playwright Mary Chase. The Tony Awards began in 1948, a year after Perry's death.

PICKERSGILL, MARY YOUNG (1776–1857) The maker of the flag that inspired "The Star-Spangled Banner," Pickersgill should be far better known than BETSY ROSS. Pickersgill learned her trade from her mother, Rebecca Flower Young, who made George Washington's 1776 flag. By the War of 1812, Pickersgill was a Baltimore manufacturer of insignia for ships, and she was commissioned by Fort McHenry's commander to make a flag "so big that the British will have no trouble seeing it" during the War of 1812. With her daughter and two nieces, she wove 1,200 square feet of wool into a seamless flag, for which she charged $405.90. It was this flag that Francis Scott Key described as withstanding "the rockets' red glare" when the British bombarded Fort McHenry; its quality was so high that it has survived for almost two centuries. The Smithsonian Institution is currently restoring Pickersgill's great work.

PINCKNEY, ELIZABETH (ELIZA) LUCAS (1732–1793) America's pioneer agriculturist, Pinckney ran three South Carolina plantations for her absent military father when she was sixteen years old. She continued her hybridization experiments after marriage and motherhood, particularly working on indigo, which is used in blue dyes. The seeds she began selling in 1744 transformed the Southern economy; exports from Charleston soared from 5,000 to 130,000 pounds in the first two years. Her contemporaries held Pinckney in such esteem that George Washington took time during his presidency to serve as her pallbearer.

PINKHAM, LYDIA (1819–1883) The first woman to become nationally known through a product she manufactured, Pinkham had an appreciable effect on women's health. Regardless of the effectiveness of her 1873 tonic for women—a botanical compound containing nineteen percent alcohol—Pinkham's sales brochures included gynecological information that was new to many women. She also employed a staff of women in Lynn, Massachusetts, who wrote personalized answers to customers' letters and understood the importance of a holistic approach to health—a century ahead of organized medicine. Her motherly image in an 1879 photograph was the first to personalize a major product, and it ensured millions of dollars in annual sales decades after her death.

"PITCHER, MOLLY" (MARY LUDWIG HAYS McCAULEY) (1754–1832) The woman known as Molly Pitcher was actually Mary Hays of Pennsylvania, who joined the army along with her husband. She had marched with Revolutionary soldiers for more than two years when she became famous in battle at Monmouth, New Jersey, in 1778. When her husband was wounded, she took over his cannon and held her position until nightfall, when the British retreated. George Washington recommended that she be commissioned as a sergeant and granted half pay for the rest of her life, which Congress accepted. Remarrying after her husband died from his wounds, she lived to age eighty-five. She is buried in Carlisle, Pennsylvania.

PLATH, SYLVIA (1932–1963) An icon to many modern feminists, Plath suffered from depression and from living in the shadow of her husband, English poet Ted Hughes. Born in Boston, she graduated summa cum laude from Smith College in 1955, after a suicide attempt that institutionalized her. She married Hughes the next year, and they lived in Massachusetts and England, while she published several books of poetry and bore two children. They separated late in 1962; their younger child was barely a year old when Plath killed herself. She is best known for an autobiographical novel based on her earlier mental breakdown, *The Bell Jar* (1963), which was initially published under a pseudonym after her death in London at age thirty.

POCAHONTAS (c. 1595–1617) Although a Hollywood-imposed image makes Pocahontas seem mythical, there is a great deal of documentation on her life. She did in fact plead for Captain John Smith when he was taken captive in Virginia by the Powhatan tribe, of which her father was chief, in 1607; in fact, it was fairly common in eastern tribes for women to make the decisions as to whether prisoners lived or died. She married John Rolfe in 1614, called herself Rebecca after she was baptized, and bore a child she named Thomas. The family went to England in 1616 to meet Rolfe's Norfolk relatives, and she attended social events in London and was presented to QUEEN ANNE. As their ship was going down the Thames River to return to Virginia, she sickened; they debarked, and she died. No legendary figure—rather a missed opportunity for unification of American Indians and English newcomers—

Pocahontas was buried at St. George's Church in the parish of Gravesend, on March 21, 1617.

PRICE, LEONTYNE (1927–) The first African American woman to achieve star status in opera, Price was born in Mississippi; she was educated at a historic black college in Wilberforce, Ohio, and at the prestigious Juilliard School of Music in New York. She debuted with New York's Metropolitan Opera in 1960 and went on to a twenty-five-year career with the Met.

PRINCE, LUCY TERRY (c. 1730–after 1797) Born in Africa, Prince argued and won a United States Supreme Court case in 1797. After being sold into slavery in Deerfield, Massachusetts, she became literate and was America's first black poet; her 1746 poem on the Deerfield Massacre (see Massachusetts) predates PHILLIS WHEATLEY's work by several decades. In 1756, she married Abijah Prince, a free black man, and they moved to Vermont, where, decades later, a neighbor disputed their property boundary. The Supreme Court rode circuit then, and she argued her case before Justice Salmon Chase, who is said to have commented that she did a better job than any Vermont lawyer could have. Indeed, one of the lawyers hired by the opposition was valedictorian at Harvard University in 1766.

QUIMBY, EDITH HINKLEY (1891–1982) Physicist Edith Quimby developed standards for radiation exposure in treating cancer and other disease. After earning a 1916 master's degree from the University of California, she worked at Memorial Hospital for Cancer in New York City. In the 1920s and 1930s, she was the only woman in the United States in nuclear medicine. She was honored with a gold medal from the Radiological Society of North America in 1941; its only previous award to a woman had gone to MARIE CURIE. Quimby worked on the Manhattan Project, which built the atomic bomb during World War II, and then researched radioactive isotopes. Despite a lifetime of potentially risky experiments, she lived to age ninety-one.

QUIMBY, HARRIET (1875?–1912) The first American woman to earn a pilot's license, Quimby was a California journalist who learned to fly just five years after the Wright brothers patented their "flying machine." When she got her license on August 1, 1911, thirty-five men and one French woman were the world's only certified pilots. She was the first woman to fly across the English Channel and was celebrated in Paris and London. On July 1, 1912, however, Quimby crashed into Boston harbor. Her male passenger, who was much bigger than she, apparently shifted his weight and overturned the plane; both pilot and passenger were killed.

RANKIN, JEANNETTE PICKERING (1880–1973) The first woman elected to Congress, Jeannette Rankin was elected before most American women could vote. She graduated from the University of Montana in 1902, was a social worker in Washington State, and, after 1910, was an employee of the National American Woman Suffrage Association. Montana enfranchised women in 1914, and Rankin built on that success, winning a statewide race for Montana's sole House seat in 1916. She ran on a peace platform, and when the United States entered World War I the next year, Rankin joined more than fifty congressmen who voted against it. When the war ended victoriously at the same time as her bid for reelection, however, voters did not reward her faithfulness to her campaign promises; she lost in 1918.

Rankin spent the 1920s and 1930s working for the Women's International League for Peace and Freedom and ran for Congress again in 1940. Again, voters responded to her pacifism and elected her. The next year, she was the only member of Congress to vote against World War II, and Montana voters once again removed her from office in 1942. Her Republican Party did not reward her with any appointments, and Rankin's late life was difficult. Spending winters in Georgia, she also worked in underdeveloped countries, participated in Mohandas K. Gandhi's nonviolent revolution in India and marched against the Vietnam War. Rankin died in California, and the ashes of this dedicated pacifist were scattered on the Pacific Ocean.

RAY, CHARLOTTE E. (1850–1911) America's first black female attorney, Ray achieved that goal in 1872, just three years after Iowa made Arabella Mansfield, a white woman, the first female attorney in the United States. Ray graduated from the law school of Washington's new Howard University and was admitted to the District of Columbia bar in 1872—without the fight that BELVA LOCKWOOD had later. This may have been an indication that male competitors did not take Ray seriously; she could not find enough clients to support herself and by 1879 had returned to teaching in New York City.

RAY, DIXY LEE (1914–1994) Elected the governor of Washington in 1976, Ray had earned a 1945 doctorate from Stanford University and taught at the University of Washington. President Richard Nixon appointed her to an oceanography task force in 1969 and then to the Atomic Energy Commission in 1972. An ardent advocate of nuclear power, she was often opposed by environmentalists, but feminists appreciated the fact that she freely credited the women's movement for her appointment. Few experts expected her to do well in her first run for office, but she won by a surprisingly large margin. Her tenure was difficult, however, especially with regard to environmental issues, and Democrats did not renominate her in 1980. Ray, who was the nation's first never-married female governor, then wrote and lectured on science policy.

REMOND, SARAH PARKER (1826–1894) Born to an African American family in Massachusetts that had been free for generations, Remond successfully sued a Boston policeman who assaulted her when she integrated an 1853 opera audience. Hired as an antislavery lecturer in 1856, she was particularly important in England: her speeches helped keep that nation from aiding the Confederacy, which its cotton-mill owners wanted to do. Remond returned to the United States in 1867, but, after losing an effort to delete "white" and "male" from the New York Constitution, spent the rest of her life in Italy. She is buried in Rome.

RENO, JANET (1938–) The first woman to serve as attorney general of the United States, Reno was appointed by President Bill Clinton in 1993. A Miami native, she graduated from Cornell University and from Harvard Law School in 1963. In 1978, she became the first female state attorney in Florida's sprawling Dade County, where she developed innovative programs to deal with domestic violence and drug addiction. She was reelected six times before becoming the nation's top law officer.

RICHARDS, DOROTHY ANN WILLIS (1933–) Governor of Texas from 1990 to 1994, Ann Richards had been elected state treasurer in 1982. A Democrat and mother of four, she defeated a conservative Republican millionaire to become the state's second female governor. She lost a reelection bid in 1994, but her exceptional wit and strong feminism has made Richards a popular speaker.

RICHARDS, ELLEN SWALLOW (1842–1911) An early systems thinker, Richards was the first woman admitted to the Massachusetts Institute of Technology (MIT), graduating with a degree in chemistry in 1873. Although MIT never awarded the doctorate she earned, it employed her in 1884, after she demonstrated expertise in a number of fields, especially metallurgy; colleagues elected her the first female member of the American Institute of Mining and Metallurgical Engineers. Her work in public health engineering set standards for air and water pollution, and she introduced biology to MIT's curriculum and was a founder of the Woods Hole Oceanographic Institution. An environmentalist long before the term existed, she conducted some of the first tests for toxins in food and home furnishings. In addition, she introduced a term, yet to be adopted, in the title of a 1912 book, *Euthenics: The Science of the Controllable Environment.* Happily married to an MIT professor, she was active in many women's causes and endowed the *Journal of Home Economics.* Too frequently, however, Richards is narrowly defined as the mother of home economics. Instead, as one male admirer wrote, "if these [men] were the 'fathers' of their individual fields, she was the 'mother' of them all."

RIDE, SALLY (1951–) The first woman in space, Ride spent six days on the 1983 space shuttle *Challenger.* She had graduated from Stanford University just a decade earlier, with a double major in physics and English, and in 1977 was one of 8,000 astronaut applicants. Six women were chosen, along with thirty-five men, and Ride became the first female space pioneer. She served on the presidential commission that investigated the 1986 *Challenger* explosion. Ride left the National Aeronautics and Space Administration in 1987 and is currently a physics professor at the University of California at San Diego; she also heads a new Web site, space.com.

ROBERTS, BARBARA SANDERS (1936–) Governor of Oregon from 1991 to 1996, Roberts first served as a legislator and as secretary of state; a Democrat, she became Oregon's first female House majority leader in 1983. She was born in Corvallis, married and had two sons, and began volunteering in government after seeking aid for her autistic child. As governor, Roberts reformed the tax system and streamlined government. She was especially known for a commitment to gay rights and to promoting women and minorities. Roberts declined to seek reelection in 1994 and joined Harvard University's Kennedy School of Government.

ROOSEVELT, ANNA ELEANOR (1884–1962) America's longest serving and most extraordinary first lady had her surname before and after marrying her cousin Franklin Roosevelt; both of them were descended from New York pioneers. They lived in New York City, and she bore six children in eleven years. World War I volunteerism exposed her to progressive women. Her husband's tenure as assistant navy secretary brought her to Washington, and in 1920 he ran for vice president. Not until polio struck him the next year, however, did she discover her political self; he never recovered the use of his legs, but she became his eyes and ears with the public. They campaigned successfully for New York's governorship and then for the presidency in 1932.

The public saw much more of Eleanor than they had of any previous first lady, and most responded like a child to a mother. The Great Depression had devastated the United States, and she was a deep well of empathy through the depression and the sorrows of World War II. More important, she grew courageous, regularly taking political risks for repressed minorities, especially blacks. She also understood the reality of the Holocaust earlier than most, and she offered continual support and endless personal networking for women. A syndicated columnist for the *New York Post,* she also wrote regularly for the *Ladies' Home Journal* and other women's magazines. Among her many books are *This Is My Story* (1937) and a second autobiography in 1961.

Although Eleanor was ready to retire when Franklin died in 1945, President Harry Truman insisted that—as a global as well as a national figure—she take a leading role in the new United Nations. Her most important achievement, in fact, may be chairing the Human Rights Commission, which not only dealt with the war's millions of displaced people but also created the Universal Declaration of Human Rights. Her service to the United Nations ended with the 1952 election of President Dwight Eisenhower, a Republican, but Democratic President Kennedy appointed Roosevelt to chair an unprecedented Commission on the Status of Women. In the last official act of her life, she worked for the Equal Pay Act, which passed just months after her death. "Mother to a generation," Eleanor Roosevelt is buried at Hyde Park, New York.

ROSE, ERNESTINE (1810–1892) Although she was born and died abroad, Rose was a great pioneer for American women. Born Siismund Potowski in Poland, she successfully sued her father in 1826 to end an arranged marriage and to get the money her mother had bequeathed to her. At age eighteen, she left for Berlin and then moved on to Paris and London, where she married and changed her name. The Roses, who never had children, immigrated to New York, and she immediately began working on women's property rights. She sent a petition on the subject to the legislature in 1836 and between 1837 and 1848—when the first women's rights convention met—addressed the legislature five times. Although English was not her native language, Rose ignored taboos on public speaking and soon was known as "queen of the platform." She spoke in Ohio in 1844 and to the legislature of frontier Michigan the next year. One of the few Jews or immigrants in the women's movement, she was popular enough by the 1854 National Women's Rights Convention to overcome objections to her atheism and was elected convention president. She had lectured in at least twenty-three states by 1869, when the Roses decided to return to England. Not nearly as active there, she died at age eighty-two in Brighton.

ROSENBERG, ANNA (later HOFFMAN) (1912–1983)

The only woman to serve as an assistant secretary of defense, Rosenberg was appointed by President Harry Truman at the special request of Defense Secretary George C. Marshall. He had observed her in World War II, when Rosenberg put her background in labor relations to work for President Franklin Roosevelt. Credited with "knowing more Army privates than anyone else," she ate military rations and slept on the ground during field trips to assess morale. In 1945 she became the first woman to receive the Medal of Freedom. Born in Budapest, she became a naturalized citizen in 1919 and the first woman to serve as a regional Social Security commissioner in 1936. That her precedent-setting Pentagon position, which she held from 1950 to 1953, is not better known may be because of the unfortunate case of the similarly named ETHEL ROSENBERG.

ROSENBERG, ETHEL GREENGLASS (1915–1953)

The only American woman ever executed for espionage, Rosenberg was far less guilty than several female Civil War spies. Her era, however, was one of profound paranoia about Communism, and in an irrational twist of post-Holocaust fate, Jews were most likely to be accused of betrayal. She was an unexceptional housewife and mother in her native New York City when her brother, David Greenglass, and then her husband were arrested in 1950 for passing secrets to the Soviets. Her arrest followed, although no charges were filed for eight months, when she was accused of "conspiracy to commit espionage"—specifically, typing secret information for her brother, who had worked at the atomic research center in Los Alamos, New Mexico, until he was fired five years earlier. He pleaded guilty to reduced charges and, with his wife, testified against the Rosenbergs, who were convicted.

Civil libertarians were shocked by the severity of the sentence—not even J. Edgar Hoover, the fervently anti-communist director of the Federal Bureau of Investigation, had recommended the death penalty. Ethel Rosenberg spent the next two years in prison at Sing Sing, while the Supreme Court and Presidents Harry Truman and Dwight Eisenhower refused to overturn her sentence. Despite worldwide protests, Ethel and Julius Rosenberg were electrocuted on the day after their fourteenth wedding anniversary. They were survived by two young sons.

ROSS, BETSY (ELIZABETH GRISCOM ROSS ASHBURN CLAYPOOL) (1752–1836)

The woman known as Betsy Ross actually had that name for less than four years; she married John Ross in November 1773, and, after he died in a gunpowder explosion during militia duty in January 1776, she remarried in June 1777. She lost her second husband to the Revolution as well and supported her family by running a Philadelphia business that specialized in upholstery. Making flags was a sideline, and Pennsylvania state records show a payment to her in May 1777 for "ship's colours, etc."—but no evidence exists that she made a federal flag for George Washington. Instead, the flag that he hoisted in January 1776, while camped in Cambridge, Massachusetts, was made by Rebecca Flower Young. The first written account of the Betsy Ross tale did not appear until almost a century later, when her grandson presented this family lore at an 1870 Philadelphia historical society meeting. Instead of being remembered as a seamstress, Betsy Ross should be known as a businesswoman who gave two husbands to the Revolution and left a valuable estate to be run by a daughter. The woman who should be known as the premier flag-maker is MARY PICKERSGILL.

ROSS, NELLIE TAYLOE (1876–1977)

The nation's first female governor, Ross was inaugurated in Wyoming two weeks before MIRIAM "MA" FERGUSON became governor of Texas. Both women were elected in 1924, the first presidential year in which American women could reasonably run for office, but Ross could have been elected much earlier; Wyoming women had voted since 1869. Born in Missouri, she moved to Wyoming in 1902, and when her husband died in the middle of his term as governor, she ran to replace him. A Democrat in a Republican state, she won twenty of twenty-three counties, but, as voters returned to party lines, she narrowly lost her bid for reelection in 1926.

When President Franklin Roosevelt took office in 1933, he appointed Ross to head the United States Mint, a position she held through the Great Depression and the paper shortage of World War II. President Harry Truman reappointed her, and she served for two decades. Ross was the first American woman to have her image on a medal made by the mint, and she is honored at the Fort Knox gold depository, which was built under her leadership. She lived on in Washington to age 101, but her death—in the same year as that of Elvis Presley—was little noted.

ROWSON, SUSANNA HASWELL (c. 1762–1824)
Rowson's 1786 novel, *Victoria*, was one of America's first; her *Charlotte Temple* (1791) was reprinted at least 200 times during its first hundred years and has never gone out of print. A playwright and actor at a time when respectable women did not appear on stage, Rowson also played the trumpet. Her work delivered an implicit feminist message, much of it based on her husband, whose illegitimate child she reared.

Rowson made a further contribution to American women in 1797, when she organized one of the nation's first academies for "young ladies." She wrote textbooks for her students and also contributed to one of the nation's first magazines, *Boston Weekly Magazine*, from its 1802 beginning. Born in England, she lived most of her life in the Boston area but performed as far away as Edinburgh.

ROYALL, ANNE NEWPORT (1769–1854) At a time when women were not supposed to travel unescorted, Royall left western Virginia and roamed the young nation, publishing ten travelogues between 1826 and 1831. She settled in Washington, where an all-male jury convicted her of "being a common scold" when she objected to street preachers outside her home; Secretary of War John Eaton paid a ten-dollar fine to save the fifty-nine-year-old woman from a sentence of dunking in the Potomac River. A strong Jacksonian Democrat, Royall published Washington newspapers until her death at age eighty-five. Some of the corrupt politicians she exposed blocked her legitimate claim to a pension as a Revolutionary War widow.

SABIN, FLORENCE (1871–1953) The first woman elected to membership in the National Academy of Sciences, Sabin researched a number of medical advances, especially in histology and the lymphatic system. An 1893 graduate of Smith College, she published *An Atlas of the Medulla and Midbrain* (1901) while still a medical student. The prestigious Johns Hopkins University hired her as a professor in 1902; in the same year, she was the first female president of the American Association of Anatomists. Sabin "retired" to her home state of Colorado in 1938, where—like FLORENCE SEIBERT in Florida—she worked in health causes.

SACAGAWEA (c. 1786–1812) More statues have been built in honor of Sacagawea (whose name is variously spelled) than for any other American woman. A Shoshone Indian from modern Idaho, she was taken captive by the Hidatsa in about 1800; when the Lewis and Clark expedition encountered her in 1804 in what is now North Dakota, she was pregnant by a Frenchman, Toussaint Charbonneau. In April 1805, with her newborn, she led the men hundreds of miles across the Continental Divide, introducing them to new plants and smoothing their way with natives. She spent the winter with her people, and, after the explorers returned from the Pacific, she guided them back through the Big Hole and Bozeman Passes of Montana. She adopted white dress while living in Saint Louis in 1810 and probably died at Nebraska's Fort Manuel Lisa in 1812.

SAMPSON, DEBORAH (1760–1827) Disguised as a man, Deborah Sampson of Massachusetts joined the army in May 1782; although this was late in the American Revolution, she served in several New York engagements and was wounded at Tarrytown. Her Middleborough church excommunicated her. She returned to conventional dress at the war's end, married, and had three children. Massachusetts gave her a pension in 1792, and Paul Revere was among those attesting to her federal pension rights, which Congress granted in 1805; in 1838, her children received retroactive payments for their mother's military service.

SANGER, MARGARET LOUISE HIGGINS (1879–1966)
Future historians may see Sanger as the twentieth century's most important woman. Her advocacy of birth control—and, thereby, population control—was fundamental to global health and quality of life. It was a lesson she learned from personal experience: first by watching her mother die after bearing eleven children and second as a nurse who saw patients die after painful attempts to end pregnancies.

Born in Corning, New York, Sanger trained as a nurse and moved to New York City, where she married an architect in 1902. She had three children but continued to be active in progressive causes and public health nursing. Increasingly convinced that women's ignorance of their bodies was the cause of much suffering, she began publishing the *Woman Rebel* in 1914; although it carefully excluded specific contraceptive information, she was arrested and indicted for obscenity by an all-male jury. Sanger fled to Europe, where she studied the Netherland's birth-control clinics; meanwhile, her husband was arrested for distributing her booklet *Family Limitation*, and her only daughter died.

Sanger returned home when criminal charges were dropped and with her sister, Ethel Byrne, opened a Brooklyn clinic in 1916. "Every child a wanted child" was their motto, and 500 women sought their services in the ten days before they were arrested. Sanger was in and out of court for years, but as she recruited physicians to take the lead in her American Birth Control League, the authorities harassed her less. A 1920 divorce and remarriage to a millionaire gave her financing for the Birth Control Clinical Research Bureau she opened in Manhattan in 1923. Sanger and her husband moved to Arizona the next year, but she continued to be active and was a founder of International Planned Parenthood in 1952. The birth-control pill went on the market in 1960, six years before her death.

SCHIFF, DOROTHY (1903–1989) The major shareholder of the *New York Post* in 1939, Schiff was not only its publisher but also chief editor from 1963 to 1976. She exerted a strong influence during an era of great change and published works by an exceptional number of women, including columnists Doris Fleeson, Sylvia Porter, and ELEANOR ROOSEVELT. Married four times and the mother of three, she maintained her business independence and succeeded when other newspapers failed after television was introduced. Retiring at age seventy-three, she left intact the *Post*'s record of continuous publication since its founding by Alexander Hamilton in 1801.

SCHNEIDERMAN, ROSE (1882–1972) Born in Polish Russia, Schneiderman began work in New York's garment industry at age thirteen; she was the main income provider for her widowed mother and siblings. After her oratorical ability made her a star of the massive 1909 strike, she organized several hundred thousand members of the International Ladies' Garment Workers Union. She was president of the Women's Trade Union League from 1926 to 1950, and President Franklin Roosevelt appointed her as the only female commissioner of the National Recovery Administration during the Great Depression.

SEIBERT, FLORENCE BARBARA (1898–1991) The developer of the skin test for tuberculosis, Seibert was disabled by childhood polio but nonetheless earned a chemistry doctorate from Yale while also inventing a method for eliminating contaminants from distilled water—a necessity for intravenous therapy. She taught mostly male medical students at the University of Chicago while doing tuberculosis research and had her test ready by 1941, but the medical community refused to accept it until a 1952 presentation to the World Health Organization. Her sister Mabel was her longtime assistant; both retired to Florida in 1958, where—like FLORENCE SABIN in Colorado—they did cancer research for another two decades. In identifying the bacillus that causes tuberculosis, Seibert benefited the world tremendously; prior to her test, millions of people died from what is now a curable disease.

SETON, ELIZABETH ANN BAYLEY (1774–1821) The first American-born saint, Mother Seton was a widow with five children when she founded the first convent of nuns in the United States. She was introduced to Catholicism on an 1804 visit to Rome and defied family and friends to take vows in 1809, when she also began her community in Emmitsburg, Maryland. The Sisters of Charity of St. Joseph expanded to Philadelphia in 1841, and at least twenty other communities grew from this beginning. Seton Hall College was named for her in 1856, and her canonization was begun in 1907; on September 14, 1975, Mother Elizabeth Ann Seton was declared a saint.

SHAHEEN, JEANNE (1947–) Governor of New Hampshire, Shaheen was elected as a Democrat in this traditionally Republican state in 1996. Born in Missouri, she was educated in Pennsylvania and Mississippi; after marriage and motherhood, she established herself in New Hampshire and was elected to the state senate in 1990. Her campaigns focused on health care and utility rates (New Hampshire's were the highest in the nation). As governor, she created the state's first industrial research center and led economic development efforts. A former teacher, she also emphasized early childhood education, prepaid college tuition, and other innovations.

SHAW, ANNA HOWARD (1847–1919) President of the national suffrage association from 1904 to 1915, Shaw earned both a divinity degree (1878) and a medical degree (1886) from Boston University. She was born in England and grew up in Michigan; her 1871 Methodist preacher license there was one of the first granted to a woman.

Shaw did not practice either of her credentialed professions but rather became a career lecturer, often sponsored by the Women's Christian Temperance Union. Although a superlative orator, she was not particularly politically astute. To Shaw's disappointment, SUSAN B. ANTHONY chose CARRIE CHAPMAN CATT as her successor. When Catt resigned to care for her ailing husband, Shaw served for a decade—during which so many members, especially younger women, rebelled against her excessive religiosity and lack of political skill that she was eventually forced to resign.

President Woodrow Wilson appointed Shaw to head the women's committee of World War I's National Defense Council, for which she received the Distinguished Service Medal. Shaw, who wintered in Florida, died at her Pennsylvania home. Her autobiography is *The Story of a Pioneer* (1915).

SMITH, BESSIE (1894–1937) A pioneer of the American music called the blues, Smith moved from her birthplace, Chattanooga, Tennessee, to Philadelphia in 1920 and sold two million copies of her first record album in 1923. She made more than 150 records, but as the Jazz Age turned into the Great Depression, and as she grew increasingly dependent on alcohol, Columbia Records failed to renew her contract in 1931. After her death in a Tennessee car accident, a legend grew that she bled to death when refused treatment at a segregated hospital, but contemporary scholars agree that her care was prompt and her injuries too serious for the available technology.

STANTON, ELIZABETH CADY (1815–1902) More than anyone else, Stanton is the mother of the women's movement. She was the link between the earlier LUCRETIA MOTT and the later SUSAN B. ANTHONY; though Anthony was the chief organizer, Stanton was the chief thinker and writer.

Stanton graduated from EMMA WILLARD's academy in 1832 and went to the 1840 World Anti-Slavery Conference in London on her honeymoon. When she, Mott, and other women were barred from the convention because they were women, she began to prioritize women's rights over her earlier abolitionism, and that priority remained central to her personal life and political philosophy. She was the chief motivator for the first women's rights convention—held in her hometown of Seneca Falls, New York, when Mott visited there in July 1848—and wrote most of its Declaration of Rights of Women. While raising seven children, Stanton publicized the movement's ideas with prolific writing for the era's newspapers.

After moving to New York City, Stanton and Anthony organized the Civil War's Loyal League. Stanton made a quixotic run for Congress in 1866, campaigned in Kansas in 1867, and with Anthony began a newspaper, the *Revolution*, in 1868; in 1869, they formed the National Woman Suffrage Association. President for most of its existence (and even after its 1890 merger with LUCY STONE's American Woman Suffrage Association), Stanton also coauthored the first four volumes of *The History of Woman Suffrage*.

A genuine social philosopher as well as a political leader, Stanton radicalized as she aged, especially in religious ideas. Her *Woman's Bible* (1895) offended many former friends, and, over Anthony's objection, the suffrage association passed a resolution of condemnation. Her autobiography is *Eighty Years and More* (1898), and she was honored on a 1948 postage stamp.

STEIN, GERTRUDE (1874–1946) Born in Pennsylvania, Stein grew up in California. She attended Radcliffe College and Johns Hopkins School of Medicine before moving permanently to France in 1902, where she wrote avant-garde literature and mentored the post–World War I "lost generation" of Americans abroad, including Ernest Hemingway. Stein's best-known book is *The Autobiography of Alice B. Toklas* (1933), in which she wrote about herself but used the name of her longtime lover. By the 1940s, she was famous enough that, unlike most Jews, she not only remained in France but also continued to publish. She and Alice Toklas are buried at Paris's Pere Lachaise cemetery.

STEINEM, GLORIA (1934–) Known especially for founding *Ms.* magazine in 1972, Steinem graduated from Smith College in 1956, studied in India, and worked as a journalist in New York City. Her articles were fundamental to the revitalization of feminism in the 1960s, and she was a cofounder of the Women's Political Caucus and other feminist groups. Her best-known book is *Outrageous Acts and Everyday Rebellions* (1983). Steinem remains a leading author and lecturer for the modern women's movement.

STEVENS, NETTIE MARIA (1862-1912) Biologist Nettie Stevens discovered that the male chromosome determines the sex of an embryo. Her 1906 breakthrough was not acknowledged until long after her death, however, and countless women continued to be blamed when their babies were not of the desired sex. A New England native, Stevens studied at Stanford and Bryn Mawr, where she also taught. She made her great discovery with research money provided by ELLEN SWALLOW RICHARDS.

STONE, LUCY (1818–1893) Primarily known for retaining her maiden name at her 1855 wedding to Henry Blackwell (brother of physicians Emily and ELIZABETH BLACKWELL), Stone made many contributions to the women's movement, most of them earlier than other leaders. When she graduated from Oberlin College in 1847, she was nearly thirty years old because she had had to support herself when her affluent father refused to fund her schooling. Stone worked as a paid abolitionist speaker during the week and spoke on women's rights on weekends, routinely enduring jeers and even assault. The star attraction at the first national women's rights convention in 1850, her speech was reprinted in England and helped internationalize the movement.

As founder of the American Woman Suffrage Association in 1869, Stone edited its *Woman's Journal* with assistance from her husband and, later, her daughter, Alice Stone Blackwell. She campaigned for women in many states, made her last speech at the International Congress of Women in 1893, and—in accordance with a lifetime of innovation—asked that she, the first female college graduate in Massachusetts, be the first woman to be cremated.

STOWE, HARRIET BEECHER (1811–1896) More than any other single factor, Stowe's *Uncle Tom's Cabin* (1852) rallied Americans to end slavery. The book probably sold more than 2.5 million copies in its first few years, but many were pirated editions from which she did not earn royalties, and Stowe wrote voluminously for the rest of her life to support her invalid husband and adult children. She also supported the women's movement, as did her relatives: her brother, the Reverend Henry Ward Beecher, served briefly as president of the American Woman Suffrage Association, and a sister, Isabella Beecher Hooker, was the organization's longtime president in Connecticut. Stowe also lived in Connecticut much of her life, although it was living in Cincinnati, where many slaves escaped across the Ohio River to freedom, that inspired her great book.

TALLCHIEF, MARIA (1925–) One of the top ballerinas of all time, Tallchief was born in Oklahoma, the daughter of a chief of the Osage tribe. Initially a pianist, she studied ballet under the Russian dancer and choreographer Bronislava Nijinska and debuted with the Ballet Russe de Monte Carlo in 1942. She joined the New York City Ballet at its 1948 beginning and danced with the company for most of her career. Married to choreographer George Balanchine between 1946 and 1952, Tallchief won critical acclaim as America's greatest virtuoso of dance. After her retirement in 1965, she founded the Chicago City Ballet, and in 1997 she published an autobiography, *Maria Tallchief: America's Prima Ballerina*.

TERRELL, MARY CHURCH (1863–1954) Perhaps the best-educated black woman in the world when she earned an 1888 master's degree from Oberlin College, Terrell was the founding president of the National Association of Colored Women in 1896. She delivered a 1904 speech in three languages at the meeting of the International Council of Women in Berlin and served on the Washington, D.C., school board from 1895 to 1911. Although she was wealthy, she radicalized as she aged and led some of the nation's first civil rights actions, including a sit-in at a segregated restaurant; she testified before the Supreme Court at age ninety and won the case while Martin Luther King, Jr., was still a student. Terrell's autobiography, *A Colored Woman in a White World* (1940), has an introduction by H.G. Wells.

THOMAS, M. CAREY (1857–1935) A pioneer educator, Martha Carey Thomas never used her first name. The University of Zurich granted her doctorate in 1882—its first to a woman and to a non-European. She spent her life at Bryn Mawr, a prestigious women's college in suburban Philadelphia, becoming its president in 1894. Unlike most of the era's academics, Thomas actively supported the suffrage movement; in 1908 she became the founding president of the college-based Equal Suffrage League.

THOMPSON, DOROTHY (1893–1961) Some of her contemporaries thought of Thompson as second only to ELEANOR ROOSEVELT in global influence. A syndicated columnist and radio commentator, she interviewed Adolf Hitler in 1931 and published a cautionary book on him the next year—long before most people understood the danger that fascism represented. Her editorship of the *Ladies' Home Journal* during the war years may have diminished her reputation in the male world, but the columns she wrote were visionary, presaging much of modern feminist thought. Marriage to Nobel Prize winner Sinclair Lewis also probably distracted from her independent image and work, especially as he descended into alcoholism. Tellingly named, *The Courage to Be Happy* (1957) was Thompson's last book.

TOMPKINS, SALLY (1833–1916) Commissioned as a Confederate captain, Tompkins ran Robertson Hospital in Richmond, Virginia. Physicians sent their worst cases there, but she was such an outstanding hospital administrator that the hospital had the lowest fatality rate of any similar institution on either side of the Civil War.

TRUTH, SOJOURNER (c. 1797–1883) Named Isabella when she was born a slave in upstate New York, her native language was Dutch—for which she was punished when sold to English speakers. In 1827, she fled to a family of Quakers, who helped her file a successful suit to recover her son from Alabama, where he had been sold in violation of state law on gradual emancipation. Adopting "Sojourner Truth" as her name in 1843, she began preaching and speaking against slavery throughout New England; abolitionists helped her write her autobiography, which she sold to support her travels.

Truth attended the first national women's rights convention in 1850, and her reputation grew the next year, when she made her famous "Ain't I a Woman?" speech in Akron. For the rest of her life, she identified herself with the movements for both women's rights and black rights; indeed, she argued publicly with Frederick Douglass over prioritization of the two. After 1872, she lived in Battle Creek, Michigan, where she attempted to vote, and although black men voted, her ballot was rejected. Buried at Battle Creek, she was honored with a postage stamp in 1987.

TUBMAN, HARRIET (c. 1820–1913) No other abolitionist—male or female, black or white—exhibited more sheer courage than Harriet Tubman, who risked her life at least nineteen times leading some 300 people out of slavery. Born a slave on Maryland's eastern shore, she escaped to Philadelphia in 1849, just before passage of the repressive Fugitive Slave Act. As a child, she had suffered a brain injury from her master that could cause her to suddenly lapse into unconsciousness; this, combined with an inability to read, made her ventures into slave territory especially dangerous. Tubman developed secret communication codes with those she intended to free and carried a gun to threaten anyone with second thoughts. Plantation owners offered as much as $40,000 for her capture, and detectives trailed her; she outwitted one by purchasing train tickets heading south, convincing him that he was following the wrong group of blacks.

During the early 1850s, she escorted many slaves all the way to her home in Saint Catharines, Ontario. After southern coastal islands fell to Union control, she did some army reconnaissance there but was never assigned a job commensurate with her ability. With help from Secretary of State William E. Seward, she began the Harriet Tubman Home for Indigent Aged Negroes after the war, supported in part by sales from an 1869 autobiography written for her by a white woman, Sarah Bradford. Her former home is open to visitors in Auburn, New York. Tubman has received many honors, including a 1978 postage stamp.

VANN, JESSIE ELLEN MATTHEWS (c. 1890–1967) The *Pittsburgh Courier*, which Vann published from 1940 to 1963, was read by almost every black leader in the United States. Because World War II integration and the postwar civil rights movement took place during the years after she inherited the paper from her husband, Vann was a national molder of public opinion until her retirement at age seventy-seven.

WALD, LILLIAN (1867–1940) Wald began her New York City settlement house in 1893, unaware of JANE ADDAMS's three-year-old Chicago model. More than others, she emphasized sending credentialed nurses into urban slums, where they not only treated disease but also taught the principles of public health to immigrant women. The founding president of the National Organization for Public Health Nursing, Wald wrote an autobiographical book, *The House on Henry Street* (1915), that was a best-seller.

WALKER, MAGGIE LENA (1867–1934) America's first black female bank president, Walker exhibited excellent entrepreneurial skills. She began running a mutual insurance society in 1899, when it was $400 in debt; by the time she died, it

had solid assets and had paid $3 million in benefits. Her bank, which she started in 1903, absorbed most Richmond banks that served blacks during the Great Depression, providing jobs and mortgages when others went bankrupt. A leader in several organizations for black women, her Richmond home is a national historic landmark.

WALKER, MARY EDWARDS (1832–1919) The only woman to win the Congressional Medal of Honor, Walker was an 1855 graduate of Syracuse Medical College; she retained her maiden name when she married that year, just months after LUCY STONE set the precedent. When her marriage failed, Walker moved to Iowa unsuccessfully seeking a state that allowed divorce, and then volunteered when the Civil War began. In Tennessee battlefields in 1863, General George "Pap" Thomas ignored his men's objections and commissioned her as an officer and surgeon. Captured by Confederates the next year, she was held as a prisoner of war in Richmond, Virginia, and—like men who endured such conditions—won the coveted medal. In World War I, however, the military upgraded the prestige of this medal and withdrew her honor; at age eighty-four, she went to Washington to protest, slipped on the steps of the Capitol, and never recovered. Meanwhile, because of petty quarrels and especially her masculine appearance, most leaders of the era's women's movement were alienated from her, and her Iowa death went largely unmourned. In 1977, feminists succeeded in getting Congress to restore the medal, and Walker was honored with a 1981 postage stamp.

WALKER, SARAH BREEDLOVE ("MADAME C.J.") (1867–1919) Probably America's first black female millionaire, Madame C.J. Walker not only developed hair products designed for black women but also created an innovative sales technique; her "Walker agents" personally marketed her system of hair styling. Both she and Annie Turbo Malone created these products in Saint Louis around 1905, but Walker claimed that her "Wonderful Hair Grower" came to her in a dream. Regardless of whether the concept was original, she successfully exploited it: by 1909, she had a manufacturing plant in Indianapolis and beauty schools all over the nation. When she died a decade later, Walker owned a New York City townhouse and a villa on the Hudson River—yet Booker T. Washington tried to prevent her from speaking to the 1912 National Negro Business League.

WARNER, SUSAN BOGERT (1819–1885) Warner's *The Wide, Wide World* (1851), which featured an adventurous girl, outsold *David Copperfield* even in England. Although it probably was the first American book to sell a million copies, copyright protection was so poor that Warner and her sister, Anna Bartlett, lived humbly on a Hudson River island near West Point, New York. Bartlett wrote as well; her most famous work was the children's song "Jesus Loves Me, This I Know."

WARREN, MERCY OTIS (1728–1814) As much a revolutionary as her husband and brother, both leaders of the American Revolution, the times did not permit Warren to be politically visible, but she anonymously published satires of the British years before the Declaration of Independence. Although she rarely had the opportunity to leave her home in Plymouth, Massachusetts, Warren carefully chronicled the war; her three volumes were finally published in 1805 as *History of the Rise, Progress, and Termination of the American Revolution.*

Presaging much feminist thought, she wrote in her old age of doing needlework while her brothers went to Harvard University and argued that such artificial limitations on human achievement harmed everyone while also violating the Revolution's natural-rights philosophy. Like ABIGAIL ADAMS, she corresponded with many of the era's most important men, and her words provide incisive views of the new nation.

WEDDINGTON, SARAH (1945–) Weddington successfully argued the landmark Supreme Court case *Roe v. Wade* (1973) when she was twenty-seven years old. Her legal experience at the time was limited to a few wills, divorces, and other simple matters, yet her reasoned arguments on the issue persuaded seven of the nine men on the court to strike down Texas laws that banned abortion. Weddington was also a state legislator at the time; elected in 1972, she was the first Austin woman in the Texas House. After three terms, she joined President Jimmy Carter's administration in 1978, where she advised him on women's issues and cochaired the U.S. delegation to the 1980 United Nations women's conference in Copenhagen. Weddington lives in Austin, where she practices law and teaches at the University of Texas. She continues as an outstanding advocate for reproductive rights and was honored as the 1992 Speaker of the Year by the National Association for Campus Activities; in the same year, Weddington published *A Question of Choice.*

WELLS-BARNETT, IDA BELL (1862–1931) Born a slave in Mississippi, Wells-Barnett became perhaps the most radical black woman in the United States at a time when leading the crusade against lynching was considered dangerously radical. As Ida B. Wells, she published a newspaper in Memphis when white riots devastated the black community there in 1892; decades ahead of Martin Luther King, Jr., she urged blacks to boycott the city's streetcars. When her life was threatened and her office looted, she moved to Chicago, and, after adopting her hyphenated surname with an 1895 marriage, she unsuccessfully lobbied President William McKinley at the White House for an antilynching law. Wells-Barnett understood sexism as well as racism, and most black leaders found her threatening. She did not receive the recognition she merited in her lifetime, but, since the 1970 publication of her autobiography, *Crusade for Justice,* her honors have included a 1991 postage stamp.

WHARTON, EDITH NEWBOLD JONES (1862–1937) One of America's most important novelists, Wharton spent much of her life in France; indeed, the American classic *Ethan Frome* was initially published in French. Although blessed with inherited wealth, she was burdened by a mentally ill husband and especially by the constraints placed on women in her society. This was the chief theme of *The House of Mirth* (1905) and *The Age of Innocence* (1920), both classics of a very different sort of Americana than *Ethan Frome.* Wharton won a Pulitzer for *The Age of Innocence,* and she also wrote a variety of nonfiction works, publishing some fifty books. Elected to the National Institute of Arts and Letters in 1930, she was buried at Versailles.

WHEATLEY, PHILLIS (c. 1753–1784) The first African American to publish a book, Wheatley came to Boston on a slave ship from Gambia as a child but was not treated as slaves usually were; the Wheatley family not only taught her to write but sent her to England in 1773, where she published *Poems on Various Subjects, Religious and Moral.* The American Revolution devastated the Wheatleys, and Phillis's 1778 marriage to a free black man proved unfortunate; she was found dead of malnutrition in an unheated room with her third dead baby. She was largely forgotten until abolitionists republished her work in 1834, but since then, her literary ability has been repeatedly honored.

WHITE, ELLEN HARMON (1827–1915) Cofounder of the Seventh-Day Adventists, White was believed by her followers to be divinely inspired; she reputedly saw visions and sometimes knew private details of her disciples' lives. The church was formalized in 1860 in Battle Creek, Michigan—where White's modern health ideas influenced Dr. John Kellogg's cereal products—and she spent most of her life there, but she devoted the 1890s to expanding the church in Australia. The author of some fifty books and 4,600 articles, she also was a popular lecturer, attracting 20,000 listeners at a Massachusetts camp meeting. Born in Maine, she died in California and was buried at Battle Creek.

WHITMAN, CHRISTINE TODD (1946–) Governor Christine Todd Whitman of New Jersey, a Republican, defeated the Democratic incumbent in 1993 even though New Jersey had voted Democratic in the previous year's presidential election. Born to a wealthy family of active Republicans, she served in local office and as an appointed utility regulator before running for the U.S. Senate in 1990; although unsuccessful, she did well enough to take on the governor. Delivering on her promises to cut taxes, Whitman was reelected in 1997. She defies many in her party by being strongly pro-choice.

WILDER, LAURA INGALLS (1867–1957) One of the most beloved of children's authors, Wilder wrote autobiographical depictions of pioneer life. The most popular are *Little House in the Big Woods* (1932), the story of her earliest years in Wisconsin; *Farmer Boy* (1933), about her husband's youth in northern New York; and *Little House on the Prairie* (1935), the basis for a television series.

WILKINSON, JEMIMA (1752–1819) The founder of a short-lived religious sect, Wilkinson called herself the "Publick Universal Friend." She emphasized tolerance and experimented with faith healing and dream interpretation. Some of her followers freed their slaves in response to her, and she led nearly 300 disciples from the coastal northeast to western New York in 1788, where they dealt with Native Americans according to her humanitarian ideas.

WILLARD, EMMA HART (1787–1870) America's first important female educator, Willard was a visionary who saw far earlier than most that girls should have an education comparable to that of boys. Decades ahead of others, she lobbied members of the New York legislature for funding in 1818, but they were scandalized by her intention to teach science, especially anatomy; residents of the town of Troy—across the Hudson River from the capital of Albany—voted to tax themselves to build her school. It soon paid off, as hundreds enrolled from all over the nation. Willard also wrote textbooks, set up a school in Greece in 1830, and represented the United States at the World's Educational Convention in London in 1854. Her Troy Female Seminary was renamed the Emma Willard

School on the twenty-fifth anniversary of her death and remains a prestigious girls' boarding school.

WILLARD, FRANCES (1839–1898) Longtime president of the Women's Christian Temperance Association, Willard was more of a feminist than the modern image of that organization implies. She was the first dean of women at Chicago's Northwestern University in 1871, when most colleges did not yet admit women. Elected president of the temperance association in 1879, Willard spent the rest of her life traveling the world to end alcohol abuse and ensure women's rights. Millions signed petitions for the vote because of her, and her autobiography, *Glimpses of Fifty Lives* (1889), was a best-seller. In 1905, Illinois honored her with one of the two statues that each state is allowed in the Capitol; hers was the first of a woman.

WINNEMUCCA, SARAH (c. 1844–1891) The most famous female American Indian of her time, Winnemucca was a Piute whose native name meant "shell flower." Fluent in English, Spanish, and three Native American languages, she served as an interpreter in Oregon, Idaho, and elsewhere. Winnemucca argued strongly for her people and especially against the corrupt Bureau of Indian Affairs; she had greater trust in army men. The federal government paid her expenses when she went to Washington in 1880, where she lobbied President Rutherford B. Hayes. She followed up with a successful lecture tour in the northeast and with *Life Among the Piutes* (1883). Married three times—twice to white men—Winnemucca was born in Nevada and died in Montana.

WOODHULL, VICTORIA CLAFLIN (1838–1927) Perhaps the most free-spirited woman of the Victorian Age, Woodhull had no match as an attention-getter in the 1870s. With her sister, Tennessee Claflin, she lived the "free love" lifestyle that she advocated. With backing from millionaire Cornelius Vanderbilt—for whom they conducted séances—the sisters opened a Wall Street brokerage and published a radical newspaper, which they used to promote Woodhull's quixotic 1872 presidential campaign. She spent election day in jail, however, charged with obscenity for publishing the story of the Reverend Henry Ward Beecher's affair with a married member of his Brooklyn congregation. Because everyone involved was active for women's rights, his resulting trial for adultery significantly harmed the movement. Woodhull moved to England, where she published *Humanitarian* magazine and again became popular and affluent.

WRIGHT, FRANCES ("FANNY") (1785–1852) One of the nineteenth century's most advanced thinkers, Wright advocated birth control and world government decades ahead of most others. A controversial but popular lecturer, she broke taboos on public speaking by women and frequently traveled between the United States and her home in Scotland. Among her books were *Views of Society and Manners in America* (1821) and an 1825 proposal for the gradual elimination of slavery. A cofounder of New Harmony, a utopian community in Indiana, she was the sole founder of a colony near Memphis for slaves she bought and freed; when this site proved too remote, she escorted some thirty blacks to Haiti in 1830, spending half her fortune. Wright died after falling on ice in Cincinnati.

YALOW, ROSALYN SUSSMAN (1921–) The second American woman (after GERTY CORI) to win the Nobel Prize in physiology or medicine, Yalow is a radiologist who pioneered nuclear medicine and immunology. A New York City native, she graduated from Hunter College in 1941 and earned a 1945 doctorate in physics at the University of Illinois. Affiliated with the Veterans Administration Hospital in the Bronx through most of her career, she was elected to the National Academy of Sciences in 1971 and was honored with the National Medal of Science, America's highest such award, in 1988. Her 1977 Nobel Prize was awarded for her role in developing tests that measure tiny amounts of enzymes, hormones, and other biological substances.

YOUNG, ANN ELIZA WEBB (1844–1908) Young became notorious in 1873 when she attempted to divorce Mormon elder Brigham Young. Billed as "the twenty-seventh wife," she toured the nation with her story of forced marriage when she was twenty-four and he sixty-eight.

The case was still in court when Brigham Young died at age seventy-six.

YOUNG, ELLA FLAGG (1845–1918) The first woman to head a major school system, Young was appointed superintendent of Chicago's public schools in 1909. The next year, she was elected the first female president of the National Education Association, a teachers' organization founded in 1870.

ZAHARIAS, MILDRED "BABE" DIDRIKSON (1911?/ 1914–1956) Sports writers voted Zaharias "outstanding woman athlete of the century" in 1949. A champion in a half-dozen sports, she won three medals at the 1932 Olympics. After turning pro, she cofounded the Ladies Professional Golf Association and was the first woman to approach a million-dollar annual income. Born in Texas, she retired to Florida but returned to Texas when diagnosed with cancer.

ZAKRZEWSKA, MARIE (1829–1902) Born in Germany, Zakrzewska earned her 1856 medical degree in Cleveland. After working with Emily and ELIZABETH BLACKWELL in New York, she took over Boston's New England Female Medical College, opening an affiliated hospital in 1862. She trained many of the nation's pioneer female physicians and professional nurses. By 1881, the school was so eminent that Zakrzewska limited her students to women who already had a medical degree.

ZWILICH, ELLEN TAAFFE (1939–) The first woman to win the Pulitzer Prize for musical composition, Zwilch's award came in 1983, forty years after the prize was established. A graduate of Florida State University and the Juilliard School of Music, she received Carnegie Hall's new composer chair in 1985.

Notable Women of World History

ADELAIDE (c. 931–999) Adelaide and her husband, Otto I, were crowned empress and emperor of the Holy Roman Empire by Pope John XII in 962. When Otto died less than a decade later, Adelaide was forced from power by her son. She founded a convent in Alsace and was so esteemed for goodness that she was canonized in 1097.

AGNES (?–c. 304) Although Agnes is one of the most famous Roman saints, the date of neither her birth nor her death is known, but a church in Rome reputedly was built in her honor in 350. Like many of the early female saints, she allegedly was martyred at around age thirteen after insisting on dedicating her life to God rather than marrying.

AGRIPPINA (c. 18–59) Agrippina's third husband was the Roman emperor Claudius. She poisoned him in 53 to make her seventeen-year-old son, the infamous Nero, the emperor—but Nero had her killed just five years later.

ALIYE, FATIMA (1862–1936) Turkish author Fatima Aliye published almost exclusively in the 1890s, after she became an adult but before the fall of the Ottoman Empire, which displaced her family. Aliye wrote both fiction and nonfiction; perhaps most important is her *History of Women of Islam* (1892).

ANGELA MERICI (1474–1540) Founder of the order that became the Company of Saint Ursula, Angela Merici was an Italian orphan who made a pilgrimage to the Holy Land, then led a group of young women who dedicated themselves to teaching; this became the specialty of Ursuline nuns. Angela was canonized in 1807.

ANNE OF AUSTRIA (1601–1666) Anne became queen of France when she married King Louis XIII at age fourteen. Accused of treason against him more than once, she became regent for their five-year-old son after the king's

1643 death. She effectively ruled France for almost two decades, during which the Thirty Years' War and other conflicts were successfully resolved.

ANNE, QUEEN OF ENGLAND (1665–1714) Anne was the last of the Tudor dynasty. She bore seventeen children, none of whom survived her—a striking illustration of poor health common to the era. Her 1702–1714 reign is distinguished for the 1707 union of Scotland and England as the United Kingdom, as well as for England's continued exploration of North America.

ANNEKE, MATHILDE FRANZISKA GIESLER (1817–1884) Early suffragist Anneke was born in Germany's Westphalia; married at age nineteen, she managed to obtain a divorce in 1838 and keep custody of her child—uncommon at the time. In 1847 she published (in German) *Woman in Conflict with Social Conditions* under her maiden name. The next year, she joined her new husband in riding into battle against Prussian forces. The Annekes fled to the United States when the revolution failed, and in 1853 she spoke in New York City to one of the first women's rights conventions. She permanently separated from her husband in 1861 and supported six children by lecturing and writing in German and English.

AQUINO, CORAZON COJUANGCO (1933–) The first female president of the Philippines, Aquino drew international headlines for much of the 1980s in her attempt to force the corrupt president Ferdinand Marcos and his wife Imelda to leave the impoverished islands. Aquino's struggle had begun in 1972, when Marcos imprisoned her husband, Benigno; the Aquinos went into exile in the United States in 1980, and Benigno was assassinated when he returned to Manila in 1983. She focused on his sacrifice for democracy and won the 1986 election. The constitution that Aquino put into effect in 1987 limits the president to one term, and she retired in 1992.

ASTOR, LADY NANCY LANGHORNE (1879–1964) The first woman to sit in the British House of Commons, Lady Astor was an American born in Danville, Virginia. She became a British citizen with her 1906 marriage to Waldorf Astor and was active in the international suffrage movement. Elected from the constituency of Plymouth in 1919, she served until 1945; while she was continually reelected to the House of Commons, her husband served in the House of Lords. Lady Astor is remembered for several feminist quotes, especially the quip "I married beneath me. All women do."

ATWOOD, MARGARET (1939–) Perhaps Canada's most recognized novelist, Atwood is especially known for her dark feminist work *The Handmaid's Tale* (1985), which depicts a society in which women are valued exclusively for their reproductive ability. A graduate of the University of Toronto, she also studied at Harvard and has held numerous teaching and writer-in-residence positions in the United States.

AUSTEN, JANE (1775–1817) The most respected of all early female novelists, England's Jane Austen is especially known for *Sense and Sensibility* (1811), *Emma* (1816), and *Pride and Prejudice* (1813), one of the most popular and acclaimed novels of all time. With elegant wit and satire, Austen consistently developed feminist themes, especially that of the constant pressure on women to marry; she herself never married. Austen also left minor works and many entertaining letters.

BANDARANAIKE, SIRIMAVO RATWATTE DIAS (1916–) The world's first female prime minister, Sirimavo R. D. Bandaranaike was elected in 1960 in Ceylon after the assassination of her husband, S. W. R. D. Bandaranaike. As Ceylon moved from its longtime status as a British colony, she promoted peace, prosperity, and especially the use of the native language and traditional Buddhism. She lost the 1965 election but returned in 1970 with strong policies: she nationalized some industries, broke up large estates to give land to the poor, and changed the nation's name from Ceylon to Sri Lanka. This time she governed for seven years, losing the election in 1977. The government that replaced her adopted major constitutional changes in 1978, including the creation of a president with the power to dismiss parliament. Bandaranaike's daughter, Chandrika Kumaratunga—who was born in 1945 and whose husband also had been assassinated—campaigned against this in 1994. She promised that if elected, she would return to the system of a ceremonial presidency and powerful prime minister; she won and immediately appointed her mother as prime minister. As the century ends, they are the world's only mother-daughter team at the head of any government.

BARROW, DAME (RUTH) NITA (1916–1995) Appointed the first female governor-general of Barbados in 1990, Barrow had a distinguished international career prior to that. She was educated in Canada, Scotland, and the United States and worked in public health in the Caribbean until her 1964 appointment as an advisor to the World Health Organization. In 1975, she became president of the World YWCA; in 1980, she was named a dame of the Order of St. Andrew, and in 1983 Dame Barrow was elected president of the World Council of Churches. She also presided over the 1985 United Nations conference on women's issues.

BATHILDE (?–680) Born in England, Bathilde was taken to France by pirates, and she eventually married Clovis II, king of the western Franks. In 657, she became regent for their son, Clothar III, and thus the effective ruler of France; she is especially notable for her opposition to slavery—more than a thousand years before this view became general. After her regency ended in about 665, she lived in the nunnery she had founded at Chelles. The Catholic Church honors her with a feast day on January 30.

BEAUVOIR, SIMONE de (1908–1986) The dominant female French intellectual of the twentieth century, de Beauvoir was a professional philosopher; she graduated from the Sorbonne in 1929 and was a founder of French existentialism. In addition to philosophy, she wrote fiction and, with existentialist Jean-Paul Sartre, published a leftist journal, *Le Temps Modernes*. She is especially known for *The Second Sex* (1949), which predated other modern feminist theory by several decades. De Beauvoir's longtime sexual relationship with Sartre—and others, including women—brought these philosophers far more than usual media attention.

BEHN, APHRA (1640–1689) English dramatist Behn was also a pioneer novelist: her 1668 *Oroonoko*, the story of a slave in Suriname (formerly Dutch Guiana), is prescient in both form and subject matter. Behn is known primarily as a playwright; the first of her eighteen known plays was *The Forc'd Marriage*, which was produced at London's Duke's Theatre in 1671. A comedy, *The Dutch Lover* (1673), followed, and Behn went on to a variety of work, often with themes centered on women.

BELL, GERTRUDE MARGARET LOWTHIAN (1868–1926) A British expert on the Middle East, Gertrude Bell was the first female student to earn honors at the

University of Oxford. Bell published travel books on the Middle East as early as 1894 and served in the British government there during and after World War I; her knowledge of unmapped areas and local politics was valuable during the war, when she worked in intelligence in Cairo. Perhaps Bell's most outstanding achievements were the establishment of the National Museum of Iraq and her insistence that archaeological artifacts stay in their native area, instead of being exported to Britain as was usual. Sometimes termed "the uncrowned queen of Iraq," Bell committed suicide at age fifty-eight in Baghdad; two volumes of her letters were published the next year.

BERGMAN, INGRID (1915–1982) One of the most acclaimed yet controversial actors of her era, Sweden's Ingrid Bergman became an international star in 1939 with an American film, *Intermezzo*. She followed that with the classic *Casablanca* (1942) and others, making more than a half-dozen major films between 1942 and 1946. Americans were scandalized by her open affair with Italian director Roberto Rossellini while still married to another man, and Bergman was able to work only in Europe until 1956. Bergman won Academy Awards in three decades: 1944, 1956, and 1974.

BERNHARDT, SARAH (1844–1923) French actor Sarah Bernhardt debuted in 1862 and, during a long career, became perhaps the era's most acclaimed woman on the international stage. She was especially noted for her 1912 performance, at age sixty-eight, as ELIZABETH I. Very popular in the United States, she began her last tour there at age seventy-two.

BESANT, ANNIE (1847–1933) English reformer and pioneer birth-control advocate Annie Besant was a giant of her era. After separating from her husband in 1873, she published *All Sorts and Conditions of Men* (1882) and joined George Bernard Shaw as a founder of the Fabian socialists. She led the fight against a law that barred atheists from Parliament, was arrested for speaking about birth control, and in 1888 organized the first British labor union for women. Besant also campaigned for suffrage, and some believed her to be the most powerful female orator in the world. Besant's persona changed in the next decade. Influenced by HELENA PETROVNA BLAVATSKY, she dropped socialism for theosophy; she spread this mystical philosophy in the United States and, after 1893, in India, where she also upset Western missionaries by encouraging native beliefs and traditions. Besant was an ardent advocate of Indian independence and befriended the young Mohandas K. Gandhi and Jawaharlal Nehru. During World War I, she was imprisoned by the British; Indians

rewarded her efforts with election as president of the Indian National Congress in 1917.

BHUTTO, BENAZIR (1953–) The first female leader of a modern Islamic nation, Pakistan's Benazir Bhutto graduated from Harvard University in 1973 and from the University of Oxford—where she was the first Asian woman elected president of the Oxford Union—in 1977. After her father (Zulfikar Ali Bhutto, who had been both president and prime minister of Pakistan) was assassinated in 1979, she joined her mother, Begum Nusrat Bhutto, in leading his democratic political party. During the next five years, she was frequently arrested and imprisoned, including during the horrifying summer of 1981, when she was confined to a desert cage and nearly died from exposure to insects and the blistering sun. Exiled to England in 1984, Bhutto returned to Pakistan in 1986 and married the next year; she has three children with Asif Ali Zardari. Supported by huge crowds, Bhutto was elected prime minister a few months after the 1988 death of corrupt president Mohammad Zia-ul-Haq. Less than two years later, however, another president deposed her; she won again in 1993, and history repeated itself, with the president removing her in 1996. During her brief periods in power, Bhutto restored civil liberties and supported progressive programs in such basics as clean water and literacy. She has received dozens of international honors.

BLAU, MARIETTA (1894–1970) Austrian nuclear scientist Marietta Blau pioneered photographic studies of cosmic radiation and, in 1925, took the first measurements of high-energy proton tracks. After earning her doctorate at the University of Vienna in 1919, Dr. Blau worked for two years in Berlin and Frankfurt, then returned to the University of Vienna from 1923 to 1938. When the Nazis took over Austria, she fled to Norway and then, in 1939, to Technical University in Mexico City. She worked in Canada from 1944 to 1948 and then was affiliated with Columbia University and the Atomic Energy Commission until 1955, but she never received the permanent appointment she merited. Although a previous Nobel Prize winner nominated Dr. Blau for the prize several times, she never won. She ended her career as an associate professor at the University of Miami, where she retired in 1960.

BLAVATSKY, HELENA PETROVNA HAHN (1831-1891) The Russian founder of the Theosophical Society, Helena Hahn married a Russian general at 16, but soon ran away. During the next three decades, she lived in Turkey, Egypt, Hungary, and possibly Tibet, learning from mystics and occultists. After teaching piano in Paris and London, she arrived in America in 1873, and the next year, established the Theosophical Society, a group that promoted belief in the supernatural; Blavatsky herself was believed to have supernatural powers. She became an American citizen in 1878, but soon sailed for India, where she converted to Buddhism. The Theosophical Society, however, continued under ANNIE BESANT.

BORGIA, LUCREZIA (1480–1519) Although her name has entered the language to denote ruthlessness, Italy's Lucrezia Borgia was actually—like most women of her era—a pawn in the power games of male relatives. The daughter of the man who would become Pope Alexander VI, she married at age thirteen; the marriage was annulled four years later so that she could marry Alfonso, duke of Bisceglie, who was strangled by one of her brother's servants in 1500. In 1503, she married Alfonso d'Este; they became the duke and duchess of Ferrara in 1505, and she lived quietly until her death at age thirty-nine. A patron of art and literature, she does not merit her cruel reputation.

BREMER, FREDRIKA (1801–1865) Swedish writer and reformer Fredrika Bremer visited Swedish émigrés in the United States in the 1850s, and her travelogues influenced the millions of Scandinavians who followed in the next decades. Bremer also met New England reformers and, upon returning to Sweden, pioneered its women's rights movement. One of Sweden's first novelists, she often dealt with women's issues, and several of her books were translated into English.

BRESHKOVSKY, CATHERINE (YEKATERINA KONSTANTINOVNA BRESHKO-BRESHKOVSKAYA) (1844–1934) Known as the Little Grandmother of the Russian Revolution, Breshkovsky rejected her aristocratic family (in what is now Belarus) at age twenty-six to join the rebellion against the despotic Russian tsar. Imprisoned in 1874, she was exiled to Siberia in 1878, and she remained there for twelve years. After her 1896 release, she founded the Social Revolutionists, and by 1900 she had to flee to Switzerland. Breshkovsky went on to the United States in 1904 but returned to Russia when the unsuccessful revolution broke out the next year. Again imprisoned in 1907, she was banished to Siberia in 1910 and remained there until the 1917 revolution, when Petrograd (Saint Petersburg) welcomed this longtime hero of change. After Bolsheviks replaced the more democratic government of Aleksandr Fyodorovich Kerensky in 1919, Breshkovsky again had to flee; she died in Czechoslovakia fifteen years later.

BRIDGET OF SWEDEN (1303–1373) A Swedish nun, Bridget founded the Order of the Most Holy Savior (the Bridgettines); her motherhouse at Vadstena became an important center of Scandinavian Christianity. She also went on at least one crusade and spent a great deal of time in Rome, where she died. Canonized in 1391, Saint Bridget was known for outspoken advice to popes on both church and political issues.

BRIGIT OF IRELAND (c. 450–c. 523) Countless Irish women have been named in honor of this beloved saint, whose popularity in Ireland is surpassed only by Saint Patrick. She formed the first group of religious women in Ireland, soon after Catholicism was introduced there, and headed the abbey at Kildare.

BRONTË sisters—CHARLOTTE (1816–1855); EMILY (1818–1848); and ANNE (1820–1849) Charlotte Brontë, born the year that JANE AUSTEN published *Emma*, was the eldest of these extremely popular English novelists. They had two older sisters who died young, as did their mother; their only brother, Branwell, attempted a literary career but failed in that and every other vocation. Although their father, a Yorkshire clergyman, provided little in the way of formal education, he did encourage the girls' lively imaginations and lifelong writing efforts. All three sisters taught or worked as governesses until an aunt's 1842 bequest allowed them to concentrate on their writing. In 1847, Charlotte published the classic *Jane Eyre* in October and Emily's equally acclaimed *Wuthering Heights* came out in December. Anne's *Agnes Grey*, also issued in December, was not up to the level of her sisters' work, but *The Tenant of Wildfell Hall*, published the next year, was more successful. None of the sisters lived long to enjoy their acclaim. Emily—whose poetry would also rank with the best—caught a cold at Branwell's September funeral and died in December, and Anne followed in May. Charlotte overcame her grief to publish two more novels and to marry, but after just nine happy months, she died from complications of pregnancy, only a few weeks before her thirty-ninth birthday.

BROWNING, ELIZABETH BARRETT (1806–1861) One of the most popular romantic poets of all time, England's Elizabeth Barrett was the eldest of twelve children and so gifted that, with no formal education, she learned French, Latin, and Greek as a child. Her first book, *The Seraphim and Other Poems* (1838), was full of the ancient allegories loved in that era, while *Poems* (1844) drew praise—followed by love letters—from poet Robert Browning. Her father, however, opposed marriage for any of his children, forcing

Barrett and Browning to marry secretly in 1846; they eloped to Italy and never returned. She bore a child at age forty-three and published her most famous book, *Sonnets from the Portuguese* (1850), the next year. Like MARGARET FULLER, Browning supported the Italian revolution, and her 1860 collection *Poems Before Congress* was highly political. She died at age fifty-five in Florence. Her husband published her *Last Poems* in 1862 after her death.

BRUNDTLAND, GRO HARLEM (1939–) Norway's first female prime minister, Gro Brundtland served in that position three times in the 1980s and 1990s, for a total of more than a decade. A physician, she earned her 1963 medical degree from the University of Oslo and added a master's degree in public health from Harvard University in 1965. Dr. Brundtland bore four children, and in 1977 she was elected to parliament, where she rose to chair the foreign affairs committee. Appointed minister of the environment in 1974, she became chair of the Labour Party in 1982. She also has held a number of international positions and has won several international honors.

BRUNHILD (550?–613) Brunhild ruled the Frankish kingdom of Austrasia after the 575 murder of her husband, Sigebert I. The wars she led became the basis for a number of Germanic legends. Her age did not protect her from an extremely violent death: when her forces lost a battle in 613, the queen was tied to a horse and dragged to death.

CAMPBELL, KIM (AVRIL PHAEDRA) (1947–) Canada's first female prime minister, Campbell served only a few months in 1993. A 1969 graduate of the University of British Columbia, she studied at the London School of Economics and, after returning to British Columbia, earned a law degree. She was elected to Parliament in 1988, served as minister for Indian affairs, and passed stronger laws against rape as attorney general. Prime Minister Brian Mulroney appointed her defense minister in January 1993, and when he resigned soon after, her Progressive Conservative Party named Campbell prime minister in June. In November, however, both she and the party were defeated by the largest margin in Canadian history; most voters said that Campbell failed to outline a platform dealing with the severe economic problems that occurred during her party's tenure. She has since taught at Harvard's Kennedy School of Government and published a 1996 memoir.

CARLOTA (1840–1927) Empress of Mexico from 1864 to 1867, Carlota was born Princess Charlotte of Belgium and married Archduke Maximilian of Austria in 1857. With support from a minority of upper-class Mexicans, Napoleon III placed them on the Mexican throne, but French forces were not strong enough to keep them there. Carlota attempted to get assistance for her husband's regime in Paris, Vienna, and Rome, but when her efforts failed she had an emotional collapse. A popular uprising resulted in the execution of Maximilian, and although Carlota had escaped to Europe, she never fully recovered her sanity.

CAROLINE (1768–1821) The trial of Queen Caroline, which absorbed the British in 1820–1821, was a clear example of moral double standards. Caroline's husband, the Prince of Wales, was notorious for his multiple mistresses and outrageous mistreatment of her, including several bungled attempts to cause her "accidental" death. They separated, and she was living abroad when her father-in-law, George III, died in 1820; when her husband was to be crowned George IV, she returned to England and claimed her rightful queenship. He invented stories of her bad behavior, and Parliament investigated but refused the king's request for a divorce. Literally barred from the coronation because she had no ticket, Caroline died three weeks later. The British people, with whom she had always been popular, insisted that her last request, to be buried in her native Brunswick, be granted; amid riots, they escorted her coffin down the Thames.

CATHERINE OF SIENA (1347–1380) Caterina Benincasa was the twenty-sixth child in her medieval family. She reputedly saw visions and attracted a large number of male and female disciples. Although illiterate, she dictated letters that became classics of Italian literature. She also played a strong role in papal politics, especially in persuading Pope Gregory XI to return to Rome from Avignon. Canonized in 1461, she is one of the most popular Catholic saints; she was declared the patron saint of Italy in 1939. Her *Dialogo* was the chief reason that Saint Catherine, along with SAINT TERESA OF ÁVILA, became one of the first women honored with the title doctor of the church in 1970.

CATHERINE THE GREAT (SOPHIE FRIEDERIKE AUGUSTE von ANHALT-ZERBST) (1729–1796) The most powerful female ruler of Russia was not Russian; she was born to minor German royals in Pomerania and educated in French, and she changed her name to Catherine. After her 1745 marriage to Peter III, Catherine II quickly became more Russian than her husband. Peter III became tsar in January 1762, but Catherine's supporters soon placed him under house arrest; the archbishop crowned

Catherine empress even before Peter's death—officially of apoplexy—that July. She transformed Russia from a European backwater to a great power during the next three decades. Exercising superlative political and military leadership, she expanded the empire's borders to the west and south, bringing in millions of subjects. The first Russian ruler to allow the private printing of books, she personally wrote plays and articles that introduced Western ideas. She encouraged the arts and learning, including Russia's first schools for girls; built hospitals and other charitable institutions; and demonstrated her faith in science by having herself and her son inoculated against smallpox. Although she never surrendered any personal power, Catherine streamlined local government and encouraged free trade, but she was careful not to jeopardize her popularity with the nobility by excessive democratization; she gave up on her early plans to gradually emancipate the serfs and in the end actually expanded serfdom to include more than a million previously free peasants. Nonetheless, her thirty-four-year reign represented a golden age of Russian progress.

CAVELL, EDITH (1865–1915) An English nurse trained in the methods of FLORENCE NIGHTINGALE, Cavell went to Brussels in 1907, where she is credited with establishing that country's first professional nursing system. When the Germans invaded in World War I, she helped both Belgians and British prisoners of war to escape. She refused to lie about this when arrested and tried, and the Germans executed her by firing squad. Her funeral in Westminster Abbey included military honors and inspired great Allied support for the war.

CHAMORRO, VIOLETA BARRIOS de (1929–) The first female president of a Central American nation, Violeta Chamorro's 1990 election in Nicaragua was greeted as a victory for international human rights. Educated in the United States, she married Pedro Chamorro in 1950, edited his democratic newspaper *La Prensa* during his frequent imprisonments, and endured exile with him; the repressive Somoza regime finally assassinated him in 1978. She continued with the newspaper and the next year joined the Sandinistas in overthrowing Somoza rule. She served in one of five positions on the executive council, but the Sandinistas soon began to adopt the tactics of the government they ousted, and she resigned. Throughout the civil war that followed in the 1980s, Chamorro continued to use *La Prensa* as a voice of reason; she campaigned in 1990 to end militarism, including the draft, and was elected by a comfortable majority. The Sandinistas

retained legislative control, however, and her term was difficult. Chamorro retired in 1996, at the end of her constitutional tenure.

CHÂTELET, GABRIELLE-ÉMILIE LE TONNELIER de BRETEUIL, MARQUISE du (1706–1749) Better educated than most French women of her era, Madame du Châtelet ignored her elderly husband and the usual social life of a marquise to pursue philosophical and scientific interests. She shared both a sexual and a scientific relationship with the great French philosopher Voltaire, and she built a laboratory that attracted Newtonian scholars. Parts of works by Voltaire and others probably are hers; her translation of Sir Isaac Newton's *Principia Mathematica*, though not published until a decade after her death from childbirth, was the first in French.

CHRISTIE, DAME AGATHA MARY CLARISSA MILLER (1890–1976) The master of murder mysteries for most of the twentieth century, Agatha Christie published her first book, *The Mysterious Affair at Styles*—which introduced the Belgian detective Hercule Poirot—in 1920. Her 1930 marriage to an archaeologist provided background for a number of mysteries set in the Middle East. In that year she also introduced the character of Miss Jane Marple, whose quiet life in an English village belied amazing deductive powers. In addition to writing dozens of books that sold millions of copies, Christie was a very successful playwright: *The Mousetrap*, first produced in 1952, holds the record for London's longest continuously running play. She was named a dame of the British Empire, the female equivalent of a knight, in 1971.

CHRISTINA (1626–1689) After her father's death, Christina became queen-elect of Sweden when she was six; she assumed the throne at age eighteen and abdicated at twenty-seven to move to Rome and study philosophy. Even while still queen, she brought famed French philosopher René Descartes to Sweden and developed a brilliant court of outstanding thinkers. Sweden made tremendous progress both culturally and economically during her short reign, but Christina preferred contemplation to power. She died in Rome thirty-five years after she stepped down.

CILLER, TANSU (1946–) The first woman without male relatives in government to be prime minister of an Islamic nation, Tansu Ciller graduated from college in Istanbul; she then studied at three American colleges, earning a doctorate in economics at the University of Connecticut. Returning to Turkey, she taught at Bogaziçi University and wrote nine books on economics while rearing two children.

She also amassed a fortune in business with her husband, who—defying Islamic practice—took her name when they married. Ciller was elected to Turkey's Parliament in 1991 and subsequently was named economic minister by her party. Just two years later, she became prime minister. As prime minister, she supported an entrepreneurial economy with ties to the European Union and especially reached out to urban women; on the other hand, she also repressed the minority Kurds. When she unwisely called for a 1995 election, another party finished first. Since then, Ciller has worked to build coalitions that would return her to office but has so far not succeeded.

CLARE OF ASSISI (1194–1253) Namesake of the nuns known as Poor Clares (also called Clarissines), Clare was a close associate of Saint Francis of Assisi. Although she belonged to a noble family, the order that she founded in 1212 depended on begging; women took a vow not to own anything, including communal property. Unlike teaching or nursing nuns, her "daughters" were strictly devoted to contemplation, and by 1630 there were some thirty-four thousand in more than nine hundred convents. Saint Clare personally started convents as far away as France, Germany, and Prague, and, despite her self-denial, she outlived Saint Francis by almost three decades. She was canonized just two years after her death.

CLEOPATRA (69–30 B.C.) One of the most famous monarchs of all time, Cleopatra VII was the last of Egypt's Ptolemaic dynasty. She and her younger brother, Ptolemy XIII, were jointly crowned upon their father's death in 51 B.C. Her brother's regents created a rebellion against her and forced her to go to Syria; she raised an army and was preparing to return to Egypt when Julius Caesar arrived at Alexandria. In a story retold many times since, she had herself rolled up in a carpet and presented to Caesar. He ruled in her favor the next day, and Ptolemy XIII and his forces were soon obliterated. Over the objections of his wife, Caesar tried to force the Roman Senate to pass a law allowing him to marry Cleopatra and to make their son his heir. Cleopatra went to Rome in 46 B.C. and lived in his palace until Caesar was assassinated two years later. She returned to Egypt, and when her younger brother died the next year, Cleopatra was widely believed to have poisoned him. Completely taking over Egypt, she also intervened in the Roman civil war that followed Caesar's death. When her allies lost, she again created a sensation by sailing to the winner, Mark Antony, in a magnificent barge; as she had done with Caesar, she captivated her would-be captor. She bore twins in 40 B.C., and, like Caesar, Antony promised to marry

her and legitimate them—but when his wife died, he married a Roman in 39 B.C. The affair with Cleopatra continued, however, and she bore his son in 36 B.C. Meanwhile, both engaged in warfare that greatly increased the size of their empires. Romans were furious with Antony, however, because of Cleopatra; ultimately, his armies lost the civil war his enemies mounted against him, and her fleet deserted to the obvious victors. In a scene made for opera, she fled to the tomb she had prepared for herself; Antony committed suicide but lived long enough to be brought to die in her arms. She followed, supposedly by allowing herself to be bit by a poisonous asp. They were buried together.

COLETTE (SIDONIE-GABRIELLE) (1873–1954) France's leading female novelist in the first half of the twentieth century, Colette was known simply by her maiden surname. Her husband, Henri Gauthier-Villars, published her first work under his pen name, "Willy," when Colette was twenty. She divorced him in 1906 and, while singing and dancing to support herself, continued to write; ultimately, Colette married twice more and published some fifty novels. The Claudine series is especially known for Colette's understanding of women's lives and emotions.

CORDAY, CHARLOTTE (MARIE-ANNE-CHARLOTTE CORDAY d'ARMONT) (1768–1793) Like most of the French, Charlotte Corday of Caen initially welcomed the revolution, but as exiles from Paris fled the country, she became concerned that it had gone too far. In June 1793, Corday went to Paris, where she gained an audience with Jean-Paul Marat, president of the Jacobin Club—a political group that used terrorism to achieve its egalitarian aims—by pretending to be a spy working on his behalf. Because of a skin infection, he took frequent medicinal baths, and it was in the bathtub that she knifed him to death on July 13. Refusing to hide or lie, she was guillotined on July 17, ten days before her twenty-fifth birthday. Marat's absence contributed to the rise of the revolutionary Robespierre and a worsening of the Reign of Terror.

CORRIGAN-MAGUIRE, MAIRÉAD (1944–) A lifelong resident of Belfast in Northern Ireland, Corrigan-Maguire was cowinner of the 1976 Nobel Peace Prize with BETTY WILLIAMS. Both women were moved by the deaths of children during violence between the Irish Revolutionary Army and Belfast authorities in August 1976. Corrigan-Maguire led Catholic women, while Williams led Protestant women, in marches to end the long conflict, which had killed some seventeen hundred people in the past decade. They formed the Community of Peace People and published a newspaper, *Peace by Peace*. The Nobel Committee awarded their 1976 prize after pressure from both sides; many longtime peace activists resented the award of this most prestigious prize to women whose activism had been relatively brief, but others, especially Norwegians, wanted it so much that they raised more than $300,000 as a "Norwegian Peace Prize."

COURT, MARGARET SMITH (1942–) Australian tennis champion Margaret Court won the grand slam of women's tennis singles—the British, U.S., Australian, and French titles—in 1970, creating a craze for the sport that resulted in better attention to women's athletics in this era of rising feminism. She had already won the 1963 doubles grand slam, and her 1970 achievement made Court the only woman to hold both titles. Born in New South Wales, she won the 1960 Australian championship as Margaret Smith, then changed her name when she got married in 1967. She ultimately held more than sixty international titles.

CRESSON, EDITH CAMPION (1934–) The first female premier of France, Cresson served for less than a year. Born near Paris, she earned a doctorate in economics, married in 1959, and was elected to the European Parliament in 1979. She also served as mayor of two towns and, in 1981, won a seat in the National Assembly. François Mitterrand, president of the Socialist Party, appointed Cresson to several positions, mostly on trade, during the next decade. He appointed her premier in May 1991, but when the Socialists suffered major losses in elections early in 1992, she was replaced in April. Although criticized as too outspoken, Cresson tried to balance a competitive economy with social reform.

CURIE, MARIE SKLODOWSKA (1867–1934) The world's only woman to win two Nobel Prizes, Curie is closely associated with France, although she was Polish. She moved to Paris from Warsaw in 1891, graduated from the Sorbonne in physics two years later, and married chemist Pierre Curie in 1895. Together they pioneered knowledge of radioactivity—a term she coined—and discovered the elements of polonium and radium in 1898. By 1902, the Curies had isolated radium in its pure form, and the next year they jointly won the Nobel Prize in physics. Pierre died in 1906, and Madame Curie, as she was known, took his position as physics professor at the Sorbonne. Curie won her second Nobel Prize in 1911 for chemistry and headed the university's new Radium Institute in 1914, where her daughter, Irène Joliot-Curie, joined her research projects. A second daughter, Ève

Curie, became an accomplished concert pianist and published a best-selling biography of her mother, *Madame Curie* (1937). Despite a lifetime of dangerous experiments, she lived to age sixty-six and remains the century's most admired female scientist.

DEBORAH (between 900 and 600 B.C.) A Hebrew military leader and judge, Deborah united several Hebrew tribes in successful warfare against the Canaanites. Her song of celebration, in Judges 5, is a classic of biblical poetry.

DELEDDA, GRAZIA (1875–1936) The 1926 Nobel Prize winner in literature, Italian novelist Grazia Deledda was born on the island of Sardinia; although she lived in Rome as an adult, many of her books feature Sardinia and its people. Her most famous book is *The Mother* (1923).

DIETRICH, MARLENE (1901–1992) German film star Marlene Dietrich had her first big success with *The Blue Angel* (1930), which was filmed in Berlin. She came to the United States and became an American citizen in 1939, when World War II began in Europe. Dietrich performed for soldiers throughout Allied territory during the war. Her most outstanding postwar films were *Witness for the Prosecution* (1957) and *Judgment at Nuremberg* (1961).

DINESEN, ISAK (KAREN CHRISTENCE DINESEN, BARONESS BLIXEN-FINECKE) (1885–1962) Author of the popular book *Out of Africa* (1937), Dinesen was born to an aristocratic Danish family. She published her first stories in 1907 under the pseudonym Osceola and then went to Kenya, where she married her cousin Baron Bror Blixen-Finecke, a Swedish nobleman. The baroness did not live like nobility, however, especially after their 1925 divorce: drought and worldwide depression forced her to sell her coffee plantation in 1931. She returned to Denmark and published *Seven Gothic Tales* in 1934. Many stories, set in both Africa and Europe, followed; some were issued under pseudonyms, and the last was published just a year before she died at age seventy-seven.

DROSTE-HÜLSHOFF, ANNETTE, BARONESS von (1797–1848) Long considered Germany's greatest female poet, Annette Droste-Hülshoff was born a noble; she never married and lived reclusively in Westphalia. Like America's later EMILY DICKINSON, she wrote modern, realistic poetry uninfluenced by the wider world. Unlike Dickinson's, her poems reflect her Catholicism, and she also wrote at least one dark novella, *Die Judenbuche* (1842).

DURAS, MARGUERITE (1914–) Prize-winning French novelist Marguerite Duras grew up in Saigon—then part of French Indochina—as Marguerite Donnadieu. She studied at the Sorbonne, was active in the Communist Party, and began to write under the pseudonym Duras while Paris was occupied by Nazis during World War II. Many of her books and plays feature Asia: her first big success, *The Sea Wall* (1950), concerns a French family in Indochina, and her most recent book is *The North China Lover* (1991).

DUSE, ELEONORA (1859–1924) Italy's Duse was considered one of the greatest women on the late nineteenth-century stage. She was born to a family of actors in Lombardy, debuted at age four in a dramatization of Victor Hugo's *Les Misérables*, and was especially popular in France. Duse retired in 1901, made an Italian film in 1916, and then, in need of money, returned to the stage in the 1920s. She died on tour in Pittsburgh.

ELEANOR OF AQUITAINE (1122–1204) One of the strongest women of the Middle Ages, Eleanor of Aquitaine (a French province) married King Louis VII of France at age fifteen and led an armed band of women on a crusade to the Holy Land with him. They divorced in 1152 at her initiative, and she married Henry Plantagenet, son of the empress MATILDA, six weeks later. When he ascended the English throne in 1154, Eleanor became the only woman in history to be queen of both France and England. She bore eight children and, in 1172, joined some of her sons in rebelling against their father; when they were defeated, Eleanor dressed in male clothing to escape but was captured and kept under house arrest until the king's death. She then served as regent while her son, Richard I—known as the Lion-Heart—went on long crusades; in her seventies, she traveled throughout England holding court and pardoning many who had been imprisoned by her husband.

ELIOT, GEORGE (MARY ANN EVANS) (1819–1880) Born Mary Ann Evans, Eliot grew up in Warwickshire, England. After her father died when she was twenty-seven, she moved to London and worked for the *Westminster Review*, a progressive journal that published Europe's first reports on America's women's rights conventions. There she met an unhappily married man, George Lewes; they fell in love, but divorce was difficult in that era. After long consideration, they began living together—initially in Germany—and then endured ostracism after returning to London. In 1856, she began writing fiction. Her first work, *Scenes of Clerical Life*, was serialized in a magazine under her pseu-

donym. The series was such a success that Charles Dickens was among those who insisted on meeting "George Eliot," and she continued to use that name as her literary reputation grew. Her major works include *The Mill on the Floss* (1860), *Silas Marner* (1861), and *Middlemarch* (1872). One of the most important English novelists of her era, Eliot shifted English literature from concentration on plot to greater character development and introspection on the ethical principles of behavior.

ELIZABETH I, QUEEN OF ENGLAND (1533–1603) One of the greatest monarchs of all time, Good Queen Bess helped make England into the world's dominant power. She ascended the throne at age twenty-five, after the 1558 death of her half sister, MARY I. Refusing to marry, Elizabeth demonstrated great maturity and judgment from the beginning of her reign. Unlike her troublesome cousin, MARY QUEEN OF SCOTS, Elizabeth did not allow her male advisors to manipulate her. While fiercely maintaining her independence, she encouraged religious toleration and created general prosperity. Under her, England built a state-of-the-art navy that conquered the Spanish Armada and established the tiny island nation as the most powerful in the world. Arts and letters flourished so well that "Elizabethan" came to define England's golden age. Elizabeth sponsored the country's first explorations of America, including Sir Frances Drake's voyages all the way to California. Many places on the North American continent, including the state of Virginia, are named for the Virgin Queen. Few monarchs have been as sincerely mourned by their subjects as Elizabeth was at the end of her forty-five-year reign.

ELIZABETH II, QUEEN OF GREAT BRITAIN (1926–) The current queen of Great Britain ascended the throne after the 1952 death of her father, whose health was strained by World War II. Twenty-six years old at the time, she was almost exactly the same age that Elizabeth I was when she had become queen, but unlike her namesake she was married: Philip Mountbatten, the son of a Greek prince and a German princess, became her husband in 1947. To the extent permitted by her nonpolitical status, Elizabeth continued England's postwar recovery. She was especially effective at creating a persona for herself that maintained loyal connections with former colonies in Asia, Africa, and elsewhere after their postwar rebellions against the mother country. The tribulations of Elizabeth's four children have been so well publicized that they threaten the existence of the monarchy; at the end of the millennium, however, she appeared to be returning the institution to stability.

ELIZABETH, EMPRESS OF AUSTRIA (1837–1898) Beloved by the Hungarians, Elizabeth was born to Bavarian nobility; she married the powerful Austrian emperor Francis Joseph I in 1854. Unlike other royals, she learned the difficult Hungarian (Magyar) language and successfully crusaded to bring Hungary to equal status with Austria in the empire that dominated southeastern Europe. She insisted on traveling and living apart from the king and spent much of her time in Budapest. Elizabeth was in Geneva when—in a precursor to the assassination that began World War I—she was stabbed to death by an Italian anarchist.

ELIZABETH, EMPRESS OF RUSSIA (1709–1762) Had she reigned as long as CATHERINE THE GREAT, Elizabeth, daughter of Peter I the Great, might well also be termed "the Great." Instead, she served as a mentor for Catherine; as Catherine did later, she essentially put herself on the throne. With help from palace guards, she overthrew the regency for the infant male tsar and was crowned in 1741. She was successful in both domestic and foreign affairs: Russia's first university and its Academy of Fine Arts were founded during her reign, and she expanded the empire into Finland and was annexing Prussia when she died. Like England's ELIZABETH I, she refused to marry; unlike the English queen, she was open about her lovers.

ELIZABETH OF HUNGARY (1207–1231) Hospitals throughout the world are named for Saint Elizabeth, who founded one of the first hospitals in 1229. Born a Hungarian princess, she was betrothed to a German prince at age four and grew up in his court at Thuringia; her six-year marriage to Ludwig IV—which ended when he died of plague—was happy. When she became queen, Elizabeth not only was exceptionally generous to the poor but also welcomed Germany's first Franciscans. After her husband's death, however, her brother-in-law forced her out of Wartburg Castle. During what remained of her brief life, she joined the Franciscans in charitable work, which included establishing the hospital in Marburg in the German state of Hessen. A favorite German saint, she was canonized just four years after her death.

ELIZABETH OF PORTUGAL (1271–1336) Named for her great aunt, ELIZABETH OF HUNGARY, Elizabeth of Portugal was born in the Spanish province of Aragon and married the Portuguese king at age twelve. She introduced extremely modern charitable institutions to Portugal, including a home for prostitutes and abused women. Also politically astute, Queen Elizabeth successfully mediated

problems with royal relatives. When the king died in 1325, she devoted herself completely to charitable work and one last act for peace: she died after going to the battlefield and successfully negotiating an end to war with Castile. Peacemaker Elizabeth was canonized in 1626.

ELIZABETH, QUEEN OF ROMANIA (1843–1916) Unlike most queens, Elizabeth of Romania is notable as an author. She was born a Prussian princess, married a Romanian prince in 1869, and became queen in 1881. The next year, she published her first book of Romanian folklore; several more books followed, including novels written under a pseudonym. Her autobiography, *From Memory's Shrine* (1911), was published just before the outbreak of World War I; she died in Bucharest during the war.

EMECHETA, BUCHI (1944–) Nigerian author Buchi Emecheta has lived most of her life in London, but her novels feature African women. Outspokenly feminist, her books include *The Bride Price* (1976), *The Slave Girl* (1977), and *The Rape of Shavi* (1983). She has also written in other genres, including nonfiction; her autobiography is *Head Above Water* (1986).

ENDER, KORNELIA (1958–) In Montreal in 1976, Kornelia Ender became the first woman to win four gold medals for swimming in one Olympic Games. She represented East Germany—then a Communist country—and broke twenty-three world records before retiring after the 1976 games, over the objections of her autocratic coaches. She has since spoken out about the repressive supervision of athletics in that culture.

ESTHER (between 500 and 200 B.C.) Although doubt exists about the historical authenticity of the biblical Esther, she has been so much a part of both the Jewish and the Christian past that these doubts are less important than the reality of Esther's influence. Allegedly a beautiful Hebrew woman married to a Persian king (Ahasuerus, or Xerxes I), she saved Jews in Persia from a pogrom planned by the king's chief minister, Haman. The Jewish festival of Purim celebrates her, and, despite objections that it does not mention God, the Book of Esther was added to the Bible in the second century A.D.

ETHELDREDA (AUDREY) (c. 630–679) Perhaps the most revered of English saints, she was the daughter of the king of East Anglia and was twice married—but after she reputedly refused to sleep with either husband, her family gave up and allowed her to take vows as a nun. She founded the monastery at Ely in about 672, and a cathedral remains at the site.

FATIMAH (606–632) Although she died at age twenty-six, Fatimah was the only child of Muhammad, the founder of Islam, to outlive him. She married a cousin, Ali, and bore two sons, Hasan and Husayn—names that, with variants, are fundamental to the modern Middle East. Hasan's sons were granted the title sharif (Arabic meaning "noble"), while Husayn's descendants had the lesser rank sayyad (Arabic meaning "sir"). Shiite Muslims particularly revere Fatimah and believe that her descendants are the rightful political and religious heirs of the great prophet.

Muslims occupied Portugal from the eighth through the twelfth centuries, and a town north of Lisbon was named Fátima. This is the only connection that the historical Fatimah has with Our Lady of Fátima, a twentieth-century Catholic phenomenon that began when three children reputedly saw the Virgin Mary in a pasture near Fátima, Portugal, in 1917. A basilica there, completed in 1944, draws large numbers of modern pilgrims.

FAWCETT, DAME MILLICENT GARRETT (1847–1929) Although she is remembered primarily for her leadership in winning the right to vote for British woman, Fawcett was also a scholar: she published her first book, *Political Economy for Beginners*, in 1870, when she was twenty-three. Elected president of the British National Suffrage Association in 1904, she was—like America's CARRIE CHAPMAN CATT—the leader of mainstream women; just as Catt opposed the militant tactics of ALICE PAUL, Fawcett objected to the lawbreaking faction led by EMMELINE PANKHURST. While crediting Pankhurst's group for ending "the conspiracy of silence . . . observed by the press," she argued that "the women's movement was an appeal against government by physical force" and that the violence promoted by Pankhurst betrayed this principle. Instead, Fawcett used reasoned speech and effective political organizing to elect supportive men, and in 1918 British women won the vote. She published a 1924 memoir and the next year was made a dame of the British Empire—the female equivalent of being knighted.

FINNBOGADÓTTIR, VIGDÍS (1930–) Iceland's first female president, Finnbogadóttir was elected in 1980. She stressed retention of native Icelandic culture and was extremely popular; reelected by wide margins for sixteen years, she announced her retirement in 1996. Since then, she has chaired the World Commission on the Ethics of Scientific Knowledge and Technology.

FONTEYN, DAME MARGOT HOOKHAM (1919–1991) English ballerina Margot Fonteyn began dancing in Asia as a child; returning to her homeland, she debuted in 1934 and went on to more than four decades with the Royal Ballet. The first Briton to be internationally acclaimed in this field, she was especially known for her dances with Russian exile Rudolf Nureyev. Fonteyn became president of the Royal Ballet in 1954, married the Panamanian ambassador to Great Britain in 1955, and was made a dame of the British Empire—the female equivalent of a knight—in 1956.

FRANK, ANNE (ANNELIES MARIE) (1929–1945) Almost every teenager in the Western world is taught *The Diary of Anne Frank*, written by a Jewish teenager trapped in an Amsterdam attic during the Nazi occupation of the Netherlands in World War II. With four other Jews, the Frank family hid above the factory owned by Anne's father for just over two years—from July 1942 to their capture in August 1944. While Dutch friends risked their lives to smuggle food to them, someone else told the Germans of their hiding place; they were deported and only Anne's father, Otto Frank, survived the concentration camps. He published her diary in 1947, and it has been translated into more than fifty languages.

FRANKLIN, ROSALIND (1920–1958) British Rosalind Franklin was a pioneer in the field of crystallography; using x-ray techniques, she took some of the first pictures of DNA in 1953. The discovery of DNA redefined biology and medical school curricula, and after her death at age thirty-eight, Franklin's coworkers won the 1962 Nobel Prize in physiology or medicine.

FREUD, ANNA (1895–1982) Anna Freud was the daughter of the founder of psychoanalysis, Sigmund Freud, and was herself the founder of child psychoanalysis. Born in Vienna, she practiced with her father and worked especially with children; she began publishing there and chaired the Vienna Psycho-Analytic Society in 1925. Forced to flee when the Nazis took over Austria in 1938, she settled in London with her father. She went on to found the Hampstead Child Therapy Course and Clinic, which she directed until her death. Anna Freud's seminal work is *Normality and Pathology in Childhood* (1968).

GANDHI, INDIRA NEHRU (1917–1984) The first female prime minister of a major nation, Indira Gandhi was elected in 1966, six years after SIRIMAVO BANDARANAIKE became prime minister of Ceylon. Gandhi's father, Jawaharlal Nehru, had died in office two years earlier, and she ran to continue his reformist policies. She won reelection by a large margin in 1980—the same year that her son was killed in a plane crash. Four years later, Gandhi was assassinated by her Sikh bodyguards.

GENEVIÈVE (c. 420–500) The patron saint of Paris, Geneviève allegedly saved the city from the Huns; her prayers were thought to cause Attila to detour from Paris to Orléans in 451. She later led a convoy up the Seine for food when Paris was under siege by the Franks and then successfully influenced King Clovis on behalf of the vanquished. A procession of Saint Geneviève's relics supposedly ended an epidemic in 1129, and pilgrims still visit the Church of Saint-Étienne-du-Mont, where the relics are enshrined.

GENTILESCHI, ARTEMISIA (1592–1652) Perhaps the first woman in the Western world to gain fame as an artist, Italian Artemisia Gentileschi is especially known for a series of Renaissance paintings dealing with rape and vengeance. They feature Judith and Holofernes, figures from the Old Testament Apocrypha. Judith allegedly was a Hebrew woman who went to the tent of Holofernes, a general of the Assyrian enemy Nebuchadnezzar, to save her city from siege. She spent the night with him, and when he fell asleep, Judith beheaded him. Gentileschi's paintings on the subject are so powerful that some critics have speculated that she was herself a rape victim.

GORDIMER, NADINE (1923–) The 1991 winner of the Nobel Prize in literature, novelist Nadine Gordimer is a South African of European descent. She published her first short story in the *New Yorker* in 1951 and has been frequently published in that magazine ever since. Her novels feature South Africa, and Gordimer has been a consistent voice against racism. She has also published in other genres, including political essays. A member of the African National Congress, Gordimer has especially encouraged black writers. *July's People* (1981) may be her best-known book.

GREER, GERMAINE (1939–) Australia's Germaine Greer became internationally known with *The Female Eunuch* (1970). Born in Melbourne, she was educated there and in England, where she earned a doctorate from the University of Cambridge in 1968. *Eunuch* was published just two years later; it was translated into a dozen languages, and Greer wittily interpreted its sophisticated feminist theory on television shows, bringing her ideas to countless people. Now living in Europe, she has published regularly in a number of genres.

HATSHEPSUT (c. 1503–1482 B.C.) Comparable in ability and power to CATHERINE THE GREAT and ELIZABETH I,

Hatshepsut predated them by three millennia and was the first known female monarch. Like the later CLEOPATRA and other Egyptians, she married her royal half brother but used her greater intelligence to displace him—as well as, after his death, his son by another wife. Her largely peaceful reign emphasized a huge building campaign, including great temples, obelisks, and other structures, some of which still survive despite the efforts of her successor to eradicate the monuments. The temple at Dayr al-Bahri contains hieroglyphics detailing her divine birth, an idea that shrewd political leaders throughout the world continued to implant in the popular mind far into the modern age.

HELEN OF TROY (c. 1200 B.C.) Like the Hebrew ESTHER, there is doubt about whether Helen (Helene in Greek) was a historical figure or the stuff of legends, but her lore is an important part of the world's collective past. Allegedly, Helen was born to Sparta's Leda, who—like the Christian Virgin Mary—bore a baby fathered by a god, Zeus. The acme of beauty and grace, Helen rejected many men before marrying Menelaus and bearing a daughter, Hermione. When Paris of Troy invaded Sparta, he took Helen back with him, and thus began the Trojan War, in which Paris was killed. Helen then married Paris's brother, Dephobus, but betrayed him to help Sparta win the war. Menelaus killed Dephobus, and Helen returned to Sparta and lived happily with him and their daughter. Variants of the story also exist, but Helen has come to symbolize all things beautiful in Greece's Hellenic Age.

HELENA (c. 255–330) Revered by Christians as a leading proponent of that religion in the Middle East, Helena was the mother of Constantine I the Great. She converted to Christianity after her husband, the Roman emperor Constantius I Chlorus, repudiated her in 292 and married THEODORA to advance his political interests. When Helena's son became emperor, she encouraged his 313 proclamation of religious toleration and devoted the rest of her life to developing Christianity in Asia Minor. After a pilgrimage to Jerusalem, she died in Nicomedia (now Turkey's Izmit).

HÉLOÏSE (1101–1164) Perhaps the most learned woman of the Middle Ages, France's Héloïse grew up in Paris, where her uncle was canon of Notre Dame. Her name is invariably linked with that of Abelard, by whom she bore a son when she was about eighteen. Both of them, however, were dedicated to the religious life—the only educational opportunity available, especially to women, at the time—and so, despite their great love, they lived in separate monastic institutions. Héloïse rose to head an abbey in Champagne, and her letters to Abelard reveal much about that period of French history.

HENIE, SONJA (1912–1969) World champion ice skater between 1927 and 1936, Norway's Sonja Henie won ten consecutive annual championships, as well as gold medals at the Olympic Games in 1928, 1932, and 1936. Born in Oslo, Henie became a professional skater in the United States after her last Olympic Games and skated in ice shows and on movie screens for another two decades. She was the first to use costumes and dance techniques to enhance figure skating, and her popularity helped advance women in professional athletics.

HERSCHEL, CAROLINE (1750–1848) Astronomer Caroline Herschel was born and died in Germany's Hanover but spent her career in London. Working with her brother, William, who discovered the planet Uranus in 1781, she had her own breakthrough in 1786, when she became the first woman to discover a comet. King George III rewarded her with a salary large enough to support good telescopic equipment, and she went on to locate seven more comets. In 1822 she published *A Catalogue of the Nebulae*, a description of some 2,500 star groups. The Royal Astronomical Society gave Herschel the rare honor of a gold medal in 1828 and, without breaking gender norms, indicated their great respect for her work by electing her to honorary membership in 1835. Perhaps the most recognized female scientist of her time, Caroline Herschel was also honored by the governments of Prussia and Ireland.

HILDEGARD (1098–1179) As head of the Benedictine convent at Rupertsberg, a town near what is now Frankfurt, Hildegard corresponded with at least four popes and two emperors, as well as other important figures. She was believed to be clairvoyant, and her *Scivias* (c. 1141) is comparable to Dante's work in its allegorical predictions of wrath. She wrote about natural science, including physiology, as well as theology; composed dozens of pieces of church music; and, most remarkably, created a language that combined Latin with German. Although some have disparaged Hildegard as "the Sybil of the Rhine" and a doomsayer, her scientific writings, with their keen observations of nature and the body, reveal a superlative mind.

HODGKIN, DOROTHY CROWFOOT (1910–1994) Winner of the 1964 Nobel Prize in chemistry, Britain's Dorothy Hodgkin is credited with the discovery of vitamin B12; using x-ray photography, she and her colleagues determined the molecular structure of this extremely complex compound. She was born to English parents in Cairo, studied at the Universities of Oxford and Cambridge, and from the 1930s taught and worked at Oxford. Specializing in proteins, she also worked on the development of penicillin and on insulin, as well as compounds essential to overcoming anemia. Dr. Hodgkin received many honors, including the British Order of Merit in 1965.

HROSVITHA (935–c. 1000) Germany's first known female author, Hrosvitha lived in Saxony's Gandersheim, where she headed the Benedictine convent. Also known as Roswitha of Gandersheim, she was an accomplished writer in Latin. In addition to didactic plays featuring early Christian martyrs, she wrote at least six Latin comedies, as well as poems and two histories on Germanic subjects. Her manuscripts, which were lost for centuries, were rediscovered in 1501 in Nuremberg.

HYPATIA (c. 370–415) An Egyptian mathematician and philosopher, Hypatia was exceptionally fortunate in that her father, an astronomer at the museum in Alexandria, sent her to Greece and Italy to be educated. After returning to Alexandria, she wrote on arithmetic, geometry, and astronomy; her philosophy similarly was rational rather than theological. She invented several scientific instruments and, as head of the Alexandria school of philosophy that was devoted to Greece's Plato, attracted many students. When Cyril became patriarch of Alexandria in 412, he conducted a campaign of forcible conversion to Christianity; Hypatia refused to convert and was brutally executed by monks.

IRENE (752–810) The first woman to rule the Byzantine Empire, based in what is now Turkey, Irene was intelligent and strong but also cruel. After the 780 death of her husband, Leo IV, she effectively assumed power as regent for her son, Constantine VI, and restored the use of religious icons, which her husband had ended. She gained church approval for her policy in 787, but the iconoclasts—who considered religious art to be false idols—violently objected; continued turmoil over this encouraged Constantine to overthrow his mother in 791. Irene mounted a countercampaign, and when she won in 797, she had her son blinded. Proclaimed emperor, she tried to expand her power by marrying Charlemagne, the Frankish king whom Pope Leo III had crowned as the first Holy Roman Emperor in 800. Instead, Irene was deposed in 802, ending the Byzantine Empire's Isaurian dynasty. Exiled to the

Greek island of Lesbos, she died a year later. The Greek Orthodox Church canonized her for her support of icons.

ISABELLA I (1451–1504) Isabella of Spain is remembered for financing Christopher Columbus's expeditions to the New World. Although she thus supported the science of her day, Isabella is less admirable in that she also supported the expulsion of Jews and introduced the Inquisition. Her 1469 marriage to Ferdinand II of Aragon was one between equals: his Aragon joined her inheritance of Castile to create the modern Spain. Because she was more than his equal in ability and energy, she largely set its domestic policy; termed "La Católica," Isabella created both a strong church and state.

JACOBS, ALETTA (1854–1929) The founder of the world's first birth control clinic and first female physician in the Netherlands, Dr. Jacobs studied in England. She founded Holland's suffrage association in the 1880s; two decades later, she was a founder of the International Woman Suffrage Association, for which she chaired the 1908 meeting in Amsterdam. She conducted a global tour for women's rights with CARRIE CHAPMAN CATT from 1911 to 1913. Dr. Jacobs' fluency in several languages was very helpful as they traveled to South Africa, the Middle East, India, China, Japan, and many other places. Their report on the status of women in these disparate places was a monumental achievement for individuals who had no governmental support.

JADWIGA, QUEEN OF POLAND (1370–1399) Polish nobles elected Jadwiga as their monarch two years after her father's 1382 death. At sixteen, she married a Lithuanian prince who took both a Polish name and the title of king, and thus her official reign lasted only from 1384 to 1386. Their marriage, however, founded one of the greatest dynasties in Europe; Christianity was introduced and Poland's golden age began under Jadwiga.

JOAN OF ARC (1412–1431) The peasant girl known in French as Jeanne d'Arc (d'Arc was her father's surname) was born in the village of Domrémy in northeastern France. Uneducated but not especially poor, she reputedly saw visions starting at age thirteen. The English controlled much of France at that time, and when they, with help from Burgundians, lay siege to Orléans in 1428, Joan's angels told her to go there and assist the French dauphin, Charles VII, in taking his rightful place as king. Dressed in men's clothing, Joan convinced military commanders and Charles that she was divinely empowered,

and on May 8, 1429, she was given command of an army sufficient to win the siege. In July, Charles was crowned with Joan at his side. Charles then abandoned her. She continued to lead the army and was wounded in an unsuccessful battle at Paris; in May 1430, Burgundians captured her at Compiègne. When Charles offered no ransom, they sold her to the English, who turned her over to the bishop of Beauvais, an enemy of Charles's. While the king did nothing to help, a church court convicted her of being a witch. On May 30, 1431, she was burned at the stake in Rouen. When Charles roused himself to rally France against the English, he revised this history to convince his people that the English had burned Joan, but it was in fact French clergymen who were most at fault. They—very belatedly—canonized the Maid of Orléans in 1920.

JOLIOT-CURIE, IRÈNE (1897–1956) Winner of the 1935 Nobel Prize in chemistry, Irène Joliot-Curie was the daughter of scientist MARIE CURIE. Educated at the Sorbonne, she worked as a nurse in World War I and then joined her mother at the university's Radium Institute. She published her first scientific paper in 1921, married Jean-Frédéric Joliet in 1926, and worked with him on radioactivity; they jointly won the Nobel Prize for their research on artificial inducement of radiation. The next year, she was invited to join the French cabinet as an undersecretary for scientific research, but she soon resigned to continue her work on chain-reaction nuclear fission. Forced to flee to Switzerland late in World War II, she also suffered from politics in the postwar era: she was forced out of the French Atomic Energy Commission because of her husband's membership in the French Communist Party. She died five years later at age fifty-nine.

JOSÉPHINE (MARIE-JOSÈPHE-ROSE TASCHER de LA PAGERIE) (1763–1814) Joséphine was crowned empress of France in 1804 with Napoleon Bonaparte, whom she had married in 1796, but the emperor famously divorced her in 1809 because she—six years his elder—seemed unable to provide him with an heir. Joséphine had borne a daughter to her first husband, a 1794 victim of the French Revolution's guillotine, and Napoleon III was her grandson. The story of Napoleon Bonaparte's reluctant divorce from a woman he loved has been frequently retold; as a Parisian salon keeper, she had brought elegance to his young life, and he continued to visit her until she died.

JULIA DOMNA (167–217) Of the several Roman empresses named for Julius Caesar, Julia Domna is striking because she went all the way to Britain with the Roman army and was with her husband, Septimius Severus, when he was killed at what is now York in 211. Her sons, Caracalla and Geta, served as joint emperors until Caracalla murdered Geta in Julia's presence in 212. Caracalla was so poor an emperor that Roman leaders presented all important documents to Julia instead of to him. When he was assassinated and she therefore lost power, Julia killed herself.

JULIA MAMAEA (190–235) More honored with titles than any other Roman woman, Julia Mamaea, who was born in Syria, effectively governed the Roman Empire as regent for her son from 211 to her death in 235. Although she led armies into battle, her soldiers objected when she tried to buy peace with the Germans; she and her son were murdered by Romans in Germany.

KAHLO, FRIDA (MAGDALENA CARMEN FRIDA KAHLO Y CALDERÓN) (1907–1954) The brightly colored paintings of Mexico's Frida Kahlo are currently enjoying greater popularity than they received in her lifetime, perhaps because her work was overshadowed by that her of husband, Diego Rivera. The couple married in 1929, separated a decade later, and remarried in 1941. In 1943—little more than a decade before she died at age forty-seven—Kahlo was appointed a professor at La Esmeralda, Mexico's school of fine arts. Although she had exhibits in New York and Paris in the 1930s, it was not until the 1950s that Kahlo was exhibited in her own land, and her diaries and letters were published only recently. Her artistry, which sometimes includes surrealistic self-portraits, is clearly Mexican in color and imagery.

KAUFFMANN, ANGELICA (1741–1807) Swiss artist Angelica Kauffmann was highly successful in three countries. She learned painting from her father, an Austrian, and was hired to do her first portrait at 13. She left Switzerland for Rome in the next decade, where she was elected to the Academy of St. Luke in 1765, and went on to London the following year. A charter member of the Royal Academy, she worked as a portraitist, engraver, and decorator. After fifteen years in London, she married a Venetian and, retaining her name, moved with him to Rome, where patrons again sought her. Also a writer, Kauffmann published *Music and Painting* (1760) when she was just 19; she died at 66 in Rome.

KENNY, ELIZABETH (1886–1952) The Australian nurse who revolutionized polio treatment in the mid–twentieth century, Sister Kenny (as she was invariably addressed) had little or no formal training. She nonethe-less began treating children with polio as early as 1911, using the simple method of applying warmth and encouraging movement. After serving in the Australian army nurse corps in World War I, she worked in New South Wales; in 1933, she became a national celebrity when her methods proved effective during a polio epidemic. "Sister Kenny Clinics" soon began, and when the United States suffered a similar epidemic a few years later, she moved to the University of Minnesota. Her treatment was once again controversial, but it was so much better than the traditional method of immobilizing the patient that she ultimately prevailed. Because she refused to adopt the subordinate position that physicians expected of nurses, she was frequently criticized, but the relevant health agencies endorsed her methods prior to her death back in Australia.

KEY, ELLEN KAROLINE SOFIA (1849–1926) Swedish author Ellen Key was perhaps Europe's most visionary writer on the egalitarian family and women's roles in the late nineteenth and early twentieth centuries. Although she wrote for a women's rights periodical as early as 1869, she taught in the Stockholm schools through the 1880s and 1890s and then began concentrating on writing. *The Century of the Child* (1900)—which opens with a chapter titled "The Right of the Child to Choose His Parents" and follows that up with headings such as "Soul Murder in the Schools"—caused great furor in both Europe and the United States. Undaunted, she championed greater independence for married women in *Love and Ethics* (1911) and other books. Although much vilified in her time, most of Key's platform was accepted in the century that followed, especially in her native Sweden.

KOLLWITZ, KÄTHE SCHMIDT (1867–1945) German artist Käthe Kollwitz is particularly known for etchings and lithographs that sympathetically depict people suffering from poverty and war. Born in Königsberg, East Prussia, she studied in Munich and began a career as an artist in 1890; a painter and sculptor as well as a printmaker and woodcutter, she became the first woman elected to the Berlin Academy of Fine Arts in 1919. The Nazis expelled her from the academy in 1933, and Kollwitz survived the horrors of World War II—including the bombing of Dresden, near where she lived—only to die a few days before the war ended.

KUMARATUNGA, CHANDRIKA BANDARANAIKE—see BANDARANAIKE, SIRIMAVO

LABÉ, LOUISE (1520–1566) French Renaissance poet Louise Labé lived her entire life in Lyon, where she wrote in both Italian and French. She never married, and some of her poetry reveals feminist inclinations—for which she was criticized by some of her era—but she also conducted an early salon that attracted male poets.

LA FAYETTE, MARIE-MADELEINE (PIOCHE de LA VERGNE), COMTESSE de (1634–1693) One of the earliest novelists, she published *La Princesse de Montpensier* in 1662, four years before APHRA BEHN's pioneer work in English. After marriage three years later made her a countess, she bore two children and continued to write. La Fayette's *La Princesse de Clèves* (1678) is often termed the first psychological novel; like many women of her era, she published the book anonymously.

LAGERLÖF, SELMA OTTILIANA LOVISA (1858–1940) The first woman to win the Nobel Prize in literature (in 1909), Lagerlöf was born in Varmland, Sweden. She was thirty when she went to Stockholm to train as a teacher—but the immediate success of her first book, published when she was thirty-three, quickly ended her teaching career. From its 1891 publication into the 1930s, Lagerlöf was one of the most popular and respected international authors. In 1914, she was the first woman elected to the Swedish Academy of Arts and Letters. Her work drew on both Scandinavian sagas and contemporary issues, and she was especially adept at exploring the psychological effect of profound change: *Jerusalem* (1901), for example, was based on Swedes who immigrated to Palestine.

LEAKEY, MARY DOUGLAS NICOL (1913–1996) Mary Leakey was probably the world's most prominent female archaeologist, especially because of her 1959 discovery of an African skull approximately 1.7 million years old. After studying at University College in London, she went to Kenya in 1931 and married colleague Louis Leakey in 1936. While rearing three children, she spent a lifetime in Africa, digging and sifting many sites; among other important finds were fossilized footprints and a 3.7 million-year-old jaw in Tanzania. The author of several books, she was also an artist who drew and painted many of her finds: *Africa's Vanishing Art* (1983) especially helped popularize that field. She died in Nairobi at age eighty-three. Her autobiography is *Disclosing the Past* (1984).

LESSING, DORIS (1919–) The work of British writer Doris Lessing has been popular for a half century. Born in Iran, she grew up in South Africa, which provided the setting for *The Grass Is Singing* (1950). Active to end apartheid earlier than most people, Lessing also has worked for peace, socialism, and feminism. These themes are woven throughout her work, which includes science fiction and fantasy. Lessing is especially known for *The Golden Notebook* (1972).

LIND, JENNY (JOHANNA MARIA) (1820–1887) Known as the Swedish Nightingale, Jenny Lind probably was the most globally popular singer in the nineteenth century. She debuted at the Swedish Royal Theatre in 1838 and went on to study opera in Paris; from 1841 on, her unusual range and dramatic soprano voice took European audiences by storm. In 1850 she left for a two-year tour of the United States, singing more popular music under the management of P. T. Barnum and earning more than $125,000. At age thirty-two, she married her pianist in Boston and moved with him to England, but she continued to perform into the 1870s. Born in Stockholm, she died in Malvern Hills, England.

LOREN, SOPHIA (SOFIA SCICOLONE) (1934–) Like Sweden's INGRID BERGMAN, Italy's Sophia Loren was known not only for film acting but also for a controversial marriage: soon after her 1957 wedding to producer Carlo Ponti—who had not legally ended an earlier marriage—they were charged with bigamy under Italy's strict divorce laws. After complicated annulment and divorce proceedings, they remarried in 1966. Although Loren was seen as a sex symbol, especially in the United States, she won her first European acclaim for a film of the famed opera *Aida* (1954); her 1961 Italian work, *La Ciociara* (known in English as *Two Women*), won her the Academy Award. She worked in both Italian and English from the 1950s through the 1970s; one of her later films was the classic *Man of La Mancha* (1972).

LOUISE, QUEEN OF PRUSSIA (1776–1810) A queen by marriage, not by birth, Louise is notable because she was unusually supportive of political reform. Germans especially revere her because she made a personal (albeit unsuccessful) appeal to Napoleon Bonaparte to spare the land and because she set up a foundation for the education of girls.

LUTHER, KATHERINA von BORA (1499–1552) German nun Katherina von Bora left a convent to marry Martin Luther in 1525, thus becoming the mother of Protestantism. Lutherans especially honor her for creating a model of happy family life; with Luther, she encouraged more recognition of children and introduced such domestic pleasantries as Christmas trees.

LUXEMBURG, ROSA (1870–1919) Revolutionary author Rosa Luxemburg was born to a Jewish family in Poland (then under Russian control) and educated at Switzerland's University of Zurich; she acquired German citizenship with her 1898 marriage but kept her maiden name. She participated in the unsuccessful Russian Revolution against the tsar in 1905 and the next year was imprisoned for advocating a general strike in Germany. The government considered her thoughts so dangerous that she published some of her many books under pseudonyms: *The Crisis in the German Social Democracy*, for example, was initially published in Switzerland under the pseudonym Junius. She also coedited a newspaper, *Red Flag*. Her opposition to World War I cost her another year in prison and house arrest until Germany's defeat. In the general collapse of government that followed, she was again arrested during street fighting in 1919; beaten to death by the police, her body was thrown into a canal.

MacDONALD, FLORA (1722–1790) Flora MacDonald became a Scottish legend for her bravery in 1746, when she enabled Charles Edward Stuart to escape to France after he lost his battle against the English at Culloden. The Stuarts, a Scottish royal family, inherited the throne of England with the death of ELIZABETH I and in the Scottish view rightfully retained it; they long supported their Bonnie Prince Charlie in his efforts to take power. MacDonald followed up on her reputation for adventure thirty years later when, in Fayetteville, North Carolina, she rallied Scottish immigrants who, as Loyalists, supported the homeland during the American Revolution.

MANDELA, WINNIE (NKOSIKAZI NOBANDLE NOMZAMO MADIKIZELA) (1934–) Perhaps the best-known African woman of the late twentieth century, Winnie Mandela is also one of the most controversial. In 1958, she wed Nelson Mandela and, at age twenty-four, dedicated herself to ending South African apartheid. When he was sentenced to life in prison in 1964, she carried on the fight for civil rights, including enduring solitary confinement in 1969–1970 and being declared a "banned person" in 1976. In 1988, however, the esteem in which she was generally held was lessened by charges that she and her bodyguards had kidnapped and beaten four black youths—one of whom was killed in her home. Nelson Mandela was freed in 1990, when the African National Congress achieved its longtime goals, and in 1993 courts

that presumably were no longer racist upheld Winnie Mandela's kidnapping conviction. Nelson Mandela nonetheless appointed her to his government when he was elected president in 1994, but she was forced to resign the next year. The Mandelas divorced in 1996.

MARGARET I (1353–1412) The first monarch to unify Scandinavia, she was queen of Denmark and Norway by birth and became the effective queen of Sweden in 1389, when her supporters ousted the incumbent and its Rikstag elected her. Although technically regent for her son and later for a grandnephew she chose, Queen Margaret was the true ruler. She purchased the Baltic Sea areas of Gotland and Schleswig and was on her way to expansion in Holstein when she died aboard ship.

MARIA THERESA (1717–1780) Austro-Hungarian Empress Maria Theresa strode over the eighteenth century much as Britain's VICTORIA did in the next century. She inherited the empire at her father's death in 1740; although she had married four years earlier, her husband stayed in the background while she made the military and political decisions for an area that included the many and diverse ethnic groups of southern and eastern Europe. Vienna became a glittering capital under Maria Theresa. She centralized government and created a modern army, including a military academy. Over the pope's objections, she ended Jesuit control of education, expanded the universities, and introduced elementary education. At the same time, however, she refused to allow the publication of uncensored books or the practice of any religion other than Roman Catholicism. Although she ended legal torture, Maria Theresa was no liberal; she never doubted her right to behave as an absolute monarch. Meanwhile, she bore sixteen babies and placed the ten who survived childhood on thrones from Germany to Spain. Her 1780 death spared her the knowledge that one, MARIE-ANTOINETTE, would be beheaded in the French Revolution.

MARIE-ANTOINETTE (1755–1793) Known by every schoolchild for suggesting "Let them eat cake" when told that her French subjects had no bread, Marie-Antoinette was the daughter of Austria's powerful MARIA THERESA. Marie-Antoinette married the future king of France at age fifteen and became queen at nineteen. She probably would have had an unexceptional royal life, but she and her husband, Louis XVI, inherited an oppressed citizenry with horrific problems. They also had the bad timing to ascend the throne in 1774, just before the American Revolution demonstrated the possibility of governance without monarchs. The queen's Austrian background made her an easy target, and she was almost immediately unpopular with the French. Indifferent to all of this, she gave her weak husband bad political advice and continued to bankrupt the nation with an extravagant lifestyle. When the revolution began, the royal family was forced in 1789 to abandon their estate at Versailles for the lesser Tuileries Palace in Paris. It seemed clear to Marie-Antoinette that they needed outside help, and she sent secret messages urging her powerful family to rescue them—an invitation to invasion that the French understandably saw as treason. Two years passed under what was essentially house arrest, and as other nobles fled the country, she convinced the king that they too should escape. Disguised as common travelers, they got as far as Varennes before their identities were discovered and they were forced back to Paris. On August 10, 1792, a mob attacked Tuileries, and the royal family was imprisoned. Louis was beheaded in January, and Marie-Antoinette, separated from her son, endured most of 1793 in the Conciergerie prison. Having matured quickly, she faced death with courage, and although she never abandoned hope of rescue, she was guillotined just days before her thirty-eighth birthday.

MARTINEAU, HARRIET (1802–1876) One of the most important writers in English during much of the nineteenth century, Harriet Martineau was widely read in a number of genres. Best known for her travelogues of the United States in the 1830s—which made her famous on both sides of the Atlantic—she was already well known in England for a monthly series begun in 1832, "Illustrations of Political Economy." She produced two novels in the 1840s, as well as an account of her travels in the Middle East and a history of England. Turning to philosophy in the 1850s, she introduced the new ideas of positivism and then, as the American Civil War developed, returned to the United States and wrote some sixteen hundred newspaper stories on abolitionism and the war. Martineau's life was so full that her *Autobiography* (1877), edited by her friend, Boston abolitionist Maria Weston Chapman, filled two volumes.

MARY I (1516–1558) The five-year reign of Mary I, between 1553 and 1558, was disastrous for England, primarily because of her excessive devotion to Catholicism and to her Catholic husband, King Philip of Spain, whom she married in the first year of her reign. The daughter of Catherine of Aragon (a Spanish province) and the notorious Henry VIII, Mary allowed herself to be exploited by others, and this weakness led to the loss of Calais,

England's last possession on the Continent, which it had held since 1347. The generally Protestant populace resented her attempts to impose Catholicism and viewed her death at age forty-one with relief. Mary is not buried with her husband, however, but instead lies in Westminster Abbey with her half sister ELIZABETH I.

MARY II, QUEEN OF ENGLAND (1662–1694) During the reign of Mary II and her husband, William of Orange, England returned to Protestantism and peace—after the public had forced King James II, a Catholic, into exile in France. New World exploration continued during their reign, as indicated by the names of several American places, including the College of William and Mary in Virginia. She died childless at age thirty-two but made her mark in other ways: especially interested in architecture, she designed Kensington Palace.

MARY, QUEEN OF SCOTS (1542–1587) The failures of Mary, Queen of Scots are especially striking in contrast to the marvelous success of her cousin, ELIZABETH I of England, in the same period. Mary became queen just days after her birth when her father died; at age five, her regents packed her off to France, where she was betrothed to its future king, Francis. She became queen of France at seventeen, but the king died the next year. A widow at eighteen, she was completely French in her upbringing and almost a total stranger to Scotland when she returned to that throne. Unlike Elizabeth, she had many tumultuous, and even murderous, relationships with men. This, plus turmoil between her Catholic supporters and Scotland's Calvinists, ultimately led to warfare—which Mary lost. Forced to abdicate in favor of her infant son James, she fled to England and asked for Elizabeth's protection—despite the fact that she had long participated in plots to take the English throne from her Protestant cousin, whose birth was considered illegitimate by Catholics. For thirteen years, Elizabeth kept Mary confined to remote castles, but as Mary continued to plot Elizabeth's assassination, the queen was forced to have her arrested. Mary was tried and convicted of conspiracy in October 1586, but Elizabeth delayed for another four months before agreeing to her execution, and Mary was beheaded at age forty-five. Her son would achieve what she could not: when Elizabeth died childless nearly two decades later, James became king of both Scotland and England.

MATA HARI (1876–1917) The term that has come to mean a female spy had its origin in the pseudonym of Margaretha Geertruida Zelle, who was executed in World War I. Born in the Netherlands, in 1895 she married a Dutch colonial officer, who took her to Java and Sumatra. Separating from him, she went to Paris in 1905 and began dancing semi-nude under the Malay name Mata Hari. She was living in The Hague in 1916, when she apparently agreed to spy for Germans who were occupying Belgium. Although the details of her presumed crime are obscure, she was arrested in Paris in February 1917, tried by a French military court in July, and sentenced to death by firing squad.

MATILDA (1102–1167) Empress of the Holy Roman Empire by marriage, Matilda was the daughter of Henry I of England, and she legitimately viewed herself as England's rightful monarch. She returned to England after her husband died in 1125 and waged a fifteen-year civil war to take its throne from her cousin, King Stephen. She ultimately was defeated, in part because of the leadership of his wife (also named Matilda), who led the war when Stephen was taken captive. Although Empress Matilda was crowned queen in 1141 during Stephen's captivity, by 1148 she had to flee to Normandy; there she brought up her son, Henry II, to be powerful enough to establish the long line of English monarchs.

MÉDICIS, CATHERINE de (1519–1589) Queen of France and the mother of three French kings, Catherine de Médicis was born to a powerful but bourgeois family in Florence. Her 1533 wedding to the future French king Henry II was performed by the pope, and after her husband's 1559 death she played a strong role in European politics as regent for her sons. The French, however, believed her loyalty was to her native Italy, and—like her compatriot Niccolò Machiavelli—she became known as a skilled but untrustworthy political manipulator.

MEIR, GOLDA (GOLDIE MABOVITCH MYERSON) (1898–1978) The first female prime minister of Israel, Golda Meir was a true citizen of the world: she was born in Kiev, grew up in Milwaukee, and moved to Israel (then Palestine) with her husband at age twenty-three. She spent the next three decades, between 1921 and 1948, working for a Zionist state in the ancient Hebrew homeland. She was a signatory of Israel's declaration of independence in 1948 and served in its first legislative assembly. Under its parliamentary system, she also served as ambassador to Russia and in 1949 became labor minister. Her husband died in 1951, and when she rose to the position of foreign minister in 1956, she changed her name from Goldie Myerson to the more Hebraic Golda Meir. After a decade as foreign minister, Meir concentrated on building the party coalition that elected her prime minister in 1969.

Widely viewed as a great success until Israel was caught off guard in the 1973 Yom Kippur War, she was forced to resign the next year. After writing a 1975 autobiography, Golda Meir, "the mother of Israel," died in Jerusalem.

MEITNER, LISE (1878–1968) Austrian theoretical physicist Lise Meitner was a pioneer of nuclear research. After earning a 1906 doctorate at the University of Vienna, she worked for the next three decades in Berlin with Max Planck and other scientists. In 1918, she and Otto Hahn discovered the element protactinium, but the collapse of the German government that year after World War I shrank their funding and slowed their work. Although it was the Italian Enrico Fermi who first demonstrated the power of uranium bombardment in 1934, Lise Meitner was the first to explicate the physical process of what she termed "nuclear fission." She also predicted atomic chain reaction at least a decade prior to its demonstration. A professor at the University of Berlin since 1926, Meitner, a Jew, was forced to resign when the Nazis began to take power. Distinguished male scientists such as Niels Bohr invited her to join them in exile, and in 1938 Meitner fled to Stockholm. Her work contributed to the development of the atomic bomb and to fission reactors now used in nuclear power plants. Dr. Meitner held visiting professorships in the United States after the war and retired to England's Cambridge in 1960. In 1997, the international governing body for chemistry recommended that element 109 be named meitnerium in her honor.

MENCHÚ, RIGOBERTA TUM (1959–) Menchú was awarded the 1992 Nobel Peace Prize for her work on behalf of Guatemala's persecuted Maya Indians. At an early age she joined her family in rebelling against Guatemala's repressive government. By age twenty, she was alone: her family had all been murdered by government forces. In 1981, Menchú fled to Mexico, where she began to speak about the genocide in her native land, and—much like escaped slaves in the abolitionist movement of the nineteenth century—she came to the attention of human-rights activists. Her book, *I, Rigoberta Menchú* (1983), was dictated to Elizabeth Burgos-Debray, a Venezuelan; it brought an international focus on the civil war in Guatemala, which at that time had killed a hundred thousand mostly indigenous people. Despite subsequent questions about the accuracy of parts of her memoir, Menchú remains an important advocate of native peoples and continues to promote their welfare as chair of the Indigenous Initiative for Peace.

MENDELSSOHN, FANNY (CÄCILIE MENDELSSOHN HENSEL) (1805–1847) Far less famous than her younger brother Felix, Fanny Mendelssohn not only composed but was acknowledged by Felix to be a superior pianist. While he received education and training, however, she was married in 1829. After her mother's 1842 death, her primary responsibility was running the Mendelssohn home in Berlin. She nonetheless managed to compose at least four hundred works, including oratorios and cantatas; although contemporary musicologists rate them as comparable to her brother's work, most were never published. She died at age forty-two, and her brother—who was openly dependent on her presence but who resisted publication of her music—died just months later.

MERCOURI, MELINA (MARIA AMALIA) (1925–1994)
Born in Athens, Mercouri studied drama at the National Theatre of Greece and became internationally known for her role as a prostitute in the film *Never on Sunday* (1960). Other films followed, but it was her political activism that made Mercouri distinctive. She spoke out strongly against the military junta that took over Greece's government in 1967; when it fell in 1974, she returned home from the United States and was elected to Parliament as a Socialist. Appointed minister of culture, Mercouri crusaded (with little success) for the return of Greek antiquities, especially the Elgin Marbles in the British Museum.

MILL, HARRIET HARDY TAYLOR (1807–1858) Many of the thoughts attributed to the great democratic philosopher John Stuart Mill were, according to him, actually those of his wife—with whom he shared a long relationship prior to the 1849 death of her first husband. She was the author of the 1850 essay published under his name in the famed *Westminster Review*, "On Enfranchisement of Women," and when he published *On Liberty* (1859) soon after her death, Mill wrote that "much of it was the work of her whom I lost." Inconsolable at her sudden death while they were traveling in Avignon, he bought a cottage in sight of her grave, and wrote in his autobiography that he was "wholly her pupil. Her bolder and more powerful mind arrived before mine at every conclusion."

MISTRAL, GABRIELA (1889–1957) The first Latin American of either gender to win the Nobel Prize for literature, Lucila Godoy Alcayaga of Chile won in 1945 under the pseudonym Gabriela Mistral. Her first book is considered her best: *Solace* (1922) was motivated by the suicide of her former fiancé. She moved to Europe in the year it was published and stayed there until the outbreak of World War II; after 1948, she taught at several North American universities. She never married, and her life

became more tragic with the suicide of an adopted son. Mistral published the collection *The Wine Press* (1954) shortly before her death at age seventy.

MODERSOHN-BECKER, PAULA (1876–1907) German painter Paula Becker, who was born in Dresden and grew up in Bremen, was educated in England and Germany. She began to draw and paint in the late 1880s, and her work became a merger of traditional Germanic style and the era's French impressionism. She frequently lived in Paris, apart from the man she married in 1901, but they were together enough that Paula Becker-Modersohn died in childbirth at age thirty-one. Her best-known work is *Self-Portrait with a Camellia*, done in the year she died.

MONTAGU, LADY MARY WORTLEY (1689–1762) Although known for the brilliant letters she wrote throughout her long life, Lady Mary also played a significant role in Western scientific history. After returning from Constantinople, where her husband was the British ambassador, she introduced the Turkish practice of inoculation for smallpox in 1718. She published *The Nonsense of Common Sense* (1737) and then left her husband in 1740. She lived the rest of her life in Italy, where the pope declared his love for her; when she rebuffed him, the two exchanged a series of caustic letters.

MONTESSORI, MARIA (1870–1952) Internationally known for her innovative approach to early childhood education, Maria Montessori was also Italy's first female physician. She graduated from medical school at the University of Rome in 1894 and, working from the university's psychiatric clinic, pioneered the twentieth century's greatest change in the way children were taught. Dr. Montessori opened her first school in Rome's slums in 1907, and educators from all over the world soon came to see children younger than five who could read and write. When her Italian schools were closed by the Fascists in 1934, she fled to Spain, where that country's civil war again forced her to flee; she went to the Netherlands, and after German fascists took over that country in World War II, she was exiled to India. The effect—though unintended—was to internationalize Montessori schools and give her more time to write. She added three books during this period to the ones she published in 1912 and 1913. She died back in the Netherlands seven years after the war's end.

MORE, HANNAH (1745–1833) English writer Hannah More had particular impact in the United States with her

1799 book, *Strictures on the Modern System of Female Education*, which early feminists admired for its advocacy of improved educational opportunity. A friend of Samuel Johnson and other literati of her day, More had her earliest success as a playwright, with her first play produced in 1774. She also wrote against slavery, established Sunday schools, and published innovative books designed to teach the poor to read. Her work in these many genres sold well enough that she became quite rich.

MORI MARI (1903–1987) The winner of three major Japanese prizes for literature in three decades, Mori Mari won her 1957 award for an essay collection; in 1961 and 1975 she was honored for her novels. Uncommonly candid about sex, including homosexuality, in a culture that encouraged female modesty, she refused to marry. Her unconventional lifestyle made her the object of considerable attention in Japan.

MURASAKI SHIKIBU (c. 978–c. 1014) The Japanese woman sometimes called Lady Murasaki wrote at a time when men of her culture slavishly followed the Chinese, while women were inventing a wholly new Japanese literature. Her *Tale of Genji*—which some have called the world's oldest novel—was written in about 1000 and depicts life and love in the imperial court. Translated into English in the 1920s and 1930s, the complex tale required six volumes. A Japanese historian writing in the 1960s termed Murasaki's work and SEI SHONAGON's *Pillow Book* "Japan's two greatest literary masterpieces."

MYRDAL, ALVA REIMER (1902-1986) Winner of the 1982 Nobel Peace Prize, Swedish Alva Myrdal shared the prize with her husband Gunnar. The Myrdals married in 1924 and worked collaboratively in economics and social science the rest of their lives. An early employee of the United Nations, she directed its Office of Social Affairs in 1949 and then served in several Swedish governmental positions, especially as its advocate for disarmament. Her books on that subject, including *Wars, Weapons and Everyday Violence* (1977), were honored with the Nobel.

NEFERTITI (c. 1390–1354 B.C.) Queen Nefertiti of Egypt, whose name meant "the beautiful lady comes," led rejection of pantheism in favor of a monotheistic sun god during her long reign with two husbands—who, in the Egyptian tradition, were also her close relatives. She is known especially for the mystery surrounding a statue of her head: excavated at Tell el-Amarna in 1913, it disappeared from a Berlin museum during World War II.

NIGHTINGALE, FLORENCE (1820–1910) Florence Nightingale is considered the founder of professional nursing—although she may be more accurately remembered as a public-health pioneer and the first military consultant to insist that troops have decent sanitation and hospital care. Born in Florence, Italy, to affluent English parents, she was named for that city. She grew up in England but traveled a great deal on the Continent with her family, making a point of visiting hospitals there and observing their management. At age thirty-one, she ignored her family's objections to spend three months at the Deaconess Institute at Kaiserswerth, Germany; that plus two weeks in Paris, both in 1853, was all the formal training Nightingale had. Just a year later, however, she led thirty-eight British nurses to the Crimean War. Her rise in the British imagination was meteoric: newspapers proclaimed her "the angel of the Crimea" and "the lady with the lamp." After the war, Nightingale compiled statistics on preventable deaths and pursued government officials until an 1857 commission was created to carry out her reforms, including such basics as proper drainage in hospitals. British donors raised a large sum that enabled her to establish the Nightingale School for Nurses in 1860, and she worked there for the rest of her life. In 1907 Nightingale became the first woman honored with the British Order of Merit.

NÜSSLEIN-VOLHARD, CHRISTIANE (1942–) Winner of the 1995 Nobel Prize in physiology or medicine, Dr. Nüsslein-Volhard was honored for her work in genetics; she shared the prize with two men doing similar research. A German, she earned a 1968 doctorate at Eberhard-Karl University of Tübingen and, after 1978, worked at the European Molecular Biology Laboratory in Heidelberg. Her research used fruit flies—which live just nine days—to study mutations by generations.

OCAMPO, VICTORIA (1890–1979) The first woman elected to Argentina's Academy of Letters, Victoria Ocampo received that belated honor in 1976—three years before the end of her long life. She wrote in many genres, publishing her first book in 1924 and her last posthumously in 1983. After studying at the Sorbonne, she lived in France until its German occupation during World War II; she then continued publication of a French literary journal from Buenos Aires. Known especially for her appealing memoirs, Ocampo received honors in England and India, as well as in France and her native Argentina.

OKU MUMEO (1895–1997) During her long life, Oku Mumeo was a leader of Japanese women; she especially encouraged them to use the right to vote, which they won with the new constitution adopted during the American occupation after World War II. She was elected to three terms in the national legislative body, where she spoke out for women, and founded the Housewives Association, the first organization for Japanese consumers.

ORCZY, BARONESS EMMUSKA (1865–1947) The author of *The Scarlet Pimpernel* (1905), the popular novel set during the French Revolution, Orczy was a Hungarian baroness by birth, not by marriage. Born in Hungary, she was educated in Paris and Brussels but lived most of her life in Britain. In addition to novels, she also wrote mysteries, some of which featured female detectives, and was an artist; her paintings were exhibited by the British Royal Academy.

PANKHURST family—EMMELINE GOULDEN (1858–1928); DAME CHRISTABEL HARRIETTE (1880–1958); (ESTELLE) SYLVIA (1882–1960) Emmeline Pankhurst and her daughters Christabel and Sylvia were Europe's most visible suffragist activists. Emmeline Pankhurst founded the Women's Social and Political Union in Manchester in 1903. She was the most militant of any international leader, and her tactics were very controversial within the International Woman Suffrage Association, which generally sided with MILLICENT FAWCETT. Moving the union's headquarters to London in 1906, Pankhurst encouraged her supporters, including her daughters, to chain themselves to public railings, interrupt politicians' speeches, and, later, deface property, set fire to opponents' mailboxes, and other tactics designed to shake polite society out of its lethargy on women's rights. Frequently imprisoned after 1908, Pankhurst went on well-publicized hunger strikes in jail between 1911 and 1913, but when World War I began she called a moratorium on attacking the government—and British women won the vote with the war's end. Emmeline Pankhurst died a decade later while campaigning for Parliament; although once a Socialist, she was running as the nominee of the Conservative Party. Christabel Pankhurst ran for Parliament in 1918 in the first election in which women could vote; although she lost, she received more votes than any other woman in that election. In 1936, she was made a dame commander of the Order of the British Empire, the nation's highest possible honor to a woman. She nonetheless lived abroad after her electoral loss, dying in Los Angeles in the 1950s. Unlike her mother and sister, Sylvia became more leftist as she aged. The author of many political books, she was quick to perceive the dangers of fascism and helped lead Ethiopians in Britain who opposed Benito Mussolini's 1935 takeover of their home-land. When the end of World War II made it possible, she moved to Ethiopia; she died in the capital, Addis Ababa, at age seventy-eight.

PARDO BAZÁN, EMILIA, CONDESA de (1851–1921) Countess Pardo Bazán defied strong conventions to achieve a career as an author and literary critic. In her era, many upper-class Spanish women considered even reading to conflict with societal demands for complete familial devotion. Her 1883 book on international literary trends introduced new ideas to Spain, and she followed that with four novels published in quick succession. Her scandalized husband promptly left her, but she established a literary journal in 1891 and continued to publish new novels. She taught at the University of Madrid and in 1916—more than three decades after her first cutting-edge publication—was rewarded with a chair in Romance literature.

PAULA (347–404) and EUSTOCHIUM (c. 368–419) A wealthy Roman widow, Paula went to Palestine (now Israel) in 385 with her daughter Eustochium. Paula spent her fortune building a Christian community for both men and women in Bethlehem; it included a hospice for pilgrims and a school. While Paula functioned primarily as an administrator, Eustochium was a scholar: Saint Jerome, who translated almost the whole Bible from its original Hebrew and Greek into Latin, gave Eustochium credit for great assistance with the three languages. Paula died shortly after a local mob burned their residence. Although neither woman was canonized, they are referred to as Saint Paula and Saint Eustochium.

PAVLOVA, ANNA (1882–1932) The greatest ballet dancer of her era, Pavlova began studying with Russia's Imperial School of Ballet in 1891 and debuted in Petrograd (then Saint Petersburg) in 1899. By 1906 she was a prima ballerina, and the next year she began the first of many tours that helped popularize the art throughout the world. Her first American appearance was at the Metropolitan Opera in 1910; she began her own touring company two years later. Between 1910 and 1925, Pavlova gave more than thirty-five hundred performances across the globe. Particularly known for a brief but magical work, The *Dying Swan*, Pavlova last performed in London in 1930, just two years prior to her death.

PERÓN, (MARIA) EVA DUARTE (1919–1952) Few twentieth-century women have been both so adored and so vilified as Argentina's Eva Perón, who was often called by the endearment Evita. After a career as an actress, she married Juan Perón in 1945, a year before he became president; together they dominated Argentina's politics for decades. Although she never held a government office, she freely distributed the country's revenues to the poor—and naturally was accused of corruption, while the country's peasantry viewed her as a near saint. She also founded the Peronista Feminist Party in 1949 and almost single-handedly won the vote for Argentine women. Even after her 1952 death from cancer, Juan evoked Eva's powerful image in his attempts to retain control. Her supporters have attempted to have Evita, a staunch Catholic, canonized.

PERÓN , ISABEL (MARIA) ESTELA MARTÍNEZ CARTAS (1931–) Like EVA PERÓN, Isabel had a career in show business before she married former Argentine president Juan Perón during his exile in Madrid in 1961. She frequently went to Argentina to campaign, and when they triumphantly returned in 1973, she became his vice president; because he was ill, she was in effect the president, and she officially gained that title when he died six months later. The first female head of a Latin American nation, she worked for moderate policies, but Argentina's economic problems were so profound that she made little progress before the military deposed her in 1976. Held under house arrest without trial for five years, she was convicted of corruption in 1981; she exiled herself in Spain and was pardoned two years later.

POMPADOUR, MADAME de (JEANNE-ANTOINETTE LE NORMANT d'ÉTIOLES) (1721–1764) Although Madame de Pompadour, the extremely influential mistress of Louis XV of France, had both another name and the title marquise, she is not referred to by either. Her marriage at age twenty introduced her to court circles, and she soon left her husband for the king, whom she met at a masked ball in 1744. Louis not only supplied her with an apartment at Versailles but also, within a few months, gave her the title by which she is known. Until her death twenty years later, no one in government exercised more power; she even succeeded in her major goal of driving Jesuit priests out of France. If her political judgments were sometimes wrong, her cultural influence was good: she established the Sèvres porcelain factories, supported many enlightened thinkers, including Voltaire and Baron Montesquieu, and is considered the founder of the École Militaire.

RAMBOUILLET, CATHERINE de VIVONNE, MARQUISE de (1588–1665) Born in Rome, at age twelve she married a future French marquis, and after 1611 she headed a famous Parisian salon that had influence throughout Europe. Among those who benefited from her patronage were Honoré de Balzac and MADELEINE DE SCUDÉRY.

REIS, MARIA FIRMINA dos (1825–1917) Although born a poor mulatto, Reis wrote Brazil's second novel by a woman and its first abolitionist novel. She is especially known for *Ursuala* (1859), the cover of which said simply that it was written by "a Brazilian." The theme of her work, which included short stories, poems, and hymns, was sympathy for slaves, including both blacks and Indians.

REITSCH, HANNA (1912–1979) The first woman awarded the German military's prestigious Iron Cross, Hanna Reitsch was an ace test pilot. She flew every type of German aircraft, including its new jets and rocket prototypes, and took the last warplane from Berlin when that capital collapsed at the end of World War II. Like other Nazi leaders, she fled from the Soviets when they invaded from the east. The U.S. Army, which captured her, valued her flying skills, as well as her information on Hitler—she shared the leadership's underground bunker in Berlin and was one of the last to see him. Imprisoned for just fifteen months, she went on to set aviation records in Europe and the United States. She lived in Ghana during the 1960s but died in Frankfurt.

ROBINSON, MARY BOURKE (1944–) The first female president of Ireland, attorney Mary Robinson was elected in 1990. Robinson studied at Harvard University in 1967, when student demonstrations against the Vietnam War and for civil rights helped develop her commitment to peace and justice. Elected to the Irish senate just two years later, she also defied her Catholic family by marrying a Protestant. After more than two decades in the senate, she surprised experts by winning the presidency. Robinson served out her six-year term working to end Ireland's longtime violence, and in 1997 she became the United Nations' high commissioner for human rights.

ROLAND (de LA PLATIÈRE), JEANNE-MARIE PHLIPON (1734–1793) The French revolutionary known as Madame Roland was born Jeanne-Marie Phlipon in Paris. At least as politically active as her husband, Jean-Marie Roland, she turned their home into a headquarters for freedom fighters, and when their faction won in 1792, he became minister of the interior. This lasted just a year, however, before the original revolutionary aims went too far in the form of Robespierre's Reign of Terror. When her husband fled to Rouen early in June 1793, Madame

Roland remained in Paris. Soon arrested, she was in prison when CHARLOTTE CORDAY was beheaded; Madame Roland went to the guillotine on November 8. Her last words became famous: "O Liberty, what crimes are committed in thy name!"

ROSE OF LIMA (1586–1617) The first saint in the Western Hemisphere, the woman known as Rose of Lima was named Isabel de Flores; the daughter of Spanish parents in Peru, she was born and died in Lima. She is called the pioneer of Latin American social work because of her assistance to slaves, Indians, and others in need. At the same time, she also engaged in the harsh, self-imposed penances—including wearing a crown of thorns and sleeping on a bed of broken glass—that earned great respect in her culture; although morbid by today's standards, that—and the resulting mystical visions—was the chief reason for her 1671 canonization.

ROSSETTI, CHRISTINA GEORGINA (1830–1894) Rossetti ranks with American EMILY DICKINSON as the top female poet of the late nineteenth century. She was born and died in London; her father, Gabriele, was an exile from the Italian revolution, and her mother, Frances Polidori Rossetti, had an Italian father and an English mother. Like Dickinson, Christina Rossetti never married, but she did break an 1850 engagement because of her fiancé's Catholicism. Unlike her brother, the poet and painter Dante Gabriel Rossetti, Christina had no opportunity for formal education. Her poetry is known for both its rich imagery and the precision and occasional striking dissonance of its words. She avoided the complex Latin allusions of her era and, like Dickinson, conveyed perceptive thoughts in clear, beautiful English. Her best-known collection, *Goblin Market and Other Poems* (1862), was her first; her last, *The Face of the Deep* (1892), came out thirty years later.

ROSWITHA OF GANDERSHEIM—see HROSVITHA

SAADAWI, NAWAL EL (1930–) An Egyptian physician and feminist, Dr. Saadawi's first book, *Women and Sex* (1971), critiqued the inferior position of women under Islam. Her most famous book, *The Hidden Face of Eve: Women in the Arab World* (1977), helped bring global attention to the practice of female circumcision. Although under constant attack in her own country—including arrest in 1981 for violating the law "for the protection of values from shame"—Saadawi writes and lectures regularly. Her nonfiction includes *Memoirs from the Women's*

Prison (1987), and her novels include *Death of the Only Male on Earth* (1976) and *The Fall of the Imam* (1987).

SACHS, NELLY (1891–1970) The 1966 winner of the Nobel Prize in literature, poet Nelly Sachs was almost at the end of her life when she was first published. Born to an affluent Jewish family in Germany, she lived with her mother; except for corresponding with 1909 Nobel Prize winner SELMA LAGERLÖF of Sweden, Sachs lived an insular life until she was forty-nine. With help from Lagerlöf, Sachs and her mother fled the Holocaust to Sweden in 1940. More than two decades later, Sachs issued the first of her poetry on Hebraic and Holocaust themes: *Journey into the Dust-Free Zone* was published in German in 1961. Two more volumes came out in 1962 and 1964, and she won the coveted prize in 1966—four years before her death.

SACKVILLE-WEST, VITA (VICTORIA MARY) (1892–1962) English writer Vita Sackville-West is known for her lifestyle as much as for her work. Although she married and had a son, she neither used her husband's name nor lived much with him; both had homosexual relationships, and hers with Violet Trefusis lasted more than three decades. Sackville-West's literary work ranged from poetry to gardening books and included biographies of women, especially European saints and pioneer writer APHRA BEHN. *All Passion Spent* (1931) is Sackville-West's classic feminist novel.

SAND, GEORGE (1804–1876) Probably the best-known French female writer of the nineteenth century, it was George Sand's lifestyle as much as her writing that made her famous. Born Amandine-Aurore-Lucile Dupin in Paris, she grew up in Nohant and married Baron Casimir Dudevant at age eighteen; unhappy with life as a baroness, she separated from him in 1831 and went to Paris. The name of her first lover, Jules Sandeau, became the basis for her pseudonym when she published her first book the next year. *Indiana* (1832) is the most feministic of her novels. Although she published virtually a book a year from the 1830s through the 1850s, her writing grew increasingly sentimental and conservative—while at the same time she sometimes dressed as a man and enjoyed a string of male lovers, including composers Frédéric Chopin and Franz Liszt. Universally respected by the time she reached old age, Sand lived comfortably on her estate as "la bonne dame de Nohant."

SAPPHO (c. 620–565 B.C.) The greatest female poet of antiquity, Sappho's work was well recognized by ancient

Greeks. Born on the island of Lesbos, she married a wealthy man, bore a daughter named Calis, and, for unexplained reasons, lived alone in Sicily before returning to Lesbos, where she taught girls. Many of her poems were written to or about these girls, leading to her association with lesbianism. Although most of her poetry has been lost, the fragments that survive earn high praise from modern literary critics.

SCHREINER, OLIVE (1855–1920) Long before better-recognized modern writers, Olive Schreiner was an enlightened voice in South Africa. Born there to Lutheran missionaries, she went to England in 1881, where she published *The Story of an African Farm* (1883). Although the book was a success, Schreiner's stronger manuscripts detailing the repressive life of Victorian colonialism remained unpublished in her lifetime. Feminists of her time knew her best for *Woman and Labour* (1911), and she developed her anti-imperialism in several books, including *Thoughts on South Africa* (1923); along with most of her fiction, it was published posthumously. Her German name caused Schreiner great pain during the last years of her life in the England of World War I, and she died thinking of herself as a failure.

SCHUMANN, CLARA WIECK (1819–1896) One of the finest pianists of the nineteenth century, Germany's Clara Wieck gave concerts at age ten and was composing by fourteen. Her father was a noted music teacher in Leipzig who had Robert Schumann as a pupil. Schumann was awed by Clara's virtuosity, and, over her father's objections, they married when she was twenty one. She continued to compose and perform, but their seven children understandably limited her independent career; one critic wrote that "her artistic genius and strength of character made him a great composer." As her husband became mentally ill, however, she had to resume her performances, and after a suicide attempt he was institutionalized near Bonn, where he died in 1856. A widow at age thirty-seven, with a large family to support, Clara returned to European concert halls, taught at the Konservatorium in Frankfurt, and composed, especially for the pianoforte. Schumann not only introduced her husband's first works but did the same for her young friend Johannes Brahms.

SCHWIMMER, ROSIKA (1877–1948) Hungarian feminist Rosika Schwimmer organized the 1913 convention of the International Woman Suffrage Alliance in Budapest—the last before the organization collapsed with the outbreak of World War I. She fled Hungary for London the next year.

Along with American CARRIE CHAPMAN CATT and others, she led the 1915 peace movement that drew a thousand women to The Hague; she then joined the Americans in crossing the U-boat–infested Atlantic to do a speaking tour of the United States, including meeting with President Woodrow Wilson. Returning to Hungary at war's end, she was appointed to the National Council of Fifteen, the governing body of its new republic, and served as ambassador to Switzerland. After Communists seized power, she returned to the United States in 1921 and remained there for the rest of her life.

SCUDÉRY, MADELEINE de (1607-1701) The earliest of French female novelists, her work, first published in 1641, is considered less meritorious than that of MARIE DE LA FAYETTE. Scudéry's novels, however, were more popular at the time, perhaps because she used celebrities as stock characters, once blending herself with SAPPHO. Never marrying, she received financial support from the state; another patron was Sweden's Queen CHRISTINA.

SEI SHONAGON (c. 966–c. 1015) While men of her time imitated what they viewed as a superior Chinese culture, women such as Sei Shonagon created fresh literature in Japanese. Her *Makurano Soshi*, which translates as *The Pillow Book*, was written in about 1000; the witty diary of her thoughts while living in Japan's imperial court, one Japanese historian termed it and a book by MURASAKI SHIKIBU "Japan's two greatest literary masterpieces."

SHELLEY, MARY WOLLSTONECRAFT (1797–1851) The author of *Frankenstein* was born in London, where her mother, pioneer feminist MARY WOLLSTONECRAFT, died giving birth; her father, political radical William Godwin, honored his wife by giving the baby her mother's name. She was not yet seventeen when she met poet Percy Bysshe Shelley in May 1814; they married in 1816, after Shelley's wife committed suicide. Just two years later, while living in Lord Byron's villa on Lake Geneva, Mary Shelley wrote her first and best book, *Frankenstein* (1818)—almost single-handedly inventing the science fiction and horror genres with her tale of a man who creates life from slaughterhouse and dissection materials. Despite her long-term impact, the rest of Mary Shelley's life was difficult. She bore four children during perpetual moves in Italy, Switzerland, and England, while her husband was entangled in financial and emotional problems that ended only with his 1823 death. With their only surviving child, Mary Shelley returned to London as a twenty-six-year-old widow. Although she supported herself and her son by writing, nothing in the second half of her life approached the creativity of the first half.

SHIPLEY, JENNY (1952) The first female prime minister of New Zealand, Shipley took office December 1997. Similar to Britain's MARGARET THATCHER in political philosophy, Shipley was burned in effigy during her earlier tenure as health minister because of social service spending cuts. A 1971 graduate of Christchurch Teachers' College, she taught school prior to marriage and motherhood and was first elected to Parliament in 1987. Shipley lost her position as prime minister to Labor's Helen Clark late in 1999.

SIDDONS, SARAH KEMBLE (1755–1831) So famous on English stages that she was known simply as Mrs. Siddons, Sarah Kemble Siddons debuted at London's Drury Lane Theatre in 1775, two years after she married at age eighteen. She was born into a large family of actors, and although fame eluded her until her late twenties, she grew to become the era's most acclaimed female performer of tragic roles. Known especially for her interpretation of Shakespeare's Lady Macbeth, Mrs. Siddons retired in 1818.

SIGNORET, SIMONE (1921–1985) Like Greece's MELINA MERCOURI, France's Simone Signoret was acclaimed for her films in the 1950s and 1960s but also used that fame for political action. She spoke against the 1953 execution of American ETHEL ROSENBERG and supported independence for French colonies, including Vietnam and Algeria. Highly controversial, she also wrote novels and an autobiography, *Nostalgia Isn't What It Used to Be* (1976).

SIMPSON, WALLIS WARFIELD SPENCER (1896–1986) "Mrs. Simpson" was in countless headlines during 1936, when Edward VIII gave up the British throne to marry her. Born in Baltimore, she divorced her first husband, an American, in 1927; she moved to London with her second husband, a Briton, the next year and was still married when the king abdicated. Parliament refused to condone such a queen, and she refused to accept the traditional role of mistress to the bachelor Edward. He surrendered his throne in December, and they married the following June, after her divorce was final. The titles duke and duchess of Windsor were created for them. Except during World War II, when they lived in the Bahamas, they spent the rest of their lives near Paris. She was especially known for her maxim that "one can never be too rich or too thin."

SMEDLEY, AGNES (c. 1892–1950) More famous in her adopted China than in her native country, the United States, Agnes Smedley spent her life working for global change. Radicalized by World War I, she taught English at the University of Berlin, lived with an Indian man, and worked for India's independence from Britain. She went to China in 1929 as a reporter for a German newspaper and participated in the Long March of 1934–1935, the six-thousand-mile trek of the Chinese Communists from southeast to northwest China, with Chou En-lai and Mao Tse-tung. Dressed in army camouflage, she moved with the Red Army as a correspondent for England's famous *Manchester Guardian* while the army fought the Japanese prior to World War II. The resultant book—one of several—was *China Fights Back: An American Woman with the Eighth Route Army* (1938). Desperately ill two years later, she returned to the United States, and because Americans then favored the Chinese over the Japanese, she was initially welcomed. That was no longer true after her predictions proved correct when the Communists began to defeat the Nationalists in China's postwar civil war. Smedley exiled herself in Oxford and died just months after the final victory of her Chinese friends. Her ashes were returned to Peking (now Beijing) and buried with honors.

SOONG CH'ING-LING (1892–1981) Born in Shanghai, Soong Ch'ing-ling graduated in 1913 from Wesleyan Female College in Macon, Georgia; she returned to China and married Sun Yat-sen, the hero of the 1911 overthrow of the Manchu dynasty. He soon was ousted by former allies. Until his 1925 death, they worked from Japan and Shanghai in an unsuccessful attempt to overthrow mainland warlords. As a widow, Madame Sun Yat-sen, as she was known in the West, not only supported the Chinese against the Japanese in the 1930s and 1940s but also backed the Chinese Communists against the Western-influenced Nationalists in the civil war that followed World War II. When her sister SOONG MEI-LING and other Nationalists retreated to Taiwan, she stayed on the mainland, where she served in several government positions, especially related to women's issues. Just prior to her death, she was awarded the title of honorary president of the People's Republic of China.

SOONG MEI-LING (1897–) Like her sister SOONG CH'ING-LING, Soong Mei-ling was educated in the United States, attending Georgia's Wesleyan Female College before graduating from Wellesley College in Massachusetts. She returned to China and met Chiang Kai-shek, a revolutionary ally of her late brother-in-law Sun Yat-sen. Chiang divorced his wife in October 1927; he and Mei-ling married in December; and he was baptized in her Methodist faith in

1930. Madame Chiang became an increasingly formidable power in Chinese politics, especially during and after World War II, when it appeared that her husband's Nationalists would lose the civil war with the Communists. She attracted much media attention as a strong but ultimately unsuccessful diplomat in the United States in the 1940s, speaking to Congress in 1943. Her husband was forced to retreat to Formosa (now Taiwan) in 1949; after his 1975 death, she moved to the United States.

STAËL, GERMAINE DE (ANNE-LOUISE-GERMAINE NECKER) (1766–1817) The most prominent European woman of her time, Madame de Staël married and quickly separated from a Swedish baron in 1786. Born in Paris to French-Swiss parents, she grew up in her mother's salon, where she met important figures such as Denis Diderot. By the outbreak of the French Revolution, her own salon was a center of liberal politics—but the excesses of the Revolution eventually forced her to flee to the family home in Switzerland in 1793. She published her first significant book three years later, and her travels throughout Europe led to a number of books of both fiction and nonfiction; an 1813 trip to Sweden helped bring that nation into the coalition against Napoleon Bonaparte, and after his downfall she settled again in Paris. Her *Reflections on the Chief Events of the French Revolution* (1816) set the standard for future historians. Madame de Staël is also recognized as a literary critic, especially for *On Literature Considered in Its Relations with Social Institutions* (1800).

SUCHOCKA, HANNA (1946–) The first female prime minister of Poland, Suchocka held that position in 1992–1993. An attorney, she was first elected to Poland's parliament in 1980; in 1992, a party coalition chose her as their leader because she was seen as fair to both Catholic conservatives and political moderates. She won the August election, but after fourteen months in office, Suchocka lost a vote of confidence in October 1993.

SU SHUEH-LIN (1895–1999) Chinese revolutionary and writer Su Shueh-lin was a leader in the 1919 uprising known as the May Fourth Movement; with other young people, she rebelled against the repressive governance of warlords who had ousted democratic Sun Yat-sen. A tireless political activist and writer, her books influenced generations of Chinese leaders, but the Communist victory in 1949 forced her into exile in Taiwan. Until her retirement in the 1960s, she taught at Cheng Kung University; the university published a fifteen-volume collection of her letters and memoirs prior to her death in Taipei at age 104.

SUTTNER, BERTHA, BARONESS von (1843–1914) The first winner of the Nobel Peace Prize, Baroness Bertha von Suttner of Austria was also a leader in the international women's suffrage movement. She won the Nobel Prize in 1905 for the pacifist stance she began with her 1889 novel, *Lay Down Your Arms!* In 1912, she joined SYLVIA PANKHURST, the countess of Warwick, and other Europeans on a tour for suffrage in the United States; her speeches were particularly effective in Milwaukee and other cities with large numbers of German speakers. She did not live to see women vote in either the United States or her native land.

SUU KYI, AUNG SAN (1947–) Winner of the 1991 Nobel Peace Prize, Aung San Suu Kyi has spent a decade under house arrest in Burma (Myanmar). She was born to politically active parents and studied at the University of Oxford in England, where she met Michael Aris, a Briton; they married in 1972. After twenty-eight years of exile, she returned home in 1988 to nurse her dying mother and quickly became the leader of a democratic movement against a military regime that seized power that year. She was placed under house arrest in 1989, but her party nevertheless won a landslide election in 1990. Neither that nor her Nobel Prize the following year has abated the government's persecution of her, and she could not visit her husband, an Oxford professor specializing in Tibet, prior to his death in March 1999. While her two sons live in England, she remains a hero to the Burmese people, who elected her but have yet to see her take office.

SZYMBORSKA, WISLAWA (1923–) Polish poet Wislawa Szymborska won the 1996 Nobel Prize in literature. She grew up in Kraków and went to school illegally as a teenager during the German occupation of Poland; at the war's end, she studied at the University of Kraków. For almost thirty years, from 1953 to 1981, Szymborska was poetry editor of a literary magazine, *Zycie literackie*, while also publishing eight volumes of her own work. The best known in English is *People on a Bridge* (1990).

TERESA OF ÁVILA (1515–1582) Along with CATHERINE OF SIENA, Saint Teresa of Ávila was one of the first two women named a doctor of the church in 1970—almost four centuries after her death. Born Teresa de Cepada y Ahumada in Ávila, in the Spanish province of Castile, she entered the local convent at about age twenty. It was a convivial place, where the sisters enjoyed both appreciable property and freedom, and in 1562 she became determined to create a more rigorous order. After establishing

St. Joseph's at Ávila, she went on to found seventeen convents throughout Spain; the nuns became known as Carmelites and spread worldwide. Also a prolific and witty author, she wrote several spiritual books, as well an autobiography in 1562.

TERESA OF LISIEUX (1873–1897) The most popular saint of the early twentieth century, Saint Teresa was born Marie-Françoise-Thérèse Martin in Lisieux, in the French province of Normandy. Her life in the local Carmelite convent was unexceptional; she became famous because of the book she wrote while dying of tuberculosis, which killed her at age twenty-nine. After heavy editing by her sister, who was also a Carmelite nun, *The Story of a Soul* was an immediate success. Translated into many languages, it attracted so many visitors to Lisieux that a larger church had to be built. Miracles throughout the world were attributed to the Little Flower, and she was canonized in 1925.

TERESA, MOTHER (AGNES GONXHA BOJAXHIU) (1910–1997) The woman internationally known as Mother Teresa and closely associated with India was born in Macedonia of Albanian heritage and educated in an Irish convent. She worked at a Calcutta high school for a decade, became an Indian citizen, and began her mission for the sick and dying in 1948. The Vatican authorized the new order for this purpose; she founded the Order of the Missionaries of Charity and opened her Home for Dying Destitutes in Calcutta's slums in 1952. She expanded her order to every continent except Europe during the next decades but remained based in India. At the same time, she has been vocally conservative on women's issues, opposing any reproductive control, divorce, and even work outside the home. For her international visibility on behalf of the poor, Mother Teresa won the Nobel Peace Prize in 1979.

TERESHKOVA, VALENTINA (1937–) As the first woman in space, Valentina Tereshkova attracted international attention for her flight on the Soviet Union's *Vostok 6* in June 1963; she orbited Earth forty-eight times during a three-day voyage. Some have disparaged this achievement because Tereshkova had no scientific background—indeed, she worked in a textile mill until joining the cosmonaut training program in 1961. Regardless of whether she was used as a publicity gimmick, however, she gave American feminists a precedent to point to in arguing for the inclusion of women in the U.S. space program. Meanwhile, Tereshkova received several major honors from the Soviet Union. She also headed the Soviet Women's Committee in the 1960s, and from the 1970s to the 1990s she served on the Presidium of the Supreme Soviet.

THATCHER, MARGARET HILDA ROBERTS (1925–) The first female British prime minister, Thatcher also was its only twentieth-century prime minister to win three consecutive elections. A student at the University of Oxford during World War II, she worked as a chemist until her 1951 marriage to Denis Thatcher, who stayed in the background during her political career. She passed the bar in 1953 and practiced tax law until her 1959 election to Parliament—but none of this seemingly feminist activity made her a supporter of traditional women's issues. Thatcher first came to public attention when her Conservative Party appointed her education minister in 1970 and she abolished free milk in schools. Conservatives elected her to lead the party in 1975, and in 1979 they won control of the government. She was praised by some for defeating Argentina in a war over South America's Falkland Islands, while others noted that unemployment nearly tripled during her first two terms. Called the Iron Lady, Thatcher privatized a number of government functions, opposed the European Union, and came to be seen as too conservative even for her Conservative Party, which forced her to resign in 1990. For many years, however, British girls had as role models two strong women, Margaret Thatcher and ELIZABETH II, at the head of the nation. The queen awarded Thatcher the Order of Merit in 1990 and made her a baroness in 1992.

THEODORA (508–548) Theodora, whose mosaic with her husband Justinian is one of the most frequently reproduced artworks of the Byzantine Empire, was a leader of sixth-century culture. She also was an important political and military strategist, once saving Justinian's throne by standing up to rioters. A few years after her death, the empire was scandalized by *Anedota* (553), which told of her relationship with Belisarius, Justinian's most valuable general.

TRISTAN, FLORA (1803–1844) An international feminist before the first women's rights organizations officially began, Flora Tristan was born in Paris, the illegitimate child of a wealthy Peruvian man. At age eighteen, she was pressured into marrying a man who later tried to kill her. She finally left him and sailed on her thirtieth birthday for Peru, where she attempted to claim an inheritance from her father. While there, she observed the oppressed status of Peruvian women and wrote her first book, *Travels of an Outcast* (1838). She predated Karl Marx and other economic theorists with her *Worker's Union* (1843); it was based on Tristan's personal efforts to organize the French working class and was published just a year prior to her death at age forty-one. This crusader for freedom and equality is often remembered—if she is thought of at all—as the grandmother of painter Paul Gauguin.

TUSSAUD, MARIE GROSHOLTZ (1760–1850) Known the world over for the wax museums that still bear her name, Madame Tussaud merits recognition as an artist who used an unusual technique to create amazingly realistic sculptures in wax. She was not the first woman to do so, but Tussaud's business skills made her the person best known for this art form. Born in France to Swiss parents, she sculpted in Paris, including for royalty. Imprisoned because of these connections during the French Revolution, she then was forced to make death masks of its guillotined victims, many of whom were her friends. She married in 1795, changing her name from Grosholtz to Tussaud, but left her husband and French political turmoil for London in 1802. Many of Tussaud's images of famous people during this era are still lifelike more than two hundred years after she created them.

TZ'U-HSI (1835–1908) Powerful Chinese ruler Tz'u-hsi never held a rank higher than empress mother, but she dominated China for almost a half century through the strength of her personality. Indeed, her dictatorial policies and ruthlessness were important factors in the final downfall of the Chinese monarchy just three years after her death. Tz'u-hsi entered the Forbidden City of Chinese royalty in 1852 as a lowly concubine, but after producing the emperor's only son she rose to the rank of concubine first class, just below his wife. When he died, she became empress mother as regent for her son—and when her son died, she continued in that position through a succession of male minors. When one rebelled against her autocratic rule and attempted to introduce reforms in 1898, he found himself imprisoned for the rest of his life. Often referred to as the Empress Dowager, her 1908 death signaled the revolution in 1911—led by Sun Yat-sen, future husband of SOONG CH'ING-LING—that ended the Manchu dynasty and thousands of years of absolute power.

UNDSET, SIGRID (1882–1949) Norwegian novelist Sigrid Undset won the Nobel Prize for literature in 1928 for her masterpiece *Kristin Lavransdatter*, a three-volume novel set in the fourteenth century. Born in Denmark, Undset grew up in Oslo, where she published her first book in 1907. A 1909 scholarship allowed her to travel to Italy; she wrote *Jenny* in 1911, married the next year, and pub-lished very little until the three volumes of *Kristin Lavransdatter* came out between 1920 and 1922. She both divorced and converted to Catholicism in 1925, and her work after that is more conservative. Undset escaped to Sweden during the Nazi occupation of Norway and died back in Lillehammer.

VICTORIA (1819–1901) The sixty-three-year reign of Queen Victoria, between 1837 and 1901, saw incredible change as she greatly expanded the British Empire and led the transformation of her English homeland from an agricultural to an industrial economy. So powerful was her influence that her name is used to denote both the era and the social standards she set.

When Victoria was born, it seemed unlikely that she would reign. She was the daughter of the duke of Kent, who had three older brothers—and yet, by the time she was seventeen, her uncles died childless, her father died, and then, on her eighteenth birthday, the king died. She was already engaged to Prince Albert of Germany; their 1840 marriage probably was the happiest of any royal family in history. Albert and Victoria had nine children, and although some of them went to war against each other when Germany and Britain clashed in World War I, their family life was emulated by the aspiring middle class throughout the world. Much of Asia and Africa came under British control during Victoria's popular reign, the longest of any monarch.

VIGÉE-LEBRUN, MARIE-LOUISE-ÉLISABETH (1755–1842) French painter Élisabeth Vigée-Lebrun is especially known for her portraits of MARIE-ANTOINETTE. Born to a family of artists, Élisabeth Vigée became a professional portraitist at age fifteen; she added Lebrun to her name with a 1776 marriage and did her first portrait of the queen in 1779, at a time when both women were young mothers. Although she was elected to the Royal Academy in 1783, Vigée-Lebrun was more politically prescient than many, fleeing her established career when the French Revolution began in 1789. She lived in exile from Naples to Moscow for most of the next three decades and portrayed many diverse subjects during her wide travels. Modern critics call her work technically expert as well as sensitive. Her best work may be a self-portrait with her daughter done in 1789, the year they fled France.

WEST, DAME REBECCA (1892–1983) A dominant force in English literature throughout her long life, Rebecca West wrote both nonfiction and fiction and lived her political liberalism. Educated in Scotland, she was born Cicily Isabel

Fairfield in Ireland; she adopted her pseudonym at age twenty from the feminist protagonist of a play by Henrik Ibsen. She wrote for feminist and Socialist periodicals and campaigned for suffrage in Britain. Her World War I novel, *The Return of the Soldier* (1918), brought her national fame at age twenty-six. Two years earlier, she had published her first book of literary criticism, a witty disparagement of male icons that brought West to the attention of H. G. Wells, with whom she had a child. Unwilling to marry at that point, she finally did so in 1930 but did not take her husband's name. West published a wide variety of work: Black Lamb and Grey Falcon, for instance, is a travelogue and history of Yugoslavia that remains relevant today. Her best-known novel may be her last, *The Birds Fall Down* (1966), which was set in the Russian Revolution.

WILHELMINA (1880–1962) Perhaps the most highly respected of modern queens, Wilhelmina became monarch of the Netherlands at her father's death when she was ten. Formally crowned in 1898, she reigned for fifty years and was especially esteemed for her roles during two world wars. In the first, she opened the Netherlands to all who sought asylum—including, at his defeat, Kaiser Wilhelm of Germany, a traditional enemy of the Dutch. Exiled in London during World War II, she actively sought American aid and in 1942 was the first reigning queen to address Congress. She returned to rebuild her country— which had been bombed by Allies during the German occupation with her approval—and dealt with the new issue of independence for Dutch colonies. Exhausted, she celebrated her fiftieth anniversary on the throne and abdicated in favor of her daughter, Juliana.

WILLIAMS, BETTY (1943–) The cowinners of the 1976 Nobel Peace Prize, Betty Williams and MAIRÉAD CORRIGAN-MAGUIRE were both motivated by the deaths of children in August 1976, during violence between the Irish Revolutionary Army and Belfast authorities. Williams—a Protestant native of Northern Ireland who had been ostracized by family and friends when she married a Catholic—led Protestant women, Corrigan-Maguire led Catholics, and they marched to end the long conflict, which had killed some seventeen hundred people in the past decade. They formed the Community of Peace People and published a newspaper, *Peace by Peace*. The women were nominated after the deadline for the 1976 prize, but the Nobel Committee awarded it to them in 1977 (as well as another for that year) after pressure, especially from Norwegians, who wanted it so much that they raised more than $300,000 as a "Norwegian Peace Prize." On the other hand, many longtime activists resented

the award of this most prestigious prize to women whose work had been relatively brief—complaints that seemed justified when Williams resigned her Community of Peace People membership in 1980.

WOLLSTONECRAFT, MARY (1759–1797) The most important pioneer feminist, Mary Wollstonecraft is famous for *A Vindication of the Rights of Woman* (1792)—published decades prior to the organized women's movement and the classic of feminist philosophy far into the next century. Her work as a governess in Ireland led to her first publication, "Thoughts on the Education of Daughters" (1787). Her first novel, *Mary, A Fiction* (1788), was followed by *The Female Reader* (1789). After her masterful *Vindication*, Wollstonecraft went from London to Paris in 1792—when most were going in the opposite direction, fleeing the French Revolution. Her time there resulted in *A Historical and Moral View of the French Revolution* (1794), as well as a daughter by an American man. They did not marry, and she overcame a suicide attempt to publish *Letters from Scandinavia* in 1796. In the same year, she developed a happy relationship with political radical William Godwin; they married in March 1797, but she died in September, soon after giving birth to MARY WOLLSTONECRAFT SHELLEY. Godwin published her memoirs the next year.

WOOLF, (ADELINE) VIRGINIA STEPHEN (1882–1941) Every feminist knows Virginia Woolf for *A Room of One's Own* (1929), a philosophical work based on her lectures to women at the Universities of Oxford and Cambridge. A Londoner all her life, as a young adult she moved with her siblings to the city's bohemian Bloomsbury section, which became known as a literary center in part because of her. She married Leonard Woolf in 1912; unlike many of the Bloomsbury set, they enjoyed a long and stable relationship, despite a series of mental breakdowns she suffered after 1916. The Woolfs formed a publishing house, Hogarth Press, and issued her first novel in 1915. In 1922, she had her first big success with *Jacob's Room*, an antiwar novel. *Mrs. Dalloway* (1925) pioneered the stream-of-consciousness technique, while *To the Lighthouse* (1927) was a popular childhood memoir. The experimental Orlando (1928) featured a time-traveling protagonist who changed from a man to a woman. With these and other works, Virginia Woolf established herself as one of the most important literary figures of the century. Bombed out of their London home in World War II, the Woolfs retreated to Sussex, which was also in the path of German planes; fearing that she was going permanently insane, Virginia Woolf drowned herself in the River Ouse. Decades later, her name spread to the masses with the play and film *Who's Afraid of Virginia Woolf?* but it has no direct connection to Woolf.

YOURCENAR, MARGUERITE (1903–1987) Belgian writer Marguerite Yourcenar wrote in French; although she became an American citizen in 1939 when World War II began, she lived all over the world. This is reflected in her work, which includes both fiction and nonfiction and ranges in subject from ancient Rome to contemporary Japan; the best known may be *L'Oeuvre au noir* (1968), which is set during the Reformation. In 1980, when the Académie Française belatedly elected its first female member, the honor went to Yourcenar.

ZOE (c. 978–1050) The extravagant habits of her three husbands had bankrupted the Byzantine Empire by the time Zoe ascended to the throne in her own right. She governed for a brief period around 1028 and then permanently after the death of her uncle, Constantine VIII. The empire was in a state of collapse, and although the people—in what now is Turkey—were fanatically loyal to Zoe and her sister, Theodora, neither woman was able to stem the empire's decline. Theodora's death in 1056 signaled the end of the Isaurian dynasty.

Timeline: Women in U.S. History

1492   Christopher Columbus uses maps that belonged to his mother-in-law, Doña Isabel Moniz.

1539   Ana Mendez and Francisca Hinestrosa sail from Cuba to Florida with Hernando de Soto. Hinestrosa dies in 1541 warfare with natives, but Mendez, who had been Doña Isabel de Soto's servant, lives to testify before a Spanish commission on her experience.

1565   North America's oldest city, Saint Augustine, Florida, is founded by the Spanish; soon about a hundred women live among twelve hundred men. None are nuns; although Spain sends many priests, three centuries will pass before any Catholic sisters go from Spain to North America.

1587   Only days after arriving on Roanoke Island in what will become North Carolina, Ellinor White Dare gives birth to the first English child born in North America, Virginia Dare.

1598   Some four hundred Spanish-speaking men, women, and children move from Mexico to what will become Texas and New Mexico.

1608   Anne Forrest and her maid, Anne Buras, join about four hundred men at Virginia's Jamestown; seven ships will bring more than a hundred English women next year. Most are sold as servants, usually for seven years, to pay for their travel expenses; some women are purchased as brides.

1619   The first African women and men arrive at Jamestown on a Dutch ship.

1620   Of the eighteen adult women on the *Mayflower*, fourteen are dead by winter's end.

1623   New Amsterdam, which will later become New York City, is settled by the Dutch. Women there retain their maiden names, sign prenuptial agreements, and engage in commerce.

1637   Members of the Boston clergy try ANNE HUTCHINSON for heresy.

1639   North America's first divorce results from the husband's bigamy; the Boston court grants his property to his local wife and banishes him back to England, where he had abandoned his first wife.

1644   Adultery is a capital crime in Puritan Boston: a young married woman and her lover are hanged.

1647   MARGARET BRENT is the effective governor of Maryland.

1649   The Maryland Toleration Act uses gender-neutral language, while Massachusetts law refers to midwives in the same class as physicians.

1650   ANNE DUDLEY BRADSTREET is America's first published poet.

1660   Boston's theocrats hang Quaker preacher MARY DYER.

1676   The Pocasset band of the Wampanoag tribe is led by a woman named Wetamoo. Only twenty-six of her three hundred warriors survive King Philip's War, and her head is displayed in Taunton, Massachusetts.

1677 On the St. Lawerence River, Kateri Tekakwitha escapes from her Mohawk tribe to join Christian Indians; in 1982, she will become the first Native American canonized as a Catholic saint.

1682 Pennsylvania is founded by Quakers, who view women as nearly equal to men.

Mary Rowlandson publishes her experience as a captive of the Wampanoag: *The Soveraignty and Goodness of God* will become a classic of American literature.

1692 Trials for witchcraft begin in Salem, Massachusetts; 141 suspected witches are arrested, and 19, most of them women, are executed.

1709 America's first female commercial artist may be Henrietta Johnston of Charleston, South Carolina.

1711 "Madame Montour" serves as interpreter at an Albany conference between the governor of New York and the chiefs of the five Iroquois Nations.

1727 North America has its second convent when French Ursuline nuns settle at New Orleans; the first was at Montreal.

1736 Ann Smith Franklin, sister-in-law of Benjamin Franklin, is the official printer for the colony of Rhode Island.

1746 Teenage LUCY TERRY (later PRINCE) writes what is probably the first poem by an African American.

1765 Mary Jemison, who was taken captive by a Shawnee war party as an adolescent and then rescued by Seneca Indians, opts for Seneca life and becomes a powerful mediator in the Lake Erie area.

Anne Catherine Hoff Green, mother of fourteen, publishes the *Maryland Gazette* and is the official printer of the colony of Maryland.

1768 Newspapers cover Lord Baltimore's rape of a respected woman. When he dies, he will designate an illegitimate son as Maryland's proprietor.

Connecticut executes its last witch. Since 1647, the colony has hanged thirty-seven people, mostly women, for witchcraft. No one is ever executed for witchcraft in southern colonies.

1772 Sculptor Patience Lovell Wright goes to London, where she will be the first American artist to have a work in Westminster Abbey.

1773 The nation's first female political network, the Daughters of Liberty, organizes support for the boycott of British goods; some of its members hold demonstrations and even physically attack Loyalists.

1775 Molly Brant, a Mohawk woman who has nine children by a recently deceased British official, assists the British in their alliance with Iroquois tribes; at the end of the Revolutionary War, they award her a sizable pension.

Only weeks before Patrick Henry delivers his "liberty or death" speech, his allegedly insane wife dies in the basement where he had confined her.

1776 Months prior to the Declaration of Independence, Massachusetts' ABIGAIL ADAMS writes to her husband, a member of the Continental Congress meeting in Philadelphia: "In the new code of laws . . . I desire you would remember the ladies. . . . If particular care and attention are not paid to the ladies, we are determined to foment a rebellion and will not hold ourselves bound to obey any laws in which we have no voice or representation."

A Staten Island commander says that court-martials for rape occur "every day" and calls the testimony "most entertaining."

Pennsylvanian MARGARET CORBIN becomes the first American woman to earn a soldier's pension.

1777 At age sixteen, SYBIL LUDINGTON makes a longer ride than Paul Revere's famed one.

Newspaper publisher Mary Katherine Goodard is also postmaster of Baltimore.

1778 Mary Hayes of Pennsylvania becomes legendary during the battle of Monmouth, New Jersey as MOLLY PITCHER.

1779 JUDITH SARGENT STEVENS (later MURRAY) writes "Essay on the Equality of the Sexes."

1780 About forty Philadelphia women go door-to-door and raise some $300,000 in continental dollars from over sixteen hundred donors to fund Washington's army.

1781 In the South Carolina wilderness, young Emily Geiger rides for two days to deliver a message between American commanders; she is briefly taken prisoner. Her fifty-mile ride is much longer and more dangerous than that of either SYBIL LUDINGTON or Paul Revere.

1782 Prostitution is so common among both the British and American armies that some prostitutes openly state their business in filing claims for wartime property losses.

1783 Yale College's admissions board interviews twelve-year-old Lucinda Foote and finds her "fully qualified, except in her sex."

1786 *Victoria* makes SUSANNA HASWELL (later ROWSON) America's first recognized novelist.

1788 JEMIMA WILKINSON leads a frontier utopian community.

1790 New Jersey's 1776 State Constitution implicitly enfranchised women; this year, the phrase "he or she" is added to clarify that the state's women do indeed have the right to vote.

In Carroll County, Maryland, four Carmelite nuns establish the first convent within the boundaries of the United States.

1792 Louisa St. Clair, daughter of General Arthur St. Clair, is so respected by natives that she goes alone to negotiate an Ohio treaty with them.

1793 Free black women form the Philadelphia Benevolent Society, which may be the nation's first organization of black women.

1795 Twelve-year-old Betsey Metcalf of Dedham, Massachusetts, devises a new method of hand-weaving straw into hats; by the 1830s, thousands of New England women earn money by making straw hats.

1797 Scottish immigrants Isabella Graham and her daughter, Joanna Graham Bethune, begin endowing several New York charities, including one of the world's first Sunday schools.

1802 Political opponents allege that Democrat Thomas Jefferson had a long sexual relationship with one of his slaves, Sally Hemings. The president does not issue a denial, and no one disputes that Hemings traveled to France when Jefferson was ambassador there.

1803 Elizabeth Patterson of Baltimore marries Napoleon Bonaparte's brother and spends her life trying to put her son on the French throne.

1807 Men wearing dresses cast illegal ballots in New Jersey, and women's suffrage is repealed.

1811 Marie Dorian of the Iowa tribe guides explorers on a longer and more perilous journey than that of SACAGAWEA. Dorian has two children and gives birth to a third during a thirty-five-hundred-mile trip.

1812 ANN JUDSON and HARRIET NEWELL sail for Asia, where they are America's first female missionaries.

Disguised as a man, Lucy Brewer serves as a marine on the *Constitution* during the War of 1812.

1813 MARY PICKERSGILL manufactures the flag that inspires the "Star-Spangled Banner"; her mother had made George Washington's 1776 flag.

1814 First lady DOLLEY MADISON rescues state documents and art acquisitions when the British set fire to Washington, D.C.

1818 Respectable women do not speak in public, so EMMA WILLARD presents *An Address...Proposing a Plan for Improving Female Education* to the New York legislature in writing.

1819 Rebecca Gratz founds the Female Hebrew Benevolent Society in Philadelphia. Many believe she is the model for Rebecca in Sir Walter Scott's *Ivanhoe*.

One of the first acts of Kaahumanu's reign in Hawaii is to break the taboo on men and women eating together; she also establishes the islands' first legal code.

1824 Women join men in the nation's first industrial strike at the textile mills of Pawtucket, Rhode Island.

Aristocratic Mary Randolph publishes *The Virginia House-wife*, which becomes America's first widely used cookbook.

Painters Anna Claypoole Peale and Sarah Miriam Peale are elected to the Philadelphia Academy of Fine Arts; both go on to great commercial success.

1825 Rebecca Pennock Lukens begins running the Pennsylvania iron foundry that will build the hull of America's first metal ship.

1826 Women are the sole strikers when the United Tailoresses declare a work stoppage in New York City.

1828 To support her five children, widow Sarah Buell Hale works as an editor. She virtually invents the women's magazine format, writes such classics as "Mary Had a Little Lamb," and pushes for as much feminism as her readers will accept.

1829 Because his recently dead wife, Rachel Donelson Jackson, was greatly hurt by bigamy accusations after her abusive first husband failed to properly divorce her, Andrew Jackson spends much of his presidency defending Peggy Eaton, the wife of his secretary of war, who is similarly slandered.

The first order of African American nuns, the Oblate Sisters of Providence, is founded in Baltimore.

Almira Lincoln (later Phelps) publishes *Familiar Lectures on Botany*, which sells more than a quarter of a million copies.

1830 New England textile mills recruit young rural women during this decade, and factory life presages college life: the women live in dormitories, organize evening classes, and publish their writing.

1831 Maria Stewart, an African American born free in Boston, writes and speaks against slavery.

1833 The first coeducational college begins: Oberlin in frontier Ohio accepts women and also blacks.

1834 Attacks by her neighbors force Prudence Crandell, a young white Quaker, to close her Connecticut boarding school for black girls.

1835 LYDIA MARIA CHILD publishes "The History and Condition of Women," in *Various Ages and Nations*.

1836 Missionaries Narcissa Whitman and Eliza Spaulding are the first white women to make the trek to the Pacific Northwest.

Georgia Female College is founded in Macon; it is arguably the nation's first women's college.

ERNESTINE ROSE sends the New York legislature a petition "to give a married woman the right to hold real estate in her own name." Just five women are courageous enough to sign it.

1837 Two hundred women from nine states go to New York City for the first Women's Anti-Slavery Convention. ABBY KELLY (later FOSTER) speaks, and several free black women also participate. It may be the first national political gathering of women, and it violates not only taboos on public speaking but also codes on integration.

Despite the nation's first serious economic depression this year, MARY LYON begins Mount Holyoke Female Seminary.

1838 Kentucky women become the first in the postrevolutionary United States to win some voting rights: widows with no children currently in school may vote in school elections.

At a time when public speaking by women is condemned, MARY GOVE (later NICHOLS) lectures on the shocking subject of women's anatomy.

SARAH GRIMKÉ writes *Letters on Equality of the Sexes and the Condition of Women*; her sister ANGELINA GRIMKÉ sets a precedent for women by testifying on slavery to a committee of the Massachusetts legislature.

1840 FRANCES WRIGHT will cross the Atlantic five times in this decade alone.

ELIZABETH CADY and Henry STANTON agree that she should omit "obey" from her wedding vows. On their honeymoon, they attend the World Anti-Slavery Convention in London; elected female delegates, including LUCRETIA MOTT, are banned from the meeting, and this will lead to the first women's rights meeting in 1848.

1842 Some five hundred Massachusetts women join the Lowell Female Labor Reform Association, one of America's earliest unions. SARAH BAGLEY is the association's president.

The world's first deaf-and-blind person to be educated, New England's Laura Bridgman, reads and communicates by touch.

1844 MARGARET FULLER becomes the nation's first professional book reviewer.

1846 *Woman as She Was, Is, and Should Be* is early feminist thought by Ohio's Hannah Tracy (later Cutler). A journalist, she goes to London in 1851 as a delegate to the World's Peace Congress.

1847 Jane McManus Storms (later Cazneau) is the only reporter to file stories from behind enemy lines during the Mexican War.

Oberlin College grants Emily Frances Fairchild a master's degree; it may be the first to a woman anywhere in the world.

Pacific pioneer Narcissa Whitman is among fourteen whites killed near Walla Walla, Washington; Cayuse tribespeople blame her and her physician husband for failing to cure their children in a measles epidemic.

DOROTHEA DIX speaks to the Tennessee legislature.

The Boston Lying-In Hospital is the nation's first to use anesthesia to ease delivery. Many clergymen object, citing the biblical mandate "in pain ye shall bring forth children."

1848 The organized women's movement begins with a meeting on July 19 and 20 in Seneca Falls, New York, when Philadelphian LUCRETIA MOTT visits ELIZABETH CADY STANTON. To their surprise, some three hundred women and men attend the barely advertised meeting. The women, inexperienced in parliamentary procedure, call on James Mott to preside, but they soon find their voices and adopt a strong Declaration of Rights for Women. Modeled by Stanton on the nation's Declaration of Independence, it calls for rights in education, employment, and the legal system; the right to vote is hotly debated but passes. Two weeks later, a follow-up meeting is held in Rochester, and this time a woman, Abigail Bush, presides.

Elizabeth Lummis Ellet is the first to publicize women's contributions to America when she issues the carefully researched two-volume *Women of the American Revolution*. Some of her work is illustrated by Lilly Martin Spencer, the era's most successful female artist; the mother of thirteen, she twice turns down $20,000 for a painting.

Astronomer MARIA MITCHELL is the first woman elected to the American Academy of Arts and Sciences.

1849 ELIZABETH BLACKWELL graduates at the top of her otherwise all-male medical school class; she is the first woman in the modern world to earn a medical degree.

HARRIET TUBMAN escapes from slavery.

Cartoonist Frances Berry Whitcher dies from childbirth; a posthumous collection of her work sells more than 100,000 copies.

Some forty utopian communities have developed in the first half of the century, but none is more controversial than Oneida in upper New York State. Its members practice "complex marriage," in which they have multiple spouses, and men are required to practice withdrawal during sex unless a woman wants to become pregnant.

1850   The first national women's rights convention is held at Worcester, Massachusetts. Organized by Paulina Kellogg Wright Davis from her Rhode Island home, it attracts attendees from nine states. The *New York Tribune* reprints much that is said, and among those influenced is English philosopher John Stuart Mill.

Philadelphia Quakers begin the Female Medical College of Pennsylvania; as Woman's Medical College of Pennsylvania after 1862, it will educate the era's most influential female physicians.

1851   At a women's rights convention in Akron, Ohio, SOJOURNER TRUTH makes her "Ain't I a Woman?" speech.

Emulating FANNY KEMBLE, Elizabeth Smith Miller wears "Turkish trousers" in Seneca Falls, New York; her cousin, ELIZABETH CADY STANTON, is among those who adopt pants. National newspapers pick up the story from AMELIA BLOOMER and use her name for the style. Women like the practicality of pants, but the public thinks their garb is immoral; because feminists decide that pants distract from their work on legal rights, most soon abandon them.

Myrtilla Miner, a white woman, opens a school for black girls in Washington against all advice—including that of abolitionist Frederick Douglass.

The second woman to graduate from an established medical school is Lydia Folger Fowler, who has already published *Familiar Lessons in Physiology* (1847).

SUSAN BOGERT WARNER publishes the first American book to sell a million copies, *The Wide, Wide World*.

1852   HARRIET BEECHER STOWE's *Uncle Tom's Cabin* may be history's most influential novel, fanning the flames of abolitionism and leading to the Civil War.

Two decades after the nation's first coeducational college opens, a second is founded, also in Ohio. The president of Antioch College is Horace Mann; his wife, Mary Peabody Mann—sister of ELIZABETH PEABODY—is an educator in her own right.

1853   "Immense audiences" from eight states and Canada go to Syracuse for the Third National Women's Rights Convention, where they pay "an admission fee of one shlling." This is the first meeting for future leader SUSAN B. ANTHONY.

African American Mary Ann Shadd (later Cary) becomes the world's first black female newspaper editor: she endures criticism from black men to publish an abolitionist weekly in Toronto. After the Civil War begins, she will return to the United States and recruit soldiers.

ANTOINETTE BROWN (later BLACKWELL) is the first woman ordained as a minister of a mainstream church.

1854   CLARA BARTON sets the first of many precedents by working in the U.S. Patent Office in Washington. Other women hired by the federal government do clerical work at home; their paychecks are mailed, and those of married women are made out to their husbands.

Massachusetts passes a model Married Women's Property Act, largely because of lobbying by Mary Upton Ferrin. She collected petition signatures for six years after realizing that her husband had legal title to property she owned prior to marriage, as well as the right to all earnings from her labor.

1855   When Henry Blackwell persuades LUCY STONE to marry him, they agree that she should retain her maiden name. He joins in her activism and will continue to hold office in women's rights organizations even after her death.

1856   In Salem, Massachusetts, Charlotte Forten may be the first African American woman to teach white students.

The presidential election is the first for the new Republican Party and the first to spotlight a potential first lady: Jessie Benton Fremont actively promotes her husband's career—even using secret information she obtained as a translator of government documents.

1857 The first Southern woman to earn a medical degree is Orianna Moon of Virginia.

1858 Responding to a petition signed by ten thousand, a committee of the Ohio legislature favorably reports amending the state constitution to give women the vote. The proposal fails on the floor with a vote of 44-44.

The tenth anniversary of women's rights conventions attracts a crowd to New York City.

1859 Jane McManus Storms Cazneau returns to the Caribbean, where she has long worked for expansion of American slave interests. She writes for New York newspapers and uses her diplomatic connections to promote various commercial schemes.

When white abolitionist John Brown is hanged for leading a slave rebellion, ex-slave FRANCES ELLEN WATKINS (later HARPER) raises money to support his family. Mary Brown is too poor to visit her husband prior to his execution.

1860 Sculptor Harriet Hosmer is the first woman to receive a major public commission for artwork when Missouri hires her to carve a statue.

Jane Grey Swisshelm speaks to the Minnesota House; she publishes a newspaper in that state, as she did earlier in Pittsburgh and will later in Washington.

1861 As the Civil War begins, Anna Ella Carroll—who supports herself as a Washington lobbyist—uses her influence with Maryland's governor to help prevent the state from seceding. This is vital to the Union, for the nation's capital would be isolated from the rest of the United States if Maryland joined the Confederacy.

Confederate spy Rose Greenhow is key to early Rebel victories; Belle Boyd and other women also spy. Elizabeth Van Lew takes similar risks for the Union, and after the war she is rewarded with the position of postmaster for Richmond.

Thousands of women, including nearly a thousand nuns, work as nurses on both sides of the war, serving under fire and on hospital ships. Among the most important Union women is MARY ANN BICKERDYKE; the nation's first woman formally appointed to a military position is DOROTHEA DIX, who is named "superintendent of the United States Army Nurses."

President Jefferson Davis commissions Sally Tompkins as a Confederate captain so that she can commandeer hospital supplies, while Ella K. Trader builds hospitals in four states. Phoebe Levy Pember runs a Richmond hospital that becomes the world's largest; in 1995, the U.S. Post Office will honor her with a stamp in its Civil War series.

Emily Edson Briggs of the *Washington Chronicle* is the first woman to report from the White House. Meanwhile, Lillie Devereux Umsted (later Blake) is a Washington correspondent for two New York papers.

As men join the military, women are hired as government employees in both the North and the South; treasury departments and mints on both sides particularly hire women, who are seen as trustworthy and detail oriented.

Kansas women win the right to vote in school elections, becoming the first American women to achieve any permanent suffrage.

1862 When the State of the Union speech is leaked to the *New York Herald* before the president delivers it, Mary Todd Lincoln is suspected of having sold an advance copy to pay her clothing bills. A congressional committee investigates, even jailing a White House aide.

JULIA WARD HOWE—who has published two plays that embarrassed her husband with their dark violence—becomes instantly famous with "The Battle Hymn of the Republic."

Mary Jane Patterson is the world's first black female college graduate; she will become a Washington educator. She graduates from Ohio's Oberlin College almost thirty years after it became the first college to admit women and blacks.

1863 The Republican Party hires orator Anna Dickinson to speak to tough audiences of northerners who oppose the war. Pennsylvania coal miners literally take shots at her.

1864 The businesswoman most successful at exploiting the war may be Adelicia Acklen, who deceives both Confederate and Union officials to take a shipload of cotton from her Louisiana plantations to the cotton-hungry mills of Liverpool, England. She sails past embargo barricades, returns with $960,000, and builds a fantastic mansion in Nashville.

Dr. Clemence S. H. Lozier, an 1852 graduate of Syracuse Medical School, begins the New York Medical College for Women. The third such institution, it predates ELIZABETH BLACKWELL's more famous one.

African American Rebecca Lee graduates from MARIE ZAKRZEWSKA's school, the New England Hospital for Women and Children. Lee becomes the first black female physician; she will practice in Richmond.

Only a few years after women began speaking in public, twenty-one-year-old Anna Dickinson is invited to address the U.S. House of Representatives, with President Lincoln in the audience.

1865 A prisoner-of-war the previous year, physician MARY WALKER is the only woman ever granted the Congressional Medal of Honor.

The play that President Lincoln is watching when he is assassinated is produced by Laura Keene, an impresario who has worked at theaters from England to Australia.

Maryland's Mary Surratt is hanged for alleged complicity in President Lincoln's assassination.

Diarist MARY CHESNUT epitomizes the suffering of Confederate women at the war's end, but her problems are complicated by childlessness: under South Carolina law, her ailing husband's estate will revert to his family when he dies.

Hundreds of white women go south to teach blacks the literacy skills that had been illegal under slavery. Many such schools depend on funds raised by women—New York's Emily Howland alone endows thirty schools—while others operate under the federal Freedmen's Bureau, which owes its existence in part to the vision of Josephine Griffing of Ohio.

At the same time that northern women teach in schools for freedmen, thousands of others begin going west to the schools of pioneer towns. The influence of these multitudinous but anonymous women is tremendous: in both the South and the West, they educate millions—but they also teach a view of the United States that stresses Pilgrim heritage to the exclusion of other cultures.

Dentist Lucy Hobbs (later Taylor) is a founder of the Iowa State Dental Society.

1866 The Young Women's Christian Association (YWCA) merges groups that responded to women's need to travel during the war. Because many hotel operators believe that any woman without a male escort is a prostitute, the YWCA provides accommodations.

At age eighteen, Vinnie Ream (later Hoxie) is the first woman to win a federal art commission. Abraham Lincoln posed for her prior to his death, and Congress pays her $10,000 for a statue that will be unveiled in the Capitol rotunda in 1871.

1867 The U.S. House decides against enfranchising women in the District of Columbia, with a vote of 49 for, 74 against, and 68 failing to vote.

Women's rights leaders converge on Kansas, where the nation's first state referendum on suffrage is held. Despite energetic campaigning, they win only about nine thousand of thirty thousand votes.

The editor of the new *Harper's Bazaar* is Mary Louise Booth. During two decades in this position, she will rise to a then-fabulous $4,000 annual salary.

1868 MYRA BRADWELL begins the *Chicago Legal News* and her long struggle to become an attorney.

New York City women form Sorosis, America's first organization for professional women, after journalist JANE CUNNINGHAM CROLY is excluded from a city press club event. At the same time, the New England Women's Club begins in Boston; President Caroline Severance will lead the successful effort to establish Girls Latin School and to elect women to the Boston school board.

In Vineland, New Jersey, 172 women, including 4 blacks, cast ballots that officials assume will not be counted. The women argue that the recently passed Fourteenth Amendment entitles them to vote.

The first organized suffrage opposition appears in Lancaster, Massachusetts, where two hundred women send a petition to the legislature saying that the vote "would diminish the purity, the dignity, and the moral influence of women."

1869 The American Equal Rights Association, which had merged abolitionists and women's rights advocates after slavery was abolished in 1866, splits over the issue of the proposed Fourteenth and Fifteenth Amendments, which grant civil rights and the vote to black men while excluding all women. SUSAN B. ANTHONY and ELIZABETH CADY STANTON form the National Woman Suffrage Association, separating from LUCY STONE and others who form the more moderate American Woman Suffrage Association. Louisa May Alcott, JULIA WARD HOWE, MARY LIVERMORE, and HARRIET BEECHER STOWE are among the literary luminaries who make a long-term success of the latter association's *Woman's Journal*.

Iowa is the first state to admit a woman, Arabella Mansfield, to the bar. She does not intend to practice law, however, and continues as a college administrator.

Women in the Wyoming Territory become the world's first to have an unqualified right to vote. Men are so eager to lure women to this frontier that they adopt a constitution assuring women of complete political and economic rights—even equal pay in public employment.

Physician Clara Swain goes to northern India, where she rides an elephant to see her patients.

1870 Utah women win the vote a few weeks after those in Wyoming, but they are the first to actually cast ballots because Utah's elections are first. Although controversy over polygamy in Utah clouds the achievement, many skeptical men become supporters of suffrage after seeing the decorum that female presence brings to frontier polls.

For the first time in the history of jurisprudence, women serve on juries—to the delight of cartoonists, who find Wyoming's precedent hilarious.

Esther Morris is the nation's first female law enforcement official: Wyoming's governor appoints her justice of the peace for South Pass City, a mining boomtown that is the territory's largest. Although lawlessness often prevails in such places, Morris is a success.

The Fifteenth Amendment uses gender-neutral language, giving women a legal argument that their enfranchisement is included along with that of former slaves. During the next two years, about 150 women from Delaware to California will attempt to vote; the first is Marilla Ricker, a wealthy young widow in Dover, New Hampshire.

1871 Missouri follows Iowa to become the second state to admit a woman to the bar. Phoebe Couzins is also admitted in Arkansas, Utah, Kansas, and the Dakota Territory, but she never builds a career.

Women in Washington, D.C., form the first anti-suffrage association; they are led by the wives of two Civil War military leaders, Mrs. William Sherman and Mrs. James Dahlgren.

1872 VICTORIA WOODHULL is the first woman to declare herself a candidate for president.

CHARLOTTE E. RAY is the nation's first black female attorney.

Although women have worked as nurses from the nation's beginning, this year marks the founding of the first formal school for training nurses in the United States. Based at Dr. MARIE ZAKRZEWSKA's Boston establishment, it is promoted by brilliant young doctor Susan Dimock. The first graduate, Linda Richards, is deemed America's first professional nurse.

Sculptor Edmonia Lewis, who has a black father and a Chippewa mother, is so successful that she employs nine male assistants in her Boston studio.

Mary Clemmer Ames becomes the highest-paid newswoman in history when she earns $5,000 annually from the *Brooklyn Daily Union.*

1873   In *Bradwell v. Illinois*, the U.S. Supreme Court rules that states may exclude a woman from practicing law even if—as is the case for Chicagoan MYRA BRADWELL—she has passed the bar exam. Citing women's "timidity and delicacy," the Court says that the Constitution's equal-protection clauses are overruled by the "law of the Creator."

Protesting "taxation without representation," sisters Julia and Abigail Smith refuse to pay property taxes in Glastonbury, Connecticut. Town officials sell their cattle, and the "Glastonbury cows" become a celebrated cause.

1874   In a case filed by VIRGINIA MINOR, the Supreme Court hands women another big defeat. The effect is to force suffragists to amend the Constitution, which requires a positive vote from two-thirds of both houses of Congress and three-quarters of the state legislatures—an overwhelming task not achieved until 1920.

Women in several midwestern states begin prayer meetings outside saloons. The Women's Christian Temperance Union will be formally organized in Cleveland next year; its first president is Annie Wittenmyer, an Iowa widow who learned organizing skills in the wartime Sanitary Commission. In five years, she recruits more than twenty-five thousand members, most of whom aim at prohibiting alcohol sales rather than strengthening women's legal protection from drunken husbands.

1875   The adultery trial of the Reverend Henry Ward Beecher makes headlines. A nationally popular preacher, former president of the American Woman Suffrage Association, and brother of HARRIET BEECHER STOWE, he had an affair with Lib Tilton, a married member of his Brooklyn congregation and a friend of many feminists. Although their relationship ended in 1869, Tilton's husband sues, and the highly publicized trial does great damage to the image of feminists, even though the all-male jury fails to reach a decision. VICTORIA WOODHULL and her sister, Tennessee Claflin, arguably suffer most: they are jailed on obscenity charges for revealing the affair in their newspaper.

The American Medical Association admits its first female member: Sarah Stevenson, who graduated at the top of her class last year at Woman's Medical College of Chicago, an institution founded by Dr. Mary Thompson in 1870. Also this year, Dr. Emeline Cleveland becomes the first-known female physician to perform major surgery; she is a mother and supports an invalid husband.

Needing money after her husband's bankruptcy, LYDIA PINKHAM begins to sell a health tonic. From the same town of Lynn, Massachusetts, but apparently unconnected, MARY BAKER EDDY begins Christian Science.

Sculptor Anne Whitney wins a commission from the state of Massachusetts—but loses it when the judges find that the piece they chose was done by a woman.

1876   A giant Centennial Exposition in Philadelphia commemorates the century since the Declaration of Independence was signed in that city. MATILDA JOSLYN GAGE writes a Declaration of the Rights of Women modeled on the 1776 declaration, and on July 4 SUSAN B. ANTHONY reads it to a surprisingly receptive crowd.

1877   Bell Telephone Company forms this year, and thousands of women will become telephone operators; many previously were telegraph operators.

The first American woman to earn a doctorate of philosophy is Helen Magill, who completes a degree in Greek at Boston University. She never obtains a position that matches her credentials.

1878 Women begin the task of overturning *Minor v. Happersett* to win the right to vote. A constitutional amendment is introduced in the U.S. Senate; the Sixteenth Amendment at this point, it will be the Nineteenth Amendment when it finally passes in 1919.

1879 The suicide of Ann Trow Lohman makes headlines. Called Madame Restell, she has practiced as an abortionist since the 1830s; the willingness of New Yorkers to use her services is clear from her million-dollar estate. Prevention of pregnancy is more controversial in this era than its termination, however, and she slits her throat on the day of her trial for selling contraceptives.

FRANCES WILLARD leads a drive that nets some 180,000 signatures on a petition to the Illinois legislature for the right of women to vote on liquor sales. Women's Christian Temperance Union members are so impressed that they elect her president, where Willard will be key to changing suffrage from a radical idea to a mainstream one. Her "Do Everything" platform includes a range of feminist goals.

Years of lobbying by attorney BELVA LOCKWOOD pay off when Congress passes legislation permitting women to practice law in federal courts. She will be the first credentialed woman to argue before the Supreme Court.

Mary Mahoney, who graduates from Dr. MARIE ZAKRZEWSKA's nursing school, is considered the world's first black professional nurse.

1880 SARAH WINNEMUCCA and SUSETTE LA FLESCHE become nationally known crusaders for American Indians during this decade. La Flesche's speaking tour inspires *Century of Dishonor* (1881) by Helen Hunt Jackson, which did more than any other book to change public opinion on American Indians.

New York women win the vote for school elections, and Lydia Sayer Hasbrouck is elected to the Middletown school board—despite decades of wearing pants and refusing to pay her taxes because she cannot vote.

1881 Eight female physicians—including Emily Blackwell and MARIE ZAKRZEWSKA, who run competing medical schools—offer Harvard $50,000 to open medical studies to women. Harvard turns them down.

Women's colleges now have a generation of graduates, and the Association of Collegiate Alumnae begins; its name later changes to the American Association of University Women.

1882 At age twenty-seven, ALICE FREEMAN (later PALMER) becomes president of Wellesley College, but she must give up the position when she marries five years later.

1883 Women in the Washington Territory are third in the nation to have full voting rights—which they lose four years later, when a court strikes down the law that enfranchised them.

Louisa Knapp Curtis edits the women's supplement of a farm magazine; she and her husband Cyrus realize that it has more readers than the "main" magazine and begin *Ladies' Home Journal*.

1884 The National Equal Rights Party, a small group primarily on the West Coast, nominates BELVA LOCKWOOD and San Francisco's Marietta L. B. Stowe in the presidential campaign.

Mary Abigail Dodge is a ghostwriter for Republican presidential nominee Senator James G. Blaine; she opposes suffrage.

1885 Sharpshooter ANNIE OAKLEY becomes an international star.

Angelia F. Newman is employed by Methodists and others to lobby against polygamy. She gets a $40,000 congressional appropriation to fund a Salt Lake City rehabilitation center for women who leave polygamist husbands.

1886 White House gossip reaches new heights when President Grover Cleveland weds twenty-two-year-old Frances Folsom.

Reclusive poet EMILY DICKINSON dies at age fifty-five, and literary critic Thomas Wentworth Higginson continues to advise against publication of her work, which he calls "too crude in form."

1887 For the first and only time in the century, a congressional vote is taken on the "Susan B. Anthony Amendment" that enfranchises women: just sixteen of seventy-five senators support it. Congress also takes away the right of Utah women to vote when it outlaws polygamy, leaving women in Wyoming as the only fully enfranchised ones in the nation. Also this year, Rhode Island is the first eastern state to hold a referendum on suffrage; it too fails.

Ethnologist Alice Cunningham Fletcher, who was instrumental in passing the Dawes Act—intended to benefit American Indians—administers the act for Nebraska's Winnebago and Idaho's Nez Percé people.

1888 The fortieth anniversary of the Seneca Falls Women's Rights Convention is meaningfully commemorated by the formation of the International Council of Women.

Louise Blanchard Bethune of Buffalo is the first woman elected to the American Institute of Architects.

1889 JANE ADDAMS and Ellen Gates Starr begin Chicago's Hull House; by the turn of the century, about a hundred settlement houses throughout the nation—most run by women—will emulate its work with immigrants. In Baltimore, Henrietta Szold begins Americanization classes that become standard for immigrants.

Hearst newspapers sell at unprecedented rates as journalist Nellie Bly lives out Jules Verne's science-fiction story *Around the World in Eighty Days* using a multiplicity of travel methods.

1890 After more than twenty years of rivalry, the American Woman Suffrage Association and the National Woman Suffrage Association merge. Alice Stone Blackwell, daughter of the AWSA's LUCY STONE, and Harriot Stanton Blatch, daughter of the NWSA's ELIZABETH CADY STANTON, play key roles in overcoming the bad feelings between their mothers' organizations. A few pioneers refuse to join the merged group, accurately predicting that the National American Woman Suffrage Association will be more con-

servative than the women's rights societies of their youth.

Two other major organizations also begin this year: the Daughters of the American Revolution and the General Federation of Women's Clubs become much larger but far less progressive forces.

A study finds just thirty black women in the entire nation who have received any university degree—only slightly more than one for each of the twenty-five years since slavery ended.

1891 The American Economics Association honors Helen Campbell for her *Prisoners of Poverty*, which shows that—regardless of the industry or skill level—women are almost invariably paid half as much as men. Meanwhile, MARY KENNY O'SULLIVAN is the first woman hired by the American Federation of Labor.

1892 Although North Dakota women will not gain the vote for decades, male voters there elect Democrat Laura J. Eisenhuth as State Superintendent of Public Instruction. She is the first woman to win a statewide office; she will be defeated in the next election by another woman, Republican Emma Bates.

The Boston Symphony Orchestra performs *Mass in E Flat Major* by twenty-five-year-old Amy Beach.

The nation's attention is riveted on the trial of Lizzie Borden, a thirty-two-year-old Massachusetts woman accused of murdering her father and stepmother with an ax. The all-male jury acquits her, despite great evidence of her guilt.

Orator Mary Ellen Lease of Kansas seconds the presidential nomination at the Populist Party convention. Some call her "Mary Yellin," and she will be remembered for telling farmers to "raise less corn and more hell." Also this year, Wyoming Republicans elect Theresa A. Jenkins as the first female delegate to a major national political convention.

On Columbus Day, a yearlong exposition celebrating the 400th anniversary of Columbus's 1492 voyage opens in Chicago. A beautiful Woman's

Building is constructed under the supervision of twenty-two-year-old Sophia Hayden, who is the Massachusetts Institute of Technology's first female architecture graduate. The Board of Lady Managers—a congressionally mandated group with a large appropriation to spend—insists that the sculptors and artists who decorate the building be women, and even the music played is composed by women. The building offers some eighty thousand exhibits by women around the world.

1893   After more than a century of operation, the U.S. Post Office issues a stamp depicting a woman—but not an American: Queen ISABELLA of Spain is honored as the Columbus anniversary year continues.

Millions of women visit the exposition before its October end. In May, a World's Congress of Women follows up on the 1888 intention of having international women's meetings every five years. May Wright Sewall of Indiana presides; she traveled for two years, recruiting 330 speakers from twenty-seven countries; over 150,000 women attend a week of simultaneous seminars.

Geologist Florence Bascom earns what may be the first doctorate of science granted to a woman.

In a campaign organized by CARRIE CHAPMAN CATT, Colorado women win full voting rights.

1894   Women are elected to a state legislature for the first time, as Clara Cessingham, Carrie Holly, and Frances Klock win races for the Colorado House of Representatives.

1895   New Jersey librarian Carolyn Wells publishes the first of some 170 books; about half are mysteries, and she will earn much credit for defining that genre.

1896   Western women continue to outpace those in the East on the suffrage front: an Idaho referendum run by CARRIE CHAPMAN CATT grants women the vote, and Colorado adds three more women to its legislature.

Women in Utah regain the vote when its male leadership—who are also officials of the Mormon Church—renounce polygamy to become a state, and Democrat Martha Hughes Cannon becomes

the nation's first woman in a state senate. A physician, Cannon is also the fourth wife of a Mormon official; they both run in an at-large race, and she wins.

Delegates from twenty-five states, representing about five thousand women, found the National Association of Colored Women in Washington; its president will be MARY CHURCH TERRELL.

Like MARY CASSATT, Philadelphian Cecilia Beaux is an impressionist painter in Paris, where her colleagues elect her to the Société Nationale des Beaux-Arts.

1897   Gertrude Stanton Käsebier opens a studio on New York's Fifth Avenue, where she will become the doyen of female photographers.

Anna Katherine Green creates what may be the nation's first female fictional detective; Amelia Butterworth. Green's first work, *The Leavenworth Case* (1878), sold a half-million copies, and Sir Arthur Conan Doyle, the creator of Sherlock Holmes, is a fan.

1898   Some sixteen hundred women contract with the army to provide nursing services during the Spanish-American War. They serve from the Caribbean to the Philippines; in Puerto Rico, Ellen May Tower of Michigan becomes the first American woman to die on foreign soil while serving her country.

African American journalist IDA WELLS-BARNETT goes to the White House to lobby President William McKinley for an anti-lynching law.

Esther Reel, who was elected as Wyoming's State Superintendent of Public Instruction in 1894, is appointed by President McKinley as National Superintendent of Indian Schools; her Senate confirmation is the first for a woman and is unanimous.

Charlotte Perkins Gilman publishes *Women and Economics* this year, but she is best known for her feminist story "The Yellow Wallpaper" (1892).

1899   In the Arizona desert, Pearl Hart robs one of the few stagecoaches still operating. She attracts intense media interest, which she uses to draw attention to the injustice of women's being punished by a legal system in which they play no part.

Fanny Bullock Workman explores India's Himalayas and is rewarded with the most prestigious medals of ten national geographic societies. She lectures at the Sorbonne and, like ANNIE SMITH PECK, uses publicity opportunities to advocate the vote.

Beatrix Jones Farrand is a cofounder of the American Society of Landscape Architects; she designs some of America's most beautiful gardens.

As the century ends, the U.S. Patent Office has granted more than eight thousand patents to women inventors.

1900 The International Ladies' Garment Workers' Union begins; the members will be mostly women and the officers mostly men.

1901 Congress creates the Army Nurse Corps, the first permanent military unit for women.

Mary Murphy sues the Chicago school system, which dismisses women when they marry. She wins, but most school boards ignore the ruling.

Revolutionaries in Macedonia kidnap missionary Ellen M. Stone; she is freed several months later for $66,000 raised by public donations.

Army Nurse CLARA MAASS dies in Havana during experiments on yellow fever.

1902 The East has its second suffrage referendum, and New Hampshire men vote it down, just as Rhode Islanders did in 1887.

1903 Mother Jones loses her job with the United Mine Workers, which sees her as too radical, while the Women's Trade Union League begins at a convention of the American Federation of Labor. The league becomes an unusual meld of working class women and affluent women who support its goals, with wealthy Mary Drier as its leader.

1904 Concern about "white slavery"—international trade in prostitutes—prompts an Ellis Island rule

that forbids the entry of a young woman into the United States unless she is accompanied by an escort whom authorities deem proper. Although well intended, the effect is to limit the free movement of women; some are forced into weddings before they are allowed to leave Ellis Island.

Ida Tarbell publishes *History of the Standard Oil Company*, which leads to major business reforms.

Indiana's Gene Stratton-Porter—who changed her name from Geneva at the suggestion of her husband—sells 1.4 million copies of the first of her nineteen ecologically oriented novels.

1905 In *Lochner v. the United States*, the Supreme Court strikes down a New York law limiting the hours of female bakery employees as an unfair burden on employers—but it will reverse itself just three years later in *Muller v. Oregon*, when it upholds an Oregon law establishing a maximum ten-hour day for women employed in laundries. Many states also ban night work for women, with exceptions for telephone operators, nurses, and other nighttime jobs considered natural to women.

Jessie Redmon Fauset graduates from Cornell University, possibly the first black woman in the world to earn Phi Beta Kappa membership; she goes on to a distinguished literary career.

Mary Calkins is the first woman elected president of the American Psychological Association; at the century's end, she will have been the only female president of both it and the American Philosophical Association.

1906 Deaf and blind HELEN KELLER authors an article for *Ladies' Home Journal* on the connection between neonatal blindness and maternal venereal disease. Shocked by the article's candor, thousands cancel their subscriptions.

1907 The founding of Jamestown three hundred years ago is noted with a stamp on which the Post Office honors POCAHONTAS.

After her financier husband dies, Margaret Slocum Sage gives away more than $80 million, making her equivalent to Andrew Carnegie and other more famous philanthropists.

1908   Congress establishes the Navy Nurse Corps.

With Bryn Mawr president M. CAREY THOMAS as its leader, the Equal Suffrage League begins on college campuses. This is the first such organization, and its formation sixty years after the 1848 women's rights convention is indicative of the tepid support that female academicians give to suffrage. Instead, middle-class housewives are the movement's backbone.

Rose Knox takes over Knox Gelatine Company, which soon dominates the national market; it will be one of very few businesses that do not lay off a single employee during the Great Depression.

1909   Chicago is the nation's first city to have a woman, ELLA FLAGG YOUNG, at the head of its school system. The city's teachers' union is headed by Margaret A. Haley.

Over twenty thousand women in New York City's garment industry go on strike; many are assaulted by police, and over seven hundred are arrested. Upper-class women, including ALVA BELMONT and future ambassador Daisy Harriman, organize a boycott against the clothing manufacturers, who are forced to concede. Next year, Chicago women strike in even greater numbers, and JANE ADDAMS plays a supportive role.

New York's theater district features *A Man's World* by Rachel Crothers. She will write forty plays during four decades, many with feminist themes.

1910   Female authors—Florence Barclay, Mary Johnston, Frances Little, Kathleen Norris, and Mrs. Humphry Ward—hold the best-seller records during five of the past ten years.

Harriot Stanton Blatch, daughter of ELIZABETH CADY STANTON, organizes twenty thousand New Yorkers into the Women's Political Union. One of several leaders unhappy with the slow pace of the National American Woman Suffrage Association, Blatch will use innovative visibility techniques, especially parades.

1911   Last year Washington women regained the vote they lost in 1887, and this year Californians run a sophisticated winning campaign. A railroad car of women is especially effective at small-town whistle-stops.

A fire in New York's non-union Triangle Shirtwaist Factory kills 146; most are immigrant women who work behind locked doors. The tragedy leads to safety reforms.

HARRIET QUIMBY is the first American woman licensed to fly.

Gertrude Bonnin, a South Dakota Sioux, leads the Society of American Indians.

Astronomer Harriet Leavitt dies, leaving an amazing scientific legacy: since beginning work at the Harvard Observatory in 1895, she has discovered some twenty-four hundred variable stars—about half of those known to exist.

1912   The premature death of Dr. Nettie Stevens ends her important research in genetics. She was the first to discover that an embryo's sex is determined by the presence of an X or a Y chromosome in the father's sperm. Her breakthrough will not be accepted until long after her death, and meanwhile countless women continue to be blamed when their babies are not the desired sex.

Mill workers in Lawrence, Massachusetts—where conditions are so bad that one-third of textile spinners die before they work a decade—strike when management cuts their pay. Among them these immigrants speak forty languages, but they unite and endure police beatings while on strike. One woman dies, and a congressional inquiry forces owners to reverse the pay cut.

Women win full voting rights in three places: Arizona, Kansas, and Oregon. Alaska is admitted as a territory, and the first act of its legislature early next year will be granting women the vote.

1913   Woodrow Wilson is the first Democratic president in two decades, and some eight thousand women, led by ALICE PAUL, use his inauguration to stage Washington's first suffrage parade.

Illinois enacts a new form of partial suffrage that allows women to vote only in presidential elections.

Anthropologist Elsie Clews Parsons, who is married to a New York congressman, uses a male pseudonym for her book on sexual behavior. She will mentor MARGARET MEAD.

1914   Publisher MIRIAM LESLIE dies and leaves $2 million to CARRIE CHAPMAN CATT to be used for the vote; it funds more sophisticated campaigns and is crucial to victory.

Annette Adams of California is sworn in as the nation's first female assistant attorney general—with President Woodrow Wilson's support and over the objections of his attorney general.

Unknown Chicagoan Margaret Anderson begins the *Little Review*; among the writers she introduces are Robert Frost, EMMA GOLDMAN, Ernest Hemingway, Amy Lowell, and GERTRUDE STEIN.

1915   JANE ADDAMS leads forty-two women across the war-imperiled Atlantic to work for peace, while EMILY BALCH meets with several foreign ministers and briefs President Wilson on her return. Later in the year, a second group—led by former International Council of Women president May Wright Sewall of Indianapolis—makes a voyage on the "Peace Ship" funded by Henry Ford.

Montana and Nevada grant full voting rights, but four referenda in eastern states fail: the men of Massachusetts, New Jersey, Pennsylvania, and New York reject suffrage. Members of the National American Woman Suffrage Association are shocked and replace President ANNA HOWARD SHAW with CARRIE CHAPMAN CATT.

1916   Using the slogan "Every child a wanted child," MARGARET SANGER and her sister-in-law, Ethel Byrne, open a birth-control clinic in Brooklyn, New York, but are soon jailed.

Montana elects the first congresswoman, JEANNETTE RANKIN.

The more radical women led by ALICE PAUL break from the mainstream suffrage association and form the National Woman's Party.

Arkansas is the first southern state to offer women any enfranchisement—for primary elections only and effectively excluding black women. Next year, Texas adopts this model.

1917   The National Woman's Party begins picketing the White House and continues until suffrage passes. Hundreds of picketers will be arrested, jailed, and force-fed in jail.

Some women, including EMMA GOLDMAN and ELIZABETH GURLEY FLYNN, speak against the war, but most support it. Tens of thousands volunteer for the Red Cross and other organizations. Women also replace men in such occupations as streetcar driver and postal worker, while others work at dangerous munitions plants.

More than a thousand women are civilian employees of the army in Europe, working as translators, telephone operators, and ambulance drivers. Some ten thousand women serve under the aegis of the Red Cross, while the YWCA sends almost thirty-five hundred, some of whom specialize in the complex legal problems of refugees. Several YWCA women will earn France's croix de guerre.

Finally, over twenty thousand women enlist in the Army and Navy Nurse Corps; more than two hundred members of the Army Nurse Corps will die, some from the mustard gas introduced in this war.

Pulitzer Prizes are first awarded this year, and a biography of JULIA WARD HOWE by her daughters wins the biography category. However, not until 1948 does another female biographer win, and no woman writing about a woman wins until 1986.

New York becomes the first eastern state to fully enfranchise women. Women now have full rights in twelve states, eleven of which are in the West.

1918   The U.S. House passes the constitutional amendment granting the vote to all women by exactly the required two-thirds, but the Senate tally is two votes short.

Venereal disease is rampant during the war, and Congress passes the Chamberlain-Kahn Act, which calls for "mandatory examination" of any woman suspected of prostitution. Near some military posts, women have a 9:00 P.M. curfew.

In August, three months before the end of World War I, the military begins enlisting women for non-nursing jobs: 12,500 women termed "yeomen (female)" join the Navy, while the Marine Corps enlists 305 "marinettes." Most serve in Washington offices.

When the war ends, three women receive the Distinguished Service Cross and twenty-three earn the Distinguished Service Medal.

1919 Members of the new Congress take office in March. In May, the House passes the Nineteenth Amendment granting women the vote, and in June the Senate follows by a two-vote margin. Illinois, Michigan, and Wisconsin are the first to ratify, and state campaigns begin across the nation.

It is a year for new organizations: state suffrage associations begin transforming themselves into the League of Women Voters, and the National Federation of Business and Professional Women's Clubs begins, as does Zonta International, a service club for women. JANE ADDAMS is the founding president of the Women's International League for Peace and Freedom.

1920 When the legislatures of West Virginia and Washington provide the thirty-fourth and thirty-fifth votes for the Nineteenth Amendment, attention focuses on Tennessee. After weeks of complex machinations, the Tennessee legislature enfranchises all American women by a one-vote margin. The amendment is formally added to the U.S. Constitution on August 26.

At age ninety-three, Charlotte Woodward Pierce is the only woman who attended the 1848 Seneca Falls Women's Rights Convention who has lived to vote in a national election.

1921 The Roaring Twenties are visibly different from any preceding time. Skirts rise inch by scandalous inch to above the knee, but unlike women during the earlier "bloomer" stage of dress reform, flappers do not necessarily hold feminist political views. Women also adopt traditionally male habits such as smoking, drinking, and driving cars. Without visible leadership or organized movement, women liberate themselves from centuries of restrictive ways.

Congress passes the Sheppard-Towner Act, which appropriates up to $1 million annually for maternity clinics aimed at lowering infant mortality rates. It is the nation's first federal spending on women's health, but it will be repealed before the decade ends.

1922 The first woman to serve on a state supreme court is FLORENCE ALLEN, while REBECCA FELTON is the first female U.S. senator.

Oklahoma Seminoles choose Alice Brown Davis as their first female chief.

Newlyweds DeWitt and Lila Bell Acheson Wallace found *Reader's Digest*; because DeWitt was recently fired from his job, they use Lila's savings.

Playwright Anne Nichols has the era's longest-running play with *Abie's Wild Rose*, about the romance between a Jewish man and an Irish woman.

Hollywood's Lois Weber, who pioneered techniques of matching sound to film, is a producer, director, and screenwriter for hundreds of films made by such studios as Paramount and Universal.

1923 ALICE PAUL's Woman's Party introduces a proposed Equal Rights Amendment to the Constitution, but the leaders of most mainstream women's groups oppose it because it would nullify protective labor laws that they champion.

President Warren Harding, whose extramarital affairs are well known, dies suddenly; when he is buried without an autopsy, some suspect that his wife, Florence, poisoned him.

Edna St. Vincent Millay is the first woman to win the Pulitzer Prize in poetry.

1924 The Pulitzer Prize in literature goes to women in four of five years. Margaret Wilson wins this year for *The Able McLaughlin*; she joins WILLA CATHER, who won it in 1923, and EDITH WHARTON, the 1921 honoree. EDNA FERBER will win next year.

Tennis champ Hazel Hotchkiss Wightman wins the Olympic gold in tennis. Her record of forty-five national championships will stand for most of the century.

Just four years after the Nineteenth Amendment is passed, NELLIE TAYLOE ROSS of Wyoming and Miriam Ferguson of Texas become governors.

1925   The first woman invited to membership in the National Academy of Sciences is FLORENCE SABIN.

Lulu Hunt Peters sets a precedent by holding the nonfiction best-seller title for two consecutive years: *Diet and Health* is the top book in both 1924 and 1925.

1926   Seattle is the first major city to elect a woman as mayor: Bertha Landes wins on a platform of cleaning up police corruption.

Violette Neatly Anderson is the first black female attorney admitted to practice before the U.S. Supreme Court—almost a half century after the first black male was admitted.

Mae West writes and stars in *Sex*. She will be the first actor to earn a million dollars in the movie business, reaching the height of celebrity after age forty.

Dorothy Parker writes her first book, *Enough Rope*, and Anita Loos her most successful play, *Gentlemen Prefer Blondes*. Both personify the era with their cynical feminist humor. Parker ultimately will be more famous, but Loos makes much more money; she has already written some two hundred scripts for silent movies.

1927   Jazz becomes popular with white audiences, and an all-black cast featuring Ethel Waters does a Broadway show, *Africana*. Meanwhile, BESSIE SMITH's recording of "Down Hearted Blues" recently set sales records.

At age twenty-five, aviator Blanche Hill is a cofounder of Avion Corporation, which builds the first all-metal aircraft.

1928   When Norwegian explorer Roald Amundsen disappears in the Arctic, Louise Boyd organizes an expedition to search for him; she is honored by the governments of Norway and France.

Songwriter Dorothy Fields begins a career in which she is the lyricist for almost five hundred songs, including "I'm in the Mood for Love" and "The Way You Look Tonight."

1929   When Congress convenes, RUTH BRYAN OWEN has to argue for her right to be seated as a representative of Florida. Because she is the widow of an Englishman, her election opponent claims that Owen, who was born in the United States, is not an American citizen.

First Lady Lou Henry Hoover (who is also an accomplished geologist) creates an uproar when she includes Mrs. Oscar De Priest, the wife of a black congressman from Chicago, at a tea for congressional wives.

Award-winning sculptor Gertrude Vanderbilt Whitney offers to donate her avant-garde art collection—as well as a wing in which to house it—to the Metropolitan Museum of Art. The museum rejects her, and she begins the Whitney Museum.

1930   The Great Depression sets in, and just one example of its devastating effect on women is in the number of college faculty and administrative positions they hold: it peaks this year at thirty-two percent and will fall to nineteen percent by 1960.

Arkansas is the first state to simultaneously have two women in the U.S. House of Representatives; next year, it elects the first in the Senate, HATTIE CARAWAY.

Jessie Daniel Ames of Texas leads white women in founding the Association of Southern Women for the Prevention of Lynching.

1931   JANE ADDAMS is the first American woman to win the Nobel Peace Prize.

DOROTHY THOMPSON interviews Adolf Hitler and publishes a book warning of the danger he represents; she is expelled from Germany.

The National Air Race opens to women—but when Phoebe Omlie wins $12,000 and a new car for her first-place finish, women are again declared ineligible.

1932　AMELIA EARHART is the first woman to fly solo across the Atlantic. Far less attention goes to Ruth Rowland Nichols, who becomes the first female airline pilot.

The Chicago Symphony Orchestra is the first to perform a symphony by a black woman, Florence Price, who is a 1906 graduate of the New England Conservatory of Music.

Swimmer Helene Madison wins three gold medals in the Olympic Games.

Women play their first major roles inside a presidential campaign when Franklin Roosevelt uses the abilities of Molly Dewson and others in his landslide victory.

1933　FRANCES PERKINS is appointed by President Roosevelt as the first woman in the cabinet. Roosevelt also names RUTH BRYAN OWEN as the nation's first female ambassador and appoints more women to high positions than any president until late in the century.

ELEANOR ROOSEVELT is the first first lady to conduct press conferences—a boon to female journalists, who scoop their male competitors on White House stories.

Driving an old jalopy, former journalist Lorena Hickok roams the country for the next three years, anonymously checking on New Deal services for the Roosevelt administration.

1934　Esther Bubley and Dorothea Lange are among the photographers hired by New Deal programs; with MARGARET BOURKE-WHITE, they chronicle Depression-era America.

1935　The first high-level position for a black woman goes

to MARY MCLEOD BETHUNE, whom President Roosevelt names to head the Office of Minority Affairs of the National Youth Administration.

Sylvia Porter masks her gender by signing her financial column as S. F. Porter; a half century later, the column runs in 450 newspapers that reach forty million readers every day.

Ma Barker dies in a machine-gun shoot-out with federal authorities; she was the brains behind a series of midwestern bank robberies. Last year, a similar shoot-out killed the Texas outlaw team of Bonnie Parker and Clyde Barrow.

1936　SUSAN B. ANTHONY is honored on the thirtieth anniversary of her death with a stamp issued by the U.S. Post Office.

MARGARET MITCHELL's *Gone With the Wind*, published this year, will become an unparalleled book and movie success. Three years later, African American actress Hattie McDaniel will become the first black person to win an Academy Award for her portrayal of Mammy.

Publisher Blanche Knopf welcomes writers censored by European fascists. In the same year, France awards the Legion of Honor to American-born Sylvia Beach, primarily for her 1922 publication of James Joyce's *Ulysses*, which was banned as obscene.

1937　Representative MARY T. NORTON chairs the House Labor Committee; with Labor Secretary FRANCES PERKINS, she is central to legislation that will become the foundation of the modern welfare state: Social Security, minimum-wage and maximum-hour laws, unemployment compensation, and more.

ANNE O'HARE MCCORMICK is the first female correspondent to win the Pulitzer Prize in journalism.

1938　PEARL BUCK wins the Nobel Prize for literature just eight years after her first book. She will remain the only female American winner for a half century.

The first black woman in a state legislature is Philadelphia's Crystal Bird Fauset, who triumphs in a largely white district. She disappoints her supporters by soon resigning to take a local New Deal job. She later moves to a position with the Democratic Party in Washington, but when she endorses the Republican candidate in the 1944 presidential election, Fauset's political career is over.

1939 The Daughters of the American Revolution refuse to rent their hall to singer MARIAN ANDERSON, prompting widespread protest.

Anthropologist Ruth Benedict coins the word racism in her *Race: Science and Politics*.

DOROTHY SCHIFF is a major newspaper publisher in New York City, as is CISSY PATTERSON in Washington.

Clara Adams makes aviation history by piloting a Pan American Clipper around the world.

When Europe erupts in war, among those there are Mary Martin Breckinridge, who broadcasts from bombed-out London; Helen Kirkpatrick of the *Chicago Daily News*, who predicts the German invasion of Belgium eight days before it happens; and photojournalist Thérèse Bonney, who later wins France's croix de guerre.

1940 Daisy Harriman, who was appointed minister to Norway by Franklin Roosevelt in 1937, endures Nazi air raids to help Americans and others escape the German invasion.

ALICIA PATTERSON begins *Newsday*, while JESSE VANN becomes publisher of the *Pittsburgh Courier*, a national newspaper for African Americans.

Two decades after all American women got the vote, twenty-six women from sixteen states have served in Congress. The South has had far more women in Congress than any other region, even though it was the least supportive of suffrage.

1941 With America still neutral, aviator JACQUELINE COCHRAN flies a bomber from Canada to England and joins the British Air Transport Authority. She recruits other American women, who pilot 120 types of planes over Britain's dangerous skies.

Representative Edith Nourse Rogers, a Republican from Massachusetts, introduces a bill to establish the Women's Army Auxiliary Corps (WAAC); after the December declaration of war, the secretary of war supports her. Congressional debate is lengthy, but the bill will pass by a wide margin next spring.

On Christmas, women in the Army Nurse Corps are bombed as the Japanese attack the Philippines. Some escape to Australia, but most serve in Bataan and Corregidor until they become prisoners of war. About five hundred American and British women will be confined to a Manila prison camp for the next three years, where they nearly starve to death.

1942 When the first troops arrive in North Africa, over two hundred women in the Army Nurse Corps move with them. By the year's end, the first non-nurse military women, the WAACs, are in North Africa, where they are highly effective in Signal Corps communication.

Congress also creates women's units in the U.S. Navy (Women Accepted for Volunteer Emergency Service, or WAVES) and the Coast Guard (the SPARs), as well as the Women Marines. By the war's end, about a half million women serve in these new units. They work in almost all noncombat jobs, including over 400 of the army's 625 occupational categories.

Eight congressional bills are introduced to emulate Britain and draft women for compulsory work in war industries. All are sponsored by Republicans or conservative Southern Democrats and opposed by the Roosevelt administration—not because it necessarily opposes drafting women but because labor shortages are local, not national. Nonetheless, more than two-thirds of Americans consistently tell pollsters that they approve of drafting women for defense jobs.

1943 Following models developed in England and Canada, the Women's Land Army replaces male agricultural workers who go to war. Usually young urban women, they wear uniforms, live in camps, and earn low wages.

Millions of women work in aircraft factories, shipyards, and other "men's jobs," often earning the highest wages of their lives. Defense plants run twenty-four hours a day, and some offer child care and take-home meals.

An explosion at a munitions plant in Elkton, Maryland, kills fifteen and injures fifty-four, mostly women. Ammunition manufacturers hire women because they are considered to be careful workers, but the work is inherently dangerous and Elkton has another explosion this year, while the arsenal at Pine Bluff, Arkansas, also has two fires in one year. A black woman, Anne Marie Young, receives the War Department's highest civilian award for her courage in rescuing coworkers there.

1944   *Collier's* publishes the story of "thirteen nurses and seventeen men of the American Army Air Forces" whose plane was shot down in the mountains of German-occupied Albania. They walked some eight hundred miles to reach a rescue ship on the Adriatic Sea, dodging bullets and enduring blizzards.

Representative Frances Bolton of Ohio arrives in Paris two days after its liberation. Her congressional colleagues see her as their authority on nurses, and she pays her own way to check on the conditions these women face. The French later award her their Legion of Honor.

The quasi-military Women's Air Service Pilots (WASPs) is disbanded: now that the war is being won, male pilots want these jobs. Since 1942, some two thousand WASPs have flown thirty million miles; a monument at their base in Sweetwater, Texas, will honor the thirty-eight who died serving their country.

The army's "flight nurses" begin operations in remote South Pacific terrain. Lone women fly on planes that—because they carry weapons into war zones—are not marked with the Red Cross and thus are vulnerable to attack. They are amazingly successful: during the war's last thirteen months, these young women evacuate thirty-seven thousand men and lose just one patient.

1945   War casualties mean a great shortage of nurses, and President Roosevelt calls for amending the Selective Service Act to "provide for the induc-

tion of nurses into the Armed Forces." A poll shows that seventy-three percent of Americans support him, and the House approves the Nurses Selective Service Act by a vote of 347-42. The Senate Military Affairs Committee recommends it, but the army soon enters Berlin and the legislation is no longer needed. Interestingly, no one argues that the Constitution protects women from the draft—a myth that will be successfully promoted by opponents of the Equal Rights Amendment in the 1970s.

As the war ends, none of the commanders of women's military units has a rank compatible with her level of responsibility. Colonel OVETA CULP HOBBY and Captain MILDRED MCAFEE especially merit higher rank: each created an entirely new corps and commanded some hundred thousand women but had a rank given to men who command as few as five hundred.

President Roosevelt appoints Barnard College president Virginia Gildersleeve, ANNE O'HARE MCCORMICK, and RUTH BRYAN OWEN to meetings that form the United Nations. After Roosevelt's death, President Harry Truman adds MARY MCLEOD BETHUNE, and when the U.N. charter is finalized, she is the world's only woman of color who has official status. Truman also insists that ELEANOR ROOSEVELT accept a leading role.

1946   The largest strike by American women occurs when 230,000 telephone operators walk off the job.

Representative Edith Nourse Rogers chairs the House Committee on Veterans Affairs, where she develops the historic GI Bill. Representative Francis Bolton chairs the Committee on Foreign Affairs Subcommittee on the Near East and Africa; next year, she will be the first woman received by the king of Saudi Arabia.

EMILY BALCH wins the Nobel Peace Prize, while MOTHER CABRINI is the first American citizen declared a saint.

1947   Martha Rountree is the cocreator and moderator of *Meet the Press*, which at the end of the century is television's longest-running program.

Academy Award winner Hattie McDaniel stars in the popular radio show *Beulah* and earns $2,000 a week. She refuses to use stereotyped black dialect.

Theater's Tony Awards are named for actor-producer Antoinette Perry Frueauff, known as Tony Perry, who died last year. Among her most successful Broadway productions was *Harvey*, which won a 1945 Pulitzer Prize for playwright Mary Chase.

1948 The Women's Armed Services Integration Act regularizes the Women's Army Corps, the WAVES, and other military women's corps. The Air Force separates from the Army, and its female unit is dubbed the Women's Air Force, or WAF. The legislation imposes a quota on women of two percent of total forces and limits their rank, benefits, and occupational categories but nonetheless is an important milestone, marking the first non-nursing women in the peacetime military.

Portland, Oregon, is the second city to elect a woman, Dorothy McCullough Lee, as mayor. Seattle was the first more than two decades earlier.

On the 100th anniversary of the first Women's Rights Convention, the U.S. Post Office issues a stamp featuring ELIZABETH CADY STANTON and LUCRETIA MOTT, who convened the event, as well as CARRIE CHAPMAN CATT, the suffragist who led the completion of the 1848 goal.

1949 Paper money has a female name on it for the first time when President Truman appoints banker Georgia Neese Clark as United States treasurer. He also names Pearl Mesta and Eugenie Moore Anderson as ambassadors to Luxembourg and Denmark. Activist India Edwards urges him to appoint these and other women but will reject his offer of the Democratic Party chairmanship for herself.

Sports writers declare MILDRED "BABE" ZAHARIAS the outstanding woman athlete of the century.

1950 President Truman appoints the century's only female assistant secretary of defense, ANNA ROSENBERG.

For the first time in American history, women are called involuntarily to military service along with men, when thirteen platoons of Women Marine Reserves are mobilized for the Korean War.

Senator Margaret Chase Smith of Maine denounces her fellow Republican, Senator Joseph McCarthy, for his abuse of those he considers "soft on communism." When McCarthy tries to take revenge by endorsing her opponent, Smith wins an amazing eighty-two percent of the vote.

The election features the first large-state Senate race between a man and a woman, and Republican Richard Nixon beats Democrat Helen Gahagan Douglas, a congresswoman since 1944. So vicious are the attacks on her and her film-star husband, Melvyn Douglas, that other women, especially Democrats, are deterred from running.

1951 Three women begin multimillion-dollar companies this year. Lillian Vernon starts a mail-order business in her home, and four decades later, almost half of American households get her company's catalog. Rose Totino bakes a pizza for a Minneapolis loan officer who does not know what pizza is; she later sells her business to Pillsbury for $22 million. Marion Donovan patents the disposable diaper; several manufacturers turn her idea down, saying production will not be cost efficient.

1952 The House Un-American Activities Committee targets Lillian Hellman, whose prize-winning plays explored topics such as women's resistance to fascism and women accused of lesbianism. Next year, the committee questions the patriotism of seventy-year-old labor expert Mary Van Kleeck, whose American heritage dates to Dutch colonial New York.

1953 Despite worldwide protests of her innocence, ETHEL ROSENBERG becomes the only woman in American history to be executed for espionage.

President Dwight Eisenhower appoints the second woman to the cabinet: OVETA CULP HOBBY heads the new Department of Health, Education, and Welfare. Eisenhower names CLARE BOOTH LUCE ambassador to Italy.

NBC's Pauline Fredrick is the first woman to have a serious television news beat, but it will be another two decades before female reporters are routine on television.

1954   The first African American woman nominated for an Academy Award for best actress is Dorothy Dandridge; she is also the first black woman to have her picture on the cover of *Life*, the nation's most popular magazine.

Dr. VIRGINIA APGAR develops a system for measuring the health of newborns that, as the Apgar score, becomes the hospital standard.

Ann Landers is the pseudonym that Esther Friedman Lederer uses for her advice column, while her twin, Pauline Friedman Phillips, goes by the name Abigail Van Buren, or "Dear Abby." They keep their kinship secret from their millions of readers for years.

In Montgomery, Alabama, seamstress ROSA PARKS refuses to give her bus seat to a white man. Her arrest is the catalyst for the Montgomery bus boycott, an early highlight of the modern civil rights movement.

1956   Long before more-famous college integrations by black men, AUTHERINE LUCY sets the southern precedent by enrolling for classes at the University of Alabama; riots break out.

McCall's has its highest single-issue sales ever with a cover story titled "The Mother Who Ran Away."

Women found the La Leche League to promote breast-feeding—something most physicians discourage. Physicians will also dissent two years later, when the Childbirth Without Pain Education Association begins to educate women on Lamaze techniques for labor and delivery.

1957   Columbia University announces that the law of parity, which had governed modern physics, has been disproved by Dr. Chien-Shiung Wu, a physicist who worked on producing fissionable uranium for the atomic bomb during World War II.

DAISY BATES, head of the Arkansas branch of the National Association for the Advancement of Colored People (NAACP), leads school integration efforts in Little Rock.

1958   African American tennis champ ALTHEA GIBSON is named woman athlete of the year by the Associated Press.

New Jersey bank president Mary Roebling is the first woman on the thirty-two-member board of governors of the American Stock Exchange.

The founding president of the American Association of Retired Persons is Ethel Percy Andrus, a retired organizer of teachers.

1959   The first black winner of the New York Drama Critics' Circle Award is LORRAINE HANSBERRY, author of *A Raisin in the Sun*.

At age forty-one, Phyllis Diller opens the door for women in late-night television with her success in stand-up comedy.

1960   The birth-control pill receives federal approval and goes on the market. The pill, which was initially researched with funds raised by MARGARET SANGER, will enable women to live with unprecedented freedom.

Two days before the filing deadline for his reelection, Senator Richard Neuberger of Oregon dies; his widow, Maurine Neuberger, files and defeats other Democrats, as well as the Republican nominee, an ex-governor.

Look magazine features Floridian Betty Skelton, who holds speed records in both airplanes and race cars; she has driven cars at more than three hundred miles per hour.

1961   President John Kennedy creates the nation's first Commission on the Status of Women; it is chaired by ELEANOR ROOSEVELT.

The Supreme Court upholds a Florida law that keeps women off most juries. Eighteen other states have versions of this law, while three—Alabama, Mississippi, and South Carolina—bar women from juries completely.

McCall's publishes a story by one of the twenty-six women who have undergone the grueling two-year program administered to male astronauts. Although half of the women pass—a rate similar to that of the men—the National Aeronautics and Space Administration (NASA) cancels the women's participation.

The Pulitzer Prize in literature goes to Harper Lee (whose full name is Nell Harper Lee) for *To Kill a Mockingbird*.

1962   Dr. Frances Oldham Kelsey of the Food and Drug Administration is honored for keeping thalidomide off the U.S. market; the tranquilizer has caused severe birth defects in Europe. More attention goes to Sherri Finkbine, a children's television personality and mother of four who discovers that her exposure to the tranquilizer thalidomide has caused her fetus to be badly deformed; her appeals for a legal abortion in Arizona are denied, and she goes to Sweden.

Although women have served in the U.S. House of Representatives for almost a half century, only now is the first appointed to the powerful Committee on Ways and Means. Democrat Martha Griffiths of Michigan will lead public hearings that reveal inequities to women in credit, insurance, and other economic areas.

RACHEL CARSON's *Silent Spring* becomes the foundation for the modern environmental movement, while *Sex and the Single Girl* is a huge seller for Helen Gurley Brown.

Dolores Huerta is a cofounder of the United Farm Workers.

1963   Congress passes the Equal Pay Act, which was first proposed during World War II.

BETTY FRIEDAN publishes *The Feminine Mystique* and quickly becomes the leader of a newly revitalized women's movement.

When the first Weight Watchers office opens in New York City, entrepreneur Jean Nidetch has to have her husband sign the lease.

1964   Texan Lyndon Johnson pushes the 1964 Civil Rights Act through a reluctant Congress soon after he assumes the presidency. The act bans discrimination based on race, religion, and other factors—and "sex" is added as an afterthought.

Although she is not the first woman to run for president, Senator Margaret Chase Smith of Maine is the first to have traditional credentials. She runs in several Republican primaries but does not come close to winning the nomination.

Civil rights leader FANNIE LOU HAMER draws national attention, while fellow Mississippian Hazel Brannon Smith, a white woman, is the first female editor to win a Pulitzer Prize for her editorial support of integration; racists bomb her Jackson office.

A weekly newspaper in suburban Ohio begins publishing humor columns by Erma Bombeck—paying her $3 for each.

1965   The Supreme Court rules in *Griswold v. Connecticut* that states may not ban the distribution of contraceptives to married people.

Septima Poinsette Clark, an African American who was fired from the school system of Charleston, South Carolina, less than a decade ago because of her NAACP membership, is elected to its school board.

President Lyndon Johnson appoints PATRICIA ROBERTS HARRIS as the first black female ambassador; next year, he will make CONSTANCE BAKER MOTLEY the first black woman on the federal judiciary.

Viola Gregg Liuzzo, a young white mother who went from Detroit to Selma to march with Martin Luther King Jr., is killed by Alabama racists.

1966   In July, Richard Speck kills eight Chicago nursing students. In August, Charles Whitman kills his wife and mother and then randomly kills twelve people, including a pregnant woman, at the University of Texas. In September, Valerie Percy, daughter of a leading Illinois politician, is stabbed to death in her home. Emulating these men, an Arizona high-school senior enters a Mesa beauty shop, forces the women to lie on the floor, and methodically shoots them; five die.

The Group, by novelist Mary McCarthy, reflects changing values among Vassar-educated women like herself. Also this year, Katherine Anne Porter wins the Pulitzer Prize for *Ship of Fools* at age seventy-six, and Anaïs Nin begins to publish a ten-volume diary that makes her a feminist cult figure.

The National Organization for Women (NOW) is founded in October; BETTY FRIEDAN becomes president.

1967 The National Education Association elects the first black president in its 106-year history, Elizabeth Koontz of North Carolina.

Lurleen Wallace is the third woman to become governor, but Alabama elects her because incumbent George Wallace is ineligible for reelection. She married him at age sixteen and makes it clear during the campaign that he will be the real governor.

1968 The only member of Congress to have voted against both world wars, eighty-eight-year-old JEANNETTE RANKIN leads some five thousand women in a Capitol Hill protest against the Vietnam War.

The 1968 Civil Rights Act passes; its primary purpose is to ensure racial equity in housing and public facilities, but it also will benefit women.

Muriel Siebert spends $445,000 and becomes the first woman to purchase a seat on the 176-year-old New York Stock Exchange.

Yale University announces that, for the first time since its 1718 formation, it will admit women at the undergraduate level. Similar change is also occurring at other Ivy League schools.

1969 SHIRLEY CHISOLM is the first African American woman in Congress.

California adopts the nation's first "no-fault" divorce law, which permits divorce by mutual consent. Other states follow so quickly that divorce reform soon moves off NOW's agenda.

1970 The military finally has its first women of top rank when Anna Mae Hays, chief of the Army Nurse Corps (which has existed since 1901), and Elizabeth P. Hoisington, director of the Women's Army Corps, are promoted to brigadier general.

New York passes a liberalized abortion law, and hospitals are swamped with out-of-state women seeking legal abortions.

To commemorate the fiftieth anniversary of the ratification of the Nineteenth Amendment, which ensured women's right to vote, NOW promotes a one-day strike by women on August 26. Some ten thousand New Yorkers march, and, for the first time in the history of women's rights parades, lesbians are openly included.

1971 The National Women's Political Caucus begins; among its founders are Representative BELLA ABZUG, Representative SHIRLEY CHISOLM, and journalist GLORIA STEINEM. Next year, Steinem begins *Ms.* magazine.

Oklahoma City elects Patience Latting as mayor.

1972 Congress passes the Equal Rights Amendment to the Constitution, which has languished since 1923. The revived feminism of the 1970s is strong enough that both the House and the Senate provide the necessary two-thirds vote without significant debate. Hawaii is the first state to ratify.

Congress also passes legislation to end historical discrimination against girls and women in education. Particular attention will focus on what becomes known as Title IX, the portion of the act that bans schools from spending more money on athletic programs for males than it does on those for females—something that has long been routine.

In a Massachusetts case, the Supreme Court expands its 1965 *Griswold v. Connecticut* decision and makes birth control available regardless of marital status.

Representative SHIRLEY CHISHOLM runs in presidential primaries and receives 151 votes at the Democratic convention—appreciably more than Senator Margaret Chase Smith's 27 votes at the Republican convention eight years ago. When Smith loses her reelection bid this year, the Senate becomes all male for the first time since 1948.

1973   By a 7-2 vote, an all-male Supreme Court hands down a decision that may have more impact on women than any single ruling in the Court's history, for it has the effect of legalizing abortion throughout the nation. The Court rules on both *Roe v. Wade*, a Texas case argued by SARAH WEDDINGTON, and *Doe v. Bolton*, a Georgia case presented by Margie Pitts Hames. *Roe* becomes the public focus because the Texas law was more severe.

The Supreme Court also supports women in other cases. In *Frontiero v. Richardson*, it says that spouses of male and female military members are entitled to equal benefits. It rules against a Pittsburgh newspaper that—like most American papers—separates jobs in classified ads by gender. Last year, the Court struck down an Idaho law giving automatic preference to men as executors of estates. At least to some extent, these and other victories negate the need for the Equal Rights Amendment.

Millions watch Billie Jean King trounce Bobby Riggs in a televised tennis match at the Houston Astrodome. He and most sports experts have proclaimed that a woman cannot beat a man.

1974   Four Episcopalian bishops ignore their church's edicts and ordain eleven women in Philadelphia.

Connecticut elects ELLA GRASSO, the first female governor whose political career is independent of any male relative.

1975   Fifteen years after the birth-control pill went on the market, seventy-nine percent of married white women of childbearing age use contraception, despite continued Catholic bans.

The last American woman killed in Vietnam is Captain Mary T. Klinker, an Air Force flight nurse who dies evacuating Vietnamese orphans when their plane crashes. About 11,500 women served in Vietnam, mostly as nurses.

The Supreme Court strikes down selection processes intended to keep women off juries. The influence of the women's movement is clear: the Court had upheld similar laws in 1961.

1976   The nation celebrates its second centennial. For women, it is a great contrast to the first, from which SUSAN B. ANTHONY and others were excluded in 1876; this year, the fact that Congress's Joint Committee on Bicentennial Arrangements is chaired by a woman, Representative Lindy Boggs of Louisiana, goes almost unnoticed.

Women lobby Congress into requiring the military to open its prestigious academies to women. Female cadets go to the U.S. Army's West Point, the Naval Academy at Annapolis, and the Air Force Academy in Colorado Springs.

Scientist DIXY LEE RAY wins the governorship of Washington.

1977   President Jimmy Carter is the first to appoint two women to his cabinet.

Indiana becomes the thirty-fifth of the necessary thirty-eight states to ratify the Equal Rights Amendment, but the amendment stalls this year. Four states refuse to ratify, while three try to rescind their previous ratifications—a situation without legal precedent.

More than a thousand female runners carry a torch from the historic birthplace of the women's movement at Seneca Falls, New York, to Houston, where the United Nations Decade of Women attracts huge crowds.

ROSALYN SUSSMAN YALOW wins the Nobel Prize in physiology or medicine, while race-car drivers Janet Guthrie and Shirley Muldowney fill the sports pages.

1978   After issuing nearly fifty stamps related to women during the eighty years since the first such stamp, the U.S. Post Office acknowledges African American women with a stamp honoring HARRIET TUBMAN.

More than fifty years after women started voting, Nancy Kassebaum of Kansas is the first female senator who did not have a husband precede her in Congress; her father, however, was the 1936 Republican presidential nominee.

Illinois, the only major northern state that has not ratified the Equal Rights Amendment, votes it down despite a strong campaign.

Although women tested as well as men in 1961, only this year does NASA include six women in its astronaut program.

1979 By the biggest margin since 1901, Chicago elects Jane Byrne as mayor; San Francisco elects Dianne Feinstein.

Mormon officials excommunicate Sonia Johnson, a former missionary with four children, because of her support of the Equal Rights Amendment.

Spousal abuse begins to be broadly discussed this year when cases in California, Massachusetts, and Oregon set precedents for wives who resist abusive husbands.

1980 President Carter proclaims the week of March 8, which includes the UN's International Women's Day, as National Women's History Week. During the next decade, March will become Women's History Month, largely because of the California-based National Women's History Project. Also this year, historian Barbara Tuchman is the first woman elected president of the American Academy of Arts and Letters.

The nation's first clinic for in vitro fertilization opens in Norfolk, Virginia, and Mothers Against Drunk Driving begins in California.

Sherry Lansing is the first female chief executive officer of a major Hollywood studio, 20th Century Fox, while the Reverend Marjorie Matthew of Michigan, a Methodist, is America's

first woman to sit on the governing board of a major religion.

The presidential campaign gives almost no attention to the fact that Ronald Reagan is divorced. A generation ago, divorce was an insurmountable political handicap.

1981 When a vacancy occurs on the U.S. Supreme Court, women lobby hard to have the first woman appointed. SANDRA DAY O'CONNOR of Arizona is unanimously confirmed by the Senate; earlier, she was the first female president of a state senate. O'Connor reveals that after graduating from law school in 1951, the only jobs she was offered were secretarial.

Female government employees in San Jose strike for the principle of "comparable worth"—reevaluating "women's jobs" based on their true skill level so that, for example, nurses earn more than garbage collectors.

President Reagan does not continue the twenty-year-old Presidential Commission on the Status of Women.

Kathy Whitmire defeats an incumbent to become mayor of Houston.

1982 The Equal Rights Amendment dies; when the ratification period expires, it is three states short of the needed three-fourths vote.

The Vietnam Veterans Memorial, designed by MAYA YING LIN, is dedicated in Washington, D.C.

What will become a long-term gender gap appears clearly this year: fifty-nine percent of women vote for Democratic congressional candidates and only thirty-eight percent for Republicans.

1983 BARBARA MCCLINTOCK wins the Nobel Prize in physiology or medicine. Other women play major roles in introducing the public to the newly discovered disease AIDS.

SALLY RIDE becomes the first American woman in space. Next year, Kathy Sullivan will be the first woman to walk in space.

For the first time since the award's 1943 inception, a woman, ELLEN TAAFFE ZWILICH, wins the Pulitzer Prize for a musical composition.

1984   The Southern Baptist Convention passes a resolution against the ordination of women.

Nurses go on strike in Minnesota.

The Democratic Party nominates GERALDINE FERRARO for vice president. Kentucky elects MARTHA LAYNE COLLINS as governor, while Vermont elects MADELEINE KUNIN.

1985   Soon after President Reagan's second inaugural, Jeane Kirkpatrick resigns as his ambassador to the United Nations. She obtains a $900,000 book advance and reveals that she felt excluded by Washington foreign-policy decision makers.

The Cherokee Nation chooses WILMA MANKILLER as its first female chief.

After years of debate, the Conservative Rabbinical Assembly admits female rabbis as members.

Dian Fossey, who has lived with African gorillas for two decades, is found murdered in Zaire.

1986   Among the seven killed when the *Challenger* space shuttle explodes are veteran astronaut Judith Resnick and science teacher Christa McAuliffe.

The Supreme Court hears its first sexual harassment case and strongly declares that demands for sexual favors on the job are illegal. It also strikes down a Pennsylvania law intended to discourage abortions by making them more difficult to obtain.

KAY ORR of Nebraska is the first Republican woman elected governor; eight Democrats have served. Two women run in a close U.S. Senate race in Maryland: Democrat Barbara Mikulski defeats Republican Linda Chavez.

1987   "Surrogate motherhood" fills the news during the "Baby M" case. A New Jersey judge allows Elizabeth Stern to adopt her husband's child,

thus enforcing the contract that Mary Beth Whitehead made with the Sterns in which Whitehead agreed to become pregnant with Stern's sperm and allow the couple to adopt the child she bore.

The National Museum of Women in the Arts opens in Washington.

1988   GERTRUDE ELION wins the Nobel Prize in physiology or medicine.

When the governor of Arizona is forced to resign, Secretary of State Rose Mofford, a Democrat, becomes governor; she serves until 1991.

President Reagan vetoes legislation intended to end gender discrimination in colleges by withholding their federal funds, but Congress overrides his veto.

Susan Estrich is the first woman to manage a presidential campaign—that of Democrat Michael Dukakis.

1989   Media attention to the Missouri case of *Webster v. Reproductive Health Services* implies that the Supreme Court is on the verge of reversing its 1973 *Roe v. Wade* decision on abortion.

Even though eighty percent of its members are women, the American Library Association, founded in 1876, only now has its first female executive director.

1990   During the two decades since the revival of the organized women's movement, women have gone from 6 percent to 27 percent of lawyers and judges, from 16 percent to 38 percent of pharmacists, from 11 percent to 22 percent of physicians, from 13 percent to 30 percent of stockbrokers, and from 14 percent to 44 percent of economists.

With the exception of 1951 cowinner Marguerite Higgins, no women won the Pulitzer Prize for international reporting during the first four decades of the prize's existence, but four won between 1981 and 1990.

Dr. ANTONIA NOVELLO, a native Puerto Rican, is the first female U.S. surgeon general. Sharon Pratt Dixon is the first female mayor of Washington, D.C., and Eleanor Holmes Norton is the city's representative in Congress; both are African Americans.

Three women—all Democrats—win elections for governor. ANN RICHARDS of Texas draws the most attention, but BARBARA ROBERTS also wins in Oregon; not only does JOAN FINNEY of Kansas upset an incumbent, but her election also makes Kansas the first state to have women as both governor and U.S. senator.

1991   In *Rust v. Sullivan*, the Supreme Court not only chips away at the right to privacy established by *Roe v. Wade* but also assails free speech by ruling that health professionals in clinics receiving government funds may not answer patients' questions on abortion except to discourage it. The only woman on the Court, SANDRA DAY O'CONNOR, dissents from the 5-4 ruling.

The United States women's soccer team wins the World Cup in China, but relatively few notice. In 1999, however, when the games are played in California, millions of Americans will watch intensely as the United States again beats China.

1992   The nation's first female poet laureate is seventy-one-year-old Mona Van Duyn of St. Louis, who won the Pulitzer Prize last year.

MAE JEMISON is the first African American woman in space.

In an election year called "the year of the woman," twenty-four women win races for the U.S. House of Representatives. California becomes the first state to simultaneously have two women, Dianne Feinstein and Barbara Boxer, in the U.S. Senate, while Illinois is the first state to elect an African American female senator, CAROL MOSELEY-BRAUN. The Senate reaches a historic peak with six women among its hundred members; all but Nancy Kassebaum of Kansas are Democrats.

1993   President Clinton appoints the most women ever to top positions: three serve as cabinet members,

including JANET RENO, who, as attorney general, is the highest-ranked woman ever in the executive branch. Several women head federal agencies, while the White House budget director is Alice Rivlin and the chair of the President's Council of Economic Advisers is Laura D'Andrea. The most prestigious diplomatic appointment goes to a woman for the first time, when Pamela Churchill Harriman becomes ambassador to France. MADELEINE ALBRIGHT is ambassador to the United Nations, Sheila Widnal is secretary of the Air Force, and later this year, Clinton appoints the second female member of the Supreme Court, RUTH BADER GINSBERG.

The nation observes its first "Take Our Daughters to Work Day."

Dr. David Gunn is killed by anti-abortion activist Michael Griffin in Pensacola, Florida. Next year, also in Pensacola, the Reverend Paul Hill will fatally shoot two older men who volunteer to protect women at clinics.

TONI MORRISON wins the Nobel Prize for literature—the first to an American woman in more than a half century.

New Jersey elects CHRISTINE TODD WHITMAN as governor; she is the thirteenth female governor and the second female Republican to be elected. Also this year, the predominantly white city of Minneapolis elects African American Sharon Sayles Belton as mayor.

1994   The American Bar Association chooses its first female president—Roberta Cooper Ramo, a New Mexican of Native American descent—and Judith Rodin of the University of Pennsylvania becomes the first woman to serve as president of an Ivy League institution.

Congress passes the Violence Against Women Act, which makes it a federal crime to cross state lines with the intent to injure, harass, or intimidate a spouse or domestic partner.

1995   Women and minorities make up fifty-eight percent of President Clinton's judicial appointments, compared with thirteen percent for the Bush administration and eight percent for the Reagan administration during the comparable period of their first two years in office.

Myrlie Evers-Williams is the first woman to head the NAACP; she ousts the incumbent after he is charged with corruption and sexual harassment.

When Representative Patricia Schroeder of Colorado announces that she will not seek reelection, her colleagues from both parties acknowledge in Congressional retirement ceremonies that "every woman in this house is walking in her footsteps." Schroeder has led almost every important advance for women during the past two decades.

1996   Shannon Lucid sets an endurance record for American astronauts during six months aboard the Russian space station, *Mir*.

The Food and Drug Administration approves the French pill known as RU-486 as a safe method of terminating early pregnancies, but pharmaceutical manufacturers are reluctant to expose themselves to anti-abortion violence and consumer boycotts.

The one-hundred member Senate reaches a historic high of nine women, and women hold 49 of 435 House seats. JEANNE SHAHEEN is elected governor of New Hampshire.

1997   The third American woman to win the Nobel Peace Prize is Vermont's Jody Williams; she shares it with the organization she created in 1991, the International Campaign to Ban Landmines, which has chapters in some sixty countries.

When the incumbent is forced to resign, Secretary of State Jane Dee Hull of Arizona becomes that state's governor. She is only the third Republican among fifteen female governing during the twentieth century.

After tireless fund-raising headed by General Wilma Vaught, the Women in Military Service to America foundation dedicates an Arlington Cemetery memorial to the nearly two million women who have served in the armed forces.

1998   The 150th anniversary of the first women's rights convention is celebrated in Seneca Falls, New York, where the movement began.

The news is absorbed with President Bill Clinton's personal life after his relationship with young Monica Lewinsky is revealed. Just before its Christmas break, the House impeaches him; early in 1999, the Senate will acquit. Women vote differently from men: eight of the nine female senators—including two of the three Republicans—vote against the charges.

1999   NASA's 95th shuttle mission into space is the first to be commanded by a woman, Colonel Eileen Collins, who in 1995 was also the first woman to pilot a spacecraft.

In what may be the most watched women's athletic event ever, the United States defeats China in World Cup Soccer.

For expansion of these and other news developments in 1999, please refer to Part One: News.

Women's History, State-by-State

Alabama

Alabama was the third state to elect a woman as governor, but its most famous woman opposed this governor. In most of the state's history, women were not a political factor.

The Creek, Choctaw, Cherokee, and Chickasaw Indians built permanent communities in which women were the primary agriculturists. Alabama saw little colonial settlement until after the War of 1812. Missionaries found native women there more willing than men to adopt European ways: Catherine Brown, for example, was a Creek who ran a school for girls in the early 1820s. When Congress passed the Indian Removal Act in 1830, however, those natives who had not already vacated Alabama were brutally moved west.

Cotton planters from the Carolinas and Virginia replaced the natives, and Alabama developed into a plantation society where black women labored in the fields along with black men; meanwhile, white women, in the absence of men busy with politics and war, exercised much more managerial ability than is usually recognized. The Civil War changed this lifestyle but did not completely end it. Some thirty-five thousand Alabama men were killed, leaving widows to bring up children in an economy that offered them few opportunities. Yet, although Montgomery was briefly the capital of the Confederacy, Alabama suffered less from the war than its neighbors did.

Iron mines around Birmingham made it the industrial center of the South in the late nineteenth century, but most of Alabama remained a nearly feudalistic agricultural society until well into the twentieth century. Its few educational opportunities were limited to the affluent, which meant that the state sometimes lost young people who went away to school and never returned—Alabama natives HELEN KELLER and ALVA BELMONT among them.

In the 1880s, Julia Strudwick Tutwiler led a reform movement that created teacher-training and vocational schools for women, and in the next decade she persuaded the University of Alabama to admit women. These institu-tions, however, were intended only for white women; the best opportunity for blacks was Tuskegee Institute, which began in 1881 and was funded largely by northern whites, many of them women. Although Tuskegee and its counterparts were coeducational, the curriculum was segregated by sex: men learned agriculture and trades such as carpentry, while women worked on sewing and other domestic skills.

The notion of female suffrage was taboo in Alabama. The first discussion did not occur until 1902, when a revision of the state constitution proposed granting the vote to women with more than $500 worth of property—but only on tax referenda. Even that idea had a brief life, and it was not until 1912—more than four decades after the Civil War—that Alabama suffragists finally organized. With Birmingham's Pattie Ruffner Jacobs as their president, they staged a determined but unsuccessful fight for the next eight years. They raised money, hired a field organizer, sent out biweekly press releases, held parades, organized a men's committee, and maintained a headquarters in Selma.

The 1950s brought Alabama's greatest change, and a woman was its greatest catalyst: ROSA PARKS electrified the nation when she went to jail rather than give up her bus seat to a white man in 1955. The next year, AUTHERINE LUCY did something equally heroic, if less recognized: before any man, she attempted to integrate a southern state university. The University of Alabama caved in to rioters, but Lucy bravely withstood them. In 1961, a white Alabamian named Nell Harper Lee published *To Kill a Mockingbird* under the name Harper Lee. Her best-seller won the Pulitzer Prize—the first to go to a woman in nineteen years—became an acclaimed film, and helped fuel a national conversation on racial justice. Racism exploded on Sunday, September 15, 1963, when dynamite went off in a Birmingham church, killing four black girls: Addie Mae Collins, Cynthia Wesley, and Carole Robertson and Denise McNair.

In 1966 Alabama became the third state to choose a woman as governor. Lurleen Wallace campaigned as a surrogate for her husband, populist segregationist George

Wallace, who was unable to run because of term limits. She defeated nine male opponents to win the Democratic primary (the only significant election at the time) with fifty-four percent of the vote. Elected at age thirty-nine, Wallace died of cancer less than three years later.

Between 1937 and 1978, four Alabama women were appointed to vacancies in Congress—two each in the House and the Senate. Currently, Alabama is one of eight states that have never elected a congresswoman.

Alaska

Alaskan women had full voting rights before most other American women—just as soon as it became a U.S. territory.

The early Inuit and Aleut inhabitants were nomadic, peaceful people whose women held a relatively high status. Although female infanticide did occur during hard times, adult women had more self-determination than in most societies. Marriage was informal, divorce was easy, and there was almost no sense of male ownership of women.

Europeans explored Alaska's coastline in 1728, but few whites settled there. Russian fur traders predominated until 1867, when the United States paid Russia $7.2 million to give up its claim to Alaska. Americans rarely moved there, though, and—even after an 1896 gold strike—the population remained so low that Alaska was not organized into a territory until 1912.

Men on America's western frontiers valued women who endured the dangers and discomforts; hoping to attract more women, they typically were quick to grant legal rights. Alaska was the most difficult of any frontier, and women seemed amazed at the ease with which they became voters in the new territorial government. Without any organized political action, two men—with constituencies fifteen hundred miles apart—arrived at the first legislative session with bills for equal suffrage. It was the first act to pass, with unanimous votes in both houses of the state legislature, and on March 21, 1913, the governor signed equal suffrage into law.

Areas of inequality remained, however. Alaskan women did not sit on juries, and all civil rights were curtailed by ethnicity. Indian women could vote only if they were married to white men or if they had "severed tribal relations." In 1920, feminists estimated that fewer than five hundred native women voted, compared with some six thousand white women and thirty thousand white men. This imbalance continued through the twentieth century.

Most Alaskan women were adventurers. They followed in the tradition of Alice Cunningham Fletcher, an ethnologist who went to Alaska in 1886 at the request of the secretary of state; Fletcher's reports on the condition of native peoples there and in the American West resulted in major legislation on Native American issues.

Alaska was vital to American security in World War II, and at war's end, Alaskans began agitating for statehood. Some natives argued for better treatment in this new state; during 1945 hearings, the moving testimony of Elizabeth Peratrovich was key to legislation ensuring access to public accommodations and fair housing to all Alaskans.

Statehood was granted in 1959, but Alaska's population remains so small that it is still entitled to just one member in the House of Representatives. This is doubtless a factor in its undistinguished record on electing women: Alaska is one of the seven states that have never been represented by a woman in Congress or as governor. The tradition of female adventurism continues, however, and in 1985 Libby Riddles made global headlines when she was the first woman to win Alaska's brutal dogsled race, the Iditarod. Susan Butcher carried on this tradition; at the end of the century, she is the only person to have won three consecutive Iditarod trophies.

Arizona

At the end of the twentieth century, Arizona was unique in that all its top state officials were women. It also was one of the two states that twice had a female governor.

The prehistoric people in what would become Arizona lived in pueblos (towns) built in canyons. Women grew corn in fields irrigated with carefully retained water and harvested wild foods and medicines from the deserts and mountains. The Spanish arrived in 1535, but the first permanent white settlement did not exist until 1776, when a military post, or presidio, was established at what would become Tucson. The United States acquired the land in 1848, and the Arizona Territory was added to the Union in 1863 during the Civil War—but its population, especially its female inhabitants, remained sparse for decades.

The negative impression Americans held of Arizona was reinforced by an 1858 best-seller, *Captivity of the Oatman Girls: Among the Apache and Mohave Indians.* In it, teenager Olive Oatman described how Indians killed her parents and four of her siblings in 1851; another sister, taken captive with Olive, starved to death during a drought that decimated the Mojave people. Life in Arizona was so harsh that few went there by choice, and most of its white women were army wives: Martha Summerhayes, who wrote *Vanished Arizona* at Fort Apache in the 1870s is one example.

Jessie Benton Frémont was Arizona's first lady from 1878 to 1882. Other notable women of the era were Pauline Cushman, who spied for the Union in the Civil War and ran Arizona hotels in the 1880s, and Nellie Cashman, who was called "the angel of Tombstone" when she shared the wealth from her mining activities. Pearl Hart attracted national attention as the last of the stagecoach robbers; at her 1899 trial, Hart delivered a feminist message on the injustice of punishing women under laws they could play no part in writing.

After speeches by Kansas suffragist Laura Johns and other women, an 1891 constitutional convention rejected suffrage by just three votes. Women immediately organized a state suffrage association, with Mrs. L.C. Hughes, the wife of a future governor, as president. When Johns returned in subsequent winters, the two women campaigned in Tucson, Yuma, Prescott, and other cities. CARRIE CHAPMAN CATT spent a month in Phoenix in 1899, when the House voted 10 to 5 for suffrage, but the leader of the upper chamber, Morris Goldwater, refused to allow a vote. In 1903, suffrage passed both houses by a two-thirds margin, but it was vetoed by territorial Governor Alexander O. Brodie.

A 1910 constitutional convention also turned women down, as did the 1911 legislature. Angry that they were excluded when Arizona entered the Union in February 1912, women in every county volunteered to gather petitions to put the question on the September ballot. Although their elected leaders snubbed women, Arizona's men followed the democratic tradition of other frontiers and enfranchised them by a vote of 13,442 to 6,202.

Unlike women in most states, those in Arizona immediately ran for office following enfranchisement. Frances Munds, president of the suffrage association, was elected to the Senate and Rachel Berry to the House, so the second legislature in the state's history included two women, and three women won legislative races in the state's third election. All were married, most were from rural areas, and most had been active in the suffrage campaign. In 1920, when the Nineteenth Amendment—which enfranchised women throughout the country—passed out of Congress, both Arizona's congressmen and its legislature supported it unanimously.

In the following decades, two Arizona women distinguished themselves in architecture and construction. Millions of tourists have seen Mary Colter's work at the Grand Canyon's Watch Tower and Marguerite Staude's Chapel of the Holy Cross at Sedona. During the Depression, Arizona elected its first woman to Congress: Isabella Greenway. After seconding Franklin Roosevelt's nomination at the 1932 Democratic National Convention, Greenway won a congressional seat in a special election in 1933. She was a respected businesswoman, and her connections brought important New Deal projects to Arizona.

In 1960 Arizona became the first state to have a woman, Lorna Lockwood, as chief justice of its supreme court. SANDRA DAY O'CONNOR became the first female majority leader in any state senate in 1972; eight years later she was the first woman appointed to the U.S. Supreme Court.

Arizona was the ninth state to have a woman as governor: Secretary of State Rose Mofford took office in 1985 when the governor resigned and served until 1991. Democrat Karan English was elected to Congress in 1992 but fell in the Republican tide of 1994, and the congressional delegation remains all male. Beginning in 1997, however, women completely took over state government. Jane Dee Hull became governor; like Mofford, she was secretary of state when Governor Fife Symington was forced to resign in the national savings-and-loan scandal. Betsey Bayless replaced Hull as secretary of state, and in 1998 Janet Napolitano became attorney general; Carol Springer, treasurer; and Lisa Graham Keegan, superintendent of public instruction. Except for the attorney general, all are Republicans.

Arkansas

Arkansas has the distinction of being the first state in the nation to elect a woman to the U.S. Senate. At the end of the twentieth century, it was among the few states to have done so twice.

Bluff dwellers in prehistoric Arkansas were replaced by mound builders; the Osage, Quapaw, and Caddo people lived there later. The first colonial settlement wasn't founded until 1722, and another century passed before there was any appreciable white population. Unlike most frontiers, Arkansas had almost no Indian warfare; most native people simply moved to the Indian Territory on its western border. Nor did it have the usual frontier imbalance of men and women, for most settlers were young families who had moved from southern states in the east for cheaper land.

Plantation owners in the state's Mississippi delta led Arkansas into the Confederacy, but the Ozark side of the state had many Union sympathizers. The experience of Arkansas women in the Civil War was atypical; they probably suffered more during Reconstruction than in the war itself. The state had its own internal civil war in the 1870s, and for more than a decade, men used a Union or Confederate cover as an excuse to rob civilians, including—perhaps especially—widows and other women whose husbands had gone to war. It was in this difficult period that suffrage was first debated: during an 1868 constitutional convention, a proposal to enfranchise women along with former slaves caused so much tumult that the meeting had to be adjourned.

Despite appreciable natural resources, Arkansas continued to be one of the poorest states. Few educational opportunities were available, especially to women, and the women's clubs that began at the turn of the century made the establishment of public libraries their highest goal. When Little Rock women formed a suffrage league in 1911, it was largely in response to a resolution for suffrage that had been introduced by two House members without any consultation with women. It attracted just six votes, but by the next legislative session, the women had affiliated themselves with the National American Woman Suffrage Association and were better prepared. After several losses, the fourth try brought success with a unique twist: sponsor John A. Riggs, who had promised his mother that he would pass a suffrage bill, came up with a compromise that worked. In 1917, Arkansas became the first southern state to grant women voting rights—but for primary elections only. This was a device to prevent black women from having an effective vote. The few blacks who dared to vote in this era thought of themselves as Republicans—members of "the party of Lincoln"—but to the white majority, Democratic primaries were the only elections that mattered.

In 1918 suffragist leader CARRIE CHAPMAN CATT spoke to "an immense audience" in Arkansas. After women voted in that year's primaries and the newspapers noted how favorably they compared with the average male voter, many legislators were eager to endorse full suffrage. Arkansas moved so dramatically ahead of other states that it was the only southern state whose entire congressional delegation supported the Nineteenth Amendment.

Arkansas soon set other precedents. It was the first state to have two women in Congress simultaneously, when Effiegene Wingo joined Pearl Oldfield in the U.S. House in 1930. Both replaced husbands who had died in office, but both won subsequent elections in their own rights. Then in 1931, Hattie Caraway became the first woman to serve in the U.S. Senate. Because she was initially appointed when her husband died in office, some dismissed her as merely a caretaking widow, but Caraway defeated seven men in the 1932 election. With particular help from women in 1938, she won a second full term. Caraway brought much-needed New Deal programs to Arkansas and set a number of precedents: she was the first woman to chair a Senate committee and to be elected Senate president pro tempore.

The fall of 1957 brought crisis in Little Rock, where national attention focused on the first big attempt to integrate southern schools. DAISY BATES, president of the Arkansas state conference of the National Association for the Advancement of Colored People, recruited six girls and three boys brave enough to attempt to enroll at Central High School. Bates was arrested, her home was bombed, her life was repeatedly threatened, her business collapsed, and she was forced into bankruptcy—but she stood fast and eventually won. Integration, with all that it meant for black women, was accomplished in the 1960s.

In the late 1970s, Arkansas elected thirty-two-year-old Bill Clinton as governor—despite his marriage to a feminist who kept her maiden name; Hillary Rodham added "Clinton" later, after her husband sought national office. A practicing attorney actively involved in state policy, she led educational reforms and helped develop lending policies that encouraged women to operate farms and businesses.

In the same year that the Clintons moved to the White House, 31-year-old Democrat Blanche Lambert Lincoln defeated an incumbent congressman. She withstood a challenge in 1994, and in 1998 won the race for the U.S. Senate. With this milestone, Arkansas became one of just four states that have elected more than one woman to the U.S. Senate.

California

The first state to send two women to the U.S. Senate simultaneously, California is the nation's most populous state and has a complex, cosmopolitan past.

The Spanish explored southern California's coastline as early as 1540. European settlement did not occur for two centuries, however, during which California's relatively small number of independent native tribes continued their way of life. Women gathered food and wove baskets but did not engage in settled agriculture.

Between 1769 and 1823, the Spanish built missions from San Diego to Sonoma. Although no nuns came with these priests, a few Spanish-speaking women accompanied the men of military presidios. In 1812, Russian fur traders established Fort Ross (meaning Russia) near San Francisco; some of them married native and Spanish women, as shown in records from the 1820s, when the women got divorces after their men returned to Russia.

The ability to sue for divorce was not the only indication of the greater freedom that these Spanish women enjoyed: it was also acceptable for them to smoke, drink, and gamble, and they often retained their maiden names and wore less restrictive clothing than American women. Yet, the cultural bias against female education was so strong that some women were forbidden to read.

California held only fifteen thousand people when the United States acquired it at the end of the Mexican War in 1848—but as many as two hundred thousand arrived during the gold rush of the next few years. Most were men, but entrepreneurial women worked in boarding houses and brothels. Eight Irish nuns established a San Francisco convent in 1854 and Ohio's Mary Atkins founded a girls' school that eventually became Mills College. When Atkins arrived in 1855, however, just ten percent of San Francisco's population was female.

Perhaps the most famous female San Franciscan at the time was actress Lotta Crabtree, who became one of the first celebrities with a national base of fans; she was especially popular in roles from works by Charles Dickens. English impresario LAURA KEENE worked in San Francisco at the same time, helping to establish women in California's entertainment industry. Other nationally known women who were in California during this pre–Civil War era were politicos Rose O'Neal Greenhow, who successfully sued the city of San Francisco over her husband's accidental death, and Jessie Benton Frémont, whose influence was a factor in California's 1850 entrance into the Union as a free state.

The Civil War had relatively little effect on remote California. The high status of its African Americans can be seen in that, just a year after the war, Mary Ellen Pleasant won her lawsuit to integrate San Francisco's streetcars. Many Californians had been abolitionists and women's rights supporters back east, and it became the first western state to form a suffrage association. Among the stars of early feminism who eventually moved to California were Abigail Bush, who had presided over the 1848 women's rights convention in Rochester, New York, and Caroline Severance, a founder of the New England Woman's Club in 1868.

San Francisco newspaper publisher Emily Pitt Stevens organized California's suffrage association in 1869. In the same year, Ellen Rand Valkenburg attempted to vote in Santa Cruz. Her lawsuit, which went to the California Supreme Court, was unsuccessful, but the decade did include the first admissions of women to state medical schools and legislation that equalized pay between male and female educators. While California women could not vote in any election, they won the right to hold school offices in 1873; men could elect women to school boards or as school superintendents.

In contrast to the rising status of white and even black women, Asian women in California would long be oppressed. The Chinese who came in the 1860s were almost entirely single men who were brought to build the railroads; most of the few Chinese women in California at the time were in brothels. During 1876 legislative hearings on Chinese immigration, one expert asserted that "the women as a general thing are held as slaves." Japanese women who arrived later in the century were more likely to be part of a family unit, but all Asians suffered from blatant discrimination—and women were oppressed from within their culture as well as from the outside.

Meanwhile, white California women continued their efforts to be recognized as full citizens. In 1882, Marietta Stowe drew attention to the issues by declaring herself a candidate for governor; two years later, when the National Equal Rights Party nominated BELVA LOCKWOOD for president of the United States, Stowe ran as her vice president.

Most suffragists, however, saw such tactics as unrealistic egocentrism. Instead, they supported the efforts of Senator A. A. Sargent of California, who, beginning in 1878, valiantly introduced a suffrage bill in every Congress.

It was not until 1896—nearly three decades after they began organizing—that California suffragists finally undertook a state campaign, but it was a big one; the national association spent more money in California than anywhere else. The women were winning until the liquor industry poured in last-minute dollars; with 247,454 votes cast, they lost by just 13,000 votes. Many women suspected that election tampering caused their defeat.

California's suffragists spent the next fifteen years lobbying unsuccessfully. When the male electorate threw out many incumbents in 1910, the women were ready. The 1911 legislature put suffrage on the ballot, and women ran a sophisticated campaign. Thousands of grassroots workers printed some four million pieces of advertising, some of it in foreign languages. Women ran a banner-bedecked railroad car through the state, drawing rural crowds with entertainment. By a statewide margin of just one vote per precinct, California women were enfranchised.

In 1914, attorney Annette Adams, who also was president of the California Democratic Women's Club, became the nation's first female assistant attorney general—a presidential appointment made over the objections of the attorney general in Washington, D.C. In 1918—before most American women could vote—Californians elected four women to the state legislature.

Mae Ella Nolan became California's first congresswoman in 1923. The fourth congresswoman in the nation, she was the first to fit the stereotype assigned to early congresswomen—that of a congressman's widow—but Nolan defeated three other candidates. Florence Kahn, elected in 1925, served more than a decade, and she was the first woman on major committees, including Military Affairs and Appropriations.

World War II transformed California. The millions who came to wartime shipyards and aircraft plants brought an economic expansion that is perhaps unmatched in any place or time. California continued to boom after the war, passing New York in the 1960s as the nation's most populous state. The entertainment industry that blossomed with movies in the 1920s continued with television in the 1950s, while the computer industry developed in the last quarter of the century. More than in the old industries of the East, women were an integral part of this new economy.

In addition to economic leadership, California has been at the forefront of social change. Hollywood's women personified liberated lifestyles, and Californians supported unconventional women—such as evangelist AIMEE SEMPLE

McPHERSON—even in such a traditional area as religion. In 1969, California adopted the first "no-fault" divorce law. In the 1970s, Berkeley women were among the first to raise the issue of sexual harassment by professors; California women also pioneered the idea of "comparable worth" in pay.

Between 1923 and 1998, California elected nineteen women to the U.S. House of Representatives—more than any other state, but not an overwhelming number given its huge population. The most memorable may have been Representative Helen Gahagan Douglas, whose Hollywood celebrity and liberal ideas made her a target for Richard Nixon when they ran against each other for the U.S. Senate in 1950. More than twenty years passed before California elected another woman to Congress—Yvonne Brathwaite Burke of Los Angeles. Burke established two new milestones: when she took office in 1973, she was one of the first three African American women in the U.S. House, and later that year she became the first congresswomen to bear a child while in office. A slow but steady stream of California congresswomen followed: one California congresswoman in the 1970s, four in the 1980s, and nine in the 1990s. By far the most striking achievement, however, came in 1992, when California sent its first two women to the U.S. Senate—both in the same election. Dianne Feinstein, mayor of San Francisco since 1979, won a special election, and Barbara Boxer, who had served in the U.S. House since 1983, won the second seat.

Achievements such as these are the focus of the National Women's History Project. This organization, which is largely responsible for the recognition of March as Women's History Month, is based in Windsor, California.

Colorado

Colorado holds a special place in the history of women in the United States: decades before most women could vote, it was the first state to elect women to its legislature. Yet when the nation's first Women's Rights Convention met in 1848, few Americans knew of Colorado; a decade later, in 1858, Denver was home to just three white women.

The lives of the area's native women were detailed in an 1853 government study, *Report of an Expedition Down the Zuni and Colorado Rivers.* They grew corn, lived in cliffside pueblos, wove cloth, and generally moved south to New Mexico as whites entered Colorado.

In 1858, abolitionist and adventurer Julia Archibald Holmes of Massachusetts scaled Pikes Peak, the first woman known to have done so. The discovery of gold that year brought a rush of men to Colorado, and when Congress authorized a territorial government in 1861, approximately five thousand women lived among the state's twenty-five

thousand men. In response to Wyoming's precedent, the 1870 legislature debated enfranchising women but defeated it by one vote. When it became clear that Colorado would become a state in 1876, women mounted another campaign, but Colorado's men voted down a statewide referendum by a two-thirds margin.

Most of the men in Colorado were young, unmarried, and fearful that female voters would close down their saloons. When women conducted another campaign twenty years later, CARRIE CHAPMAN CATT kept out suffragists with links to Prohibition, and this time suffrage passed. In 1893 Colorado became the second state in the nation in which women had full voting rights—and in the very next election, three women won races for the state legislature. Clara Clessingham, Carrie Holly, and Frances Klock were elected in 1894, more than a quarter century before most American women voted. Another three women won elections in 1896.

The turn of the century brought union organizer Mother Mary Jones to Colorado, where she led a strike of male coal miners. A strike in 1914 was deadly; women were among those killed in what was known as the Ludlow Massacre. Women also went to Washington to testify on the injustices of life in the coal camps.

In 1913, Colorado became the second state to elect a woman, Helen Ring Robinson, to its state senate. Four years later, when Agnes Riddle was chosen, it became the first state to have elected two women to this position. When suffrage was extended to all U.S. women in 1920, Colorado feminists proudly filed a report showing that they had moved far beyond women in other states: among other things, they wrote that "the office of State Superintendent of Public Instruction has been filled by a woman since 1894 and no man has been nominated for it." One of these women, Mary Bradford, was also was elected president of the National Education Association.

Later in the twentieth century, Colorado became one of the few states to honor a woman with one of the two statues that each state is allowed in the U.S. Capitol. The statue commemorated Dr. FLORENCE SABIN, a medical researcher and public health activist who, in 1925, was the first woman to become a member in the National Academy of Sciences.

As the feminist movement became revitalized in 1972, Denver elected the woman who would champion more feminist legislation than anyone. When attorney Patricia Schroeder went to Congress as a representative, her children were preschoolers; when she retired in 1996, they had graduated from college. Meanwhile, Schroeder pushed innumerable advances for women and girls. As a senior member of the House Armed Services Committee, she especially worked to end sexual harassment and to promote women in the military. Denver replaced Schroeder with another woman, Diana DeGette.

Connecticut

Connecticut was the first state to elect a female governor who had not been preceded by her husband—on the other hand, it also was one of very few urban states that refused to ratify the Nineteenth Amendment enfranchising women.

One of the nation's oldest states, Connecticut was settled by New Englanders who vanquished the native Pequot in 1637—in warfare that some men, influenced by ANNE HUTCHINSON, refused to join. Many of Connecticut's founding fathers were religious dissidents from Massachusetts; nevertheless it quickly became a theocracy. Quaker missionary MARY DYER was banished from New Haven in 1658, and from 1647 to 1738, the colony hanged 37 "witches."

Connecticut women generally supported the Revolutionary War, but one in particular should be far more famous than she is. When the British burned the town of Danbury in 1777, sixteen-year-old SYBIL LUDINGTON rode through the night to rally resistance, galloping forty miles through Connecticut and New York.

In the postrevolutionary world, Sarah Pierce wrote textbooks and began Litchfield Female Academy, which served as an educational model for female leadership in the United States and Canada. Among her students was HARRIET BEECHER STOWE, who became Connecticut's most famous woman after the 1852 publication of *Uncle Tom's Cabin*; the novel outsold any book of the century and profoundly affected the onset of the Civil War.

When the national suffrage associations began in 1869, Connecticut women joined. Their league would be headed by Isabella Beecher Hooker for more than thirty years. Although she was a half sister to Harriet Beecher Stowe and the immensely popular Reverend Henry Ward Beecher, Hooker's celebrity connections did little to advance her political cause, as year after year the legislature defeated suffrage bills. Nor were lawmakers moved by two 1873 demonstrations of the principle of "no taxation without representation." When abolitionist ABBY KELLY FOSTER and her husband refused to pay taxes because Abby could not vote, the authorities sold their farm, but supporters bought it and returned it to the Fosters. Similarly, when sisters Julia and Abigail Smith of Glastonbury refused to pay, authorities not only sold their land but also confiscated their cattle; the "Glastonbury cows" provided cartoon fodder throughout the nation, as most people considered the Smiths' sacrifice amusing.

Connecticut was slow to open higher education to women; Yale University, begun in 1701, remained closed to women far into the twentieth century. Connecticut women finally achieved a property rights bill in 1877—decades later than neighboring states—and, in 1893, the right to vote in school elections. As the century turned and its leadership aged, the suffrage association diminished to the point that its 1903 "convention" was small enough to be held in Hooker's home.

A Hartford speech by British militant EMMELINE PANKHURST in 1909 attracted younger women to the suffrage movement; membership in and donations to suffrage organizations soared, with Katharine Houghton Hepburn, the mother of future star KATHARINE HEPBURN, serving as suffrage association president in this era. The legislature, however, remained obdurate. The women filed bills for various forms of suffrage in every annual session, but except for granting the vote on library taxes in 1909, lawmakers defeated bills at every opportunity between 1884 and 1919.

In 1920, Connecticut had a historic opportunity to be the last state needed for ratification of the Nineteenth Amendment, which enfranchised all women, but Governor Marcus A. Holcomb allowed that privilege to go to Tennessee. Despite rallies and petitions, he refused to call the legislature into session. After Tennessee made the amendment official on August 26, Holcomb belatedly called a September session, the sole point of which was to appease the newly enfranchised women in the hope that they would forgive Republican incumbents by November.

The state elected its first woman to Congress, CLARE BOOTH LUCE, in 1942—the same year that the Coast Guard's World War II women's division, the SPARS, began. SPARS officers set a precedent when they trained along with male cadets at the U.S. Coast Guard Academy in New London. The postwar world offered fewer opportunities, and when the top 1954 graduate of Yale Law School was Ellen A. Peters, not one law firm offered her a job. After many years of teaching, Peters rose to become chief justice of the state supreme court in 1984.

Connecticut conservatism also can be seen in a landmark 1965 case: the U.S. Supreme Court ruled in *Griswold v. Connecticut* that the state could not ban distribution of contraceptives to married people (the extension to unmarried people would not occur until 1972). The case was brought by Estelle Griswold, who was arrested when she opened a birth-control clinic.

The era brought other momentous change. Female undergraduates were finally admitted to Yale in 1968 and six years later, Connecticut voters elected Ella Tambussi Grasso as governor. Not only was she the first governor whose husband had no political base, she also overcame the disadvantage of being a Democrat in a traditionally Republican state.

A graduate of single-sex Mount Holyoke College, she married in 1942 and, despite having two children, was elected to the legislature in 1952, to Congress in 1970, and became governor in 1974. The nation's Democratic governors chose her to chair their organization in 1979, but cancer forced her to resign the next year. She died just five weeks later.

Since Luce's 1942 election, Connecticut has sent five women to Congress. Democrat Barbara Kennelly, elected in 1982, was the first woman to serve on the House Intelligence Committee and championed such legislation as enforcement of child support and insurance coverage of mammograms; she ran for governor in 1998 but lost. Republican Nancy Johnson, elected in 1983, rose to chair the House Ethics Committee in 1995. Finally, Democrat Rosa DeLauro was elected in 1990 after serving as head of the feminist fund-raising organization EMILY's List.

Delaware

Delaware is one of the few states that have never elected a woman to Congress or to the governorship. It also failed to ratify the Nineteenth Amendment, which gave women the vote, but it was a Delaware senator who provided one of the two crucial votes that enfranchised American women.

Delaware was settled in 1638 by Swedish families, who introduced the log cabin to America, and were joined by Finns in the next decade. Delaware's small size and peninsular position protected it from much harm in the American Revolution.

An 1803 bill to abolish slavery failed on a tie vote, and—in contrast to other northern states—legislative votes on this issue grew more conservative with time. Delaware remained a slave state until after the Civil War, despite the best efforts of female abolitionists such as Elizabeth Chandler and Mary Parker Welch. Chandler won a prize for her poem "The Slave-Ship" in 1825, and she wrote for an abolitionist newspaper from then until her premature death in 1834. Welch's approach was more political, and when moral arguments failed to bring change, she appealed to economics—arguing that Delaware is so far north that maintaining slaves through the winter was not financially advantageous—but still in vain. The state did prohibit slave trading, and the majority of its blacks were emancipated prior to the Civil War, but some eighteen hundred had to wait until the Thirteenth Amendment abolished slavery late in 1865.

When the Fifteenth Amendment was interpreted to have enfranchised male ex-slaves but not women, Delaware women were among those who tested its gender-neutral language. The movement there remained tiny, however. The legislature did adopt a women's property-rights bill in 1873, but despite the presence of ELIZABETH CADY STANTON,

SUSAN B. ANTHONY, and other luminaries, an 1881 suffrage bill garnered just two votes.

Except for Wilmington women, who gained the vote for school elections, Delaware suffragists largely gave up that effort to concentrate instead on educational opportunity. The state's leading feminist, Mary A. Stuart, wrote in 1886: "Delaware College, the only institution of the kind in the State, was open to girls for thirteen years, but owing to a tragedy committed by the boys in hazing . . . the doors were thereafter closed to girls, although they were in no way directly or indirectly implicated in the outrages." For almost three decades, access to college was the chief concern of Delaware feminists; finally, in 1914, Delaware became the second-to-last state in the nation to open the doors of its public college to women.

In 1918, when the suffrage amendment failed to pass the U.S. Senate by just two votes, CARRIE CHAPMAN CATT targeted Delaware and three other states to elect new, pro-suffrage candidates; the chosen states were all small and eastern, and efforts in two of the four succeeded. Delaware women did their part impressively. Lacking the vote, they campaigned among men and managed to replace their anti-suffragist senator with a supporter, L. Heisler Ball. With his vote, the Nineteenth Amendment passed out of Congress and went to the states. Ironically, Delaware's ratification was one of the hardest; although the Senate ratified, after weeks of lobbying, the House defeated it 24 to 10.

The state's most notable women may have been Emily P. Bissell, a 1907 founder of the Anti-Tuberculosis Society, which introduced Christmas seals as a highly successful fund-raising method, and Mrs. Wilmer Steele, who developed the "broiler" method of raising chickens in 1923, which revolutionized both American agriculture and the national diet. World Wars I and II brought opportunity to the state's women in the form of jobs in chemical and munitions plants. In the postwar era, Delaware's tax structure attracted the corporate headquarters for many out-of-state firms, which created white-collar jobs.

Delaware's current lieutenant governor is Ruth Ann Minner; the attorney general is M. Jane Brady.

Florida

The first southern state to elect a woman to Congress, the Spanish flag flew over Florida longer than the U.S. flag has.

At least one woman was with Ponce de León when he landed in 1513, and in 1539 Ana Mendez and Francisca Hinestrosa sailed with explorer Hernando de Soto when he explored the southeastern coast. Saint Augustine, settled in 1565, is the nation's oldest city; its settlers included some one hundred Spanish women—many more women than there were at Plymouth.

Spanish conquistadors also raped, enslaved, and killed, and Florida's Tocobaga, Calusa, and other tribes soon were decimated. By 1708, ten thousand natives had been sold into slavery in the Carolinas—and at the same time, blacks were welcomed to Florida: a 1693 royal edict granted "liberty to all . . . the men as well as the women." Spain was motivated not so much by humanitarian concerns as by a desire to economically harass the British colonies; nonetheless, Florida's Fort Mose was the first free black community in what would become the United States.

After Spain ceded Florida in 1819, military forts continued to be the centers of settlement long into the nineteenth century. Two future first ladies, Rachel Donelson Jackson and Margaret Smith Taylor, were among the women who passed through these forts during three wars with the Seminoles, a tribe made up of Indians driven from the north. The federal government offered a reward for eliminating them: Seminole women were worth a $200 bounty while the men were worth $500.

The last Seminole war ended just two years before the Civil War began, adding more troubles for women who lived with Florida's malarial mosquitoes and other difficulties. The population began to grow after the war's end, and some of those who arrived on the new railroads brought ideas from the national women's movement. Florida's first suffrage official was a Massachusetts woman, Dr. Esther Hill Hawks, who came along with the Union army. Both a physician and an educator, Dr. Hawks became the National Woman Suffrage Association's vice president for Florida. Two decades later, transplanted Ohioan Julia Tuttle, a clever real estate developer, bought a square mile of land in 1891 and became "the mother of Miami."

When the National American Woman Suffrage Association had its first convention in the South in 1895, SUSAN B. ANTHONY warmly introduced the president of the Florida chapter, Eleanor McWilliams Chamberlain. The two-year-old affiliate had about a hundred members, but when Chamberlain moved to the Midwest in 1897, it died.

The Spanish-American War of 1898 brought more newcomers. Troops bound for Cuba departed from Florida, and along with such men as Theodore Roosevelt, there were well-known women, including Red Cross chief CLARA BARTON. Female journalists were among the national media, and other women contracted with the Army to work as nurses on hospital ships and at convalescent centers in Florida. At least one woman spied on the Spanish at the Army's request. Nuns turned their schools into barracks, and Cuban women in Key West and Tampa raised funds to support Cuban independence from Spain. Paulina Pedroso was the chief female revolutionary in exile, and the great Latin American leader José Martí headquartered his U.S. activities in Pedroso's home—even though he was white and she was black.

Various forms of suffrage were introduced in every legislative session between 1912 and 1919, and each lost, often on a technicality or by a slim margin. This was true despite the fact that Florida's movement attracted more well-known leaders than those in many states. Orlando minister Dr. Mary A. Safford, who had been Iowa's 1911 suffrage president, was quickly elected to the same position in Florida and was supported by prominent Floridians. Orlando's mayor organized a pro-suffrage Men's League almost before the women organized themselves. Two wives of former governors were highly visible activists, and Mary Baird Bryan, Miami retiree and wife of presidential nominee William Jennings Bryan, received star political billing.

Some male voters were more progressive than legislators, and between 1915 and 1920, twenty-three cities granted women the vote in municipal elections. One town unanimously elected a woman as mayor, while another sent its proposed charter to Tallahassee with the names of the city commissioners already filled in—all were women. Perhaps because of the Bryans' influence with congressional Democrats, Florida's U.S. House delegation was one of just two southern ones to cast favorable votes on the Nineteenth Amendment.

When Congress sent the amendment to the states for ratification in June 1919, the legislature was one of the few still in session, and the governor begged it to make Florida "the first state in the sisterhood of states to ratify this great movement." The lawmakers, however, were ready to adjourn- and the suffragists were too wary of them to risk a defeat only hours after the national campaign had begun.

Although Florida failed on suffrage, it was the first southern state to elect a woman to Congress: with the help of her activist mother, Mary Baird Bryan, RUTH BRYAN OWEN was elected just eight years after women got the vote. Other significant Florida women of the 1930s and 1940s include Carita Doggett Corse, one of the few women to head a state Federal Writers' Project, as well as authors Marjorie Kinnan Rawlings, MARJORY STONEMAN DOUGLAS, and ZORA NEALE HURSTON. In the same era, educator and Roosevelt adviser MARY MCLEOD BETHUNE of Daytona may have been the most prominent African American woman in the world.

World War II transformed Florida. The Women's Army Corps (WAC) trained at Daytona, while the U.S. Navy's female auxiliary, the WAVES (Women Accepted for Volunteer Emergency Service) and the Army's Air WACs ran air-traffic control towers and repaired planes at bases from Pensacola to the Keys. Yet, state law remained conservative:

for example, women did not serve on juries until the late 1940s, and then only if they actively solicited the duty. Not until 1975 were male and female jurors treated equally, and then only because of a U.S. Supreme Court decision.

Recent significant Florida women include Paula Hawkins, Florida's first female U.S. senator, who served one term in the 1980s; ELLEN T. ZWILICH, who in 1983 became the first female winner of the Pulitzer Prize for musical composition; and two 1993 presidential appointees: Carol Browner, head of the Environmental Protection Agency, and JANET RENO, U.S. attorney general—who was then the highest-ranked female Cabinet member in history.

Georgia

The first state to have a female U.S. senator, Georgia also can claim the nation's first women's college.

Georgia was the last of the Atlantic coast colonies, founded in 1732 as a refuge for felons freed from English jails. The American Revolution began just four decades later. Georgia's most notable female patriot may have been Nancy Morgan Hart, who served a meal to demanding Tories, then drew a gun and held them for hanging. The decade after the Revolution brought a crucial change for the South: the cotton gin, although invented by Connecticut visitor Eli Whitney, had its genesis in the ideas of his Georgia landlady, Catherine Littlefield Greene.

When cotton prices soared in the 1820s, many Cherokee women began working in cloth production. Like other native societies, that of the Cherokee was matrilineal; men lived with their wives' families, and women owned any noncommunal property. Despite adoption of the new economy, however, the Indian Removal Act of 1830 forced the Cherokee into Oklahoma.

For white women, the era's great precedent was the 1836 establishment of Georgia Female College in Macon, one of the world's earliest institutions of higher education for women. Women studied advanced mathematics and science, and Latin and French were required; in 1840, the college granted the first bachelor of arts degrees to women. When its name changed to Wesleyan Female College in 1843, it had two hundred students. Its graduates formed the world's first alumnae organization in 1859.

Among the era's most notable blacks were Ellen and William Craft, who escaped from slavery and lectured in England on *Running a Thousand Miles for Freedom*, a book about their experiences. Susie King Taylor fled to the Union-held seacoast islands and later wrote *Reminiscences of My Life in Camp*. Among white women, Georgia widow PHOEBE LEVY PEMBER ran history's largest hospital, Chimborazo

Hospital in Richmond, Virginia. After the war, CLARA BARTON began the first systematic identification of the missing and dead by marking some thirteen thousand graves at Georgia's notorious Andersonville prisoner-of-war camp.

The "New South" of the postwar world brought textile plants that employed large numbers of white women. On the other end of the economic scale, Agnes Scott College, which was named for a donor, began in Decatur in 1890; the next year, Athens women formed what was later termed the nation's first garden club. In 1895, the National American Woman Suffrage Association held its first convention in the South. Although some preachers warned people not to attend, hundreds of the curious, including many men, crowded the Atlanta hall where SUSAN B. ANTHONY presided.

In 1900 African American Gertrude Pridgett debuted in Columbus; as "Ma" Rainey, she became the most important female jazz innovator of the era. In 1902, Martha Berry turned her thirty-five-thousand-acre plantation near Rome into a school that enabled poor white students to earn their tuition by working; the school survives as Berry College today. Georgia's most significant woman of the era doubtless was JULIETTE GORDON LOW, who organized the nation's first Girl Scout troop in Savannah in 1912.

While suffrage was the burning issue elsewhere, Georgia women dared not dream of the vote. The state's first suffrage association was formed in 1890, but women could not find legislators willing to sponsor their bills to encourage public schooling or to raise girls' age of sexual consent above ten. They persisted, though; suffragists filed legislation in every session from 1895 on, although no form of the vote moved beyond committee hearings. Their only victory was the election of U.S. Senator William J. Harris, who provided one of the two crucial votes that moved the Nineteenth Amendment out of Congress in 1919. In the same year, a progressive city council enfranchised Atlanta women for municipal elections—but used wording that allowed only affluent white women to vote.

This history makes it all the more ironic that Georgia was the first state to have a female U.S. senator—in 1922, just two years after women were barred from the national election. When a senator died at election time, the governor appointed eighty-seven-year-old newspaper columnist and political advisor REBECCA LATIMER FELTON, the sister of suffrage leader Mary McLendon, to the interim seat. Although it was clearly an honorary appointment, she traveled to Washington for the first day of the session, was sworn in, spoke, resigned, and returned home—where she continued to write for the *Atlanta Journal* until she died at age ninety-four.

Georgia's most notable women of this era were literary. A 1934 5 Prize went to Caroline Miller (later Ray) for *Lamb in His Bosom*, a novel about south Georgia pioneers. Three years later, MARGARET MITCHELL's *Gone With the Wind* became one of the century's most popular books and a movie phenomenon. In the 1940s, CARSON MCCULLERS won major prizes after she wrote *The Heart is a Lonely Hunter* at age twenty-three. The 1944 best-seller *Strange Fruit* was a story of interracial love by Lillian Smith, a white, rural Georgian.

World War II brought change, as military bases opened across the state. Fort Oglethorpe, near Macon, was the third of the Women's Army Corps training camps, and it was the only Army training center commanded by a woman, Elizabeth Strayhorn. Georgia also elected its first two women to Congress during the war, while Atlanta became one of the first big cities to have a woman as its superintendent of schools.

In 1961, a year prior to the highly publicized admission of a black man to the University of Mississippi, young Charlayne Hunter quietly integrated the University of Georgia. As Charlayne Hunter-Gault, she went on to a career in print and broadcast journalism. Georgia's literary genius of this era was Flannery O'Connor, whose critical acclaim grew after her premature death.

In the 1970s and 1980s, several Georgia court cases were feminist landmarks. *Doe v. Bolton* predated *Roe v. Wade*; in both, an anonymous woman seeking an abortion sued a state official. Margie Pitts Hames successfully argued against Georgia's statute before the U.S. Supreme Court; the court ruled on both cases at the same time, but the *Roe* case has become more famous because Texas law was more severe. In 1980, female professors at Georgia Southwestern College won back pay for discrimination, while a male professor at the University of Georgia was jailed when he refused to testify in a woman's tenure case.

In 1983 Georgia native Alice Walker became the first black woman to win a Pulitzer Prize in letters, for her novel *The Color Purple*. Georgia elected its first African American woman, Cynthia McKinney, to Congress in 1992. In 1999 Celestine Sibley, a writer with the *Atlanta Journal-Constitution* for 55 years, received the Lifetime Achievement Award of the National Society of Newspaper Columnists just weeks prior to her death at age 85; she was only the second woman in the U.S. so honored.

Hawaii

The newest state, Hawaii has an old tradition of women in leadership positions. It also was the first state to ratify the Equal Rights Amendment.

When American missionaries arrived in Hawaii in 1819, they found powerful women. Queen Kaahumanu held the reins of government until her death in 1832. She shattered taboos based on gender, including one that had kept men and women from eating together, and during the next decade she established the islands' first legal code, which included jury trials. A contemporary of hers was political and religious leader Kapiolani, who converted to Christianity and demonstrated the power of her new god over the old ones by climbing into a sacred volcano in 1824.

A woman was Hawaii's monarch when American businessmen overthrew the native government in 1893. Queen Liliuokalani was displaced from her throne by sugar and pineapple growers who funded a rebellion when she tried to reassert powers that her brother, who died two years earlier, had surrendered. They placed Liliuokalani under house arrest and applied for annexation of Hawaii to the United States; President Grover Cleveland refused them, but by the time the queen traveled to Washington to plead her case in 1896, Cleveland was on his way out. Republican William McKinley was more sympathetic to the imperialists, and the Spanish-American War in 1898 sealed Hawaii's fate. Liliuokalani had no choice but to return to Honolulu, where she was granted a modest pension and lived until 1917.

Under Sanford B. Dole, president of the Hawaiian Republic, it was American business interests that truly held power. Not surprisingly, the government was hostile to suffrage. Although the national association called for enfranchisement of women from the time that Hawaii became a U.S. territory in 1899, Honolulu women did not organize until 1912. Their league included both native Hawaiians and mainlanders (especially missionary women), CARRIE CHAPMAN CATT spoke to a large, receptive audience there as part of her world tour. With persistent lobbying from the national association, Congress authorized suffrage, and President Woodrow Wilson signed the 1918 bill—but Hawaii's legislature never implemented it.

Women were enfranchised with the Nineteenth Amendment in 1920, and the first female Hawaiian legislator was elected in 1925. The status of women had declined so much during this period of colonialism that Representative Rosalie Keliinoi had to concentrate on the passage of a bill allowing women to retain control of their property after marriage.

It was the attack on Hawaii's Pearl Harbor, of course, that began American involvement in World War II and tremendously changed the islands. A civilian, Cornelia Fort, was in the air teaching a student pilot on the Sunday morning when the Japanese planes appeared. Hawaii was the nation's first point of defense in the Pacific, and its loyalty was rewarded with statehood in 1959. Statehood's chief opponents were southern congressmen who objected to Hawaii's uncommon racial mixture and tolerance of diversity.

Even before statehood, a woman represented Hawaii in Congress: Mary Farrington, who served from 1954 to 1957, was a journalist and broadcaster who championed statehood. Just five years after statehood, Hawaiians chose Patsy Mink for one of their two seats in Congress. Born Patsy Matsu Takemoto, she was an attorney who had served in both houses of the Hawaiian legislature; in Congress, she took the lead on women's issues and was one of the first to argue against the Vietnam War. She lost her quest for a Senate seat in 1976, but President Jimmy Carter appointed Mink as an assistant secretary of state; in 1990, she returned to Congress, where she still serves.

Hawaii was the first state to ratify the Equal Rights Amendment in 1972. It also elected a woman, former state senator Jean King, as its lieutenant governor in 1978. In 1987, Patricia Fukuda Saiki joined Mink in Congress; the first Republican to represent Hawaii in the U.S. House since statehood, she lost a 1990 U.S. Senate race.

For more than a century, many Hawaiians have been educated with funds left by the last native female chief, Bernice Pauchi Bishop; she died in 1884, but the Bishop Estate remains an important philanthropy for Hawaiian youth. Hawaiians are the only Americans to enjoy a state-sponsored system of free health care, a benefit of particular importance to women and their children.

Idaho

Although it was one of the first states to grant women the vote, Idaho also was one of a handful of states that rescinded their ratification of the Equal Rights Amendment.

Women played significant roles in the exploration of what would become Idaho. SACAGAWEA took the Lewis and Clark expedition to her tribe's camp there in the winter of 1805–1806; despite having recently borne a child, she escorted these men from the Dakota prairie into the Rocky Mountains. A member of the Iowa tribe, Marie Dorian made an even more impressive trek through this land in 1811. Although less known, she traveled farther and suffered greater hardships than Sacagawea.

Idaho's first non-native child was born to Henry and Eliza Spaulding, missionaries to the Nez Percé, in 1836. She and her contemporary, Narcissa Whitman, were the first white female settlers in the Pacific Northwest. Spaulding set up a school for Indian women and girls on the western edge of modern Idaho, and other female missionaries joined her as early as 1838. She was so popular that when the Cayuse tribe killed whites in 1847, members of the Nez Percé tribe protected her.

The mission had to be abandoned, however, and European settlement slowed. As late as 1878, there was

major Indian warfare in the area. SARAH WINNEMUCCA, perhaps the most famous Native American woman of her era, scouted for the army in the Bannock War; despite nearly impassable mountain terrain, she led a successful search for Paiutes who had been captured by other Indians.

In 1887, Oregon's Abigail Scott Duniway addressed Idaho's territorial legislature on behalf of suffrage; as publisher of *The New Northwest*, she also influenced many readers there. Perhaps the most powerful woman of the era, however, was ethnologist Alice Cunningham Fletcher, who arrived in 1889 to administer the Dawes Act, legislation she helped create that Congress intended to end mistreatment of Indians. The Interior Department hired her to implement the law, and although the Nez Percé people were highly suspicious, Fletcher worked with them until 1893, doing everything in her power to make the act function to their benefit.

Idaho became a state in 1890, and women were enfranchised almost as soon as they requested the ballot. The first suffrage meeting was in 1893; in 1895, the Senate passed their resolution for a referendum unanimously, and in the House just two members voted against it. Led by National American Woman Suffrage Association field organizer CARRIE CHAPMAN CATT and others, Idaho women proved amazingly successful. Only three of the state's sixty-five newspapers opposed them, and in November 1896, Idaho men voted almost two to one in favor of suffrage.

In the very next election, three women, all married, were elected to the state legislature: a Republican, a Democrat, and a Populist. In 1900, Permeal French became one of the nation's first female winners of a statewide election, and she and other women would consistently hold the office of superintendent of schools in the future. Many women were elected county school superintendents, while others served on the board of regents for the state's coeducational colleges. Idaho further defied stereotypes with three female deputy sheriffs in 1900, and four women were elected county treasurers.

As in other states in this era, women formed civic improvement clubs; with suffrage won, they especially concentrated on the reforms advocated by the Women's Christian Temperance Union. These early political gains, however, were not maintained. By 1920, only three more women had been added to the three legislators elected in 1898. Although their female constituents had been voting for a quarter century, six state senators voted against the Nineteenth Amendment, which enfranchised all American women.

Idaho finally elected its first woman to Congress in 1953, more than a half century after women began voting. Gracie Bowers Pfost defeated the incumbent by a tiny margin; she went on to chair the Interior Affairs Committee's subcommittee on public works. The Democratic nominee for U.S. senator in 1963, she lost the general election.

In the 1970s, while feminism grew elsewhere, Idaho became more conservative. The state's defense of an anachronistic law in 1972 had to be struck down by the U.S. Supreme Court: it ruled in *Reed v. Reed* that Idaho's preference of men over women as executors of estates was unconstitutional. In 1977 Idaho rescinded its previous ratification of the Equal Rights Amendment, a situation so historically uncommon that legal experts could not agree on its effect.

Idaho elected its second woman to Congress in 1995: Republican Helen Chenoweth defeated an incumbent to win one of the state's two House seats.

Illinois

The first state to elect an African American woman to the U.S. Senate, Illinois has a long history of exceptional women.

By the time of the American Revolution, it had several thousand white and black residents. In the War of 1812, Mrs. Heald, the wife of the Army commander at Chicago, joined men in fighting on horseback. Illinois became a state in 1818.

Springfield's Mary Todd Lincoln is the best known of Illinois' Civil War–era women. Galesburg's MARY ANN BICKERDYKE saw more combat than most soldiers while she nursed General William Tecumseh Sherman's troops across the country. MARY LIVERMORE, the Midwestern head of the Army's Sanitary Commission, organized three thousand local units of women to supply military needs. The Sisters of the Holy Cross operated the huge U.S. General Hospital at Mound City, while other women nursed on ships that brought thousands of wounded men up the Mississippi.

Former Civil War nurse MYRA BRADWELL filed one of the century's most significant court cases in 1869. The publisher of the nationally read *Chicago Legal News*, she passed the bar exam, but the state supreme court refused to admit her. In 1873 Bradwell's case reached the U.S. Supreme Court, which ruled that states could bar female lawyers and that the Constitution's equal protection did not apply to women. While the case was being heard, however, the Illinois legislature had removed the word "male" from its statutes on attorneys, and an unmarried woman, Alta M. Hulett, had been admitted to the bar in 1872.

Illinois women made easier progress as physicians. Dr. Mary Harris Thompson, who was educated by female physicians in Boston and New York, arrived in Chicago during the Civil War; after working with the Sanitary Commission, in 1865 she opened the Chicago Hospital for Women and Children, which soon expanded into a medical college. One of her students, Dr. Sarah Stevenson, became the first female member of the American Medical Association.

Dr. Thompson's medical school was absorbed into Northwestern University in 1870, and the University of Illinois became coeducational the same year. Northwestern's first dean of women, FRANCES WILLARD, went on to international fame as head of the Woman's Christian Temperance Union, while the first female dean of the University of Chicago, ALICE FREEMAN PALMER, maintained a commuter marriage with her husband in Boston. Coeducational from its 1891 beginning, the university's graduate school offered unusual opportunities to women.

Many women associated with the University of Chicago also worked with Illinois' most famous woman of the era, JANE ADDAMS. With Ellen Starr Gates, Addams began Hull House in 1889 and soon developed this immigrant settlement house into a model of innovative social work. Among those who contributed to Hull House were sociologist GRACE ABBOTT; economist EMILY BALCH; child specialist JULIA LATHROP, one of the first women confirmed by the U.S. Senate for a federal position; physician and toxicologist ALICE HAMILTON; attorney Florence Kelley, who became Illinois' chief factory inspector; and Sophonisba Breckinridge, the world's first woman to be awarded a doctorate in political science.

Illinois's suffrage assocation was begun in 1855 in the town of Earlville by Susan Hoxie Richardson, a cousin of SUSAN B. ANTHONY. Mary Livermore organized a state association in 1868, but progress was slow: women won the right to hold school office in 1874 and to vote in school elections in 1891. In 1894, Lucy L. Flower defeated Julia Holmes Smith for a seat on the University of Illinois board of trustees, and in the next election, eleven of eighteen candidates for the board were women.

In 1892–1893, more than twenty-one million visitors came to Chicago for a giant fair honoring the 400th anniversary of Christopher Columbus's expedition, and women played a major part. The 150-member Board of Lady Managers for the event was headed by Chicago businesswoman BERTHA HONORÉ PALMER, who traveled the world to collect some eighty thousand exhibits by women, which were displayed in a building designed by architect Sophia Hayden. African American women, however, had to fight to participate; led by IDA WELLS-BARNETT, they finally won some opportunities—but Wells-Barnett was pointedly excluded.

At the turn of the century, Illinois women again made important advances in the field of education. In 1901, Mary Murphy sued the Chicago school board when she was fired after getting married—a common practice at the time. The court ruled that "marriage is not misconduct" and that married women could not automatically be fired. Murphy was supported by Margaret A. Haley, business agent for the Chicago Teachers' Federation and, later, a founder of the American Federation of Teachers. Chicago was the nation's first major city to have a woman head its school system when ELLA FLAGG YOUNG became superintendent in 1909. Dr. Young went on to be the first female president of the National Education Association.

In the same year that Young became superintendent, some forty thousand Chicago women went on strike against the garment industry. Among the working-class leaders were Bessie Abramowitz and Agnes Nestor; their upper-class supporters included Mary McDowell, president of the Women's Trade Union League. After four months and intervention by the esteemed Jane Addams, management settled.

In 1913, the Illinois legislature devised a variation on partial suffrage: women won the right to vote for president but for no other (nonschool) offices. Several other eastern states quickly emulated this compromise. Illinois rushed to support the Nineteenth Amendment in 1919. All congressmen voted for it, and the legislature was one of three to ratify on the first possible day.

In 1921, Illinois became the third state to elect a woman to the U.S. House. Winnifred Mason Huck defeated challengers from both parties but, too liberal for her time, lost the next election. Other precedents were set in 1924, when the University of Chicago's Edith Abbott was the founding dean of the nation's first graduate school of social work; in 1926, when Chicago's Violette Neatly Anderson became the first black woman to argue before the U.S. Supreme Court; and in 1928, when RUTH HANNA MCCORMICK, a former suffrage leader, was elected to Congress.

The Chicago Symphony Orchestra set a milestone in 1932 by performing work by a black female composer, Florence Price. Earlier in the century, publisher Margaret Anderson introduced many important writers, and in 1950, GWENDOLYN BROOKS won the Pulitzer Prize in poetry.

The Equal Rights Amendment of the 1970s saw major battles in Illinois, which became the only major northern state that failed to ratify; with opposition led by Phyllis Schlafly, the legislature rejected it seven times. Meanwhile, Illinois' ban on the use of Medicaid funds for abortions became a national test case, and the same was true for its parental-consent law in the next decade.

In the seven decades between 1920, when women got the vote, and 1990, Illinois sent nine women to the U.S. House—including the state's first black congresswoman, Cardiss Collins, in 1973. Jane Byrne made international headlines in 1979 when she was elected mayor of Chicago; she was the first woman to head a city of that size. Finally, in 1992, Illinois became the first state to elect a black woman, Carol Moseley-Braun, to the U.S. Senate. Its twenty-member House delegation in 1996 was the largest with no women, but two were elected in 1998—the same year that Moseley-Braun lost her bid for reelection.

Indiana

The last state to ratify the Equal Rights Amendment, Indiana also was home to some of the nation's first women's rights conventions.

Indiana's first European settlers were French fur traders who arrived in the late 1600s. Many French men developed long-term relationships with Indian women and were absorbed into their matrilineal culture. When Anna Symmes Harrison arrived with Indiana's first territorial governor, William Henry Harrison, Vincennes—Indiana's first city, settled in 1702—was very much a wilderness. She bore nine children and, like other women, managed the family business while her husband traveled. She stayed in Indiana all her life, for she had not yet moved to Washington when her husband died soon after his 1841 presidential inauguration.

Frontier Indiana spawned several of the era's utopian societies. Followers of "MOTHER" ANN LEE created a Shaker colony in 1808, and internationalist FRANCES WRIGHT publicized the commune at New Harmony, where she lived in the 1820s. The radical ideas promoted by these societies began to dissipate, but in Bloomington in 1841, there were women unconventional enough to form a club for their intellectual improvement. Calling themselves the Edgeworthalean Society—a combination of the names of Maria Edgeworth, a popular British author, and Thalia, the Greek muse of comedy—they defied ridicule to meet once a week and discuss the papers they wrote.

The women's rights movement expanded to Indiana soon after its 1848 start in Seneca Falls, New York. The Indiana Women's Rights Society began in Wayne County's Dublin at an 1851 convention. Their leader, Amanda Way, went on to work for women's rights in Kansas and California, but in 1859, she joined Sarah E. Underhill in publishing the *Women's Tribune* out of Indianapolis. That year, people packed the capitol to hear Dr. Mary F. Thomas read a petition signed by a thousand citizens calling for equal property rights for married women, as well as for suffrage. Legislators listened respectfully while Mary Birdstall spoke, but then declared that "legislation on this subject is inexpedient."

Amanda Way gave up the *Women's Tribune* to work as a nurse in the Civil War, and other women similarly contributed. The Sisters of Providence ran a large military hospital in Indianapolis, and the governor authorized African American newspaper editor Mary Ann Shadd Cary to recruit black soldiers. After black men won the vote in 1870, women redoubled their crusade. Indiana legislators were among the first to vote on the issue, but they defeated it 51 to 22 in 1877. Women tried again in 1882, but the liquor lobby, fearful of the pro-temperance element among suffragists, persuaded the legislature to reject suffrage again.

Indianapolis became home to what was probably was the largest business run by an African-American woman in 1905, when Madame C. J. Walker built a plant to manufacture cosmetics for black women. Innovative sales methods made her America's first black female millionaire. At the same time, Gene Stratton-Porter—whose husband suggested changing her name from "Geneva"—sold more than a million copies of her first book, *Freckles* (1904). Her novels sold at rates comparable to those of men such as Charles Dickens and Sir Walter Scott.

The women's rights movement dwindled after its nineteenth-century defeats, but a 1906 convention in Kokomo began the revitalization, and women submitted a bill for municipal suffrage to the 1907 legislature. It and subsequent forms of the vote were defeated, but finally, in 1917, the legislature passed a complex bill giving women the vote in municipal and presidential elections, as well as the elections for some other offices. Tens of thousands of women had registered to vote when the courts began ruling parts of the act unconstitutional. A confused series of decisions made their way to the Indiana Supreme Court, which, in the end, took the vote away from women.

Suffragists brought in a Chicago attorney, Catharine Waugh McCulloch, to draft a presidential suffrage bill modeled on Illinois's precedent, and it passed the next year. In 1920, the governor insisted that suffragists have pledges from two-thirds of both houses of the legislature before he would call a session to ratify the Nineteenth Amendment. Years of grassroots organizing paid off: they won ratification, with just three senators voting no and a unanimous House vote.

Indiana elected its first woman to Congress in 1932, when Democrat Virginia Jenckes defeated male incumbents in both the primary and the general election. A farmer and widow, she worked for New Deal agricultural and flood-control programs. After her 1938 defeat, Jenckes became an employee of the Red Cross and she made the news again in 1956 when, well into her seventies, she helped priests escape from war-torn Hungary. Indiana's second congresswoman, Cecil Murray Harden was elected in 1948 to represent the same district as Jenckes and, though a Republican, worked toward many of the same goals through the 1950s.

In 1977, Indiana became the thirty-fifth of the thirty-eight states needed to ratify the Equal Rights Amendment. That same year, the city of Gary sent the state's first African American woman to Congress; although Katie Beatrice Hall served only one term, it was her bill that made Martin Luther King Jr.'s birthday a federal holiday. In 1988, Democrat Jill Long pulled off a surprise victory to win the seat vacated by Vice President Dan Quayle, and in 1992, African American Pam Carter was elected attorney general. Indiana's current ten-member congressional delegation includes one woman, Democrat Julia Carson. Republican Sue Ann Gilroy lost her reelection bid as mayor of Indianapolis to a Democratic man in late 1999.

Iowa

Iowa was the first state to admit women to the practice of law and to its public university, but it currently is one of just eight states that have never elected a woman to Congress.

When Iowa became a state in 1846, one-fifth of Iowans were foreign born. These immigrants were relatively prosperous northern Europeans attracted to Iowa's excellent land. Their women, especially the Scandinavians, were better educated than many Americans. Norwegians Gro Svendson and Elisabeth Koren are two examples of women who wrote of life in early Iowa.

Such female literacy was promoted in 1858, when Iowa was the first state to integrate women into its public university. At the same time, however, this frontier was no more liberal than eastern states for women seeking a divorce—as Dr. MARY WALKER discovered when she moved there in 1855, vainly hoping to dissolve her New York marriage. Iowa also attracted some of the era's utopian communities, but its Amana and Amish settlements were extremely conservative groups that clung to a seventeenth-century lifestyle. One of the leaders of the Amana colony was Barbara Heinemann, who was considered a prophet and near saint.

The Amana colony was settled in 1859, and the Civil War started two years later. One anonymous woman joined Iowa's Fourteenth Regiment and, when her gender was discovered, put a revolver in her mouth and killed herself in full view of the regiment. More conventional women joined the U.S. Sanitary Commission that supplied soldiers, but unlike other states, Iowa paid its "state sanitary agents." They traveled the Mississippi on hospital ships and served under fire at Vicksburg and other battles. Their leader was Annie Wittenmyer, who in 1874 became the first president of the Women's Christian Temperance Union.

Women set other milestones at the war's end. When the Iowa State Dental Society had its founding meeting in 1865,

Lucy Hobbs, a practicing dentist for several years, was included. Perhaps because these men considered her a peer, the Ohio College of Dental Surgery reconsidered her 1861 application, and the next year she became America's first female dental graduate. After her 1867 marriage, Lucy Hobbs Taylor taught dentistry to her husband, and they practiced together in Kansas.

In 1869, Iowa became the first state to admit a woman to the bar. In contrast to MYRA BRADWELL's situation in Illinois, in which she was denied the right to practice law although she had passed the bar, Judge Francis Springer persuaded Arabella Mansfield to take the bar exam—even though Mansfield was an Iowa Wesleyan professor who did not intend to practice law. Three judges passed Mansfield with high honors and ruled the statute's masculine language irrelevant. Medicine offered opportunities to women also; Iowa's medical college became coeducational in 1870, and aspiring female physicians from the East went there. Meanwhile Carrie Lane graduated first in her 1880 class at Iowa State Agricultural College, and within a few years she was superintendent of schools for Mason City. As CARRIE CHAPMAN CATT, she went on to became perhaps the greatest feminist leader of the early twentieth century.

Meanwhile, AMELIA BLOOMER, whose name had become part of the language, had been quietly living in Iowa since 1855. She supported her husband in his position as mayor of Council Bluffs while retaining her interest in women's rights: she was a founding president of the Iowa Woman Suffrage Association.

From its 1870 founding onward, Iowa's suffrage association filed bills in every legislative session, but its only victory was extremely minor: in 1894, Iowa women were permitted to vote in municipal elections, but only on bond referenda. At the same time, men showed ironic confidence in the abilities of some women; in 1884, for example, twenty-three women were elected county or city school superintendents and almost a hundred served as officers of school boards.

Iowa's suffrage association built a permanent headquarters at the state fair in 1886, and longtime leader Mary J. Coggeshall published the *Woman's Standard* from 1886 to 1911. Iowa hosted such luminaries as LUCY STONE and SUSAN B. ANTHONY and gathered a hundred thousand signatures on a 1900 suffrage petition. In 1908, responding to speeches by Carrie Chapman Catt and British women, they conducted what may have been the nation's first suffrage parade in Boone.

Still, legislators remained obdurate until 1916, when they finally allowed a referendum. Officially it lost by some ten thousand votes of over 330,000 cast, but the evidence of fraud was overwhelming. The *Des Moines Register* said that in fifteen counties, more ballots were cast than there were voters—and that was one of many irregularities. A Republican leader candidly explained that they could not allow the "machine" of this one-party state to be "thrown out of gear" by women voters.

A second referendum was promised for 1921, but the events of 1919 made it irrelevant: in April, the legislature adopted presidential suffrage; in May, ten of Iowa's eleven House members voted for the Nineteenth Amendment; and in June, both senators did. Emboldened by this near unanimity of their congressional colleagues, Iowa lawmakers responded to the governor's call for a special session, and on July 2, with no Senate opposition and just five negative House votes, Iowa ratified the federal amendment.

Iowa's legislators honored well-known sculptor Vinnie Ream Hoxie with a 1906 commission for one of the two statues that each state is allowed in the U.S. Capitol; native daughter Nellie Verne Walker did the second one. In 1936, Carrie Chapman Catt unveiled a monument, also by Walker, in the state capitol, dedicated to suffragists. Famous Iowans include photographer Gertrude Stanton Käsebier and the creator of fictional teen detective Nancy Drew, Mildred Wirt Benson, who wrote for decades under the pseudonym Carolyn Keene.

In World War II, the first installation of the Women's Army Corps began at an obsolete Des Moines cavalry post. So many women were eager to join that their "barracks" soon overflowed to hotels and apartments, but Iowans welcomed them more hospitably than was the case for many military women elsewhere.

Iowa ratified the Equal Rights Amendment, and its 1974 legislature made it a crime to discriminate against women in housing or credit. In 1986, Linda Neuman became the first woman on the Iowa Supreme Court in its 148-year history. Roxanne Conlin won the Democratic nomination for governor in 1982, as did Attorney General Bonnie Campbell in 1994, but Iowa has never had a woman in its governorship or in either house of Congress.

Kansas

The site of the nation's first big suffrage campaign, Kansas also was the first state to have women simultaneously in its governorship and in the U.S. Senate.

When whites negotiated an 1825 treaty with the Kansa people, they noted that this tribe accorded women a high status. In this matrilineal culture, women not only owned the family property and passed on their names but also performed sacred ceremonies. Fort Leavenworth, established in 1827, was intended to protect the Kansa and Osage from illegal white settlers; some whites, including the family of LAURA INGALLS WILDER, had to move.

"Bleeding Kansas" aptly described the civil war that absorbed the territory long before the Civil War began. An 1854 act allowed (male) voters to decide whether Kansas would be a slave state or a free state, and thousands of men and women on both sides flocked there to participate. New England women organized support for abolitionist "emigrants" to Kansas. Among them were Julia Archibald Holmes of Massachusetts, who became the first woman to climb Pikes Peak; SUSAN B. ANTHONY's brother Daniel, a Lawrence newspaper editor whose influence was helpful to women; and CLARINA HOWARD NICHOLS, who moved from Vermont and persuaded the territorial governor and others to support suffrage at an 1855 constitutional convention.

Kansas became a free state with the beginning of the Civil War in 1861, and its women set a milestone by winning the first permanent voting rights in the nation—for school elections only. When the war ended, they aimed to expand this to full suffrage and conducted the first statewide campaign. LUCY STONE and her husband, Henry Blackwell, went to Kansas in 1867 and sent back excited letters that convinced Anthony, the Reverend Olympia Brown, ELIZABETH CADY STANTON, and others to join them. In the end, they won less than a third of the vote.

On the other hand, Kansas admitted Phoebe Couzins, the nation's first female law school graduate, to the bar in 1871, and in the same decade, it welcomed thousands of African Americans who fled southern states when Reconstruction ended. Again, New England women organized aid: black Bostonian Josephine St. Pierre Ruffin led the Kansas Relief Association, which sent supplies to charities overwhelmed by needy newcomers. The most celebrated woman of Kansas in the 1880s and 1890s was orator Mary Ellen Lease. Denigrated by some as "Mary Yellin," she was the most popular woman affiliated with the new Populist Party and made the presidential nomination seconding speech at its 1892 convention. The main attraction for "Kansas Day" at the World's Fair, she is remembered for urging farmers to raise "less corn and more hell."

Twenty years after their failed effort for full suffrage, Kansas women conducted a second campaign and added the right to vote in municipal elections to their school-election rights. This 1887 expansion was vital to the temperance movement, because crucial "wet" or "dry" decisions are made at the local level. Many temperance advocates, however, came to believe that their votes had been manipulated. The saloons stayed open, and in 1900, CARRY NATION took the state's unenforced liquor laws into her own hands. Beginning in Kiowa, she wielded a hatchet in saloons. After six months of destroying property, she was arrested for breaking up the bar of a Wichita hotel favored by politicos. Nation went on a national tour—with some of the income going to support a Kansas City shelter for the families of alcoholics, one of the nation's first such havens.

In 1912, Kansas suffragists conducted their third campaign and won full voting rights—more than a half century after forming their first women's rights society in 1859. Kansas was the seventh state to fully enfranchise women, and its men gave women their biggest margin of victory thus far. The suffrage association stayed in business to help women in other states, and in 1919, the governor called a special legislative session to ratify the Nineteenth Amendment just eleven days after Congress sent it to the states. Representative Minnie J. Grinstead introduced the unanimously passed joint resolution.

Although its abolitionist heritage made Kansas a largely Republican state, Democrat Kathryn O'Laughlin became its first congresswoman when she defeated an incumbent in the 1932 Roosevelt landslide. Roosevelt's successor, Harry Truman of small-town Missouri, appointed small-town Kansas banker Georgia Neese Clark as United States treasurer; since her 1949 precedent, this position has traditionally gone to a woman.

In the next decade, a Kansas case brought racial integration to the nation's attention. Young Linda Brown was the plaintiff in *Brown v. Board of Education of Topeka* in 1954. She lived in a white neighborhood and had to travel past nearer schools to attend an elementary school for blacks. The U.S. Supreme Court ruling on her behalf absorbed the nation for decades, as many school systems resisted it.

In 1976, Representative Martha Keys of Topeka, a Democrat who was the state's second congresswoman, became the nation's first to marry a colleague. Keys was elected in 1974 and appointed to the powerful Ways and Means Committee. The third woman to represent Kansas in the U.S. House was Republican Jan Meyers, who has been continuously reelected since 1984.

It was Nancy Kassebaum, however, whom most Americans would associate with Kansas. The daughter of 1936 presidential nominee Alf Landon, she won the 1978 U.S. Senate race. Although her experience was limited to a small-town school board, she defeated eight men in the Republican primary and won the general election with fifty-six percent of the vote. More than fifty years after women started voting, she was the first female senator who did not have a husband preceding her in Congress.

The nation's eyes were on Kansas again in 1982, when Kansas City reporter Christine Craft sued television executives after they fired her for being "too old" and "not deferential enough to men." A federal jury awarded her

$500,000, thus raising awareness among employers that discrimination could cost them.

In 1990, Democrat Joan Finney upset the incumbent Republican governor, making Kansas the first state to have women as both governor and U.S. senator (with Nancy Kassebaum still in that position). Kassebaum became chair of the Labor and Human Resources Committee in 1995, and she retired in 1998. Governor Finney did not run in 1994, and as the century turns, Kansas has no women in these top positions. Women recently have held the offices of attorney general, treasurer, and insurance commissioner.

Kentucky

The first state to grant women partial suffrage, Kentucky is also is one of eleven states that have elected a female governor.

In 1775, well before land west of the Appalachians was legally open to white settlers, Rebecca Bryan Boone joined her husband Daniel in the Kentucky wilderness. The next year, their daughter Jemina and her friends Betsey and Frances Calloway were ambushed by Shawnee Indians who overtook their canoe, and their rescue was nationally publicized. Soon after, the American Revolution intensified conflict with natives. At Bryan's Station in 1782, women were credited with saving the garrison by supplying water, and in 1787—after the war was officially was over—Bourbon County's "Widow Scraggs" was featured in national publications defending her home from Indian attack.

Kentucky became a state in 1792, and in 1805, Frenchwoman Mary Menessier Beck opened a Girls' Academy in Lexington, where future first lady Mary Todd Lincoln was one of her students. At the same time, Shaker followers of "MOTHER" ANN LEE established a commune at Pleasant Hill, and, between 1812 and 1822, three Catholic sisterhoods established Kentucky missions. In the 1830s Kentucky became the era's only state to grant voting privileges—albeit limited ones—to women: widows who had no school-age children could vote in school elections.

Kentucky provided the setting for HARRIET BEECHER STOWE's 1852 book *Uncle Tom's Cabin*, and thousands of escaped slaves used that route across the Ohio River to freedom. This border location made it one of the few states to stay neutral in the Civil War. Women were on both sides: Ella K. Trader, for example, managed Confederate hospitals and supply depots in Kentucky, while MARY LIVERMORE did the same for the Union.

Kentucky's best-known postwar woman was Sarah Bryan Piatt. From the same pioneer family as Rebecca Bryan Boone, and the mother of seven, she published seventeen volumes of poetry and was especially acclaimed

abroad; English critics ranked her with Christina Rosetti and Elizabeth Barrett Browning. The 1907 fictional bestseller was *The Lady of the Decoration* by Frances Little, a pseudonym for Kentucky native Fannie Caldwell Macaulay. And everyone knows "Happy Birthday," a song published by Kentucky sisters Mildred and Patty Hill in 1900.

Sophonisba Breckinridge became Kentucky's first female attorney in 1895; in 1900, the University of Chicago awarded her a doctorate in political science—the world's first granted to a woman. She was a member of a politically powerful family that, like Kentucky's Clay family, also included feminists. Mary B. Clay headed Kentucky's suffrage movement in the 1870s. Her sisters Anne Clay and Sally Clay Bennett were newspaper columnists, and a fourth sister, Laura, became president of the suffrage association in 1880.

Although their political connections allowed the suffragists to conduct meetings in the state legislative chambers, the legal rights of women in Kentucky were far behind those in most states. "An infinitesimal number of women had a bit of School suffrage," Desha Breckinridge wrote in 1888, but "Kentucky was the only State that did not permit a married woman to make a will; a wife's wages might be collected by a husband; . . . fathers were the sole guardians of their children and at death could appoint one even of a child unborn . . . and it was legal for a girl to marry at 12."

In this context, full enfranchisement seemed impossible, and indeed, women actually went backwards: in 1894, the legislature repealed the limited school suffrage of women in three cities where it deemed that too many black women voted. Not until 1912 did suffragists manage to overturn this repeal. Although they never truly tried to expand their state suffrage, by the time that Congress passed the Nineteenth Amendment, their educational campaign was effective enough that ten of twelve congressmen supported it. More remarkably, the legislature ratified by strong margins on the first day of the session in January 1920. Because it was not yet clear that the amendment would be ratified in time for the November election, the legislature also passed presidential suffrage in March.

Meanwhile, Laura Clay formed an organization to oppose the Nineteenth Amendment. She insisted on states' rights instead of a federal mandate, and after four decades of national feminist leadership, joined Kate Gordon of Louisiana in lobbying against ratification.

The newspapers were a liberalizing factor. Suffragist Desha Breckinridge owned the state's second-largest paper, the *Lexington Herald*, and the largest, the *Louisville Courier-Journal*—which also supported suffrage—was taken over by the Bingham family. It remained a Kentucky power through the century, with Sallie Bingham and Eleanor Bingham Miller making national headlines in the 1980s as they tried to wrest control of the paper from their brother.

Family conflict was also at the heart of Kentucky's first female congressional race. Representative John Wesley Langley, a Republican, was reelected in 1924 while in prison for selling liquor during Prohibition. When his appeals ran out, Katherine Langley was elected to her husband's seat on a platform of vindicating his reputation. President Calvin Coolidge, also a Republican, pardoned him with the proviso that he never again run for office. He betrayed both the president and his wife when, without informing her, he announced his candidacy for the next term; she refused to withdraw, and the Democrat won.

Other notable women of this era were Mary Breckinridge, whose Frontier Nursing Service inspired the formation of the American Association of Nurse-Midwives, and Georgia Madden Martin, a married white woman who called herself "George" in nationally published magazine articles and worked in vain for the teaching of black history.

Kentucky was the site of Bowman Field, which trained women to nurse on World War II airplane evacuations. These "flight nurses" were so well trained at Bowman Field that they moved thirty-seven thousand men from remote Pacific battles and lost just one patient.

The status of Kentucky women reached its apex in 1983, with the election of Governor Martha Layne Collins. A Democrat, she pioneered tax incentives to bring new industries to a state that had barely modernized. Due to term limits on governors, however, and she could not run for reelection. Over six decades after Katherine Langley's disastrous 1930 race, Kentucky elected a second woman to Congress: Republican Anne M. Northup was elected from Louisville in 1996.

Louisiana

The only state whose legal system is based in the French Napoleonic Code, Louisiana also is one of seven states that currently have a woman in the U.S. Senate.

New Orleans was settled in 1718 by French colonists, and very soon after, in 1727, Ursuline nuns began the first convent within the boundaries of the future United States. They operated a New Orleans hospital, orphanage, and school and were guardians for young women who came from France to marry lonely men.

German speakers from the Rhineland also arrived, but the most distinctive settlers came from Canada: French families known as Acadians (now called Cajuns) were expelled from Nova Scotia when the British took power in 1755.

They settled in remote bayous and contributed greatly to the unique culture of their adopted home. Louisiana became a state with the beginning of the War of 1812.

More than a century after its first convent was formed, New Orleans' second was established in 1833 by the Congregation of Our Lady of Mt. Carmel. Two decades prior to the Civil War, there were enough free blacks in New Orleans in 1842 to form what became the largest order of African American nuns: the Sisters of the Holy Family.

Some participants in the exodus from Ireland in this era came to Catholic Louisiana, and one, Margaret Gaffney Haughery, became known as "the bread woman" of New Orleans. She went from poverty to great success and in 1858 opened a steam-powered bakery; among other innovations, she introduced packaging for crackers that kept them dry in the Louisiana humidity. Adelicia Acklen was an equally successful businesswoman. Probably the richest southern woman of her era, she owned six Louisiana plantations, and, during the Civil War, she deceived officials to sail past embargo barricades; Liverpool mills desperate for cotton paid her almost a million dollars.

Louisiana's Civil War experience also was unique: the Union had control of the Mississippi River, and New Orleans surrendered on May 1, 1862—three years before the war ended. Rebellion lived on, however, and numerous prominent women were arrested. Among them was Eugenia Levy Phillips, who was confined to Ship's Island because she laughed during a Union funeral procession. An Irish-American woman from Baton Rouge named Mrs. William Kirby stole supplies for Rebels; caught with Union rifles under her dress, she was also was confined on Ship's Island, where she died.

After the war, northern women came south to teach ex-slaves, and the largest of their schools was the Abraham Lincoln School in New Orleans. Resentful whites attacked blacks in New Orleans in 1868, and black teachers particularly risked their lives. A recently graduated teacher, Julia Hayden, was killed three days after arriving in Hartsville.

No college in Louisiana would be open to black women for decades, and higher education for white women also was slow. Sophie Newcomb Memorial College opened under Tulane University in 1887 because of an endowment from Josephine Louise Newcomb in memory of her daughter; a Baltimore investor, Newcomb eventually gave more than $3 million to the college. As the twentieth century began, Louisiana was one of three states that did not admit women to its public university.

Dr. Sara Tew Mayo, who began the New Orleans Hospital for Women and Children in 1905, had been educated at Woman's Medical College of Pennsylvania, but even without formal education, some women succeeded. Eliza J. Nicholson, owner of the New Orleans *Daily Picayune* in 1895, hired her neighbor, Elizabeth Meriwether Gilmer, who under the pen name Dorothy Dix largely invented the advice-column genre; when she retired a half century later, she was read by thirty million people daily. Grace King's fiction based on Creole life won her election as a fellow of the Royal Society of Arts and Sciences in England. Kate Chopin, who lived in Louisiana's bayous in the 1870s, also published fiction set there; her 1899 novel *The Awakening*, with its exploration of female sexuality, was so criticized that she stopped writing at age forty-eight.

The women's rights movement—with its English, Protestant, and abolitionist roots—was slow to develop. Louisiana's first agitation came in 1879, when St. Anna's Asylum, which was run by women, had to cede an endowment to the state because no man had witnessed the female donor's will. As a result, Elizabeth Lyle Saxon and Caroline E. Merrick drew up a petition for suffrage; along with Dr. Henriette King, Saxon and Merrick spoke to a convention revising the state constitution, but without success. Louisiana's first suffrage association began in 1896, almost a half century after the nation's first. Even then, its members wanted the vote limited to educated, taxpaying women.

A form of this partial suffrage was quickly achieved, largely because of yellow fever, which had killed twenty thousand Mississippi Valley people in 1878 and appeared again in 1898. New Orleans was by then a city of three hundred thousand with no sanitation system, and government officials desperate for revenue believed that women would support them. In a carefully organized campaign led by Kate Gordon, property-owning women were granted the vote for tax referenda only. Many women, according to Gordon, "had not the courage to go to the polls" and instead cast proxy ballots, which required two male observers because a woman could not legally witness any document.

This limited suffrage would be the height of Louisiana success. Although the National American Woman Suffrage Association held its 1903 convention in New Orleans, the first state convention was not held until 1913. Jean Gordon became president that year, while her sister Kate led the formation of the Southern States Woman Suffrage Conference, a group that excluded blacks. Like most southerners, these aristocratic white women strongly believed in states rights and were therefore ambivalent about the national suffrage association's federal strategy.

Louisiana's sole suffrage campaign was in 1918, and it was the only one of four state campaigns that year to lose. When the federal amendment passed out of Congress the next year, Louisiana suffragists split. While the Gordons lob-

bied against the federal amendment, others worked for either ratification or state suffrage.

Louisiana's first woman in Congress was Rose McConnell Long, who briefly took her husband's Senate seat after his 1935 assassination. Four decades passed before a second woman went to Washington, and that was also for a short Senate term resulting from the death of the incumbent: Elaine Edwards was appointed by her husband, the governor, in 1972.

The next year, Corinne Claiborne Boggs—known as Lindy—became Louisiana's first female House member after her husband's plane disappeared in Alaska. Boggs was reelected until her 1990 retirement; she presided over the 1976 Democratic National Convention, another precedent for women. Currently, she is also known as the mother of political commentator Cokie Roberts.

Representative Boggs was joined in 1985 by Catherine Small Long, who defeated four others to win an election brought about by her husband's death. Two of Louisiana's four female congresswomen thus were members of the powerful Long family, but Representative Long did not run for reelection. Mary Landrieu set a precedent when she was elected to the U.S. Senate in 1996: more than seven decades after women got the vote, she was Louisiana's first to win a seat that was not left vacant by the death of a man.

The unequal status of women was highlighted again in 1975, when it was necessary for the U.S. Supreme Court to strike down the state's routine exemption of women for jury service. Organizations supporting the Equal Rights Amendment in that decade pulled their conventions from New Orleans because of Louisiana's failure to ratify, and in 1979, the Supreme Court ruled in favor of a woman who sued a Louisiana congressman for discrimination.

The 1991 legislature passed perhaps the nation's most harsh antiabortion law, threatening physicians who performed abortions with ten years at hard labor. In this political environment, the election of pro-choice Democrat Mary Landrieu to the U.S. Senate in 1996 was particularly noteworthy. The same year, Democrat Kathleen Blanco became lieutenant governor in a state where that post is elected independently from the governor.

Maine

Maine is one of the two states that have women in both U.S. Senate seats at the turn of the century. It also elected a strong female senator decades ahead of most states.

Although its coast was explored by Europeans in the late 1400s, Maine's climate kept the population so low that it was part of Massachusetts until 1820. In 1846, it became the first state to pass a law prohibiting alcohol sales, and temperance advocates in other states—many of them women—frequently cited the Maine Law as a model. Maine also supported the abolitionist cause earlier than other states, and its anti-slavery society hired a black lecturer, FRANCES ELLEN WATKINS (later HARPER), in 1854. HARRIET BEECHER STOWE wrote *Uncle Tom's Cabin* in her Maine kitchen.

In 1863, Bates College in Lewiston was chartered as a coeducational institution. Although this precedent was well established in the Midwest and South, Bates was the first college in the East to grant degrees to women. Colby College followed in 1871.

The threads of Prohibition, abolition, and education wove together in the women's rights movement, and attendees from Maine were at national meetings as early as 1855. The state's first suffrage association didn't start until 1868, however, and it was a man, John Neal, who issued the call. Suffrage was the chief goal, for property-rights laws had been reformed during the previous two decades. Married women could sign contracts and thus practice law: while MYRA BRADWELL's Illinois case was wending its way to the U.S. Supreme Court, Maine quietly admitted a married woman, Clara Hapgood Nash, to its bar in 1872. She was New England's first female attorney.

That year Maine's legislature became one of the first to vote on suffrage, but no debate was allowed and both houses defeated it. In 1875, the state passed a bill allowing women to hold school office—after several had already been elected superintendent by male voters. The suffrage association then lapsed until 1885.

Meanwhile, several Maine women developed careers as nationally popular writers. Fannie Hardy Eckstrom specialized in nature and in Maine's Penobscot Indians, while Harriet Prescott Spofford published hundreds of imaginative short stories in the era's best magazines. Mary Abigail Dodge wrote nonfiction, primarily under the pseudonym Gail Hamilton, and was a political ghostwriter for Republicans; initially a feminist, she became increasingly conservative and opposed suffrage. The writer most identified with Maine, however, was Sarah Orne Jewett, whose 1896 *Country of the Pointed Firs* became a classic of regional literature.

The suffrage association made its final push for the municipal vote in 1903 and then lapsed into inactivity for more than a decade. In 1917, the legislature allowed a referendum for full suffrage; despite an energetic campaign and endorsements from President Woodrow Wilson and former president Theodore Roosevelt, Maine's men voted women down almost two to one. The legislature, however, quickly ratified the Nineteenth Amendment in November 1919.

Twenty years later, Maine elected its first woman to the U.S. House; Margaret Chase Smith would personify the state for years thereafter. Voters elevated her to the Senate in 1948, making her the first woman to have served in both houses of Congress. The first female Republican senator, she voted with the Democratic Party more often than many of the era's Democrats. Smith was the chief sponsor of the U.S. Navy's women's corps, the WAVES, and was especially known for her 1950 speech against the violations of civil liberties committed by her Republican colleague Joseph McCarthy. He vowed revenge, but in the election that followed, eighty-two percent of Maine's Republicans supported Smith over McCarthy's preferred candidate.

In 1960, Maine featured the first Senate race between two women when Democrats nominated Lucia Cormier to run—in vain—against Smith. Four years later, Senator Smith received twenty-seven votes for president at the convention that nominated Barry Goldwater. After thirty-two years of never losing an election, she was finally defeated in 1972.

Six years later, in 1978, Maine elected its second woman to the House, Olympia Snowe; as they had done with Smith, voters elevated her to the Senate in 1994. Snowe split from her Republican colleagues to support abortion rights and oppose cutting aid to unwed mothers.

In 1996 Maine voters chose Susan Collins, the 1994 Republican gubernatorial nominee, to join Snowe in the Senate—making Maine and California the only states that have ever had simultaneous female senators. Collins and Snowe were also two of the five Republicans who voted against the impeachment of President Bill Clinton in February 1999. Maine is the only state that has elected three women to the U.S. Senate.

Maryland

Few states opposed women's enfranchisement as strongly as Maryland, but currently it is one of seven states represented by women in the U.S. Senate.

Maryland was founded by Catholic families from England in 1634. Annapolis was named for Anne Arundel, whose dowry supported Lord Baltimore after she married him at age thirteen; she bore nine children before dying at thirty-four. Lord Baltimore gave MARGARET BRENT a huge land grant, and because she was the executor of the governor's will, she effectively became governor at his death in 1647. Maryland's legislature backed her during a crisis with rebellious soldiers, resolving that without her, "all would have gone to ruin." The colony set a precedent in 1695, when Dinah Nuthead became an Annapolis printer—probably the first woman printer in the Americas.

Maryland continued to be a proprietary colony of Baltimore lords, who set poor examples in their treatment of women. When the fourth Lord Baltimore died in 1715, his mistress, Mrs. Grove, continued in the same role with his son—while Lady Baltimore, according to contemporary records, was treated with "barbarous cruelty." The status of women can also be seen in the era's newspapers, which carried almost as many advertisements seeking runaway wives as for escaped slaves.

The American Revolution was strongly supported by many Maryland women. The mother of fourteen, Anne Catherine Hoff Green became Maryland's official printer in 1767; she inherited both the *Maryland Gazette* and the governmental contract when her husband died, and she risked this business to publish news favoring rebellion. Mary Katherine Goddard's *Maryland Journal* also editorialized for revolution and published the first copy of the Declaration of Independence that included the signers' names. She also was postmistress of Baltimore from 1775 to 1789; many residents objected when a man replaced her.

In 1790, Carmelite nuns established the first convent within the boundaries of the United States at Port Tobacco. After an 1831 move to Baltimore, many sisterhoods grew from it. Maryland's most famous Catholic was ELIZABETH ANN SETON, a young widow with five children who established the Sisters of Charity of St. Joseph in western Maryland in 1809. Mother Seton was canonized in 1975, becoming the first American-born saint of either gender.

HARRIET TUBMAN was Maryland's most famous exile. She escaped from an eastern-shore plantation to Philadelphia in 1849 but returned nineteen times, imperiling her life to lead some three hundred other slaves to freedom—with the exception of her husband, who refused to take the risk.

Anna Ella Carroll also grew up on an eastern-shore plantation, where overinvestment in slaves was a factor in her father's bankruptcy. The Carrolls were politically powerful, though, and beginning in 1845 she became a behind-the-scenes lobbyist and political ghostwriter. She rendered the Union an incomparable service when she persuaded the governor not to call legislators into session; had they seceded, the nation's capital would have been in enemy territory.

As a border state, Maryland suffered tremendously from the Civil War. On one side was ninety-six-year-old Barbara Frietschie of Frederick, who flew the Union flag as Rebels surrounded her—inspiring the John Greenleaf Whittier poem that includes the line "Shoot, if you must, this old gray head." On the other side was Mary Surratt of Clinton, whose civil liberties were grossly violated when she was hanged for alleged complicity in Lincoln's assassination.

Maryland's first equal-rights society began in 1868 with ten white and four black women, who met at a facility owned by blacks. In 1870, they presented a petition with 150 signatures to the legislature, and three Baltimore women tested the Fifteenth Amendment by attempting to vote. The society soon lapsed, and the first woman to represent Maryland at a National Woman Suffrage Association meeting was Sarah T. Miller in 1889.

Educational progress was also slow. No Maryland college admitted women until 1885, when Methodist women managed to open Goucher College. The Johns Hopkins University—named for a descendant of Margaret Johns Hopkins, who was a contemporary of Margaret Brent—did not admit women, although M. CAREY THOMAS and JANE ADDAMS took classes there unofficially.

In 1889, Henrietta Szold pioneered Americanization classes in Baltimore for the era's many immigrants, and in 1912 she founded Hadassah, which became the largest organization for Jewish women. She mentored Rebecca Kohut, also of Baltimore, who became the 1923 president of the World Congress of Jewish Women.

As the twentieth century dawned, Maryland had yet to make the kind of progress other states had. No suffrage bill had been introduced. A mother had no right to her children, and fathers could name new guardians in wills. In 1901—decades after other states allowed women as attorneys—Maryland courts upheld the bar's rejection of Miss Etta Maddox, a graduate of Baltimore College of Law. Only two of Maryland's nine colleges accepted women in 1900, and all Johns Hopkins departments rejected them—except its medical school, which was open to women because Mary E. Garrett had insisted on it when she donated more than half of its initial endowment.

The legislature defeated suffrage bills from 1910 onward, the only victory being a 1918 grant of presidential suffrage, which became irrelevant at election time because the Nineteenth Amendment had eclipsed it. Maryland not only rejected the Nineteenth Amendment but went further: the legislature sent seven members to West Virginia to speak against ratification, and it authorized the attorney general to file suit against the amendment if other states added it to the Constitution. In 1920, suffragist pioneer Olympia Brown cast her ballot in Baltimore at age eighty-five, and anti-suffragists indeed filed suit. They symbolically challenged the registration of one white woman and one black one and, despite losses at lower levels, pushed the case all the way to the U.S. Supreme Court. Months after women voted, the Court declared the Nineteenth Amendment to have been legitimately ratified and to be applicable to Maryland.

Notable women of the next decades were Dr. FLORENCE SEIBERT, a Goucher College graduate who developed the tuberculosis test; GERTRUDE STEIN, who spent four years as a Johns Hopkins medical student before embarking on her extraordinary life in Paris; and WALLIS SIMPSON, a Baltimore divorcée for whom a British king gave up his throne.

A 1943 explosion at a World War II munitions plant in Elkton killed fifteen and injured fifty-four, most of them women. Maryland elected its first congresswoman during the war, but even though ELEANOR ROOSEVELT campaigned for Katherine Edgar Bryon, she did not run for reelection after completing her late husband's term. In 1978, her daughter-in-law, Beverly Butcher Byron, also replaced her husband in the House and enjoyed a long tenure.

Maryland in the 1970s was a huge contrast to its earlier political history. Marjorie Sewell Holt, Gladys Spellman, and Barbara Mikulski had solid House careers, serving as models for Helen Bentley and Constance Morella in the 1980s. In 1986, both parties nominated women for the U.S. Senate: Democratic Representative Barbara Mikulski defeated Republican Linda Chavez, the controversial former head of the U.S. Civil Rights Commission. At the turn of the century, she continues to represent Maryland in Washington, while Kathleen Kennedy Townsend is lieutenant governor.

Massachusetts

The first national women's rights convention—whose 150th anniversary is October 2000—was held in Massachusetts.

The Pilgrim families of the *Mayflower* arrived in December 1620, and of the eighteen women aboard, fourteen died in their first winter. A second colony developed at Salem in 1626, and major migration to Boston began in 1630. These settlers were more affluent than Plymouth's Pilgrims. Known as Puritans because they tried to purify the Church of England, they set up a theocracy in which church and state were synonymous. In 1637, they tried ANNE HUTCHINSON for heresy, and she and MARY DYER were banished; after Dyer converted to Quakerism and returned to preach the new faith, Puritan fathers hanged her.

During King Philip's War of 1676, the Pocasset band of Wampanoag Indians was led by a woman named Wetamoo; her men were annihilated, and her head was displayed in Taunton. Mary Rowlandson, one of dozens of women taken captive, wrote about her experience in 1682; her narrative, *The Soveraignty and Goodness of God . . . a Narrative of the Captivity and Restauration of Mrs. Mary Rowlandson*, became a classic of colonial literature.

America's first published poet was ANNE DUDLEY BRADSTREET, a mother of eight whose work appeared in

1650. Other colonial women worked as barbers, made ropes and eyeglasses, and ran slaughterhouses. Massachusetts law referred to midwives in the same category as physicians and surgeons—but women would be excluded from Harvard College, founded in 1636, for more than three centuries.

In 1704, Abenaki natives attacked Deerfield; the majority of its 268 residents were slain or marched as prisoners to Canada, where women endured extreme cruelty. Lucy Terry Prince wrote a poem about this event in 1746, making her America's first black poet. PHILLIS WHEATLEY, who came to Boston as a child on a slave ship in 1761, went to London in 1773, where she published *Poems on Various Subjects*.

That year, Sarah Bradlee Fulton became known as "the mother of the Boston Tea Party" because of her role in organizing and executing the raid. Massachusetts women strongly objected to the quartering of British soldiers in their homes, and the Daughters of Liberty—an informal network that was America's first female political-action group—enforced the boycott of British goods.

Like other wives of signers of the Declaration of Independence, Abigail Adams ran a farm and endured the war alone. She corresponded with many of the new nation's famous men, but a 1776 letter to her husband is most famous: "In the new code of laws," she wrote, "remember the ladies. . . . If particular care and attention are not paid to the ladies, we are determined to foment a rebellion."

Many Massachusetts women set trends for the new nation's culture. JUDITH SARGENT STEVENS MURRAY wrote "Essay on the Equality of the Sexes" in 1779. Hannah Adams became America's first successful female author of nonfiction; her first book, a 1784 reference work on the era's religions, stayed in print for decades. Sarah Apthorp Morton anonymously published *The Power of Sympathy*, which some call the nation's first novel, in 1789.

Deborah Skinner of Waltham was the first woman to run a power loom in the factories that sprang up in the early nineteenth century. Taunton women were among the nation's first to go on strike in 1829, and female shoemakers in Lynn and Saugus struck in 1833—but it was Lowell that came to epitomize female employment. Factory women there published magazines and hired professors to instruct them in a wide range of subjects, enjoying a golden age depicted in memoirs by Lucy Larcom and Harriet Robinson.

Abolitionism was born in Boston, with women as leaders from the beginning. Maria Stewart, who wrote against slavery in 1831, was probably the first black woman to do so. Despite threats to her life, Maria Weston Chapman founded the Boston Female Anti-Slavery Society in 1832. Established author LYDIA MARIA CHILD published an abolitionist book in 1833 and forfeited so many fans that the children's magazine she had published since 1826 went bankrupt. Massachusetts clergymen issued an 1837 pastoral letter condemning the "unnatural" public speaking of abolitionist women—but ANGELINA GRIMKÉ nonetheless spoke to a committee of the Massachusetts legislature in 1838, setting another milestone.

The Boston Lying-In Hospital, the nation's first obstetric hospital, was founded in 1832, and unlicensed physician Harriot K. Hunt began her very successful practice in 1835. MARY LYON opened her innovative school at Mount Holyoke in 1837; ELIZABETH PEABODY began publishing some of the nation's most important male writers in 1840; and DOROTHEA DIX's work for the mentally ill, begun in 1841, had no model anywhere in the world. Astronomer MARIA MITCHELL became the first woman elected to the American Academy of Arts and Sciences when she discovered a comet in 1847. Yet, in the same year, LUCY STONE had to go to Ohio to become the first female college graduate from Massachusetts.

Stone was the star of the first national women's rights convention, held at Brinley Hall in Worcester on October 23 and 24, 1850. Sarah H. Earl greeted delegates from nine states, who formed a half-dozen committees to follow up on the convention's resolutions. The 1854 legislature reformed property laws, largely in response to Mary Upton Ferrin, who collected petition signatures for six years after realizing that her husband had legal title to property she owned before marriage, as well as all income from her labor.

Massachusetts women continued to define the nation's cultural scene. A first novel by Maria Susanna Cummins, *The Lamplighter*, sold an unprecedented forty thousand copies shortly after its 1854 publication. Sculptor Harriet Hosmer became the first woman to receive a major public commission for artwork in 1860, and in the next decade, mixed-race Edmonia Lewis developed a successful career as a Boston sculptor. EMILY DICKINSON quietly produced more than 350 finely crafted poems in 1862 alone.

During the Civil War, Worcester readers were the first to respond to CLARA BARTON's newspaper pleas for necessary supplies. In Boston, the Young Women's Christian Association (YWCA) was organized in response to women's need to travel during the war: hotels often rejected unescorted women, so the YWCA provided rooms. Many Massachusetts women went south to work as nurses, including Louisa May Alcott, whose first successful book was *Hospital Sketches* (1863). The state's most famous wartime woman was probably JULIA WARD HOWE—although her immensely popular "Battle Hymn of the Republic" threatened to overshadow a lifetime of literary work and feminist leadership.

The New England Women's Club began in Boston in 1868; with support from celebrities such as Alcott and Howe, President Caroline Severance led the establishment of Girls Latin School and other progressive efforts. Stone, Howe, and others—including men, especially Stone's ardently feminist husband, Henry Blackwell—formed the American Woman Suffrage Association in 1869. Based in Boston, its publication was the *Woman's Journal*, a high-quality, long-lasting magazine initially edited by MARY LIVERMORE.

Massachusetts suffragists, including the Grimké sisters, tested the Fifteenth Amendment by attempting to vote in 1870. Although their ballots were rejected, women did persuade male voters to elect four women to the Boston school board in 1873; one of them, Kate Gannett Wells, held this powerful elective office while opposing her own right to vote. The nation's first opposition from women to their own enfranchisement began in 1868, when two hundred Lancaster women sent a petition to the legislature saying that they did not want the vote. Until final enfranchisement in 1920, Massachusetts was the national center of anti-suffragists. Most were members of wealthy families; many said that they opposed the vote because they did not wish their servants to be able to outvote them.

More progressive women, however, continued to surmount barriers. Although the state medical society refused to admit Dr. Susan Dimock—who graduated with high honors from the University of Zurich in 1871—Dimock trained LINDA RICHARDS, who pioneered professional nursing at Massachusetts General Hospital. ELLEN SWALLOW RICHARDS, the first woman admitted to the Massachusetts Institute of Technology (MIT) in 1870, was never awarded the doctorate that she earned there—although MIT employed her (sometimes without pay) for the rest of her life.

Single-sex education was an attractive option for many. Wellesley College began in 1870, and, unlike other prestigious women's schools, it had female presidents from its earliest years. Smith College opened in Northampton the next year and was the first major college endowed by a woman, Sophia Smith. With the earlier Mount Holyoke and the Harvard affiliate Radcliffe College, four of the elite Seven Sisters schools were in Massachusetts.

Beginning in 1869, the state legislature held annual hearings on suffrage, and women won the right to vote in school elections in 1879; after that, however, a variety of attempts to expand the vote were defeated, often by wide margins. In lieu of winning political battles at home, Massachusetts women were national pacesetters. Helen Hunt Jackson's *Century of Dishonor* (1881), the first widely read documentation of the nation's wrongs toward its natives, induced Congress to pass new legislation. The Harvard Observatory hired WILLIAMINA FLEMING to do mathematical calculations in 1881, and she developed a brilliant career in astronomy. On the other hand, also in 1881, eight female physicians—including Emily Blackwell and Marie Zakrzewska, who ran competing medical schools—offered Harvard $50,000 to open medical studies to women but were rejected.

The World Woman's Christian Temperance Union formed in Boston in 1891, but it was the 1892 murder trial of Lizzie Borden that captured public attention. Also that year, the Boston Symphony Orchestra performed a work by twenty-five-year-old Amy Beach, who became an internationally known composer.

Immigrants from southern and eastern Europe joined the earlier ones from Ireland in huge numbers during the latter part of the century. By 1912, forty languages were spoken in Lawrence mills, where one of the nation's most violent strikes erupted; police beat picketing women, and one, Annie LoPezzi, was fatally shot.

The Massachusetts legislature put full suffrage on the 1915 ballot. Campaigners worked tirelessly, attracting five hundred thousand people to their last big parade—but the saloons offered coupons for free drinks if suffrage was defeated. It went down 295,489 to 163,406, the greatest loss of any comparable campaign in the nation.

Giving up on state change, suffragists concentrated on Congress and the state's antisuffrage senators, Henry Cabot Lodge and John W. Weeks. When Weeks came up for reelection in 1918, suffragists campaigned against him, and he was replaced by David I. Walsh, a former governor who strongly supported women's rights. Walsh provided one of the two votes needed for Senate passage of the Nineteenth Amendment. On June 25, 1919, the legislature made Massachusetts the eighth state to ratify.

EDITH WHARTON carried on the state's literary tradition by becoming the first woman to win the Pulitzer Prize in literature in 1921. Massachusetts elected its first congresswoman soon after women got the vote: Edith Nourse Rogers established the record for female longevity in Congress, serving from 1925 to 1960 and dying in office.

During World War II, Navy WAVES trained at Smith College; their commander, MILDRED MCAFEE, had been president of Wellesley College. The war also transformed the life of Boston native JULIA CHILD, who was introduced to exotic foods in Ceylon, where she worked in wartime intelligence. In 1946, EMILY GREENE BALCH became the second American woman to win the Nobel Peace Prize.

Boston's puritanical image returned in the 1950s, when among the books banned there were Lillian Smith's *Strange Fruit* and Kathleen Windsor's *Forever Amber*. Massachusetts also initially banned birth-control pills; it was a feminist man,

Bill Baird, whose 1972 U.S. Supreme Court case, *Eisenstadt v. Baird*, made them available without regard to marital status. In *Bellotti v. Baird* (1979), the Court struck down a state law that required unmarried minors seeking abortions to obtain the consent of both parents or a judge.

The second congresswoman from Massachusetts was Margaret Heckler, who defeated a former Speaker of the House in the 1966 Republican primary. When she lost to a more liberal man in 1982, President Ronald Reagan appointed her head of the Department of Health and Human Services and then made her ambassador to Ireland. Meanwhile, between 1970 and 1972, Louise Day Hicks, a member of the Boston school board and an avowed segregationist, served one congressional term.

In 1988, Susan Estrich became the first female manager of a presidential campaign, for candidate Michael Dukakis. President Bill Clinton appointed Jean Kennedy Smith, sister of former president John F. Kennedy, as ambassador to Ireland in 1993. At the turn of the century, however, no women serve in these top state positions or in the ten-member congressional delegation, and many states with much smaller populations have elected more congresswomen than Massachusetts, which has had a total of three.

Michigan

Michigan held one of the first suffrage elections, but it is also currently one of the largest of the states that have never elected a woman as governor or U.S. senator.

Few women came with the fur traders who built the area's first permanent settlement at Sault Sainte Marie in 1668, and almost two centuries passed before Michigan's population merited statehood in 1837. Just eight years later—three years before the first women's rights convention—Polish immigrant ERNESTINE ROSE came from New York to deliver a series of lectures in Michigan on women's rights.

Kalamazoo College, a private school under the leadership of A. B. and Lucinda Stone, opened to women in the 1830s, but public colleges did not follow. In 1852 and 1853, the University of Michigan rejected several applications from Augusta Chapin and Olympia Brown because they were women. After attending a national women's rights convention, Sarah Burger organized a dozen women who applied in vain in 1858.

After the Civil War began, African American journalist Mary Ann Shadd Cary, who had fled to Canada, returned to recruit black soldiers. White Quaker abolitionist Elizabeth Comstock addressed the state senate in 1862 and went on to meet with two presidents: she prayed with Abraham Lincoln and lobbied James Garfield for aid to postwar blacks.

SOJOURNER TRUTH also met Lincoln; in 1864, the famed orator went from Battle Creek, where she had lived for the past decade, to be honored at the White House.

Battle Creek also was home to the Seventh Day Adventists; co-founder ELLEN WHITE, whom many believed to be a prophet, was an unquestioned authority in church structure. The Unitarian Church granted credentials to Olympia Brown and Augusta Chapin during the 1860s; both became career pastors and women's rights leaders, serving as models for ANNA HOWARD SHAW, who was licensed by Michigan Methodists in 1871.

In 1870, almost two decades after Chapin's first rejection, the University of Michigan, including its medical school, admitted women—something that was still uncommon in the East. Still, when Amanda Sanford became both the university's first female graduate and valedictorian of her class, she was pelted with spitballs.

An 1867 constitutional revision gave taxpaying women the right to vote in school elections; in 1870, women formed an association for full suffrage, and several tested the Fifteenth Amendment's gender-neutral language. A Detroit registration official rejected Catherine A. F. Stebbins but registered her friend Nanette Gardner on the grounds that Gardner was a widow. Gardner cast a ballot in 1871 and went on voting in municipal elections for years. Sojourner Truth joined the crusade the next year but, though an unmarried property owner, was unsuccessful—making it clear that the Fifteenth Amendment's enfranchisement of ex-slaves meant only male ones.

The legislature had considered suffrage petitions since the days of Ernestine Rose's visit, and in 1874 it placed the question on the ballot, but Michigan's men voted it down. The disappointed suffrage association lapsed for a decade. Some cities even rescinded school suffrage, but Eva R. Belles successfully sued Flint officials who refused her 1888 school ballot. Perhaps encouraged by this, Detroit women organized the next year and elected Sophronia O. C. Parsons to the school board, and by the turn of the century hundreds of women served on school boards.

Notable women of this era were Sarah Logan Fraser, who became the state's first black female medical-school graduate in 1876; Bertha Van Hoosen, founding president of the American Medical Women's Association and developer of the anesthetic known as "twilight sleep"; and Ellen May Tower, who, during the Spanish-American War, became the first American nurse to die on foreign soil.

Women were surprised when the legislature unexpectedly put suffrage on the 1912 ballot, but they organized quickly and probably won: the governor and most newspapers agreed that ballot boxes disappeared after early returns showed women winning. A three-week recount finally resulted in a loss. Indignant but also encouraged, women went back to the polls the next year, but they lost by an even greater margin after the liquor lobby, fearful that suffrage would bring Prohibition, worked hard to get immigrant men to the polls. Men adopted Prohibition themselves in 1916, however, making the alcohol issue moot. Finally, in 1918, women won their fourth statewide campaign. The next year, Michigan was one of three states that ratified the Nineteenth Amendment on the first possible day.

The automotive industry transformed Michigan in the following decades. The Women's Emergency Brigade was a vital part of the 1937 sit-down strikes, when the United Auto Workers closed down the assembly lines—and the state's economy—with 125,000 strikers. While men camped out in the factories, women defied armed guards to bring them food and supplies. Women's marches were a chief media focus in the successful strike.

As the auto plants switched to manufacturing weaponry during World War II, women got jobs in huge numbers. Ford, for instance, broke a forty-year precedent of never hiring women for assembly lines and employed some twelve thousand at its Willow Run plant alone. Management desperate for workers adopted such enlightened ideas as on-site child care, but when the war ended, so did most innovations.

Three decades after enfranchisement, Michigan elected its first woman to Congress in 1950: Republican Ruth Thompson, a lawyer in her sixties, also became the first woman on the House Judiciary Committee. Democrat Martha Griffiths, who joined her in Congress in 1954, not only became the first on the Ways and Means Committee but also was the era's feminist champion. The chief sponsor of the 1963 Equal Pay Act and the 1964 Civil Rights Act's important Title VII, she also led the petition drive that forced the Equal Rights Amendment out of the Judiciary Committee, where it had languished for almost a half century. Griffiths retired after twenty years in the House but later served as lieutenant governor.

Other notable women of the era include Viola Gregg Liuzzo, a young white mother of five who was killed in Alabama after Martin Luther King Jr.'s 1965 civil rights march, and the Reverend Marjorie S. Matthew, whose 1980 election as a bishop of the United Methodist Church made her the first woman on the governing body of a major religious denomination.

Despite the success of Michigan's first congresswomen, no more were elected until the 1990s, when four Democrats won. Barbara-Rose Collins was the first African American; elected in 1990, she was replaced by Carolyn Kilpatrick in 1996. Michigan's sixteen-member delegation also includes

Ann Arbor's Lynn Rivers, one of the few Democratic women to win in 1994, and Lansing's Debbie Stabenow, who replaced Dick Chrysler in 1996.

Minnesota

Minnesota was the first state to create a coeducational public university.

The native women of Minnesota harvested wild rice, tapped maple trees, and fished through the ice in winter. Some lived with French fur traders, whose explorations began in the 1650s, but Minnesota was not accurately mapped until the 1830s. Non-native women, including black slaves, had been there a decade by then: in 1819, women came with the army to Saint Anthony, which became Minneapolis. The diary of Pennsylvanian Eliza Taliferro recorded life in this frigid frontier.

An 1848 boom brought many newcomers, including Sarah Judd, who established a daguerreotype business in Stillwater. She tapped a fertile market: immigrants were eager to use this early form of photography, as grandparents far away probably would never see their grandchildren.

As the territory moved to statehood, an 1857 constitutional convention considered enfranchising married women, but the idea was quickly dropped. In the same year, Pittsburgh's Jane Grey Swisshelm moved to Minnesota and began the *St. Cloud Visiter* [*sic*]. Her abolitionist editorials initially outraged local men, who destroyed her printing press, but just two years later she spoke to the Minnesota House; the Senate invited her in 1862.

Abolitionists supported Eliza Winston, a Mississippi slave brought to Minneapolis by her owner, who sued her owner for her freedom in 1860 on the grounds that Minnesota was a free state. State courts ignored the Supreme Court's *Dred Scott* decision and emancipated her, and Winston escaped to Canada following an attack on the house where she was staying by an anti-abolitionist mob.

During the Civil War, Dakota Sioux in western Minnesota took advantage of the military's absence to kill some four hundred settlers. Women were raped and held for ransom; near Saint Peter, thirty women were herded into a house that was set on fire. Lavina Eastlick's *A Personal Narrative of Indian Massacres* told of being forced to watch her two children be beaten to death by a woman. On the other hand, many Indians, especially Ojibwa, protected whites, and a Dakota woman, Aza-ya-man-ka-wan (Berry Picker), was honored for her humanitarianism.

The University of Minnesota had been open to women from its 1851 beginning, as Sarah Burger Stearns—who vainly organized female applicants to the University of Michigan in 1858—found when she moved to the state. In 1867, Stearns and Mary J. Colburn addressed the legislature, and a suffrage bill failed by just one vote the next year. The two led the first suffrage organization in Rochester in 1869. A second club at Kasson, formed in 1872, attracted national speakers, including SUSAN B. ANTHONY, JULIA WARD HOWE, and FRANCES WILLARD. An 1875 referendum allowed women to vote in school elections, and some soon were on school boards, including Stearns, who won a Duluth seat.

An 1877 referendum to allow women to vote on issues related to alcohol sales lost, however, motivating the first statewide suffrage association, which began in 1881 in Hastings. Women set up a headquarters at the state fair, which they maintained until 1920, and gathered 31,228 petition signatures during their first year. The American Woman Suffrage Association held its 1885 convention in Minneapolis; LUCY STONE and, later, ELIZABETH CADY STANTON and other national leaders visited. Except for gaining the right to vote on library matters, however, women repeatedly lost their campaigns.

Other areas saw more progress. Martha Angle Dorsett became the state's first female attorney in 1877—after the legislature overruled her exclusion from the bar. In 1875, Minneapolis women established the Bethany Home for women in crisis; Dr. Martha G. Ripley, a suffrage association president, founded Maternity Hospital; and musicologist Frances Densmore documented Ojibwa music with the new technique of sound recording. By the turn of the century, forty-three women were elected county school superintendents. Minneapolis hosted the 1901 national suffrage convention, but perhaps the bigger news was that, despite the Catholic church's general antipathy to suffrage, Archbishop John Ireland signed their petition at the state fair. In 1907, ELIZABETH GURLEY FLYNN organized miners in the Iron Range. The Scandinavian Woman Suffrage Association began the same year; its members aimed for the same status as their sisters in Finland, Denmark, and Norway, who by 1906 had more voting rights than those in Minnesota.

Following the immigrants' lead, black women, working women, and college women also organized. Thousands marched in Saint Paul in 1914, a Minneapolis headquarters was established in 1915, and in 1916 the women went on a "suffrage barge" to Saint Louis for the Democratic National Convention. In 1919 the House raced the Senate to be the first to ratify the Nineteenth Amendment; of 191 votes in both houses, only 11 were negative.

Minnesota elected four women to its legislature at its first opportunity in 1922. In the same era, Lila Bell Acheson Wallace cofounded *Reader's Digest*, Lorena Hickok went from the Sunday editorship of the *Minneapolis Tribune* to being an advisor to President Franklin Roosevelt, and artist Wanda Gág illustrated and translated *Tales from Grimm* and *Snow White and the Seven Dwarfs* into English.

In 1942 Minneapolis welcomed Australian nurse ELIZABETH KENNY, who introduced new techniques to treat polio. Eugenie Moore Anderson set a diplomatic milestone in 1949, when she was appointed ambassador to Denmark; under President John F. Kennedy, she represented the United States in Bulgaria. In 1958, Minnesota became the second state to honor a woman, university professor Maria Sanford, by placing her statue in the U.S. Capitol.

Minnesota elected its first congresswoman in 1954, when Democrat Coya Gjesdal Knutson defeated an incumbent; she became the first woman on the House Agriculture Committee. It was her 1958 defeat, however, that is most memorable: she lost after Republicans distributed "Coya, Come Home," a letter allegedly written by her husband. A postelection House investigation revealed that her husband had not written it and that its accusation of romance with an aide was false. Minnesota has yet to elect another congresswoman. The state's only other female representative was Muriel Humphrey, appointed in 1978 to the unexpired Senate term of her late husband, former Vice President Hubert Humphrey.

Minnesota has provided feminist models in other areas. Its 1975 rape law was copied in other states, and its 1982 study of comparable worth was one of the best: the legislature appropriated $22 million to raise the pay levels of social workers and others in historically underpaid "women's jobs" to be comparable to those of "men's jobs." Such equity was the motivation for the Minnesota nurses' strike in 1984 and for the nationally publicized strike of bank tellers in Wilmar.

President Bill Clinton appointed Hazel O'Leary to head the Department of Energy in 1993, and later that year the largely white voters of Minneapolis elected Sharon Sayles Belton, an African American, as mayor. Minnesota's current lieutenant governor is Mae Schunk.

Missouri

A Missouri law school was the first to admit women, and some of women's most important court cases were filed in this state.

French fur traders, who came in the late 1600s, had amicable relations with Missouri's natives, the Osage, Sauk, and Fox. When Rebecca Bryan Boone came with her husband Daniel in 1798, Missouri was Spanish territory; it was American in 1808, when SACAGAWEA briefly adopted white women's clothing in Saint Louis. Saint Louis was also the beginning point of Madame Marie Dorian's 1811 expedition, in which Dorian, a member of the Iowa tribe, led explorers to the West Coast.

Sacred Heart nuns settled in the wilderness of Saint Charles in 1817. Sister Rose Philippine Duchesne came from France and began a dozen schools. By 1818, Saint Louis had a German aid society, and during the next decades, tens of thousands of immigrant families came up the Mississippi River from New Orleans. One immigrant, Jette Bruns, left remarkable letters of her experience in Westphalia, Missouri, which Catholics from Saxony colonized in the 1830s.

Because no eastern school would accept her, Boston sculptor Harriet Hosmer went to Saint Louis in 1850, where she and Missourian Jane Peck were the first women to study anatomy at Missouri's medical college.

When Missouri became a state in 1821, its admittance as a slave state was paired with that of Maine as a free one. The conflict was personified in Jessie Benton Frémont: her father, U.S. Senator Thomas Hart Benton, supported the status quo, while her husband, John Charles Frémont, was supported by abolitionists when he became the first nominee of the new Republican Party in 1856. The presidential election was the first to promote a potential first lady, with advertisements featuring "Frémont and our Jessie." In 1860, Missouri honored retired senator Benton with a statue—by Harriet Hosmer. It was the first state art commission granted to a woman.

The Civil War began the next year. Officially part of the Union, Missouri was also the first locus for hospital ships coming up the Mississippi, and hundreds of women worked there as nurses.

Phoebe Couzins was one of those nurses, and in 1868, Saint Louis men recruited her to begin coeducation at the law school of Washington University. She and Lemma Barkaloo of Brooklyn, New York, were the first female law students anywhere. Barkaloo was admitted to the Missouri bar in 1870 and was the first woman to try a case, but she died soon after. Couzins, admitted to the bar in 1871, worked in the women's movement; in eastern Missouri in 1887, she briefly was the nation's first female federal marshal.

VIRGINIA L. MINOR's 1872 suit against the Saint Louis official who refused to register her to vote was the century's most crucial court case for women. With her husband, Francis Minor, as her attorney, she argued in *Minor v. Happersett* that the Fifteenth Amendment's gender-neutral language should enfranchise women as well as male ex-slaves, and the Minors pursued the case to the U.S. Supreme Court. The Court's 1874 ruling was a huge setback for suffragists; it meant they had no choice except to either conduct state-by-state campaigns or win extraordinary majorities to amend the federal Constitution.

British militants reenergized Missouri on the vote: beginning in 1910, young Saint Louis women brought the celebrated PANKHURSTS and other speakers from England. They opened a headquarters in 1914; and one of them, politically astute Helen Guthrie Miller, became the top vice president of the national association. When the Democratic National Convention met in Saint Louis in 1916, some seven thousand women lined the route that male delegates took between their hotel and meeting hall—and for the first time, a party platform included suffrage. The legislature passed presidential suffrage in 1918, and when Congress sent the Nineteenth Amendment to the states, most of Missouri's delegation supported it. Its governor called one of the first special sessions, and legislators ratified resoundingly: just 7 of 161 were opposed.

In the Roaring Twenties, Marie Meyer's Flying Circus astonished crowds with daredevil acts; Meyer stood on the plane's wing while her husband flew between Saint Louis buildings. St. Louis native Josephine Baker became the toast of Paris in the Jazz Age, dancing with the Folies-Bergère and posing for Pablo Picasso. As radio developed, Missouri journalist and author Mary Margaret McBride set the national standard for talk shows aimed at women.

The World War II advisory committee of the Women's Army Corps was chaired by Margaret A. Hickey, successful owner of a Saint Louis business school and national president of the Business and Professional Women's Clubs. The war brought thousands of women to Saint Louis factories, while sleepy towns such as Neosho were transformed by military camps.

In 1947, biochemist GERTY RADNITZ CORI became the first woman to win the Nobel Prize in physiology or medicine. She shared it with her husband, who had ignored warnings that her presence in the laboratory was damaging his career, and Washington University finally granted her full faculty rank. President Harry Truman, a fellow Missourian, appointed Dr. Cori to the new National Science Foundation. During Truman's last year in office, Missouri elected its first congresswoman: Democrat Leonor K. Sullivan of Saint Louis defeated an incumbent, won reelection twelve times, and created the nation's food-stamp program.

A century after *Minor v. Happersett*, Missouri feminists were back at the U.S. Supreme Court—with better results in 1976. In *Planned Parenthood of Central Missouri v. Danforth*, the Supreme Court struck down a state law requiring a married woman to obtain her husband's permission for an abortion and—by a bare majority—a mandate that a minor obtain her parents' consent. Litigation continued, however, and 1989's *Webster v. Reproductive Health Services* upheld Missouri's ban on abortions in public hospitals.

Almost four decades passed between the elections of Leonor Sullivan and Missouri's second congresswoman: although Democratic nominee Harriet Woods ran a close race for the U.S. Senate in 1986, no women won until 1990, when Democrat Joan Kelly Horn won a House seat by fifty-four votes—which she lost after census reapportionment. Democrats Pat Danner and Karen McCarthy won in 1992 and 1994. Republican Jo Ann Emerson joined them in 1996, replacing her husband in office.

For the first time ever, the Library of Congress named a woman as the nation's poet laureate in 1992, Mona Van Duyn of Saint Louis. She carried on the poetic tradition of two Missouri natives, Sara Teasdale and Marianne Moore, when she won the 1991 Pulitzer Prize for *Near Changes*.

Montana

Montana elected the first woman in Congress—before most American women could vote.

The state's name—Spanish for mountain—and its far-north location were key to its slow settlement. Not even French fur traders went there until 1743, and they did not stay. The land was truly unfamiliar to white men in 1806, when SACAGAWEA helped lead the Lewis and Clark expedition through Montana's Bitterroot Mountains.

A gold strike in 1862 attracted many men, and after the Civil War many displaced Rebels fled there. Lynchings and robberies were common, and with more Indian warfare in the 1870s, Montana was so near anarchy that Congress only reluctantly accepted it as a state in 1889.

Women had received limited voting rights for some school and tax elections under the territorial government that was organized in 1864, but full suffrage hinged on how women might vote on alcohol sales. In Montana's overwhelmingly male environment, an 1883 visit from FRANCES WILLARD, president of the Women's Christian Temperance Union, may have done more harm than good.

Yet LUCY STONE's husband, Henry Blackwell, nearly succeeded. So devoted to women's rights that he came from Massachusetts to address the new state's constitutional convention, he pointed out that neighboring Wyoming—which granted full suffrage when it became a territory in 1869—had found suffrage to be a positive influence on government. The convention rejected him 34-29, however, and just weeks later, a follow-up bill in the legislature died on a tie vote.

In 1892, the Populist Party—a major party in western states—nominated Ella Knowles for attorney general. She ran five thousand votes ahead of the rest of the slate, and it took three weeks of vote counting before officials finally proclaimed the Republican, H. J. Haskell, the winner. He appointed her assistant attorney general, and they later married. In 1896, Ella Haskell was a delegate to the Populists' national convention, where she was instrumental in making it the first party to endorse suffrage.

A suffrage association formed in 1895. Their bill that year passed the House by a wide margin but failed in the Senate. Yet, by 1900 male voters had elected women as school superintendents in every county in the state.

At the turn of the century, ELIZABETH GURLEY FLYNN and Mother Jones organized Montana miners, and Fannie Sperry won the 1907 national bucking-horse contest, making her a major draw on the professional rodeo circuit. CARRY NATION met the beginning of her end in Montana, at the hands of a woman; after a decade of destroying bars while men watched aghast, a female saloon operator beat her so badly that she died six months later.

A House bill in 1903 passed 41-23—one vote short of the necessary two-thirds. The disappointed women drifted for a decade, until Missoula's JEANNETTE RANKIN assumed leadership. Although her chief opponent tried to dismiss her with a violet bouquet when she spoke to the legislature in 1911, her message sank in by the following session. The legislature put full suffrage on the 1914 ballot, and women conducted an energetic campaign and—overcoming organized opposition from national anti-suffragists and the liquor industry—won narrowly. Perhaps most effective was a Helena parade featuring as many men as women, including the national president of the Men's Suffrage League.

These women then set the model for the League of Women Voters by forming a Good Government Club. They won every one of the goals adopted at their first meeting, including electing a woman to Congress at the first opportunity, Jeannette Rankin in 1916. When Montana ratified the Nineteenth Amendment, a female legislator introduced it.

But such progress did not last. Montanans defeated Rankin in 1918 because—along with fifty male House members—she kept her campaign promise and voted against World War I. In the 1920s and 1930s, the Great Depression affected rural Montana sooner and more deeply than it did eastern states, with inevitable loss of opportunity. A noteworthy Montana native of this era was Rose Hum Lee, one of the Chinese Americans whose families had been recruited for dangerous mining jobs, often as strikebreakers. When Japanese bombed Canton in 1937, she was working as a businesswoman in China and helped organize refugee aid.

That bombing presaged World War II, but Montanans were not committed to the war when they again elected Jeannette Rankin on a peace platform in 1940. More than two decades later, her personal history repeated itself: she

kept her campaign promise, was the only member of Congress to vote against the war, and lost the next election.

At the turn of the century, Rankin remains the only Montana woman elected to high office. Democrats nominated State Representative Dorothy Bradley for governor in 1992, but she lost narrowly. The current lieutenant governor is Republican Judy Martz.

Nebraska

Nebraska is one of the few states that have elected a female governor and, albeit briefly, had two women as U.S. senators.

Although located in America's heartland, Nebraska was settled comparatively late. Growth was so slow that the huge territory's population was less than three thousand when the government was organized in 1854—with parts of five future states in its borders. The very next year, legislators invited AMELIA BLOOMER of neighboring Iowa to address them, and the House voted 14-11 to fully enfranchise women. The upper chamber did not follow suit, and Nebraska missed its chance to be the first territory to give women the vote; instead, the Wyoming Territory set the precedent fourteen years later.

The army pushed Indians west and north, after the 1862 Homestead Act brought the first farms to the area, and there were enough whites to justify statehood in 1867. SUSAN B. ANTHONY and ELIZABETH CADY STANTON lectured in Omaha that year, on their way to the Kansas campaign, and in 1869 the legislature granted women school suffrage. In 1871, the University of Nebraska opened on a coeducational basis. When Anthony returned that year, the legislature invited her to speak. With the governor's wife leading the drive, women gathered a thousand petition signatures—but the Senate killed their bill in a 6-6 vote. Suffrage regressed in 1875, when the right of married women to vote in school elections was repealed, but the 1882 legislature put full suffrage on the ballot. The national associations held their conventions in Omaha, but to no avail: women lost badly.

Nebraska's population more than doubled in the 1880s. Nearly equal numbers of women and men came, especially German speakers from eastern provinces, but with the exception of the Bohemians, they tended to be culturally conservative; most opposed women's rights.

In the same year as the losing suffrage campaign, ethnologist Alice Cunningham Fletcher went to Washington, D.C., where she drafted legislation aimed at improving life for American Indians; she administered the Dawes Act with Nebraska's Omaha and Winnebago natives. She also promoted Omaha leaders SUSETTE and SUSAN LA FLESCHE, who toured the nation as "Bright Eyes," to educate people on Indians' desperate status. Susette's younger sister Susan graduated at the top of her 1889 class at Women's Medical College of Pennsylvania and became the first Native American female physician. After their father's death, she was effectively chief of the Omaha tribe.

Angelia F. Newman of Lincoln worked to outlaw polygamy; a national leader in missionary and temperance organizations, she presented Congress with 250,000 petition signatures in 1886. In 1888, Mary Baird Bryan, wife of future presidential nominee William Jennings Bryan, was admitted to the Nebraska bar. This was unusual because not only was Bryan a married woman, but also a mother—her daughter Ruth, a future Florida congresswoman, was three.

Throughout the 1880s and 1890s, suffrage leader Clara Colby published her *Woman's Tribune*, and SUSAN B. ANTHONY made her sixth visit to the state in 1894. The national association sent organizers in 1899, who held some three hundred meetings that resulted in thirty-eight clubs—but the era had grown conservative and the legislature obdurate. Bills for various forms of suffrage were introduced at every opportunity, but none passed.

As the century turned, Nebraska's Abbott sisters began their national careers. GRACE ABBOTT was a pioneer sociologist and EDITH ABBOTT earned a 1905 doctorate in economics; much later, she saw many of her ideas implemented in Franklin Roosevelt's New Deal program. By far the best-known Nebraska native was WILLA CATHER, whose Nebraska-based novels became classics of American literature.

When a new law made it possible to bypass the legislature and go directly to male voters, women began a 1914 campaign, soon collecting upward of fifty thousand petition signatures from men in sixty-three counties—many more than required. But the national anti-suffrage organizations also made a major effort, especially among German Catholics. Men in the brewers' association threatened the businesses of suffragists' husbands, forcing many to curtail their public support. Women lost 100,842 to 90,738—but suffragists went back to work and, in 1917, the legislature granted them the vote for president.

Even this compromise was too much for opponents, who collected petition signatures to repeal it. Nineteen activists filed suit, and the evidence of fraud was so overwhelming that the secretary of state refused to put the repeal on the ballot. When the governor called a special session to ratify the Nineteenth Amendment, both legislative houses voted for it unanimously.

The decades that followed were especially hard for the rural economy. In 1934, Nebraska adopted a one-house legislature as a Depression-era cost-cutting tool—but the fact that there were fewer seats in this unique unicameral body made it even harder for women to win one. Perhaps as a means of escape, disproportionate numbers of Nebraska women volunteered for the military in World War II.

In 1954, Nebraska briefly had female representation in the U.S. Senate. After the incumbent's death, Republican rancher Eva Kelly Bowrig was appointed in April; a technicality in state law meant that she could not continue after the November election, and Hazel Hempel Abel served the two months that remained in this session of Congress. A businesswoman, she defeated eighteen candidates for her short term, during which she cast a historic vote to censure fellow Republican senator Joseph McCarthy. Abel placed second in the 1960 Republican primary for governor.

Republican Virginia Dodd Smith became Nebraska's first female member of the U.S. House in 1974; she was reelected until her 1990 retirement. In 1977, Nebraska was one of three states that rescinded their earlier ratification of the Equal Rights Amendment, but a decade later it became the eighth state to have a woman as governor. The campaign set two precedents: It was the nation's first gubernatorial race to have women as nominees of both major parties, and the winner, Kay Orr, was the nation's first female Republican governor. She defeated Helen Boosdis, a former mayor of Lincoln. Nebraska's current highest-ranking woman is Auditor of Public Accounts Kate Witek.

Nevada

The last western state to grant women the vote, Nevada was the first in the nation where a woman campaigned for the U.S. Senate.

The state's Shoshone, Paiute, and Washoe tribes were undisturbed longer than most; the first white men to venture there were Americans who arrived in the 1820s. The first white women came with the Bidwell-Bartleson group in 1841. Mexico ceded the area to the United States in 1848, but Nevada's white population was so small that more than a decade passed before it was even organized into a territory. The 1859 discovery of silver deposits brought thousands of newcomers, and Virginia City boomed into one of the largest—and most male—towns in the West. Some women mined, but prostitution was a more common female occupation; one popular woman reputedly charged $1,000 a night.

Congress granted territorial status to Nevada as the Civil War loomed in 1861, with statehood following in 1864—even though it had less than one-sixth of the required population. Unlike that of neighboring Utah, its citizenry remained overwhelmingly male and irreligious, but like those of other western states it was open to new ideas. Nevada's legislature welcomed California suffragists in 1871, and after a speech by Laura de Force Gordon, a proposal for full enfranchisment lost by just two votes.

SARAH WINNEMUCCA was doubtless Nevada's most famous native. A Piute called "Shell Flower," she went to Washington, D.C., in 1880 and lobbied President Rutherford B. Hayes for reform of the corrupt Bureau of Indian Affairs. Locally, perhaps the era's most notable woman was Hannah K. Clapp, who disguised her gender to win the bid to produce the ironwork that still adorns the state capitol grounds.

Clapp also led an 1883 suffrage effort that passed in the Senate but failed in the House. Nevada's first suffrage association finally formalized a decade later, when SUSAN B. ANTHONY and the Reverend ANNA HOWARD SHAW visited. Anthony returned the next year with CARRIE CHAPMAN CATT, and with Elda A. Orr as their president, women lobbied the legislature. The process was extraordinarily difficult: Nevada required a two-thirds vote from both houses in two successive biannual sessions. Each time, victory narrowly eluded the suffragists. Unlike those in many states, Nevada women did not even have school suffrage. However, Nevada women did have the right to easily obtain a divorce: at the turn of the century, a husband who failed to exert "ordinary industry" to support his family could be divorced after just one year.

The suffrage association lapsed during the first decade of the twentieth century, but a 1911 reorganization met quick success. After speeches by Mrs. Henry Stanislawsky and Miss Felice Cohn (whose surnames were unusual in the Anglo-dominated suffrage movement), both houses passed the amendment by the necessary two-thirds vote. The rule requiring two successive sessions meant that the process had to be repeated again in 1913, and only then did the amendment go to a referendum. When male voters finally cast their ballots in 1914, Nevada was known to national suffragists as "the only black spot in the West" because all other western states had enfranchised women by then.

President Anne Martin of the Equal Franchise Society led the issue to victory. With a master's degree from Stanford University, Martin founded the history department at the University of Nevada and joined the suffrage movement while studying in England. JANE ADDAMS and CHARLOTTE PERKINS GILMAN also campaigned, and with endorsements from labor unions, Democrats, and minor parties, "the most male state in the nation," as Martin called Nevada, enfranchised women by a vote of 10,936 to 7,257.

Martin repeated her campaign in a 1918 race for the U.S. Senate; running as an Independent, she won twenty percent of the vote. Sadie D. Hurst became the first female state legislator that year, and in 1920 she presided when Nevada ratified the Nineteenth Amendment.

Drought and depression in the 1920s and 1930s turned once-prosperous communities into ghost towns; the population of mined-out Virginia City plummeted from its heyday of thirty thousand to five hundred. To attract new people, the legislature legalized gambling and further relaxed divorce laws. Most states, even in the post–World War II era, severely limited grounds for divorce, and Nevada became the great marital-breakup state. Affluent couples who wished to end their marriages but who had no grounds for divorce would send one partner (usually the woman) to Nevada (usually Reno), where she would establish the required six weeks of residency and legally terminate the marriage.

In 1971 Nevada became the only state to legalize prostitution. The law excluded the counties containing Reno and Las Vegas, giving other counties the option of voting on it; by 1999, 12 of 17 counties had implemented it. Many feminists supported legalization, arguing that it increased occupational freedom and protected women from exploitative pimps and selective law enforcement.

Republican Barbara Vucanovich was the first congresswoman from Nevada, elected in 1982. A survivor of breast cancer, she championed that cause until her 1998 retirement. Mayor Jan Laverty Jones of Las Vegas lost a 1994 Democratic primary race against the incumbent governor, while Secretary of State Cheryl Lau lost the Republican gubernatorial primary—but in 1998, Democrat Shelley Berkley, an attorney with two children, won the Las Vegas congressional district.

New Hampshire

New Hampshire is one of the few states that currently has a woman as governor.

Its first English settlement was near the coastal town of Rye in 1623, settled just three years after Plymouth Colony in Massachusetts; the colony was closely bound to Massachusetts, often with common governance. Its natives, who were organized into the Pennacook Confederacy, went north to Canada as whites entered the south, but nevertheless warfare with natives was a part of life. In 1697, for example, the Massachusetts General Assembly granted twenty-five pounds sterling to Hannah Dustin of the border town of Haverhill as a reward for scalping nine Indians. She and midwife Mary Neff had been taken captive just a week after Dustin's twelfth baby was born, and during a hundred-mile march into New Hampshire, she attacked her sleeping captors. New Hampshire became a separate state at the time of the American Revolution.

In the 1820s, before MARY LYON founded Mount Holyoke, her famous women's college in Massachusetts, she taught at Adams Academy in Londonderry, where her friend Zilpah (Polly) Grant established a precedent by issuing diplomas to women. Both resigned in 1827, when the male board of trustees insisted that they teach "music and dancing" instead of the innovative science curriculum that Lyon created. The next year, Sarah Buell Hale, a New Hampshire widow with five young children, became editor of America's first important magazine for women, which after 1837 was called *Godey's Lady's Book*.

In the same era, women conducted the nation's second major textile-mill strike: more than three hundred Dover women walked away from their looms in an 1828 effort to win higher pay for workers in this still-new industry. In the 1840s, New Hampshire women supported the New England Working Men's Association—a misnamed union, given that many more women than men worked in Nassau, Manchester, and other towns where fast-moving rivers provided power in the preelectric age.

When Charles Dickens visited America in 1842, one of his priorities was to meet Laura Bridgman of Hanover, who was then twelve. Deaf and blind since a fever at age two, her ability to read and communicate by touch made her perhaps the world's first disabled celebrity.

Hanover was the home of Dartmouth College, established in 1769, but no women were admitted to any state college until 1893. That injustice was a motivation for Sarah and Parker Pillsbury, who faithfully represented New Hampshire at many national women's rights conventions, since the first in 1850.

In addition to Parker Pillsbury, several of the state's most active feminists were men. New Hampshire native Stephen Symonds Foster, husband of ABBY KELLY FOSTER, cared for their child while she went on lecture tours; his brother Galen sponsored property-rights reform in the state legislature. The four men and one woman of Milford's Hutchinson family were nationally known political songsters; for decades, Abby Hutchinson and her brothers gave concerts to raise funds for abolition, women's rights, and other causes.

These activists organized a suffrage association in 1868, with Armenia S. White as president. The male editor of the *Concord Monitor* joined JULIA WARD HOWE and others who spoke to the legislature in 1870, but their only success was a law allowing women to be elected to school boards. A more notable 1870 precedent was when Marilla M. Ricker, a wealthy young widow, became the nation's first woman to test the Fifteenth Amendment; Dover officials initially accepted her ballot but then rejected it. Ricker went on to become an attorney who spent her winters in Washington,

D.C., where she practiced law and supported women's legislative campaigns.

New Hampshire was the first eastern state to grant women a form of the vote. In 1878, women won the vote for school issues, a victory owed primarily to Armenia White and her politician husband, Nathaniel. Although U.S. Senator Henry W. Blair was one of women's rights greatest stalwarts in Washington—even lobbying for appointment of Marilla Ricker as minister to Colombia in 1897—little progress was made on the state or national level.

Women regrouped in 1901, when CARRIE CHAPMAN CATT visited with another pioneer male feminist, Henry Blackwell; Blackwell, widower of LUCY STONE, rallied New Hampshire's suffragists several times. The next year they succeeded in putting the issue on the ballot. The referendum at this 1902 election, despite decades of activism, was only the second in the East. As in Rhode Island in 1887, however, New Hampshire men soundly rejected the vote for women.

Membership in the suffrage association more than doubled in the following year, and—especially after a 1911 visit from British militant SYLVIA PANKHURST—New Hampshire women paraded, worked the state fair, and in 1915 sent four hundred valentines to the state's uncommonly large legislature, along with tickets to a feminist movie. They filed bills for various forms of suffrage in each biannual session between 1905 and 1917, but none succeeded. Their work paid off the next year: the governor and his council called a special session and on September 9, 1919, the House ratified the Nineteenth Amendment by a 212-143 vote; the Senate followed more closely, 14-10.

During World War II New Hampshire's coastline, though short, was busy with shipyards offering women new jobs, and in the postwar world new technical industries spread north from Boston. In the next decades, New Hampshire developed the nation's earliest presidential primary: every four years, the most powerful politicians and media representatives in the United States spend time in its small towns, giving New Hampshire women and men an extraordinary opportunity to influence the future.

New Hampshire's best-known woman of this era doubtless was science teacher Christa McAuliffe, who died at age thirty-seven in the 1986 Florida explosion of NASA's *Challenger* space shuttle. She had won a fierce competition to be the first "ordinary citizen" in space, and her hometown of Concord became the focus of national mourning.

The state's unusually large House of Representatives has helped more women to be elected than in other states, but its small population means that it has few members in the U.S. Congress. Currently, New Hampshire is one of eight states that have never sent a woman to Washington.

Yet, it is one of the thirteen states that have had women in their top job: Governor Jeanne Shaheen was elected in 1997. Although New Hampshire has long been a Republican state, Shaheen is a Democrat, and in a new function for a "first gentleman," her husband Bill heads Vice President Al Gore's New Hampshire campaign.

New Jersey

The only state to follow up the American Revolution by granting women the vote, New Jersey also was the first eastern state to elect a woman to Congress.

The area's first European settlers came from the Netherlands, arriving in 1623 at modern Jersey City. In 1635, Penelope Van Princes was the only survivor when natives, probably of the Delaware tribe, attacked her Dutch ship as it landed near Monmouth. English Quakers in the area predated those in Pennsylvania, and with Swedes and Finns across the Delaware River, the area began its long tradition as a mixing bowl of ethnicities.

Its location between the two largest cities, Philadelphia and New York, meant that New Jersey was a major Revolutionary battlefield, with approximately a hundred conflicts. In 1776, Annis Stockton risked her life to retrieve seditious papers when Princeton was under siege. MOLLY PITCHER's gunnery ability at the Battle of Monmouth is legendary, and other women also contributed. Margaret Vliet Warne, who practiced as a physician, rode through the area treating soldiers and their families.

New Jersey was more willing to acknowledge women than other new states, however, and its 1776 constitution granted the vote to "all free inhabitants." This was not a thoughtless phrasing, for when Quaker Representative Joseph Cooper spelled out the intent in 1790 by adding "he or she," only three men voted negatively. Most women, however, did not take advantage of the vote. When Elizabethtown women marched to the polls in 1797 and nearly defeated the power structure's candidate, politicians began considering disenfranchisement. After men dressed as women cast illegal ballots in 1807, the legislator whom the women almost defeated led the repeal of this historic right.

Some of the nation's first factories were at Paterson, and in 1828 the entire workforce of the textile mills—an industry dominated by women—went on strike. Women who had to support themselves were especially likely to be mill workers in New Jersey, because the state was slow to build educational facilities. The school board of Bordentown allowed CLARA BARTON to begin one of the state's first tuition-free schools—in 1852, later than most northern states. Enrollment soared, but Barton resigned

when the board decided that a man should supervise her successful work.

Soon after marrying Henry Blackwell, LUCY STONE moved to Orange and began organizing. After forming the suffrage association in 1867, she and her mother-in-law, Hannah Blackwell, unsuccessfully went to the polls. This led to the first major test of women's right to vote: in November 1868, 172 Vineland women, including 4 blacks, voted under the "equal protection" of the Fourteenth Amendment. Nervous officials accepted their ballots but, assuming that the votes would not be counted, put them in a separate box.

Stone moved away in 1869, just after ELIZABETH CADY STANTON came to Tenafly—but although Stanton lived there for twenty years, she was a national figure who participated very little with the state group. Keenly aware of their 1807 loss of rights, suffragists unsuccessfully petitioned the legislature for restoration several times. Women became eligible to hold school office in 1873, and Ann H. Connely almost single-handedly pushed through an 1871 bill giving mothers equal child custody in divorce—a rare policy at that time.

The Women's Club of Orange organized an evening school for girls after school officials proved unwilling to give young working women the same opportunity for evening study that was offered to men. The Vineland women organized the Woman's Political Science Club in 1879 to discuss topics such as the banking system. Even more unconventionally, Ericka C. Jones supervised male prisoners as the Hudson County jail warden, a position she inherited when her husband died—and which local officials unanimously supported, despite the state attorney general's disapproval.

After a decline in the 1880s, Lucy Stone's sister-in-law, the Reverend ANTOINETTE BROWN BLACKWELL, became president of New Jersey's suffrage association in 1891; she was followed by Florence Howe Hall, the daughter of JULIA WARD HOWE. Throughout the 1890s, they were preoccupied with another complex repeal issue: the legislature granted school suffrage for rural areas in 1887, but an 1894 court ruling restricted this still further, allowing women to vote only on school appropriations. Many interpreted this to mean a complete loss of rights, and Vineland women were forcibly prevented from depositing ballots. Three different legislatures restored the right, but male voters—particularly German immigrants—rescinded it in an 1897 referendum.

Meanwhile, Claytonia Dorticus invented a chemical bath for developing photographic prints in 1875; she went on to patent other photography equipment, as well as devices for dyeing leather. In 1895, librarian Carolyn Wells, who is credited with defining the mystery genre, published the first of her 170 books. While Passaic County's medical society admitted Sarah F. MacKintosh in 1871, the state bar resisted female lawyers. Women's rights leaders, including Florence Howe Hall, had to go to the legislature and lobby through a bill that permitted Mary Philbrook to be the first—in 1894, decades after the issue was settled in other states.

New Jersey's most important leader in the early twentieth century was ALICE PAUL, a Mount Laurel native who directed the more radical suffragists of the Congressional Union, and later, the National Woman's Party.

By 1915 New Jersey had four suffrage associations, just one of which had fifty thousand members in 215 branches. That year, they overcame the difficulties of the state's constitutional-amendment process, which required passage by two successive legislatures to put the issue on the ballot, but suffragists won just forty-two percent of the vote. With the slogan "Delayed But Not Defeated," women then concentrated on the federal amendment. Unlike those of many states, New Jersey's major suffrage association put the president of the State Federation of Colored Women's Clubs, the Reverend Florence Randolph, on its board. New Jersey's women were especially important in getting their former governor, President Woodrow Wilson, to endorse the Nineteenth Amendment. When it came to Trenton for ratification, women posted a petition with 140,000 names. The Senate ratified it 18-2, and—after a postmidnight filibuster—the House approved it 34-24.

In 1917, suffrage president Florence Howe Hall shared the first Pulitzer Prize with her sisters for a biography of their mother. The following year, New Jersey women—who had long bemoaned the fact that women were not admitted to Princeton University or any other college in the state—rejoiced when New Jersey finally offered higher education to women. After almost a decade of lobbying, Mabel Smith Douglass and her College Women's Club pressured Rutgers University into making this public institution "coeducational" with nearby gender-segregated classes.

Atlantic City boosters developed the Miss America contest in 1921; contrastingly, Alice Paul drafted the Equal Rights Amendment at her New Jersey home in 1923. In 1924, New Jersey became the first eastern state to elect a woman to Congress, MARY T. NORTON. Reelected until her 1950 retirement, she was one of the era's most powerful members of Congress.

Princeton's Institute for Advanced Study, where Albert Einstein and other great thinkers worked, began with a 1933 endowment from Carrie Frank Fuld. In 1937, Clara Adams made aviation history in Newark, setting a speed record in a Pan American Clipper flight around the world.

New Jersey rebounded from the Great Depression with huge defense plants in World War II, and its blue-collar immigrant and second-generation women found good new jobs. Women also joined postwar strikes: New Jersey's telephone operators were among those arrested during the largest strike by American women, when 230,000 women walked out in 1946. In the next decade, New Jersey's Mary Roebling became the first woman on the board of governors of the American Stock Exchange.

The state's second congresswoman, elected in 1956, was Republican Florence Price Dwyer. In Washington, she championed consumer rights and sponsored the Equal Rights Amendment. She retired in 1972, and New Jersey elected two women in 1974. Democrat Helen Stevenson Meyner, a journalist and the wife of a former governor, defeated an incumbent and served until her 1978 defeat. Much more attention went to liberal Republican and former *Vogue* editor Millicent Fenwick, who won Princeton's congressional seat. The model for Lacey Davenport of the *Doonesbury* comic strip, she lost a 1982 Senate race.

The U.S. Justice Department filed its first gender-based fair-housing suit in 1976, saying that New Jersey businesses required higher standards from unmarried women than from men or married couples. Two other local stories made national headlines during much of the 1970s and 1980s: the right-to-die case of Karen Ann Quinlan and the surrogate-motherhood case of Mary Beth Whitehead versus Elizabeth Stern.

In 1993, Republican Christine Todd Whitman defeated the incumbent governor with a promise to reduce taxes. Her win brought the number of female sitting governors to a high of four. Whitman, who is pro-choice, was reelected in 1997. The only woman on the state's current eleven-member delegation is Marge Roukema, elected in 1980. A pro-choice Republican, she sponsored the Family and Medical Leave Act.

New Mexico

New Mexico was the only western state that failed to grant women any significant voting rights before the Nineteenth Amendment, but its current three-member U.S. House delegation includes a woman.

The state's native people included Navajo, Apache, and Pueblo tribes. The Spanish explored in the 1530s, and the first non-native settlement was in 1598, when Juan de Ornate led some four hundred men, women, and children from Mexico. In the seventeenth century, Spanish priests and soldiers built missions and presidios, or military posts. A Pueblo revolt resulted in the deaths of more than four hundred Spanish settlers, including women.

The rebellion was crushed in the 1690s, and the Spanish ruled through the early 1800s. Growth was slow because deserts in the south and arid mountains in the north kept settlers out. As their foremothers had done, women lived in adobe homes and supported their families by carrying water to irrigate crops, butchering and drying meat, and crafting pottery and baskets.

Mexico won independence from Spain in 1821 but ceded New Mexico to the United States in 1848, at the end of the Mexican War. Abolitionists, including LYDIA MARIA CHILD, opposed this war because they feared expansion of slavery, which the Mexican government had forbidden. In contrast, journalist Jane McManus Storms advocated the war, translating for Americans in Mexico City and venturing into enemy territory at Veracruz. After an 1849 marriage, Jane McManus Storms Cazneau settled in southern New Mexico, where, despite being 150 miles from a mail route, she reported for the *New York Tribune* and other papers.

Congress made New Mexico a territory in 1850, but statehood was not attained until 1912. Julia Archibald Holmes moved to Taos from Kansas—on foot—in 1858. She replaced Cazneau as *New York Tribune* correspondent and introduced many readers to New Mexico's unfamiliar culture. Ethnologist Matilda Stevenson did the same: from the 1870s onward, she worked with the Zuni tribe and brought hundreds of unclassified southwestern plants to the Smithsonian Institution.

The vote for women was discussed during an 1888 revision of the territorial constitution, but with little support. The first suffrage group began at Albuquerque in 1893, the same year that New Mexico's northern neighbor, Colorado, granted full voting rights. After appreciable work by the presidents of the Minnesota and Kansas associations, a statewide suffrage association formed in 1896, but it soon lapsed. New Mexico remained an isolated frontier, and lacking railroads and telephones, it was hard for women to organize. The state constitution in 1912 was a huge disappointment: women's limited school suffrage could be repealed at the local level, and amendments were designed to be so difficult that women had virtually no hope of achieving one.

ANNE MARTIN, who led Nevada's successful campaign, worked in New Mexico in 1917, and in 1918 the state's U.S. House members unanimously supported the Nineteenth Amendment. CARRIE CHAPMAN CATT's Albuquerque appearance in December 1919 got favorable statewide press, motivating Governor Octaviano Larrazolo to call a special session to ratify the amendment. On February 16, 1920, with men on both sides of the issue, the Senate ratified 17-5 and the House 36-10.

After Mary Austin's *Land of Little Rain* (1903) brought her lifelong fame, she popularized Santa Fe as an art and literary colony. WILLA CATHER lived in Austin's adobe home while writing her southwestern novel, *Death*

Comes for the Archbishop (1927). Avant-garde New Yorker Mabel Dodge came to Taos in 1918; marriage to a Pueblo Indian changed her name to Luhan, and she recruited others to the area, especially with her book *Winter in Taos* (1935). Painter GEORGIA O'KEEFFE began visiting in 1929 and moved to the mountains of northern New Mexico in 1949.

New Mexico elected its first congresswoman, Georgia Lee Lusk, in 1947. A widowed rancher and long-time educator, she was state superintendent of schools in the 1930s and 1940s. After she lost the 1948 Democratic primary, President Harry Truman appointed her to the War Claims Commission.

Women of both parties have been New Mexico's secretary of state from the 1960s onward. Three ran for Congress during the 1980s, but none won.

In 1994, the American Bar Association chose Roberta Cooper Ramo, a New Mexican of Native American descent, as its president-elect. The first woman to preside over this elite group, she could not get a job when she graduated from law school in 1967.

Heather Wilson became New Mexico's second congresswoman when she won a special election in June 1998 for the Albuquerque district. A Republican, she is a graduate of the Air Force Academy—an institution that did not admit women until feminists raised the issue in the 1970s.

New York

New York was the birthplace of the women's rights movement, and it was the first eastern state to grant full voting rights.

The area's first European settlers came from the Netherlands, whose women probably had the world's highest status: they often retained maiden names, made prenuptial agreements, and participated in commerce. New Amsterdam was founded in 1623: Tryntje Jonas began practicing medicine in 1629; Annettje van Cortlandt paved America's first street in 1648; Margaret Hardenbroeck owned a successful import-export and shipping business. The religiously tolerant New Netherlands colony attracted an eclectic mix of people, including freethinkers banished from New England such as ANNE HUTCHINSON and Lady Deborah Moody, who settled Coney Island. The English soldiers who appeared in 1664, however, were so formidable that New Netherlands surrendered without a fight and became New York.

Sara Roeloef, who spoke Dutch, English, and Algonquian, was employed as an interpreter for area natives; in 1711, "Madame Montour" interpreted at an Albany conference between New York's governor and chiefs of the five

Iroquois Nations. Near the Canadian border, Kateri Tekakwitha endured stoning to be baptized in 1677; in 1982, she became the first Native American saint. "MOTHER" ANN LEE, who was imprisoned in England for dissident preaching, began the first of several Shaker colonies at Watervielt in 1774.

The American Revolution began soon after, and New Yorkers were on both sides. The British paid Molly Brant, a Mohawk who had nine children by a recently deceased British official, to keep Indians loyal to the Crown. On the other side, Catherine van Rensselaer Schuyler, who supported fourteen children while her husband went to war, set fire to her wheat crop rather than allow the British to harvest it.

The new state named Elizabeth Hunter Holt as its official printer in 1784. Her daughter, Elizabeth Oswald, followed Holt as publisher of the *Independent Gazette*. A mother-daughter team, Scottish immigrants Isabella Graham and Joanna Graham Bethune, began the nation's first Sunday school in New York City in 1803. After the 1818 legislature refused to fund EMMA WILLARD's proposed school for girls, the town of Troy sponsored it; within a decade, hundreds of girls showed that they wanted to learn science and math. In 1827, just three years after America's first industrial strike, the United Tailoresses declared the first strike solely of women in New York City. In the same year, a slave called Isabella—later known as SOJOURNER TRUTH—fled her upstate master and filed a successful suit to recover her son from Alabama, where he had been sold in violation of New York's gradual-emancipation law.

When Paulina Kellogg Wright Davis held an 1835 anti-slavery meeting, a mob attacked her Utica home—but two hundred women from nine states attended the first Women's Anti-Slavery Convention in New York City in 1837. MARGARET FULLER became the nation's first professional book reviewer in 1844 at the *New York Tribune*. ELIZABETH BLACKWELL'S 1847 graduation from Geneva Medical College in western New York made her the first credentialed female physician in the world.

The next year rural New York distinguished itself by becoming the birthplace of women's rights. Philadelphian LUCRETIA MOTT joined ELIZABETH CADY STANTON to call a meeting in Stanton's town of Seneca Falls on July 19 and 20, 1848. Some three hundred people came to discuss "the social, civil, and religious rights of women." They adopted a Declaration of Rights for Women modeled on the Declaration of Independence, and the only debate occurred on the topic of women's right to vote, which passed by a close margin. A follow-up meeting was held in Rochester two weeks later.

In 1851, Susan Bogert Warner's *The Wide, Wide World* became the first American book to sell a million copies. In the same year, Central Medical College of Rochester graduated Lydia Folger Fowler and hired her to teach obstetrics and gynecology, making Dr. Fowler the world's first female medical professor. The next year, Clemence S. H. Lozier graduated with highest honors from Syracuse Medical College; in 1864, she opened her own New York City medical school. Doctors Emily and ELIZABETH BLACKWELL opened the New York Infirmary for Women and Children in 1855 and later expanded with a medical school.

As the Civil War began, HARRIET TUBMAN led an assault on Troy police, enabling a fugitive slave to escape to Canada. SUSAN B. ANTHONY and ELIZABETH CADY STANTON established the Loyal League in New York City during the war: they recruited five thousand members who gathered almost four hundred thousand petition signatures averring loyalty to the Union, while also pushing for stronger action to end slavery.

Vassar College opened after the war, and Wells College followed in western New York—but Brooklyn's Lemma Barkeloo had to go to Missouri to find a law school that admitted women. New York's first professional women's club, Sorosis, began in 1868 after female writers were excluded from a dinner for Charles Dickens. Its first president was Phoebe Cary, who ran a literary salon along with her sister Alice.

In 1873, almost four hundred attended the founding meeting of the Association for the Advancement of Women, which aimed to improve female educational opportunity, in New York City; astronomer MARIA MITCHELL, who taught at Vassar College, was a leader of this organization. Women also founded the Bellevue Hospital Training School for Nurses that year, emulating the work of Britain's FLORENCE NIGHTINGALE, and Josephine Shaw Lowell became the first woman appointed to the State Board of Charities.

New York women won the right to vote in school elections in 1880, and Lydia Sayer Hasbrouck was elected to the Middletown school board, despite her radical attire: pants. The 1880s also marked the beginning of a huge wave of immigration, including many women who worked in New York factories to support families back in Europe. Upper-class women and men began to serve their needs at the Lower East Side's University Settlement House in 1887—a precedent JANE ADDAMS was unaware of when she began Chicago's more famous Hull House two years later.

An 1893 depression was so severe that starvation was common, and EMMA GOLDMAN was arrested for a speech that encouraged stealing bread. LILLIAN WALD began her Henry Street Settlement House, which largely developed the concept of public-health nursing, that year. Dr. Anna Wessels Williams, a New York City Department of Health employee, isolated a diphtheria bacillus in 1894, while Dr. MARY PUTNAM JACOBI published *"Common Sense" Applied to Woman Suffrage*, a refutation of physicians' arguments against equality. The next year, the New York State Association Opposed to Woman Suffrage began.

As the century turned, Gertrude Käsebier took avant-garde photographs in New York City; a 1906 exhibit with Jessie Tarbox Beals included photos by thirty-two women. Sculptor Gertrude Vanderbilt Whitney did her initial work under pseudonyms so that judges would not be influenced by her famous name; later, she built New York City's Whitney Museum. In 1907, Margaret Slocum Sage began giving away the $80 million she inherited—an amount that should rank her with famous philanthropist Andrew Carnegie.

The International Ladies' Garment Workers' Union was founded in 1900, and in 1903 the Women's Trade Union League (WTUL) began as a support group for women in all industries. Over twenty thousand garment workers went on strike at New York factories in 1909, and the WTUL spent an average of $1,000 per day on bail, as police arrested hundreds of women for picketing. Among the most important worker leaders were ROSE SCHNEIDERMAN, Leonora O'Reilly, and MARY ANDERSON; their upper-class supporters included Mary Drier and ALVA VANDERBILT BELMONT. It was the 1911 Triangle Shirtwaist Factory fire, however, that truly drew attention to the need for labor reform: locked in, 146 workers—mostly young female immigrants—burned to death.

Nora Stanton Blatch DeForest, granddaughter of Elizabeth Cady Stanton, became the first woman in the American Society of Engineers in 1909. By then, the suffrage organization founded in 1902 by her mother, Harriot Stanton Blatch, had grown to twenty thousand members; her Women's Political Union reached out to working-class women and used the visibility techniques of British suffragists. New York banker James Lee Laidlow founded the Men's Suffrage League, probably the world's first male auxiliary to a female political organization, and New Yorkers held the nation's first suffrage parade in 1910.

MARGARET SANGER was arrested for writing about birth control in 1914. She and her sister-in-law, Ethel Byrne—both credentialed nurses—were imprisoned when they began a Brooklyn clinic in 1916. Five hundred women sought contraceptive advice in the ten days before the government closed it down. When Sanger fled to Europe, MARY WARE DENNETT headed the National Birth-Control League.

Four eastern states finally held their first suffrage referenda in 1915; all lost, with fifty-eight percent of New York's men rejecting the measure. Suffragists changed leadership, with New York City resident CARRIE CHAPMAN CATT as president of the chief national association. Meanwhile, the nation entered World War I. Although some New York women visibly opposed the war, Catt argued that women's war work entitled them to the vote. New York's wartime leaders included Julia Stimson, who led Red Cross nurses in Europe and won the Distinguished Service Medal; feminist biographer Rheta Dorr, a syndicated war correspondent; Daisy Harriman, who chaired the federal Committee on Women in Industry; and Jane Delano, a former Bellevue nursing chief and Army Nurse Corps commander, who died in France. A parade shortly before the 1917 election featured a giant petition signed by a million women doing war work, and the strategy succeeded: this time, New York's nearly two million registered male voters passed suffrage by about a hundred thousand votes.

Even after they had the vote, New York women were leaders in the fight for the federal Nineteenth Amendment that would apply to all states. Lucy Burns of Brooklyn was one of the Woman's Party contingent that picketed the White House for years; first arrested in 1913, she was proud to have served more jail time than any other suffragist. When Congress sent the Nineteenth Amendment to the states in 1919, New York's legislature ratified unanimously less than two weeks later.

In 1925, Ruth Pratt became the first woman on the New York City Board of Aldermen, and in 1928 she defeated an incumbent to become the state's first congresswoman. Also in the 1920s, playwright Anne Nichols set a record for the longest-running play with *Abie's Wild Rose*, Anita Loos made a fortune with *Gentlemen Prefer Blondes*, and Lila Bell Acheson Wallace cofounded *Reader's Digest*. *New York Herald Tribune* owner Helen Rogers Reid promoted the work of many women, including influential book reviewer Irita van Doren and later journalists Dorothy Thompson and Marguerite Higgins.

When Franklin Roosevelt was elected president in 1932, he named women from his home state to a number of positions. Secretary of Labor FRANCES PERKINS, the first woman on the cabinet, was most visible, but others included Mary Anderson, Rose Schneiderman, and Molly Dewson. The incomparable ELEANOR ROOSEVELT, of course, exerted global influence for women, and New York elected her friend Carolyn O'Day to Congress in 1934.

Suffragist MARY BEARD published three histories of American women in the 1930s, while Columbia University's RUTH BENEDICT joined MARGARET MEAD and Elsie Clews Parsons as a social-science pioneer. Rose Knox of Knox Gelatine Company was the first woman elected to the board of directors · of the Grocery Manufacturers Association; she managed her Johnstown company so well that it suffered no cutbacks in the Great Depression. Meanwhile, Sylvia Porter disguised herself as "S. F. Porter" when she began writing on finance at the *New York Post*—before editor DOROTHY SCHIFF took over in 1939.

Florence (Daisy) Jaffray Harriman was an early World War II hero: as the U.S. minister to Norway, she sheltered Norwegians, including royalty, when the Nazis invaded. The Navy's WAVES trained at Hunter College, and many New York women worked in nontraditional jobs, especially those related to massive shipping. A number of women worked as war correspondents for New York newspapers and magazines; some endured combat and were expelled from foreign countries. Several women, including Barnard College president Virginia Gildersleeve, were involved in the postwar United Nations, and President Truman appointed ANNA ROSENBERG as assistant secretary of defense.

Meanwhile, avant-garde poet Marianne Moore—who lived with her mother in Greenwich Village and taught Sunday school—won the 1951 Pulitzer Prize. In 1953, New York City native ETHEL ROSENBERG became the only woman in American history to be executed for espionage. In a more positive milestone, Josephine Bay became the first woman to head a major Wall Street brokerage.

LORRAINE HANSBERRY was the first award-winning black playwright; her *Raisin in the Sun* (1959) was also a financial success, and she moved from the Lower East Side to Croton-on-Hudson. President Johnson made Manhattan's CONSTANCE BAKER MOTLEY the first black woman on the federal judiciary in 1966, and two years later New York elected the nation's first black congresswoman, SHIRLEY CHISHOLM.

Ten thousand New York women marched in celebration of the fiftieth anniversary of the Nineteenth Amendment on August 26, 1970, and in the same year BELLA ABZUG defeated a congressional incumbent. Betty Holtzman and GERALDINE FERRARO also were elected in the 1970s, making New York's congresswomen the nation's most outstanding on women's issues.

Other barriers fell in 1975, when Sarah Caldwell conducted the New York Philharmonic, and 1977, when New York City physicist Janet Guthrie raced in the Indianapolis 500 and Dr. ROSALYN SUSSMAN YALOW, a radiologist, won the Nobel Prize in physiology or medicine. Geraldine Ferraro drew national attention as the Democratic nominee for vice president in 1984. Seven more women were elected to the U.S. House of Representatives between 1986 and 1996, bringing New York's historic total to eighteen, slightly behind California's twenty-one. Six of those eighteen women are currently serving; in the context of New York's large population, however, they constitute less than twenty percent of its representation.

North Carolina

North Carolinians formed what may be considered the first political organization of American women.

Days after her 1587 arrival on Roanoke Island off the North Carolina coast, Ellinor White Dare delivered the first English baby in North America. One of 17 women among 116 colonists, she sailed in the advanced stages of pregnancy on a ship captained by her father. He returned to Europe, and when he came back three years later, everyone in this "Lost Colony" had vanished. His infant granddaughter, VIRGINIA DARE—named for the reigning virgin queen ELIZABETH I—became legendary.

Many of the English women who emigrated in the 1600s came as indentured servants—a near-slave status—or intended to sell themselves as brides. African women were brought as slaves, and in 1708 Florida's Spanish governor reported that some ten thousand Indians had been sold into slavery in the Carolinas. Natives of the area, which later became North and South Carolina, were primarily of the Cherokee tribe, in which women played strong decision-making roles, but by the 1700s, they were being displaced.

After long domination from Charleston, North Carolina separated from South Carolina in 1712. By 1770, the governor's wife, Margaret Wake Tryon, presided over Tryon Palace, which some called "the most beautiful public building in North America," but resentment of the governor's near-royal lifestyle was a factor in the growing rebellion. In 1765—more than a decade prior to the Declaration of Independence—Edenton's Society of Patriotic Ladies wrote a declaration supporting revolution. Decades before women were supposed to organize politically, these women did so.

The University of North Carolina was chartered in 1789, but education was reserved for elite males. No public schools existed prior to 1840, and the state's population shrank as young families sought better opportunities. North Carolina lost a disproportionate number of men in the Civil War; with almost one of every four Confederate deaths, the state was left with tens of thousands of widows and young women who had no chance to marry.

Through her legislator son, New Bern journalist Mary Bayard Clarke reformed guardianship law after the Civil War. Among the era's notable women were Harriet Morrison Irwin of Charlotte, who used national publications to sell architectural drawings for a hexagonal house designed for invalids like herself. Marion A. Williams was president of the State National Bank at Raleigh; she may have been the nation's first woman in this position. The most famous North Carolina woman of the late nineteenth century was probably Dr. Susan Dimock from the town of Washington:

the state was so proud of this internationally educated young physician that its medical society awarded her honorary membership in 1872.

Dr. Dimock practiced out of state, however, and three decades passed before North Carolina had its own female physician. After the turn of the century, Delia Dixon-Carroll practiced at Raleigh's private Meredith College. North Carolina finally opened a public college for women in 1897, but even then the Greensboro institution was a "normal school" for teacher training; not until 1918 did it become North Carolina College for Women.

Unlike those of most southern states, North Carolina's Agricultural and Mechanical College was initially for black men only, leaving black women with no option. Although the African Methodist-Episcopal Conference ordained Raleigh's Sarah A. Hughes, most black women had to leave the state to succeed. The nation's first female African American college graduate, MARY JANE PATTERSON, had fled to Ohio in the 1850s from a Raleigh plantation.

Asheville's mayor offered his home as the meeting place when the first suffrage organization formed in 1894. North Carolina native Lillie Devereux Blake spoke to the 1895 legislature on the suffrage question, but a bill to allow men to put women on school boards was defeated. The legislature further insulted women by sending its only nineteenth-century suffrage bill, introduced in 1897, to the Committee on Insane Asylums.

North Carolina suffragists reorganized in 1913, and their first convention featured a resolution against "militancy," but they joined ANNA HOWARD SHAW in speaking to the 1915 legislature. When their bill lost by wide margins in both houses, the more radical Woman's Party sent workers to North Carolina; as a result, the state's small Republican Party endorsed the Nineteenth Amendment in 1918. The Democratic Party was the real battleground, however, and after a long fight, its state convention endorsed the amendment in April 1920, and the governor called a special session to ratify it on August 13. Although they were aware that they might be surrendering a historic opportunity to Tennessee—which in fact became the last state to ratify two weeks later—lawmakers voted 25-23 to defer action.

A politically successful woman of the 1920s was Harriet Moorehead Berry, whose Good Roads Association lobbied for improvements vital to the age of the automobile; the year after women got the vote, the legislature passed her multi-million-dollar bond authorization. At the end of the decade, a strike among Gastonia's primarily female textile workers exploded; Ella May Wiggins, mother of nine, was killed in 1929 when vigilantes fired at the unarmed strikers.

During World War II, the state's textile-mill workers produced more army materiel than those in any other state. Although strikes were banned during the war, a few erupted, including one by black women working in North Carolina cigarette plants. Because cigarettes were included in military rations, literally millions were manufactured each day.

The state's first congresswoman served for only a few months in 1946. Eliza Jane Pratt was a congressional aide, and when a congressman died in office, the Democratic Executive Committee nominated her as a replacement.

A more significant election occurred in 1967, when more than a million members of the National Education Association voted for Elizabeth Koontz, the first African American president in their 106-year history. In 1973, President Richard Nixon appointed Elizabeth Hanford to the Federal Trade Commission; she married Senator Robert Dole of Kansas in 1975, and Republican presidents continued to appoint Elizabeth Dole to head federal agencies.

North Carolina's first genuinely elected congresswoman was Eva Clayton, a black Democrat who has been resoundingly reelected from her coastal district since 1992. With Charlotte's Republican mayor Sue Myrick joining her in 1994, two of North Carolina's eleven House seats are held by women.

North Dakota

North Dakota's male voters were the first to elect a woman to statewide office.

With its extremely cold and often dry climate, North Dakota's land was unattractive to early French explorers. The region's ten tribes of natives were diverse, including nomads such as the Dakota and Crow; semi-nomadic people, including the Cheyenne and Cree; and agriculturists such as the Mandan and Hidatsa. Women's status was lower in the nomadic tribes, whose men sometimes practiced polygamy.

Although the Hidatsa took SACAGAWEA away from her native Shoshone, they and the Mandan also assisted her and the rest of the Lewis and Clark expedition. Dakota was not organized as a territory until 1861, and not until Chief Sitting Bull surrendered in 1881 did large numbers of whites come to the vast Dakota Territory.

Many of these newcomers were foreign-born families recruited by railroads, and especially those from eastern Europe tended to be culturally conservative. Even though one-third of the population came from the more liberal Norway—whose women got the vote prior to those of the United States—North Dakota's women's movement was almost wholly Anglo American.

In 1872, three years after Wyoming's territorial legislature enfranchised women, Dakota's came within one vote of doing so. The 1879 legislature granted school suffrage, but it varied between counties and was difficult to use effectively.

The Homestead Act recognized household heads regardless of gender, and by 1887, more than a third of the territory's land belonged to women. Divorces could be obtained after just six months of residency, and some women held offices, especially clerk of court. In 1892, male voters became the nation's first to elect a woman to statewide office, when they chose Laura J. Eisenhuth as state superintendent of public instruction. The University of North Dakota was coeducational from its 1883 beginning, and Dr. Janette Hill Knox, an active suffragist, was vice president of private Red River Valley University.

The territorial legislature passed a full suffrage bill in 1885, but it was vetoed by the governor. That same year, Dakota women attended the American Woman Suffrage Association's convention in Minneapolis, and when North Dakota and South Dakota entered the Union as separate states in 1889, LUCY STONE's husband, Henry Blackwell, lobbied on behalf of suffrage among the delegates in Bismarck who wrote the new constitution, but he was unsuccessful. A full suffrage bill passed both houses in 1893, but Speaker of the House George Walsh refused to sign it.

The Women's Christian Temperance Union was North Dakota's oldest and largest organization of women, and as Prohibition goals were reached, they worked for suffrage. CARRIE CHAPMAN CATT visited in 1898, but the 1911 tour by British radical SYLVIA PANKHURST signaled greater change. Led by Dr. Cora Smith Eaton, women got suffrage on the 1914 ballot and ran a winning campaign, but again, it was not quite enough—although women won a small majority, they lost when unmarked ballots were counted as negative votes.

In the next election, women helped defeat the governor and lieutenant governor who had opposed them. Politicians noticed, and in 1917 women won municipal and presidential suffrage. North Dakota's five congressmen all voted for the Nineteenth Amendment in 1918, and on December 2, 1919, a near-unanimous legislature ratified it. The state already had put full suffrage on the 1920 ballot, however, and so women enfranchised by the federal amendment ended up voting on their right to vote.

The Nonpartisan League, a farmers' union that won a majority of the 1918 legislature and helped turn the suffrage issue around, also successfully pushed economic reforms that indirectly benefited women. Nonetheless, life in the Dust Bowl of the 1920s and 1930s was very hard, and people left North Dakota in droves. Meanwhile, the legislature created more than a dozen elective state officer positions. With this greater opportunity, women won such positions as tax commissioner and treasurer decades earlier than in other states.

North Dakota's legislature not only ratified the Equal Rights Amendment in 1975 but also stuck to that decision despite pressure: the amendment's opponents went all the way to the U.S. Supreme Court, which struck down their argument that the legislature must get voter approval for ratification. Feminists demonstrated the need for legal equality with a 1977 case in which the North Dakota Supreme Court ruled that the state must stop sending women to out-of-state prisons; because North Dakota had so few female criminals, it never built a prison for them, making it more difficult for families and lawyers to visit. Its courts also were among the first to strike down restrictive abortion laws.

In contrast, not until 1988 was a woman finally appointed as a circuit judge. North Dakota elected its first female lieutenant governor, Ruth Meier, in 1984. Still largely a rural area, it has long been the nation's slowest-growing state. The current population entitles it to just one U.S. House member, and it has never elected a woman to that position. Jocelyn Burdick served briefly in the Senate when the governor appointed her after her husband's 1991 death.

Ohio

It is hard to overstate Ohio's importance as an incubator for the early women's rights movement—especially its Oberlin College, the world's first coeducational college.

The first white woman to see the Ohio River was Mary Draper Ingles, who was heavily pregnant when she was captured by the Shawnee in 1755; leaving her baby behind, she escaped with a Dutch woman who went insane during the seven hundred miles back to Virginia. The first white families settled Cincinnati in December 1788. Ohio's first territorial governor had been appointed the previous year, and by 1792, his daughter, Louisa St. Clair, was so respected that she went alone to negotiate a treaty with natives.

Ohio became a state in 1803, and the next decades began its tradition as an incubator for new ideas. Several utopian communities developed, including one started by disciples of Shaker ANN LEE. Early pioneers in women's education introduced their innovations in Ohio: Catharine Beecher, the sister of HARRIET BEECHER STOWE, began the Western Female Institute in Cincinnati in 1831; she later pioneered the field of home economics. In 1833, Oberlin College became the world's first college to admit blacks and women, and in 1841 it granted the first bachelor's degrees ever earned by women. Emily Frances Fairchild received what may have been the world's first master's degree granted to a woman in 1847—the same year that LUCY STONE and ANTOINETTE BROWN BLACKWELL graduated.

ELIZABETH BLACKWELL and her influential siblings grew up in Cincinnati in this era, as did Alice and Phoebe Cary, sisters who became prominent in New York's literary world. Years before the first women's rights convention, both ABBY KELLY FOSTER and ERNESTINE ROSE lectured on women's rights in the backwoods of Ohio. When Hannah Tracy Cutler became principal of the female department of Columbus's new high school in 1850, she had already published a prescient feminist work, *Woman as She Was, Is, and Should Be.* Meanwhile, Marietta's Lilly Martin Spencer developed into perhaps the era's most successful female artist: the National Academy of Design exhibited her paintings, which were the primary source of income for her thirteen children; Spencer twice turned down $20,000 for one of her paintings.

Ohio was the first state to follow up on western New York's 1848 women's rights conventions. In April 1850, Ohio women met in Salem, where Oliver and Mariana Johnson published the *Anti-Slavery Bugle* and supported women's rights. In contrast to the 1848 Seneca Falls meeting, where women asked a man to preside, at the Salem meeting men were forbidden to speak. An Akron convention in 1851 was the site of SOJOURNER TRUTH's famous "Ain't I a Woman?" speech.

Revolution in Europe in 1848 brought many immigrants, especially Germans, to Ohio. Because beer was basic to their culture, however, and because the women's movement so closely paralleled the temperance movement, even these liberals—like most immigrants—usually voted against women's rights.

Oberlin's experiment with coeducation remained unique for almost two decades, until Ohio developed a second institution, Antioch College, which began near Dayton in 1852. Like Oberlin, Antioch encouraged reform and hosted controversial speakers. Its president was famed Horace Mann; his wife, educator Mary Peabody Mann, was the sister of publisher and educator ELIZABETH PEABODY. Suffrage leader Reverend Olympia Brown was an early graduate, and the progressive faculty included mathematician and astronomer Lucretia Crocker.

In the same year that Antioch College began, FRANCES WRIGHT—perhaps the most innovative female thinker of her time—died in Cincinnati. HARRIET BEECHER STOWE's *Uncle Tom's Cabin* also was published in 1852; she obtained much of the background for this book while living in Cincinnati.

AMELIA BLOOMER continued publishing the *Lily*, which first advocated wearing pants, when she moved to Ohio in 1853. That year's women's rights convention was presided over by Frances Dana Gage, an immensely popular newspa-

per columnist whose influence led to reform of women's property rights. Caroline Severance followed up with a petition to the state senate urging that married women be able to control their own wages and inheritance. Ohio adopted property reforms, and in 1858 its senate took the nation's first vote on suffrage, which ultimately failed.

As attention turned to the looming Civil War, feminists concentrated on black freedom. Cleveland women organized the nation's first soldiers' aid society just five days after guns began firing. Josephine Griffing, a paid agent of the Western Anti-Slavery Society since 1856, not only worked through the war but made the welfare of black people the focus of her entire life through the Freedmen's Bureau. During the war, Oberlin College produced the nation's first black female college graduate, MARY JANE PATTERSON, and Hallie Q. Brown, an 1873 graduate of Ohio's Wilberforce College, became a longtime leader of African American women.

Six women running on an equal-rights slate took over Toledo's library board in 1869, the same year that the state suffrage association formally organized. Ohio women were among the midwestern temperance advocates who protested in front of saloons, and in 1874 Cleveland was the founding site of the Women's Christian Temperance Union. Women raised money to support a Cincinnati clinic begun by doctors Ellen M. Kirk and M. May Howells in 1879, and the same year, a long fight for the admission of women to Cincinnati's Pulte Medical College finally succeeded.

The 1880s and 1890s were a more conservative time. Although suffrage bills were introduced in almost every annual session, women won only a limited form of school suffrage in 1894—and spent the rest of the decade defending it in a court case and a repeal drive.

Dr. Susan Smith Steward, the third African American woman to graduate from medical school, began practicing at Wilberforce in 1897; in 1911, she was a featured speaker at the World Congress of Races. Also in 1911, the Society of American Indians organized at Ohio State University with women as leaders.

Revisions to the state constitution in 1912 gave women the opportunity to put suffrage on the ballot. In the biggest election yet, more than a half-million men voted; suffragists spent $40,000, but the liquor lobby spent $120,000 and soundly defeated suffrage. Undaunted, suffragists tried again in 1914, but again they lost. Women concentrated on municipal suffrage after that, and—after a court case successfully argued by young attorney FLORENCE ALLEN—went on to win the city vote in Columbus. The legislature emulated nearby states and granted presidential suffrage in 1917, but women then had to fight a campaign to repeal. Although signatures gathered in saloons were so obviously fraudulent that officials in some counties threw out thousands of names, the repeal went on the ballot, and Ohio men took away the right women had won.

However, suffragists lobbied their congressmen with great success. In 1918, only eight of twenty-two Ohio House members voted for suffrage, but in 1919 just two voted against it. The legislature ratified the Nineteenth Amendment by wide majorities, despite aggressive opposition from antisuffragists.

Harriet Taylor Upton, president of the Ohio suffrage association from 1899 to 1920, deserves credit not only for this victory but also for her dedication at the national level. When the movement was at its low point at the turn of the century, the national headquarters was actually in her rural Warren home. She also kept Ohio's suffrage network together after the Nineteenth Amendment. In 1922 suffragists led the successful election campaign of Florence Allen to the Ohio Supreme Court—the first woman in the world to serve in this position. Allen set a second milestone in 1934, when Franklin Roosevelt appointed her to the U.S. court of appeals, just below the Supreme Court.

Frances Bolton won a special election when her congressman husband died, and when Republican powers refused to support her in the 1940 race, she organized Cleveland women who led her winning campaign. A representative for three decades, she especially worked for legislation to benefit nurses. In 1952, Ohioans set another milestone when they elected her son to an adjoining district, making the Boltons the first mother-child team in Congress.

Bolton finally lost at age eighty-three, when anti-incumbent feeling exploded after the National Guard shot Vietnam War protesters at Kent State University. The same anti-incumbent sentiment helped Jo Ann Davidson replace Ohio's House Speaker, the nation's longest-serving, in 1970. Voters also elected Lieutenant Governor Nancy Putnam Hollister and Attorney General Betty D. Montgomery that year; both stayed in office for the next quarter century.

The 1970s also brought the Cincinnati ordination of Sally Priesand, the nation's first female rabbi. In 1976, Cleveland elected Democrat Mary Rose Oakar to Congress, where she championed the coverage of mammograms by health insurance, and Democrat Marcy Kaptur defeated a Toledo incumbent to join Oakar in 1982. Oakar lost her 1992 primary, but Columbus elected pro-choice Republican Deborah Pryce. In 1998 Stephanie Tubbs Jones became the third female member of Ohio's congressional delegation.

For a few days in 1999, Republican Nancy Hollister was governor: the incumbent lieutenant governor, she took office on New Years Eve, when the governor resigned to begin a term in the U.S. Senate. She left on January 11, when the governor-elect took office.

Oklahoma

Oklahoma was the second state to elect a woman to Congress, which was especially remarkable because at the time it had been a state for just thirteen years.

The state's natives were of two types: buffalo hunters such as the Comanche and Kiowa and agriculturists such as the Caddo and Wichita. Spanish explorers came in the 1540s, but the population remained small until Congress passed the 1830 Indian Removal Act, which forced the Cherokee in southeastern states onto the Trail of Tears that led to the region. Choctaw, Creek, and Chickasaw Indians from the midsouth followed, and in 1858 Seminole natives sailed from Florida after losing three wars. These Five Civilized Tribes valued education; they reestablished mission schools in Oklahoma and often sent their children, including girls, to distant schools at tribal expense. Western Indians were also deported to Oklahoma, and by the 1950's, the state had remnants of sixty-seven tribes.

During the Civil War, the situation in Oklahoma was much like that in neighboring Arkansas and Missouri: with divided loyalties, an internal civil war promoted lawlessness long after the war officially ended. Judges from bordering states also exiled criminals there, making it a haven for outlaws such as Belle Starr, "the Bandit Queen" of Indian Territory, until someone shot her in 1883. Oklahoma also was a refuge for African Americans fleeing post-Reconstruction oppression. Entire congregations of black churches in Memphis, for example, moved there after white mobs destroyed their homes.

Federal soldiers not only escorted unwilling Indians to Oklahoma but also forced whites out—until 1889, when Congress succumbed to homesteader pressure for access to one of the last remaining desirable regions. On April 22, women joined men in a land rush; within twenty-four hours, some fifty thousand settlers claimed two million acres of former Creek and Seminole territory. Several more "runs" in the 1890s took other reservation land, and a 1901 lottery opened settlement in the far southwest, which had belonged to the Apache. Although a vast number of modern Indians live in Oklahoma, the state's reservations are gone.

When Congress authorized the Oklahoma Territory in 1891, members of the newly organized Women's Christian Temperance Union spoke to the first territorial legislature. They won school suffrage, but full suffrage lost the House by three votes. Because the territory was formed late in the women's rights movement, its property laws were more equitable than those of older areas, and divorces could be obtained after just ninety days of residency. Indefatigable Kansas activist Laura Johns developed Oklahoma's suffrage association in 1895; in 1897, the House voted 13-9 for full suffrage, but it died in the upper chamber.

By the turn of the century, however, eleven of twenty-three counties had female school superintendents, and about a hundred women were notaries public and one a deputy U.S. marshal. Oklahoma also awarded a commission to sculptor Vinnie Ream in 1906; her work stands in the U.S. Capitol today. On the other hand, although women ran a strong campaign for inclusion in the constitution when Oklahoma became a state in 1907, they were rejected. Undaunted, women launched repeated efforts to get suffrage on the ballot, but not until 1918 did a more progressive legislature authorize an election.

The national suffrage association sent more money to Oklahoma than to any state in the past because women had to overcome extraordinary hurdles: any ballot unmarked on this issue would be counted as voting against it, and thousands had been mailed to World War I soldiers without the question on them, all of which would be counted negatively.

Suffragists believed that Aloysius Larch-Miller, a young woman from Shawnee, gave her life for the cause: though ill, she debated Oklahoma's attorney general at a Democratic convention, won that vote, and died days later. Yet even after the congressional delegation unanimously voted for the Nineteenth Amendment in 1918 and 1919, and after the 1920 legislature ratified it nearly unanimously, the attorney general still intended to force a referendum on ratification—until the U.S. Supreme Court ruled against that in an Ohio case.

Oklahomans showed themselves to be more enlightened than their attorney general. They not only elected a woman to both houses of the state legislature but sent the nation's second woman to Congress: Alice Mary Robertson, running as a Republican in a Democratic state, defeated the Democratic incumbent. She disassociated herself from suffragists and opposed the League of Women Voters' goals. She also lost the next election, but not before establishing another precedent—as the first woman to preside over the U.S. House.

Robertson was defeated in 1922—the same year that the Oklahoma Seminole chose educator Alice Brown Davis as their first female chief. Indians gained some power by default in the Dust Bowl days of the 1920s and 1930s, as poor whites departed in numbers. Congressional seniority brought federal dollars in the 1940s: land-locked Oklahoma had thirteen naval bases, as well as twenty-eight army camps,

during World War II. These, plus public-works projects in the 1950s, offered women better jobs. President Harry Truman set a precedent in this period when he appointed Oklahoman Beth Campbell Short as head of the White House Office of Correspondence in 1949.

Oklahoma City was the nation's third large municipality to elect a woman to its top job: Patience Latting became mayor in 1971. PATRICIA ROBERTS HARRIS, the first black woman to represent the nation abroad, was Oklahoma's best-known woman in this era.

In 1985, the 150,000-member Cherokee Nation chose WILMA MANKILLER as its first female chief; governing from the capital of Tahlequah, she was reelected for a decade. In 1987, the American Historical Association honored Angie Debo just prior to her death at age ninety-eight. Debo chronicled midwestern history; *And Still the Waters Run* (1966) is considered to be a classic on the Five Civilized Tribes.

University of Oklahoma law professor Anita Hill drew huge media attention with her 1991 testimony on Supreme Court nominee Clarence Thomas. Legislator Betty Boyd's proposal to fund research on breast cancer with a one-percent tax on entertainment also was nationally publicized, but voters rejected it in 1994.

At the turn of the century, Alice Robertson's one congressional term represents the highest elective position held by an Oklahoma woman. No woman has recently won a major office other than lieutenant governor.

Oregon

At the turn of the century, Oregon is one of just four states that have elected women as both governor and U.S. senator.

Spanish explorers visited the area in the 1540s, but the first overland journey was the Lewis and Clark expedition in 1805. Led by Native American SACAGAWEA, the expedition did not go all the way to the Pacific. Few Americans are aware of the woman who did: on a thirty-five-hundred-mile trek to Astoria in 1811, Marie Dorian of the Iowa tribe interpreted Native American languages, gave birth in midwinter, endured starvation, and saw her infant die along the way.

Narcissa Prentiss Whitman and Eliza Hart Spaulding settled just outside the boundaries of what is now Oregon in 1836. The American Missionary Board sent four more women in the next few years, but it was the 1841 opening of the Oregon Trail that transformed the Pacific Northwest. During the next three decades, some five hundred thousand people took that route. Women, like men, walked much of the distance from Independence, Missouri. Thousands died along the way, and the death rate rose as time passed.

Oregon's Land Donation Act of 1850 predated the Homestead Act by twelve years and—with a ratio of four men to every woman in the territory—was designed to attract women. It offered a single woman 320 acres of free land; a married couple was entitled to 640 acres, with the wife eligible to hold her half separately. At a time when eastern states were only beginning to consider reforming property laws, Oregon offered women great independence. When the Washington Territory split off in 1853 and Oregon became a state in 1859, however, it was still too soon to expect that women would be included as voters.

One of the most influential feminists of her era, Abigail Scott Duniway came to Oregon as a teenager in 1852; her mother died on the trail, leaving nine children. Duniway herself bore six children, supporting them and her disabled husband by publishing the *New Northwest*; from its 1871 beginning, the newspaper circulated widely in Oregon and surrounding states. The previous year, Duniway had founded the Oregon Equal Rights Society. She also arranged an 1871 tour for SUSAN B. ANTHONY; the two women traveled the region and spoke on women's rights as far away as British Columbia.

Duniway and Dr. Mary Sawtelle, one of the early female physicians on the West Coast, addressed Oregon's legislature in 1872 on the suffrage issue; women won suffrage for school board elections in 1878 and an equal-custody bill in 1880. They hoped to emulate the Washington Territory's full enfranchisement in 1884, but they lost by a vote of 28,176 to 11,223. The 1885 legislature passed a bill enabling women to practice law, but this was later than in many states. Despite the legislation, officials continued to delay the bar admission of Mary Gysin, who practiced in nearby Washington; having been tried and acquitted of murdering her husband, she had great empathy for female clients.

In 1896 and again in 1898, Oregonians held a Congress of Women that featured regional achievers in education, art, science, and more. One of the most significant was Frances Fuller Victor, who wrote several works of western history, including some attributed to the eminent H. H. Bancroft. Legislators honored Abigail Scott Duniway on the fortieth anniversary of statehood, and in 1900 they again put suffrage on the ballot: this time it failed by just four percent.

Dozens of nationally prominent women visited Portland in 1905, when the National American Woman Suffrage Association held its convention there. When women lost their third suffrage referendum, Duniway became convinced that the presence of outside activists—and especially their links to Prohibition—were holding suffrage back. Indeed, her animosity for the Reverend ANNA HOWARD SHAW was so great that Duniway threatened to have Shaw arrested if Shaw returned to Oregon. Soon after the death of

her old friend Susan Anthony, Duniway led Oregon out of the national suffrage association.

A 1911 victory for suffrage in California left Oregon as the only unenfranchised western state, and a reenergized movement won a close vote in 1912. The 1920 legislature ratified the Nineteenth Amendment unanimously and honored not only Duniway, who died in 1915, but also former Kansas resident Helen Ekin Starrett—the only woman in the nation who attended both the first National Woman Suffrage Association convention in 1869 and the last in 1920.

In 1936, Oregon elected its first congresswoman: Democrat Nan Wood Honeyman won a three-way race but lost a close reelection bid. She had gone to finishing school with ELEANOR ROOSEVELT, and her constituents vacillated between appreciating and resenting this connection.

In the first summer of World War II, the Women's Land Army—modeled on British and Canadian programs to utilize female labor—provided as many as sixty percent of Oregon's agricultural workers. Women accounted for at least a third of workers in Portland shipyards, and Kaiser defense plants were especially innovative in attracting women with in-house child care and take-home meals. Soon after the war ended, Portland elected Dorothy McCullough Lee as mayor, becoming the second major city headed by a woman.

Edith Starrett Green worked as a Portland radio announcer during the war, and in 1955 she was elected to Congress. During almost a quarter century in Washington, D.C., she served on major committees and wrote much of the legislation that created federal aid to education, including the first college scholarships. A Democrat, she particularly promoted equal pay for women.

When Senator Richard Neuberger died just two days before his 1960 reelection filing deadline, his widow (and former state legislator), Maurine Brown Neuberger, quickly filed and then defeated not only other Democratic candidates but also the Republican nominee, an ex-governor. Neuberger supported the President's Commission on the Status of Women, which President Kennedy appointed in 1961; she was less successful with her attempt to allow tax deduction of child-care expenses.

Oregon legalized most abortions prior to the 1973 Supreme Court decision on this issue, and an Oregon case captured national attention in 1979, when prosecutors charged John Rideout with raping his wife. He was eventually acquitted, but the court's acceptance of the premise that a husband could be guilty of raping his wife was a major feminist milestone. Within five years more than twenty states eliminated marriage as a defense against rape.

In 1990, Oregon joined the nine states that had elected women as governors: Democrat Barbara Roberts, a former legislator and secretary of state, served for the next four years. Portland epitomized the 1992 "year of the woman" by sending vintner Elizabeth Furse, a leftist Democrat, to Congress with an astonishing sixty percent of the vote. A strong champion of women and especially girls, she survived a close 1994 race but chose not to run again in 1998.

Oregon dominated national news in 1995, when Republican Robert Packwood was forced to leave the U.S. Senate after dozens of women testified to his history of sexual harassment. On a more positive note, the district that includes Oregon State University elected Democrat Darlene Hooley to Congress in 1996.

Rhode Island

Although a small state, Rhode Island's independent tradition made it the first eastern state to vote on suffrage.

Just two years after religious dissenter Roger Williams founded Rhode Island in 1636, ANNE HUTCHINSON—forty-seven years old and in her thirteenth pregnancy—was tried for heresy in Massachusetts and banished to Providence, and MARY DYER soon followed. Although Hutchinson moved away, Dyer lived in Newport for most of the next decades, until Bostonians hanged her for religious heresy in 1660.

Women played powerful roles in the state's native tribes: during King Philip's War of 1675–1676, Sogonate Wampanoag were headed by Awashonks, the widow of a chief; although Philip was her cousin, she kept her people out of the worst of his warfare. In contrast, Pocasset warriors were led by Wetamoo, who replaced her husband as sachem, or chief, after his 1661 death. Only twenty-six of her three hundred warriors survived the war, and her head was displayed in Massachusetts.

In 1736, Ann Smith Franklin became Rhode Island's official printer, and Sarah Updike Goddard began publishing the *Providence Gazette* in 1762. When the nation's first textile factory began at Pawtucket in 1791, women immediately went to work—and were also the first to go on strike in 1824. Frances Green promoted abolitionism with her 1838 *Elleanor Eldridge*, a novel based on an actual black woman; Green also wrote nonfiction, including a botany textbook. Providence had one of the nation's first coeducational high schools, and an 1846 graduate, Sarah Doyle, promoted women's admission to the esteemed Rhode Island School of Design at its 1877 beginning.

Paulina Kellogg Wright Davis was the state's most significant women's rights pioneer. With a mannequin imported from Paris, she daringly lectured on female anatomy in the 1840s. The first national women's rights convention in 1850 was organized from her Providence home, and in 1853 she began publishing *Una*, arguably the first newspaper to focus on women's rights. Over a thousand people attended the meeting she called to organize Rhode Island's suffrage association in 1868. With Elizabeth B. Chace as president, suffragists not only petitioned the legislature but also supported four women who ran for the Providence school board in 1873; despite an endorsement from the *Providence Journal*, they lost. The state House voted for school suffrage in 1880, but the senate rejected it.

The best-known Rhode Island woman in this era was Ida Lewis, who took over the Lime Rock lighthouse from her disabled father. Although the government did not recognize her as an official lighthouse keeper, national publications praised her rescue of two sailors in an 1869 storm. Lewis had already saved at least eight others during that decade, and finally, after she rescued more men, Congress honored her with a gold medal when she was almost forty. Lewis saved her last life at age sixty-four.

SUSAN B. ANTHONY and LUCY STONE were among the speakers when the state suffrage association met in the House of Representatives in 1884. Two successive legislative sessions passed a full-suffrage amendment by the necessary two-thirds vote, and when it went on the ballot in 1887, Rhode Island men were the first east of the Mississippi to vote on the issue. Women ran a campaign from their headquarters in Providence, and JULIA WARD HOWE, MARY LIVERMORE, and others came to speak—but Susan Anthony declined, proclaiming the cause to be hopeless. Indeed, it lost 21,957 to 6,889, and no eastern state held another election during the century.

Rhode Island women did not even have school suffrage, but they nonetheless took up Henry Blackwell's visionary presidential suffrage idea and introduced a bill for it in 1892—long before Illinois's 1913 model. Attorney Mary A. Greene led a significant revision of family law in 1893, and by the turn of the century women frequently served on school boards. The Pawtucket city charter actually required one of the three members of the school board to be a woman, and the legislature mandated women's appointments on governing boards of state-run charities. A woman even was jailer in Kent County.

Brown University, founded for men in 1764, offered the state's only college degrees; a women's affiliate, later called Pembroke College, opened in 1891, after suffragists led a decade of agitation. No other college had such a direct link to suffragists; the women also offered essay prizes and sponsored students in debates with all-male colleges.

Women introduced their presidential suffrage bill fifteen times before it finally passed in 1917. They made full use of an endless stream of supportive celebrities who visited

Newport, including Julia Ward Howe—one of the era's most popular women—who died in 1910 at her Rhode Island summer home. Multimillionaire ALVA BELMONT began a summer headquarters in 1912 and opened her mansion to the Woman's Party after its 1916 formation. Mary Anthony operated a Newport "suffrage shop" that supplied campaign materials and, after the vote was in sight, taught a civics course. This activity helped create a nearly unanimous vote to ratify the Nineteenth Amendment on January 6, 1920.

The 1920 state Democratic convention nominated suffragist Elizabeth Upham Yates for lieutenant governor, but Rhode Island's best-known woman was mountain climber Annie Smith Peck, who scaled a five-thousand-foot peak in 1932—when she was eighty-two. Peck had also made headlines back in 1911, when she posted a "Votes for Women" banner at the top of a twenty-one-thousand-foot mountain in Peru. Also in this era, Providence sculptor Nancy Elizabeth Prophet, of Narraganset and African heritage, integrated the Rhode Island School of Design.

Rhode Island's only congresswoman was Claudine Schneider. Elected in the 1980 Reagan landslide, she was the first Republican representative in forty years; after a decade in the House, she lost a Senate race. Democrats nominated state legislator Linda Kushner for the U.S. Senate in 1994, but she also lost.

South Carolina

South Carolina is home to some of the most important, yet unrecognized, women of early America.

In 1568, Spanish families from Florida colonized Santa Elena in what would become South Carolina. A century later, a hundred women and men sailed from London to Charles Town (later Charleston), where English families from Barbados soon joined them. Large numbers of slaves were brought from both the West Indies and Africa after 1690, and, during most of the area's history, blacks outnumbered whites.

Perhaps Charleston's most unusual early settler was Mary Fisher Cross. A Quaker banished from Boston to England in 1656, she returned to America and settled in South Carolina in 1682; meanwhile, she had done missionary work in Europe, including an attempt to convert a Turkish sultan. In the early 1700s, Henrietta Johnston sold portraits to supplement the income of her husband, Charleston's Anglican rector. She used a new technique for pastels, and many notable men posed for her.

Johnston may have been America's first female professional artist, but ELIZA LUCAS PINCKNEY was South Carolina's most famous woman of the period. While running

three plantations as a teenager, she began botanical experiments in 1739. The nation's first agriculturist, she was so esteemed that George Washington took time away from the presidency to be a pallbearer at her funeral.

Away from the coast, Carolina was Cherokee country. In that Native American society, women played such strong roles that Chief Attacullaculla expressed surprise when no white women attended a 1757 treaty council. Ten years later, Anglican clergymen also testified to what they saw as the low status of South Carolina women: some men, they said, "Swapped away their Wives and Children, as they would Horses or Cattle."

The Cherokee people were pushed permanently west after their British allies lost the American Revolution. Among the South Carolina women who supported the war were Mary Gill Mills, who organized women to harvest crops for absent men, and Rebecca Motte, who set her plantation mansion on fire to drive the occupying British toward the attacking Americans. The woman who deserves the most fame, though, was a teenager in a Dutch settlement of Orangeburg County: Emily Geiger delivered a message from General Nathanael Greene to General Thomas Sumter by riding two days in the British-occupied wilderness. Her fifty-mile ride was much longer and more dangerous than that of Paul Revere.

In the next decades, slavery became so entrenched in South Carolina's economy that the few women who objected to it did not dare say so. SARAH GRIMKÉ hid when she disobeyed the law and taught slaves to read in 1813; after her younger sister, ANGELINA GRIMKÉ (WELD), wrote a supportive letter to an abolitionist newspaper in 1829, hostility against the sisters became so strong that they never again dared to visit their Charleston family.

Confederates in South Carolina began the Civil War by firing on Fort Sumter, but the state nevertheless escaped most of the warfare that devastated areas further north. Federal troops quickly took over its seacoast, and many women worked with newly freed slaves there; among the whites were Dr. Esther Hill Hawks and educator Cornelia Hancock. HARRIET TUBMAN was authorized to use military transportation for army reconnaissance in South Carolina, and African American writer Charlotte Forten brought national attention to these refugees. Dr. Rebecca Cole, the nation's second credentialed black female physician, began practicing in Columbia soon after the war ended.

A few black women, protected by federal troops and inspired by the Fifteenth Amendment, cast ballots in 1870. The first women's rights meeting was on December 20 of that year. An 1871 statement from the Reconstruction attorney general was extremely feminist, and a joint committee of the 1872 legislature recommended suffrage—but these were "carpetbaggers" who did not represent most South Carolinians. When Reconstruction ended in 1877, the nascent women's movement also ended.

In 1890 Fairfax newspaper editor Virginia Durant Young formed a suffrage organization, and the 1892 senate voted on her suffrage proposal for taxpaying women, which failed 14-21. The next year Young presented Henry Blackwell's presidential suffrage idea to the legislature.

At the turn of the century, South Carolina law was far behind that of other states in terms of women's rights: divorce was unobtainable and women were not permitted to practice law. The state university opened to women in 1894, but when freshmen elected Laura Bateman class president in 1897, administrators insisted she resign. The only office women were eligible to hold was state librarian, a position elected by the legislature.

The national suffrage association sent workers to organize this last state in 1914, and three years later they had three thousand members in twenty-five leagues. Still, most South Carolinians remained very conservative. Legislatures from 1914 onward buried suffrage bills, and just four senators voted for the Nineteenth Amendment in 1920; the House voted 93-20 to specifically reject it. South Carolina women got the vote only because other states gave it to them.

Orangeburg's Julia Peterkin won a 1929 Pulitzer Prize for her third novel, *Scarlet Sister Mary*; among her fans were Carl Sandburg and H. L. Mencken. Although she owned a cotton plantation, many of her novels portrayed the hard lives of black workers.

In 1938, South Carolina became the second state to simultaneously have two women in the U.S. House. Elizabeth Gasque and Clara McMillan briefly replaced their late husbands; the same was true of Willa Lybrand Fulmer in the 1940s and Corrine Boyd Riley in the 1960s.

While other coastal states gained population during World War II, South Carolina did not: many of its black residents left for better jobs elsewhere. After the war, South Carolina was the only state in the nation with no provision for divorce. Women did not serve on juries until the 1970s.

An African American woman set an activist example. By 1919, Charleston's Septima Poinsette Clark had gathered ten thousand petition signatures for educational equity: she taught 132 students and earned $35 monthly, while a white teacher across the street received $85 for teaching 3 students. After forty years, Clark was fired in 1956 because she belonged to the National Association for the Advancement of Colored People—but she organized and, less than a decade later, was elected to the school board. Clark accompanied Martin Luther King Jr. when he accepted the Nobel Peace Prize, and in 1979 President Jimmy Carter honored her at the White House.

Democrat Elizabeth J. Patterson was South Carolina's first congresswoman who did not replace her husband. A former Peace Corps volunteer, she won a Republican district in 1988 but lost in 1992. Currently, South Carolina's only statewide elected female official is Superintendent of Education Inez Moore Tenenbaum.

Conservatives resisted Shannon Faulkner's application to The Citadel, a tax-supported military school, but in 1995 the U.S. Supreme Court ruled in her favor. Exhausted by the legal battle, Faulkner soon dropped out, but she paved the way for others: with forty-one women among eighteen hundred male cadets, Nancy Mace became the first woman to graduate from the 153-year-old school in May 1999.

South Dakota

South Dakota women worked hard for political equality, conducting six statewide campaigns before finally winning the vote in 1918.

South Dakota's original inhabitants were Arikara who lived in permanent earthen lodges, but the nomadic Sioux displaced them in the 1750s. Marie Dorian, a member of the Iowa tribe, led American men through the Black Hills in 1811, but the first permanent settlements, at Yankton and Vermillion, did not exist until 1859; territorial government began in 1861.

The Civil War, and especially the 1862 uprising of Minnesota Sioux, further discouraged white settlers. An influx of gold miners in the 1870s brought many lone men and a few adventurous women such as Calamity Jane, whose exploits with Wild Bill Hickock made colorful stories in the national press. The population more than tripled in the 1880s, as agents for newly built railroads recruited homesteaders in northern Europe. Most of the newcomers were Scandinavian, but some came from as far east as Russia and as far south as Bohemia. Almost all immigrated as families.

The territorial legislature granted school suffrage to women in 1879, and women pushed for full suffrage in the three constitutional conventions that met prior to separation from North Dakota and statehood in 1889. MATILDA JOSLYN GAGE, whose daughter lived at Aberdeen, toured the territory in 1883 and gathered a thousand petition signatures to omit the word male from the new constitution. That did not happen, but women were promised a referendum on full suffrage immediately after statehood. National leaders, including SUSAN B. ANTHONY, ANNA HOWARD SHAW, and Olympia Brown, campaigned there during the summer of 1890. Anthony later wrote bitterly about the Republican convention, which excluded women "although Indians in blankets were welcomed." Women won only thirty-five percent of the vote.

An 1898 rerun of women's full-suffrage campaign was nearly victorious—it lost 22,983 to 19,698. Other indicators also suggested that women's status was advancing: the state university was coeducational from its 1882 beginning, Day County had a female deputy sheriff in 1885, and divorce could be obtained with just six months of residency. By 1900, the legislature had passed a maximum ten-hour work-day for women, eleven women were county school superin-tendents, and the governor was required to appoint women as inspectors of penal and charitable institutions.

South Dakota suffragists had operated from the begin-ning under the aegis of the Women's Christian Temperance Union, but they finally created a separate organization in 1909. A third referendum in 1910 lost by a bigger margin than in 1898, but they charged onward. Male voters were more obdurate, though, and women lost elections in 1914 and 1916 before finally winning in 1918 by a close margin. The legislature, in contrast, unanimously ratified the Nineteenth Amendment at the earliest possible time that state law would allow.

South Dakotans of this era took pride in mathematician Anna Wheeler: the daughter of Swedish immigrants, she graduated from the University of South Dakota in 1903, studied at prestigious universities, and then taught women at Bryn Mawr. Far into the twentieth century, Wheeler was the only woman whose research won honors from the American Mathematical Society. The best-known woman in the state, however, was Gladys Pyle. The daughter of a suffragist leader, she was the state's first female legislator in 1922, and in 1926 she became secretary of state. Encouraged by the winning gubernatorial campaigns of Wyoming's NELLIE TAYLOE ROSS and Texas's Miriam Ferguson, she ran for governor in 1930—but decades would pass before voters anywhere accepted an unmarried woman as governor. In 1938, Pyle won a special election for a U.S. Senate seat vacated by the death of an incumbent, but because Congress did not go into session during her two-month term, she was never sworn in.

During the Depression, drought and a grasshopper infestation compounded the problems of a state in which almost everyone farmed, forcing a third of South Dakotans to ask for New Deal benefits in the 1930s; in one county, eighty percent of the people were on relief. Author Rose Wilder Lane saw that the time was right for nostalgia, and *Let the Hurricane Roar* (1933), based on her pioneer Dakota childhood, became a classic of Americana.

South Dakota's second female senator also never went to Washington: Vera Cahalan Bushfield was appointed to replace her recently dead husband in October 1948, while the Senate was in an election-year recess. Although South Dakota did not elect as many state officers as North Dakota, many women followed Gladys Pyle as secretary of state, and occasionally women held such offices as state auditor and school superintendent.

While feminists elsewhere demonstrated in the 1970s, the headlines from South Dakota were focused on Indian rights—especially in 1973, when some two hundred mem-bers of the American Indian Movement laid siege to Wounded Knee for ten weeks, killing federal officials. Although women participated in this rebellion, they were not leaders, and according to the treaty under dispute in the Black Hills, Sioux women were not even eligible to vote. One female participant is better known now than at the time, for the 1975 murder of twenty-seven-year-old Anna Mae Pictou-Aquash remains under investigation. Some believe Aquash was killed by the FBI, but dissident Indian groups have also accused each other of her murder.

Women were more visible in less militant tribal eco-nomic development efforts that followed the uprising—but one indication of how far behind they were came in 1988, when Sophie Marrs Schmidt was the first Indian to gradu-ate from the University of South Dakota Medical School.

In 1979 Republican Governor William Janklow led the legislature in rescinding South Dakota's previous ratification of the Equal Rights Amendment. He also lost two libel suits against national publications that wrote of his alleged 1969 rape of a fifteen-year-old on the Rosebud Sioux reservation.

South Dakota remains so sparsely populated that it currently is entitled to just one member in the U.S. House; although the state had more seats in the past, no woman has ever been elected to this position. At the turn of the century, it is one of eight states that have yet to pass this milestone. Charlene Haar was the Republican nomi-nee for U.S. Senate in 1992, but she lost badly. The cur-rent lieutenant governor is Carole Hillard, and Joyce Hazeltine is secretary of state.

Tennessee

As the last state needed to ratify the Nineteenth Amendment, Tennessee gave all American women the right to vote.

Once home to Creek, Shawnee, and other natives, only the Cherokee remained in Tennessee when whites pushed across the Appalachians during the American Revolution. As the war drew to an end in 1781, a Cherokee leader named Nancy Ward conducted treaty negotiations; she also had a record as a warrior, having replaced her dying husband dur-ing battle in 1755.

Nashville was settled in 1779 by Virginians, including young Rachel Donelson, who later married Andrew Jackson. Cherokee attacked their boats as they rowed the Tennessee River, and Charlotte Robertson led other women in beating the Indians back with oars. The group nearly starved because, during much of the four-month journey, no one could go ashore for game.

By 1790, Rachel Donelson Robards had grown up, married, and fled her abusive husband. Divorce was a rare procedure in which women had no power, and only after she married Andrew Jackson did they discover that the process was incomplete. Bigamy charges plagued them throughout their lives; while Andrew went on to the presidency, Rachel Jackson hid from society—but ran their plantation successfully and built an aptly named mansion, The Hermitage.

She died shortly before Andrew's 1829 inauguration—the same year that Eliza McCardle married another future president, Andrew Johnson. At the time, however, Johnson was an illiterate tailor and she was a teacher. She taught him while he sewed, and they went on to the White House, where she continued to write his daily news summary.

Near Memphis FRANCES WRIGHT developed Nashoba, a colony for slaves she bought and then freed—in 1825, long before other emancipation efforts. The area was still a wilderness, however, and when the freed slaves could not support themselves, she financed their 1830 move to Haiti.

Tennessee legislators invited mental-health reformer DOROTHEA DIX to speak to them in 1847. In 1851, Mary Sharp College began in Winchester—again, much earlier than most women's colleges. Requiring both Latin and Greek, its curriculum was that of a true college, not merely a finishing school.

In 1853, at age thirty-three, Adelicia Acklen—probably the richest woman in the South—built a Nashville mansion with a bowling alley and running water. She owned huge amounts of land in Texas and Louisiana and even profited from the Civil War by sailing cotton past naval embargoes.

The war had the opposite effect for most women. Some 450 battles were fought in Tennessee; officially part of the Confederacy, it also had many Union supporters, and tens of thousands of women lost loved ones and property.

Ella K. Newsom Trader of Winchester was a parallel to the North's CLARA BARTON: a wealthy young widow, she showed tremendous executive ability in procuring goods that armies lacked, often buying a railroad car of food or blankets, and developing hospitals in four states. Prominent Union women also worked in Tennessee, among them surgeon MARY WALKER and MARY ANN BICKERDYKE, the only nurse for some two thousand casualties at Lookout Mountain. Pauline Cushman, one of several women employed to spy for

the Union, was sentenced to death in a military trial at Shelbyville; a Union victory a few days later saved her, and she was honored with the rank of major.

Fisk University, founded in Nashville the year after the war ended, offered black women and men their first higher educational opportunity. Meharry Medical College, also in Nashville, followed in 1876; although women were channeled into nursing while men became physicians, it eventually educated more black health-care professionals than any institution in the world.

The era's feminist progress was personified by journalist Elizabeth Avery Meriwether and her friend Elizabeth Lyle Saxon. Although they were the sole signers, they nonetheless circulated hundreds of copies of a suffrage petition to men at the 1876 Democratic National Convention. They also waged a seven-month war on the Memphis school board after it fired three female teachers for—in the board's words—"having too many of Mrs. Meriwether's views." The teachers got their jobs back, and Memphis got a new school board and superintendent.

Memphis mobs attacked blacks so severely in 1892 that many fled the state. When African American journalist IDA WELLS-BARNETT editorialized for civil rights, her property was looted and her life threatened; she went to England and organized a boycott of Memphis cotton that persuaded civic leaders to apologize. At the White House in 1898, she less successfully lobbied President William McKinley for an anti-lynching law.

At the turn of the century, the status of Tennessee women ran decades behind that of women in other states. Married women still could not sign a contract or file suit. Property law was heavily weighted in favor of husbands and the legal age for girls to marry was twelve. After some Tennessee women became attorneys, the state supreme court struck down their right to practice law in 1901.

Southern suffragists convened at an 1897 Nashville exposition, and there was a regional meeting at the Peabody Hotel in Memphis in 1906, but with little effect on Tennessee. Determined to energize southerners, national suffragists held their 1914 convention at Nashville's Ryman Auditorium, and soon afterward younger, more demanding women formed a rival suffrage organization. Competition between the two groups greatly increased membership, and they merged in 1918 for the final drive.

Tennessee's labor federation had already endorsed suffrage in 1908, and both the Democratic and Republican state conventions endorsed it in 1916. Women finally ran their first legislative campaign in 1917, when a bill for presidential and municipal suffrage passed the House but not the senate; the same bill passed both at the next session in 1919. Anti-suffragists sued, and the state supreme court sided with them, but the U.S. Supreme Court overruled in July, in time for women to vote in Nashville and Knoxville elections; about twenty-five hundred black women who voted in Nashville.

When Connecticut, Vermont, and Delaware failed to ratify the Nineteenth Amendment in the summer of 1920, national suffragists focused on Tennessee as the last necessary state. The U.S. Supreme Court ruled Tennessee's technical requirements for ratification unconstitutional, and President Woodrow Wilson pressured its Democratic governor to call the legislature into session. Legislators and lobbyists on both sides of the issue poured into Nashville, as the last act of a decades-long drama began.

Democratic leaders urged legislators, most of whom were Democrats, to vote for suffrage, arguing that the party would suffer in the coming presidential election if ratification failed. The senate promptly ratified by a wide margin, but the House pandered to anti-suffragists. Lobbyists used everything from liquor to kidnapping threats to delay action, and when the vote was taken on August 18, it was 48-48. The deciding vote was then cast by twenty-four-year-old Harry Burn, who had originally voted against it but had promised his mother that if there was a tie, he would vote yes.

Unwilling to acknowledge defeat, opposing legislators moved to reconsider and then, to prevent a quorum, holed up in Decatur, Alabama, for more than a week while the Speaker tried to force supporters to switch sides. All stayed loyal, and the opponents' attempts to prevent the governor and secretary of state from finalizing the bill also failed. The amendment was formally added to the U.S. Constitution on August 26.

Willa Eslick became Tennessee's first congresswoman in 1932; she was listening to her husband's speech when he collapsed and died in the U.S. House. Although she defeated three men to replace him, legal technicalities prevented her from running for a full term.

Some thirty-five hundred Tennessee women joined the military during World War II, while others worked in secret atomic laboratories at Oak Ridge. In the middle of the war, Nashville's Ryman Auditorium became home to the Grand Ole Opry, where women proved to be as popular as men in country music. Mother Maybelle Carter especially influenced dozens of female stars, while Minnie Pearl broke ground for female comedians.

Two women replaced their husbands in Congress in the 1960s, but Democrat Marilyn Lloyd became the first congresswoman elected in her own right in 1974, when she defeated the Republican incumbent. Representing the Oak Ridge district, she served on the Space and Technology Committee. Two years after her election, Tennessee rescinded its earlier ratification of the Equal Rights Amendment.

Representative Lloyd chaired a subcommittee on aging in 1990 and retired after twenty years in Congress in 1994. At the end of the century, Tennessee's most prominent woman may be the nation's "second lady," Tipper Gore. No women currently hold statewide office or any of nine congressional seats.

Texas

Texas is the only state that has elected two women as governor, as well as a U.S. senator.

Families from Mexico settled at El Paso in 1598, and Texas, like California and Florida, has a Spanish history that is longer than its American history. Between the late 1600s and 1700s, the Spanish built more than thirty missions for at least a dozen native tribes, but they sent few women. Except at San Antonio, most of these communities died. Mexico declared its independence from Spain in 1813, and in 1820 Jane Herbert Wilkinson Long of Maryland settled near Galveston. Remembered as "the mother of Texas," she almost single-handedly held off Indian attacks in the winter of 1821–1822—while also bearing the first Anglo child in the area. The Mexican governor of Texas gave permission for some three hundred American families to settle in 1821 at Brazoria, on the Gulf of Mexico. Others followed, and they soon outnumbered the Spanish. The cultures clashed: Spanish women, for example, drank, gambled, and kept their maiden names. After battles including the Alamo, Texas became an independent nation in 1836. It immediately began waging war on its natives, and again cultures collided. In Limestone County, young Cynthia Ann Parker was taken by Comanche natives; when Texas Rangers recaptured her in 1860, the only English word she remembered was her name. Her son became the last Comanche chief to surrender to the United States.

Twenty-one ships from Bremen and Antwerp docked at Galveston in 1845. Carrying 3,084 families recruited by promoters of a Germanic state, they were joined by some thirteen thousand German speakers in the next two years. Many were Bohemians—and Bohemian women led all European women as freethinkers. Norwegians also came; one of them, Elise Waerenskjold, left valuable letters describing her independent frontier life.

Abolitionists, including LYDIA MARIA CHILD, opposed the admission of Texas to the United States and collected forty-five thousand petition signatures against this huge expansion of slave territory; Jane McManus Storms, who traveled between her New York home and the Texas land she had held since 1832, led the opposite side. Texas was admitted in 1845, but because Mexico had never ceded its claim to the territory, war broke out again. Sarah Borginnis became "the heroine of Fort Brown" (now Brownsville) when she resupplied soldiers under siege, and General Zachary Taylor rewarded her with the rank of brevet colonel. Jane McManus Storms went to Mexico City in 1847, where she translated for diplomats and was the only newspaper reporter behind enemy lines.

Just over a decade after admission, Texas seceded from the Union; in a statewide election, its men voted overwhelmingly to join the Confederacy. Compared with the rest of the South, the area was little affected by the Civil War. On women's issues, Texas was more like the West than it was like the South: property rights under its 1845 constitution were more favorable to women than those in most states, and a committee of the 1868 constitutional convention that returned Texas to the Union described voters as "he or she." Sarah W. Hiatt led the lobbying of the committee, and even though the full convention rejected its recommendation, she was, in her own words, "not discouraged." In 1875, she wrote that "there is hardly a State in the Union that has such just and excellent laws concerning . . . women as Texas. . . . The unusual number of widows here, due to the incursions of Indians during and since the war, has made . . . the ownership of property by women so common a thing as to attract no notice."

The University of Texas was coeducational from its 1882 beginning, and the 1885 legislature proved amazingly progressive, mandating that at least half of state clerical jobs go to women. Several women ran huge sheep and cattle ranches, including Henrietta King, known as "the cattle queen of the world," with a million acres. Two women successfully practiced dentistry in the 1880s, and by 1900 two had been bank presidents. The era's most notable woman probably was Elisabet Ney, a German-born sculptor who came to Texas in 1872; she carved the statues of Stephen Austin and Sam Houston that stand in the U.S. Capitol.

The state's first suffrage meeting was in Dallas in 1893 and was led by Rebecca Henry Hayes—who traveled nine thousand miles in the next two years, organizing the 360 counties in Texas. Women conducted a ten-year crusade to build the State Industrial College for Girls, which taught not only domestic science but also such traditionally male courses as blueprint drafting. One of the speakers at the world's fair in 1892–1893 was Sue Huffman Brady of Fort Worth, the first female superintendent of schools in Texas, and three women were appointed to the board of regents in 1901.

Houston suffragists sponsored speeches by CARRIE CHAPMAN CATT, ANNA HOWARD SHAW, and Charlotte Perkins Gilman in 1903 and 1904, but their efforts soon lapsed. In 1911, Jovita Idar formed the Mexican Feminist League, which not only advocated equality for women but also opposed lynching. Two other achievers of the era were sisters Katherine and Marjorie Stinson. In 1912, Katherine was the second American woman licensed as a pilot; Marjorie got her license the next year, and, with their mother, the sisters ran an aviation school.

San Antonio women led a 1912 revitalization of the suffrage movement, and the state association had twenty-one branches, including a Men's Suffrage League, by 1915. Texas women joined demonstrations at the 1916 national conventions of both parties and in 1918 they won primary-election suffrage. They had just seventeen days between the time that the law went into effect and the election, but over 386,000 women registered to vote. Suffragists endorsed a slate of candidates, including Annie Webb Blanton for superintendent of public instruction and Governor William P. Hobby, who had helped them; all won by wide margins.

Both of Texas's U.S. senators and half its House voted for the Nineteenth Amendment in 1919. Governor Hobby called a special session to vote on ratification less than three weeks later; the House voted for it 96-20 and the senate 18-9, making Texas the ninth state to ratify.

Most suffragists were appalled when Miriam "Ma" Ferguson—a vehement opponent of suffrage—was elected governor; they saw her as a surrogate for her husband, previous governor James "Pa" Ferguson, who was barred from office after a 1917 corruption conviction. She lost her 1926 reelection campaign but won again in 1932, at the worst point of the Great Depression. Her second term was more successful: she ordered banking reforms before President Roosevelt did and convinced the legislature to pass a tax on oil for the benefit of schools.

Notable Texan women of this period include aviator BESSIE COLEMAN and Jessie Daniel Ames, a white woman who dedicated her life to ending the practice of lynching. At the same time, Ruth Baldwin Cowan was a successful political writer in Austin—until an Associated Press official came to congratulate "R. Baldwin Cowan" on his work, discovered Cowan's gender, and fired her. In 1929 the Texas legislature formally objected to first lady Lou Henry Hoover's inclusion of the wife of a black congressman at a congressional wives' tea. Also in this era, Dallas native Bonnie Parker made national headlines until law officers fatally ended the bank-robbing career of Bonnie and Clyde.

During World War II, the Women's Air Service Pilots flew from Houston and later from Avenger Field in Sweetwater, where a monument commemorates the thirty-eight who died. Tens of thousands of women defied military advice and went with their husbands to training camps in

Texas, and many stayed permanently. Both civilian and military women worked in multiple military installations, while others found new jobs at Beaumont, Port Arthur, and other Gulf of Mexico shipyards.

Houston's OVETA CULP HOBBY did such a superlative job as commander of the Women's Army Corps that President Dwight Eisenhower appointed her the second woman in the cabinet in 1953. Another prominent Texas woman was MILDRED "BABE" DIDRIKSON ZAHARIAS, whom sportswriters voted the outstanding woman athlete of the century in 1949. Bronco-riding champion Jackie Worthington began the National Girls' Rodeo Association in 1947, and a woman was the protagonist of EDNA FERBER's sweeping saga of Texas history, *Giant*, which was a 1952 best-seller. In 1955, Caro Brown of the *Daily Echo* in Alice won the newly created Pulitzer Prize for local reporting; her story ended the career of a corrupt politician who terrorized this Mexican-border area.

In response to efforts by Austin atheist Madalyn Murray O'Hair, the U.S. Supreme Court ruled in 1963 that school-sponsored Bible reading and prayer are unconstitutional violations of students' religious freedom. After enduring public approbation for decades, she and several supporters disappeared in the late 1990s; some believe they were murdered.

Although Texas had elected a woman as governor at the first opportunity, it has been slow to send them to Congress. The first was in 1966, when Lera Millard Thomas replaced her recently dead husband; more unconventionally, that year BARBARA JORDAN, a thirty-year old Houston lawyer, became the only woman and the only African American in the state senate. She went on to Congress in 1972, where she quickly became a national celebrity.

The U.S. Supreme Court's 1973 ruling that overturned state abortion laws was based on the Texas case of *Roe v. Wade*. Attorney Sarah Weddington, aged twenty-seven, successfully argued that laws that mandate pregnancy are unconstitutional. In the same year, the National Women's Political Caucus met in Houston, billing the gathering as the first political convention of women since VICTORIA WOODHULL'S 1872 event. It was headed by Texas gubernatorial candidate Frances Farenthold, who had won votes for vice president at the 1972 Democratic convention. Houston also was the site of a 1977 International Women's Year event; female runners carried a torch from Seneca Falls, New York—the site of the first women's rights convention—to the Houston gathering.

Texas elected its second female governor in a bitter 1990 election: ANN RICHARDS, the first female state treasurer in 1982, defeated a Republican millionaire who ran a negative—even slanderous—campaign. In 1993, Texas became the second state (after Kansas) to simultaneously have women as governor and U.S. senator when Republican Kay Bailey Hutchinson won a special election.

Eddie Bernice Johnson, who was the first black woman elected to office in Dallas, won her 1992 congressional race with seventy-four percent of the vote; she is one of three nurses in the U.S. House. In 1994 Houston added African American Sheila Jackson Lee, a Yale-educated attorney who serves on the prestigious Judiciary Committee, but Governor Ann Richards lost to George W. Bush, son of the former president. In 1996, Kay Granger became Texas's first Republican congresswoman; mayor of Fort Worth from 1991 to 1995, she sits on the Committee on Appropriations.

Utah

Utah women were the nation's first to vote—a half century ahead of most American women.

The area's natives were primarily Ute and Paiute, who lived in the small groups best suited for their food-gathering desert life; the introduction of horses around 1700 made them more nomadic and warlike, with a probable reduction in the status of women. Arid and mountainous, with cold winters, Utah was not attractive to settlers and remained largely uninhabited until members of the Church of Jesus Christ of Latter-day Saints made it their earthly Zion.

Much of the state's history actually began in western New York, where Joseph Smith published the *Book of Mormon* in 1830. His followers, called Mormons, adopted the communal style of property ownership that other utopian societies also accepted—but, much more controversially, they believed in the polygamy of the Old Testament. They soon moved on to the greater freedom of the Midwest, but in 1847 violence forced them from their home in Nauvoo, Illinois, and they went on to the Great Salt Lake of Utah. There they established a theocracy in which church and state were one. In 1852, Smith's successor, Brigham Young, publicly proclaimed the church's acceptance of polygamy and personally became a model: he married at least seventy women, although some of his marriages did not involve a physical relationship. When he died in 1877, Young left seventeen widows and forty-seven children. This introduction of Old Testament practice into modern society made Utah a hot debate topic for the rest of the century.

The Mountain Meadows massacre worsened the controversy. On September 7, 1857, 134 women, children, and men were killed when their wagon train was attacked. Who was responsible became a subject of great dispute: the Indians involved insisted that they were hired by Mormons, while the Mormons argued that this was another outrageous calumny against their religion. Twenty years later, one man—a dissident Mormon—was executed for the crime.

Meanwhile, tens of thousands of people converted to the faith. Mormon missionaries sought converts in Europe, and from England to Switzerland, emigrants went to Utah. While some women regretted their conversion and wrote painfully of it—as did Fanny Stenhouse in her 1872 *Exposé of Polygamy*—others promoted the lifestyle as more independent. Women often maintained their own farms and lived much of the time without a man present; they enjoyed a genuine sorority, with cooperative enterprises such as beekeeping and silk making. Nor did everyone practice polygamy: many couples stayed monogamous, or the man took a second wife only after the first was past her childbearing years. It was church elders and the wealthy—after the end of Utah's initial communalism—who had multiple wives, and again, some women preferred this opportunity to share household work. They especially argued that the lifestyle gave them greater independence and improved political and educational status.

In 1850, for example, the two-year-old colony established the University of Deseret, which admitted women long before eastern colleges did. When Brigham Young University began in 1874, women served on its board of trustees. The Woman's Relief Society was founded while the Mormons were still in Illinois in 1842 and grew to be perhaps the oldest and largest of any female-run charity; in a true sisterhood, women cared for their own needs.

Mormons governed themselves as the state of Deseret, but Utah also was part of the vast Southwest that the United States acquired at the end of the Mexican War in 1848. Congress created the Utah Territory in 1850, but federal troops fought both Mormons and Indians during the next two decades. The discovery of mineral deposits in the late 1860s brought many non-Mormons, mostly male. In January 1870 Mormon leadership granted the vote to women; although designed to tip votes in favor of the Mormons, the move also lent credibility to the view that polygamy might be good for women. Sarah M. Kimball, appointed by Brigham Young and subsidized by the church, became the longtime liaison to the National Woman Suffrage Association.

Although Wyoming's women were the first to receive the right to vote, Utah's were the first to cast ballots because their territory held municipal elections earlier. Observers noted that female voters made the election process more orderly and solemn: the usually rowdy miners behaved themselves in the presence of women. ELIZABETH CADY STANTON and SUSAN B. ANTHONY visited the state in 1871, but most suffragists did not greet this enfranchisement with the enthusiasm they had for Wyoming's; many believed that

Mormon women were tools for theocrats, and—even if the Mormons were independent thinkers—their controversial lifestyle was such an embarrassment that most suffragists ignored Utah's precedent.

The status of Utah's women was atypical and complex. Feminists cheered when Utah admitted Phoebe Couzins to the bar in 1871, but 1873's headlines were highly negative: Ann Eliza Webb Young created a sensation by filing for divorce from patriarch Brigham Young and speaking against polygamy on a national tour, saying she was pressured into the marriage when she was twenty-four and he was sixty-eight. Few noticed the point that Young, unlike many women, at least could file for divorce.

Emmeline B. Wells discovered the complex status of Utah women in 1878, when her party convention nominated her for treasurer of Salt Lake City, but officials refused to put her name on the ballot; when the legislature passed a bill granting women the right to hold office, the territorial governor vetoed it. Wells went on to be the most prominent of Mormon women; a Massachusetts native and original pioneer, she was the seventh wife of a church elder. The church sponsored her as a Washington lobbyist in the mid-1880s.

Angelia F. Newman, who represented the Methodists, was Wells's nemesis. In 1885, Newman got Congress to appropriate $40,000 to build a Salt Lake City rehabilitation center for women who left their marriages, creating a precedent for what was, in effect, a center for displaced homemakers. Newman also led a Women's Christian Temperance Union (WCTU) drive that garnered 250,000 signatures against polygamy—and urged Congress to rescind Utah women's right to vote. Even though most WCTU members supported suffrage, they believed that in this case, men used the multiple votes of their wives against women's best interests.

Congress agreed, and in 1887—a year in which Wells did not lobby—it both outlawed polygamy and took away the vote that Utah women had had for seventeen years. Many Mormons were so angered by this governmental interference with their lifestyle that they moved to Mexico. Women concerned about the legitimacy of their children were especially likely to do so, but the migration also included monogamists.

Emmeline Wells immediately organized a suffrage association and expanded the coverage of the *Woman's Exponent*, which she—signing herself "Aunt Em"—had edited since 1877. She was part of a delegation to the White House that discussed suffrage with First Lady Lucy Hayes in 1879.

Church leaders capitulated on the issues that prevented statehood—issuing a manifesto that abolished polygamy in 1890—and with statehood in 1896, women regained the vote. In the same year, they elected Sarah A. Anderson and Eurithe LeBarthe to the Utah House, while other women won races for county treasurer, auditor, and other offices. Women also were immediately appointed to the boards of all state institutions, including the board of regents.

Martha Hughes Cannon not only became the nation's first female state senator in 1896—she defeated her husband. After earning an 1880 medical degree at the University of Michigan, she became the fourth wife of a Mormon official and even exiled herself to England to prevent his arrest for polygamy—but when they both ran in an at-large race, Mr. Cannon, a Republican who was appreciably her elder, lost.

Even after they regained the vote, the Utah Council of Women continued to support the national suffrage association, traveling long distances to eastern meetings. They noted that Utah had an incomparable number of taxpaying female heads of households, and they could refute those who argued that women did not want the vote by pointing to their analysis of the 1900 election, which showed that women registered and voted in larger numbers than men did. On Susan B. Anthony's eightieth birthday, they gave her a dress produced by their own silkworms; Anthony called it "the finest dress this former Quaker lady ever owned," and it can still be seen at her Rochester home.

Not only were Utah women delegates to both national party conventions in 1900; Elizabeth M. Cohen seconded the nomination of Democrat William Jennings Bryan. Legislator Mary G. Coulter set a milestone when she chaired the House Committee on the Judiciary in 1903, and in 1908 Margaret Zane Cherdon was the nation's first woman to serve in the electoral college, which officially elects the president. By 1920, eighteen women had served in the legislature and several held statewide offices. Not surprisingly, when Senator Elizabeth A. Hayward presented the Nineteenth Amendment, it took less than thirty minutes for unanimous ratification in both houses. Utah women held a jubilee to celebrate not only the amendment's passage in 1920 but also their own fifty-year anniversary of the vote.

It was a high point, and as the twentieth century advanced, the status of Utah women declined. The Great Depression was particularly hard on the state, for its resources could not sustain its large birth rate. Many left, and Utah's per capita income fell far below the national average. This era's greatest achiever was probably Elise Furer Musser, who emigrated from Switzerland in 1897; a former state senator, she was the only woman appointed by President Franklin Roosevelt as a delegate to the Inter-American Conference for the Maintenance of Peace in 1936.

Democrat Reva Beck Bosone became Utah's first congresswoman in 1948; in 1952, this former judge was defeated for being "soft on communism." No women followed her for decades, as the 1950s and 1960s were especially regressive in Utah.

In 1992, Salt Lake City made Democrat Karen Shepard the state's second congresswoman, but the 1994 revolution replaced her with Republican Enid Greene Waldholtz. Recently married, she became the second woman in congressional history to give birth while in office, and the Republican leadership showcased her on the powerful Committee on Rules—the first freshman to be so favored in seventy years. Waldholtz was in office less than a year when officials issued a warrant for her husband's arrest, after he disappeared rather than answer questions about his role as her campaign treasurer. Though a Mormon who campaigned on a platform of family values, she filed for divorce and, not surprisingly, lost the 1996 election. Utah currently has no women in any high office.

Vermont

Vermont is one of thirteen states that have had a woman as governor.

Native Algonquian and Iroquois people—in whose cultures women had significant power—kept whites out of the area until the end of the French and Indian War. Settlers from older colonies came in the next decades, including LUCY TERRY PRINCE. Born in Africa, she and her husband, both free blacks, farmed near Sunderland, where a white neighbor disputed their property boundary. In 1797, when the U.S. Supreme Court still rode circuit, Prince argued and won her case. Justice Samuel Chase is said to have commented that she did a better job than any Vermont lawyer could have.

Vermonters were early abolitionists, with the first society forming in 1819. Women's rights grew naturally out of that, and CLARINA HOWARD CARPENTER NICHOLS was the superlative leader of the movement in Vermont. A Brattleboro journalist, her editorials inspired a property-rights law in 1847—long before most states—and she spoke to the legislature for school suffrage in 1852. She and New York physician Lydia Folger Fowler traveled on an 1853 lecture tour as far away as Wisconsin, and she went on to pioneer women's rights in Kansas.

Vermont women worked in freedman schools after the Civil War ended, among them Anna M. Kidder, who helped build schools from Virginia to Florida. Three years after the war ended, suffragists formally organized; the initial officers of Vermont's suffrage organization were all men. A committee of an 1870 constitutional convention invited supporters to speak, including JULIA WARD HOWE, LUCY STONE, and

Stone's feminist husband, Henry Blackwell. Nonetheless, the full convention flatly rejected enfranchisement.

The University of Vermont, founded in 1791, opened its doors to women in 1871—earlier than the public universities of many states. The 1872 senate almost granted school suffrage to female taxpayers; it lost 13-14. In 1877, Thyrza F. Pangborn was sworn in as a notary public and became a Burlington probate official. Progress continued in 1880, when the legislature enacted school suffrage and authorized women to hold some town and school offices; by 1885, thirty-three women had been elected school superintendent in eleven of Vermont's fourteen counties.

The male-led suffrage society soon lapsed, and the New England Woman Suffrage Association led an 1883 reorganization by hiring lecturer Hannah Tracy Cutler. From 1884 onward, women sponsored a municipal suffrage bill in every legislative session: in 1894, it failed in the House 106-108, and in 1900 the senate also rejected it by two votes. When the women responded by requesting an exemption from all but school taxes—where they could vote—their petition was referred to the Committee on the Insane.

In 1900, Jessie Tarbox Beals became the world's first female news photographer when she sold pictures published in Vermont newspapers. Vermonters held their thirtieth suffrage convention that year. They continued to come close to legislative victories: a 1906 bill to substitute the word "person" for "male" in statutes passed the House and lost the senate by just six votes, arousing anti-suffragists, who appeared in force in future years. The 1910 debate lost by two votes, and the Speaker of the House broke his desk gaveling for order. After a failed attempt in 1915, both houses passed a 1917 municipal suffrage bill, which the governor quickly signed. Coming a few months before New York's full suffrage, Vermont became the first eastern state whose women could vote in school and city elections.

A different governor vetoed presidential suffrage in 1919, and he also refused to call a special session to ratify the Nineteenth Amendment. During a cold rain, four hundred women marched in Montpelier, sixteen hundred sent telegrams, and even the Republican Party convention of this very Republican state endorsed it, but to no avail. Vermont's legislature never went into session, and the opportunity of being the last state to ratify passed to Tennessee.

Dorothy Canfield Fisher was Vermont's most nationally known woman during this era. The first woman appointed to the state board of education, she introduced MARIA MONTESSORI's innovative educational techniques in 1911. A prolific author, she published fiction under the name Canfield and nonfiction under the name Fisher.

A second Vermont woman took the nation by storm in 1939, when New York's Museum of Modern Art exhibited paintings by Anna Robertson Moses, who, at eighty, became known as GRANDMA MOSES. During the two decades that remained of her long life, she became nationally known and was considered the artistic world's leading primitivist.

A Vermont senator was the lead sponsor of World War II's National Service Act, which called for compulsory registration of women aged eighteen to fifty, who then would be required to work at whatever industrial or agricultural job they were assigned. The measure never passed, but it garnered enough support to demonstrate that Congress considered itself capable of drafting women for war service. Vermont's most famous World War II personality was probably Austrian baroness Maria von Trapp, who settled there with her large family after escaping from the Nazis; her life was the basis of *The Sound of Music.*

Vermont's small population means that it elects just one member of the U.S. House, and it is one of eight states that have never sent a woman to either branch of Congress. In 1984, however, the traditionally Republican state elected Democrat Madeleine Kunin; she was the state's first female governor, as well as its first Jewish one. Kunin erased a deficit, increased education funds, passed strong environmental legislation, and was twice reelected.

Finally, Annie Proulx won the 1994 Pulitzer Prize in literature for *The Shipping News*; she had published her first novel, *Postcards*, just two years earlier at age fifty-seven.

Virginia

Home to America's first English-speaking women, Virginia has a rich history—but also is the largest state that has never sent a woman to Congress.

Virginia was named for ELIZABETH I, the virgin queen who reigned over England's golden age. Its first women came in 1608, just a year after men settled Jamestown; they were Anne Forrest and her thirteen-year-old maid, Anne Buras, who married John Laydon at fourteen and bore a child named Virginia. In 1609, seven ships brought more than a hundred women, many of whom died in the 1610 "starving time."

The colony's financiers initially gave free land to women but stopped when they discovered that this reduced female willingness to wed. Thereafter, about one of every three newcomers was a woman. Many were indentured servants, a slavelike status that bound them until their fare was repaid; men greeted arriving ships to buy women as brides. Although a "boundwoman" could redeem her indenture by working (usually for seven years), few jobs were available, and there was great societal pressure to wed and reproduce.

POCAHONTAS married an Englishman in 1614, changed her name to Rebecca Rolfe, and went to England, where she was received at the court of James I; she died on the return trip. Had she lived, she would have been an exceptional mediator between Virginia's natives and newcomers.

A Dutch ship brought about twenty African women and men, the first in North America, to Jamestown in 1619. They were initially treated much like white indentured servants, with limitations on work and hope of freedom, until chattel slavery was legalized three decades later.

Indian women arguably had a higher status than white women: Virginia officials presented a medal to Cockacoeske of the Pamunkey tribe after she signed a 1676 treaty, but no white women were admitted to the College of William and Mary (named for MARY II) for two centuries after its 1693 founding. Only weeks before Patrick Henry delivered his famed "liberty or death" speech in 1775, his wife died in the basement of their home—where he had confined the allegedly insane woman.

Clementina Rind became Virginia's official printer in 1773; a widow with five children, she also published the *Virginia Gazette*, a Williamsburg paper in which she included science news. Many women contributed to the Revolution—none more than Martha Washington, who cared for her husband's soldiers in winter, managed the family plantation in summer, and kept an optimistic attitude throughout, despite the death of all four children she bore in her first marriage. No one was more aware of the importance of women than General George Cornwallis, who made Britain's final surrender in Virginia: "We may destroy all the men in America," he said, "and we shall still have all we can do to defeat the women."

The Revolution's rhetoric encouraged some women to think that they, too, were entitled to liberty and equality. Hannah Lee Corbin wrote her brother Richard Henry Lee, a Virginia representative in the Continental Congress, saying that "no taxation without representation" should mean she could vote—and he agreed. Just as ABIGAIL ADAMS asked her husband to "remember the ladies" in the new Constitution, Lucy Ludwell Paradise begged Jefferson to "remember my sex . . . and introduce [the] Marriage Settlement for to preserve my Sex from want in case of Bad behavior of their husbands."

In 1823, aristocratic Mary Randolph published the first popular American cookbook, *The Virginia House-wife*. Enterprising Richmond women formed a stock company in 1838 and raised $5,000, which they used to buy materials for dressmakers—thus providing work to poor women while profiting from the garments. The first female southern physician was Orianna Moon, who practiced in Charlottesville.

She earned her medical degree in 1857, the same year that Hollis College began in Roanoke; many of the South's most prominent women are graduates of the still-extant college.

With only the Potomac River between Virginia's border and the Union capital—Robert E. Lee and Abraham Lincoln could see each other's homes—more battles raged in Virginia than in any other state, and countless women were involved. Confederate President Jefferson Davis commissioned Sally Tompkins as an army captain, enabling her to commandeer supplies for the hospital she ran in her Richmond mansion; it had the lowest death rate of any similar facility even though physicians sent her their worst cases. PHOEBE LEVY PEMBER ran Chimborazo Hospital, which became history's largest, with more than fifteen thousand male patients; she was depicted on a 1995 postage stamp.

Confederate victories early in the war were strongly influenced by women: Rose Greenhow's sophisticated spy ring was crucial to the disastrous 1861 Union loss at Bull Run, while Belle Boyd successfully reconnoitered in the Shenandoah Valley. Both women were repeatedly arrested and finally banished. Meanwhile, Elizabeth Van Lew spied for the Union; she also sheltered prisoners of war and rendered other services so valuable that, after the war, President Ulysses S. Grant made her postmaster of Richmond.

Union women also worked in Virginia. CLARA BARTON got her start there, for instance, and MARY WALKER was a Richmond prisoner of war. At the war's end, abolitionist women went to Virginia, where they established Hampton Institute and other assistance for former slaves. New York's Emily Howland was particularly generous: she not only taught but also endowed some thirty southern schools, including Virginia's Howland School. Rebecca Lee, who became America's first credentialed black female physician in 1864, practiced in postwar Richmond.

The National Woman Suffrage Association began holding January meetings in Washington in 1869, and the very next year, Richmond's Anne Bodecker invited Paulina Wright Davis and MATILDA JOSLYN GAGE to come the hundred miles south and speak—in a U.S. courthouse offered by a supportive federal judge. Virginia's suffrage association began there, and SUSAN B. ANTHONY came in 1871. With the judge's support, Bodecker was one of the first women to test the Fifteenth Amendment: her November 1871 ballot was deposited not in the ballot box, however, but in the judicial archives instead.

Randolph-Macon Woman's College opened in 1890; like Hollis, it educated many southern leaders. Both colleges were private, though, and no taxpayer-supported higher education for women existed. Virginia's government was regressive in other ways: the governor vetoed an 1898 bill that would have allowed women to serve as notaries public, and not until 1900 did the legislature address property rights that other states reformed decades earlier.

Frances Hodgson Burnett, who moved from England to western Virginia, published *Little Lord Fauntleroy* in 1886 and *The Secret Garden* in 1911. The nation's 1900 best-seller was *To Have and to Hold*, a Jamestown historical novel by Mary Johnston. Decades later, MARGARET MITCHELL emulated Johnston's carefully researched settings in *Gone With the Wind*—but Mitchell never felt that her work met Johnston's standards.

The early suffrage organization, which was dominated by Reconstruction outsiders, soon dissolved, and, uniquely, Virginia's twentieth-century movement was led by authors. Johnston and ELLEN GLASGOW, along with writers Kate Langley Bosher and Sally Nelson Robins, called a 1911 meeting that featured the president of William and Mary College. In defiance of southern tradition, women demonstrated on the capitol steps in 1914 and held "street meetings" in a half-dozen cities the next year. By 1919, they had thirty-two thousand members in 175 locations. However, legislators saw suffrage as a Yankee idea, and the first bill, introduced in 1912, failed 84-12. Although the margin improved during the next four biannual sessions, there were not enough converts to keep Virginia from rejecting the Nineteenth Amendment in 1920—but legislators were so confident other states would ratify that they adopted procedures for women to register and vote.

President Woodrow Wilson's second wife was Virginian Edith Galt Wilson; although no friend to suffrage, she was nonetheless accused of usurping authority and excluding the vice president after her husband suffered a debilitating stroke. Suffragists pointed with more pride to Virginia-born NANCY LANGHORNE ASTOR; a British citizen since her 1906 marriage, Astor became the first woman elected to Parliament in 1919.

African American MAGGIE L. WALKER ran for superintendent of instruction on the "Black Lily" ticket in 1921. Although she had almost no chance of winning, she wanted black women to use their new political rights. The founding president of a Richmond bank in 1903, Walker was an astute entrepreneur; when most banks crashed in 1929, she consolidated the Richmond ones that served blacks and provided hundreds of jobs and mortgages to people who would otherwise have been destitute.

Norfolk's population soared sixty-one percent during World War II, when many women found nontraditional jobs in its shipyards. When the War Department built its new Pentagon in northern Virginia, it also built more than twelve thousand dormitory-like rooms for the women who toiled there. Women worked as "computers" for the National Advisory Committee for Aeronautics at Langley Field, doing complex mathematical calculations. Fifty years later, NASA honored these women for their virtually error-free work, which was faster than the electronic computers of the period.

Virginia's Mary Lee Settle wrote *All the Brave Promises* about her experience in the British military before the United States entered the war; in 1977, she won the National Book Award for *Blood Ties*. University of Virginia poet RITA DOVE won the 1987 Pulitzer Prize in poetry, and in 1993 she become the nation's first black poet laureate, as well as its youngest.

Virginia had the nation's first in vitro fertilization clinic in 1980. That and controversy about women on Norfolk's naval ships absorbed headlines in the 1980s, while in the 1990s the hot topic was admission of women to Virginia Military Institute. The courts finally insisted that this tax-supported school—founded in 1839—could no longer exclude female students, and in 1999 Chin-Yuan Ho became the first woman to graduate.

Attorney General Mary Sue Terry was the 1992 Democratic gubernatorial nominee, but she lost the election. At the turn of the century, Virginia's eleven-member congressional delegation is by far the largest that has never included a woman.

Washington

Washington women were the nation's third to win full voting rights—which they lost and had to regain. It is one of four states that have elected a woman as both governor and U.S. senator.

Supported by ELIZABETH I, Sir Francis Drake explored the coast in 1579, but two centuries passed before whites returned. The first white woman to visit did not stay: Jane Barnes, a barmaid from Portsmouth, England, sailed in on the *Isaac Todd* in 1814, rejected marriage proposals from both white and native men, and returned home.

The British claimed "Oregon Country," and as late as 1839, only about 150 Americans lived in the Pacific Northwest. Along with Idaho's Eliza Spaulding, Narcissa Prentiss Whitman was one of the first white women to come overland in 1836. Sponsored by the American Missionary Board, she and her physician husband settled at Walla Walla and ministered to Cayuse—who, blaming them for an 1847 epidemic, killed the Whitmans and twelve others.

Settlers poured in after the Canadian border was settled in 1846. The Washington Territory was organized in 1853, and the first of twenty-two eventual Indian reservations began in 1859. In 1852, Oregon's Abigail Scott Duniway and Washington's Mary Olney Brown were part of the same wagon train; after establishing their families, they led the women's movement in the two territories.

The 1867 legislature passed an act granting the vote to "all white American citizens over the age of 21 years," and Brown—accompanied by a supportive husband, daughter, and son-in-law—went to the polls, but officials rejected her. In 1870, her sister, Charlotte Olney French, led women who voted in Grand Mound; when all went well, they alerted Black River women, who also voted.

SUSAN B. ANTHONY visited the next year, and the legislature invited both her and Abigail Duniway, whose Portland newspaper, the *New Northwest*, was popular in the region, to speak. Washington Territory granted equal child custody to men and women in 1879—earlier than most states—and a committee of a constitutional convention came close to adopting suffrage in 1878: by a vote of 8-7, they rejected Duniway's plea to omit the word *male* in the relevant clause. The House passed suffrage early in the 1883 session, but the territorial council delayed until late in the year, after most women—and most opponents—had gone home. Only Duniway was watching when, to her surprise and joy, the bill passed, making Washington the third territory (after Wyoming and Utah) to enfranchise women.

More than twelve thousand women voted in 1884, but the victory did not last: in 1887, the territorial supreme court struck it down in *Harlan v. Washington*. Harlan was a convicted felon who argued that his verdict should be reversed because women were on his jury, and they ruled in his favor, sweeping away women's new rights with nineteen other bills. The 1888 legislature restored suffrage, but opponents persuaded a female saloonkeeper, Nevada Bloomer, to file another suit, and the court agreed that the territorial legislature had no right to enfranchise women. Washington became a state in 1889 with its women disenfranchised.

The first state legislature conferred school suffrage and passed protective legislation for working women. It finally put full suffrage on the 1898 ballot—but even though most newspapers and all labor and farm unions endorsed it, male voters rejected it 30,540 to 20,658.

The disappointed women's movement stalled. Abigail Scott Duniway had long pleaded with the national suffrage association to come west, and they held conventions in Portland in 1905 and Seattle in 1909. Railroads offered reduced rates for the Alaska-Yukon-Pacific Exposition in 1909, and the exposition ran a Woman Suffrage Day with buttons, balloons, and a huge kite marked "Votes for Women." The very next year, Washington men granted women the vote, ending the malaise of suffragists, who had not seen a victory since Idaho in 1896.

Above all, it was Emma Smith DeVoe who won the vote for Washington women. Living in a rented house in Olympia, DeVoe quietly lined up legislators, and the proposed constitutional amendment passed by wide margins and went on the ballot in 1910. Consciously avoiding a campaign of outside celebrities, DeVoe organized two thousand women, and made a special effort to convert preachers—particularly Washington's many Scandinavian Lutherans—and even employed a man "to travel and engage men in conversation . . . on trains, boats, and in hotel lobbies and lumber camps." Moneyed antisuffragists overlooked this grassroots campaign, and women won by a nearly two-to-one margin, carrying every city and county.

Washington women formed the State Legislative Federation—composed of 140 women's clubs with a total membership of fifty thousand—which maintained an Olympia headquarters and passed bills to benefit women and children. Representative Frances Axtell of Bellingham successfully sponsored a minimum-wage law, Representative Frances Haskell of Tacoma equalized pay for male and female teachers, and King County judge Reah Whitehead led reforms for unwed mothers.

Women had voted for a decade by 1920, but they had to persuade a reluctant governor to call a special session to ratify the Nineteenth Amendment. When he finally overcame his fear that legislators would use the opportunity for extraneous bills, legislators ratified unanimously and then honored Emma Smith DeVoe.

Just six years later, Seattle became the first major city to have a woman mayor. Republican Bertha Landes was elected to the city council in 1921 with the backing of suffragist friends, and while serving as acting mayor in 1924 she fired the police chief. Her victorious 1926 campaign stressed her intention to clean up a police force that took bribes for ignoring vice, especially illegal alcohol. She ran an efficient administration and improved revenue; labor and the newspapers endorsed her for reelection, but Landes lost in 1928.

World War II made a profound impact on Washington. Women worked in giant aircraft factories that sent planes to war in the Pacific; naval bases and shipyards dotted the state's coastline, and women found well-paid jobs as welders and riveters. Some defense plants were so eager to attract women that they offered child care, take-home meals, and other services (which disappeared at the war's end). Washington also was one of a handful of states that offered relatively easy divorce, and as postwar marital-breakup rates soared, some women went there to end their marriages.

The postwar era brought the first congresswoman: the rural area around Yakima elected Catherine Dean May in 1958. A divorced writer and broadcaster, she was a liberal Republican who sponsored the food-stamp program and served on the Agriculture and Atomic Energy committees until her 1970 defeat. Democrat Julia Butler Hansen's congressional career closely paralleled May's: the rural area on the Pacific elected her in 1960, and she served until 1974. Hansen served on the Education and Labor committees and chaired an Appropriations subcommittee for a decade.

Representative Hansen was still in Congress in 1972, when President Richard Nixon surprised University of Washington professor DIXY LEE RAY—a marine biologist who knew little about nuclear energy—by appointing her to the Atomic Energy Commission. She learned, however, and chaired the commission the next year. With this credential, she returned home and, running as a Democrat in 1976, surprised experts by winning the governorship. The nation's fifth female governor, Ray was the first unmarried woman to hold the job. She attracted great media attention, but an image as an outsider made her tenure difficult, and after alienating environmentalists she lost the next Democratic primary.

In the 1990s, Washington sent four more women to the U.S. House. The southeastern district elected Democrat Jolene Unsoeld in 1988; a feminist and environmentalist, she lost to Linda Smith in the Republican landslide of 1994. Democrat Maria Cantwell won Seattle's northeastern suburbs in 1992 but lost to a Republican man in 1994. Republican Jennifer Dunn, also elected in 1992, represents the largely rural district east of Seattle, leaving women with two of the state's nine seats.

The big victory, however, was the 1992 election of Washington's first female U.S. senator: Democrat Patty Murray defeated men in both parties to win a healthy fifty-four percent. She won by amassing small donations from many people, especially women; her average contributor gave a mere $35. The election gave women six of a hundred Senate seats, a historic high.

West Virginia

West Virginia ratified the Nineteenth Amendment in a setting that could not have been more dramatic.

Long part of Virginia, West Virginia was a hunting ground for northern Iroquois and southern Cherokee. When whites began moving across the Appalachians with the American Revolution, Fort Henry, near Wheeling, was attacked in 1781; young Betty Zane became a hero as she dodged bullets running between the fort and her home to resupply ammunition. This inspired her descendant, Zane Grey, to write the first of his best-selling western thrillers, *Betty Zane* (1903).

Mountains promoted isolation, and the area remained a wilderness much longer than surrounding states. Nuns from France established a Wheeling convent in 1848, but, except for some Irish railroad construction workers, few Catholics settled. The area also had few Quakers or members of other Protestant sects that promoted liberal ideas; nor did it develop the individualistic ideology of the Far West. Because its terrain did not support a plantation economy, there was relatively little slavery, and it had a disproportionate (though still small) number of free blacks, which may explain why white abolitionist John Brown chose Harpers Ferry to stage his 1859 uprising. He intended to establish a free state for escaped slaves, and his plans included a leadership role for HARRIET TUBMAN, whom he called "General Tubman." Tubman's methods, however, were both less rash and more successful, and she was not among the sixteen executed when the plot failed.

This mountain culture was so different from the tidewater that few were willing to die for the Confederate capital back east. When Virginia seceded from the Union, West Virginia seceded from Virginia, and Congress adopted it as a state in 1863. Yet, despite the fact that nearby Ohio and Pennsylvania had held women's rights conventions for more than a decade, the new state's constitutional convention never considered these issues.

A Reconstruction legislator, Samuel Young, introduced an 1867 bill granting the vote to women who could read "the Declaration of Independence intelligently, write a legible hand, and have actually paid tax," but the sole affirmative vote was his own. Two years later, his resolution asking Congress to enfranchise all women got eight of twenty-four votes, and the legislature invited Pennsylvanian suffragist Anna Dickinson to speak—but West Virginia women did nothing to support their supporters.

When a suffrage association finally formed in 1895, it was one of the last in the nation. CARRIE CHAPMAN CATT spoke in 1897 and, with the Reverend ANNA HOWARD SHAW, preached in a Wheeling church. Suffragists worked the state fair that year, and Shaw spoke to the next legislature. West Virginia law needed reform: in 1900, a man had total control of his wife's property, and the "age of protection" for girls, at which a man could legally claim that she consented to sex, was twelve.

Suffragists' big victories in the late 1890s were a law requiring employers to provide seats for female employees and a reform school for girls; previously, girls went to prison for the same offense that sent boys to reform school. After much opposition, the state university became coeducational in 1897. West Virginia's conservatism reflected a southern, not western, heritage—but, like that of some Western states, its law prohibited female miners.

Its most notable native in this era may have been photographer Frances Benjamin Johnston. A cousin of First Lady Frances Folsom Cleveland, she published the first interior photographs of the White House. In 1899 she became the only American woman invited to an international photographic gathering in Paris.

West Virginia was an early state to consider presidential suffrage, but the 1901 bill lost 31-25, and the future got worse instead of better. A 1905 senate bill to put a suffrage amendment on the ballot got just two votes, Wheeling women lost a 1910 attempt for the municipal vote, and—despite active help from the bar association—women even narrowly lost a 1910 effort to allow them to serve as notaries public and court clerks and on state boards.

Virginia author Mary Johnston revived the suffrage movement with a Charleston appearance in 1912. She spoke to the 1913 legislature, and—by one vote—they accepted a referendum that, after reconfirmation by the 1915 legislature, went on the ballot in 1916. Defying southern tradition, suffragists spoke to a Parkersburg circus crowd and ran automobile parades; they raised $25,000, hired a male professional publicist, formed an amazing four hundred local groups, and conducted fifteen hundred meetings. They brought in celebrity speakers, distributed two hundred thousand copies of *Congressional Record* speeches, and sent four monthly issues of the Boston-based *Woman's Journal* to sixteen hundred clergymen. Nevertheless, they lost 161,607 to 63,540—the largest negative margin of any election in the history of the movement.

West Virginia's House ratified the Nineteenth Amendment 47-40, but the senate deadlocked 14-14. Supporters called on Senator Jesse A. Bloch, who was away in California; Bloch made the long railroad trip across the country while suffragists worked to hold their votes. Parliamentary maneuvers continued for almost two weeks, but on March 10, 1920, Bloch took his seat amid cheers; another senator, seeing that he would be on the losing side, switched his vote and made the final tally 16-13. West Virginia became the thirty-fourth of the necessary thirty-six states.

Mother Jones was arrested in 1913 for alleged illegal activity in organizing miners; she was sentenced to twenty years in prison, but the governor pardoned her. Others who spent time in West Virginia's federal prison for women were Mildred Gillars, also known as "Axis Sally," who broadcast for the Nazis in World War II, and leftist orator ELIZABETH GURLEY FLYNN, who spent her sixty-fifth birthday in prison during the anti-Communist hysteria of 1955.

West Virginia's only congresswoman was Democrat Maude Simpkins Kee, who was elected six times in the 1950s and 1960s. Ardently pro-labor, she also chaired a subcommittee on veterans. President Lyndon Johnson appointed Virginia Mae Brown—whose mother was a West Virginia bank president—to the powerful Interstate Commerce Commission in 1964; Brown also was the nation's first female state commissioner of insurance. In the next decade, country singer Loretta Lynn did much to popularize West Virginia, especially with her filmed autobiography, *Coal Miner's Daughter* (1979).

West Virginia elects its supreme court, and Margaret L. Workman became the first woman to win a statewide race in 1988. Robin Jean Davis followed her to the court in 1996, but no women hold top state offices or congressional seats.

Wisconsin

Wisconsin was the first state to ratify the Nineteenth Amendment, which granted all American women the vote.

Although French men explored the region as early as 1634, most settlement waited until after the 1832 Black Hawk War—during which Juliette Kinzie wrote *Wau-Bun*, about her pioneer life. Wisconsin became a state in 1848, the year of the women's rights convention in Seneca Falls, New York; far earlier than other states, its constitutional convention discussed suffrage without regard to color or gender. That same year, Lucy Parsons founded the Milwaukee Female Seminary.

A failed European revolution brought unusual immigrants to the Midwest, especially Milwaukee. Educated radicals, they included such nonconformists as MATHILDE ANNEKE: after riding into unsuccessful combat against Prussians, she fled to Milwaukee, separated from her husband, and supported six children by lecturing and writing in German and English. Great numbers of more conventional Catholic and Lutheran Germans and Scandinavians also arrived in the next decades, including Norwegian Linka Preus, whose diary of life in Spring Prairie dates to 1851.

Vermont newspaper editor CLARINA HOWARD NICHOLS and New York physician Lydia Folger Fowler traveled nine hundred miles in Wisconsin during 1853, lecturing as paid agents for its temperance society. Dr. Fowler addressed alcohol's physiological effects, and Nichols emphasized the issue of women's rights in an era when the law did not protect women from drunken husbands. A large church was too small for the throng that came to hear the women speak in Milwaukee—but they could not find any minister willing to introduce female speakers.

Dr. Fowler was probably an inspiration to Milwaukee's Laura Ross Wolcott, who graduated from Woman's Medical College of Pennsylvania, and in 1858 became the first female physician in any western state. The governor appointed Dr. Wolcott to represent Wisconsin at the 1867 World's Exposition in Paris, and she and Mathilde Anneke were among the German and American women and men who founded the suffrage association in 1868 at Janesville.

Wisconsin's progressive legislators reformed property rights in 1858, and—decades ahead of other states—they passed a maximum-hours law for women in 1867. SUSAN B. ANTHONY, MARY LIVERMORE, and ELIZABETH CADY STANTON attended the 1869 suffrage convention, held in Milwaukee's city hall, and follow-up meetings were held in Madison and Janesville, with the latter featuring Lilia Peckham, a student at the University of Wisconsin. Founded in 1848, the university admitted women in 1867 but limited their curriculum. Still, in this era eastern states did not typically admit women to any tax-supported colleges.

Wisconsin was progressive in other areas as well. Stockholders of private Milwaukee Female College elected three women to its board of trustees in 1870, and male voters elected women as county school superintendents after the legislature made them eligible in 1869. Lavinia Goodell became Wisconsin's first female attorney in 1874; when her bar admission was questioned, the legislature amended statutes to ensure women's inclusion. Within a few years, Kate Kane in Milwaukee, Angie J. King in Janesville, and Cora Hurtz in Oshkosh were practicing law. Ella Wheeler Wilcox published *Poems of Passion* in 1883; she achieved immortality with the line, "Laugh, and the world laughs with you; weep, and you weep alone."

The Reverend Olympia Brown moved to Racine in 1877 and retired from her successful pastorate in 1884 to become president of the suffrage association. The next year male voters approved a constitutional amendment that granted women the vote on "school matters." Suffragists began the *Wisconsin Citizen* in 1887, hoping to expand their voting rights, but instead the movement stalled.

By 1885, Wisconsin had more immigrants per capita than any other state and was the nation's second most Catholic state, as Hungarians, Poles, and Czechs joined the earlier German Catholics. Beer drinking was integral to the culture and to Wisconsin's economy, and the suffrage association suffered internal dissension over its association with Prohibition. It may have been fatal to progress, for the legislature enacted no more vote expansions. Instead, the Reverend Brown spent the next decade in lawsuits, unsuccessfully arguing that "school matters," broadly interpreted, should include other elections.

The University of Wisconsin awarded the first doctorate in history granted to a woman, Kate Ernest Levi, in 1893. In the same year, geologist Florence Bascom was the first woman awarded a doctorate of philosophy by Johns Hopkins University; she also was the first woman elected to membership in the American Geological Society. By the turn of the century, women sat on many school boards, and eighteen had served simultaneously as county superintendents. The board of regents had its first female member in 1901.

That year, Janesville's Carrie Jacobs Bond published the century's standard wedding song, "I Love You Truly." A successful songwriter, she sold more than five million copies of "The End of a Perfect Day." EDNA FERBER graduated from high school in Appleton in 1902 and began her writing career at seventeen with the *Milwaukee Journal*. In 1905, Oshkosh sculptor Helen Farnsworth Mears was commissioned by Illinois to carve a statue of FRANCES WILLARD; it was the first of a woman in the U.S. Capitol.

MAUDE WOOD PARK organized college women to work for suffrage in 1908; suffragists brought in such speakers as JANE ADDAMS and BELVA LOCKWOOD, and the legislature put the question on the 1912 ballot. Suffragists conducted an innovative campaign, with a banner-bedecked boat cruising rivers and a broad range of supportive celebrities, including German speakers such as BARONESS BERTHA VON SUTTNER of Austria. But the issue was placed on a special pink ballot, enabling brewers and other opponents to coach even illiterate men into marking it "No," and women lost 227,054 to 91,318. The only supportive area was near Lake Superior; the Milwaukee margin was extremely negative.

The legislature granted presidential suffrage in January 1919. In June, both senators and eight of eleven congressmen voted for the Nineteenth Amendment, and the legislature raced Illinois to be the first to ratify. Wisconsin finished voting—with one negative senate vote and two in the House—at 11:00 a.m. Illinois finished at 10:00 a.m., but they made a technical error and had to re-ratify, allowing Wisconsin to claim to be the first.

Zona Gale of Portage was one of the most active suffragists, and in 1921 she became the first woman to win the Pulitzer Prize in drama for *Miss Lulu Bett*. In 1922, the first year in which women could run for legislative office, Wisconsin Democrats set a national precedent by nominating suffragist Jessie Jack Hooper for the U.S. Senate. The honor was that of sacrificial lamb, however, for she ran against popular liberal Republican Robert La Follette and lost in a landslide—except for the Democratic stronghold of Milwaukee, which she won despite her opposition to beer.

LAURA INGALLS WILDER published her classic reminiscence of frontier Wisconsin, *Little House in the Big Woods*, in

1932. In 1934, physician Lillie Rosa Minoka-Hill was finally licensed by the state—thirty-five years after graduating from Woman's Medical College of Pennsylvania. A Mohawk and the widow of Oneida, she supported six children by practicing medicine, but her patients were too poor for her to pay the license fee. In 1947, after decades at the *New York Herald-Tribune*, Wisconsin native Helen Rogers Reid became the newspaper's publisher.

The founding meeting of the National Organization for Women in October 1966 was chaired by University of Wisconsin professor Kathryn Clarenbach. The university also employed the incomparable Gerda Lerner, whose *Woman in American History* (1971) gave impetus to the new field of women's studies. Wisconsin took special pride in the 1969 inauguration of Israel's new prime minister: Golda Meir, born Goldie Myerson, grew up in Milwaukee.

Susan Engeliter was the Republican nominee for the U.S. Senate in 1988, but no woman won until 1998, when the university town of Madison made Tammy Baldwin the first openly gay U.S. representative to be elected as a non-incumbent.

Wyoming

Wyoming women not only were the world's first to be fully enfranchised—they also have a heritage of other female "firsts."

Few whites entered the region prior to 1800, when at least eight native tribes driven from the east lived there. The first American women there were probably missionaries Eliza Spaulding and Narcissa Whitman in 1836, and Jessie Benton Frémont wrote much of her husband's report of his 1842 exploration. Mormon women followed in 1847, and in the next decades, thousands stopped at Fort Laramie, but an 1851 treaty required them to stay on the Oregon Trail and leave Wyoming to natives.

An 1862 Montana gold strike nonetheless brought many settlers—mostly unmarried men, who were eager to attract women to the area. More egalitarian and open to change than easterners, Wyoming's men were ready to reward women who endured frontier life. When the territory organized in 1869, Julia Bright persuaded her husband, president of the territorial council, to introduce a suffrage bill; partly because of partisan gamesmanship, it passed. Cheyenne women headed by Amalia Post, whose husband was the territory's delegate to Congress, persuaded Governor John Campbell to sign it, and on December 10, 1869, Wyoming women became the world's first to have an unrestricted right to vote.

Wyoming's legal code also spelled out that all women, married or not, could sue, own and control property, enter into contracts, make wills, and conduct business on the same terms as men. The only gender difference made a woman "exempt from . . . the debts of her husband." Wyoming even provided equal pay for women and men in public employment, including teachers; most other states did not pay male and female teachers equally until after World War II.

On February 14, 1870, Esther Morris became the nation's first female law enforcement official when the governor appointed her justice of the peace for the mining town of South Pass City. Her statue, which was placed in the U.S. Capitol in 1960, is one of a half dozen depicting women.

The remarkable winter of 1869–1870 continued into March. For the first time in the history of jurisprudence, women served on juries—to the delight of many eastern cartoonists, who found the idea hilarious. Local reaction was the opposite. The first all-female grand jury met in Laramie for three weeks and heard cases from murder to illegal branding. Despite the incredulity of newsmen who reported the story by telegraph, law-enforcement officials proclaimed the experiment a success. Seven women were included in the follow-up petit jury, and Laramie's sheriff appointed a female bailiff: Martha Boies was the first woman in the world to hold this position. Pennsylvanian Eliza Stewart opened Laramie's first public school that winter.

In November 1870, Laramie opened its polls early so that Eliza A. Swain could be the world's first woman to vote in a general election: a seventy-five-year-old Quaker, she was an inspiration to SUSAN B. ANHTONY and ELIZABETH CADY STANTON, who grew up in the Quaker faith. The legislature had second thoughts and repealed suffrage in 1871, but the governor vetoed the bill and no more repeal attempts occurred.

When Wyoming became a state in 1890, its women again were the only ones in the world with full rights; Utah and Washington women had lost the vote they once enjoyed by 1890. Moreover, Wyoming's representatives fought hard for women at statehood: so many congressmen opposed admitting Wyoming to the Union with women as voters that the House debated the issue for three days. When Wyoming's delegate telegraphed home that it looked as though women would have to be abandoned for statehood to pass, the legislature wired back, "We will remain out of the Union a hundred years rather than come in without woman suffrage."

The House conceded in March by a vote of 139-127; the Senate dallied until June and then voted 29-18, with 37 absent. President Benjamin Harrison signed the bill, and Wyoming rejoiced. Some ten thousand people came to celebrate in Cheyenne, where they honored Esther Morris and

Grace Raymond Hebard, author of the state constitution's suffrage clause. A University of Iowa graduate in civil engineering, Hebard was a draftsman for the office of the surveyor general and later became Wyoming's first female attorney. She also was heavily involved with its university, which opened in 1886 and not only was coeducational but also had women on its board of trustees.

In 1892, Republicans made Theresa A. Jenkins a delegate to their national convention. The first woman so honored, Jenkins was a University of Wisconsin graduate who went west in 1877; she gave hundreds of speeches during suffrage campaigns in Colorado and Kansas. Esther Reel was elected state superintendent of public instruction in 1894, receiving more votes than any candidate in the state's past. In 1898 President William McKinley appointed her as national superintendent of Indian schools. Reel's unanimous confirmation by the U.S. Senate was another first.

Wyoming was slow to send women to its legislature, however. More than a decade after Colorado and Utah set the precedent, Laramie elected Mary Godat Bellemy in 1910; among other bills, she successfully supported an eight-hour workday for women. Two women won in 1913: Anna Miller, a Laramie merchant, and Nettie Traux, a Sundance teacher who almost immediately chaired the education committee. Because Wyoming's liberal property laws made marriage less legally onerous than in other states, they—along with Morna Wood, elected in 1915—successfully led the opposition to easier divorce.

On November 7, 1910, Wyoming became the first state to commission a woman in the National Guard, albeit in unusual circumstances. When the secretary to the governor resigned late in his term, he appointed his daughter—and, according to state law, "the Governor's Secretary shall have the rank of Major." Jean Willard Brooks thus was sworn in as a major; she performed the duties of acting governor when both her father and the secretary of state went out of state at the same time.

The Nineteenth Amendment was a non-issue in Wyoming, but the governor called a special session; the legislature ratified unanimously and went on to celebrate the fiftieth anniversary of Wyoming women's enfranchisement. Later in 1920, Jackson Hole elected an all-female slate of city officers: the mayor, council, and executive offices were won by women who campaigned on a platform of paving roads and building a park.

In 1921, the University of Wyoming awarded its first honorary degree: the recipient, appropriately for this first suffragist state, was CARRIE CHAPMAN CATT. In the same era, Wyoming commissioned Gertrude Vanderbilt Whitney to carve a statue of William "Buffalo Bill" Cody that stands in Cody.

By far the most important event, however, was the 1924 election of NELLIE TAYLOE ROSS as governor. Replacing her recently dead husband, Ross won twenty of twenty-three counties—especially impressive because she was a Democrat in a largely Republican state. Although Texas elected Miriam "Ma" Ferguson at the same time, Ross was termed "the first woman governor" because she was sworn in two weeks earlier. She lost her 1926 reelection by fewer than fourteen hundred votes but then served in the legislature. Soon after President Franklin Roosevelt took office in 1933, he made fellow Democrat Ross the first woman to head the U.S. Mint; she served there for two decades.

Wyoming women volunteered for World War II in numbers disproportionate to its population: 456 women joined the army and 213 the navy, but modern women have not built on the heritage their pioneers gave them.

Nellie Tayloe Ross went almost unmourned when she died in 1999 at age 101, and not until 1994 did Wyoming send its first woman to Congress. The population remains so small that Wyoming has only one U.S. House seat: Republican Barbara Cubin from Casper won the statewide race.

Timeline: Women in World History

B.C.

5700 Paintings at Çatal Hüyük, in what will later become Turkey, often feature women giving birth or breast-feeding.

3000 In Sumerian society, both women and men are priests; on the other hand, training as a scribe—key to the society's most powerful positions—is open only to boys, not girls.

2000 Although many tribes in Africa and the Americas are matrilineal societies, in which children and property are traced through the mother, those in the "cradle of civilization," in what will later become the Middle East, are patriarchal. Egyptian women have more rights than those in Mesopotamia; for instance, married women retain their property in Egypt.

c. 1792 Hammurabi's Code in Babylonia is the first codification of law; its largest section concerns marriage and the family. Marriages are arranged by parents, and women have a distinctly inferior position. A woman guilty of "neglecting her house [and] humiliating her husband" may be drowned, and husbands may sell their wives to pay debts. At the same time, some Babylonian women engage in commerce and even become priests.

1500 Egyptians practice birth control: According to one prescription on papyrus: "To make a woman cease to become pregnant for one year . . . tips of acacia and dates are triturated with honey. Seed wool is moistened therewith and placed in her vulva." Meanwhile, the royal family is incestuous, and the rulers of Egypt may be brother and sister as well as husband and wife.

c. 1473 HATSHEPSUT is the first female ruler in history. Her reign over Egypt features less warfare and more construction than those of most pharaohs.

1354 Queen NEFERTITI of Egypt dies; her reign promoted monotheism and sun worship.

c. 1250 The destruction of Troy in Asia Minor in the Trojan War is attributed to conflict that began when legendary beauty HELEN left her Greek husband and escaped to Troy with Paris, the son of the Trojan king. During the ten-year war, one of Troy's allies is allegedly Penthesilea, queen of the Amazons.

900 Polygamy is the common practice among Hebrews and other Middle Eastern peoples. One Persian king fathered 115 sons—daughters were not counted.

811 As regent for her young son, Queen Samuramat (also spelled Sammu-ramat) reigns over Assyria. She will become legendary through Greek historians, who call her Semiramis; they credit her with building Babylon.

c. 700 SAPPHO of Lesbos writes Greek poetry from which the word "lesbian" is ultimately coined.

c. 690– 638 Hebrew leader DEBORAH unites neighboring tribes in a successful attack against aggressive Canaanites. She is aided by Jael, a Kenite woman who kills the Canaanite commander.

600 Warriors in the Greek state of Sparta live in military barracks while their wives remain at home, which gives Spartan women a great deal of independence. Girls are educated similarly to boys;

they train in athletics and, like boys, wrestle and throw the javelin while naked. In Athens and other Greek cities, however, formal education of all types is reserved for boys. Girls marry in their early teens, and women are expected to remain in the home except when accompanied by a man. Although wealthy women supervise both male and female slaves, legally all women are perpetual minors. Athenian widows are not even eligible to inherit their husbands' property.

c. 500   The Chinese language defines the inferior position of women: the character for the word "man" merges the symbols for "rice field" and "strength," while that for "woman" is a submissive figure. Chinese women are limited not only by their sex but also by age. Until a woman bears children—especially sons—she is a virtual slave to her husband's extended family. A childless woman can expect to be abused, and she may be returned to her family, who also will view her as an economic burden.

c. 400   The legendary Jewish queen of Persia, ESTHER, prevents a plotted pogrom of Hebrews there.

331   When Alexander the Great destroys the Persian palace at Persepolis, the attacking procession is led by an Athenian courtesan, Thais, who had suggested the attack during a drunken feast. Female musicians perform while Thais joins the king in setting fire to the palace.

300   India's caste system is well developed. Societal rank is determined by male occupation and ranges from elite warriors and priests to untouchables; women are at all levels, depending on the men in their lives. An upper-caste woman pays for her privilege with her life, for when her husband dies, she is expected to practice suttee—allowing herself to be burned alive by the fire that cremates her husband.

247   Antiochus II, who reigns over Asia Minor, is killed by his wife, Berenice.

200   Divorce is introduced in the Roman Empire and becomes fairly easy for either a woman or a man to obtain. Upper-class women enjoy property rights and are much less confined than Greek women. Meanwhile, the legal age for Roman girls to marry is twelve.

47   The armies of CLEOPATRA defeat those of her brother, and she becomes one of the most forceful female military and political leaders of all time.

43   While Roman leader Mark Antony dallies with Cleopatra in Alexandria, his wife, Fulvia, raises an army and attacks Octavius Caesar in Rome.

c. 40   The status of women in southeast Asia is much higher than that in China. During warfare between the two countries, Vietnamese sisters Trung Trac and Trung Nhi recruit an army of men and women. At least three dozen of the army's officers are women. The army defeats the Chinese, and the Trungs jointly rule the new independent state for several years, until the Chinese again invade. Then, rather than allow themselves to be captured, the sisters drown themselves.

A.D.

c. 45   Ban Zhao (also spelled Pan Chao) is a well-known historian of China's Han dynasty. Even she writes, however, that a woman's most important function is servitude to her husband.

54   AGRIPPINA the Younger poisons her husband, the Roman emperor Claudius; her son Nero becomes ruler and has her executed five years later. Nero will also have his wife, Octavia, killed.

177   Among several Christians tortured to death by Romans at Lyons, in what will later become France, are an unidentified woman and her slave, Blandina.

235   Although she has been more honored than any other Roman woman, JULIA MAMAEA, mother and regent of the young Roman emperor Severus Alexander, is assassinated by her own soldiers.

304   AGNES, a young Roman, becomes a Christian martyr; her persecution—like that of many female saints—is based on her refusal to marry. She will be far more famous than another woman martyred in this same year: Crispina of Numidia,

in northern Africa, who is put to death even though she is the mother of several children.

415 Greek philosopher and mathematician HYPATIA is savagely killed by a mob incited by Alexandria's Christian bishop.

523 BRIGIT dies at Kildare, where she had founded the first religious community of women in Ireland; she will rank alongside Saint Patrick as the country's most beloved patron saint.

548 The Byzantine empress THEODORA dies. She has much influenced her husband, Justinian the Great, and tremendously improved the status of women in the empire.

589 Theodelinda, queen of the Lombards, promotes Christianity in what will later become northern Italy.

c. 600 The status of Japanese women begins to decline: vestiges of matriarchy—such as newly married couples living with the bride's household—begin to disappear, while inheritance and other property rights are lost as male domination becomes complete.

613 Although she probably is past sixty, Visigoth ruler BRUNHILD is brutally executed in Burgundy (later part of France) by Chlotar II, the Merovingian king.

622 The Islamic calendar begins this year with Muhammad's move to Medina. His first wife, Khadijah, was his first convert to the new religion of Islam, which ultimately will prove highly inhibiting to women. At the beginning, however, Muhammad raises women's status by limiting men to four wives.

632 FATIMAH, daughter of the prophet Muhammad, dies; her descendants become the Fatimids, a dominant dynasty in North Africa and the Middle East.

657 In England's Northumbria, Hilda founds what will later be called Whitby Abbey, which includes both men and women. Five future bishops will be educated under her supervision.

665 BATHILDE ends her regency in France, during which she has opposed slavery.

683 Wu Hou rules China after forcing her son into exile; she will reign until the year 705.

735 Frideswide founds an abbey at Oxford in England and eventually becomes the patron saint of this university town. Like several other female saints, she allegedly gave up her position as a princess and fled from her family to avoid marriage.

755 Emperor Hsüan Tsung of China is so in love with a commoner that he scandalizes his society by continually sending runners the fifteen hundred miles to Canton to bring back litchis for her.

780 IRENE becomes a strong ruler of the Byzantine Empire.

c. 800 The Rom people, later known as gypsies, move out of northern India and head west toward Europe. In gypsy society, women play roles similar to those of men. Fortune-tellers who see the future through crystal balls and tarot cards, their women are especially known for reading palms and tea leaves. Despite determined eradication efforts by men ranging from scientists to theologians to Adolf Hitler, the ancient culture will survive—perhaps because it holds women in high esteem, and other women are therefore attracted to it.

The Maya civilization on Mexico's Yucatán peninsula begins to decline. Women in this society did most of the farming, while men were engaged in warfare. Men who lost in battle were most likely to be the victims of the society's human sacrifices.

Japan's Fujiwara family becomes extremely powerful by positioning itself so that it supplies all the wives and concubines of future emperors.

852 Natalia and Liliosa, Christians in Córdoba, Spain, are beheaded by Muslims when they refuse to wear veils.

c. 900 In Islamic society there is a maxim that a woman should go beyond her house just three times in her life: when she is led from her parents' household to that of her husband, when her parents die, and when she herself dies.

c. 910   As mistress to Pope Sergius III, Marozia becomes the mother, grandmother, and aunt of future popes.

913   Aethelflaed (also called Ethelfleda), daughter of King Alfred the Great, begins construction of Warwick Castle in England.

c. 960   Saxony's HROSVITHA writes plays, poems, and German histories.

999   ADELAIDE, who was jointly crowned with Otto the Great as head of the Holy Roman Empire, dies in the Alsatian convent she founded.

c. 1000   All Japanese literature during this period is written by women; at least a hundred are authors during a time when Japanese men scorn writing as "women's work." Two women, MURASAKI SHIKIBU and SEI SHONAGON, write the first Japanese classics. Murasaki's complex multivolume novel is still considered a literary masterpiece.

1050   ZOE, followed by her sister Theodora, governs the Byzantine Empire.

1074   The Roman Catholic Church begins to excommunicate married priests, forcing men to choose between their wives and the church. In the Greek and Russian Orthodox Churches, priests may be married, but this does not create a superior status for women.

1126   A long civil war begins in England between two women named MATILDA, both of whom are entitled to be queen.

1152   One of the most powerful women of her era, ELEANOR OF AQUITAINE divorces the king of France and marries the king of England.

1173   The body of Euphrosyne of Polotsk—who had spent her life copying and selling books—is returned to Kiev for burial after she dies in Jerusalem on a pilgrimage.

c. 1200   Upper-class Chinese families begin binding girls' feet so that they grow to only a fraction of normal length. At age five, a girl's feet are wrapped so tightly in cloth that the toes curve under, the arch breaks, and the foot comes to resemble a lotus blossom. Bound feet are considered beautiful, and by the Ming dynasty of the 1300s and 1400s, more than half of Chinese girls have bound feet. Peasant women, whose work in the fields would be compromised by binding, are exempted from the practice; some become servants to wealthy women who cannot walk unassisted.

1215   The world's first democratic document, the Magna Carta, owes its origin in part to the fact that England's King John has weakened himself by divorcing Avisa of Gloucester to marry Isabella of Angouleme.

1236   Tolls on the London waterway known as Queenhithe have gone to the queen for centuries, and when Eleanor of Provence (in southern France) becomes queen of England this year, she will force more cargo to go through that wharf. Some individuals resent her so much that when civil war breaks out, they assault the boat that carries Eleanor and her ladies past London Bridge. Throwing stones and garbage, they shout, "Drown the witch," but she escapes and eventually reigns as regent for her son.

c. 1300   Women in East Africa begin to marry Arab men, intermingling the two cultures. The growth of Islam is slow, however, in part because African women do not accept the restrictive clothing and lifestyle it imposes on them.

A Japanese man may divorce his wife for reasons grave and trivial—because she has a serious illness or because she talks too much.

1317   Law is adopted in France that forbids women from reigning; unlike most of its European neighbors, France will never have a woman who is queen by birth, as opposed to by marriage.

1326   Isabella of France, queen of England, has been treated so badly by her husband, Edward II, that she feels justified in raising an army against him; with her lover, Roger Mortimer, she ousts the king.

1384   Polish nobles choose JADWIGA as their monarch.

c. 1400   Midwives among Mexico's Aztecs tell baby boys that they are warriors, while at birth girls are told, "As the heart stays in the body, so you must stay in the house." Some upper-class girls, however, become educated religious leaders.

1431   After successfully leading France in battle against England, JOAN OF ARC is burned at the stake in Rouen.

1445   International trade is sufficiently developed that Margaret of Anjou receives a lion as a wedding present when she marries King Henry VI of England. The royal couple keep the animal in the Tower of London and complain about the cost of feeding it.

c. 1450   Inca territory stretches across an area bounded by the future countries of Colombia and Chile, but marriages are limited to partners within the immediate tribe. Women are highly skilled weavers, and when the Spanish arrive, some note that Inca women carry their weaving tools wherever they go. Women also serve as priests.

In Africa's Congo, both boys and girls live with their mother until age six, when girls go to the "house of the women" and boys to the "house of the men." Both have rites of passage at puberty.

1453   The Byzantine Empire falls to the Ottoman Turks this year, and Muslims replace Orthodox Christians in power at Constantinople (later Istanbul). Turkish sultans generally do not marry but keep a harem (which means "sacred place") of women; after they have borne sons, four of the women—the maximum allowed by Muhammad—are named favored concubines. The mother of a sultan can become quite powerful. Nonroyal women in the Ottoman Empire generally have more rights than other Islamic women: they can own property and control their dowries, and a few will even be government officials.

1455   Margaret of Anjou personally leads soldiers of the house of Lancaster into combat during England's War of the Roses. Although she ultimately is defeated, during her time as queen, Margaret also encour-

ages women's participation in the development of the silk and wool industries and founds Queens College of Cambridge University. No woman will be admitted to the college for centuries.

1489   Caterina Cornaro, queen of Cyprus, is forced by the king of Venice to surrender her island country.

1490   Isabella d'Este begins her patronage of Raphael and other Italian artists and intellectuals.

1492   Queen ISABELLA of Spain—who rules jointly with her husband, Ferdinand II—supports the historic voyage of Christopher Columbus, an Italian, thereby proving to be her husband's superior in scientific curiosity.

1497   Beatrice, duchess of Milan, dies in childbirth, prematurely ending what could have been a brilliant career in both politics and art.

c. 1500   As travelers from the north begin to arrive in Africa, they are surprised to discover matrilineal societies; one writes that "a man does not pass on inheritance except to the sons of his sister." Europeans also are astonished at the ability of women to balance large objects on their heads, leaving their hands free for other tasks.

As the Spanish expand into South America, one observer praises native women in battle, saying that women "fired the crossbows and guns while the men lay down seeking a bit of shade in which to die." When they retreated, "it was the women who hoisted the sails and set the course upriver, rowing and rowing without complaint."

During this century and the next, as many as a hundred thousand Europeans will be prosecuted as witches. By far the majority of those accused are women; many are tortured until they "confess." Women serve as neither judge nor jury—and this will continue to be the case in all trials until far into the twentieth century.

1508   Margaret of Austria joins France and Spain in an attack on Venice; when these members of the League of Cambrai (an anti-Venetian alliance) negotiate a 1529 treaty, it is known as the Paix des Dames, or "Ladies' Peace."

1509   When Venetians capture the husband of Isabella d'Este, who rules Mantua (an area between Milan and Venice), she refuses to ransom him by surrendering their son. Despite angry letters from her husband, she does not give in, and she eventually wins his release without endangering the child. She also creates one of Italy's best libraries.

1514   A Portuguese fleet arrives in China this year, and a Spanish man later writes that women are "very secluded . . . it was a very rare thing for us to see a woman." One reason, of course, is that the Chinese tradition of foot binding limits female mobility.

1519   When Spanish conquistador Hernán Cortés arrives in Mexico, Maya chiefs present him with slaves, including an Aztec woman named Marina (also called Malinche). She quickly learns Spanish and acts as an interpreter for Cortés with both the Maya and Aztec peoples. As POCAHONTAS did for John Smith in North America, Marina at least once saves Cortés from death.

1525   Italian poet Vittoria Colonna writes a lamentation, *Canzoniere*, after the death of her husband, the marquis of Pescara. She also befriends Michelangelo.

German nun Katherina von Bora leaves her convent to marry Martin Luther. She will be seen as the mother of Protestantism.

1529   Although the history of drama dates back to the ancient Greeks, only now do women appear in female roles; the innovation takes place in Italy.

1533   King Henry VIII of England secretly weds pregnant Anne Boleyn while still legally married to the queen, Catherine of Aragon. He will accuse Boleyn of witchcraft and behead her in 1536. In less than a decade, he will marry four more times, also executing his fifth wife, young Catherine Howard.

1549   Margaret of Angoulême, wife of Henry II of Navarre, writes *The Mirror of a Sinful Soul*, along with other work. At the same time, Teresa de Cepeda y Ahumada, a Spanish nun also known as Saint TERESA OF ÁVILA, is another accomplished writer.

c. 1550   The Nigerian kingdom of Benin has special reverence for queen mothers, some of whom are depicted in bronze. On the other hand, in Yoruba, the king's family is expected to commit suicide at his death.

Catholic missionaries serve as a mitigating influence in South America, making slavery there less harsh than in most places. Racial intermarriage—usually between Spanish or Portuguese men and Indian or even African women—is permitted. The children of European men and native South American women are called "mestizos," and women are key to blending the two cultures into a uniquely Latin American society.

Just as relatively few women emigrate from Spain to South America, women in France are not encouraged to go with their men to North America. Especially in the area that becomes Canada and the northern United States, French men often marry native women and sometimes are absorbed into their wives' culture.

1553   Lady Jane Grey is queen of England for nine days. She will be beheaded after MARY I takes the throne.

1566   While serving as regent of the Netherlands, Margaret of Austria abolishes the Inquisition that Spanish rulers had imposed there.

1572   CATHERINE DE MÉDICIS pressures her son, Charles IX of France, into massacring thousands of Protestants.

1575   Flemish poet Anna Bijns, who founded a school in Antwerp, dies. One of the first female writers who is neither a nun nor nobility, her work is firmly on the Catholic side of the Protestant Reformation that roars around her.

1587   ELIZABETH I of England reluctantly orders the execution of her cousin MARY, QUEEN OF SCOTS, who has long plotted to take the English throne.

1600   Catherine de Vivonne marries at age twelve; as the marquise de Rambouillet, she will head a Parisian salon that has intellectual influence throughout Europe. Among those who benefit from her patronage are Honoré de Balzac and MADELEINE DE SCUDÉRY.

1603 ELIZABETH I dies. Among the many achievements of her remarkable reign is the solidification of England's dominance in Europe and a great increase in international commerce, including such New World products as tomatoes and coffee. At the same time that imports improve the quality of European life, Elizabeth encourages exports and personally sends an organ as a gift to the Turkish sultan.

c. 1615 The Mughal Empire, in the area that will later become Pakistan and India, is effectively ruled by Nur Jahan, a native of Persia who is one of the wives of Jahangir, who rules the empire. She spends lavishly, especially on her Persian family, but also endows new charity projects. Women in this society may inherit land and commonly engage in business. Mughals, who practice Islam, also unsuccessfully attempt to abolish the Hindu custom of suttee (cremation of widows).

1619 Dutch sailors who arrive in Jakarta this year find that women have a higher status in Southeast Asia than they do in much of Europe: couples share property, daughters inherit equally with sons, women can divorce, and a newly married man often joins his wife's clan.

Marie de Médicis leads an unsuccessful rebellion against her son, Louis XIII of France.

1628 India's Shah Jahan begins building the fabulous Taj Mahal as a memorial to his favorite wife, Mumtaz Mahal, who died bearing her thirteenth child.

1640 Some women vote in an election for high sheriff of Suffolk County in England. Taxpaying women also vote for such offices as overseer of the poor.

1643 As regent for her son, ANNE OF AUSTRIA effectively rules France.

1648 The Society of Friends, commonly called Quakers, begins in England. Margaret Fell works closely with founder George Fox, keeping the minutes of the first meetings and later marrying him. The most egalitarian of any religion to date, it grants women a status nearly equal to that of men: women preach, are ordained, and govern their own church meetings. Quaker women control their finances and will establish countless schools, hospitals, and other charitable institutions throughout the world. They also will play a strong role in the abolition of slavery.

c. 1650 Germans in particular follow up on the astronomical work done by Galileo, and a number of women join male relatives in making telescopic observations. Women are especially likely to be assigned work as "computers"—doing the tedious mathematical calculations that measure distances. Most are accused of neglecting their households, and even though the work requires that they stay awake all night, they are ridiculed because they sleep late.

1654 Queen CHRISTINA of Sweden abdicates the throne; although her reign has been an economic and cultural success, she opts to concentrate on her studies of philosophy.

1656 "Mrs. Coleman" may be the first woman to appear on an English stage when she appears in the opera *The Siege of Rhodes*.

1666 Margaret Lucas Cavendish, the duchess of Newcastle, publishes *Observations upon Experimental Philosophy*. A friend of Thomas Hobbes and other British philosophers, she has already published at least two other works on physical science and the nature of the universe.

1671 ROSE OF LIMA is canonized as the Western Hemisphere's first Roman Catholic saint.

The Forced Marriage is the first of APHRA BEHN's plays to be produced in London. She is the first English woman known to earn a living from her writing.

1679 Maria Sibylla Merian publishes *The Wonderful Metamorphosis and Strange Flower-Food of Caterpillars*. A pioneer entomologist, she was trained as an illustrator in her native Frankfurt; she now lives in Holland, perhaps the world's most liberated place for women in business. Retaining her maiden name, she employs other women who do scientific illustrations, especially of insects, and travels to the Dutch colony of Suriname in South America for new specimens.

1681 The Paris Opera showcases its first female dancers.

1689 Sophia, who has governed Russia during the minority of her half brother, Peter I (known as Peter the Great), is deposed when Peter reaches legal age. Her reign was remarkable enough that Peter learns to respect the ability of women, and prior to his 1724 death he will crown his wife, Catherine I, as his successor.

1695 Sor Juana Inés de la Cruz dies; during a lifetime as a Mexican nun, she has become a great Latin American poet.

c. 1700 Prussian noblemen are forbidden by law from marrying women who are commoners.

1702 Germany's Maria Winkelmann is probably the first woman to discover a comet, but her husband receives the credit. When he dies in 1710, she appeals in vain for a job as an assistant astronomer—even though she has been invited to address Prussian royalty on her observations of sunspots. One of the few who support her is the great philosopher Gottfried Wilhelm Leibniz, who manages to get the Berlin Academy to recognize her with a medal in 1711.

1709 *The Ladies' Diary*, which began five years earlier as an annual periodical for English women, initially ran mostly articles on domesticity. After the male editor receives hundreds of responses to mathematical puzzles, however, he changes the format this year to deal exclusively with enigmas in math and science. The *Diary* will continue for more than a century.

1714 Prussia abolishes witchcraft as a criminal charge.

1718 LADY MARY WORTLEY MONTAGU, wife of the British ambassador to Turkey, introduces the Turkish practice of inoculation against smallpox into Europe; the first royal children to be vaccinated are the daughters of Queen Caroline the Good. The credit for this lifesaving idea, however, will ultimately go to Edward Jenner, who later develops it.

1720 Ulrica is the second queen of Sweden who chooses to abdicate.

1725 At the death of her husband Peter the Great, Catherine I ascends to the throne as empress of Russia.

The Italian Renaissance has given its intellectual women a higher status than in most places, and this year the University of Bologna awards a doctorate to Laura Bassi. She will be affiliated with the university as a physics professor for more than four decades; a member of Bologna's Academy of Sciences, Bassi specializes in the mechanics of fluids and experiments with electricity.

1735 France's Gabrielle-Émilie Le Tonnelier de Breteuil, marquise du Châtelet, rails against "the prejudice that excludes [women] so universally from all the sciences. . . . I would reform an abuse that cuts off . . . half the human race."

1736 Lutheranism is the official state faith of Sweden, and this year the Swedish parliament grants women the vote in church matters.

1740 Empress Anna of Russia invites German theater impresario Caroline Neuber to Moscow.

1741 British novelist Eliza Fowler Haywood mocks Samuel Richardson's *Pamela* with her more realistic *Anti-Pamela*.

1743 MARIA THERESA is crowned at Prague; she will reign very successfully over the diverse Balkan peoples.

1746 FLORA MACDONALD becomes a Scottish legend when she leads Charles Edward, the Young Pretender—claimant to the British throne from the house of Stuart—safely out of the United Kingdom.

1748 Italian mathematician and philosopher Maria Gaetana Agnesi publishes *Analytical Institutions for the Use of Italian Youth*.

1749 The Parisian salon that Marie-Thérèse Rodet Geoffrin begins this year becomes so distinguished that intellectuals vie for invitations. Women who maintain salons are much more than hosts; they render an important service in networking the era's thinkers and, indeed, function rather like educational administrators conducting seminars. Madame Geoffrin, for instance, finds that evenings are more productive if they are specialized: she invites artists on Mondays and philosophers (who are more nearly scientists in this era) on Wednesdays.

c. 1750 Robes for the first empress of China's Emperor Qianlong (also spelled Ch'ien-lung) are so laden with pearls and precious materials that it takes more than two years to complete one.

In both China and Japan, marriages are arranged and girls meet their husbands for the first time at the wedding; they move in with his family and often are treated brutally by mothers-in-law whose own lives are frustratingly unhappy. In both societies, a woman is likely to have a more egalitarian life in the lower classes—unless her family is so poor that she is sold into prostitution or killed at birth.

1766 Catherine II of Russia—later known as CATHERINE THE GREAT—issues a proclamation of religious toleration.

1767 An anonymous editor briefly publishes a feminist periodical, the *Woman's Journal and Friday Society*, in Copenhagen. More than a century later, Danish women use "Friday" to denote freedom.

1775 SARAH KEMBLE SIDDONS makes her London stage debut; "Mrs. Siddons" will become the era's most esteemed woman in drama.

1783 Painter ÉLISABETH VIGÉE-LEBRUN is elected to France's Royal Academy.

1784 The first woman to ascend into the air is Marie Elisabeth Thible, a French opera singer who soars in a balloon over Lyon.

1786 German astronomer CAROLINE HERSCHEL, working in London, is the first woman credited with discovering a comet.

1789 Women lead the mob that forces MARIE-ANTOINETTE and the French royal family from their grand estate at Versailles into Paris. Some women have genuine weapons with which to meet the king's men, but many are armed only with pitchforks or clubs—plus decades of anger.

1791 As the French Revolution develops, Marie de Gouges expands its *Declaration of the Rights of Man* with her *Declaration of the Rights of Women*. Among other points, she declares that if "woman has the right to mount the scaffold" for execution, then she also should have "the right to mount the rostrum" as a public speaker. Although many women play strong roles in the Revolution, rewarding them with the vote is never seriously considered—and, indeed, France will be among the last European nations to grant women the vote.

1792 The English writer MARY WOLLSTONECRAFT publishes *A Vindication of the Rights of Woman*, which becomes a feminist classic.

1793 The French Revolution's Reign of Terror reaches its height as tens of thousands are executed. Among those guillotined this year are MARIE-ANTOINETTE, CHARLOTTE CORDAY, Madame du Barry, MADAME ROLAND, and Marie de Gouges, whose ringing call to liberty of just two years earlier is silenced.

1794 MARY WOLLSTONECRAFT adds to her record as a broad social thinker with *A Historical and Moral View of the French Revolution*.

1796 Ireland's Maria Edgeworth and France's GERMAINE DE STAËL publish their first books this year; both will be major literary forces in fiction and nonfiction.

1799 England's HANNAH MORE publishes *Strictures on the Modern System of Female Education*.

c. 1800 Almost all of Africa also falls under European domination during this century, ranging from Belgians in the central Congo to Dutch, German, and Portuguese colonies in the south and east. French influence is strongest in the northwest, while British power ranges from Egypt in the far northeast to the southern tip of the huge continent. British women are the most likely to immigrate; some establish families that live in Africa for generations, but many more return to Europe after careers as missionaries or as the wives of men who run coffee plantations, diamond mines, or commercial activities that rarely welcome women. Interracial marriage is strongly discouraged, and—unlike the French experience in North America or the Spanish in South America—the society is rigidly segregated.

In southern Africa, girls are sent to work in gold mines, allegedly because their smaller size enables them to work in narrow crevices below ground. The Japanese pearl-diving industry does not bother with such justification. Without any breathing equipment, girls dive into dark, frigid water and search for pearl-bearing oysters; they are employed because the work is dangerous, and their lives are expendable.

1802 MARIE TUSSAUD leaves France, where she has been forced to make wax death masks of friends guillotined in the Revolution.

1803 The Canadian Parliament begins at York (what later will become Toronto) and in its first session passes a bill making it easier for a married woman to sell property she owns. Although women still need judicial permission for such transactions, the intent of the law is to protect a woman from coercion by her husband.

1804 The Napoleonic Code cancels freedoms, especially in divorce, that France's women won earlier in the Revolution. The code treats women as perpetual minors, favors sons over daughters in inheritance, and even proclaims the court testimony of women to be less trustworthy than that of men. It will have long-term effect in the French colonial empire throughout the world: in Louisiana a century later, for example, a woman's clothing will belong to her husband because of the Napoleonic Code.

1812 On the Indian Ocean island of Mauritius, HARRIET ATWOOD NEWELL dies of pregnancy complications; she was America's first female missionary, along with ANN HASSELTINE JUDSON, who goes from Calcutta to Rangoon in the next year. Thousands of American and European women will emulate them, and most provide the first educational opportunity that women in Asia and Africa have ever had. Millions of Western women will join missionary societies that supply funds for countless schools, hospitals, and other charities.

1816 Like all women, France's Sophie Germain largely has educated herself; when she briefly took correspondence courses from the new École Polytechnique in Paris, she used a male pseudonym. Nonetheless, her contributions in mathematics and science are so clearly the work of genius that this year she wins the grand prize of the Academy of Sciences. Although she works in many areas, Germain will be known for mathematical descriptions of vibrating surfaces and sound waves.

1818 Writing in Switzerland, England's MARY WOLLSTONECRAFT SHELLEY presages the science-fiction genre with *Frankenstein*.

1820 The marriage of King George IV and Queen CAROLINE of England is so bad that she is refused admittance to his coronation.

1826 Polish courts are liberal enough that, at age 16, Siismund Potowski (later ERNESTINE ROSE) successfully argues against the arranged marriage her father has planned and wins the inheritance that her mother left her.

Scotland's Mary Fairfax Somerville writes *The Mechanism of the Heavens*, which will be the most popular of several scientific books. Last year, she presented a paper to the Royal Society called "The Magnetic Properties of the Violet Rays of the Solar Spectrum"; her last book, *Molecular and Microscopic Science* (1869), will be published when she is 89. As a girl, she had just one year of formal education.

1829 The British outlaw the practice of suttee—the burning of widows on their husbands' funeral pyres—in India.

Two-thirds of the employees of textile factories in Britain are female.

1832 Mary Smith of Stanhope in England's York County sends a petition to Parliament insisting that unmarried taxpaying women such as herself should be entitled to vote for their representatives. She also points out that women are subject to the death penalty but never have a jury of their female peers.

1837 Queen VICTORIA begins a reign over the British Empire that will last into the twentieth century.

1839 Far ahead of other nations, Great Britain allows the mother to have custody of her children in cases of divorce—but only of children up to age seven. Maternal custody is not extended up to age 16 until 1873.

1840 FRANCES WRIGHT, a native of Scotland, continues to move between Europe and America, crossing the Atlantic five times in this decade alone; in 1830, she paid the expenses of some thirty American slaves whom she took to freedom in Haiti. Among Wright's many prescient books is an 1848 work that envisions world government.

The World Anti-Slavery Convention that meets in London this year expels elected U.S. delegates because they are women. Both sides of the male debate on this cite Queen VICTORIA in their favor: while liberals argue that women should be welcomed in a nation governed by a female monarch, conservatives point out that the queen's antislavery views are offered via her husband, Prince Albert.

1842 Long before most people can even envision the idea of amicable divorce, Norwegian journalist Elise Waerenskjold manages to divorce her husband, a sea captain, without any cause beyond her desire to do more than "iron shirts and darn socks." She moves to Texas, where she farms and builds a Norwegian Lutheran community; their divorce is so uncommonly friendly that four decades later, when she is an impoverished widow of another marriage, he sends her $400.

1843 France's FLORA TRISTAN publishes *Worker's Union*, predating similar economic theory by men who become more famous.

1845 Sweden makes sons and daughters equal in inheritance rights; next year, women will be authorized

to conduct business in their own names. Property law is inherently complex and variable, however, and it will not be until 1874 that the Swedish parliament passes laws entitling a woman to her own wages, as well as the right to "control that part of her private property set aside for her personal use in the marriage contract."

1847 The British Parliament adopts a maximum ten-hour day for women in British factories.

Germany's FANNY MENDELSSOHN dies after composing some 500 musical works.

1848 Revolutions throughout Europe this year include a feminist element; Germans MATHILDE ANNEKE and Louise Otto-Peters are among the eastern European leaders.

1849 ELIZABETH BLACKWELL, an American who is the world's first credentialed female physician, goes to Paris and London for postgraduate studies; she is the first to overcome a number of educational barriers, but she cannot gain admittance to a gynecology department—the area that drew her to medicine.

1850 Denmark's Mathilde Fibiger publishes feminist ideas but suppresses her identity by calling her work "Letters from Clara Raphael."

1851 The first organization for the vote forms in England. Anne Knight, a Quaker, leads the Sheffield Female Political Association, which issues a proclamation on February 26 unequivocally arguing that women should have voting rights equal to those of men. Women in Newcastle upon Tyne soon follow.

1852 England's countess of Lovelace, Augusta Ada King, dies at age thirty-six. A gifted mathematician who is sometimes called "the first computer programmer" because of her work with Charles Babbage, she will be honored a century and a half later when the computer language Ada is named for her.

1853 Anesthetic for childbirth pain comes into general use when Queen VICTORIA receives it for her seventh delivery. Many Christian clergymen preach against this, however, quoting the biblical mandate to Eve: "In pain, ye shall bring forth children."

1854   FLORENCE NIGHTINGALE begins to professionalize nursing during Britain's involvement in the Crimean War, an international conflict between Russia, Turkey, and other forces near the Black Sea.

1855   French feminist GEORGE SAND publishes an autobiography of her unconventional life in twenty volumes.

1856   Unmarried taxpaying women in the Westphalia region of Germany may send a male proxy to vote for them in local elections.

1859   Sweden's Baroness Leyonhufoud and Rosalie d'Olivecrona found the *Home Review*, which—despite its innocuous name—advocates women's rights.

The Canadian Parliament passes the Married Women's Property Act, which assures a woman of her independent property free of her husband's encumbrances; it also allows a married woman to be a stockholder of a bank or other corporation as if she were unmarried.

1861   *Mrs. Beeton's Book of Household Management* sets domesticity standards throughout the British Empire.

1862   The Austro-Hungarian Empire grants limited voting rights to women who are large-property owners; the actual ballot must be cast by a male proxy.

Unmarried taxpaying women in Sweden win the right to vote in all elections except those choosing the members of parliament.

1863   As the international women's movement begins to build, Dublin native Frances Power Cobb publishes *Essay on the Pursuits of Women*. Two decades later, she corresponds with ELIZABETH CADY STANTON's son Theodore when he surveys the status of European women. Cobb says, "Of all the movements . . . of past ages, not one is so unmistakably tide-like . . . as that which has taken place within living memory among the women of almost every race on the globe."

Finland grants taxpaying women the right to vote in rural areas; the right to vote in city elections follows in 1872.

1865   The General Association of German Women is formed in Leipzig, with writer Louise Otto-Peters as its leader. Emulating the American women's rights organizations, the association holds annual conventions, sends petitions to the Reichstag, and publishes a journal, *New Paths*. A Berlin group, the Lette Society, is founded in the same year but is more conservative.

1867   Hungary begins to encourage schooling for girls. Although years will pass before Hungarian women are admitted to universities, vocational and teacher-training colleges are developed for them.

Influenced by his late wife, HARRIET TAYLOR MILL, British philosopher John Stuart Mill, who serves in Parliament this year, introduces a bill to enfranchise women. Almost 14,000 petition signatures support it, and its 73-194 loss is seen as something of a victory. Two years later, female heads of households begin voting in English municipal elections.

The Australian province of New South Wales grants municipal suffrage to women; Victoria follows in 1869 and West Australia in 1871.

1868   Revolutionaries oust Queen Isabella II of Spain, and she exiles herself in France.

1869   Mary Muller writes *An Appeal to the Men of New Zealand*, arguing for women's rights in that pioneer land.

1870   An Italian women's movement develops this year; its first aim is access to education, and among its leaders are Aurelia Cimino Folliero de Luna, Laura Mantegazza, Alessandrina Ravizza, and the marchioness Brigida Tanari.

Lydia Becker is the first English woman elected to office, winning a seat on the Manchester school board; she is continually reelected until her death in 1890. In the 1880s, she edits the *Women's Suffrage Journal*.

Isabella Thoburn, an American missionary, arrives in Bombay, where she builds the first institution of higher learning for women in Asia.

1871 Anna Hierta Retzius and Mrs. E. Anckarsveld form a women's rights society in Sweden. By the next decade, Sweden offers the greatest educational opportunity for women of any European nation. Women are admitted to all universities and enjoy scholarship funds at some; other institutions range from dairy schools to the national academies of music and fine arts.

Kvinindesamfund is the first women's rights organization in Denmark.

1872 Japan's first railroad is built, and as manufacturing is developed, Japanese women repeat the history of their Western sisters by becoming the major labor force in silk mills.

Switzerland's Marie Goegg successfully petitions Geneva's city council for the admission of women to its university. Four years earlier, she had founded the Woman's International Association in Geneva; although the organization's existence is precarious, Goegg personally carries on. Other Swiss universities follow Geneva's precedent, and by 1883, a professor at Bern says that thirty-five women have earned medical degrees there.

Girton College in Cambridge is Great Britain's first higher educational opportunity for women. Others quickly follow in this decade and the next; although some do not grant women full degrees, by the turn of the century the United Kingdom will have more than two thousand female college graduates.

1874 Madeleine Andrzejkowicz founds an industrial school for women in Warsaw, while Marie Ilnicka publishes a widely read newspaper there. Although girls have no opportunity for public education beyond primary school, the Russian legal code that governs Poland is fairly liberal: adult women may buy, sell, and own property without any male guardianship.

Berthe Morisot participates in an exhibit with pioneer French impressionists; her first art instructor had discouraged her from painting outdoors because it was considered inappropriate for women.

Although women are not officially admitted to Germany's University of Göttingen, Russian native Sonya Kovalevsky does such gifted work on partial differential equations that her thesis advisor persuades the university to award her a doctorate. She later teaches at the University of Stockholm and wins a major French prize in mathematics.

1876 Dr. Emily Stowe, a Canadian native educated in New York, begins to practice medicine in Toronto. She also leads the nascent women's rights movement there.

Great Britain's Parliament passes a bill permitting medical degrees to be conferred on women; the London School of Medicine for Women was founded the previous year.

Japanese women form an unprecedented Freedom and People's Rights Movement. In doing so, they defy a culture shaped by a woman's "three obediences": duty first to her father, then to her husband, and finally to her son.

Queen VICTORIA takes the title "empress of India," and vast India becomes known as "the jewel in the crown."

1878 The International Women's Rights Congress—the first event of its kind—assembles in July and August during a Paris trade exposition. Men also attend, including several French public officials. At the last session, a dozen nations are represented, including Russia, the United States, and even isolated Romania.

Secondary schools begin in Ireland; they are initially intended only for boys but after debate in Parliament, girls are included.

Finland gives female university students equal status with male ones, even in student organizations.

1879 Thousands of Danish women successfully petition their legislature for a law ensuring that they have the right to their own wages.

1880 Three women win prizes for musical composition in Vienna, but the Academy of Fine Arts nonetheless remains closed to female students. Indeed, diplomas awarded to young women who have finished secondary school explicitly say that they are not eligible to go on to Austria's universities. At the same time, however, these universities sometimes allow foreign women to attend.

The first women enter the University of Brussels. Although their numbers remain very small, others follow at Belgium's Liège and Ghent Universities.

The province of South Australia grants municipal suffrage. When Tasmania and Queensland follow in 1884 and 1886, respectively, women throughout Australia can vote in all local—but not provincial or national—elections.

1881 Italian feminists meet in Rome. Anna Mozzoni, who heads the Milan Society for the Promotion of Woman's Interests, leads a successful drive for the endorsement of suffrage.

1882 Dr. ALETTA JACOBS begins the world's first birth-control clinic in Amsterdam.

Scottish women win the right to vote in municipal elections; their most visible leader is Elizabeth Pease Nichol of Edinburgh.

English women have voted in school elections for more than a decade, and Henrietta Muller is a member of the London school board.

At the same time that Norway's Henrik Ibsen—who is married to Suzannah Thoresen—writes his unprecedented feminist plays, Cecilie Thoresen carries on a crusade for admission to the university at Christiana (later Oslo). University officials debate the issue for almost two years, until the local representative puts the question to the Norwegian parliament; the bill for admission of women passes nearly unanimously.

Copenhagen's *Woman's Review*, edited by Elfride Fibiger, is the first Danish periodical to endorse suffrage.

Iceland grants municipal suffrage to female heads of households. In 1886, all women become eligible to vote in parish elections that choose clergy.

1883 Portugal's parliament laughingly debates the lack of any higher educational opportunity for women and does nothing about it.

America's SUSAN B. ANTHONY spends two months visiting Germany, France, Switzerland, and Italy. A few days after her arrival in Berlin, an American diplomat brings her a package of materials that she had intended to use; it is covered with stamps saying that "such sentiments cannot pass through the post-office in Germany." Nevertheless, when Anthony departs from Liverpool, women give her a farewell reception and begin plans for an international meeting to be held in five years.

Women in the Canadian province of Nova Scotia win the right to vote in city elections, while hundreds of miles to the west, the Canadian Suffrage Association organizes in Toronto, with the city's mayor presiding. The next year, Ontario women win municipal suffrage.

1884 France ends its ban on divorce. The chief reformers responsible are Hubertine Auclert and Léon Richer, a woman and a man who publish separate monthly magazines on women's rights. Other French feminists of the era are Olympe Audouard, who crusades against the power of the Catholic church; Maria Deraismes, who works to end legalized prostitution; and Emilie de Morsier, who concentrates on expanding educational opportunity.

The Royal University of Ireland issues its first degrees to nine women.

Norway's first suffrage association forms in Christiania (later Oslo), and women win some school election rights next year. The leader is Gina Krog, who also edits a women's monthly, *Nylande*.

1885 Bohemia—in what will later become the Czech Republic—differs so greatly from the European tradition that the English language uses the word "bohemian" to denote unconventionality. Although women are not admitted to universities there, they enjoy voting rights from the local to the national level. The law is nonetheless complex: women must be taxpayers in their own right, a man must take the woman's ballot to the polls and cast it for her, and women in Prague are excluded.

Calliope A. Kechayia, head of a women's college in Constantinople (later Istanbul), writes that the "condition of the Greek women in the Orient is . . . not inferior to that of women in many parts of Europe," and in the case of educational opportunity for "girls of the lower class, it is much superior."

Spanish author Concepción Arenal is active in the Madrid Association for the Education of Women. She reports that the nation's universities currently have twelve female students; three have finished medical school and passed their examinations but are barred from practicing because they are women.

1886 An expert on Slavic peoples says that women in the Balkans see Russia as a "second paradise" for women—America, by common consent, being the first. Some Russian women, however, have stronger voting rights than some Americans: taxpaying women vote in local elections, although a male relative goes to the polls for them. Russia also has some 250 female physicians; although they mostly treat women and children, at least twenty worked in Russia's recent war with Turkey. Its chemical and legal associations also have female members, and a contemporary compares the work of a woman who writes under the pseudonym Krestowsky to that of Leo Tolstoy.

1887 Holland's new constitution expressly forbids women from voting. It is a direct response to Dr. ALETTA JACOB's 1882 attempt to register to vote in Amsterdam.

1888 The founding meeting of the International Council of Women is held in Washington, D.C., and women from Ireland to India pack all six-teen sessions of an eight-day gathering; the president of the United States, Grover Cleveland, also attends the conference. The meeting is the result of SUSAN B. ANTHONY's 1883 European tour, but the platform adopted falls short of her most important goal, an endorsement of suffrage. Nonetheless, the women pass a range of resolutions on educational and economic barriers, as well as problems of marital and family law, and the speakers include women of color. They resolve to meet again in five years.

1889 Tokyo's School of the Fine Arts, which is founded this year, is intended to bring about a return to native art forms—but at the same time, some Japanese women perform music on Western instruments while wearing Western dress.

1891 New Zealand women roll out a petition for suffrage that stretches seventy yards long on the floor of Parliament; legislators walk down its sides, unsuccessfully searching for duplicate signatures. A bill passes the lower house but fails by two votes in the upper house.

1892 Annie Moore, a fifteen-year-old girl from County Cork, Ireland, is the first immigrant to enter America's Ellis Island processing station.

Canada's French-speaking province of Quebec lags behind its English-speaking ones: it is the last province to grant school and municipal suffrage—and even that is limited to unmarried women and specifically excludes them from holding office.

The Woman's Alliance Union of Finland is organized; its president, Annie Furuhjeim of Helsingfors, will go on to serve in Finland's parliament.

1893 New Zealand becomes the first nation to grant all women full enfranchisement, and they very quickly register and vote. In elections that are held this year, 90,290 women vote, compared with 124,439 men—an extremely high turnout in a frontier situation, where men always outnumber women. Moreover, in the Auckland area, where the aboriginal Maori live, nearly half the votes registered are those of Maori women.

1894 The province of South Australia almost accidentally grants full suffrage: opponents amend a bill to strike a clause that prohibits women from sitting in Parliament, thinking that this improbability will kill it, but supporters surprise them by accepting it. Women thus win full enfranchisement, as well as the right to hold legislative office.

1895 The Women's Alliance forms in Iceland; although it soon collects 3,000 signatures for suffrage, the movement stalls when the parliament fails to respond.

1896 The Canadian province of New Brunswick makes it mandatory that two women sit on each school board.

MARIA MONTESSORI graduates from medical school at the University of Rome; she will begin revolutionizing childhood education a decade later.

1898 Norwegian men won universal suffrage last year, and the women's activism that had been centered in Oslo expands. The National Woman Suffrage Association forms with Mrs. F.M. Qvam as president; although her home is almost at the Arctic Circle, she will serve until final victory is achieved. Taxpaying women win local rights in 1901, and ninety-eight women are almost immediately elected to town councils.

Great Britain, which granted municipal voting rights to English women in 1869 and to Scottish women in 1882, finally confers the privilege on Irish women.

1899 The third meeting of the International Council of Women is held in London. Chaired by the countess of Aberdeen, it receives a good deal of favorable press—especially when Queen VICTORIA invites the women to tea at Windsor Castle. They resolve to meet biannually in the future.

1900 As the century turns, women's rights continue to be highly variable by geography. In Belgium, Italy, Luxembourg, and Romania, for instance, a husband may vote at local elections by right of taxes paid by his wife; in the case of widows, this right belongs to the eldest close male relative. Although the constitution of Germany says

"every German" older than twenty-five may vote in parliamentary elections, no woman has ever been permitted to do so. Moreover, most German states have laws that effectively prohibit the formation of suffrage organizations.

Although the czar still holds nearly absolute power in Russia, there is appreciable democracy on local issues, and women are assertive. A report this year says that it is common to see a wife replace her husband at "elections and village and country meetings of all kinds." At the other end of the scale, "property-owning women of the nobility may vote by proxy in the assemblies of the nobility."

1901 Vida Goldstein begins publishing a periodical, *The Australian Woman's Sphere*, in Melbourne. Meanwhile, the six states of Australia form a commonwealth this year, and one of the first acts of Parliament is to grant women both national suffrage and eligibility for Parliament. State rights, however, are mixed: women have full rights in Western Australia, South Australia, and New South Wales, but Victoria, Queensland, and Tasmania wait several years before granting women's suffrage. In several cases, bills pass a state's lower house but fail by small margins in the upper house, whose members are chosen not by popular vote but by aristocratic men. Many aristocratic women are active suffragists, however: Lady Windeyer is suffrage association president in New South Wales and Lady Onslow in South Australia.

Germany's first suffrage association forms in Hamburg, one of three so-called free cities where restrictions on women's participation in political meetings do not apply. The other free cities, Bremen and Frankfurt, soon follow.

Canada's McGill University awards its first master's degree to a woman, and physicist Harriet Brooks (later Pitcher) goes on to do pioneer work in radioactivity.

1902 Women from nine nations—including Australia, Chile, Russia, and Turkey as well as European countries—meet in Washington, D.C., to plan an organization more radical than the International Council of Women. These plans will evolve into the International Woman's Suffrage Alliance in 1904.

The Woman's Enfranchisement League forms in Durban, South Africa—leaving unstated the founders' intention to enfranchise only white women.

1903 EMMELINE PANKHURST founds the Women's Social and Political Union in Manchester, England; it becomes the militant wing of British suffragism, while mainstream women stay with MILLICENT GARRETT FAWCETT and the British National Suffrage Association.

MARIE SKLODOWSKA CURIE, who was born in Poland but works in France, wins the Nobel Prize in physics, just two years after the prizes are first awarded.

1904 The largest political meeting of women ever held takes place in Berlin. The International Woman Suffrage Alliance splits from the more conservative International Council of Women, whose members cannot bring themselves to endorse suffrage. Delegates are astounded by African American MARY CHURCH TERRELL, who addresses them in English, German, and French.

After their parliament rejects several attempts to expand the voting rights that they won in 1862, Swedish women form a suffrage association and network with more than sixty existing societies. By 1914, 350,000 supporters, including novelist SELMA LAGERLÖF, will have signed their petition.

1905 Women's Union College begins in Peking (now Beijing). Its president is American missionary Luella Miner, who has lived in China since 1887; she will confer the first college degrees earned by Chinese women.

Russian women form the Union of Defenders of Women's Rights, which soon has ten thousand members in eighty branches. Although activity slows when the tsar dissolves Russia's new parliament, they hold the empire's first Women's Congress in 1908 in Saint Petersburg, with the mayor and other government officials welcoming the women.

Unlike those in Austria and most of Germany, women in Hungary are not prohibited from political assembly. ROSIKA SCHWIMMER, who attended last year's international meeting in Berlin, becomes Hungary's longtime women's rights leader.

Austria's BARONESS BERTHA VON SUTTNER wins the first Nobel Peace Prize.

Teresa Labriola—who lectures on law at the University of Rome, despite the fact that Italian women cannot practice that profession—organizes the presentation of a suffrage petition to the premier. He rejects it on the grounds that women cannot vote until they have full civil rights.

1906 *The Wreckers*, an opera by England's Ethel Smyth, opens in Leipzig, Germany.

The International Woman Suffrage Alliance meets in Copenhagen, with representatives from twelve nations ranging from Australia to Iceland. They begin a monthly paper, *Jus Suffragii*, which is published in English from Rotterdam, with Martina Kramers as its longtime editor.

Finland follows New Zealand as the second nation—the first in Europe—to grant women equal suffrage. The victory is a direct result of women's participation in Finnish resistance against Russian rule: women were leaders in a general strike the previous October, and the parliament includes them in a full suffrage bill—which is signed by the Russian tsar, who fears further conflict.

Austria grants universal suffrage to men and eliminates the partial voting rights that some wealthy women had long possessed. Defying a law that bans political meetings, women recently formed a suffrage association.

1907 Norway, which separated from Sweden in 1905, is the third nation to grant women the vote; the debate lasts just two hours and passes 96-23. It requires payment of minimal taxes, but that language is removed in 1910.

The Association for Women's Rights forms in Iceland. Women win municipal voting rights the next year, and Reykjavik, the nation's largest city, elects four women to the city council.

Suffragists in the Netherlands have made little progress since the 1894 formation of their association; this year, they have the ironic situation of presenting their case to the queen.

1908   The International Woman Suffrage Alliance meets in Amsterdam. Twenty nations are represented, and the six-day gathering ends with fireworks that flash "Jus Suffragii" across the sky.

Germany—host of the International Woman Suffrage Alliance four years earlier—finally ends its internal ban on women's participation in political meetings. Women celebrate with an immense meeting in Frankfurt, with speeches by British militants Annie Kenny and Mrs. Pethink Lawrence.

Women in the Canadian province of British Columbia lose the right to vote in municipal elections, which they had won years earlier. They organize and, almost a decade later, finally win full rights in a 1917 referendum.

Denmark's parliament grants the vote to unmarried taxpaying women and to women whose husbands are taxpayers. At the first election, suffragists distribute eighteen thousand brochures to women at the polls, urging expansion of the vote to all women. Seven Danish women are elected to city councils.

American Annie Smith Peck reaches the highest point that any man or woman has climbed in the Western Hemisphere; the 22,205-foot mountain in Peru is later named for her.

1909   Sweden's SELMA LAGERLÖF is the first woman to win the Nobel Prize for literature.

The French Union for Woman Suffrage, founded this year, is France's first such organization.

Canadian women present to Parliament a hundred thousand signatures favoring suffrage. They are led by Dr. Augusta Stowe Gullen, daughter of Dr. Emily Howard Stowe, who founded Canada's suffrage association in 1883. Although the crowd's numbers are so great that some officials cannot get into their offices, Parliament does nothing; in 1906, suffrage was voted down 69-2.

Holland's Lutheran and Mennonite Churches grant women the vote in church matters—before the state grants it for political ones.

The International Woman Suffrage Alliance meets ahead of schedule in London, where the hot topic is the militant tactics of British suffragists, who chain themselves to fences outside government buildings, disrupt speeches, deface property, and otherwise bring attention to their cause with behavior that provokes arrest; ultimately, many will go on hunger strikes and be fed by force.

1910   Although Swedish women still do not have full voting rights, thirty-seven are elected to thirty-four town councils this year. The number rises to sixty-four in the next election, but the upper house will block a full suffrage bill until 1919.

1911   Women participate in the revolution that overthrows China's monarchy, which had existed for thousands of years. The custom of female foot-binding is outlawed, and not only do women vote, but some are even elected to China's first parliament.

Dr. ALETTA JACOBS and CARRIE CHAPMAN CATT, officials of the International Woman Suffrage Alliance, embark on a two-year global tour to promote women's rights. They hold hearings with women in Egypt, Palestine, India, Burma, China, Japan, Java, and the Philippine and Hawaiian Islands. "Behind the veils and barred doors and closed sedan chairs," Catt reports, "there has been rebellion in the hearts of women all down the centuries." Catt and Jacobs also travel some four thousand miles in South Africa, where their presence doubles the number of women's rights societies from eleven to twenty-two. Again, the assumption is that only white women are included in expansion of rights there.

Iceland passes a constitutional amendment giving the vote to all women and making them eligible for all offices, including those of the church. The victory is soon diluted, however: Iceland is still governed by Denmark, and to make the amendment acceptable to the Danish king, Iceland accepts language that initially requires female voters to be at least forty years old. This is the most extreme of the age requirements adopted in several European nations, most of which gradually reduce women's minimum voting age until it is the same as that for men—usually twenty-five.

MARIE CURIE becomes the only woman to win two Nobel Prizes: in physics in 1903 and in chemistry this year.

Women from twenty-six nations attend the International Woman Suffrage Alliance convention in Stockholm—while the Swedish parliament debates full suffrage.

1912 Women march in German streets for the first time during a Women's Congress in Munich.

During discussion of expanding suffrage to illiterate men, Italy's parliament quickly defeats any reform concerning women, who lack all civil rights.

Although most Bohemian (Czech) women cannot vote, two parties nonetheless nominate a woman for parliament this year. Mrs. Viokova-Kuneticka, a prominent writer and suffragist, is elected, but because of World War I she cannot take her seat until six years later.

1913 When the International Woman Suffrage Alliance meets in Budapest, many delegates travel together by train and stop for rallies in Berlin, Dresden, Prague, and Vienna. The Chinese Woman Suffrage Society is admitted to membership, along with organizations in Portugal, Romania, and South Africa. Women from Galicia, who are not permitted to form organizations, nonetheless attend, and Persian women send a supportive telegram. Perhaps the most successful such meeting ever, it is organized by Hungary's ROSIKA SCHWIMMER.

Annie Furuhjelm, who founded Finland's women's union in 1892, is elected to its parliament. Since women were first elected in 1907, as many as twenty-five have served in each biannual session of the two-hundred-member body. They have passed a number of bills benefiting women and children—but, while Finland

remains under Russian control, all are vetoed by the tsar. Finland will become independent of Russia with the end of World War I.

Both men and women participate in an international conference on "white slavery"—prostitution rings in which women are transported across national boundaries to brothels. Pimps usually use seduction to induce women into the trade but often keep them there by force. Letters between men in this business speak of buying and selling women using the same language as the slave trade.

1914 World War I begins with the assassination of Austrian royals Ferdinand and Sophia. The war introduces women on both sides to new jobs, including telephone operator, translator, ambulance driver, and munitions maker. Even traditional battlefield nursing changes, as this is the bloodiest war yet fought. Women also sell war bonds, work as recruiters and entertainers, and run farms and businesses, and all of this brings new respect and new rights.

The International Woman Suffrage Association moves its headquarters from Rotterdam to London and manages to publish *Jus Suffragii*, now subtitled *International Suffrage News*, throughout the war.

Dr. Emily Howard Stowe, founder of Canada's suffrage association, is commemorated by a bronze statue in Toronto's city hall—the first official memorial in honor of a Canadian woman—despite the fact that Canadian women do not yet have the right to vote.

1915 Street demonstrations are forbidden in the wartime Netherlands, but when women's rights are about to be excluded from a new constitution, women defy the law to march in Amsterdam and The Hague. Thousands of women station themselves in front of the parliament to no avail.

Germans execute British EDITH CAVELL in Belgium.

France needs women's labor in factories enough to adopt a minimum-wage law for women; in 1917, it will mandate equal pay for men and women. Nonetheless—as in other nations—women's average wage remains about half that of men.

The Panama-Pacific Exposition brings Latin American women to San Francisco, where they join women from the United States in meetings on the vote and other issues.

Feminism in Germany and Scandinavia is published by Katharine Anthony, the American niece of SUSAN B. ANTHONY.

A thousand women from both sides of the Atlantic meet at The Hague in an effort to promote peace. Some go on to Scandinavia and Russia, where they confer with high-ranking government officials; the American women personally brief President Woodrow Wilson on their efforts after they return across the U-boat–infested ocean.

1916 Manitoba is the first Canadian province to grant full suffrage; Alberta and Saskatchewan follow just weeks later. When British Columbia gives women the vote next year, women have full rights from Ontario to the Pacific Ocean. As is the case in the United States, the Canadian West is more liberal than its East.

The genocide of Christian Armenians by Islamic Turks continues; as many as a million Armenians died last year. While men are likely to be killed outright, many women are raped and then killed or driven into the desert to starve. The massacre goes on for years, while World War I prevents even those who are capable of immigrating from crossing the Atlantic.

1917 The French execute Dutch MATA HARI, who is presumed to be a German spy.

Russia's women light the spark that overthrows the tsar: in March, about ten thousand women protest the appalling conditions that the war with Germany has brought to their country. Not only are they and their children hungry; they know that millions of their men are being slaughtered by the vastly better equipped German army. The women follow through with a general strike, and soon the revolution is under way. As the revolution proceeds, women are almost immediately elected to office, including the city councils of major cities.

Canada enfranchises about six hundred thousand women so that they can vote in a referendum on the military draft during World War I; the government expects that "women having relatives in the war would vote to compel other men to go." In return, most Canadian women win full rights the following April—except in French-speaking Quebec, which will defeat bills to enfranchise women in state elections for many years.

British authorities in India imprison ANNIE BESANT; the Indian people will later reward her by electing her president of the Indian National Congress.

1918 After fifty years of effort, British women win full voting rights. The final margin in the House of Commons is immense, and members of the Conservative Party pressure the House of Lords into a comfortable positive margin. Royal assent is granted on February 6, and seventeen women run for Parliament in the fall. Only one is elected: Countess Makievicz—a Sinn Féin supporter who is Irish by birth—had run as a statement of Irish rebellion; most people believe that she is no longer a British citizen because of her Polish husband, and she declines to fight for her seat. In the next year, LADY NANCY ASTOR will become Britain's first female member of Parliament.

The first two women elected to a legislature in the British Empire are Canadians: Mrs. L. M. McKinney and Lieutenant Roberta McAdams, a military nurse, are elected in Alberta.

With the postwar breakup of the Austro-Hungarian Empire, the Austrian Union of Suffrage Societies and its National Council of Women rapidly succeed in adding full electoral rights to the new constitution. In elections next February, more than two million Austrian women vote for the first time; 8 are elected to the national assembly, 12 to Vienna's city council, and 126 to other local offices. Hungarian women, although organized earlier than the Austrians, win fewer rights. With the empire's end this year, all men over twenty-one are voters, but women must be twenty-four and must demonstrate that they can read and write. One woman will be elected to Hungary's parliament next year.

Taxpayer qualifications were removed from Denmark's suffrage law in 1915, and in this first election in which all women can vote, nine are elected to the national legislative body. Within two years, they pass bills to open all professions to women, provide equal status in marriage, and—far ahead of most nations—mandate equal pay.

Austria's LISE MEITNER discovers chemical element 109; eventually, in 1997, it is officially named meitnerium in her honor.

1919   KÄTHE KOLLWITZ is the first woman elected to the Berlin Academy of Fine Arts. Meanwhile, socialist ROSA LUXEMBURG is killed by police during Germany's postwar revolution.

As World War I ends, women are expected to give up the jobs they were urged to take during the war. In Great Britain, more than six hundred thousand women are unemployed, and those who continue to work are forced to accept wage cuts. Despite women's participation in general strikes, many economic gains are lost. The situation is especially dire in Germany, where the war's loss brings rampant inflation. Women—the usual purchasing agents for their families—struggle with prices that rise daily. These problems are especially severe for widows and women whose husbands were disabled in the war.

France's lower house passes a suffrage bill amid great enthusiasm. In the upper house, however, the situation is different: women representing hundreds of organizations are received in cold silence, and even a bill to enfranchise women whose male relatives were killed in the war is rejected.

The Italian parliament passes the Sacchi bill, which was first proposed before the war began. It abolishes the authority of the husband, which had been absolute, and grants women the right to control their property, enter professions, and have equal child custody. It does not, however, grant the vote.

Women in the Netherlands hold a mass demonstration at The Hague, and a few months later, both houses of the Dutch parliament adopt full suffrage. Male voters have already elected a woman to each house, and more than a hundred women serve on municipal councils.

Luxembourg's parliament grants full voting rights to all women. Two women run for parliament in the fall elections, and one wins.

New Zealand, which in 1893 was the first nation in the world to grant women full voting rights, finally allows women to be elected to Parliament.

Rhodesia (later Zimbabwe) grants the vote to white women; next year, a woman will be elected to parliament.

Some 10,000 women in the Philippines sign a petition for suffrage. Three women address the senate, which passes suffrage almost unanimously, but the House fails to act.

1920   Without any organized movement to do so, European and American women begin shortening their dresses, cutting their hair, abandoning hats, and rejecting restrictive clothing such as corsets. Many drive cars, smoke cigarettes, drink cocktails, and otherwise engage in behavior previously limited to men.

Europe's first radio broadcast is a London concert featuring soprano Nellie Melba. Radio greatly changes women's lives in this decade, as it brings the world into isolated kitchens.

Germany's new government quickly adopts complete rights for women. When elections are held in January, women win 39 seats in the national assembly, 117 seats in state bodies, and more than 1,400 local offices.

After the breakup of the Austro-Hungarian Empire, the new republics of Czechoslovakia and Yugoslavia form. Czechs—formerly known as Bohemians—adhere to their progressive traditions and not only enact full suffrage but also elect sixteen women in both houses of their parliament. Yugoslavia, in contrast, defeats a suffrage proposal, as do Bulgaria, Romania, and Serbia.

Belgium's situation is unusual: Catholics support suffrage, while secular interests oppose it, fearing the influence of the church. The two sides compromise in April on language that enfranchises "all widows of soldiers . . . or, where there is no widow, the mother," as well as "all women condemned or imprisoned for patriotic acts during the enemy occupation." In July, the parliament votes 89-74 to reject any expansion of these parameters.

Poland joins other nations in granting women the vote, and eight women are elected to parliament this year.

Women in Western Australia—who were enfranchised in 1899—finally win the right to hold state office. The right still does not exist in Tasmania and Queensland, which granted the vote in 1905.

For the first time since the 1913 meeting in Budapest, the International Woman Suffrage Association assembles in Geneva. Jubilant delegates celebrate their postwar victories, announcing that women are now enfranchised in twenty-one nations; nine women attend who are elected legislators in their home countries. For the first time, women from India and China address the group; a woman comes from Japan and a Tatar woman from Crimea.

Latin American women also attend the Geneva conference: women are now organized in Argentina, Brazil, Chile, Paraguay, and Uruguay. Brazil's senate defeats a suffrage bill this year, but the fact that the bill was voted on is seen as a victory. Dr. Paulina Luisi of Uruguay and Dr. Alicia Moreau of Argentina report that Mexico's revolutionary government has enfranchised women, but political turmoil is so bad that, except in the Yucatán province, no elections have been held.

When the League of Nations forms, Sweden appoints Anna B. Wicksell as a delegate, while Denmark sends Henni Forchhammer. The league is the forerunner of the modern United Nations, and its founding documents proclaim the political equality of women. Its officials will work closely with the International Woman Suffrage Association on women's issues.

1921   Marie Stopes opens her first birth-control clinic in London.

Although Sweden was the first nation to grant women municipal voting rights back in 1862, expansion of those rights has been very slow, and only now does Sweden finalize universal suffrage without regard to marital or taxpayer status. King Gustav V makes the official proclamation in January, and in September, five women are elected to parliament.

Queen Sophia of Greece decorates Madame Parron, president of the Greek Women's Congress, for a lifetime of work.

Women have won various forms of the vote throughout India during recent years; the Women's Indian Association also works to improve education for women. Despite the leadership of longtime feminist ANNIE BESANT as president of the National Home Rule League for India, the 1918 British bill on self-government excluded women as voters— but Indian women organize massive protests and win rights in Bombay, Madras, and other areas.

Agnes McPhail is the first woman in Canada's House of Commons.

1922   World War I has changed the status of women in the British Empire so much that South Africa has the distinction of being—in the words of its suffragists—"the only English-speaking nation that has not enfranchised its women." Women there have won several parliamentary victories but consistently fall short of winning the right to vote. Politicians blame "the almost insurmountable objection to the colored vote."

Although the war brought enfranchisement for most women in northern Europe, progress flags to the south: women still lack the vote in France, Italy, Portugal, Spain, Switzerland, and Greece. Some Turkish women vote and hold office, and Jewish women in Palestine have been elected to the national assembly, as well as to local office.

Japanese women are not allowed to attend political meetings, but, through the auspices of the Women's Christian Temperance Union, some keep in touch with the global women's rights movement. Recent international attention to peace has made it acceptable for Japanese women to be seen at gatherings for that cause.

1923 OLIVE SCHREINER publishes her prescient *Thoughts on South Africa*.

Switzerland is the only European nation to follow the model of many American states in submitting the question of women's enfranchisement to male voters. When the cantons, or states, of Neuchâtel, Basel, and Zurich voted last year, women lost overwhelmingly, and the same is true this year in Geneva.

1924 With the fall of the Ottoman Empire, Turkish women win equal property and marital rights. Like many revolutionary governments, however, that of Kemal Atatürk fails to understand individual freedom: in an effort to modernize the land, he frees women from mandatory Islamic dress but forbids those who prefer it from wearing veils. Next year, Persia's shah does the same thing. Middle Eastern women are also influenced by Jewish women who emigrate from western nations after the 1922 creation of Palestine by a League of Nations mandate.

1925 Austrian nuclear scientist MARIETTA BLAU takes the first measurements of high-energy proton tracks.

Predating the love story of Britain's Edward VIII and WALLIS SIMPSON, the king of Romania gives up his throne and his wife, a Greek princess, for exile with Magda Lupescu.

1926 Italian novelist GRAZIA DELEDDA is the second woman to win the Nobel Prize for literature; the first was SELMA LAGERLÖF in 1909.

After founding the National Museum of Iraq, GERTRUDE BELL kills herself in Baghdad.

1927 Another change wrought in the West by the Roaring Twenties is increased participation of women in athletics. Norway's SONJA HENIE, who wins the world championship for ice skating this year, personifies the trend; Helen Wills of the United States does the same in tennis with her win at England's Wimbledon this year.

1928 Norway's SIGRID UNDSET is the third woman to win the Nobel Prize for literature.

Great Britain lowers the minimum age for women voters from 30 to 21.

1929 The Great Depression, which has already affected much of the world's economy, becomes official with the collapse of the American stock market. Those jobs that exist usually go to men, sinking women back into the economic dependence of the past and making political progress much more difficult. Although women now have the right to run for office, for example, many cannot afford to do so, and the general public sentiment is that political jobs, like others, should be reserved for men.

Another effect of the prolonged depression is a population decline: Western women simply stop having as many babies. Almost all are forced to figure out how to achieve this goal on their own, however, for few physicians or public agencies will speak to the question of birth control. Meanwhile, as Joseph Stalin consolidates power in the Soviet Union, women lose their right to abortion.

When Nigerian women protest taxes on the goods they sell in outdoor markets, British soldiers fire on them, killing fifty.

Thousands of women in India join Mohandas K. Gandhi's march to the sea to protest taxes on salt.

In the same year that Margaret Bondfield becomes the first woman on Britain's Privy Council, VIRGINIA WOOLF issues the feminist classic *A Room of Her Own*.

1930 Governments in Latin American nations follow those in Europe and North America in granting women the vote during this decade and the next two. It is not until the 1950s, however, that South American women are generally enfranchised.

1931   In the same year that Britain's MARY LEAKEY goes to Kenya, Baroness Karen Blixen-Finecke, later known as ISAK DINESEN, sells her coffee farm there and returns to Denmark.

English writer Vita Sackville-West publishes her feminist novel *All Passion Spent*. The year's best-seller, *The Good Earth*, focuses on Chinese women; author Pearl Buck has lived longer in China than in her native United States.

1932   France awards the Cross of the Legion of Honor to American AMELIA EARHART, whose May solo flight across the Atlantic Ocean set another precedent for women. Her route took her from Newfoundland to Ireland.

KAREN HORNEY leaves Germany for the United States, where she will become the first psychiatrist to challenge Freudian assumptions about women's mental health.

1933   Adolf Hitler seizes power in Germany. Many women, like men, admire Hitler, even though he and other fascists are clear about their belief in the fundamental inequality of women; German women and girls join Nazi groups in large numbers.

In Italy, where the fascist Benito Mussolini took power prior to Germany's Hitler, fewer women join fascist organizations. Many are greatly devoted to Mussolini, however, as shown by the fact that they donate their wedding rings to be melted down for gold—which helps pay Italian forces that terrorize Ethiopia.

Australia's Sister ELIZABETH KENNY begins to revolutionize the treatment of polio.

1934   Turkey opens all educational and professional opportunities to women and grants them the vote. Some women successfully run for office.

Evangeline Booth, a native of England, ousts her brother to become worldwide commander of the Salvation Army.

As Chinese communists begin to prevail in China's long civil war, AGNES SMEDLEY is a trusted ally of Mao Tse-tung and other leaders.

1935   A survey in China finds that even in urban areas, the majority of marriages are arranged by parents. In one rural village, only 3 of the 170 residents had even heard of the Western practice of a young couple deciding on their own to get married.

France's IRÈNE JOLIOT-CURIE wins the Nobel Prize in chemistry.

1936   Women participate in the Spanish Civil War. Women of Spanish descent in the Americas raise money and march in demonstrations, vainly supporting Spain's fragile democracy against its military. When Francisco Franco wins, the dictatorship that follows will force women into a regressive status for decades.

King Edward VIII gives up the British throne to marry WALLIS SIMPSON.

1937   The Japanese invasion of mainland Asia includes widespread rape, among other horrors. Korean women especially will be forced into sexual bondage during the next decade: tens of thousands will be unpaid "comfort women" in brothels for Japanese men.

Denmark's ISAK DINESON publishes *Out of Africa*, based on her life in Kenya.

1938   Although Jews in Germany have suffered since Adolf Hitler took power five years ago, Kristallnacht ("night of crystal") marks the clear beginning of the worst pogrom the world has ever seen. Tens of thousands of women, including scientist LISE MEITNER, are forced to flee. As the fascists consolidate their power, they also insist on a traditional status for "Aryan" women, whose primary role is to produce children to support the state and military. German women lose jobs they previously held, and married women in particular are no longer allowed to practice professions or teach at universities.

Hitler also annexes Austria this year; among those who flee is Maria von Trapp, whose story is told in the popular musical *The Sound of Music* decades later.

1939   World War II begins in Europe with Germany's invasion of Poland; Denmark, the Netherlands,

Belgium, Norway, and northern France fall the next year. The Nazis treat women as fully equal to men in terms of the pain they inflict.

1940 Thousands of women are prisoners of war, as European civilians who live in far-flung colonies are imprisoned when those areas fall. British, Dutch, French, and other women from North Africa to Malaysia go to prison camps, and as the war worsens they will be fed less and less. The Japanese are not as brutal to women as they are to men, but many prisoners will suffer illnesses caused by starvation during the long years of not knowing whether they ever would be freed.

Australia is the place of freedom in the Pacific Rim; some British and American women manage to escape there instead of ending up in prison camps to the north. Australian women are particularly important in agriculture: their cattle and sheep feed and clothe millions of Allied soldiers.

In this year prior to involvement by the United States and after the surrender of most of Europe, Britain stands alone against fascism. Women are involved in every arena: they join—or are conscripted for—both industry and the military. In addition to the traditional military nurse corps, Britain develops the Women's Auxiliary Air Force, the Women's Royal Navy, and the Auxiliary Territorial Service. By this year, women in the Air Transport Auxiliary have already flown 120 types of planes, while the Women's Land Army runs farms that must feed both the nation and its troops around the globe.

1941 Germany bombs Britain so relentlessly that it is as dangerous to be a housewife in London as to be a soldier in many other parts of the empire. Even in less industrialized Scotland, the destruction is awesome: on one March night, thirty-five thousand of the forty-seven thousand residents of Clydebank lose their homes.

Hitler breaks his pact with the Soviet Union and invades Russia. Leningrad will be under long, starving siege; from the Ukraine in the south to Estonia in the north, millions of women join men in resisting. As the war worsens, Russian women participate in every sort of manual labor

and even serve in combat, including piloting both bomber and fighter planes. One woman, for example, is a railroad engineer who runs her ammunition-laden train out of a populated area during bombing by German planes.

When the Japanese bomb the U.S. naval base of Pearl Harbor on the island of Oahu, Hawaii, in December, the United States finally joins the world conflagration. Within a year, American women will serve in army units that range from Africa to Scotland; by the end of the war, their service will encircle the globe from the Middle East to the South Pacific. Some even serve at remote stations in India and Iran.

1942 Queen WILHELMINA of the Netherlands appeals to the U.S. Congress to liberate her occupied country.

Even as the Nazis begin to lose crucial battles, Hitler insists that German women remain at home, while his industries largely depend on the slave labor of women from conquered nations. Unlike the British and American women who work to supply the Allies, these women have no interest in quality production; some even manage to deceive inspectors into sending out munitions and other goods that will kill the Nazi user instead of his intended victim.

1943 The American *Ladies' Home Journal* urges women to obey rationing laws that attempt to distribute food fairly, saying "we still get ten times as much beef a week as people in England, twenty times as much as they get in Russia, and fifty times as much as the lucky ones get in China."

With most of their men gone to war, more than eighty-five percent of students in Russian medical schools are women. After the war's end, a majority of physicians in the Soviet Union will continue to be women.

1944 French-speaking Violette Bushell Szabo is among the British women who volunteer to serve as saboteurs. She parachutes into France and kills several German soldiers before being captured, tortured, and sent to the Ravensbrück concentration camp near Berlin. She and other captured female agents are executed by the Germans the following year.

When Allied forces liberate France, Italy, and other previously occupied areas this year, women who have collaborated with the Nazis are sometimes shot; others are humiliated by having their heads shaved.

The German occupation of the Netherlands is almost over on August 22, when a Nazi sympathizer earns a few guldens by telling the Gestapo where ANNE FRANK's family is hiding.

In the fall—with Germany just months away from ultimate defeat in the spring—only three hundred thousand more German women are in its workforce than when the war began. In contrast, every Allied nation has millions of women in traditionally male industrial jobs; in the Soviet Union, two of every three workers is female. Japan has made the same mistake: its fascist leaders also believe that a Japanese woman's natural place is at home. Like Germany, it depends on the slave labor of conquered peoples. Although his military loses ground daily, Tojo Hideki, Japan's virtual dictator, still speaks out against the employment of Japanese women.

1945 As was the case with British women early in the war, German housewives now find their lives in great peril. The February bombing of Dresden is the most severe: a two-day firestorm kills as many as a hundred thousand civilians.

German jet test pilot HANNA REITSCH is one of the last to see Adolf Hitler as the Nazi government collapses.

When the war in Europe ends in May, thirty million people are homeless. Large numbers of women will assume leadership roles in international agencies such as the Red Cross and the YWCA (Young Women's Christian Association) and work through the decade to assist these "displaced persons."

China executes Yoshiko Kawashima, who, disguised as a man, has spied for Japan since 1932.

As governments are reconstituted in France and Italy, women there finally win the vote.

Chile's GABRIELA MISTRAL wins the Nobel Prize for literature.

1946 Women, who are almost always the ones responsible for their families' meals, will deal with food shortages and ration systems for years into the future. A Christian magazine reports that "food supplies in the British and American zones in Germany . . . have recently been reduced again and are within a couple of hundred calories of the rations in the terrible Belsen concentration camp. . . . India is entering what is likely to be the worst famine in its history; in great sections of China the population is already living on grass and clay."

Trials begin for women who betrayed the Allies during the war: several English-speaking women, for example, called themselves "Tokyo Rose" and broadcast morale-damaging radio shows in the Pacific, while "Sally Axis" did the same in Berlin. None of the women will be severely punished, however, and entertainers in particular—such as Egyptian dancer Hekmath Fathmy, who spied on the British in Cairo—are given short prison sentences. Others, including Norwegian singer Kirsten Flagstad, will be cleared of collaboration charges.

Tens of thousands of women have established relationships with some of the millions of soldiers who served around the globe. Many women in war-torn areas are naturally eager to escape from such devastated places as Italy and Germany, and ships full of war brides head especially to the United States. These women may be less than welcome in their new homes: some British women, for example, find it particularly hard to accept a German daughter-in-law. Postwar marriages between Allies also are common; thousands of Australian and British women go with their new husbands to the United States and Canada.

Although it is easy to agree that peace is desirable, the details of making it work are much harder. When the Women's International League for Peace and Freedom meets—without representation from either former enemies Germany and Japan or former allies in the Soviet Union—the delegates find it hard to reach a consensus. Resolutions on the Nuremberg trials and on treatment of vanquished peoples are especially difficult and even painful to discuss.

1947   So many Soviet men died in the war that women remain the greater part of its labor force—but two years after the war's end, Russian production is back to prewar levels. Few women are rewarded with top positions in either industry or politics.

Japan's new constitution, imposed by American occupation forces, grants Japanese women their first civil liberties, including the right to vote and to divorce. Relatively few women, however, will run for office or otherwise engage in either the political or the professional arena.

Women in the new nation of Pakistan must adhere to Islamic codes, but British and Indian influence, especially in the upper class, will make women's lives less restrictive there than in most Islamic societies of the Middle East.

GERTY RADNITZ CORI, who was born in Prague but now works in the United States, wins the Nobel Prize in physiology or medicine.

1948   On December 10, the General Assembly of the United Nations adopts the Universal Declaration of Human Rights. Former American first lady ELEANOR ROOSEVELT chairs the committee that has spent the previous two years drafting the declaration. After a United Nations women's caucus pointed out the need, Roosevelt ensures that its language is gender neutral. It reads in part: "All human beings are born free and equal. . . . Everyone is entitled to rights and freedoms . . . without regard to distinction of any kind, such as race, color, sex. . . . Everyone has the right to life, liberty, and security of person."

1949   France's SIMONE DE BEAUVOIR publishes the feminist classic *The Second Sex.*

When the Chinese Communists defeat the Nationalists, SOONG CH'ING-LING stays on the mainland, while her sister, SOONG MEI-LING, retreats to Taiwan.

1950   China's new government enacts major revisions in laws affecting women. Women not only have equal political rights, including the right to vote and to hold office, but also for the first time can sue for divorce. Polygamy is outlawed, and arranged marriages are discouraged. Actual behavior will be slow to change, but political support for women's equality is unequivocally proclaimed. China's official documents on women's rights are more forward-thinking than anything in Chinese history.

India's new constitution ensures women's rights. It forbids discrimination based on gender or caste; outlaws polygamy, child marriage, and dowries; and opens education and employment to women. During the second half of the century, the status of Indian women quickly improves from one of the most inferior in the world to one of Asia's most liberated. Many are educated in the West and return to practice professions in India, but—as in other revolutionary cultural change—rural areas lag behind. Discrimination against women there will remain profound.

Outside Asia, this year marks the beginning of a decade of regression for women, especially as measured by official recognitions: no women win Nobel or other major prizes, nor are there political or legal victories comparable to those women won during and after World War I. After two decades of depression and war, Western women concentrate on their personal lives and especially on pregnancies, which create a population boom. Women do win important economic security in European countries, almost all of which will adopt social welfare programs that ensure adequate health care and financial assistance to mothers.

As African colonies gain their independence from European governments during this decade and the next, women are granted the vote and other political rights along with men. Few African women, however, will run for office or make other significant changes in economic or social status. Arranged marriages and even polygamy will remain common into the future, and, even among educated Africans, women are discouraged from roles other than those in the home. This is true in the Islamic eastern and northern areas as well as in the non-Islamic nations of western and southern Africa.

1951 War in Korea brings nurses, nuns, and military women from several United Nations affiliates. Korean women live with death and destruction; as in World War II, many of them marry soldiers and move to the West.

1952 At age 26, ELIZABETH II becomes queen of Great Britain.

AGATHA CHRISTIE, whose murder mysteries sell millions of copies, is also a playwright: *The Mousetrap* begins its decades-long run in London.

1953 The United Nations follows up its Universal Declaration of Human Rights with a proclamation on the political rights of women, which asserts such civil rights as the vote, elective office, and "all public functions…on equal terms with men, without any discrimination." Not even all Western nations, however, will ratify the convention.

British crystallographer ROSALIND FRANKLIN pioneers the study of DNA.

1956 Prima ballerina MARGOT FONTEYN becomes president of Britain's Royal Ballet.

Margaret Gazo leads black women in Pretoria, South Africa, in a demonstration against a law that requires blacks to carry passes limiting their movement. For this and other activities, Gazo will be sentenced to five years in prison.

1957 Europe has a long tradition of welcoming black entertainers who are barred in their native United States. This year, MARIAN ANDERSON goes on a twelve-nation tour that—unlike her earlier ones—is sponsored by an American government trying to erase its racist image.

1958 The Great Leap Forward—China's campaign to organize its population to meet its industrial and agricultural needs—suffers a disaster, as fifteen million starve when weather catastrophes complicate collectivist economic policies. The practice of female infanticide returns, and girls are more likely than boys to die in the famine.

Tennis begins to lose its white Anglo image: two of the winners at England's Wimbledon championships this year are Althea Gibson, an African American, and Maria Audion Bueno of Brazil.

1959 Black South African women protest apartheid by attempting to enter a "whites-only" building. Police beat them back.

1960 Ceylon (which will later become Sri Lanka) elects the world's first female prime minister, SIRIMAVO BANDARANAIKE. The next three decades will bring a wave of women as elected heads of state.

1961 Queen ELIZABETH II makes a twenty-one-thousand mile tour from India to Ghana.

Thousands of birth defects in Europe are traced to the prescription drug thalidomide, a tranquilizer that had been prescribed to many pregnant women.

1962 A United Nations study emphasizes that the great majority of the world's babies are delivered not by physicians but by women assisting other women. In the Sudan, for instance, there is one physician per seventy-two thousand residents. The World Health Organization undertakes programs to better train and equip midwives, many of whom travel to their patients by camel or canoe.

1963 VALENTINA TERESHKOVA of the Soviet Union is the first woman in outer space.

German native MARIA GOEPPERT MAYER, who is now an American citizen, becomes the second woman to win the Nobel Prize in physics. The first, MARIE CURIE, won sixty years earlier.

1964 France pays its mothers, whether married or unmarried, $64 per child per month—typical of European socialist programs.

Britain's DOROTHY CROWFOOT HODGKIN wins the Nobel Prize in chemistry.

1965   As the American military presence in the civil war in Vietnam increases, Vietnamese women suffer immensely during the conflict. Some of the millions of tons of bombs will destroy their homes and farms, forcing many to move to cities and enter prostitution to support themselves and their often fatherless children. Although Vietnamese women are legally equal to men and have long held a status superior to that of most Asian women, neither the North Vietnamese nor the South Vietnamese government has any significant representation of this half of the population.

1966   India follows the lead of nearby Ceylon, becoming the second modern nation to have a woman in its top office with this year's election of INDIRA GANDHI. Gandhi not only is a new role model of an improved status for Indian women; she also understands that the key to reducing the country's dire poverty is ending overpopulation. Gandhi offers monetary rewards for having fewer children, and—for the first time in the history of national attempts to increase or decrease population—she puts the public-policy burden particularly on men. Males who irresponsibly father an excessive number of children are sometimes forced to have vasectomies. The policy is not popular, and India's population continues to rise.

Poet NELLY SACHS, who fled her native Germany for Sweden during World War II, wins the Nobel Prize for literature.

Queen ELIZABETH II surprises the public by honoring young Mary Quant, designer of the miniskirt—which has come to symbolize the sexual revolution—with the Order of the British Empire.

Portugal's elderly dictator, António de Oliveira Salazar, is under increasing pressure to liberalize his nation's policies on women. He allows revision of the 1867 code on married women's property rights, bringing this area in line with what most European nations granted decades ago.

1967   Jiang Qing joins her husband, Mao Tse-tung, in leading China's Cultural Revolution—a revolution of conservatism. Universities are closed; Western books, music, and other influences are banned; and women and men who demonstrate any sort of intellectual freedom receive severe discipline, including corporal punishment and banishment to menial labor on distant farms. When Mao dies less than a decade later, however, the situation reverses: Jiang—whose name is also spelled Chiang Ch'ing—is publicly humiliated and sentenced to life in prison.

1968   Student rebellions throughout Europe and the Americas include a feminist element. Part of this is a more relaxed standard of clothing and appearance, part is a demand for greater equity in education and employment, and much focuses on changed relationships between men and women. Formal organizations begin that are aimed at electing more women to office and removing legal barriers to equality, but much important change also happens in "consciousness-raising" sessions of the informal "women's liberation movement." Unlike earlier movements, this one especially focuses on private life: more women openly engage in sex without marriage; they insist on reproductive freedom, including access to legal abortion and the new birth-control pill; and they force men to participate in homemaking and the rearing of children.

The massacre of women and children at My Lai turns many against the war in Vietnam. Although years will pass before the United States disengages itself from war in Southeast Asia, photographs of these victims are a powerful indictment against the military. Meanwhile, as in other wars, tens of thousands of women immigrate with new husbands; many others are left to support children alone when their fathers depart.

1969   GOLDA MEIR is elected prime minister of Israel.

Also this year, Liberia's Angie Brooks is president of the 24th Assembly of the United Nations, and much media attention goes to 21-year-old Bernadette Devlin, a leftist from Northern Ireland elected to Britain's House of Commons.

1970   With Mao Tse-tung and Jiang Qing still in control, China begins its policy of one child per marriage. The nation is overpopulated and resources are few, and therefore couples who have more than one child are fined. Some farming families value child labor enough that they opt to pay the penalties, but in both farm and city economies, the result is more female infanticide; although birth control and abortion are legal, many poor women go through the pain of pregnancy and delivery and then feel forced to kill their babies if they are girls.

1971 Most westerners are astonished to realize that, long after women in other European countries were enfranchised, Swiss women still lack the vote. Male voters finally pass a suffrage referendum in February; in October, eight women are elected to parliament. In a few conservative cantons, however, women still are not eligible to vote in local elections.

Australia's GERMAINE GREER publishes *The Female Eunuch*.

The Roman Catholic Church names Spain's TERESA OF ÁVILA and Italy's CATHERINE OF SIENA as its first female doctors of the church.

1972 The United Nations proclaims 1975 as International Women's Year and begins planning an international gathering on women's issues.

1973 The communist government of East Germany begins an advertising campaign aimed at improving the status of women and especially encouraging men to help with family work. Legislation passed this year permits abortion on demand during the first three months of pregnancy; like all health care, both medical costs and sick leave from work are paid by the state. Almost eighty percent of employment-age women work, and this year their paid vacation is raised to a minimum of twenty-one days.

Chile's military attacks the presidential palace, resulting in the death of president Salvador Allende, who won the 1970 election. His wife, Hortensia Bussi Allende, survives and leads a vain effort to halt the coup. She accuses the United States of authorizing and financing the coup, and intelligence officers later admit as much. Her outspokenness is risky, for the Pinochet regime that replaces her husband tortures and kills thousands.

1974 Argentina's ISABEL PERÓN is the first female president of a Latin American nation.

While hundreds watch, high-caste Hindu men invade a Harijan (also known as untouchable) home and drag out four women, whom they strip naked and sexually assault with red-hot probes. Despite INDIRA GANDHI's efforts, this sort of crime is not exceptional: also this year, an Indian court exonerates twenty-three wealthy men who burned alive forty-two Harijan women and children.

1975 Almost a century after the first International Congress of Women, the United Nations hosts its first conference focusing exclusively on women's issues. It is held in Mexico City, and six thousand attend from all over the world. The official thirteen hundred representatives of more than a hundred countries approve an action plan for the next decade that includes improving women's economic position and promoting political participation by women.

The Anglican Church of Canada leads the way on ordination of women as priests: the mother church, back in England, will not sanction female priests until 1992.

MAIRÉAD CORRIGAN-MAGUIRE and BETTY WILLIAMS of Northern Ireland share the Nobel Peace Prize.

Japan's Junko Tabei is the first woman to climb to the top of Mount Everest.

1976 Islam is proclaimed the state religion of Algeria, and women lose some freedoms they had enjoyed since French colonialism. Although dowries are abolished, Algerian women will be notably more oppressed than their sisters in neighboring Morocco.

The progressive president of West Africa's Ivory Coast creates a ministry on women's issues; Jeanne Gervais, who heads the ministry, is the first woman at a top level of the nation's government.

The European Court of Justice forces a Belgian airline to make pension payments for female flight attendants, just as it does for men in that job.

1977 When General Mohammad Zia-ul-Haq seizes power in Pakistan, women's rights disappear.

Islamic codes replace secular law, and violators are publicly whipped.

Greek women organize against a bill their government proposed last year that would draft them into military service. They argue that they do not have equality in other areas and should not be drafted until they do. Next year, they win a compromise that makes female military service voluntary except during times of war.

The Japan Women's Party is a political manifestation of a new and still-small women's liberation movement. The party fields some candidates for office but does not win any seats.

1978 Women in the African nation of Guinea demonstrate against police who harass them while they run their open-air markets; they win governmental attention to their grievances.

Israel, which is surrounded by hostile Arab nations, drafts women as well as men for its military. This year its parliament makes it easier for Orthodox women to avoid conscription; although both the Ministry of Defense and secular women object, the measure passes 54-45.

1979 When the shah of Iran is deposed and Islamic clerics take power, the level of female freedom plummets in the new theocracy. Western clothing is no longer permitted for women, who are flogged if they are seen without veils that cover them from head to toe. Women are fired from government jobs and professions; divorce is outlawed, and the punishment for adultery is stoning. Other Islamic countries follow, and women are similarly restricted as far west as Algeria.

Albanian native MOTHER TERESA wins the Nobel Peace Prize for her longtime work in India.

MARGARET THATCHER becomes prime minister of the United Kingdom.

1980 The decade marks an economic high point for Japan: during the years since it was devastated by World War II, it has rebounded to become a global commercial superpower. Women, howev-

er, are largely excluded from the highest levels of this success; even though they make up almost half of Japanese workers, they are relegated to stereotypical women's jobs and earn an average wage half that of men. The cultural ideal is that married women devote themselves to one or two children.

Iceland elects VIGDÍS FINNBOGADÓTTIR as its first female president.

In December, the United Nations approves the Convention on the Elimination of All Forms of Discrimination Against Women. It is the result of a Copenhagen conference earlier in the year that marked the midpoint of a United Nations–declared Decade of Women.

1981 In a campaign to raise its literacy rate from fifteen percent, Saudi Arabia opens more schools, but they are largely for male students. Those women who do manage to obtain an education will be restricted to careers in which they work only with other women.

Over the objections of conservatives, Spain legalizes divorce. A woman, Soledad Becerril, is named minister of culture this year; next year, eighteen women will be elected to parliament and two will become provincial governors. An abortion bill also makes legislative progress.

Switzerland, which lagged decades behind the rest of Europe in granting the vote to women, passes an equal rights amendment to its constitution that, among other things, ensures equal pay for equal work. Of Switzerland's twenty-six cantons, nine vote against the measure.

1982 ALVA MYRDAL is the first Swedish woman to win the Nobel Peace Prize, despite that nation's longtime leadership role for peace.

Although she is a paraplegic, Neoli Fairhill of New Zealand wins the gold medal in archery at the Commonwealth Games.

1983 Dame Mary Donaldson is the first female lord mayor of London in that city's eight-hundred-year history.

When Pakistani women demonstrate against the imposition of theological law that officially proclaims men to be superior to women, they are attacked by police; several are injured and imprisoned.

1984 A new code of family law in Algeria is seen as a liberalization because it puts some limits on polygamy. A first wife is permitted to seek divorce when her husband marries another woman, and subsequent wives are protected by a provision that all be must be treated equally. Women also gain some rights to their children in divorces, but the most significant change is in birth control: because the government wants to limit the population, promotion of "planned parenthood" begins on television.

Switzerland elects the first woman to its federal council: a feminist and environmentalist, Elisabeth Kopp will become Switzerland's first female vice president in 1989.

Jeanne Sauve, who became Canada's first female Speaker of the House in 1980, is named its governor-general, also a first. A broadcast journalist who is fluent in French and English, Sauve's new duties include quarterly meetings with Queen ELIZABETH II.

1985 The United Nations marks the end of the Decade of Women that began with the 1975 conference in Mexico. Some seventeen thousand people attend a meeting in Nairobi, Kenya—about three times as many as attended the earlier conference.

1986 Filipinos elect CORAZON AQUINO as president, while Norway's GRO BRUNDTLAND serves the first of her three terms as prime minister.

RITA LEVI-MONTALCINI, who was born in Italy but now is an American citizen, wins the Nobel Prize in physiology or medicine.

1987 The Canadian province of Ontario is the first to pass "comparable worth" legislation. The concept is designed to go beyond the "equal pay for equal work" principle by instead comparing the value of jobs stereotyped by gender: nurses, for example, should earn at least as much as garbage collectors. Ontario's law is very progressive in that it applies to both private and public employers, who are given six years to implement new pay scales.

Courts in Kenya deal a blow to women's rights when they refuse to allow Virginia Wambui Otieno to bury her husband's remains in Nairobi, where he had lived for many years as a westernized Christian. Instead, the jurists support his rural clansmen—who also win his inheritance.

The Church of England authorizes its first female deacons.

Korean nuns are among those who participate in pro-democracy demonstrations in Seoul.

1988 BENAZIR BHUTTO is elected prime minister of Pakistan.

Anglican bishops representing 164 nations gather in Canterbury, England, where they vote to allow national churches to decide on whether to ordain women.

Sophia Kawawa leads the nascent women's movement in Zanzibar, Tanzania, which is governed by Islamic law. Through her husband, a political leader, she manages to introduce a proposal for greater equality, but a large crowd demonstrates against it; police fire on the demonstrators, killing two.

1989 While many Middle Eastern governments insist that women wear various degrees of Muslim dress, Turkey—though largely Muslim—is constitutionally secular and forbids women from covering their heads in the traditional way. This year, university students in Istanbul demonstrate for the right to wear conservative Muslim attire.

The Greek Women's March Home Movement is dedicated to returning to the members' former home in an area of Cyprus now controlled by Turkey. When the Greek women try to cross the border, the Turkish Cypriot Women's Action Committee—supported by police—confronts them. Some fifty are arrested and turned over to United Nations peacekeepers.

1990 As the last decade of the twentieth century begins, about two-thirds of working-age women in westernized countries are employed. Although most are still in stereotypical "women's jobs," it is a huge change from the century's beginning, when women rarely worked outside the home except in dire need.

A study of rural India shows that one in every four girls dies before reaching age fifteen—often from deliberate malnourishment, while boys are fed.

Three women set precedents as the first female heads of state in their nations: NITA RUTH BARROW in Barbados, MARY ROBINSON in Ireland, and VIOLETA CHAMORRO in Nicaragua. Chamorro's victory is especially important for democracy in that war-torn area. She is also the first woman to head a Central American nation.

1991 Two women are Nobel Prize winners: novelist NADINE GORDIMER, a white South African, wins the prize for literature, and the Nobel Peace Prize goes to AUNG SAN SUU KYI, who continues to suffer for democracy in her homeland of Burma (later Myanmar).

Swiss women make up for their earlier feminist lag: on June 14, some five hundred thousand join a national strike day, and the government pays attention. Legislation is adopted that puts the burden of proof on the employer, rather than the grievant, in pay discrimination cases; marital rape is declared a crime; and the last canton that has barred women from its legislature is forced to accept them. The city of Bern even adopts a rule that neither gender may compose more than sixty percent of council seats.

EDITH CRESSON is premier of France.

1992 For the first time since the 1905 creation of the Nobel Peace Prize, women win it in consecutive years. This year's winner is Guatemala's RIGOBERTA MENCHÚ.

HANNA SUCHOCKA is the first female prime minister of Poland.

The president of South Korea appoints women to his cabinet for the first time in that nation's history.

1993 Canada's prime minister is KIM CAMPBELL, while TANSU CILLER is elected to the same office in Turkey.

Bangladesh bans a novel by Taslima Nasreen in which Muslim men rape Hindu women. Like the far better known Salman Rushdie, she is condemned to death by religious fundamentalists; they offer a bounty for her head that is more than five times the average annual income in this poor country (formerly East Pakistan), and Nasreen flees to Sweden.

1994 In Africa's Rwanda, Hutu women join men in slaughtering members of the Tutsi tribe. Approximately half a million people are massacred—many hacked apart alive by the machetes of tribal opponents who share their race and gender.

Peaceful elections are held in Panama, and a woman, Mireya Moscoso de Gruber, comes in second for the presidency.

1995 The Fourth World Conference on Women, the United Nations conference on women's issues, is held in Beijing. Critics complain that this condones China's poor human-rights record but fail to acknowledge that earlier conferences were held in Mexico and Kenya—nations that also do not have stellar human-rights records.

A congressional investigation in Brazil reports that as many as 180 Rio de Janeiro "death squads"— usually hired by businessmen who claim to be enforcing law and order—regularly kill apparently homeless children. The Mothers of Cinelandia hold weekly plaza gatherings, where they sadly display photographs of the "disappeared."

Germany's CHRISTIANE NÜSSLEIN-VOLHARD wins the Nobel Prize in physiology or medicine.

1996 Polish poet WISLAWA SZYMBORSKA wins the Nobel Prize for literature.

An ultraconservative Muslim minority known as the Taliban begins to consolidate power in Afghanistan. Women, who had been fairly liberated, are plunged into the most appalling oppression of the late twentieth century. Girls are forbidden to attend school, and women cannot hold jobs or even venture outside the home without a male relative; they must cover themselves from head to toe, with a thick mesh over their eyes to see through. Widows and others who lack male support literally starve because they are not allowed to work.

1997 JENNY SHIPLEY becomes the first female prime minister of New Zealand.

Liberals win a landslide in Great Britain, including the election of 120 women to Parliament, 101 of whom were chosen by the Labour Party as candidates for winnable seats. They predict great change in the House of Commons, which has very few women's restrooms. Cherie Blair, wife of new prime minister Tony Blair, also is a feminist who intends to continue practicing law.

The Southern African Development Community, meeting in Malawi, adopts a resolution that commits member states to including women in economic development.

1998 Education in Africa remains a male preserve: women constitute fewer than one of every five students at the higher levels. No nonwhite African woman has won a Nobel Prize in any field, nor has any of its dozens of nations had a woman as its chief of state. While married women in cities sometimes maintain a separate income and property, few men assist with housework.

A study reveals that Portugal is the only Western European nation in which wage earners are more likely to be women than men. While most hold menial jobs, there is hope for the future in that women also make up more than half of the country's university students.

1999 Panama elects its first female president, Mireya Moscoso, who follows Nicaragua's VIOLETA CHAMORRO as the second woman to head to a Central American nation. In December, Moscoso presides over perhaps the most important event in the nation's history, as control of the Panama Canal passes peacefully from the United States to Panama.

Indonesians elect Megawati Sukarnoputri to head their 1,300-island nation in June, but after powerful incumbent men proved unwilling to accept her, she steps down to the vice presidency at the fall inauguration.

War in Kosovo again brings discussion of the need to expand the definition of human rights to include women's rights, as United States officials seek to prosecute soldiers for rape—something that traditionally has been accepted as an unfortunate but expected aspect of war.

For expansion of these and other news developments in 1999, please refer to Part One: News.

Bibliography

Adolescence and Education

American Association of University Women. *Gender Gaps: Where Schools Still Fail Our Children*. New York: Marlowe, 1998.

Ashby, Ruth, and Deborah G. Ohrn, eds. *Herstory: Women Who Changed the World*. New York: Viking Penguin, 1995.

Carlip, Hillary. *Girl Power: Young Women Speak Out*. New York: Warner Books, 1995.

Davis, Sara N., Mary Crawford, and Jadwiga Sebrechts, eds. *Coming Into Her Own: Encouraging Educational Success in Girls and Women*. San Francisco: Jossey-Bass, 1999.

Debold, Elizabeth, Idelisse Malave, and Marie Wilson. *Mother Daughter Revolution: From Good Girls to Great Women*. New York: Bantam Doubleday Dell Publishing, 1994.

Drill, Esther, Heather McDonald, and Rebecca Odes. *Deal With It!: A Whole New Approach to Your Body, Brain, and Life as a gURL*. New York: Pocket Books, 1999.

Eisenmann, Linda, ed. *Historical Dictionary of Women's Education in the United States*. Westport, Conn.: Greenwood Press, 1998.

Furger, Roberta. *Does Jane Compute?: Preserving Our Daughters' Place in the Cyber Revolution*. New York: Warner Books, 1998.

Gilligan, Carol. *In a Different Voice: Psychological Theory and Women's Development*. Cambridge, Mass.: Harvard University Press, 1982.

Green, Karen, and Tristan Taormino, eds. *A Girl's Guide to Taking over the World: Writings from the Girl Zine Revolution*. New York: St. Martin's Press, 1997.

Luttrell, Wendy. *Schoolsmart and Motherwise: Working-Class Women's Identity and Schooling*. New York: Routledge, 1998.

Madaras, Lynda with Area Madaras. *The What's Happening to My Body? Book for Girls: A Growing Up Guide for Parents and Daughters*. Rev. ed. New York: Newmarket Press, 1997.

Mann, Judy. *The Difference: Discovering the Hidden Ways We Silence Girls: Finding Alternatives That Can Give Them a Voice*. New York: Warner Books, 1996.

Nelson, Pamela, ed. *Cool Women: The Reference*. Los Angeles: Girl Press, 1998.

Orenstein, Peggy. *Schoolgirls: Young Women, Self Esteem, and the Confidence Gap*. New York: Doubleday, 1995.

Pipher, Mary Bray. *Reviving Ophelia: Saving the Selves of Adolescent Girls*. New York: Ballantine Publishing, 1998.

Schlachter, Gail A., and R. David Weber. *Directory of Financial Aid for Women, 1997–99*. San Carlos, Calif.: Reference Service Press, 1997.

Shandler, Sarah. *Ophelia Speaks: Adolescent Girls Write About Their Search for Self*. New York: HarperCollins, 1999.

Snortland, Ellen. *Beauty Bites Beast: Awakening the Warrior Within Women and Girls*. Pasadena, Calif.: Trilogy Books, 1998.

Aging

Ahern, Kathleen Dee. *The Older Woman: The Able Self*. New York: Garland Publishing, 1996.

Alexander, Jo, et al., eds. *Women and Aging: An Anthology by Women*. Corvallis, Ore.: Calyx Books, 1986.

Arber, Sara. *Gender and Later Life: A Sociological Analysis of Resources and Constraints*. Newbury Park, Calif.: Sage Publications, 1991.

Barusch, Amanda Smith. *Older Women in Poverty: Private Lives and Public Policies*. New York: Springer Publishing, 1994.

Bell, Marilyn J. *Women As Elders: The Feminist Politics of Aging*. New York: Harrington Park Press, 1987.

Bonita, Ruth. *Women, Aging, and Health: Achieving Health Across the Life Span*. Geneva: World Health Organization, 1996.

Browne, Colette. *Women, Feminism, and Aging*. New York: Springer Publishing, 1998.

Coplon, Jennifer K. *Single Older Women in the Workforce: By Necessity, Or Choice?* New York: Garland Publishing, 1997.

Coyle, Jean M., ed. *Handbook on Women and Aging*. Westport, Conn.: Greenwood Press, 1997.

Day, Alice T. *Remarkable Survivors: Insights into Successful Aging Among Women*. Washington, D.C.: Urban Institute Press, 1991.

Doress-Worters, Paula B., and Diana L. Siegal. *The New Ourselves Growing Older*. New York: Peter Smith, 1996; New York: Simon & Schuster, 1996.

Greer, Germaine. *The Change: Women, Aging, and the Menopause*. New York: Fawcett Book Group, 1993.

Komesaroff, Paul A., Philipa Rothfield, and Jeanne Daly, eds. *Reinterpreting Menopause: Cultural and Philosophical Issues*. New York: Routledge, 1997.

Lock, Margaret. *Encounters With Aging: Mythologies of Menopause in Japan and North America.* Berkeley: University of California Press, 1993.

Nordquist, Joan. *Women and Aging: A Bibliography.* Santa Cruz, Calif.: Reference and Research Services, 1994.

Paoletti, Isabella. *Being an Older Woman: A Study in the Social Production of Identity.* Mahwah, N.J.: Lawrence Erlbaum, 1998.

Pearsall, Marilyn, ed. *The Other Within Us: Feminist Explorations of Women and Aging.* Boulder, Colo.: Westview Press, 1997.

Roberto, Karen A. *Relationships Between Women in Later Life.* New York: Harrington Park Press, 1996.

Thone, Ruth Raymond. *Women and Aging: Celebrating Ourselves.* New York: Harrington Park Press, 1992.

Turner, Barbara F., and Lillian E. Troll. *Women Growing Older: Theoretical Perspectives in the Psychology of Aging.* Thousand Oaks, Calif.: Sage Publications, 1993.

Wyatt-Brown, Anne M., and Janice Rossen. *Aging and Gender in Literature: Studies in Creativity.* Charlottesville: University Press of Virginia, 1993.

The Arts

Adair, Christy. *Women and Dance.* New York: New York University Press, 1992

Betterton, Rosemary. *An Intimate Distance: Women, Artists, and the Body.* New York: Routledge, 1996.

Borzello, Frances. *Seeing Ourselves: Women's Self-Portraits.* New York: Harry N. Abrams, 1998.

Briscoe, James R., ed. *Contemporary Anthology of Music by Women.* Bloomington: Indiana University Press, 1997.

Chadwick, Whitney, ed. *Mirror Images: Women, Surrealism, and Self-Representation.* Cambridge, Mass.: MIT Press, 1998.

———. *Women, Art, and Society.* London: Thames and Hudson, 1997.

Cook, Pam, and Philip Dodd, eds. *Women and Film: A Sight and Sound Reader.* Philadelphia: Temple University Press, 1993.

Cook, Susan C., and Judy S. Tsou, eds. *Cecilia Reclaimed: Feminist Perspectives on Gender and Music.* Urbana: University of Illinois Press, 1994.

Cowie, Elizabeth. *Representing the Woman: Cinema and Psychoanalysis.* Minneapolis: University of Minnesota Press, 1997.

Davis, Angela Y. *Blues Legacies and Black Feminism: Gertrude "Ma" Rainey, Bessie Smith, and Billie Holiday.* New York: Pantheon Books, 1998.

Dickerson, James. *Women on Top: The Quiet Revolution That's Rocking the American Music Industry.* New York: Watson-Guptill Publications, 1998.

Dow, Bonnie J. *Prime-Time Feminism: Television, Media Culture, and the Women's Movement Since 1970.* Philadelphia: University of Pennsylvania Press, 1997.

Erens, Patricia, ed. *Issues in Feminist Film Criticism.* Bloomington: Indiana University Press, 1991.

Ericson, Margaret. *Women and Music: A Selective Annotated Bibliography on Women and Gender Issues in Music, 1987–1992.* New York: G. K. Hall, 1996.

Fischer, Lucy. *Cinematernity: Film, Motherhood, Genre.* Princeton, N.J.: Princeton University Press, 1996.

Gaar, Gillian G. *She's a Rebel: The History of Women in Rock and Roll.* Seattle, Wash.: Seal Press, 1992.

Gaze, Delia, ed. *Dictionary of Women Artists.* Chicago: Fitzroy Dearborn Publishers, 1997.

Grant, Barry, ed. *Dread of Difference: Gender and the Horror Film.* Austin: University of Texas Press, 1996.

Grattan, Virginia L. *American Women Songwriters: A Biographical Dictionary.* Westport, Conn.: Greenwood Press, 1993.

Gray, Anne. *The Popular Guide to Women in Classical Music.* New York: Macmillan Library Reference, 1996.

Green, Lucy. *Music, Gender, Education.* New York: Cambridge University Press, 1997.

Greer, Germaine. *The Obstacle Race: The Fortunes of Women Painters and Their Work.* New York: Farrar, Straus & Giroux, 1980.

Guerrilla Girls Staff. *The Guerrilla Girls' Bedside Companion to the History of Western Art.* New York: Viking Penguin, 1998.

Handy, D. Antoinette. *Black Women in American Bands and Orchestras.* Lanham, Md.: Scarecrow Press, 1998.

Haskell, Molly. *From Reverence to Rape: The Treatment of Women in the Movies.* Chicago: University of Chicago Press, 1987.

Hollinger, Karen. *In the Company of Women: Contemporary Female Friendship Film.* Minneapolis: University of Minnesota Press, 1998.

Jezic, Diane. *Women Composers: The Lost Tradition Found.* New York: Feminist Press at the City University of New York, 1994.

Kaplan, E. Ann. *Looking for The Other: Feminism, Film, and the Imperial Gaze.* New York: Routledge, 1997.

Kuhn, Annette. *Women's Pictures: Feminism and Cinema.* 2d ed. New York: Verso, 1994.

———, ed. *The Women's Companion to International Film.* Berkeley: University of California Press, 1994.

Locke, Ralph P., and Cyrilla Barr, eds. *Cultivating Music in America: Women Patrons and Activists Since 1860.* Berkeley: University of California Press, 1997.

Lutyens, Elisabeth. *The Choral Music of Twentieth-Century Women Composers.* Westport, Conn.: Greenwood Press, 1997.

Matheopoulos, Helena. *Diva: The New Generation*. Boston: Northeastern University Press, 1998.

Mayne, Judith. *The Woman at the Keyhole: Feminism and Women's Cinema*. Bloomington: Indiana University Press, 1990.

Meskimmon, Marsha. *The Art of Reflection: Women Artists' Self-Portraiture in the Twentieth Century*. New York: Columbia University Press, 1996.

Mulvey, Laura. *Visual and Other Pleasures*. Bloomington: Indiana University Press, 1989.

Neuls-Bates, Carol, ed. *Women in Music: An Anthology of Source Readings from the Middle Ages to the Present*. Boston: Northeastern University Press, 1995.

O'Brien, Lucy. *She Bop: The Definitive History of Women in Rock, Pop, and Soul*. New York: Viking Penguin, 1996.

Paglia, Camille. *Sexual Personae: Art and Decadence from Nefertiti to Emily Dickinson*. New York: Vintage Books, 1991.

Pendle, Karin, ed. *Women and Music: A History*. Bloomington: Indiana University Press, 1991.

Penley, Constance, ed. *Close Encounters: Film, Feminism, and Science Fiction*. Minneapolis: University of Minnesota Press, 1991.

Plackskin, Sally. *Jazzwomen: Century of Women Performers, Composers, and Producers*. New York: Macmillan Publishing, 1998.

Pollock, Griselda, ed. *Generations and Geographies in the Visual Arts: Feminist Readings*. New York: Routledge, 1996.

Pribram, E. Diedre, ed. *Female Spectators: Looking at Film and Television*. New York: Verso, 1988.

Rich, Ruby B. *Chick Flicks: Theories and Memories of the Feminist Film Movement*. Durham, N.C.: Duke University Press, 1998.

Robertson, Pamela. *Guilty Pleasures: Feminist Camp from Mae West to Madonna*. Durham, N.C.: Duke University Press, 1996.

Robinson, Jontyle T. *Bearing Witness: Contemporary Works by African American Women Artists*. New York: Rizzoli International Publications, 1996.

Sadie, Julie A., and Rhian Samuels, eds. *The Norton-Grove Dictionary of Women Composers*. New York: W. W. Norton, 1994.

Schor, Mira. *Wet: On Painting, Feminism, and Art Culture*. Durham, N.C.: Duke University Press, 1997.

Silverman, Kaja. *The Acoustic Mirror: The Female Voice in Psychoanalysis and Cinema*. Bloomington: University of Indiana Press, 1988.

Smelik, Anneke. *And the Mirror Cracked: Feminist Cinema and Film Theory*. New York: St. Martin's Press, 1998.

Smith, Patricia J. *En Travesti: Women, Gender Subversion, Opera*. New York: Columbia University Press, 1995.

Story, Rosalyn M. *And So I Sing: African-American Divas of Opera and Concert*. New York: Warner Books, 1990; Upland, Vt.: DIANE Publishing, 1998.

Trasker, Yvonne. *Working Girls: Gender and Sexuality in Popular Cinema*. New York: Routledge, 1998.

Unterberger, Amy L., ed. *Women Filmmakers and Their Films*. Detroit, Mich.: St. James Press, 1998.

Walker-Hill, Helen. *Music by Black Women Composers: A Bibliography of Available Scores*. CBMR Monographs No. 5. Chicago: Columbia College, Center for Black Music Research, 1995.

Feminism

Adam, Alison. *Artificial Knowing: Gender and the Thinking Machine*. London and New York: Routledge, 1998.

Alexander, Jacqui, and Chandra Talpade Mohanty, eds. *Feminist Genealogies, Colonial Legacies, Democratic Futures*. New York and London: Routledge, 1997.

Bowles, G., and R. Duelli-Klein, eds. *Theories of Women Studies*. London: Routledge and Kegan Paul, 1982.

Butler, Judith P. *Bodies That Matter: On the Discursive Limits of "Sex."* New York: Routledge, 1994.

———. *Gender Trouble: Feminism and the Subversion of Identity*. New York: Routledge, 1999.

Cassell, Joan. *A Group Called Women: Sisterhood and Symbolism in the Feminist Movement*. Prospect Heights, Ill.: Waveland Press, 1989.

Clark, L. M. G., and L. Lange, eds. *The Sexism of Social and Political Theory*. Toronto: University of Toronto Press, 1979.

Cole, Eve Browning, and Susan Coultrap-McQuin. *Exploration in Feminist Ethics: Theory and Practice*. Bloomington: Indiana University Press, 1992.

Collins, Patricia Hill. *Black Feminist Theory: Knowledge, Consciousness, and the Politics of Empowerment*. Cambridge, Mass.: Unwin Hyman, 1990.

Conover, P. J., and V. Gray. *Feminism and the New Right*. New York: Praeger Publishers, 1983.

Daly, Mary. *Gynecology, the Metaethics of Radical Feminism: With a New Intergalactic Introduction*. Boston: Beacon Press, 1990.

———. *Quintessence . . . Realizing the Archaic Future: A Radical Elemental Feminist Manifesto*. Boston: Beacon Press, 1999.

Davis, Angela Y. *Women, Race, and Class*. New York: Random House, 1981.

DeBeauvoir, Simone. *The Second Sex*. New York: Alfred A. Knopf, 1952.

de Lauretis, Teresa, ed. *Feminist Studies/Critical Studies*. Bloomington: Indiana University Press, 1986.

Delphy, C. *Close to Home: A Materialist Analysis of Women's Oppression*. Amherst: University of Massachussetts Press, 1984.

di Leonardo, Micaela, ed. *Gender at the Crossroads of Knowledge.* Berkeley: University of California Press, 1991.

Donovan, Josephine. *Feminist Theory: The Intellectual Traditions of American Feminism.* New York: Continuum Publishing, 1992.

Dworkin, Andrea. *Woman Hating.* New York: E. P. Dutton, 1974.

Echols, Alice. *Daring to Be Bad: Radical Feminism in America.* Minneapolis: University of Minnesota Press, 1989.

Faludi, Susan. *Backlash: The Undeclared War Against American Women.* New York: Doubleday, 1992.

Faulkner, Sue, Stevi Jackson, and Jane Prince, eds. *Women's Studies: Essential Readings.* New York: New York University Press, 1994.

Fausto-Sterling, Anne. *Myths of Gender: Biological Theories About Women and Men.* New York: Basic Books, 1985.

Ferber, Marianne A., and Julie A. Nelson, eds. *Beyond Economic Man: Feminist Theory and Economics.* Chicago: University of Chicago Press, 1993.

Findlen, Barbara, ed. *Listen Up: Voices from the Next Feminist Generation.* Seattle, Wash.: Seal Press, 1995.

Firestone, Shulamith. *The Dialectic of Sex: The Case for Feminist Revolution.* New York: William Morrow, 1970.

Freeman, Jo, ed. *Women: A Feminist Perspective.* Palo Alto, Calif.: Mayfield, 1979.

Friedan, Betty. *The Feminine Mystique.* New York: Dell Publishing, 1984.

Fuss, D. *Essentially Speaking: Feminism, Nature, and Difference.* New York: Routledge, 1989.

Greer, Germaine. *The Female Eunuch.* New York: Bantam Books, 1972.

———. *Sex and Destiny.* New York: HarperTrade, 1985.

———. *The Whole Woman.* New York: Alfred A. Knopf, 1999.

Hanen, Marsha, and Kai Nielson. *Science, Morality, and Feminist Theory.* Calgary, Alberta: University of Calgary Press, 1987.

Haraway, Donna. *Simians, Cyborgs, and Women: The Reinvention of Nature.* New York: Routledge, 1991.

Held, Virginia. *Feminist Morality: Transforming Culture, Society, and Politics.* Chicago: University of Chicago Press, 1993.

Herndl, Diane P., and Robyn R. Warhol, eds. *Feminisms: An Anthology of Literary Theory and Criticism.* New Brunswick, N.J.: Rutgers University Press, 1997.

Hesse-Biber, Sharlene. *Feminist Approaches to Theory and Methodology.* New York: Oxford University Press, 1999.

Hite, Shere. *Women As Revolutionary Agents of Change: The Hite Reports and Beyond.* Madison: University of Wisconsin Press, 1994.

hooks, bell. *Ain't I a Woman: Black Women and Feminism.* Boston: South End Press, 1981.

———. *Feminist Theory: From Margin to Center.* Boston: South End Press, 1984.

———. *Talking Back: Thinking Feminist, Thinking Black.* Boston: South End Press, 1989.

Hull, Gloria T., Patricia Bell Scott, and Barbara Smith, eds. *All the Women Are White, All the Blacks Are Men, but Some of Us Are Brave.* Old Westbury, N.Y.: Feminist Press, 1982.

Humm, Maggie, ed. *Modern Feminisms: Literary, Political, Cultural.* New York: Columbia University Press, 1992.

Ireland, Patricia. *What Women Want.* New York: N A L Dutton, 1997.

Irigaray, Luce. *Speculum of the Other Woman.* Translated by Gillian C. Gill. Ithaca, N.Y.: Cornell University Press, 1990.

James, S. M., and A. P. A. Busia. *Theorizing Black Feminisms.* London: Routledge, 1993.

Jamieson, Kathleen H. *Beyond the Double Bind.* New York: Oxford University Press, 1997.

Jarrett-MacAuley, Delia, ed. *Reconstructing Womanhood, Reconstructing Feminism.* New York: Routledge, 1995.

Katzenstein, Mary F. *Faithful and Fearless: Moving Feminist Protest Inside the Church and Military.* Princeton, N.J.: Princeton University Press, 1998.

Lewis, Paula G., ed. *Traditionalism, Nationalism, and Feminism.* Westport, Conn.: Greenwood Publishing, 1985.

Lorber, Judith. *Paradoxes of Gender.* New Haven, Conn.: Yale University Press, 1995.

MacKinnon, Catharine A. *Toward a Feminist Theory of the State.* Cambridge, Mass.: Harvard University Press, 1989.

Malveaux, J. M., and M. Simms, eds. *Slipping Through the Cracks: The Status of Black Women.* New Brunswick, N.J.: Transaction Books, 1986.

Miller, Connie. *Feminist Research Methods.* Westport, Conn.: Greenwood Publishing, 1991.

Montagu, Ashley. *The Natural Superiority of Women.* Thousands Oaks, Calif.: Sage Publications, 1999.

Morgan, Robin, ed. *Sisterhood Is Powerful: An Anthology of Writings from the Women's Liberation Movement.* New York: Vintage Books, 1970.

Muscio, Inga. *Cunt: A Declaration of Independence.* Seattle, Wash.: Seal Press, 1998.

Nagle, Jill, ed. *Whores and Other Feminists.* New York: Routledge, 1996.

Naples, Nancy A. *Community Activism and Feminist Politics.* New York: Routledge, 1997.

Nicholson, L., ed. *Feminism/Postmodernism.* New York: Routledge, Chapman and Hall, 1990.

Nussbaum, Martha C. *Sex and Social Justice.* New York: Oxford University Press, 1998.

Ortner, Sherry B. *Making Gender.* Boston: Beacon Press, 1996.

Reinharz, Shulamit. *Social Research Methods, Feminist Perspectives.* Newark, N.J.: PPI, 1993.

Richardson, Laurel Walum. *The Dynamics of Sex and Gender.* Boston: Houghton Mifflin, 1981.

Roiphe, Katie. *The Morning After: Fear, Sex, and Feminism on Campus.* New York: Little, Brown, 1994.

Ruth, Sheila. *Issues in Feminism.* Palo Alto, Calif.: Mayfield Publishing, 1994.

Schneir, Miriam, ed. *Feminism: The Essential Historical Writings.* New York: Vintage Books, 1971.

Showalter, Elaine. *The New Feminist Criticism: Essays on Women, Literature, and Theory.* New York: Pantheon Books, 1985.

———. *Speaking of Gender.* New York: Routledge, 1989.

Smith, Barbara, ed. *Home Girls.* New York: Kitchen Table/ Women of Color Press, 1983.

Smith, Valerie. *Not Just Race, Not Just Gender: Black Feminist Readings.* New York: Routledge, 1998.

Sommers, Christina Hoff. *Who Stole Feminism?: How Women Have Betrayed Women.* New York: Simon & Schuster, 1995.

Steinem, Gloria. *Moving Beyond Words.* New York: Simon & Schuster, 1995.

———. *Outrageous Acts and Everyday Rebellions.* New York: Henry Holt, 1999.

Stoller, Robert J. *Sex and Gender: The Development of Masculinity and Femininity.* London: Karnac Books, 1994.

Tobias, Sheila. *Faces of Feminism: An Activist's Reflections on the Women's Movement.* Boulder, Colo.: Westview Press, 1997.

Tong, Rosemarie Putnam. *Feminist Thought: A More Comprehensive Introduction.* Boulder, Colo.: Westview Press, 1998.

Walker, Rebecca, ed. *To Be Real: Telling the Truth and Changing the Face of Feminism.* New York: Doubleday, 1995.

Wolf, Naomi. *Fire With Fire.* New York: Fawcett Book Group, 1994.

Wollstonecraft, Mary. *A Vindication of the Rights of Woman.* Mineola, N.Y.: Dover Publications, 1996.

Young, Cathy. *Ceasefire!: Why Women and Men Must Join Forces to Achieve True Equality.* New York: The Free Press, 1999.

Health

Adams, Diane L. *Health Issues for Women of Color: A Cultural Diversity Perspective.* Thousand Oaks, Calif.: Sage Publications, 1995.

American Medical Association Staff. *American Medical Association Complete Guide to Women's Health.* New York: Random House, 1996.

Baron-Faust, Rita. *Being Female: What Every Woman Should Know About Gynecological Health.* New York: William Morrow, 1998.

Berger, Karen, and John Bostwick III. *A Woman's Decision: Breast Care, Treatment, and Reconstruction.* New York: St. Martin's Press, 1998.

Bonnick, Sydney L. *The Osteoporosis Handbook: Every Woman's Guide to Prevention and Treatment.* Dallas, Tex.: Taylor Publishing, 1997.

Boston Women's Health Book Collective. *Our Bodies, Ourselves for the New Century.* New York: Touchstone Books, 1998.

Budoff, Penny Wise. *No More Hot Flashes . . . and Even More Good News.* New York: Time Warner, 1998.

Bullough, Vern L., and Bonnie Bullough. *Contraception: A Guide on Birth Control.* Amherst, Mass.: Prometheus Books, 1997.

Carlson, Karen J., Stephanie A. Eisenstat, and Terra Ziporyn. *The Harvard Guide to Women's Health.* Cambridge, Mass.: Harvard University Press, 1996.

Christen, Joan A., and Arden G. Christe. *The Female Smoker: From Addiction to Recovery.* Indianapolis, Ind.: Dental Tobacco Cessation Consultants, 1998.

Crawford, Amanda McQuade. *Herbal Remedies for Women.* Rocklin, Calif.: Prima Publishing, 1997.

Donchin, Anne, ed. *Feminist Perspectives on Bioethics.* Lanham, Md.: Rowman and Littlefield, 1998.

Finn, Susan C. *American Dietetic Association Guide to Women's Nutrition for Healthy Living.* New York: Berkeley Publishing, 1997.

Furst, Lilian R. *Women Healers and Physicians: Climbing a Long Hill.* Lexington: University Press of Kentucky, 1997.

Futterman, Lori A., and John E. Jones. *The PMS and Perimenopause Sourcebook: A Guide to the Emotional, Mental, and Physical Patterns of a Woman's Life.* Los Angeles: Lowell House, 1998.

Goldfarb, Herbert A. *The No-Hysterectomy Option: Your Body . . . Your Choice.* New York: John Wiley & Sons, 1998.

Goldstein, Nancy, and Jennifer L. Manlowe, eds. *The Gender Politics of HIV/AIDS in Women: Perspectives on the Pandemic in the United States.* New York: New York University Press, 1997.

Hartouni, Valerie. *Cultural Conceptions: On Reproductive Technologies and the Remaking of Life.* Minneapolis: University of Minnesota Press, 1997.

Hirschmann, Jane R. *When Women Stop Hating Their Bodies: Freeing Yourself from Food and Weight Problems.* New York: Fawcett Book Group, 1997.

Kendall, Stephen R. *Substance and Shadow: Women and Addiction in the United States.* Cambridge, Mass.: Harvard University Press, 1996.

Kloser, Patricia, and Jane M. Craig. *The Woman's HIV Sourcebook: A Guide to Better Health and Well-Being*. Dallas, Tex.: Taylor Publishing Co., 1994.

Krotoski, Danuta, ed. *Women with Physical Disabilities: Achieving and Maintaining Health and Well-Being*. Baltimore, Md.: Brookes Publishers, 1996.

Lawson, Erma J., and Rose LaFrancis Rogers, eds. *Black Women's Health: Research and Social Policy*. Newark, N.J.: Traces Institute Publications, 1997.

Leavitt, Judith Walzer, ed. *Women and Health in America: Historical Readings*. 2d ed. Madison: University of Wisconsin Press, 1999.

Link, John. *The Breast Cancer Survival Manual: A Step-By-Step Guide for the Woman with Newly Diagnosed Breast Cancer*. New York: Henry Holt, 1998.

Litt, Iris F. *Taking Our Pulse: The Health of America's Women*. Stanford, Calif.: Stanford University Press, 1997.

Long, Lynellyn D., and E. M. Ankrah. *Women's Experiences with HIV/AIDS: An International Perspective*. New York: Columbia University Press, 1996.

Love, Susan M. *Dr. Susan Love's Breast Book*. Reading, Mass.: Addison-Wesley, 1995.

McGinn, Kerry A. *Women's Cancers: How to Prevent Them, How to Treat Them, How to Beat Them*. 2d ed. Alameda, Calif.: Hunter House, 1997.

Northrup, Christane. *Women's Bodies, Women's Wisdom: Creating Physical and Emotional Health and Healing*. Rev. ed. New York: Bantam Books, 1998.

Notelovitz, Morris. *The Essential Heart Book for Women*. New York: St. Martin's Press, 1997.

Perry, Angela. *The AMA Essential Guide to Menopause*. New York: Pocket Books, 1998.

Poirier, Laurinda, and Katharine Coburn. *Women and Diabetes: Life Planning for Health and Wellness*. New York: Bantam Books, 1998.

Roth, Nancy L., and Katie Hogan, eds. *Gendered Epidemic: Representations of Women in the Age of AIDS*. New York: Routledge, 1998.

Samuels, Mike, and Nancy Samuels. *The New Well Pregnancy Book*. New York: Simon & Schuster, 1996.

Shangold, Mona M., and Gabe Mirkin, eds. *Women and Exercise: Physiology and Sports Medicine*. New York: Oxford University Press, 1998.

Stabiner, Karen. *To Dance with the Devil: The New War on Breast Cancer*. Cambridge, Mass.: Harvard University Press, 1997.

Stark, Evan, and Anne Flitcraft. *Women at Risk: Domestic Violence and Women's Health*. Thousand Oaks, Calif.: Sage Publications, 1996.

Stevens, Sally L., and Harry K. Wexler, eds. *Women and Substance Abuse: Gender Transparency*. Binghamton, N.Y.: Haworth Press, 1998.

Thompson, Becky W. *A Hunger So Wide and So Deep: A Multicultural View of Women's Eating Problems*. Minneapolis: University of Minnesota Press, 1996.

Tong, Rosemary. *Feminist Approaches to Bioethics: Theoretical Reflections and Practical Applications*. Boulder, Colo.: Westview Press, 1997.

Underhill, Brenda, and Dana G. Finnegan, eds. *Chemical Dependency: Women at Risk*. Binghamton, N.Y.: Haworth Press, 1996.

Villarosa, Linda, ed. *Body and Soul: The Black Women's Guide to Physical Health and Emotional Well-Being*. New York: HarperCollins, 1994.

White, Jocelyn C., and Marissa C. Martinez. *The Lesbian Health Book: Caring for Ourselves*. Seattle, Wash.: Seal Press, 1997.

Winikoff, Beverly, and Suzanne Wymelemberg. *The Whole Truth About Contraception: A Guide to Safe and Effective Choices*. Washington, D.C.: National Academy Press, 1997.

Health (Mental Health)

Ballou, Mary B., and Nancy W. Gabalac. *A Feminist Position on Mental Health*. Springfield, Ill.: Thomas, 1985.

Bernay, Toni, and Dorothy Cantor, eds. *The Psychology of Today's Woman: New Psychoanalytic Visions*. Hillsdale, N.J.: Analytic Press, 1986; Cambridge, Mass.: Harvard University Press, 1989.

Brodsky, Annette M., and Rachel T. Hare-Mustin, eds. *Women and Psychotherapy: An Assessment of Research and Practice*. New York: Guilford Press, 1986.

Brown, Laura S., and Mary Ballou, eds. *Personality and Psychopathology: Feminist Reappraisals*. New York: Guilford Press, 1992.

Chesler, Phyllis. *Women and Madness*. San Diego, Calif.: Harcourt Brace Jovanovich, 1997.

Comas-Diaz, Lillian, and Beverly Greene, eds. *Women of Color: Integrating Ethnic and Gender Identities in Psychotherapy*. New York: Guilford Press, 1994.

Davis, Dona L., and Setha M. Low. *Gender, Health, and Illness: The Case of Nerves*. New York: Hemisphere, 1989.

Denmark, Florence L., and Michele A. Paludi, eds. *Psychology of Women: A Handbook of Issues and Theories*. Westport, Conn.: Greenwood Press, 1993.

Formanek, Ruth, and Anita Gurian, eds. *Women and Depression: A Lifespan Perspective*. New York: Springer Publishing, 1987.

Frankenhaeuser, Marianne, Ulf Lundberg, and Margaret Chesney. *Women, Work, and Health*. New York: Plenum Press, 1991.

Fulani, Lenora, ed. *The Politics of Race and Gender in Therapy*. New York: Haworth Press, 1988.

Gallant, Sheryle J. et al, eds. *Health Care for Women: Psychological, Social, and Behavioral Influences*. Washington, D.C.: American Psychological Association, 1997.

Greenspan, Miriam. *A New Approach to Women and Therapy*. 2d ed. New York: McGraw-Hill, 1993.

Jack, Dana Crowley. *Silencing the Self: Women and Depression*. Cambridge, Mass.: Harvard University Press, 1991; New York: HarperCollins, 1993.

Lerner, Harriet Goldhor. *Women in Therapy*. Northvale, N.J.: J. Aronson, 1988; New York: HarperCollins, 1989.

McGoldrick, Monica, Carol M. Anderson, and Froma Walsh, eds. *Women in Families: A Framework for Family Therapy*. New York: W. W. Norton, 1991.

Miles, Agnes. *The Neurotic Woman: The Role of Gender in Psychiatric Illness*. New York: New York University Press, 1991.

Mirkin, Marsha Pravder. *Women in Context: Toward a Feminist Reconstruction of Psychotherapy*. New York: Guilford Press, 1994.

Rieker, Patricia Perri, and Elaine H. Carmen, eds. *The Gender Gap in Psychotherapy: Social Realities and Psychological Processes*. New York: Plenum Press, 1984.

Rosewater, Lynne B., and Lenore Walker. *Handbook of Feminist Therapy: Women's Issues in Psychotherapy*. New York: Springer Publishing, 1985.

Russell, Denise. *Women, Madness, and Medicine*. Cambridge, Mass.: Polity Press, 1995.

Russo, Nancy Felipe, ed. *A Women's Mental Health Agenda*. Washington, D.C.: American Psychological Association, 1985.

Schuker, Eleanor, and Nadine A. Levinson, eds. *Female Psychology: A Psychoanalytic Annotated Bibliography*. Hillsdale, N.J.: Analytic Press, 1991.

Ussher Jane M., and Paula Nicholson, eds. *Gender Issues in Clinical Psychology*. New York: Routledge, 1992.

Walsh, Mary Roth. *The Psychology of Women*. New Haven, Conn.: Yale University Press, 1987.

Young, Glenell S., and Janet Sims-Wood. *The Psychology and Mental Health of Afro-American Women: A Selected Bibliography*. Temple Hills, Md.: Afro Resources, 1984.

History (United States)

Anderson, Karen. *Changing Woman: A History of Racial Ethnic Women in Modern America*. New York: Oxford University Press, 1996.

Anthony, Susan B., and Ida Husted Harper, eds. *History of Woman Suffrage*, Vol 4. 1902. Reprint, New York: Arno Press, 1969.

Baxandall, Rosalyn, Linda Gordon, and Susan Reverby. *America's Working Women: A Documentary History, 1600 to the Present*. New York: Vintage Books, 1976.

Beard, Mary Ritter. *Woman as a Force in History*. New York: Macmillan, 1945.

Brownmiller, Susan. *In Our Time: Memoir of a Revolution*. New York: Delacorte, 1999.

Buhle, Mari Jo. *Women and American Socialism, 1870–1920*. Urbana: University of Illinois Press, 1981.

Camhi, Jane Jerome. *Women Against Women: American Anti-Suffragism, 1880–1920*. Brooklyn, N.Y.: Carlson Publishing, 1994.

Catt, Carrie Chapman, and Nettie Rogers Schuler. *Woman Suffrage and Politics: The Inner Story of the Suffrage Movement*. New York: Charles Scribner's Sons, 1923.

Cott, Nancy. *The Grounding of Modern Feminism*. New Haven, Conn.: Yale University Press, 1987.

Crawford, Vicki L., Jacqueline Anne Rouse, and Barbara Woods, eds. *Women in the Civil Rights Movement: Trailblazers and Torchbearers, 1941–1965*. Brooklyn, N.Y.: Carlson Publishing, 1990.

Cullen-DuPont, Kathryn, ed. *The Encyclopedia of Women's History in America*. New York: Facts On File, 1996.

Degler, Carl. *At Odds: Women and the Family in America*. New York: Oxford University Press, 1981.

DuBois, Ellen Carol, and Vicki L. Ruiz, eds. *Unequal Sisters: A Multicultural Reader in U.S. Women's History*. New York: Routledge, 1994.

Evans, Sara M. *Born for Liberty: A History of Women in America*. New York: The Free Press, 1989.

———. *Personal Politics: The Roots of Women's Liberation in the Civil Rights Movement and the New Left*. New York: Random House, 1980.

Faderman, Lillian, and John Radziewicz, eds. *To Believe in Women: What Lesbians Have Done for America, a History*. New York and Boston: Houghton Mifflin, 1999.

Flexner, Eleanor, and Ellen Fitzpatrick. *Century of Struggle: The Woman's Rights Movement in the United States*. Cambridge, Mass.: Belknap Press of Harvard University Press, 1996.

Giddings, Paula *When and Where I Enter: The Impact of Black Women on Race and Sex in America*. New York: William Morrow, 1996.

Giele, Janet Zollinger. *Two Paths to Women's Equality*. Old Tappan, N.J.: Macmillan Library Reference, 1995.

Glenn, Evelyn Nakano. *Issei, Nisei, War Bride: Three Generations of Japanese-American Women in Domestic Service*. Philadelphia: Temple University Press, 1986.

Gordon, Ann D. *African American Women and the Vote, 1837–1965*. Amherst: University of Massachusetts Press, 1997.

Harper, Ida Husted, ed. *History of Woman Suffrage*. Vols. 5 & 6. New York: National American Woman Suffrage Association, 1922.

Hartmann, Susan M. *From Margin to Mainstream: American Women and Politics Since 1860.* New York: Alfred A. Knopf, 1989.

Harvey, Anna L. *Votes Without Leverage: Women in American Electoral Politics, 1920–1970.* New York: Cambridge University Press, 1998.

Hine, Darlene Clark, ed. *Black Women in United States History.* 16 vols. Brooklyn, N.Y.: Carlson Publishing, 1990.

Hine, Darlene Clark, Elsa Barkley Brown, and Rosalyn Terborg-Penn, eds. 2 vols. *Black Women in America: An Historical Encyclopedia.* Brooklyn, N.Y.: Carlson Publishing, 1993; Bloomington: Indiana University Press, 1994.

Hyman, Paula, ed. *Jewish Women in America: An Historical Encyclopedia.* 2 vols. New York: Routledge, 1998.

Jones, J. *Labor of Love, Labor of Sorrow: Black Women, Work, and the Family from Slavery to the Present.* New York: Basic Books, 1985.

Katz, Esther, and Anita Rapone, eds. *Women's Experience in America: An Historical Anthology.* New Brunswick, N.J.: Transaction Books, 1980.

Kerber, Linda, and Jane Sherron De Hart. *Women's America: Refocusing the Past,* 4th ed. New York: Oxford University Press, 1995.

Kerber, Linda K., Alice Kessler-Harris, and Kathryn Kish Sklar, eds. *U.S. History as Women's History.* Chapel Hill: University of North Carolina Press, 1995.

Kessler-Harris, Alice. *Out to Work: A History of Wage-Earning Women in the U.S.* New York: Oxford University Press, 1982.

Kinnard, Cynthia D. *Antifeminism in America: An Annotated Bibliography.* Boston: G. K. Hall, 1986.

Langley, Winston E., and Vivian C. Fox, eds. *Women's Rights in the United States: A Documentary History.* Westport, Conn.: Greenwood Press, 1994.

Lerner, Gerda. *Black Women in White America: A Documentary History.* New York: Vintage Books, 1973.

Litoff, J. B. *American Midwives: 1860 to the Present.* Westport, Conn.: Greenwood Press, 1978.

Lunardini, Christine A. *From Equal Suffrage to Equal Rights: Alice Paul and the National Woman's Party, 1910–1928.* New York and London: New York University Press, 1986.

Marshall, Susan E. *Splintered Sisterhood: Gender and Class in the Campaign Against Woman Suffrage.* Madison: University of Wisconsin Press, 1997.

O'Neill, William L. *Everyone Was Brave: A History of Feminism in America.* Chicago: Quadrangle Books, 1971.

Orleck, Annelise. *Common Sense and a Little Fire: Women and Working Class Politics in the United States, 1900–1965.* Chapel Hill: University of North Carolina Press, 1995.

Osborne, Martha Lee, ed. *Woman in Western Thought.* New York: Random House, 1979.

Roosevelt, Eleanor, and Lorena Hickok. *Ladies of Courage.* New York: G.P. Putnam's Sons, 1954.

Rothman, Sheila M. *Woman's Proper Place: A History of Changing Ideals and Practices, 1870 to the Present.* New York: Basic Books, 1978.

Rupp, Leila J., and Verta Taylor. *Survival in the Doldrums: The American Women's Rights Movement, 1945 to the 1960s.* New York: Oxford University Press, 1987; Columbus: Ohio State University Press, 1990.

Ryan, Mary P. *Womanhood in America: From Colonial Times to the Present.* New York: New Viewpoints, 1979.

Schneir, Miriam, ed. *Feminism in Our Time: The Essential Writings, World War II to the Present.* New York: Vintage Books, 1994.

Scott, Anne F., and Andrew M. Scott. *One Half the People: The Fight for Woman Suffrage.* Philadelphia: J. B. Lippincott, 1975.

Smith, Jessie Carney, ed. *Notable Black American Women.* Detroit, Mich.: Gale Research, 1992.

Solomon, Barbara Miller. *In the Company of Educated Women.* New Haven, Conn.: Yale University Press, 1985.

Solomon, Irvin D. *Feminism and Black Activism in Contemporary America: An Ideological Assessment.* Westport, Conn.: Greenwood Press, 1989.

Stanton, Elizabeth Cady. *Eighty Years and More.* New York: European Publishing, 1898.

Stanton, Elizabeth Cady, Susan B. Anthony, and Matilda Joselyn Gage, eds. *History of Woman Suffrage,* Vols. 1–3. 1881–1886. Reprint, New York: Arno Press, 1969.

Steinem, Gloria. *The Reader's Companion to U.S. Women's History.* Boston: Houghton Mifflin, 1999.

Sterling, Dorothy, ed. *We Are Your Sisters: Black Women in the Nineteenth Century.* New York: W. W. Norton, 1984.

Strauss, Sylvia. *Traitors to the Masculine Cause: The Men's Campaigns for Women's Rights.* Westport, Conn.: Greenwood Press, 1982.

Terborg-Penn, Rosalyn. *African American Women in the Struggle for the Vote, 1850–1920.* Bloomington: Indiana University Press, 1998.

Venet, Wendy H. *Neither Ballots Nor Bullets: Women Abolitionists and Emancipation During the Civil War.* Charlottesville: University Press of Virginia, 1991.

Ware, Susan. *Beyond Suffrage: Women in the New Deal.* Cambridge, Mass.: Harvard University Press, 1981.

Weatherford, Doris. *A History of the American Suffragist Movement.* Denver, Colo.: ABC-CLIO, 1998.

———. *Milestones: A Chronology of American Women's History.* New York: Facts On File, 1997.

Wertheimer, Barbara Mayer. *We Were There: The Story of Working Women in America.* New York: Pantheon Books, 1977.

Yellin, Jean F., and John C. Van Horne. *The Abolitionist Sisterhood: Women's Political Culture in Antebellum America.* Ithaca, N.Y.: Cornell University Press, 1994.

History (World)

Ackelsberg, Martha A. *Free Women of Spain: Anarchism and the Struggle for the Emancipation of Women.* Bloomington: Indiana University Press, 1991.

Agrippa, Henricus Cornelius. *Declamation on the Nobility and Preeminence of the Female Sex.* Trans. and ed. by Albert Rabil, Jr. Chicago: University of Chicago Press, 1996.

Ahmed, Leila. a *Border Passage: From Cairo to America—A Woman's Journey.* New York: Farrar, Straus, & Giroux, 1999.

———. *Women and Gender in Islam: Historical Roots of a Modern Debate.* New Haven, Conn.: Yale University Press, 1993.

Alexander, Gemma, ed. *The Mammoth Book of Heroic and Outrageous Women.* New York: Carroll and Graf Publishers, 1999.

Alvarez, Sonia E. *Engendering Democracy in Brazil: Women's Movements in Transition Politics.* Princeton, N.J.: Princeton University Press, 1990.

Ashby, Ruth, and Deborah G. Ohrn, eds. *Herstory: Women Who Changed the World.* New York: Viking Penguin, 1995.

Badran, Margot. *Feminists, Islam, and Nation: Gender and the Making of Modern Egypt.* Princeton, N.J.: Princeton University Press, 1995.

Basu, Amrita, ed. *The Challenge of Local Feminisms: Women's Movements in Global Perspective.* Boulder, Colo.: Westview Press, 1995.

Beckles, H. McD. *Natural Rebels: A Social History of Enslaved Women in Barbados.* London: Zed Books, 1989.

Beckman, Peter, and Francine D'Amico. *Women, Gender, and World Politics: Perspectives, Policies, and Prospects.* Westport, Conn.: Bergin and Garvey, 1994.

———. *Women in World Politics: An Introduction.* Westport, Conn.: Bergin and Garvey, 1996.

Birnbaum, Lucia Chiavola. *Liberazione Della Donna: Feminism in Italy.* Middletown, Conn.: Wesleyan University Press, 1986.

Brosius, Maria. *Women in Ancient Persia, 559–331 B.C.* New York: Oxford University Press, 1998.

Buckley, Mary, ed. *Perestroika and Soviet Women.* New York: Cambridge University Press, 1992.

Burton, Antoinette M. *Burdens of History: British Feminists, Indian Women, and Imperial Culture, 1865–1915.* Chapel Hill: University of North Carolina Press, 1994.

Carlson, Marifran. *Feminismo!: The Woman's Movement in Argentina from Its Beginnings to Eva Peron.* Chicago: Academy Chicago Publications, 1988.

Caudhuri, Najama, and Barbara J. Nelson, eds. *Women and Politics Worldwide.* New Haven, Conn.: Yale University Press, 1994.

Cook, Rebecca J. *Human Rights of Women: National and International Perspectives.* Philadelphia: University of Pennsylvania Press, 1994.

Duby, Georges, and Genevieve Fraisse, eds. *A History of Women in the West: Emerging Feminism from Revolution to World War.* Vol. 4. Cambridge, Mass.: Belknap Press of Harvard University Press, 1995.

Duchen, Claire. *Feminism in France: From May '68 to Mitterand.* Boston: Routledge and Kegan Paul, 1986.

Fisher, Jo. *Out of the Shadows: Women, Resistance, and Politics in South America.* New York: Monthly Review Press, 1993.

Hufton, Olwen. *The Prospect Before Her: A History of Women in Western Europe, 1500–1800.* New York: Random House, 1998

Hutson, Lorna. *Feminism and Renaissance Studies.* New York: Oxford University Press, 1999.

Jayawardena, Kumari. *Feminism and Nationalism in the Third World.* London: Zed Books, 1986.

Kimball, Michelle. *Muslim Women Throughout the World: A Bibliography.* Boulder, Colo.: Lynne Rienner, 1996.

Landes, J. B. *Women in the Public Sphere: In the Age of the French Revolution.* Ithaca, N.Y.: Cornell University Press, 1988.

Leitinger, Ilse A., ed. *The Costa Rican Women's Movement: A Reader.* Pittsburgh, Penn.: University of Pittsburgh Press, 1997.

Lezreg, Marnia. *The Eloquence of Silence: Algerian Women in Question.* New York: Routledge, 1994.

Morgan, Robin, ed. *Sisterhood Is Global: The International Women's Movement Anthology.* New York: Feminist Press at City University of New York, 1996.

Peters, Julie, and Andrea Wolper. *Women's Rights, Human Rights: International Feminist Perspectives.* New York: Routledge, 1995.

Pugh, Martin. *Women and the Women's Movement in Britain.* New York: Marlowe, 1994.

Radcliffe, Sarah A., and Sallie Westwood, eds. *"Viva": Women and Popular Protest in Latin America.* New York: Routledge, 1993.

Randall, Margaret. *Sandino's Daughters Revisited: Feminism in Nicaragua.* New Brunswick, N.J.: Rutgers University Press, 1994.

Rodriguez, Jeanette. *Our Lady of Guadalupe: Faith and Empowerment Among Mexican-American Women.* Austin: University of Texas Press, 1994.

Sievers, Sharon L. *Flowers in Salt: The Beginnings of Feminist Consciousness in Modern Japan.* Stanford, Calif.: Stanford University Press, 1983.

Smith, Harold L., ed. *British Feminism in the Twentieth Century.* Amherst: University of Massachusetts Press, 1990.

Stites, Richard. *The Women's Liberation Movement in Russia: Feminism, Nihilism, and Bolshevism, 1860–1930.* Princeton, N.J.: Princeton University Press, 1978.

Language

Bate, Barbara, and Judy Bowker. *Communication and the Sexes.* Prospect Heights, Ill.: Waveland Press, 1997.

Cameron, Deborah. *Feminism and Linguistic Theory.* New York: St. Martin's Press, 1992.

———. *Feminist Critique of Language: A Reader.* 2d ed. New York: Routledge, 1998.

Coates, Jennifer. *Women, Men, and Language: A Sociolinguistic Account of Sex Differences in Language.* 2d ed. White Plains, N.Y.: Longman Publishing, 1993.

———, ed. *Language and Gender: A Reader.* Malden, Mass.: Blackwell Publishers, 1998.

Crawford, Mary. *Talking Difference: On Gender and Language.* Thousand Oaks, Calif.: Sage Publications, 1995.

Doyle, Margaret. *The A-Z of Non-Sexist Language.* London: Women's Press, 1997.

Frank, Francine Wattman. *Language, Gender, and Professional Writing: Theoretical Approaches and Guidelines for Nonsexist Usage.* New York: Commission on the Status of Women in the Profession, Modern Language Association of America, 1989.

Glenn, Cheryl. *Rhetoric Retold: Regendering the Tradition from Antiquity Through the Renaissance.* Carbondale: Southern Illinois University Press, 1997.

Hall, Kira. *Gender Articulated: Language and the Socially Constructed Self.* New York: Routledge, 1995.

Hendricks, Christina, ed. *Language and Liberation: Feminism, Philosophy, and Language.* Albany: State University of New York Press, 1999.

Kalbfleisch, Pamela J., and Michael J. Cody, eds. *Gender, Power, and Communication in Human Relationships.* Hillsdale, N.J.: Lawrence Erlbaum, 1995.

Key, Mary Ritchie. *Male/Female Language.* Lanham, Md.: Scarecrow Press, 1996.

Kotthoff, Helga, ed. *Communicating Gender in Context.* Philadelphia: John Benjamins North America, 1997.

Livia, Anna, and Kira Hall, eds. *Queerly Phrased: Language, Gender, and Sexuality.* New York: Oxford University Press, 1997.

Lorraine, Tamsin E. *Gender, Identity, and the Production of Meaning.* Boulder, Colo.: Westview Press, 1990.

Mariniello, Silvestra. *Gendered Agents: Women and Institutional Knowledge.* Durham, N.C.: Duke University Press, 1998.

McConnell-Ginet, Sally, Ruth Borker, and Nelly Furman, eds. *Women and Language in Literature and Society.* New York: Praeger Publishers, 1980.

Miller, Susan. *Assuming the Positions: Cultural Pedagogy and the Politics of Commonplace Writing.* Pittsburgh, Penn.: University of Pittsburgh Press, 1997.

Mills, Sara. *Feminist Stylistics.* New York: Routledge, 1995.

Penfield, Joyce, ed. *Women and Language in Transition.* Albany: State University of New York Press, 1987.

Perry, Linda A.M., Lynn H. Turner, and Helen M. Sterk, eds. *Constructing and Reconstructing Gender: The Links Among Communication, Language, and Gender.* Albany: State University of New York Press, 1992.

Poynton, Cate. *Language and Gender: Making the Difference.* New York: St. Martin's Press, 1995.

Roman, Camille, Suzanne Juhasz, and Cristanne Miller, eds. *The Women and Language Debate: A Sourcebook.* New Brunswick, N.J.: Rutgers University Press, 1994.

Tannen, Deborah. *Gender and Discourse.* New York: Oxford University Press, 1994.

———. *You Just Don't Understand: Men and Women in Conversation.* New York: William Morrow, 1990.

———, ed. *Gender and Conversational Interaction.* New York: Oxford University Press, 1994.

Taylor, Jill M. *Between Voice and Silence: Women and Girls, Race and Relationship.* Cambridge, Mass.: Harvard University Press, 1997.

Valentine, Carol Ann, and Nancy Hoar, eds. *Women and Communicative Power: Theory, Research, and Practice.* Annandale, Va.: Speech Communication Association, 1988.

Law

Bartlett, Katharine T., and Angela P. Harris. *Gender and Law: Theory, Doctrine, Commentary.* 2d ed. New York: Panel Publishers, 1998.

Berry, Dawn B. *The 50 Most Influential Women in Law.* 2d ed. Los Angeles: Lowell House, 1997.

Boumil, Marcia M., and Stephen C. Hicks. *Women and the Law.* Littleton, Colo.: Fred B. Rothman, 1992.

Chan, Anja A. *Women and Sexual Harassment: A Guide to the Legal Protections of Title VII and the Hostile Environment Claim.* New York: Haworth Press, 1994.

Cornell, Drucilla. *At the Heart of Freedom: Feminism, Sex, and Equality.* Princeton, N.J.: Princeton University Press, 1998.

DeCoste, F. C., K. M. Munro and Lillian MacPherson. *Feminist Legal Literature: An Annotated Bibliography.* New York: Garland Publishing, 1991.

Drachman, Virginia G. *Sisters in Law: Women Lawyers in Modern American History.* Cambridge, Mass.: Harvard University Press, 1998.

Epstein, Cynthia F. *Women in Law.* 2d ed. Urbana: University of Illinois Press, 1993.

Fineman, Martha A., and Isabelle Karpin, eds. *Mothers in Law: Feminist Theory and the Legal Regulation of Motherhood*. New York: Columbia University Press, 1995.

Fineman, Martha A., and Martha T. McCluskey. *Feminism, Media, and the Law*. New York: Oxford University Press, 1997.

Frug, Mary J. *Postmodern Legal Feminism*. New York: Routledge, 1992.

Gillespie, Cynthia K. *Justifiable Homicide: Battered Women, Self-Defense, and the Law*. Columbus: Ohio State University Press, 1990.

Goldstein, Leslie F., ed. *Feminist Jurisprudence: The Difference Debate*. Lanham, Md.: Rowman and Littlefield, 1992.

Guinier, Lani, Michelle Fine, and Jane Balin, eds. *Becoming Gentlemen: Women, Law School, and Institutional Change*. Boston: Beacon Press, 1998.

Heinzelman, Susan S., and Zipporah Wiseman, eds. *Representing Women: Law, Literature, and Feminism*. Durham, N.C.: Duke University Press, 1994.

Merlo, Alida V. *Women, Law, and Social Control*. Englewood Cliffs, N.J.: Prentice Hall, 1994.

Olsen, Frances, ed. *Feminist Legal Theory*. 2 vols. Vol. 1, *Foundations and Outlooks*; Vol. 2, *Positioning Feminist Theory Within the Law*. New York: New York University Press, 1995.

Robson, Ruthann. *Sappho Goes to Law School: Fragments in Lesbian Legal Theory*. New York: Columbia University Press, 1998.

St. Joan, Jacqueline, and Annette B. McElhiney, eds. *Beyond Portia: Women, Law, and Literature in the United States*. Boston: Northeastern University Press, 1997.

Smart, Carol. *Feminism and the Power of Law*. New York: Routledge, 1989.

Smith, J. Clay. *Rebels in Law: Voices in History of Black Women Lawyers*. Ann Arbor: University of Michigan Press, 1998.

Smith, Patricia, ed. *Feminist Jurisprudence*. New York and Oxford: Oxford University Press, 1993.

Weisberg, D. Kelly, ed. *Women and the Law: The Social Historical Perspective*. Vol. 1, *Woman and the Criminal Law*; Vol. 2, *Property, Family, and the Legal Profession*. Cambridge, Mass.: Schenkman Books, 1982.

Parenting and Family

Aglietti, Susan, ed. *Filtered Images: Women Remembering Their Grandmothers*. Orinda, Calif.: Vintage '45 Press, 1992.

Allen, Katherine R. *Single Women/Family Ties: Life Histories of Older Women*. Newbury Park, Calif.: Sage Publications, 1989.

Anderson, Carol M., Monica McGoldrick, and Froma Walsh, eds. *Women in Families: A Framework for Family Therapy*. New York: W. W. Norton, 1989.

Baber, Kristine M., and Katherine R. Allen. *Women and Families: Feminist Reconstructions*. New York: Guilford Press, 1992.

Brody, Elaine M. *Women in the Middle: Their Parent-Care Years*. New York: Springer Publishing, 1990.

Coontz, Stephanie. *The Way We Really Are: Coming to Terms with America's Changing Families*. New York: Basic Books, 1997.

Delphy, Christine, and Diana Leonard. *Familiar Exploitation: A New Analysis of Marriage in Contemporary Western Societies*. Cambridge, Mass.: Polity Press, 1992.

DeVault, Marjorie, and Catharine L. Stimpson. *Feeding the Family: The Social Organization of Caring As Gendered Work*. Chicago: University of Chicago Press, 1994.

Dornsbusch, Sanford M., and Myra H. Strober, eds. *Feminism, Children, and the New Families*. New York: Guilford Press, 1988.

Fineman, Martha Albertson. *The Neutered Mother, the Sexual Family, and Other Twentieth Century Tragedies*. New York: Routledge, 1995.

Franklin, Donna L. *Ensuring Inequality: The Structural Transformation of the African American Family*. New York: Oxford University Press, 1997.

Friedan, Betty, and Brigid O'Farrell. *Beyond Gender: The New Politics of Work and Family*. Baltimore, Md.: Johns Hopkins University Press, 1997.

Gerson, Kathleen. *Hard Choices: How Women Decide About Work, Career, and Motherhood*. Berkeley: University of California Press, 1985.

Hertz, Rosanna. *More Equal Than Others: Women and Men in Dual-Career Marriages*. Berkeley: University of California Press, 1986.

Hochschild, Arlie. *The Time Bind: When Work Becomes Home and Home Becomes Work*. New York: Henry Holt, 1997.

Johnston, Carolyn. *Sexual Power: Feminism and the Family in America*. Tuscaloosa: University of Alabama Press, 1992.

Ludtke, Melissa. *On Our Own: Unmarried Motherhood in America*. New York: Random House, 1997.

McMahon, Martha. *Engendering Motherhood: Identity and Self-Transformation in Women's Lives*. New York: Guilford Press, 1995.

Mulroy, Elizabeth A. *The New Uprooted: Single Mothers in Urban Life*. Westport, Conn.: Auburn House, 1995.

Potuchek, Jean L. *Who Supports the Family: Gender and Breadwinning in Dual-Earner Marriages*. Stanford, Calif.: Stanford University Press, 1997.

Rothman, Barbara Katz. *Recreating Motherhood: Ideology and Technology in a Patriarchal Society*. New York: W. W. Norton, 1990.

Seligman, Milton, and Rosalyn B. Darling. *Ordinary Families, Special Children: A Systems Approach to Childhood Disability*. 2d ed. New York: Guilford Press, 1997.

Shelton, Beth Anne. *Women, Men, and Time: Gender Differences in Paid Work, Housework, and Leisure.* Westport, Conn.: Greenwood Press, 1992.

Sidel, Ruth. *Women and Children Last.* New York: Viking Penguin, 1986.

Sollie, Donna L., and Leigh A. Leslie, eds. *Gender, Families, and Close Relationships: Feminist Research Journeys.* Thousand Oaks, Calif.: Sage Publications, 1994.

Vannoy-Hiller, Dana, and William W. Philliber. *Equal Partners: Successful Women in Marriage.* Newbury Park, Calif.: Sage Publications, 1989.

Politics (United States)

Bacchi, Carol L. *The Politics of Affirmative Action: Women, Equality, and Category Politics.* Newbury Park, Calif.: Sage Publications, 1996.

Bashevkin, Sylvia. *Women on the Defensive: Living Through Conservative Times.* Chicago: University of Chicago Press, 1998.

Beard, Patricia. *Growing Up Republican.* New York: HarperCollins, 1996.

Boxer, Barbara. *Strangers in the Senate: Politics and the New Revolution of Women in America.* Washington, D.C.: National Press Books, 1993.

Braden, Maria. *Women Politicians and the Media.* Lexington: University Press of Kentucky, 1996.

Brenner, Johanna, and Yesim Arat, eds. *Rethinking the Political.* Chicago: University of Chicago Press, 1995.

Cohen, Cathy, Kathleen B. Jones, and Joan C. Tronto, eds. *Women Transforming Politics: An Alternative Reader.* New York: New York University Press, 1997.

Darcy, R., Susan Welch, and Janet Clark. *Women, Elections, and Representation.* Rev. ed. Lincoln: University of Nebraska Press, 1994.

Duerst-Lahti, Georgia, and Rita M. Kelly. *Gender Power, Leadership, and Governance.* Ann Arbor: University of Michigan Press, 1995.

Earnshaw, Doris, and Maria E. Raymond, eds. *American Women Speak: Voices of American Women in Public Life.* Davis, Calif.: Alta Vista Press, 1996.

Flammang, Janet A. *Women's Political Voice: How Women Are Transforming the Practice and Study of Politics.* Philadelphia: Temple University Press, 1997.

Foerstel, Karen, and Herbert N. Foerstel. *Climbing the Hill: Gender Conflict in Congress.* Westport, Conn.: Greenwood Publishing, 1996.

Gertzog, Irwin N. *Congressional Women: Their Recruitment, Integration, and Behavior.* Westport, Conn.: Greenwood Publishing, 1995.

Gill, Laverne M. *African American Women in Congress.* New Brunswick, N.J.: Rutgers University Press, 1997.

Githens, Marianne, Pippa Norris, and Joni Lovenduski, eds. *Different Roles, Different Voices: Women and Politics in the United States and Europe.* New York: HarperCollins College, 1994.

Handlin, Amy H. *Whatever Happened to the Year of the Woman?: Why Women Aren't Making It to the Top in Politics.* Denver, Colo.: Arden Press, 1998.

Hewitt, Nancy A., and Suzanne Liebsock. *Visible Women: New Essays on American Activism.* Urbana: University of Illinois Press, 1993.

Hirschmann, Nancy J., and Christine DiStefano. *Revisioning the Political: Feminist Reconstructions of Traditional Concepts in Western Political Theory.* Boulder, Colo.: Westview Press, 1996.

Jeffreys-Jones, Rhodri. *Changing Differences: Women and the Shaping of American Foreign Policy, 1917–1994.* New Brunswick, N.J.: Rutgers University Press, 1995.

Kahn, Kim. *The Political Consequences of Being a Woman: How Stereotypes Influence the Conduct and Consequences of Political Campaigns.* New York: Columbia University Press, 1996.

Karl, Marilee. *Women and the Political Process.* Atlantic Highlands, N.J.: Humanities Press International, 1995.

McClintock, Anne, Aamir Mufti, and Ella Shohat, eds. *Dangerous Liaisons: Gender, Nation, and Postcolonial Perspectives.* Minneapolis: University of Minnesota Press, 1997.

McGlen, Nancy E., and Karen O'Connor. *Women, Politics, and American Society.* 2d ed. Paramus, N.J.: Prentice Hall, 1998.

Martin, Mary. *Almanac of Women and Minorities in American Politics.* Boulder, Colo.: Westview Press 1998.

Melich, Tanya. *The Republican War Against Women: An Insider's Report from Behind the Lines.* Rev. ed. New York: Bantam Books, 1998.

Meyer, Cheryl. *The Wandering Uterus: Politics and the Reproductive Rights of Women.* New York: New York University Press, 1997.

Nelson, Barbara J., and Najma Chowdhury. *Women and Politics Worldwide.* New Haven, Conn.: Yale University Press, 1994.

Neuman, Nancy M. *A Voice of Our Own: Leading American Women Celebrate the Right to Vote.* San Francisco: Jossey-Bass, 1996.

Norris, Pippa. *Women, Media, and Politics.* New York, Oxford University Press, 1996.

Phillips, Anne. *The Politics of Presence: Democracy and Group Representation.* New York: Oxford University Press, 1995.

Rule, Wilma, and Joseph F. Zimmerman, eds. *Electoral Systems in Comparative Perspective: Their Impact on Women and Minorities.* Westport, Conn.: Greenwood Press, 1994.

Sainsbury, Diane, ed. *Gendering Welfare States: Combining Insights of Feminist and Mainstream Research.* Thousand Oaks, Calif.: Sage Publications, 1994.

Schultz, Jeffrey D., and George Kurian. *Encyclopedia of Women in American Politics*. Phoenix, Ariz.: Oryx Press, 1998.

Sullivan, Patricia A., and Lynn H. Turner. *From the Margins to the Center: Contemporary Women and Political Communication.* Westport, Conn.: Praeger Publishers, 1996.

Thomas, Sue, and Clyde Wilcox, eds. *Women and Elective Office: Past, Present, and Future*. New York: Oxford University Press, 1998.

Towery, Matt. *Powerchicks: How Women Will Dominate America.* Oakland, Calif.: Bookpeople, 1998.

Witt, Linda, Karen M. Paget, and Glenna Matthews. *Running As a Woman: Gender and Power in American Politics*. New York: Simon & Schuster, 1995.

Zepatos, Thalia, and Elizabeth Kaufman. *Women for a Change: A Grassroots Guide to Activism and Politics*. New York: Facts On File, 1995.

Politics (World)

Afkhami, Mahnaz, and Erika Friedl. *Muslim Women and the Politics of Participation: Implementing the Beijing Platform.* Syracuse, N.Y.: Syracuse University Press, 1997.

Ashfar, Haleh. *Women and Politics in the Third World*. New York: Routledge, 1996.

Al-Mugni, Haya. *Women in Kuwait: The Politics of Gender.* London: Saqi Books, 1993.

Aretxaga, Begona. *Shattering Silence: Women, Nationalism, and Political Subjectivity in Northern Ireland*. Princeton, N.J.: Princeton University Press, 1997.

Basu, Amrita, and Patricia Jeffery. *Appropriating Gender: Women's Agency, the State, and Politicized Religion in South Asia.* New York: Routledge, 1997.

Beckman, Peter R., and Francine D'Amico, eds. *Women, Gender, and World Politics: Perspectives, Policies, and Prospects.* Westport, Conn.: Bergin and Garvey, 1994.

Brill, Alida. *A Rising Public Voice: Women in Politics Worldwide.* New York: Feminist Press, 1995.

Bush, Julia. *Organizing for Empire: Edwardian Ladies and Imperial Power*. Herndon, Va.: Books International, 1998.

Carter, Sarah A. *Capturing Women: The Manipulation of Cultural Imagery in Canada's Prairie West*. Buffalo, N.Y.: University of Toronto Press, 1997.

Charlton, S. E., J. Everett, and K. Staudt, eds. *Women, the State, and Development*. Albany, N.Y.: State University of New York Press, 1989.

Chen, M. *A Quiet Revolution: Women in Transition in Rural Bangladesh.* Cambridge, Mass.: Schenkman Books, 1983

D'Amico, Francine, and Peter R. Beckman. *Women in World Politics: An Introduction*. Westport, Conn.: Bergin and Garvey, 1995.

Dandavati, Annie G. *The Women's Movement and the Transition to Democracy in Chile*. New York: Peter Lang Publishing, 1996.

Dore, Elizabeth, ed. *Gender Politics in Latin America: Debates in Theory and Practice*. New York: Monthly Review Press, 1997.

Eisenstein, Hester. *Inside Agitators: Australian Femocrats and the State.* Philadelphia: Temple University Press, 1996.

Elman, Amy, ed. *Sexual Politics and the European Union: The New Feminist Challenge.* Providence, R.I.: Berghahn Books, 1996.

Emmett, Ayala H. *Our Sisters' Promised Land: Women, Politics, and Israeli-Palestinian Coexistence*. Ann Arbor: University of Michigan Press, 1996.

Enloe, Cynthia. *Bananas, Beaches, and Bases: Making Feminist Sense of International Politics*. Berkeley: University of California Press, 1990.

French, John D., and Daniel James. *The Gendered Worlds of Latin American Women Workers: From Household and Factory to the Union Hall and Ballot Box*. Durham, N.C.: Duke University Press, 1997.

Galligan, Yvonne. *Women and Politics in Contemporary Ireland: From the Margins to the Mainstream*. Herndon, Va.: Books International, 1998.

Gardiner, Frances, ed. *Sex Equality Policy in Western Europe*. New York: Routledge, 1997.

Grant, Rebecca, and Kathleen Newland, eds. *Gender and International Relations*. Bloomington: Indiana University Press, 1991.

Hale, Sondra. *Gender Politics in Sudan: Islamism, Socialism, and the State*. Boulder, Colo.: Westview Press, 1996.

Jaquette, J., ed. *The Women's Movement in Latin America.* Boston: Unwin Hyman, 1989.

Jeansonne, Glen. *Women of the Far Right: The Mothers' Movement and World War II*. Chicago: University of Chicago Press, 1996.

Jharta, Bhawana. *Women and Politics in India*. Columbia, Mo.: South Asia Books, 1996.

Johnson-Odim, Cheryl, and Nina E. Mba. *For Women and the Nation: Fumilayo Ransome-Kuti of Nigeria*. Champaign: University of Illinois Press, 1997.

Kandiyoti, Deniz, ed. *Gendering the Middle East: Emerging Perspectives*. Syracuse, N.Y.: Syracuse University Press, 1996.

Kawar, Amal. *Daughters of Palestine: Leading Women of the Palestinian National Movement*. Albany: State University of New York Press, 1996.

Kim, Hyun Sook, ed. *Dangerous Women: Gender and Korean Nationalism*. New York: Routledge, 1997.

Maloof, Judy, ed. *Voices of Resistance: Testimonies of Cuban and Chilean Women*. Lexington: University Press of Kentucky, 1999.

Mayer, Ann Elizabeth. *Islam and Human Rights: Tradition and Politics*. Boulder, Colo.: Westview Press, 1995.

Mayer, Tamar, ed. *Women and the Israeli Occupation: The Politics of Change*. New York: Routledge, 1994.

Mernissi, F. *Beyond the Veil: Male and Female Dynamics in Modern Muslim Society*. Cambridge, Mass.: Schenkman Books, 1975. Revised ed. Bloomington: Indiana University Press, 1987.

Mikell, Gwendolyn, ed. *African Feminism: The Politics of Survival in Sub-Saharan Africa*. Philadelphia: University of Pennsylvania Press, 1997.

Monk, Janice, and Maria Dolors, eds. *Women of the European Union: The Politics of Work and Daily Life*. New York: Routledge, 1995.

Narayan, Uma. *Dislocating Cultures: Third World Feminism and the Politics of Knowledge*. New York: Routledge, 1997.

Nelson, Barbara J., and Najma Chowdhury, eds. *Women and Politics Worldwide*. New Haven, Conn.: Yale University Press, 1994.

Oyewumi, Oyeronke, ed. *African Women and Feminism: Reflecting on the Politics of Sisterhood*. Lawrenceville, N.J.: Africa World Press, 1997.

Pettman, Jan J. *Worlding Women: Feminist International Politics*. New York: Routledge, 1996.

Pietila, Hilkka, and Jeanne Vickers. *Making Women Matter: The Role of the United Nations*. London: Zed Books, 1996.

Reynolds, Sian. *France Between the Wars: Gender and Politics*. New York: Routledge, 1996.

Rule, Wilma, and Norma Noonan, eds. *Russian Women in Politics and Society*. Westport, Conn.: Greenwood Publishing, 1996.

Rupp, Leila. *Worlds of Women: The Making of an International Women's Movement*. Princeton, N.J.: Princeton University Press, 1998.

Sales, Rosemary. *Women Divided: Gender, Religion, and Politics in Northern Ireland*. New York: Routledge, 1997.

Sarkar, Tanika, and Urvashi Butalia, eds. *Women and Right-Wing Movements: Indian Experiences*. London: Zed Books, 1996.

Scott, Joan W., Cora Kaplan, and Debra Keates, eds. *Transitions Environments Translations: International Feminisms in Contemporary Politics*. New York: Routledge, 1997.

Staudt, Kathleen A. *Women, International Development, and Politics: The Bureaucratic Mire*. Philadelphia: Temple University Press, 1997.

Steans, Jill. *Gender and International Relations*. New Brunswick, N.J.: Rutgers University Press, 1998.

Stichter, Sharon B., and Jean Hay. *African Women South of the Sahara*. 2d ed. White Plains, N.Y.: Longman Publishing, 1996.

Tickner, J. Ann. *Gender in International Relations: Feminist Perspectives on Achieving Global Security*. New York: Columbia University Press, 1993.

Waylen, Georgina. *Gender in Third World Politics*. Boulder, Colo.: Lynne Rienner Publishers, 1995.

Winslow, Anne, ed. *Women, Politics, and the United Nations*. Westport, Conn.: Greenwood Publishing, 1995.

Wood, Elizabeth A. *The Baba and the Comrade: Gender and Politics in Revolutionary Russia*. Bloomington: Indiana University Press, 1997.

Reference

Barrett, Jacqueline K., ed. *Encyclopedia of Women's Associations Worldwide: A Guide to Over 3,400 National and Multinational Nonprofit Women's and Women-Related Organizations*. Detroit, Mich.: Gale Research, 1998.

Davidson, Cathy N., and Linda Wagner-Martin, eds. *Oxford Companion to Women's Writing in the United States*. New York: Oxford University Press, 1995.

Fast, Timothy, and Cathy Carroll Fast. *The Women's Atlas of the United States*. Rev. ed. New York: Facts On File, 1995.

Fister, Barbara. *Third World Women's Literatures: A Dictionary and Guide to Materials in English*. Westport, Conn.: Greenwood Press, 1995.

Harlan, Judith. *Feminism: A Reference Handbook*. Santa Barbara, Calif.: ABC-CLIO, 1998.

Hauser, Barbara R., with Julie A. Tigges, eds. *Women's Legal Guide*. Golden, Colo.: Fulcrum, 1996.

Humm, Maggie. *The Dictionary of Feminist Theory*. Columbus: Ohio State University Press, 1995.

Kester-Shelton, Pamela, ed. *Feminist Writers*. Detroit, Mich.: St. James Press, 1996.

Mankiller, Wilma ed. *The Reader's Companion to U.S. Women's History*. Boston: Houghton Mifflin, 1998.

Morgan, Robin, ed. *Sisterhood Is Global: The International Women's Movement Anthology*. New York: Feminist Press at City University of New York, 1996.

National Museum and Archive of Lesbian and Gay History. *The Lesbian Almanac*. New York: Berkley Books, 1996.

Neft, Naomi. *Where Women Stand: An International Report on the Status of Women in Over 140 Countries, 1997–1998*. New York: Random House, 1997.

Rosoff, Ilene, ed., and Launch Pad. *The Woman Source Catalog and Review: Tools for Connecting the Community of Women*. Berkeley, Calif.: Celestial Arts Publishers, 1997.

Ryan, Barbara. *The Women's Movement: Reference and Resources*. New York: G. K. Hall, 1996.

Slavin, Sarah, ed. *U.S. Women's Interest Groups: Institutional Profiles*. Westport, Conn.: Greenwood Press, 1995.

Stromquist, Nelly P., ed. *Women in the Third World: An Encyclopedia of Contemporary Issues*. New York: Garland Publishing, 1998.

Taeuber, Cynthia M., comp. and ed. *Statistical Handbook on Women in America*. 2d ed. Phoenix, Ariz.: Oryx Press, 1996.

Tierney, Helen, ed. *Women's Studies Encyclopedia*. Westport, Conn.: Greenwood Publishing, 1999.

Religion and Spirituality

Augsburg, Mary McClintock. *Changing the Subject: Women's Discourses and Feminist Theology*. Minneapolis, Minn.: Fulkerson Fortress, 1994.

Beck, Evelyn Torton, ed. *Nice Jewish Girls: A Lesbian Anthology*. Watertown, Mass.: Persephone Press, 1982.

Carroll, J. W., B. Hargrove, and A. T. Lummis. *Women of the Cloth*. San Francisco: Harper & Row, 1981.

Christ, C. P., and J. Plaskow, eds. *Womanspirit Rising*. New York: Harper & Row, 1979.

Coll, Regina A. *Christianity and Feminism in Conversation*. Mystic, Conn.: Twenty-Third Publications, 1995.

Daly, Mary. *Beyond God the Father: Toward a Philosophy of Women's Liberation*. Boston: Beacon Press, 1973.

Dame, Enid, and Henny Wenkart, eds. *Which Lilith?: Feminist Writers RE-Create the World's First Woman*. Northvale, N.J.: Jason Aronson, 1998.

Davis, Philip G. *Goddess Unmasked: The Rise of Neopagan Feminist Spirituality*. Dallas, Tex.: Spence Publishing, 1998.

Dresser, Marianne, ed. *Buddhist Women on the Edge: Contemporary Perspectives from the Western Frontier*. Berkeley, Calif.: North Atlantic Books, 1996.

Falk, Nancy Auer, and Rita M.Gross. *Unspoken Worlds: Women's Religious Lives in Non-Western Cultures*. San Francisco: Harper & Row, 1980.

Fernea, Elizabeth Warnock. *In Search of Islamic Feminism: One Woman's Global Journey*. New York: Bantam Doubleday Dell Publishing, 1998.

Fioerenza, Elisabeth S. *In Memory of Her: A Feminist Theological Reconstruction of Christian Origins*. New York: Crossroad Publishing, 1984.

Goldstein, Elyse. *ReVisions: Seeing Torah Through a Feminist Lens*. Woodstock, Vt.: Jewish Lights Publishing, 1999.

Johnson, Elizabeth A. *Friends of God and Prophets: A Feminist Theological Reading of the Communion of Saints*. New York: Continuum Publishing, 1999.

——. *She Who Is: The Mystery of God in Feminist Theological Discourse*. New York: Crossroad Publishing, 1993.

King, Ursula. *Women and Spirituality: Voices of Protest and Promise*. New York: New Amsterdam, 1989.

Lacugna, Catherine Mowry, ed. *Freeing Theology: The Essentials of Theology in Feminist Perspective*. San Francisco: Harper San Francisco, 1993.

Murphy, Cullen. *The Word According to Eve: Women and the Bible in Ancient Times and Our Own*. Boston: Houghton Mifflin, 1999.

Noble, Vicki. *Shakti Woman: Feeling Our Fire, Healing Our World: The New Female Shamanism*. San Francisco: Harper San Francisco, 1991.

Plaskow, Judith. *Standing Again at Sinai: Judaism from a Feminist Perspective*. San Francisco: Harper San Francisco, 1991.

Ramshaw, Gail. *Under the Tree of Life: The Religion of a Feminist Christian*. New York: Continuum Publishing, 1998.

Ruether, Rosemary Radford. *Sexism and God-Talk: Toward a Feminist Theology*. Boston: Beacon Press, 1993.

Stanton, E. C. *The Woman's Bible*. New York: European Publishing, 1895.

Welter, Barbara. *The Original Feminist Attack on the Bible (The Woman's Bible)*. New York: Arno Press, 1974.

Winter, Miriam Therese, and Meinrad Craighead. *WomanWitness: A Feminist Lectionary and Psalter: Women of the Hebrew Scriptures*. Part One, Vol. 1. New York: Crossroad Publishing, 1991.

Science

Abir-Am, Pnina G., and Dorinda Outram, eds. *Uneasy Careers and Intimate Lives: Women in Science, 1789–1979*. New Brunswick, N.J.: Rutgers University Press, 1987.

Alic, Margaret. *Hypatia's Heritage: A History of Women in Science from Antiquity Through the Nineteenth Century*. Boston: Beacon Press, 1986.

Ambrose, Susan A., Kristin L. Dunkle, Barbara B. Lazarus, Indira Nair, and Deborah Harkus. *Journeys of Women in Science and Engineering: No Universal Constants*. Philadelphia: Temple University Press, 1997.

Bailey, Martha J. *American Women in Science: A Biographic Dictionary*. Santa Barbara, Calif.: ABC-CLIO, 1994.

Barr, Jean, and Lynda I. Birke. *Common Science?: Women, Science, and Knowledge*. Bloomington: Indiana University Press, 1998.

Bleier, Ruth. *Science and Gender*. New York: Pergamon Press, 1984.

——, ed. *Feminist Approaches to Science*. New York: Pergamon Press, 1986.

Bonta, Marcia M. *Women in the Field: America's Pioneering Women Naturalists*. College Station: Texas A and M University Press, 1992.

Breton, Mary Joy. *Women Pioneers for the Environment*. Boston: Northeastern University Press, 1998.

Cole, Jonathan R. *Fair Science: Women in the Scientific Community*. New York: Columbia University Press, 1987.

Creese, Mary R. S. *Ladies in the Laboratory?: American and British Women in Science: A Survey of Their Contributions to Research*. Lanham, Md.: Scarecrow Press, 1998.

Gates, Barbara T., and Ann B. Shteir, eds. *Natural Eloquence: Women Reinscribe Science*. Madison: University of Wisconsin Press, 1997.

Haas, Violet B., and Carolyn C. Perrucci, eds. *Women in Scientific and Engineering Professions*. Ann Arbor: University of Michigan Press, 1984.

Harding, Sandra G. *Is Science Multicultural?: Postcolonialisms, Feminisms, and Epistomologies*. Bloomington: Indiana University Press, 1998.

———. *Whose Science? Whose Knowledge?: Thinking from Women's Lives*. Ithaca, N.Y.: Cornell University Press, 1991.

Harding, Sandra G., and Jean F. O'Barr, eds. *Sex and Scientific Inquiry*. Chicago: University of Chicago Press, 1987.

Kahle, Jane Butler. *Double Dilemma: Minorities and Women in Science Education*. West Lafayette, Ind.: Purdue University Press, 1982.

Kass-Simon, G., and Patricia Farnes, eds. *Women of Science: Righting the Record*. Bloomington: Indiana University Press, 1990.

Keller, Evelyn Fox. *Reflections on Gender and Science*. New Haven, Conn.: Yale University Press, 1986.

Keller, Evelyn Fox, and Helen E. Longino, eds. *Feminism and Science*. New York: Oxford University Press, 1996.

Merchant, Carolyn. *The Death of Nature: Women, Ecology and the Scientific Revolution*. San Francisco: Harper & Row, 1990.

Morse, Mary. *Women Changing Science: Voices from a Field in Transition*. New York: Plenum Publishing, 1995.

Nelson, Lynn H., and Jack Nelson. *Feminism, Science, and the Philosophy of Science*. Boston: Kluwer Academic Publishers, 1997.

Noble, David F. *A World Without Women: The Christian Clerical Culture of Western Science*. New York: Oxford University Press, 1993.

Ogilvie, Marilyn Bailey, and Kerry L. Meek. *Women and Science: An Annotated Bibliography*. New York: Garland Publishing, 1996.

Pattatucci, Angela M. *Women in Science: Meeting Career Challenges*. Thousand Oaks, Calif.: Sage Publications, 1998.

Rosser, Sue Vilhauer. *Biology and Feminism: A Dynamic Interaction*. New York: Twayne, 1993.

———. *Re-Engineering Female Friendly Science*. New York: Teachers College Press, 1997.

———, ed. *Feminism Within the Science and Health Care Professions: Overcoming Resistance*. New York: Pergamon Press, 1988.

Rossiter, Margaret W. *Women Scientists in America: Struggles and Strategies to 1940*. Baltimore, Md.: Johns Hopkins University Press, 1984.

Schiebinger, Londa L. *The Mind Has No Sex?: Women in the Origins of Modern Science*. Cambridge, Mass.: Harvard University Press, 1990.

———. *Nature's Body: Gender in the Making of Modern Science*. Boston: Beacon Press, 1995.

Zuckerman, Harriet, Jonathan R. Cole., and John T. Bruer, eds. *The Outer Circle: Women in the Scientific Community*. New Haven, Conn.: Yale University Press, 1993.

Sexual Abuse

Barry, K. *Female Sexual Slavery*. Englewood Cliffs, N.J.: Prentice Hall, 1979.

Bart, Pauline B., and Eileen G. Moran, eds. *Violence Against Women: The Bloody Footprints*. Newbury Park, Calif.: Sage Publications, 1993.

Bass, Ellen, and Laura Davis. *The Courage to Heal: A Guide for Women Survivors of Child Sexual Abuse*. New York: HarperCollins, 1993.

Benedict, Helen. *Virgin or Vamp: How the Press Covers Sex Crimes*. New York: Oxford University Press, 1992.

Bergen, Raquel Kennedy. *Wife Rape: Understanding the Response of Survivors and Service Providers*. Thousand Oaks, Calif.: Sage Publications, 1996.

Buzawa, Eva Schlesinger, and Carl G. Buzawa, eds. *Domestic Violence: The Changing Criminal Justice Response*. Thousand Oaks, Calif.: Sage Publications, 1996.

Classen, Catherine ed. *Treating Women Molested in Childhood*. San Francisco: Jossey-Bass, 1995.

Cuklanz, Lisa M. *Rape on Trial: How the Mass Media Construct Legal Reform and Social Change*. Philadelphia: University of Pennsylvania Press, 1995.

Elliott, Michele, ed. *Female Sexual Abuse of Children: The Ultimate Taboo*. New York: Guilford Press, 1994.

Francis, Leslie, ed. *Date Rape: Feminism, Philosophy, and the Law*. University Park: Pennsylvania State University Press, 1996.

Gilmartin, Pat. *Rape, Incest, and Child Sexual Abuse: Consequences and Recovery*. New York: Garland Publishing, 1994.

Gonsiorek, John C., ed. *Breach of Trust: Sexual Exploitation by Health Care Professionals and Clergy*. Newbury Park, Calif.: Sage Publications, 1995.

Gordon, Margaret T., and Stephanie Riger. *The Female Fear: The Social Cost of Rape*. Urbana: University of Illinois Press, 1991.

Hall, Liz, and Siobhan Lloyd. *Surviving Child Sexual Abuse: A Handbook for Helping Women Challenge Their Past*. Bristol, Penn.: Taylor and Francis, 1993.

Hamberger, L. Kevin, and Claire Renzetti, eds. *Domestic Partner Abuse*. New York: Springer Publishing, 1996.

Hosken, F. P. *The Hosken Report: Genital and Sexual Mutilation of Females*. Lexington, Mass.: Women's International Network News, 1979.

Human Rights Watch/Women's Rights Project Staff. *All Too Familiar: Sexual Abuse of Women in U.S. State Prisons*. New Haven, Conn.: Yale University Press, 1997.

Kirschner, Sam, et al. *Working with Adult Incest Survivors: The Healing Journey*. New York: Brunner-Mazel, 1993.

Lamb, Sandra. *Rape in America: A Reference Handbook*. Santa Barbara, Calif.: ABC-CLIO, 1995.

Lawrence, Bonita. *The Exclusion of Survivors' Voices in Feminist Discourse on Violence Against Women*. Ottowa, Ont.: Canadian Research Institute for the Advancement of Women/Institut Canadien de Recherches sur les Femmes, 1996.

Leone, Bruno, ed. *Rape on Campus*. San Diego, Calif.: Greenhaven Press, 1995.

Levy, Barrie. *Dating Violence: Young Women in Danger*. Seattle, Wash.: Seal Press, 1991.

Nordquist, Joan. *Violence Against Women: A Bibliography*. Santa Cruz, Calif.: Reference and Research Services, 1992.

Parrot, Andrea, and Laurie Bechhofer, eds. *Acquaintance Rape: The Hidden Crime*. Rev. ed. New York: Rosen Group, 1991.

Pendergrast, Mark. *Victims of Memory: Incest Accusations and Shattered Lives*. Hinesburg, Vt.: Upper Access, 1996.

Roth, Susan. *Naming the Shadows: A New Approach to Individual and Group Psychotherapy for Adult Survivors of Childhood Incest*. New York: The Free Press, 1997.

Rush, Florence. *The Best Kept Secret: Sexual Abuse of Children*. New York: McGraw-Hill, 1991.

Russell, Diana E. H. *Rape in Marriage*. Rev. ed. Bloomington: Indiana University Press, 1990.

Sanday, Peggy Reeves. *A Woman Scorned*. New York: Doubleday, 1996.

Searles, Patricia, and Ronald J. Berger, eds. *Rape and Society: Readings on the Problem of Sexual Assault*. Boulder, Colo.: Westview Press, 1995.

Spohn, Casia. *Rape Law Reform: A Grassroots Revolution and Its Impact*. New York: Plenum Publishing, 1992.

Wiehe, Vernon R. *Sibling Abuse: Hidden Physical, Emotional, and Sexual Trauma*. Thousand Oaks, Calif.: Sage Publications, 1997.

Wiehe, Vernon R., and Ann L. Richards. *Intimate Betrayal: Understanding and Responding to the Trauma of Acquaintance Rape*. Thousand Oaks, Calif.: Sage Publications, 1995.

Wilson, Melba. *Crossing the Boundary: Black Women Survive Incest*. Seattle, Wash.: Seal Press, 1994.

Wurtele, Sandy K. *Preventing Child Sexual Abuse*. Lincoln: University of Nebraska Press, 1992.

Sexuality

Abelove, Henry, Michele Aina Barale, and David Halperin, eds. *The Lesbian and Gay Studies Reader*. New York: Routledge, 1993.

Allen, Jeffner, ed. *Lesbian Philosophies and Cultures*. Albany: State University of New York Press, 1990.

Alpert, Rebecca. *Like Bread on the Seder Plate: Jewish Lesbians and the Transformation of Tradition*. New York: Columbia University Press, 1997.

Beemyn, Brett. *Creating a Place for Ourselves: Lesbian, Gay, and Bisexual Community Histories*. New York: Routledge, 1997.

Blasius, Mark, and Shane Phelan. *We Are Everywhere: A Historical Sourcebook of Gay and Lesbian Politics*. New York: Routledge, 1997.

Bright, Susie, and Jill Posener. *Nothing But the Girl: The Blatant Lesbian Image*. New York: Freedom Editions, 1996.

Case, Sue-Ellen. *The Domain-Matrix: Performing Lesbian at the End of Print Culture*. Bloomington: Indiana University Press, 1996.

Cooey, Paula M., Sharon A. Farmer, and Mary Ellen Ross. *Embodied Love: Sensuality and Relationship as Feminist Values*. San Franciso: Harper & Row: 1987.

D'Emilio, John, and Estelle B. Freedman. *Intimate Matters: A History of Sexuality in America*. New York: Harper & Row, 1988.

Daly, Meg, ed. *Surface Tension: Love, Sex, and Politics Between Lesbians and Straight Women*. New York: Simon & Schuster, 1995.

Davis, Elizabeth. *Women, Sex, and Desire: Exploring Your Sexuality at Every Stage of Life*. Alameda, Calif.: Hunter House, 1995.

Duberman, Martin, ed. *Queer World: The Center for Lesbian and Gay Studies Reader*. New York: New York University Press, 1997.

Ehrenreich, Barbara, Elizabeth Hess, and Gloria Jacobs. *Re-Making Love: The Feminization of Sex*. Garden City, N.Y.: Doubleday-Anchor, 1986.

Eng, David L., ed. *Q and A: Queer in Asian America*. Philadelphia: Temple University Press, 1998.

Faderman, Lillian. *Chloe Plus Olivia: An Anthology of Lesbian and Bisexual Literature from the Seventeenth Century to the Present*. New York: Viking Penguin, 1995.

Foucault, Michel. *A History of Sexuality*. New York: Vintage Books, 1990.

Franzen, Trisha. *Spinsters and Lesbians: Independent Womanhood in the United States*. New York: New York University Press, 1996.

Gluckman, Amy, and Betsy Reed. *Homo Economics: Capitalism, Community, and Lesbian and Gay Life*. New York: Routledge, 1997.

Greer, Germaine. *The Female Eunuch*. New York: Bantam Books, 1972.

Griffin, Gabriele, and Sonya Andermahr, eds. *Straight Studies Modified: Lesbian Interventions in the Academy*. London: Cassell Academic, 1997.

Halberstam, Judith. *Female Masculinity*. Durham, N.C.: Duke University Press, 1998.

Harris, Laura, and Elizabeth Crocker. *Femme: Feminists, Lesbians, and Bad Girls*. New York: Routledge, 1997.

Heller, Dana, ed. *Cross-Purposes: Lesbians, Feminists, and the Limits of Alliance*. Bloomington: Indiana University Press, 1997.

Lacan, Jacques, and Juliet Mitchell, eds. *Feminine Sexuality*. New York: W. W. Norton, 1984.

Leong, Russell. *Asian American Sexualities: Dimensions of the Gay and Lesbian Experience*. New York: Routledge, 1996.

Lewin, Ellen. *Recognizing Ourselves: Ceremonies of Lesbian and Gay Commitment*. New York: Columbia University Press, 1998.

———, ed. *Inventing Lesbian Cultures in America*. Boston: Beacon Press, 1996.

Lorde, Audre. *Every Woman I've Ever Loved: Lesbian Writers on Their Mothers*. San Francisco: Cleis Press, 1997.

Martin, Biddy. *Femininity Played Straight: The Significance of Being Lesbian*. New York: Routledge, 1997.

Martindale, Kathleen. *Un/Popular Culture: Lesbian Writing After the Sex Wars*. Albany: State University of New York Press, 1997.

Martinez, Elena M. *Lesbian Voices from Latin America: Breaking Ground*. New York: Garland Publishing, 1996.

McGarry, Molly, and Fred Wasserman. *Becoming Visible: An Illustrated History of Lesbian and Gay Life in Twentieth-Century America*. New York: Viking Penguin, 1998.

McKinley, Catherine E., and L. Joyce DeLaney. *Afrekete: An Anthology of Black Lesbian Writing*. New York: Doubleday, 1995.

Merck, Mandy. *Coming Out of Feminism?* Malden, Mass.: Blackwell Publishers, 1998.

Miller, Diane H. *Freedom to Differ: The Shaping of the Gay and Lesbian Struggle for Civil Rights*. New York: New York University Press, 1998.

Mintz, Beth, ed. *Lesbians in Academia: Degrees of Freedom*. New York: Routledge, 1997.

Moore, Lisa C., ed. *Does Your Mama Know? An Anthology of Black Lesbian Coming Out Stories*. Decatur, Ga.: Redbone Press, 1997.

Moraga, Cheri. *Waiting in the Wings: Portrait of Queer Motherhood*. Ithaca, N.Y.: Firebrand Books, 1997.

Nardi, Peter M., and Beth E. Schneider. *Social Perspectives in Lesbian and Gay Studies: A Reader*. New York: Routledge, 1998.

National Museum, and Archive of Lesbian and Gay History. *The Lesbian Almanac*. New York: Berkley Books, 1996.

Patterson, Charlotte, ed. *Lesbian, Gay, and Bisexual Identities in Families: Psychological Perspectives*. New York: Oxford University Press, 1998.

Phelan, Shane, ed. *Playing with Fire: Queer Politics, Queer Theories*. New York: Routledge, 1997.

Queen, Carol, and Lawrence Schimel, eds. *PoMoSexuals: Challenging Assumptions About Gender and Sexuality*. San Francisco: Cleis Press, 1997.

Raffo, Susan, ed. *Queerly Classed: Gay Men and Lesbians Write About Class*. Cambridge, Mass.: South End Press, 1997.

Reinfelder, Monika. *Amazon to Zami: Towards a Global Lesbian Feminism*. London: Cassell, 1997.

Robson, Ruthann. *Sappho Goes to Law School: Fragments in Lesbian Legal Theory*. New York: Columbia University Press, 1998.

Roof, Judith. *Come As You Are: Sexuality and Narrative*. New York: Columbia University Press, 1996.

Rosenbloom, Rachel. *Unspoken Rules: Sexual Orientation and Women's Human Rights*. New York: Cassell, 1996.

Rothblum, Esther D., ed. *Classics in Lesbian Studies*. New York: Harrington Park Press, 1997.

Schlager, Neil, ed. *The St. James Press Gay and Lesbian Almanac*. Detroit, Mich.: St. James Press, 1998.

Schwartz, Adria E. *Sexual Subjects: Lesbians, Gender, and Psychoanalysis*. New York: Routledge, 1997.

Sedgwick, Eve Kosofsky. *Epistemology of the Closet*. Berkeley: University of California Press, 1992.

Stein, Arlene. *Sex and Sensibility: Stories of a Lesbian Generation*. Berkeley: University of California Press, 1997.

Tyrkus, Michael, ed. *Gay and Lesbian Biography*. Detroit, Mich.: St. James Press, 1997.

Vicinus, Martha, ed. *Lesbian Subjects: A Feminist Studies Reader*. Bloomington: Indiana University Press, 1996.

Vida, Ginny ed. *The New Our Right to Love: A Lesbian Resource Book*. New York: Touchstone Books, 1996.

Weed, Elizabeth, and Naomi Schor, eds. *Feminism Meets Queer Theory*. Bloomington: Indiana University Press, 1997.

Weinstock, Jacqueline S., and Esther D. Rothblum, eds. *Lesbian Friendships: For Ourselves and Each Other*. New York: New York University Press, 1996.

Whisman, Vera. *Queer by Choice: Lesbians, Gay Men, and the Politics of Identity*. New York: Routledge, 1996.

Zimmerman, Bonnie, and Toni A. H. McNaron, eds. *The New Lesbian Studies: Into the Twenty-First Century*. New York: Feminist Press at the City University of New York, 1996.

Sports

Adrian, Marlene J. *Woman in Motion*. Las Vegas, Nev.: Women Diversity, 1995.

Berlage, Gai J. *Women in Baseball: The Forgotten History*. Westport, Conn.: Praeger Publishers, 1994.

Birrell, Susan, and Cheryl L. Cole, eds. *Women, Sport, and Culture*. Champaign, Ill.: Human Kinetics Publishers, 1994.

Cahn, Susan K. *Coming on Strong: Gender and Sexuality in Twentieth Century Women's Sport.* New York: The Free Press, 1994.

Cohen, Greta L., ed. *Women in Sport: Issues and Controversies.* Newbury Park, Calif.: Sage Publications, 1993.

Costa, D. Margaret, and Sharon R. Guthrie, eds. *Women and Sport: Interdisciplinary Perspectives.* Champaign, Ill.: Human Kinetics Publishers, 1994.

Creedon, Pamela J., ed. *Women, Media, and Sport: Challenging Gender Values.* Thousand Oaks, Calif.: Sage Publications, 1994.

Cylkowski, Greg J., and Kathleen Staiffer. *The Womansport Directory: The Women's Sport Bible.* Little Canada, Minn.: Athletic Achievements, 1995.

Festle, Mary J. *Politics and Apologies in Women's Sports.* New York: Columbia University Press, 1996.

Greenberg, Judith E. *Getting into the Game: Women and Sports.* New York: F. Watts, 1997.

Gregorich, Barbara. *Women at Play: The Story of Women in Baseball.* San Diego, Calif.: Harcourt Brace Jovanovich, 1993.

Guttmann, Allen. *Women's Sports: A History.* New York: Columbia University Press, 1992.

Hall, M. Ann. *Feminism and Sporting Bodies: Essays on Theory and Practice.* Champaign, Ill.: Human Kinetics Publishers, 1996.

Layden, Joseph. *Women in Sports: The Complete Book of the World's Greatest Female Athletes.* Santa Monica, Calif.: General Publishing Group, 1997.

Oglesby, Carole A., ed. *Women and Sport: From Myth to Reality.* Ann Arbor, MI: Books on Demand, 1978.

Oglesby, Carole A., and Doreen L Greenberg, eds. *Encyclopedia of Women and Sports in America.* Phoenix, Ariz.: Oryx Press, 1998.

Remley, Mary L. *Women in Sport: An Annotated Bibliography and Resource Guide.* New York: Macmillan, 1991.

Shangold, Mona M., and Gabe Mirkin, eds. *Women and Exercise: Physiology and Sports Medicine.* New York: Oxford University Press, 1993.

Smith, Lissa. *Nike Is a Goddess: The History of Women in Sport.* New York: Atlantic Monthly Press, 1998.

Tokarz, Karen. *Women, Sports, and the Law: A Comprehensive Research Guide to Sex Discrimination in Sports.* Buffalo, N.Y.: W.S. Hein, 1986.

Woolum, Janet. *Outstanding Women Athletes: Who They Are and How They Influenced Sports in America.* Phoenix, Ariz.: Oryx Press, 1998.

Women of Color

Allen, Paula Gunn. *Off the Reservation: Reflections on Border-Busting, Border-Crossing Loose Canons.* Boston: Beacon Press, 1998.

———. *The Sacred Hoop: Recovering the Feminine in American Indian Traditions.* Boston: Beacon Press, 1992.

———. *Spider Woman's Granddaughters: Traditional Tales and Contemporary Writing by Native American Women.* New York: Fawcett Book Group, 1990.

Amott, Teresa L. *Race, Gender, and Work: A Multicultural Economic History of Women in the U.S.* Rev. ed. Boston: South End Press, 1996.

Anderson, Karen. *Changing Woman: A History of Racial Ethnic Women in Modern America.* New York: Oxford University Press, 1996.

Angelou, Maya. *I Know Why the Caged Bird Sings.* New York: Random House, 1970.

Anzaldúa, Gloria. *Borderlands/La Frontera: The New Mestiza.* San Francisco: Aunt Lute Books, 1987.

———, ed. *Making Face, Making Soul/Hacienda Caras: Creative and Critical Perspectives by Women of Color.* San Francisco: Aunt Lute Books, 1990.

Bell-Scott, Patricia, ed. *Double Stitch: Black Women Write About Mothers and Daughters.* Boston: Beacon Press, 1991.

———. *Flat Footed Truths: Telling Black Women's Lives.* New York: Henry Holt, 1998.

Blea, Irene I. *U.S. Chicanas and Latinas Within a Global Context.* New York: Praeger Publishers, 1997.

Collins, Patricia Hill. *Fighting Words: Black Women and the Search for Justice.* Minneapolis: University of Minnesota Press, 1998.

Dasgupta, Shamita Das, ed. *Patchwork Shawl: Chronicles of South Asian Women in America.* New Brunswick, N.J.: Rutgers University Press, 1998.

Davis, Angela Y. *Women, Race, and Class.* New York: Random House, 1983.

DuBois, Ellen Carol, and Vickie Ruiz, eds. *Unequal Sisters: A Multicultural Reader in U.S. Women's History.* 2d ed. New York: Routledge, 1994.

Giddings, Paula. *When and Where I Enter: The Impact of Black Women on Race and Sex.* New York: William Morrow, 1984.

Golden, Marita, and Susan R. Shreve, eds. *Skin Deep: Black Women and White Women Write About Race.* New York: Doubleday, 1996.

Hine, Darlene Clark, and Kathleen Thompson. *A Shining Thread of Hope: History of Black Women in America.* New York: Broadway Books, 1998.

hooks, bell. *Ain't I a Woman: Black Women and Feminism.* Boston: South End Press, 1981.

———. *Feminist Theory: From Margin to Center.* Boston: South End Press, 1984.

———. *Talking Back: Thinking Feminist, Thinking Black.* Boston: South End Press, 1989.

————. *Yearning: Race, Gender, and Cultural Politics.* Boston: South End Press, 1990.

Hurtado, Aida. *The Color of Privilege: Three Blasphemies on Race and Feminism.* Ann Arbor: University of Michigan Press, 1996.

Jones, Jacqueline. *Labor of Love, Labor of Sorrow: Black Women, Work, and the Family from Slavery to the Present.* New York: Random House, 1986.

Lerner, Gerda. *Black Women in White America: A Documentary History.* New York: Random House, 1992.

Lim, Shirley Geok-lin, and Mayumi Tsutakawa, eds. *Forbidden Stitch: An Asian American Women's Anthology.* Corvallis, Ore.: Calyx Books, 1988.

Ling, Amy. *Between Worlds: Women Writers of Chinese Ancestry.* New York: Teachers College Press, 1990.

Martin, Patricia Preciado, ed. *Songs My Mother Sang to Me: An Oral History of Mexican-American Women.* Tuscon: University of Arizona Press, 1992.

Moraga, Cheríe, and Gloria Anzaldúa, eds. *This Bridge Called My Back: Writings by Radical Women of Color.* New York: Kitchen Table/ Women of Color Press, 1984.

Morrison, Toni, ed. *Race-Ing Justice, En-Gendering Power: Essays on Anita Hill, Clarence Thomas, and the Construction of Social Reality.* New York: Pantheon Books, 1992.

Niethammer, Carolyn. *Daughters of the Earth: The Lives and Legends of American Indian Women.* New York: Macmillan Publishing, 1977.

Ruiz, Vicki L. *From Out of the Shadows: Mexican Women in Twentieth Century America.* New York: Oxford University Press, 1998.

Shah, Sonia, ed. *Dragon Ladies: Asian American Feminists Breathe Fire.* Boston: South End Press, 1997.

Wilson, Midge. *Divided Sisters: Bridging the Gap Between Black Women and White Women.* New York: Doubleday, 1996.

Women of the South Asian Descent Collectives. *Our Feet Walk the Sky: Women of the South Asian Diaspora.* San Francisco: Aunt Lute Books, 1993.

Wong, Diane Yen-Mei, ed. *Making Waves: An Anthology of Writings By and About Asian American Women.* Boston: Beacon Press, 1989.

Work

Aisenberg, Nadya, and Mona Harrington. *Women of Academe: Outsiders in the Sacred Grove.* Amherst: University of Massachussetts Press, 1988.

Benet, M. K. *The Secretarial Ghetto.* New York: McGraw-Hill, 1972.

Cain, M., and R. Dauber, eds. *Women and Technological Change in Developing Countries.* Boulder, Colo.: Westview Press, 1981.

Daniels, Arlene Kaplan. *Invisible Careers.* Chicago: University of Chicago Press, 1988.

Epstein, C. *Woman's Place: Options and Limits in Professional Careers.* Berkeley: University of California Press, 1970.

Friedan, Betty. *Beyond Gender: The New Politics of Work and Family.* Baltimore, Md.: Johns Hopkins University Press, 1997.

Gerson, Kathleen. *Hard Choices: How Women Decide About Work, Career, and Motherhood.* Berkeley: University of California Press, 1985.

Harkess, S., and A. Stromberg, eds. *Women Working.* Palo Alto, Calif.: Mayfield, 1978.

Jamieson, Kathleen Hall. *Beyond the Double Bind: Women and Leadership.* New York: Oxford University Press, 1997.

Kanter, Rosabeth Moss. *Men and Women of the Corporation.* New York: Basic Books, 1977.

Katzman, David. *Seven Days a Week: Women and Domestic Service in Industrializing America.* New York: Oxford University Press, 1978.

Leacock, E., H. Safa, et al. *Women's Work: Development and the Division of Labor by Gender.* South Hadley, Mass.: Bergin and Garvey, 1986.

Lopata, Helene Z. *Occupation: Housewife.* New York: Oxford University Press, 1971.

Miller, Eleanor. *Street Women.* Philadelphia: Temple University Press, 1986.

Remy, Dorothy, and Karen B. Sacks, eds. *My Troubles Are Going to Have Trouble with Me.* New Brunswick, N.J.: Rutgers University Press, 1984.

Rollins, Judith. *Between Women: Domestics and Their Employers.* Philadelphia: Temple University Press, 1985.

Sokoloff, Natalie. *Between Money and Love: The Dialectics of Women's Home and Market Work.* New York: Praeger Publishers, 1980.

Organizations

Education and Professional Organizations

American Association of University Women
1111 Sixteenth Street, N.W.
Washington, DC 20036
Phone: (800) 326-AAUW
E-mail: info@aauw.org
www.aauw.org/home.html

American College of Nurse-Midwives (ACNM)
818 Connecticut Avenue, N.W.,
  Suite 900
Washington, DC 20006
Phone: (202) 728-9860
Fax: (202) 628-9897
E-mail: info@acnm.org
www.acnm.org

American College of Obstetricians and Gynecologists
409 12th Street, S.W.
Washington, DC 20024-2188
Phone: (202) 683-5577
www.acog.org

American Medical Women's Association
801 North Fairfax Street, Suite 400
Alexandria, VA 22314
Phone: (703) 838-0500
Fax: (703) 549-3864
E-mail: info@amwa-doc.org
www.amwa-doc.org/index.html

American Society for Reproductive Medicine (ASRM)
1209 Montgomery Highway
Birmingham, AL 35216-2809
Phone: (205) 978-5000
Fax: (205) 978-5005
E-mail: asrm@asrm.org
www.asrm.org

American Society of Women Accountants (ASWA)
National Headquarters

60 Revere Drive, Suite 500
Northbrook, IL 60062
Phone: (800) 326-2163
Fax: (847) 480-9282
E-mail: aswa@aswa.org
www.aswa.org

Association for Women in Science
1200 New York Avenue, Suite 650
Washington, DC 20005
Phone: (202) 326-8940
Fax: (202) 326-8960
E-mail: awis@awis.org
www.awis.org

Association of Reproductive Health Professionals
2401 Pennsylvania Avenue, N.W.,
  Suite 350
Washington, DC 20037-1718
Phone: (202) 466-3825
Fax: (202) 466-3826
E-mail: arhp@arhp.org
www.arhp.org

Association of Women's Health, Obstetric and Neonatal Nurses
2000 L Street N.W., Suite 740
Washington, DC 20036
Phone: (800) 673-8499 (U.S.) or (800) 245-0231 (Canada)
Fax: (202) 728-0575
www.awhonn.org

Association of Women Surgeons
414 Plaza Drive, Suite 209
Westmont, IL 60559
Phone: (630) 655-0392
Fax: (630) 655-0391
E-mail: info@womensurgeons.org
www.womensurgeons.org

Black Women in Publishing
P.O. Box 6275
FDR Station
New York, NY 10150
Phone: (212) 772-5951
www.bwip.org

Black Women in Sisterhood for Action (BISA)
P.O. Box 1592
Washington, DC 20013

Phone: (301) 460-1565
E-mail: bisa@erols.com
www.feminist.com/bisas1.htm

Business and Professional Women/USA
2012 Massachusetts Avenue, N.W.
Washington, DC 20036
Phone: (202) 293-1100
Fax: (202) 861-0298
www.bpwusa.org

Catalyst
120 Wall Street
New York, NY 10005
Phone: (212) 514-7600
Fax: (212) 514-8470
E-mail: info@catalystwomen.org
www.catalystwomen.org/home.html

Computer Professionals for Social Responsibility (CPSR)
P.O. Box 717
Palo Alto, CA 94302
Phone: (650) 322-3778
Fax: (650) 322-4748
E-mail: webmaster@cpsr.org
www.cpsr.org

HerStory For Futures Unlimited (HFFU)
2123 Marineview Drive
San Leandro, CA 94577
Phone: (510) 483-4246
Fax: (510) 351-3383
E-mail: milli@dnai.com
www.herstory-hffu.org

The International Alliance (TIA). An Organization of Professional and Executive Women
P.O. Box 1119
Sparks-Glencoe
Baltimore, MD 21152
Phone: (410) 472-4221
Fax: (410) 472-2920
E-mail: info@t-i-a.com
www.t-i-a.com

International Federation of University Women
IFUW Headquarters
8 rue de l'Ancien-Port CH-1201

Geneva, Switzerland
Phone: (41.22) 731 23 80
Fax: (41.22) 738 04 40
E-mail: info@ifuw.org
www.ifuw.org

International Women's Media Foundation
1726 M Street N.W., Suite 1002
Washington, DC 20036
Phone: (202) 496-1992
Fax: (202) 496-1977
E-mail: iwmf@aol.com
www.iwmf.org

Jacobs Institute of Women's Health
409 12th Street, S.W.
Washington, DC 20024-2188
Phone: (202) 863-4990
Fax: (202) 488-4229 or (202) 554-0453
www.jiwh.org

Melpomene Institute
1010 University Avenue
St. Paul, MN 55104
Phone: (651) 642-1951
Fax: (651) 642-1871
E-mail: health@melpomene.org
www.melpomene.org

National Association for Female Executives (NAFE)
P.O. Box 469031
Escondido, CA 92046-9925
Phone: (800) 634-NAFE
E-mail: nafe@nafe.com
www.nafe.com

National Association for Women in Education
1325 18th Street, N.W., Suite 210
Washington, DC 20036
Phone: (202) 659-9330
Fax: (202) 457-0946
E-mail: webweaver@nawe.org
www.nawe.org/index.html

National Association of Nurse Practitioners in Reproductive Health
1090 Vermont Avenue, Suite 800
Washington, DC 20005
Phone: (202) 408-7025
Fax: (202) 408-0902
E-mail: nanprh@nurse.org
www.nanprh.org

National Association of Women Artists, Inc.
41 Union Square West, #906
New York, NY 10003-3278
www.anny.org/orgs/0231/
000f0231.htm

National Association of Women Business Owners (NAWBO)
1100 Wayne Avenue, Suite 830
Silver Spring, MD 20910
Phone: (301) 608-2590
Fax: (301) 608-2596
E-mail: national@nawbo.org
www.nawbo.org/nawbo/nawbostart.nsf

National Association of Women Lawyers (NAWL)
American Bar Center
750 North Lake Shore Drive
Chicago, IL 60611
Phone (312) 988-6186
Fax: (312) 988-6281
www.kentlaw.edu/nawl/index.htm

National Council for Research on Women
11 Hanover Square
New York, NY 10005
Phone: (212) 785-7335
Fax: (212) 785-7350
E-mail: ncrw@ncrw.org
www.ncrw.org

National Lesbian and Gay Law Association (NLGLA)
P.O. Box 180417
Boston, MA 02118
Phone: (508) 982-8290
E-mail: NLGLA@aol.com
www.nlgla.org

National Women's Business Center, Inc.
1001 Connecticut Avenue, N.W.,
    Suite 312
Washington, DC 20036
Phone: (202) 785-4WBC (4922)
Fax: (202) 785-4110
E-mail: info@womensbusinesscenter.org
www.womenconnect.com/
    womensbusinesscenter

National Women's Business Owners Corporation
1100 Wayne Avenue, #830
Silver Spring, MD 20910
Phone: (561) 848-5066
Fax: (561) 881-7364
E-mail: info@wboc.org
www.wboc.org

National Women's Hall of Fame
76 Fall Street
P.O. Box 335
Seneca Falls, NY 13148
Phone: (315) 568-8060
Fax: (315) 568-2976
E-mail: greatwomen@greatwomen.org
www.greatwomen.org

The National Women's History Project
7738 Bell Road
Windsor, CA 95492
Phone: (707) 838-6000
Fax: (707) 838-0478
E-mail: nwhp@aol.com
www.nwhp.org

National Women's Studies Association
University of Maryland
7100 Baltimore Boulevard, Suite 500
College Park, MD 20740
Phone: (301) 403-0525
Fax: (301) 403-4137
E-mail: nwsa@umail.umd.edu
www.nwsa.org

9to5 National Association of Working Women
655 Broadway, Suite 300
Denver, CO 80203
Phone: (303) 628-0925 or
    (800) 522-0925
Fax: (303) 628-3888
www.9to5naww.qpg.com

Professional Women of Color
P.O. Box 5196
New York, NY 10185
Phone: (212) 714-7190
E-mail: PWCinsight@aol.com
www.pwconline.org

Schomberg Center for Research in Black Culture
515 Malcolm X Boulevard
New York, NY 10037-1801
Phone: (212) 491-2200
www.nypl.org/research/sc/sc.html

Society of Women Engineers (SWE)
120 Wall Street, 11th Floor
New York, NY 10005-3902
Phone: (212) 509-9577
E-mail: hq@swe.org
www.swe.org

Susan B. Anthony University Center
4-145 Dewey Hall, Box 270435
University of Rochester
Rochester, New York 14627-0435
Phone: (716) 275-8799
Fax: (716) 242-5810
E-mail: njoh@uhura.cc.rochester.edu
www.rochester.edu/SBA

The Tucker Center for Research on Girls & Women in Sport
University of Minnesota
203 Cooke Hall
1900 University Avenue, S.E.

Minneapolis, MN 55455
Phone: (612) 625-7327
Fax: (612) 626-7700
E-mail: crgwsAtc.umn.edu
www.kls.coled.umn.edu/crgws/
default.html

Wider Opportunities for Women (WOW)
815 15th Street, N.W., Suite 916
Washington, DC 20005
Phone: (202) 638-3143
Fax: (202) 638-4885
E-mail: info@w-o-w.org
www.w-o-w.org

Women Marines Association
9608 North May Avenue, PMB 265
Oklahoma City, OK 73120-2798
E-mail: WMA1stVP@aol.com
www.womenmarines.org

Women Officers Professional Association
P.O. Box 1621
Arlington, VA 22210
Phone: (202) 685-0882
E-mail: flather.jennifer@nsw.navy.mil
www.wopa.org

Women Veterans Association (WVA)
National Headquarters
680 Southwest 18th Court
Boynton Beach, FL 33426
Phone: (561) 732-4596
Fax: (561) 732-4596

Women's Educational Equity Act
WEEA Equity Resource Center
Education Development Center
55 Chapel Street
Newton, MA 02158-1060
Phone: (617) 969-7100
E-mail: weeactr@edc.org
www.edc.org/WomensEquity

Women's National Book Association
160 Fifth Avenue
New York, NY 10010
Phone: (212) 675-7805
Fax (212) 989-7542
E-mail: skpassoc@internetmci.com
(membership info)
www.he.net/~susannah/wnba.htm

Women's Philanthropy Institute
6314 Odana Road, Suite 1
Madison, WI 53719
Phone: (608) 270-5205
Fax: (608) 270-5207
E-mail: andrea@women-philanthropy.org
www.women-philanthropy.org

Women's Research and Education Institute (WREI)
1750 New York Avenue, N.W.,
Suite 350
Washington, DC 20006
Phone: (202) 628-0444
E-mail: wrei@wrei.org
ww.wrei.org

Health

AGING

Alliance for Aging Research
2021 K Street N.W., Suite 305
Washington, DC 20006-1003
Phone: (202) 293-2856
Fax: (202) 785-8574
E-mail: info@agingresearch.org
www.agingresearch.org

Alzheimer's Association
919 North Michigan Avenue,
Suite 1000
Chicago, IL 60611-1676
Phone: (800) 272-3900
Fax: (312) 335-1110
E-mail: info@alz.org
www.alz.org

Alzheimer's Disease Education and Referral Center (ADEAR)
8630 Fenton Street, #1125
Silver Spring, MD 20907-8250
Phone: (301) 495-3311 or
(800) 438-4380
E-mail: adear@alzheimers.org
www.alzheimers.org

American Menopause Foundation, Inc. (AMF)
350 Fifth Avenue, Suite 2822
New York, NY 10118
Phone: (212) 714-2398

American Society on Aging (ASA)
833 Market Street, Suite 511
San Francisco, CA 94103
Phone: (415) 974-9600
Fax: (415) 974-0300
E-mail: info@asa.asaging.org
www.asaging.org

Gerontological Society of America (GSA)
1275 K Street, N.W., Suite 350
Washington, DC 20005-4006
Phone: (202) 842-1275
E-mail: webmaster@geron.org
www.geron.org

Gray Panthers
733 15th Street, N.W., Suite 437
Washington, DC 20005
Phone: (202) 737-6637 or
(800) 280-5362
Fax: (202) 737-1160
E-mail: info@graypanthers.org
www.graypanthers.org

National Council on Aging (NCOA)
409 Third Street, S.W., Suite 200
Washington, DC 20024
Phone: (202) 479-1200
Fax: (202) 479-0735
E-mail: info@ncoa.org
www.ncoa.org

National Institute on Aging (NIA)
Public Information Office
Building 31, Room 5C27
31 Center Drive, MSC 2292
Bethesda, MD 20892
Phone: (301) 496-1752
www.nih.gov/nia

National Osteoporosis Foundation
1232 22nd Street, N.W.
Washington, DC 20037-1292
Phone: (202) 223-2226
www.nof.org

North American Menopause Society
P.O. Box 94527
Cleveland, OH 44101
Phone: (440) 442-7550
Fax: (440) 442-2660
E-mail: info@menopause.org
www.menopause.org

National Association of Area Agencies on Aging
927 15th Street, N.W., 6th Floor
Washington, DC 20005
Phone: (202) 296-8130
Fax: (202) 296-8134
www.n4a.org

Older Women's League (OWL)
666 11th Street, N.W., Suite 700
Washington, DC 20001
Phone: (202) 783-6686

AIDS/HIV

American Social Health Association
P.O. Box 13827
Research Triangle Park, NC 27709
Phone: (919) 361-8400
Fax: (919) 361-8425
www.ashastd.org

Association for Women's AIDS Research and Education
San Francisco General Hospital

Building 90, Ward 95, 955 Potrero
San Francisco, CA 94110
Phone: (415) 476-4091

Boston Women's AIDS Information Project
464 Massachusetts Avenue
Boston, MA 02118
Phone: (617) 859-8689

Centre for AIDS Services of Montreal (Women)
84 Notre Dame West, Suite 101
Montréal, Québec, Canada H2Y 1S6
Phone: (514) 843-3636
Fax: (514) 843-5098
E-mail: casm@netrover.com
netrover.com/~casm

Elizabeth Glazer Pediatric AIDS Foundation
2950 31st Street, #125
Santa Monica, CA 90405
Phone: (310) 314-1459
Fax: (310) 314-1469
E-mail: info@pedAIDS.org
www.pedaids.org

Mother's Voices
165 West 46th Street, Suite 701
New York, NY 10036
Phone: (212) 730-2777
Fax: (212) 730-4378
www.mvoices.org

National Pediatric and Family HIV Resource Center
University of Medicine and Dentistry
of New Jersey
30 Bergen Street - ADMC #4
Newark, NJ 07103
Phone: (973) 972-0410 or
(800) 362-0071
Fax: (973) 972-0399
www.pedhivaids.org

UNAIDS
20, Avenue Appia
CH-1211 Geneva 27, Switzerland
Phone: (4122) 791 3666
Fax: (4122) 791 4187
E-mail: unaids@unaids.org
www.unaids.org

Women Alive
1566 Burnside Avenue
Los Angeles, CA 90019
Phone: (323) 965-1564
Fax: (323) 965-9886
E-mail: info@women-alive.org
www.women-alive.org

Women and AIDS Resource Network
30 Third Avenue, Suite 25
Brooklyn, NY 11217

Women's AIDS Network
3543 18th Street, Suite 11
San Francisco, CA 94110
Phone: (415) 621-4160
E-mail: lorene@sonic.net
www.womens-aids-network.com

CANCER

African American Breast Cancer Alliance
P.O. Box 8987
Minneapolis, Minnesota 55408
Phone: (612) 731-3792

American Cancer Society: Breast Cancer Network
1599 Clifton Road
Atlanta, GA 30329,
Phone: (800) ACS-2345
www2.cancer.org/bcn/index.html

Breast Cancer Action Nova Scotia
P.O. Box 34091
Halifax, Nova Scotia, Canada B3J 3S1
Phone: (902) 465-2685
E-mail: bcans@bca.ns.ca
www.bca.ns.ca

Breast Cancer Resource Committee
1949 Calvert Street N.W., Suite B
Washington, DC 20009
Phone: (202) 463-8040
Fax: (202) 463-8015

CancerCare Inc.
National Office
275 Seventh Avenue
New York, NY 10001
Phone: (212) 221-3300
(Administration); (212) 302-2400 or
(800) 813-HOPE (4673) (Services)
Fax: (212) 719-0263
E-mail: info@cancercare.org
www.cancercare.org

The Celebrating Life Foundation
P.O. Box 224076
Dallas, TX 75222-4076
Phone: (800) 207-0992
E-mail: clf@cyberramp.net
www.celebratinglife.org/home.htm

Gilda's Club®, Inc.
195 West Houston Street
New York, NY 10014
Tel: (212) 647-9700
Fax: (212) 647-1151
www.gildasclub.org

Gynecologic Oncology Group
1234 Market Street, Suite 1945
Philadelphia, PA 19107
Phone: (215) 854-0770
www.gog.org/index.html

Living Beyond Breast Cancer
10 East Athens Avenue, Suite 204
Ardmore, PA 19003
Phone: (610) 645-4567
Fax (610) 645-4573
E-mail: llbbc@earthlink.net
www.lbbc.org

The Mautner Project for Lesbians With Cancer
1707 L Street, N.W., Suite 500
Washington, DC 20036
Phone: (202) 332-5536
Fax: (202) 332-0662
E-mail: mautner@mautnerproject.org
www.mautnerproject.org

National Alliance of Breast Cancer Organizations
9 East 37th Street, 10th Floor
New York, NY 10016
Phone: (888) 80-NABCO
E-mail: NABCOinfo@aol.com
www.nabco.org

National Black Leadership Initiative on Cancer
University of Illinois at Chicago
2121 West Taylor Street, Suite 512
Chicago, IL 60612
Phone: (800) 799-2542

National Breast Cancer Coalition
1707 L Street, N.W., Suite 1060
Washington, DC 20036
Phone: (202) 296-7477 or
(800) 935-0434
Fax: (202) 265-6854
www.natlbcc.org

National Cancer Institute
31 Center Drive
MSC 2580, Building 31, Room 10A16
Bethesda, MD 20892-2580
Phone: (800) 4-Cancer
www.nci.nih.gov

National Cervical Cancer Coalition
16501 Sherman Way, Suite 110
Van Nuys, CA 91406
Phone: (818) 909-3849
www.nccc-online.org

National Coalition for Cancer Survivorship (NCCS)
1010 Wayne Avenue, Suite 505
Silver Spring, MD 20910
Phone: (301) 650-8868 or

(877) NCCS YES (877-622-7937)
Fax: (301) 565-9670
E-mail: info@cansearch.org
www.cansearch.org

National Ovarian Cancer Coalition
P.O. Box 4472
Boca Raton, FL 33429
Phone: (561) 393-0005 or
 (888) OVARIAN
Fax: (561) 393-7275
E-mail: NOCC@ovarian.org
www.ovarian.org

Oncology Nursing Society (ONS)
501 Holiday Drive
Pittsburgh, PA 15220
Phone: (412) 921-7373
Fax: (412) 921-6565
E-mail: member@ons.org
www.ons.org

Women's Cancer Resource Center
1815 East 41st Street, Suite C
Minneapolis, MN 55407-3425
Phone: (800) 908-8544
Fax: (612) 729-0591
E-mail: wcrc@mr.net
www.givingvoice.org

Y-Me National Association for Breast Cancer
212 West Van Buren Street
Chicago, IL 60607
Phone: (800) 221-2141
www.breastcancerinfo.com

CHILDBEARING AND REPRODUCTIVE HEALTH

The Alan Guttmacher Institute
120 Wall Street
New York, NY 10005
Phone: (212) 248-1111
Fax: (212) 248-1951
E-mail: info@agi-usa.org
www.agi-usa.org/index.html

American Society for Reproductive Medicine
1209 Montgomery Highway
Birmingham, AL 35216-2809
Phone: (205) 978-5000
Fax: (205) 978-5005
E-mail: asrm@asrm.org
www.asrm.org

Center for Reproductive Law and Technology
120 Wall Street
New York, NY 10005
Phone: (212) 514-5534
Fax: (212) 514-5538

E-mail: info@crlp.org
www.crlp.org

Childbirth And Postpartum Professional Association (CAPPA)
310 Sweet Ivy Lane
Lawrenceville, GA 30043
Phone: (888) 548-3672
E-mail: askcappa@yahoo.com
www.childbirthprofessional.com

Citizens for Midwifery
P.O. Box 82227
Athens, GA 30608-2227
Phone: (888) CfM-4880
www.cfmidwifery.org

Family Health International
P.O. Box 13950
Research Triangle Park, NC 27709
Phone: (919) 544-7040
Fax: (919) 544-7261
www.fhi.org

La Leche League International
1400 North Meacham Road
Schaumburg, IL 60173
Phone: (800) LALECHE
Fax: (847) 519-0035
www.lalecheleague.org

Midwifery Education and Accreditation Council
220 West Birch
Flagstaff, AZ 86001
Phone: (520) 214-0997
www.mana.org/meac

National Association of Childbearing Centers
3123 Gottschall Road
Perkiomenville, PA 18074
Phone: (215) 234-8068
Fax: (215) 234-8829
E-mail: ReachNACC@BirthCenters.org
www.birthcenters.org

National Family Planning and Reproductive Health Association, Inc.
1627 K Street, N.W., 12th Floor
Washington, DC 20006
Phone: (202) 293-3114
Fax: (202) 293-1990
E-mail: info@nfprha.org
www.nfprha.org

National Healthy Mothers, Healthy Babies Coalition (HMHB)
121 North Washington Street, Suite 300
Alexandria, VA 22314
Phone: (703) 836-6110
Fax: (703) 836-3470
www.hmhb.org

Planned Parenthood Federation of America
810 Seventh Avenue
New York, NY 10019
Phone: (212) 541-7800
FAX: (212) 245-1845
E-mail: communications@ppfa.org
www.plannedparenthood.org

EATING DISORDERS

American Anorexia/Bulimia Association
165 West 46th Street, #1108
New York, NY 10036
Phone: (212) 575-6200
www.aabainc.org

Anorexia Nervosa and Related Eating Disorders
P.O. Box 5102
Eugene, OR 97405
Phone: (503) 344-1144
E-mail: jarinor@rio.com
www.anred.com

Eating Disorders Awareness and Prevention, Inc. (EDAP)
603 Stewart Street, Suite 803
Seattle, WA 98101
Phone: (206) 382-3587 or
(800) 931-EDAP
Fax: (206) 829-8501
www.edap.org

National Association of Anorexia Nervosa and Associated Disorders (ANAD)
P.O. Box 7
Highland Park, IL 60035
Phone: (847) 831-3438
Fax: (847) 433-4632
E-mail: anad20@aol.com
www.anad.org

National Eating Disorders Organization
Harding Hospital
445 East Granville Road
Worthington, OH 43085
Phone: (614) 436-1112

Overeaters Anonymous
P.O. Box 44020
Rio Rancho, NM 87124-4020
Phone: (505) 891-2664
Fax: (505) 891-4320
E-mail: overeatr@technet.nm.org
www.overeatersanonymous.org

Vancouver Anti-Anorexia/ Anti-Bulimia League
303-1212 West Broadway

Vancouver, BC, Canada V6H3VI
Phone: (604) 731-7304

HOLISTIC MEDICINE

American Holistic Health Association (AHHA)
P.O. Box 17400
Anaheim, CA 92817-7400
Phone: (714) 779-6152
E-mail: ahha@healthy.net
www.ahha.org

American Holistic Medical Association/Foundation
2727 Fairview Avenue East
Seattle, WA 98102
Phone: (206) 322-6842

International Association of Holistic Health Practitioners
3419 Thom Boulevard
Las Vegas, NV 89106
Phone: (712) 873-4542

MENTAL HEALTH

National Alliance for the Mentally Ill
Colonial Place Three
2107 Wilson Boulevard, Suite 300
Arlington, VA 22201-3042
Phone: (703) 524-7600
Fax: (703) 524-9094
www.nami.org

National Depressive and Manic Depressive Association
730 North Franklin Street, Suite 501
Chicago, IL 60610
Phone: (312) 988-1153 or
    (800) 826-3632
Fax: (312) 642-7243
www.ndmda.org

National Institute of Mental Health
NIMH Public Inquiries
6001 Executive Boulevard, Room 8184,
MSC 9663
Phone: (301) 443-4513
Fax (301) 443-4279
E-mail: nimhinfo@nih.gov
www.nimh.nih.gov

National Mental Health Association
1021 Prince Street
Alexandria, VA 22314-2971
Phone: (703) 684-7722
Fax: (703) 684-5968
www.nmha.org

Screening for Mental Health
One Washington Street, Suite 304
Wellesley, MA 02181-1706
Phone: (781) 239-0071
www.nmisp.org

Substance Abuse & Mental Health Services Administration/Women, Children and Families Team
Room 12-105 Parklawn Building
5600 Fishers Lane
MSC80-30, Room 7C-02
Rockville, MD 20857
Phone: (301) 443-4795
Fax: (301) 443-0284
www.samhsa.gov

SEXUAL ASSAULT

The Healing Woman Foundation
P.O. Box 28040-W
San Jose, CA 95159
Phone: (408) 246-1788
Fax: (408) 247-4309
E-mail: HealingW@healingwoman.org
www.healingwoman.org

National Clearinghouse on Marital and Date Rape
2325 Oak Street
Berkeley, CA 94708
Phone: (510) 524-1582

National Coalition Against Sexual Assault
125 North Enola Drive
Enola, PA 17025
www.ncasa.org

National Domestic Violence Hotline
P.O. Box 161810
Austin, TX 78716
Phone: (800) 799-SAFE
E-mail: ndvh@ndvh.org
www.ndvh.org

Partnerships for Survival (PFS)
353 North Country Road
Smithtown, NY 11787
Phone: (516) 265-7202
Fax: (516) 265-8676
E-mail: cforgash@worldnet.att.net

RAINN: Rape, Abuse, and Incest National Network
635-B Pennsylvania Avenue, S.E.
Washington, DC 20003
Phone: (800) 656-HOPE
Fax: (202) 544-3556

Rape Victim Advocacy Program
320 South Linn Street
Iowa City, IA 52240
Phone: (319) 335-6001
Crisis Hotline: (800) 284-7821
Fax: (319) 339-7710
E-mail: rvap@uiowa.edu
www.uiowa.edu/~rvap

Sexual Assault & Trauma Resource Center
300 Richmond Street, Suite 205
Providence, RI 02903
Phone: (401) 421-4100
Crisis hotline: (800) 494-8100
Fax: (401) 454-5565
E-mail: info@satrc.org
www.satrc.org

SOAR: Speaking Out Against Rape
One North Orange Avenue, Suite 500
Orlando, Florida 32802
Phone: (407) 295-1789
Fax: (407) 295-3367
E-mail: SOAR99@worldnet.att.net
www.soar99.com

SUBSTANCE ABUSE

Substance Abuse & Mental Health Services Administration/Women, Children and Families Team
Room 12-105 Parklawn Building
5600 Fishers Lane
MSC80-30, Room 7C-02
Rockville, MD 20857
Phone: (301) 443-4795
Fax: (301) 443-0284
www.samhsa.gov

Women for Sobriety, Inc.
P.O. Box 618
Quakertown, PA 18951
Phone: (215) 536-8026
www.womenforsobriety.org

OTHER

CenterWatch, Inc.
22 Thomson Place, 36T1
Boston, MA 02210-1212
Phone: (617) 856-5900 (editorial offices)
Fax: (617) 856-5901 5900
    (editorial offices)
E-mail: cntrwatch@aol.com
www.centerwatch.com/main.htm

International Women's Health Coalition
24 East 21st Street
New York, NY 10010
Phone: (212) 979-8500
Fax: (212) 979-9009
E-mail: iwhc@igc.apc.org
www.iwhc.org

National Heart, Lung, and Blood Institute, Women's Health Initiative (WHI)
6705 Rockledge Drive, Suite 300
Bethesda, MD 20892
Phone: (301) 402-2900

National Women's Health Resource Center, Inc.
120 Albany Street, Suite 820
New Brunswick, NJ 08901
Phone: (732) 828-8575
Toll Free: (877) 986-9472 (98-NWHRC)
Fax: (732) 249-4671
E-mail: NatlWHRC@aol.com
www.healthywomen.org/index.html

The Native American Women's Health Education Resource Center
P.O. Box 572
Lake Andes, SD 57356
Phone: (605) 487-7072
Fax: (605) 487-7964
E-mail: nativewoman@igc.apc.org
www.nativeshop.org/nawherc.html

PMS Access
P.O. Box 9326
Madison, WI 53715
Phone: (800) 222-4767

W.H.E.R.E. (Women for Healthcare Equity through Reform and Education)
105 14th Avenue, Suite 3-A
Seattle, WA 98122
Phone: (206) 325-7928
Fax: (206) 325-8221
E-mail: web@womens-health-equity.org
www.womens-health-equity.org

Politics

About-Face
P.O. Box 77665
San Francisco, CA 94107
Phone: (415) 436-0212
E-mail: pinniped@about-face.org
www.about-face.org

Association for Women in Development (AWID)
666 11th Street, N.W. Suite 450
Washington, DC 20001
Phone: (202) 628-0440
Fax: (202) 628-0442
E-mail: awid@awid.org
www.awid.org

Captive Daughters
10410 Palms Boulevard
Los Angeles, CA 90034
Phone: (888) 300-4918 (voice mail)
Fax: (310) 815-8739
E-mail: captive@cloud9.net
www.captive.org/index.htm#
CAPTIVE DAUGHTERS

Catholics for a Free Choice
1436 U Street, N.W., Suite 301
Washington, DC 20009-3997
Phone: (202) 986-6093
Fax: (202) 332-7995
www.cath4choice.org

Center for American Women and Politics
Eagleton Institute of Politics
Rutgers, The State University of
New Jersey
191 Ryders Lane
New Brunswick, NJ 08901-8557
Phone: (732) 932-9384, ext. 224
Fax: (732) 932-6778
E-mail: cawp@rci.rutgers.edu
www.rci.rutgers.edu/~cawp

The Clothesline Project
Box 727
East Dennis, MA 02641
Phone: (508) 385-7004
www.now.org/issues/violence/
clothes.html

Dataline
848 California Street
San Francisco, CA 94108
Phone: (415) 882-7320
Fax: (415) 397-8984
E-mail: Anee@ClarkeRonce.com
www.cyberwerks.com/dataline

Disabled Peoples' International Women's Committee
101-7 Evergreen Place
Winnipeg, Manitoba, Canada R3L 2T3
Phone: (204) 287 8010
Fax: (204) 453-1367
E-mail: dpi@dpi.org
www.escape.ca/~dpi/women.html

EMILY's List ("Early Money Is Like Yeast")
805 15th Street, N.W., Suite 400
Washington, DC 20005
Phone: (202) 326-1400
Fax: (202) 326-1415
emilyslist@emilyslist.org
www.emilyslist.org

Equal Rights Advocates
1663 Mission Street, Suite 550
San Francisco, CA 94103
Phone: (415) 621-0672
Fax: (415) 621-6744
E-mail: info@equalrights.org
www.equalrights.org

Family Violence Prevention Fund (FVPF)
383 Rhode Island Street, Suite #304

San Francisco, CA 94103-5133
Phone: (415) 252-8900
Fax: (415) 252-8991
E-mail: fund@fvpf.org
www.fvpf.org

Feminists for Animal Rights (FAR)
P.O. Box 8869
Tucson, AZ 85738
Phone: (520) 825-6852
E-mail: far@envirolink.org
www.enviroweb.org/far

Feminists for Free Expression
2525 Times Square Station
New York, NY 10108-2525
Phone: (212) 702-6292
Fax: (212) 702-6277
E-mail: freedom@well.com
www.well.com/user/freedom

Feminist International Radio Endeavor (FIRE)
P.O. Box 239-6100
Costa Rica
Phone and Fax: (506) 249-1993
E-mail: fuegocr@sol.racsa.co.cr
www.fire.or.cr/indexeng.htm

The Global Alliance Against Trafficking in Women (GAATW)
The International Coordination Office
P.O. Box 1281, Bangrak Post Office
Bangkok 10500, Thailand
Phone: (662) 864-1427
Fax: (662) 864-1637

The Global Fund for Women
425 Sherman Avenue, Suite 300
Palo Alto, CA 94306-1823
Phone: (650) 853-8305
Fax: (650) 328-0384
E-mail: gfw@globalfundforwomen.org
www.globalfundforwomen.org

Institute for Women's Policy Research
1400 20th St., N.W., Suite 104
Washington, DC 20036
Phone: (202) 785 5100
Fax: (202) 833-4362
E-mail: iwpr@iwpr.org
www.iwpr.org

International Gay and Lesbian Human Rights Commission
1360 Mission Street, Suite 200
San Francisco, CA 94103
Phone: (415) 255-8680
Fax: (415) 255-8662
E-mail: iglhrc@iglhrc.org
www.iglhrc.org

League of Women Voters
1730 M Street N.W., Suite 1000

Washington, DC 20036-4508
Phone: (202) 429-1965
Fax: (202) 429-0854
www.lwv.org/index.html

LLEGO (The National Latina/o Lesbian, Gay, Bisexual & Transgender Organization)
1612 K Street, N.W. Suite 500
Washington, DC 20006
Phone: (202) 466-8240 or
   (202) 466-8530
Fax: (202) 466-8530
www.llego.org

Ms. Foundation for Women
120 Wall Street, 33rd Floor
New York, NY 10005
Phone: (212) 742-2300
Fax: (212) 742-1653
E-mail: info@ms.foundation.org
www.ms.foundation.org

Muslim Women's Help Network
United Muslim Movement Against
Homelessness/Helping Hands
166-26 89th Avenue
Jamaica, NY 11432
Phone: (718) 658-8210
Fax: (718) 658-3434
E-mail: mwhn@muslimsonline.com
www.home.earthlink.net/~hanan/
   mwhelpnet.htm

National Committee on Pay Equity
1126 16th Street, N.W., Suite 411
Washington, DC 20036
Phone: (202) 331-7343
Fax: (202) 331-7406
E-mail: fairpay@aol.com
www.feminist.com/fairpay

The National Council of Negro Women, Inc.
633 Pennsylvania Ave., N.W.
Washington, DC 20004
Phone: (202) 737-0120
E-mail: info@nenw.com
www.ncnw.com

National Organization for Women
733 15th Street N.W., 2nd floor
Washington, DC 20005
Phone: (202) 628-8669 (628-8NOW)
Fax: (202) 785-8576
E-mail: now@now.org
www.now.org

National Partnership for Women & Families
1875 Connecticut Avenue, N.W.,
   Suite 710
Washington, DC 20009

Phone: (202) 986-2600
Fax: (202) 986-2539
E-mail: info@nationalpartnership.org
www.nationalpartnership.org

National Women's Political Caucus
1211 Connecticut Avenue, N.W.,
   Suite 425
Washington, DC 20036
Phone: (202) 785-1100
Fax: (202) 785-3605
www.nwpc.org

NOW Legal Defense and Education Fund
General Information:
395 Hudson Street
New York, NY 10014
Phone: (212) 925-6635
Fax: (212) 226-1066
E-mail: ademarco@nowldef.org
Policy Office:
119 Constitution Avenue, N.E.
Washington, DC 20002
Phone: (202) 544-4470
Fax: (202) 546-8605
E-mail: nowldef_de@nowldefdc.org
www.nowldef.org/index.htm

Office for Women's Initiatives and Outreach
The White House
Room 15, O.E.O.B.
Washington, DC 20502
Phone: (202) 456-7300
Fax: (202) 456-7311
E-mail: Women's_Office@who.eop.gov
www.whitehouse.gov/women

Office of Justice Programs
Violence Against Women Office
U.S. Department of Justice
810 Seventh Street, N.W.
Washington, DC 20531
www.ojp.usdoj.gov/vawo

The President's Interagency Council on Women
U.S. Department of State
2201 C Street, N.W., Room 6936
Washington, DC 20520
Phone: (202) 647-6227
Fax: (202) 647-5337
www.secretary.state.gov/www/picw/index.
   html

Silent Witness National Initiative
7 Sheridan Avenue South
Minneapolis, MN 55405
Phone: (612) 377-6629
Fax (612) 374-3956
E-mail: info@silentwitness.net
www.silentwitness.net

The Sisterhood Is Global Institute
4343 Montgomery Avenue, Suite 201
Bethesda, MD 20814
Phone: (301) 657-4355
Fax: (301) 657-4381
E-mail: sigi@igc.apc.org
www.sigi.org

South Asian Women for Action
E-mail: sawa@way.net
www.way.net/sawa

Sweatshop Watch
310 Eighth Street, Suite 309
Oakland, CA 94607
E-mail: sweatwatch@igc.apc.org
www.sweatshopwatch.org

Third Wave
116 East 16th Street, 7th Floor
New York, NY 10003
Phone: (212) 388-1898
Fax: (212) 982-3321
E-mail: ThirdWaveF@aol.com
www.feminist.com/3dwave.htm

Tibetan Women's Association
Bhagsunag Road
P.O. McLeod Ganj 176 219
Dharamsala, District Kangra 176 219,
   India
Phone: 0091-1892-22527
Fax: 0091-1982-22374
E-mail: twa@dsala.tibet.net
www.tibet.com/Women/twa.html

Voters For Choice
1010 Wisconsin Avenue, N.W., Suite 410
Washington, DC 20007-9301
Phone: (202) 944-5080
Fax: (202) 944-5081
E-mail: vfe@ibm.net
www.voters4choice.org

Womankind Worldwide
3, Albion Place
Galena Road
London W6 0LT, England
Phone: (44) 181 563 8607
Fax (44) 181 563 8611
E-mail: info@womankind.org.uk
www.oneworld.org/womankind

WomenAction
E-mail: info@womenaction.org
www.womenaction.org

Women, Law, and Development (WLD) International
1350 Connecticut Avenue N.W.,
   Suite 407
Washington, DC 20036
Phone: (202) 463-7477
Fax: (202) 463-7480

E-mail: wld@wld.org
www.whrnet.org/resources.html

Women of the World
9707 N.W. 73rd Terrace
Kansas City, MO 64152-3733
Phone: (816) 746-6869
E-mail: wownow@wownow.org
www.wownow.org

Women's Educational Equity Act Resource Center
Education Development Center
55 Chapel Street
Newton, MA 02158-1060
Phone: (617) 969-7100
www.edc.org/WomensEquity/index.html

Women's Environment & Development Organization (WEDO)
845 Third Avenue, 15th Floor
New York, NY 10022
Phone: (212) 759-7982
Fax: (212) 759-8647
E-mail: wedo@igc.apc.org
www.gopher.igc.apc.org/00/orgs/
wedo/about

Women's Institute for Leadership Development (WILD) for Human Rights
340 Pine Street, Suite 302
San Francisco, CA 94104
Phone: (415) 837-0795
Fax: (415) 837-1144
E-mail: wild@igc.apc.org
www.wildhr.org

Women's International Center
P.O. Box 880736
San Diego, CA 92168-0736
Phone: (619) 295-6446
Fax: (619) 296-1633
E-mail: info@wic.org
www.wic.org

Women's International League for Peace and Freedom
1213 Race Street
Philadelphia, PA 19107
Phone: (215) 563-7110
Fax: (215) 563-5527
E-mail: wilpf@wilpf.org
www.wilpf.org

World Council of Muslim Women Foundation
Box 128
Seba Beach, Alberta, Canada, T0E 2B0
Phone and Fax: (780) 439-5088
E-mail: wcomwf@connect.ab.ca

Religion and Spirituality

Brethren/Mennonite Council for Lesbian and Gay Concerns
P.O. Box 6300
Minneapolis, MN 55406
Phone: (612) 722-6906
E-mail: BMCouncil@aol.com
www.webcom.com/bmc

Canadian Council of Muslim Women
Le Conseil Canadien des Femmes Musulmanes
2400 Dundas Street, West, Suite 513
Mississauga, Ontario, Canada, L5K 2R8
E-mail: jaff1@telusplanet.net
www.ccmw.com

The Center for Women and Religion (CWR)
Graduate Theological Union
2400 Ridge Road
Berkeley, CA 94709
Phone: (510) 649-2490
Fax: (510) 649-1730
E-mail: cwr@gtu.edu
www.gtu.edu/Centers/cwr/index.html

Christian Lesbians Out
CLOUTreach Editor and Administrative Coordinator
P.O. Box 5853
Athens, Ohio 45701
E-mail: clout@scorf.ohiou.edu
www.geocities.com/WestHollywood/
Village/1305

Covenant of the Goddess
Correspondence Officer
P.O. Box 1226
Berkeley, CA 94701
E-mail: info@cog.org
www.cog.org

Fellowship of Isis
The Crossroads Lyceum
Dept. INT3
P.O. Box 19152
Tucson, AZ 85731
E-mail: isislyceum@aol.com
members.aol.com/isislyceum/file.html

Ma'yan
15 West 65th Street
New York, NY 10023
Phone: (212) 580-0099
Fax: (212) 580-9498
E-mail: mayanjcc@aol.com
www.mayan.org

National Council of Jewish Women
53 West 23rd Street, 6th Floor
New York, NY 10010
Phone: (212) 645-4048
Fax: (212) 645-7466
E-mail: actionline@ncjw.org
www.ncjw.org

Sakyadhita International: The International Association of Buddhist Women
1143 Piikoi Place
Honolulu, HI 96822
E-mail: tsomo@hawaii.edu

Women's Alliance for Theology, Ethics, and Ritual
8035 13th Street
Silver Spring MD 20910-4803
Phone: (301) 589-2509
Fax: (301) 589-3150
E-mail: water@hers.com
www.his.com/~mhunt

Women's Theological Center
P.O. Box 1200
Boston, MA 02117-1200
Phone: (617) 536-8782
E-mail: WTC@world.std.com
www.world.std.com/~wtc/

Young Women's Christian Association (YMCA) of the U.S.A.
Empire State Building
350 Fifth Avenue, Suite 301
New York, NY 10118
Phone: (212) 273-7800
Fax: (212) 465-2281
E-mail: jchesnutt@ywca.org

Web Sites

The following sites offer a sampling of some of the portals, online communities, and repositories of information for and about women available on the Internet.

The Ada Project
www.cs.yale.edu/~tap/tap.html
A collection of links to other online resources relating to women and computing, this site includes resources on conferences, projects, discussion groups and organizations, fellowships and grants, and notable women in computer science.

Advancing Women
www.advancingwomen.com/index.html
An online international business and career community, Advancing Women provides advice, resources, feature articles, and links in categories such as Workplace, Networking, International Women, and Women and Society.

Aegis: Aids Education Global Information System
www.aegis.com
This web site offers a searchable database, as well as an "HIV/AIDS Encyclopedia," which provides a concise list of key topics, such as the Science of HIV, Women's Issues, and Treatment.

Amazon City Online
www.amazoncity.com
An online community for women with chat rooms, special services, and discussion forums.

Archives for Research on Women and Gender Project
www.lib.utsa.edu/Archives/links.htm
This site contains a state by state listing of archival collections that provide information on records, manuscripts, diaries, oral tapes, and art relating to the history and lives of women.

AsiangURLs
www.asiangurls.com/index.html
A web community for women of Asian cultures, AsiangURLs offers feature articles, news, polls, links, announcement mail, a discussion mailing list, and bulletin board.

Association of Cancer Online Resources
www.acor.org
This site offers access to 79 electronic mailing lists, which function as public online support groups for people looking for information on cancer and related topics.

Breast Cancer Information Center, Feminist Majority Foundation
www.feminist.org/other/bc/
    bchome.html
The Breast Cancer Information Center includes information and resources in the following categories: What You Need to Know, What You Can Do, Breast Cancer Internet Resources, Breast Cancer Clinical Trials, and Breast Cancer Hotlines.

Bust
www.bust.com
This site offers sample stories from past magazine issues of Bust, a database of travel tips from Let's Go Girls, a chat room called "The Lounge," and links to other web sites divided into categories such as Girly and Pop Culture.

chickclick
www.chickclick.com
Organized by categories called "chicklounge," "shewire," and "hip moms," chickclick offers feature articles, news, daily polls, and quotable sound bites. Also provides links to and descriptions of its sister sites.

Critical Path AIDS Project: Hypertext Edition
www.critpath.org
This site includes links organized by news, prevention, calendar events, research, clinical trials, publications, alternative treatments, and international and national organizations.

Cybergrrl
www.cybergrrl.com/explorer.htm
This site provides original content divided into three categories: Tech (with tips and discussions of technical issues), Views (offers features on love, career, family, etc.), and Fun (with news on entertainment, books, travel, etc.).

ElectraPages
www.electrapages.com
An extensive online directory, searchable by geographic location, type, or name, that provides contact information for over 9,000 feminist organizations.

Femina
www.femina.cybergrrl.com/explorer.htm
A searchable directory of links to female-oriented information and web sites.

Feminist Activist Resources on the Web
www.igc.apc.org/women/feminist.html
A searchable guide to women's resources on the Internet, with links pertaining to domestic violence, women of color, health, global issues, and politics.

Feminista!
www.feminista.com
Feminista! is a monthly electronic feminist journal that publishes essays, editorials, fiction, poetry, interviews, and book and movie reviews.

Feminist.com
www.feminist.com
Feminist.com places a strong emphasis on activism, providing weekly news updates and maintaining a calendar of events. Other features include a women-owned business section, a classifieds section, and links to articles, speeches, and other sites.

Feminist Majority Foundation Online
www.feminist.org
This site provides up-to-date news of issues affecting women and a collection of informative resources such as a Feminist Career Center, a Feminist Arts, Literature & Entertainment Center, and a directory of women's organizations.

gURL
www.gurl.com

This colorful site offers articles, polls, contests, and stories under category listings such as Sports, Mouthpiece, FuturegURL, "Deal With It!," and MusicgURL. Members of the gURL Connection can participate in chats, listen to poetry shoutouts, and find a fellow gURL pen pal.

Her Health Online
www.herhealth.com
A holistic health site for women of all ages, Her Health Online provides health news, tips of the day, feature articles, community bulletin boards, mailing lists, and chat rooms.

Herspace
www.herspace.com
Herspace includes links to a diverse collection of women's sites, all a part of the Herspace Network. This site also offers feature articles, chats, and forums.

Hindu Women Universe
www.hinduwomen.org
A comprehensive site dealing with both women's issues and Hinduism. The Hindu Women Resource section contains articles about a variety of topics, including spirituality, family, customs, issues and politics, and the workplace.

HIV InfoWeb
www.infoweb.org
This online library with HIV and AIDS related information on topics such as Clinical Trials, Women and HIV, HIV Resources Worldwide in Other Languages, and Treatment, as well as information on agencies, calendar events, and housing for the New England area.

HIVWoman
www.hivwoman.com
Created for women living with HIV/AIDS, this site offers advocate services, up-to-date health and medical information, advice on methods of prevention and low risk activities, and chat rooms and bulletin boards.

iVillage
www.ivillage.com
iVillage provides solutions for daily living, with expert advice, feature articles, and helpful tools. Members can obtain free private E-mail accounts, enter sweepstakes, and enter discussions during live chat events.

JAMA HIV/AIDS Information Center
www.ama-assn.org/special/hiv/hivhome.htm
This site provides up-to-date information and resources relating to HIV/AIDS, such as abstracts of major HIV/AIDS articles, treatment updates, education and support groups, prevention fact sheets, and policy updates.

Jewish Feminist Bookstore
www.jew-feminist-resources.com
A Jewish feminist resource, with information on recipes, holidays, music, books, rituals, Torah, and calendar events.

Journeywoman
www.journeywoman.com
An online travel resource for women, Journeywoman provides travel tips, classifieds, recommended travel books, "Gal-Friendly City Sites," and travel tales.

Making Face, Making Soul . . . A Chicana Feminist Homepage
www.chicanas.com/huh.html
Created by, for, and about women of Mexican descent in the United States, this site addresses issues of family, class, sexuality, youth, and race and ethnicity. Also includes a research resource, entitled "Academica," which features statistics, bibliographies, and a listing of Chicana scholars.

Maven: The Jewish Portal (Women & Feminism)
www.maven.co.il
Lists links dealing with Judaism, women, and feminism, which can be sorted alphabetically, by date, or by popularity among other visitors.

Military Woman
www.Militarywoman.org
Created for women in the military, women contemplating military service, and women veterans, this site offers advice, articles on health issues, an online buddy search system, a message center, and information on harassment, discrimination, and other issues.

Muslim Women's Homepage
www.jannah.org/sisters
This site provides information on gender issues and the role of women in Islam with articles on marriage, Islamic dress and behavior, famous Muslim women, as well as a listing of Islamic organizations and resources.

National Alliance of Sexual Assault Coalitions
www.connsacs.org/alliance.htm
This site provides a brief hisotry of the Alliance, plus contact information and links to Sexual Assault Coalitions at the state level.

Oxygen
www.oxygen.com
Oxygen Media's web site provides original feature articles on topics such as friendship and marriage, dining, games, shopping, and books. Also provides links to Oxygen's other sites: Thriveonline (www.thriveonline.com), Moms Online (www.momsonline.com), Oprah (www.oprah.com), ka-Ching (www.ka-ching.com), Electra (www.electra.com), and Girls On (www.girlson.com).

RiotGirl
www.riotgrrl.com
This site offers original articles that change weekly, as well as regular features such as "Feed the Supermodel." You can also join an E-mail mailing list, participate in conversations in RiotGrrl Interact, or peruse "The Archive" to find the best of RiotGrrl.

Russian Feminism Resources
www.geocities.com/Athens/2533/russfem.html
A directory of online resources about Russian women, women's studies and the women's movement in the former Soviet Union.

Senior Women Web
www.seniorwomen.com/index.htm
Celebrating the lives of women over 55, Senior Women Web presents information on women's political, medical, financial, and legal issues, as well as leisure, home and garden, travel, education, grandchildren, and sex.

Sister Spirit
www.ethoscape.com/sistersp
A site devoted to women's spirituality, Sister Spirit includes many traditions: Dianic, Wicca, Pagan, Women's Spirituality, Goddess, Feminist, Interfaith, Earth Centered, Creation Spirituality, Christian, Jewish, Sufi, and New Age. It includes news, rituals, calendar events, spiritual links, and articles from *Spirited Women Online*.

Spiderwoman
www.spiderwoman.org
A site for women web designers,

Spiderwoman includes design tips, feature articles, a directory of web consultants and developers, and web forums on topics such as women in technology and Java.

South Asian Women's NETwork
www.umiacs.umd.edu/users/sawweb/
    sawnet/index.html
A forum for South Asian women's issues, this site features news links, a women-only mailing list, and information organized by categories such as children's books, legal issues, and domestic violence.

Teengrrl
www.teengrrl.com
Written by teenage girls specifically for and about teenage girls, this site provides regular features such as "theBUZZ," "actionGRRL," and "grrl'seyeVIEW," as well as a chat room and an E-mail mailing list.

University of Wisconsin System Women's Studies Librarian: Magazines and Newsletters on the Web (Women-Focused)
www.library.wisc.edu/libraries/
    WomensStudies/mags.htm
Provides links for finding magazines and periodicals on the web, as well as an extensive A–Z listing of links to women-focused periodicals.

University of Wisconsin System Women's Studies Librarian: Subject Listing of Women and Gender Resources
www.library.wisc.edu/libraries/
    WomensStudies/othsubj.htm
Organized according to subject and academic disciplines, this site offers numerous links.

WAiB Pages: Women Active in Buddhism
members.tripod.com/~Lhamo
An extensive collection of resources and links on contemporary Buddhist women, the WAiB Pages features individual bios of women activists, teachers, scholars; information on women's ordination; listings of Buddhist groups for women; and more.

WiredWomen
www.wiredwoman.com
Explores how technology affects women's lives, providing information on joining the Wired Women Society and viewing meetings of the society on Wired Women TV. Also offers columns

on Art & Culture and Careers & Education.

A Woman's Space
www.wospace.cnation.com/
    TableContents.html
Provides a space for women as mothers, professionals, wives and homemakers, members of the community, and poets and artists, to find information on health, nutrition, work issues, and consumerism.

Women.com
www.women.com
With a wide variety of topics including career, health, pregnancy and baby, and tech and internet, this site provides feature articles, services, community message boards, and expert advice.

Women Connect
www.womenconnect.com
A source for women in business, this site offers feature articles on business, money, health, career advice, and entertainment/leisure time.

Women in World History Curriculum
www.womeninworldhistory.com
This site, primarily geared to teachers, parents, and students, provides information and resources about women's experiences in world history.

Women Leaders Online
www.wlo.org/home.htm
An online women's activist group with current news, action alerts, voter education, and discussion lists.

Women Online Worldwide (WOW)
www.wowwomen.com
Celebrating the "spirit of womankind," WOW features live chat areas, message boards, interactive games, an e-zine called Tapestry, and Visibilities, an online lesbian magazine.

Women's Human Rights Net (whrNET)
www.whrnet.org
Supported by an international coalition of women's organizations, whrNET is divided into the following categories: Women's Human Rights Issues; Advocacy/Strategies; News and Urgent Action Alerts; UN/Regional Systems; and Capacity Building.

Women's Sports Foundation
www.lifetimetv.com/WoSport
Devoted to increasing opportunities for girls and women in sports and fitness, this site features information on sports-

related issues; training and fitness; grants, funding, and scholarships; and a resource library.

Women's Village
www.minorities-jb.com/women.html
This site includes career advice, networking information, and departments on work and family, sexual harassment and discrimination, and business and finance. Also offers access to the Minorities Job Bank, which aims to provide "career and self development information to all minorities."

WomenWatch
www.un.org/womenwatch
Devoted to working toward the advancement and empowerment of women in response to the Fourth World Conference on Women in Beijing, WomenWatch provides information on UN global conferences, international agencies, worldwide statistics on women, up-to-date news, and calendar events.

Women Writers
www.womenwriters.net
This literary site devoted to women writers, organized by categories such as 19th century, 20th century, criticism sources, and nonfiction, offers over 300 links to sites listed alphabetically by author, as well as original articles, poetry, and fiction.

Women-Writers.com
www.womenbooks.com/wwriters/
    index.html
An entire site devoted to women writers and community, Women-Writers.com features book reviews, frequently asked questions, authors on the Internet listed by genre, as well as links divided by categories such as Book Clubs and Bookstores, Freelance Editors and Writers, Lesbian Writing, Publishers, and Women Studies.

WWWomen®
www.wwwomen.com
Organized by general categories, such as Mothers and Family, Diversity Among Women, and Health and Safety Issues, this site provides links to information and web sites for and about women.

WWW Women's Sports Page
www.fiat.gslis.utexas.edu/~lewisa/
    womsprt.html
An index of websites related to women and sports.

Calendar of Historical Anniversaries

JANUARY

9   CARRIE CHAPMAN CATT's birthday, 1859.

10 The National Woman's Party began its years of picketing the White House for suffrage, 1917.

15 In Washington, D.C., women peace activists marched against the Vietnam War, calling themselves the Jeannette Rankin Brigade, 1968.

16 Twenty-one-year old orator Anna Dickinson addressed Congress, with President Abraham Lincoln in the audience, 1864.

22 Anniversary of *Roe* v. *Wade* U.S. Supreme Court decision, which legalized abortion in 1973.

29 ELIZABETH BLACKWELL's graduation from medical school, 1849.

FEBRUARY

3   Liberation of Army Nurse Corps women who had been Japanese prisoners of war for three years, 1945.

9   First censorship of MARGARET SANGER; the Post Office refused to deliver a magazine containing her article on syphilis, 1913.

14 Appointment of the nation's first female law enforcement official, Justice of the Peace Esther Morris of Wyoming, 1870.

14 ANNA HOWARD SHAW's birthday, 1847.

15 SUSAN B. ANTHONY's birthday, 1820.

18 The National Woman Suffrage Association and the American Woman Suffrage Association merged, 1890.

19 America's first female missionaries, HARRIET ATWOOD NEWELL and ANN HASSELTINE JUDSON, sailed for India, 1812.

MARCH — WOMEN'S HISTORY MONTH!

3   ALICE PAUL led the first national suffrage march in Washington, D.C., 1913.

4   JEANETTE RANKIN of Montana was the first woman sworn into Congress, 1917.

4   Secretary of Labor FRANCES PERKINS became the first woman named to the Cabinet, 1933.

8   Women's History Week proclaimed by President Jimmy Carter, 1979.

21 POCAHONTAS was buried in England, 1617.

25 146 garment workers, mostly immigrant women, died in a fire at New York City's Triangle Factory, 1911.

APRIL

2   VICTORIA WOODHULL declared her candidacy for president, 1870.

9   Opera singer MARIAN ANDERSON gave a concert at the Lincoln Memorial, after being denied the right to sing at Constitution Hall because of her race, 1939.

26 Anniversary of the midnight ride of SYBIL LUDDINGTON, 1777.

28 Take Our Daughters to Work Day first celebrated, 1993.

MAY

1   Wedding of Henry Blackwell and LUCY STONE, 1855.

10 Wedding of Henry and ELIZABETH CADY STANTON, in which they omitted her vow of obedience, 1840.

15–22 The International Congress of Women drew 150,000 women from 27 nations to Chicago, 1893.

15 Establishment of the Women's Auxiliary Army Corps, 1942.

21 The House of Representatives passed the Nineteenth Amendment; it granted all American women the vote, 1919.

JUNE

1   Quaker preacher MARY DYER was hanged, 1660.

4   By a two vote margin, the U.S. Senate passed the Nineteenth Amendment; it granted all American women the vote, 1919.

7   In *Griswold* v. *State of Connecticut*, the U.S. Supreme Court ruled that laws prohibiting the use of contraception are unconstitutional, 1965.

11 The U.S. Army promoted its first women to the rank of general, 1970.

15 Arabella Mansfield was the first woman admitted to the bar, 1869.

18 SALLY RIDE became the first American woman in space, 1983.

30 Time expired for ratification of the Equal Rights Amendment, 1982.

30 Founding meeting of the National Organization for Women, 1966.

JULY

2 Disappearance of aviator AMELIA EARHART, 1937.

4 SUSAN B. ANTHONY read a Declaration of the Rights of Women at the nation's first centennial, Philadelphia, 1876.

7 Mary Surratt hanged for alleged complicity in Lincoln's assassination, 1865.

12 Democrat GERALDINE FERRARO was the first woman nominated for vice president by a major party, 1984.

19–20 The first women's rights convention held in Seneca Falls, New York, 1848.

19 Death of MARGARET FULLER, perhaps the most important feminist of her era, in a shipwreck, 1850.

AUGUST

1 HARRIET QUIMBY became the first American woman licensed to fly, 1911.

13 The first non-nursing women join the U.S. Navy, 1918.

18 VIRGINIA DARE's birthday, 1587.

26 Women's Equality Day: the anniversary of final ratification of the Nineteenth Amendment; it granted the vote to all American women, 1920.

SEPTEMBER

3 Aviator Bessie Coleman staged the first public flight by an African-American woman in America, 1922.

15 Anniversary of ANTOINETTE BROWN BLACKWELL's ordination, the first of a woman as minister of a mainstream church, 1853.

20 BILLIE JEAN KING defeated male tennis champion Bobby Riggs, 1973.

22 The last execution of women for witchcraft in Salem, Massachusetts, 1692.

25 SANDRA DAY O'CONNOR sworn in as the first woman on the U.S. Supreme Court, 1981.

OCTOBER

1 MARIA MITCHELL discovered a comet, 1847.

23–24 The first national women's rights convention, Worcester, Massachusetts, 1850. The year 2000 marks its 150th anniversary.

NOVEMBER

1 Colorado elected the first women in a state legislature, 1894.

13 HATTIE CARAWAY of Arkansas began her career as the first long-term female U.S. senator, 1939.

21 Honorary appointee REBECCA FELTON of Georgia was the first woman sworn into in the U.S. Senate, 1922.

30 Death of labor activist Mother Jones at age 100, 1930.

DECEMBER

1 ROSA PARKS arrested in Montgomery, Alabama, for refusing to give her bus seat to a white passenger, 1955.

3 Classes began at the nation's first coeducational college, Oberlin College in Oberlin, Ohio, 1833.

10 Women in the Wyoming Territory became the nation's first to have an unrestricted right to vote, 1869.

10 The United Nations adopted the Universal Declaration of Human Rights, including women's rights, 1948.

25 Pilgrims landed at Plymouth, 1620; of the 18 women aboard, 14 died before winter's end.

31 The first graduation ceremony of the first medical school for women, Female Medical College of Pennsylvania, 1851.

APPENDIX TWO:

Women in Government

World

WOMEN LEADERS WORLDWIDE (as of 2000)

Country	Name	Role	Year Role Assumed
Bangladesh	Sheikh Hasina Wajed	Prime Minister	1996
Denmark	Margrethe II	Queen	1972
Finland	Tarja Kaarina Halonen	President	2000
Indonesia	Megawati Sukarnoputri	Vice President	1999
Ireland	Mary McAleese	President	1997
Latvia	Vaira Vike-Freiberga	President	1999
Netherlands	Beatrix	Queen	1980
New Zealand	Helen Clark	Prime Minister	1999
Panama	Mireya Moscoso	President	1999
San Marino	Domenica Michelotti	Captain Co-regent	4/2000 – 10/2000
Sri Lanka	Sirimavo Bandaranaike	Prime Minister	(1st term 1970–77), current term from 1994
Sri Lanka	Chandrika Bandaranaike Kumaratunge	President	1994
Switzerland	Ruth Dreifuss	President of Federal Council	1999
United Kingdom	Elizabeth II	Queen	1952

United States

WOMEN IN THE U.S. CABINET (as of 2000)

Name	Title	Year Appointed
Madeline Albright	Secretary of State	1996
Janet Reno	Attorney General	1993
Donna Shalala	Secretary of Health and Human Services	1993

WOMEN IN U.S. SENATE (as of 2000)

State	Name	Affiliation	Dates of Service
Arkansas	Blanche Lincoln	D	1/6/99 – present
California	Dianne Feinstein	D	11/10/92 – present
California	Barbara Boxer	D	1/5/93 – present
Louisiana	Mary Landrieu	D	1/7/97 – present
Maine	Olympia Snowe	R	1/4/95 – present
Maine	Susan Collins	R	1/7/97 – present
Maryland	Barbara Ann Mikulski	D	1/3/87 – present
Texas	Kay Bailey Hutchison	R	6/14/93 – present
Washington	Patty Murray	D	1/5/93 – present

WOMEN IN U.S. HOUSE OF REPRESENTATIVES (as of 2000)

State	Name	Affiliation	Dates of Service
California	Mary Bono	R	4/21/98 – present
California	Lois Capps	D	3/17/98 – present
California	Anna Eshoo	D	1/5/93 – present
California	Barbara Lee	D	4/21/98 – present
California	Zoe Lofgren	D	1/4/95 – present
California	Juanita Millender-McDonald	D	4/16/96 – present
California	Grace Napolitano	D	1/6/99 – present
California	Nancy Pelosi	D	6/9/87 – present
California	Lucille Roybal-Allard	D	1/5/93 – present
California	Loretta Sanchez	D	1/7/97 – present
California	Ellen Tauscher	D	1/7/97 – present
California	Maxine Waters	D	1/3/91 – present
California	Lynn Woolsey	D	1/5/93 – present
Colorado	Diana DeGette	D	1/7/97 – present
Connecticut	Rosa DeLauro	D	1/3/91 – present
Connecticut	Nancy Johnson	R	1/3/83 – present
District of Columbia	Eleanor Holmes Norton	D	1/31/91 – present
Florida	Corrine Brown	D	1/5/93 – present
Florida	Tillie Fowler	R	1/5/93 – present
Florida	Carrie Meek	D	1/5/93 – present
Florida	Ileana Ros-Lehtinen	R	9/6/89 – present
Florida	Karen Thurman	D	1/5/93 – present
Georgia	Cynthia McKinney	D	1/5/93 – present
Hawaii	Patsy Takemoto Mink	D	1/3/65 – 1/3/77 and 9/27/90 – present
Idaho	Helen Chenoweth-Hage	R	1/4/95 – present
Illinois	Judy Biggert	R	1/6/99 – present
Illinois	Jan Schakowsky	D	1/6/99 – present
Indiana	Julia Carson	D	1/7/97 – present
Kentucky	Anne Meagher Northup	R	1/7/97 – present
Maryland	Constance Morella	R	1/3/87 – present
Michigan	Carolyn Cheeks Kilpatrick	D	1/7/97 – present
Michigan	Lynn Rivers	D	1/4/95 – present
Michigan	Debbie Stabenow	D	1/7/97 – present
Missouri	Pat Danner	D	1/5/93 – present
Missouri	Jo Ann Emerson	R	11/25/96 – present
Missouri	Karen McCarthy	D	1/4/95 – present
Nevada	Shelley Berkley	D	1/6/99 – present
New Jersey	Marge Roukema	R	1/3/81 – present
New Mexico	Heather Wilson	R	6/25/98 – present
New York	Sue Kelly	R	1/4/95 – present
New York	Nita Lowey	D	1/3/89 – present
New York	Carolyn Maloney	D	1/5/93 – present

WOMEN IN U.S. HOUSE OF REPRESENTATIVES (as of 2000) (*cont.*)

State	Name	Affiliation	Dates of Service
New York	Carolyn McCarthy	D	1/7/97 – present
New York	Louise Slaughter	D	1/3/87 – present
New York	Nydia Velazquez	D	1/5/93 – present
North Carolina	Eva Clayton	D	11/4/92 – present
North Carolina	Sue Myrick	R	1/4/95 – present
Ohio	Stephanie Tubbs Jones	D	1/6/99 – present
Ohio	Marcy Kaptur	D	1/3/83 – present
Ohio	Deborah Pryce	R	1/5/93 – present
Oregon	Darlene Hooley	D	1/7/97 – present
Texas	Kay Granger	R	1/7/97 – present
Texas	Eddie Bernice Johnson	D	1/5/93 – present
Texas	Sheila Jackson Lee	D	1/4/95 – present
Virgin Islands	Donna Christian-Green	D	1/7/97 – present
Washington	Jennifer Dunn	R	1/5/93 – present
Wisconsin	Tammy Baldwin	D	1/6/99 - present
Wyoming	Barbara Cubin	R	1/4/95 – present

WOMEN IN CONGRESSIONAL LEADERSHIP ROLES (106th Congress)

State	Name	Affiliation	Role
SENATE			
California	Barbara Boxer	D	Deputy Minority Whip
Maine	Olympia Snowe	R	Secretary of the Senate Republican Conference
Maryland	Barbara Mikulski	D	Secretary of the Senate Democratic Conference
Texas	Kay Bailey Hutchison	R	Deputy Majority Whip
HOUSE OF REPRESENTATIVES			
California	Lynn Woolsey	D	Deputy Minority Whip
Colorado	Diana DeGette	D	Deputy Minority Whip
Connecticut	Rosa DeLauro	D	Assistant to the Democratic Leader
Florida	Tillie Fowler	R	Vice Chairman of the House Republican Conference
New York	Nita Lowey	D	Minority Whip At-Large
New York	Louise Slaughter	D	Minority Whip At-Large
Ohio	Deborah Pryce	R	Republican Conference Secretary
Texas	Kay Granger	R	Assistant Majority Whip
Texas	Eddie Bernice Johnson	D	Democratic Deputy Whip
Wyoming	Barbara Cubin	R	Deputy Majority Whip
CONGRESSIONAL CAUCUS ON WOMEN'S ISSUES			
California	Juanita Millender-McDonald	R	Co-Vice Chair
New York	Sue Kelly	D	Co-Chair
New York	Carolyn Maloney	D	Co-Vice Chair
Texas	Kay Granger	R	Co-Chair

WOMEN IN STATEWIDE ELECTIVE EXECUTIVE OFFICES

State	Name	Affiliation
GOVERNORS		
Arizona	Jane Dee Hull	R
New Hampshire	Jeanne Shaheen	D
New Jersey	Christine Todd Whitman	R
LIEUTENANT GOVERNORS		
Alaska	Fran Ulmer	D
Connecticut	M. Jodi Rell	R
Delaware	Ruth Ann Minner	D
Hawaii	Mazie K. Hirono	D
Illinois	Corrine Wood	R
Iowa	Sally Pederson	D
Louisiana	Kathleen Blanco	D
Maryland	Kathleen Kennedy Townsend	D
Massachusetts	Jane Swift	R
Minnesota	Mae Schunk	RP*
Mississippi	Amy Tuck	D
Montana	Judy Martz	R
Nevada	Lorraine Hunt	R
New York	Mary Donohue	R
North Dakota	Rosemarie Myrdal	R
Ohio	Maureen O'Connor	R
Oklahoma	Mary Fallin	R
South Dakota	Carole Hillard	R
Utah	Olene S. Walker	R
SECRETARIES OF STATE		
Arizona	Betsey Bayless	R
Arkansas	Sharon Priest	D
Colorado	Donetta Davidson	R
Connecticut	Susan Bysiewicz	D
Florida	Katherine Harris	R
Georgia	Cathy Cox	D

State	Name	Affiliation
SECRETARIES OF STATE *(cont.)*		
Indiana	Sue Anne Gilroy	R
Michigan	Candice S. Miller	R
Minnesota	Mary Kiffmeyer	R
Missouri	Rebecca M. Cook	D
New Mexico	Rebecca Vigil-Giron	D
North Carolina	Elaine Marshall	D
South Dakota	Joyce Hazeltine	R
Vermont	Deborah Markowitz	D
ATTORNEYS GENERAL		
Arizona	Janet Napolitano	D
Delaware	M. Jane Brady	R
Kansas	Carla J. Stovall	R
Michigan	Jennifer Granholm	D
Nevada	Frankie Sue Del Papa	D
New Mexico	Patricia Madrid	D
North Dakota	Heidi Heitkamp	D
Ohio	Betty Montgomery	R
Utah	Jan Graham	D
Washington	Christine O. Gregoire	D
STATE TREASURERS		
Alabama	Lucy Baxley	D
Arizona	Carol Springer	R
Arkansas	Jimmie Lou Fisher	D
Connecticut	Denise Nappier	D
Illinois	Judy Baar Topinka	R
Massachusetts	Shannon O'Brien	D
Minnesota	Carol Johnson	D
North Dakota	Kathi Gilmore	D
Pennsylvania	Barbara H. Hafer	R
Wyoming	Cynthia Lummis	R

* RP = Reform Party.

Index

Note: Page citations in boldface indicate main discussions of topic. Those in italic indicate illustrations. The page citation following each country name indicates a statistical analysis for that country.